A Companion to
Crime Fiction

Blackwell Companions to Literature and Culture

This series offers comprehensive, newly written surveys of key periods and movements and certain major authors, in English literary culture and history. Extensive volumes provide new perspectives and positions on contexts and on canonical and post-canonical texts, orientating the beginning student in new fields of study and providing the experienced undergraduate and new graduate with current and new directions, as pioneered and developed by leading scholars in the field.

Published Recently

The Editors

Charles J. Rzepka is Professor of English at Boston University, where he teaches and writes on British Romanticism, popular culture, and detective and crime fiction. His publications include *The Self as Mind* (1986), *Sacramental Commodities* (1995), *Detective Fiction* (2005), and *Essays: Inventions and Interventions* (2010).

Lee Horsley is Reader in Literature and Culture at Lancaster University, where she teaches two specialist crime courses. Her publications include *Political Fiction and the Historical Imagination* (1990), *Fictions of Power in English Literature 1900–1950* (1995) *Twentieth-Century Crime Fiction* (2005), and an expanded paperback edition of the 2001 publication *The Noir Thriller* (2009).

WILEY-BLACKWELL

A COMPANION TO

CRIME FICTION

Edited by Charles J. Rzepka and Lee Horsley

This cutting edge *Companion* brings together
a series of forty-seven original essays from
some of the world's leading authorities to
provide the definitive guide to crime fiction
from its origins in the eighteenth century to its
phenomenal present day popularity.

Part one of the volume follows the
development of crime fiction over the last
three centuries, examining the traditions and
conventions of the genre, as well as its cultural
and social contexts, before moving on, in part
two, to explore the different types of genres
and subgenres that have emerged. The final
chapters profile twenty of the most significant
crime writers and film makers – from William
Godwin to Arthur Conan Doyle to Agatha
Christie to Martin Scorsese – examining
the ways in which they have shaped and
influenced the field.

WILEY-
BLACKWELL

A COMPANION TO

CRIME FICTION

EDITED BY

CHARLES J. RZEPKA AND LEE HORSLEY

WILEY-BLACKWELL

A John Wiley & Sons, Ltd., Publication

Library of Congress Cataloging-in-Publication Data

A companion to crime fiction / edited by Charles J. Rzepka and Lee Horsley.
    p. cm. – (Blackwell companions to literature and culture)
  Includes bibliographical references and index.
  ISBN 978-1-4051-6765-9 (alk. paper)
    1. Detective and mystery stories–History and criticism.   2. Crime in literature.   3. Detective and mystery films–History and criticism.   I. Rzepka, Charles J.   II. Horsley, Lee, 1944–
  PN3448.D4C557 2010
  809.3′872–dc22

                                        2009050999

A catalogue record for this book is available from the British Library.

Set in 11 on 13 pt Garamond 3 by Toppan Best-set Premedia Limited

1   2010

Contents

List of Figures

Notes on Contributors

Frankie Bailey is an Associate Professor, School of Criminal Justice, State University of New York at Albany (SUNY). With Steven Chermak, she is co-series editor of the Praeger series, Crime, Media, and Popular Culture. Her own books include *African American Mystery Writers: A Historical and Thematic Study* (McFarland, 2008) and *Wicked Albany: Lawlessness & Liquor in the Prohibition Era* (The History Press, 2009). Bailey is the author of a mystery series and the 2009–2010 Executive Vice President of Mystery Writers of America.

Joel Black teaches film and comparative literature at the University of Georgia. He is the author of *The Aesthetics of Murder: A Study of Romantic Literature and Contemporary Culture* (The Johns Hopkins University Press, 1991) and *The Reality Effect: Film Culture and the Graphic Imperative* (Routledge, 2002), as well as numerous essays on cultural and media studies. He is currently completing a study of the rise of criminal culture during the Prohibition era.

Alicia Borinsky is a scholar, fiction writer and poet. She writes in Spanish and in English and has been widely published in Europe, Latin America and the United States. Her most recent titles are *Low Blows/Golpes Bajos* (fiction) (University of Wisconsin Press, 2008), *Frivolous Women and Other Sinners/Frívolas y pecadoras* (poetry) (Swan Isle Press, 2009). *One Way Tickets, Contemporary Cultures of Migration and Exile* is due out in 2010 at Trinity University Press. She is the recipient of several awards, among them the Latino Award for Fiction (1996), and is Professor of Romance Studies and Director of the Writing in the Americas Program at Boston University.

Ray B. Browne, author and editor of some seventy books on American Culture and Folklore and crime fiction, co-founded the Popular Culture Association, and founded and edited the *Journal of Popular Culture*. He also founded the American Culture Association and edited the *Journal of American Culture*. He is currently Book Review Editor of the *Journal of American Culture*.

Ed Christian is an Assistant Professor of English at Kutztown University of Pennsylvania and has been teaching detective fiction for a decade. He has written or spoken on Dorothy L. Sayers, Chester Himes, and Ellis Peters, among many others. He published *Joyce Cary's Creative Imagination* in 1988 and edited *The Post-Colonial Detective* (Palgrave's Crime Files, 2001). He has taught English to graduate students in Beijing, served as a surgical supervisor of a hospital in Rwanda, and been a Fulbright Scholar at Oxford. In addition to detective fiction, he teaches courses in biblical literature and apocalyptic fiction.

Sarah Dauncey is an independent researcher. She received her PhD from the University of Warwick and specializes in the transactions between literature and forensic science. She is currently writing a monograph called *These Bones Can Talk: Twentieth Century Forensic Narratives*, which scrutinizes the role of forensic science in twentieth-century popular and literary fiction, and is co-editing a volume of essays entitled *Corpse Life: The Contemporary Preoccupation with Human Remains*.

Malcah Effron is a final year doctoral student at Newcastle University, England. Her thesis examines forms of self-referentiality in the detective genre. Her broader research interests include the intersection of narrative theory, metafiction and textuality in detective fiction. She has co-founded the Crime Studies Network in the North (CSNN) of England. Her publications include contributions to *The Encyclopedia of Popular Fiction* (2009) and an article forthcoming in *The Journal of Narrative Theory*.

Karen Fang is the author of *John Woo's* A Better Tomorrow, one of the "New Hong Kong Cinema" series from Hong Kong University Press (2004). An Associate Professor of English at the University of Houston, she also writes on British Romantic literature, and is currently at work on a book on policing in Hong Kong cinema.

Arthur Fried is a professor of English at Plymouth State University in New Hampshire, where he teaches courses in literature and film. He has taught at Plymouth State since 1982. He is interested in the historical development of the various popular media, and in relating their development to the social, political and economic trends of their time. He has been a fan of comic books and comic strips since he learned to read.

Philippa Gates is an Associate Professor in Film Studies at Wilfrid Laurier University, Canada. Her recent publications include *Detecting Men: Masculinity and the Hollywood Detective Film* (SUNY Press, 2006) and the co-edited collection *The Devil Himself: Villainy in Detective Fiction and Film* (Greenwood Press, 2002), as well as articles on aging action stars, the female detective in film noir, the film versions of *The Maltese Falcon*, and the contemporary Hollywood war film.

Adrienne E. Gavin is a Reader in English at Canterbury Christ Church University. Author of *Dark Horse: A Life of Anna Sewell*, she has edited Caroline Clive's *Paul Ferroll*, and is co-editor with Christopher Routledge of *Mystery in Children's Literature: From the Rational to the Supernatural* and with Andrew Humphries of *Childhood in Edwardian*

Fiction: Worlds Enough and Time. She is currently editing C. L. Pirkis's *The Experiences of Loveday Brooke, Lady Detective.*

Lauren Gillingham is Assistant Professor of English at the University of Ottawa. Her research focuses on nineteenth-century popular fiction such as the Newgate novel, silver-fork novel, and sensation fiction, with a particular interest in the figure of the criminal. She has a recent article in SEL on Jack Sheppard.

John Gruesser is Professor of English and Program Coordinator of the MA in Liberal Studies at Kean University. He has published articles on detective fiction by Edgar Allan Poe, Mark Twain, Pauline Hopkins, Chester Himes, Walter Mosley, and Valerie Wilson Wesley; is the author of three books, most recently *Confluences: Postcolonialism, African American Literary Studies and the Black Atlantic*; and has edited several books, including *The Black Sleuth* by John Edward Bruce and *However Improbable: Eighteen Great Stories of Detection, 1841–1940* (forthcoming from McFarland).

Nick Haeffner is Senior Lecturer in Communications at London Metropolitan University, where he teaches film and photography, and teaches Boston University students in the London Internship Programme. He is the author of *Alfred Hitchcock* (Pearson, 2005) and co-curator of *Re-Possessed*, a travelling new media exhibition inspired by Hitchcock's *Vertigo*. He is also currently an editor of *Vertigo* magazine.

Jasmine Yong Hall wrote her dissertation on women in crime fiction and published a seminal essay on Hammett ("Jameson, Genre, and Gumshoes: *The Maltese Falcon* as Inverted Romance") in *The Cunning Craft* (1990). She is Professor of English at Elms College, Massachusetts. Her fields of interest are Victorian and modern British fiction, literary criticism, and popular culture. She has published and presented papers in *Dickens Studies Annual* and *Studies in Short Fiction*, as well as in collections on Victorian literature and detective fiction.

Louise Harrington received a PhD in Renaissance Literature from Cardiff University in 2004. She has since taught at Cardiff University and the University of Glamorgan. A lifelong fan of crime fiction, she is now pursuing a career in librarianship.

John A. Hodgson is the Dean of Forbes College at Princeton University. His publications include *Sherlock Holmes: The Major Stories with Contemporary Critical Essays* (Bedford Books of St Martin's Press, 1994) as well as books on Wordsworth and on Coleridge and Shelley. He is currently writing a book – "Venting: Ventriloquism Becomes American" – on the rise of ventriloquism as a performing art.

Lee Horsley is Reader in Literature and Culture at Lancaster University, where she teaches two specialist crime courses and co-supervises numerous PhD students in both English Literature and Creative Writing. Her publications include *Political Fiction and the Historical Imagination* (Macmillan, 1990), *Fictions of Power in English Literature 1900–1950* (Longman, 1995) and *Twentieth-Century Crime Fiction* (Oxford University Press, 2005). An expanded paperback edition of *The Noir Thriller* (Palgrave, 2001) is being published in mid-2009. Lee also created and edits (jointly with

Katharine Horsley) one of the largest websites devoted to crime fiction and film, crimeculture.com.

Maurice S. Lee is an Associate Professor of English at Boston University. He is the author of *Slavery, Philosophy, and American Literature, 1830–1860* (Cambridge University Press, 2005) and the editor of *The Cambridge Companion to Frederick Douglass* (Cambridge University Press, 2009). He has published in such journals as *American Literature, PMLA, Raritan, and African American Review* and is currently working on a book about chance and nineteenth-century American literature.

Merja Makinen is Principal Lecturer at Middlesex University and Director of Programmes for the English Studies group. She works on twentieth-century fiction, particularly women's writing, gender and popular fiction. Her last few books include *Agatha Christie: Investigating Femininity* (Palgrave, 2006), *The Novels of Jeanette Winterson* (Palgrave, 2005), and *Feminist Popular Fiction* (Palgrave, 2001).

Andrew Mangham is a Lecturer in English literature at the University of Reading. He is the author of *Violent Women and Sensation Fiction: Crime, Medicine and Victorian Popular Culture* (2007) and editor of both *Wilkie Collins: Interdisciplinary Essays* (2007) and *The Female Body in Medicine and Literature* (2010).

Carl Malmgren teaches courses in the modern novel and literary theory at the University of New Orleans. He has written book-length studies of modern and postmodern fiction, science fiction, and mystery and detective fiction. He has just completed a mystery novel set in Paris in the 1920s.

William Marling is the author of five scholarly books, including *Dashiell Hammett* (1983), *Raymond Chandler* (1986), and *The American Roman Noir* (1996). His work on James M. Cain was featured in a BBC documentary. He is currently Professor of English at Case Western Reserve University in Cleveland, Ohio, USA.

Patricia Merivale, Professor [Emer.] of English and Comparative Literature at the University of British Columbia, Vancouver, BC, is the author of *Pan the Goat-God: His Myth in Modern Times* (Harvard University Press, 1969); co-editor of *Detecting Texts: The Metaphysical Detective Story from Poe to Postmodernism* (University of Pennsylvania Press, 1999); and author of three dozen articles on comparative topics. Current interests include, but are not limited to, Holocaust detective fictions, and Artist- and Eco-Parables of the Apocalypse.

Peter Messent is the Head of the School of American and Canadian Studies at the University of Nottingham. He edited the 1997 Pluto Press collection, *Criminal Proceedings: The Contemporary American Crime Novel*, and has written on Thomas Harris and Patricia Cornwell (among others). He also works – and has published widely – in the fields of late nineteenth-century and twentieth-century American literature and culture, and his latest book is on *Mark Twain and Male Friendship* (Oxford University Press, 2009).

Esme Miskimmin is an Honorary Fellow at the University of Liverpool with research interests in crime fiction and Renaissance drama. She is currently working on a monograph on Dorothy L. Sayers for the Liverpool University Press.

Alexander Moudrov received a PhD in Comparative Literature from The City University of New York's Graduate Center in 2009. His dissertation, *The Rise of the American Culture of Sensationalism: 1620–1860*, traces the formation of the American literary tradition by emphasizing its reliance on various forms of scandalous and provocative rhetoric. He teaches in the Department of Comparative Literature at Queens College (New York).

Jonathan Munby teaches in the Department of Media, Film and Cultural Studies at Lancaster University. He is the author of *Public Enemies, Public Heroes: Screening the Gangster Film from Little Caesar to Touch of Evil* (University of Chicago Press, 1999). His most recent publications focus on criminal self-representation in African-American popular culture.

Sue Neale is a doctoral student in the Department of French Studies at Warwick University. Her research concentrates on the alternative visions of French society in the fictions of archaeozoologist Fred Vargas. Sue has previously published papers on Daniel Pennac and Fred Vargas, and given papers at crime fiction conferences in Limerick (2007) and Newcastle (2008). In her spare time she is involved on the British editorial team of europolar.eu – a European crime fiction website.

Mark Desmond Nicholls is a Senior Lecturer in Cinema Studies at the University of Melbourne, Australia. He is author of *Scorsese's Men: Melancholia and the Mob* (Pluto Press and Indiana University Press, 2004) and recently published articles on Martin Scorsese, Luchino Visconti, Shakespeare in film and film and the Cold War. Mark writes a weekly film column in the *Melbourne Age* newspaper and is active as a theatre writer, director and producer.

Bran Nicol is Reader in Modern and Contemporary Literature at the University of Portsmouth, where he is also Director of the Centre for Studies in Literature. Recent publications include *Stalking* (Reaktion, 2006), an analysis of stalking in literature and film and *The Cambridge Introduction to Postmodern Fiction* (Cambridge University Press, 2009). He is currently working on *The Private Eye: Detectives in the Cinema* (Reaktion) and co-editing the collection *Crime Culture: Figuring Criminality in Literature and Film* (Continuum).

LeRoy Lad Panek is Professor of English at McDaniel College in Westminster, Maryland. He has written nine books on popular fiction, two of which have received Edgar Allan Poe Awards from the Mystery Writers of America. He has also received the George Dove Award for contributions to the serious study of popular fiction from the Popular Culture Association of America. He and a colleague are currently engaged in editing more than 700 pieces of short fiction printed in the US before 1891 to be published online as The Westminster Detective Library.

Andrew Pepper is the author of *The Contemporary American Crime Novel* (Edinburgh University Press, 2000) and co-author of *American History and Contemporary Hollywood Film* (Edinburgh University Press, 2005). He has written a series of crime novels set in mid-nineteenth century London including *The Last Days of Newgate* (Orion Books, 2006), *The Revenge of Captain Paine* (Orion Books, 2007) and *Kill-Devil and Water* (Orion Books, 2008). He is Lecturer in English and American literature at Queen's University Belfast.

Christopher Pittard is Senior Lecturer in English Literature at the University of Portsmouth. He has published widely on Victorian and popular culture, including contributions to *The Oxford History of the Novel in English 1880–1940* (2010), *Victorian Periodicals Review, Clues: A Journal of Detection* and *Women: A Cultural Review*. His work on Victorian crime narratives won the 2006 VanArsdel Prize for Victorian periodicals research, and will appear in his forthcoming book *Purity and Contamination in Late Victorian Detective Fiction* (Ashgate, 2011).

Heta Pyrhönen is Professor of Comparative Literature at the University of Helsinki. Her books include *Murder from an Academic Angle* (Camden House, 1994), *Mayhem and Murder: Narrative and Moral Problems in the Detective Story* (University of Toronto Press, 1999) and *Bluebeard Gothic: Jane Eyre and its Progeny* (forthcoming, 2010). Her essays have been published in such journals as *Mosaic, Textual Practice, Contemporary Women's Writing, Sign Systems Studies*, and *Cambridge Companion to Narrative*.

Christopher Routledge is a freelance writer, editor and lecturer based in Lancashire, UK. He is currently co-editing *100 American Crime Writers* and *100 British Crime Writers* for Palgrave's Crime Files series. He is online at http://chrisroutledge.co.uk.

Susan Rowland is Professor of English and Post-Jungian Studies at the University of Greenwich, UK. She is author of *From Agatha Christie to Ruth Rendell* (Palgrave, 2001) and publishes on detective fiction, myth, Jung, literature, and gender. As well as a study of detective fiction and myth forthcoming in *Clues*, she will publish a book on *Jung and the Humanities* in 2010.

Charles J. Rzepka is Professor of English at Boston University, where he teaches and writes on topics in British Romanticism, popular culture, and detective and crime fiction. His books include *The Self as Mind* (Harvard University Press, 1986), *Sacramental Commodities* (University of Massachusetts Press, 1995), and *Detective Fiction* (Polity Press, 2005). In addition to editing the *Blackwell Companion*, he is currently at work on two book-length projects: a history of the emergence the ethnic detective in the early twentieth century, and a study of the relationship between the genre of detection and lyrical "difficulty" in Romantic, Victorian, and early Modernist poetry.

David Schmid is an Associate Professor in the Department of English at the University at Buffalo, where he teaches courses in British and American fiction, cultural studies, and popular culture. He has published on a variety of subjects, including the nonfiction novel, celebrity, and film adaptation and is the author of *Natural*

Born Celebrities: Serial Killers in American Culture (University of Chicago Press, 2005). He is currently working on a book entitled *From the Locked Room to the Globe: Space in Crime Fiction.*

David Seed holds a chair in American Literature at Liverpool University. He has published *American Science Fiction and the Cold War* (Edinburgh University Press, 1999) and *Brainwashing* (Kent State University Press, 2004) including books on a number of individual writers such as Heller and Pynchon. In 2005 he edited the *Blackwell Companion to Science Fiction.*

Philip Shaw is Professor of Romantic Studies at the University of Leicester. His publications include: *Patti Smith: Horses* (Continuum, 2008), *The Sublime* (Routledge, 2006), *Waterloo and the Romantic Imagination* (Palgrave Macmillan, 2002), as editor, *Romantic Wars: Studies in Culture and Conflict, 1789–1822* (Palgrave Macmillan, 2000) and, as co-editor with Vincent Newey, *Mortal Pages, Literary Lives: Studies in Nineteenth-Century Autobiography* (Scolar Press, 1996). At present he is working on a book-length art historical study entitled *Suffering and Sentiment in Romantic Military Art* and is a co-investigator for the AHRC-funded Tate Research project *The Sublime Object.* He is Reviews Editor of *The Byron Journal* and in 2008 was elected a Fellow of the English Association.

Alain Silver wrote *The Samurai Film*, with Elizabeth Ward *Raymond Chandler's Los Angeles* and *The Film Director's Team*, a dozen other books with James Ursini, and co-edited six Readers on film noir, horror and gangster films as well as four editions of *Film Noir: An Encyclopedia Reference.* His articles have appeared in *Film Comment, Movie, Wide Angle*, anthologies on *The Philosophy of Film Noir, Kurosawa*, and the Hummer and the online magazines *Images* and *Senses of Cinema.* His produced screenplays include Dostoevsky's *White Nights* and the Showtime MOW *Time at the Top.* He has also produced a score of independent feature films and over forty soundtrack albums. His commentaries may be heard and seen on numerous DVDs discussing the classic period of noir, Raymond Chandler, *Double Indemnity, The Dirty Dozen, The French Connection* and the gangster film. His PhD in motion picture critical studies is from UCLA.

Philip Simpson received his doctorate in American Literature from Southern Illinois University in 1996. He serves as Associate Provost at the Palm Bay campus of Brevard Community College in Florida. Before that, he was a Professor of Communications and Humanities at the Palm Bay campus of Brevard Community College for eight years and Department Chair of Liberal Arts for five years. He also served as President of the Popular Culture Association and Area Chair of Horror for the Association. He received the Association's Felicia Campbell Area Chair Award in 2006. He sits on the editorial board of the *Journal of Popular Culture.* His book, *Psycho Paths: Tracking the Serial Killer through Contemporary American Film and Fiction*, was published in 2000 by Southern Illinois University Press. He is the author of numerous other essays on film, literature, popular culture, and horror.

Stephen Soitos is a writer and artist living in Western Massachusetts. He has an MFA and PhD from the University of Massachusetts. He is the author of *Blues Detective: A Study of African American Detective Fiction* and many essays on American writers and artists. He can be contacted at stephensoitos@yahoo.com or at Soitos.com.

Catherine Spooner is Senior Lecturer in English Literature at Lancaster University, UK. She is the author of *Fashioning Gothic Bodies* (Manchester University Press, 2004), *Contemporary Gothic* (Reaktion, 2006) and the co-editor, with Emma McEvoy, of *The Routledge Companion to Gothic* (Routledge, 2007). She is currently working on a series of articles about Gothic, fashion and consumer culture from the Victorian period to the present.

James Ursini co-wrote *The Noir Style, L.A. Noir, The Vampire Film, More Things than Are Dreamt Of, Film Noir* (Taschen) and directed studies of David Lean, Robert Aldrich, and Roger Corman with Alain Silver. His other books include *Modern Amazons, Cinema of Obsession*, and monographs on Bogart, Dietrich, Elizabeth Taylor, Mae West, and Robert DeNiro for the Taschen Icon series. A bilingual reprint of his seminal book on Preston Sturges was published by the San Sebastián Film Festival. Articles have appeared in *Photon, Cinefantastique, Midnight Marquee*, and the *DGA Magazine*. His DVD commentaries include *Out of the Past, The Dark Corner, Nightmare Alley, Lady in the Lake, Kiss of Death, Brute Force* and *Crossfire*. He holds a Masters from UCLA, has been a producer on feature films and documentaries, and lectured on film-making at UCLA and at other colleges in the Los Angeles area where he works as an educator.

Heather Worthington is Senior Lecturer in English Literature at Cardiff University, where she teaches nineteenth- and twentieth-century crime fiction and children's literature. The author of *The Rise of the Detective in Early Nineteenth-Century Popular Fiction* (Palgrave, 2005), she is currently working on a second monograph, *Shadowing Sherlock Holmes: Crime Fiction 1850–1900*. She has also written on T. H. White's *The Once and Future King*, Bulwer-Lytton's early fiction, and Chesterton's *The Man Who Was Thursday*.

Introduction: What Is Crime Fiction?

Charles J. Rzepka

To say that crime fiction is fiction about crime is not only tautological, it also raises a host of problems, beginning with the definitions of "crime" and "fiction." Do all stories in which crimes are featured qualify? Incest and patricide and infanticide are crimes, but not many theorists of the genre would argue for reading Oedipus or Medea mainly as characters in a work of crime fiction. Brother Ambrosio, diabolical antihero of Matthew Lewis's *The Monk* (1798), rapes and murders with impunity and, like Oedipus, discovers only as his soul is about to be cast into hell that in doing so he has also committed incest and matricide. Yet *The Monk*, while clearly part of a tradition closely allied to crime fiction (see Spooner, chapter 19 in this volume), falls just outside our categorical understanding of the genre. The identifying features of Gothic and crime fiction overlap in substantial ways, but the traditions are not coterminous. Some crime fiction is Gothic, but not all Gothic literature is crime fiction. Closer to our own place and time, *Tess of the D'Urbervilles* traces the circumstances driving its eponymous heroine to a gruesome murder, for which she is arrested, tried, and hanged. Yet, you will not find *Tess* mentioned anywhere else in this book. Transgressions alone do not crime fiction make. Sin does not rate, generally, or violent or even illegal acts, per se, but the degree to which their illegality features in the plot. Tess's arrest, trial, and execution are almost perfunctory in Thomas Hardy's desolate novel. In crime fiction, the state penal code matters more than the Ten Commandments, and the threat of arrest and punishment more than the prospect of hell.

And what about "fiction"? The dozens of "confessions," testimonies, and court-proceedings appearing in the oft-reprinted *Newgate Calendar* and its knock-offs throughout the eighteenth century and well into the nineteenth, along with the hundreds of ephemeral broadsides and printed ballads hawked at public hangings in England (until such events were sequestered behind prison walls in 1868), confirm the enduring appeal of true crime narratives. Heather Worthington, writing on the early origins of the genre, is not the only contributor to this *Companion* to reflect on the feedback loop between "true" and fictional crime narratives. In the New World,

Alexander Moudrov tells us, seventeenth-century Puritan ministers sowed the seeds of a flourishing American crop of crime literature with their monitory execution sermons and pamphlets (chapter 9). True crime is a "pop culture phoenix" (Schmid, chapter 15), waxing and waning in popularity, but never going out of style. Perhaps its popularity has something to do with the legendary aura it inevitably lends its celebrities, elevating them, like the heroes of ancient epic, to something approaching mythic status: transcending human history, they seem hybrids of gods (or demons) and men. This liminal status is what made villains and outlaws like Eugene Aram and Jack Sheppard so easily appropriated by the writers of Newgate novels described by Lauren Gillingham in these pages, and helps explain the "fear of social contamination and instability" they generated among more censorious critics as they strode from the pubs and gin palaces of a proletarian readership into the genteel drawing rooms of the educated middle-class. "The potential for identification with criminal heroes" like Jack Sheppard, explicitly affirmed by B. F. Courvoisier after he murdered Lord William Russell (Gillingham, chapter 6), seems a perpetual one. This too, of course, is a phenomenon too universal to be confined within clearly delineated generic boundaries. "The dream was teaching the dreamers how to live," wrote Joan Didion in *Esquire* as late as 1964, noting how closely the murder of a San Bernardino dentist conformed to the novels of James M. Cain (Didion 1968: 17).

Perhaps "Crime Writings" would better fit the remit for this *Companion*. It would allow us to include, without apology or casuistic hair-splitting, essays like Thomas De Quincey's seminal "Murder Considered as One of the Fine Arts," neither fiction nor a true crime "tale," but perhaps the earliest, if facetious, theoretical reflection on our attraction to, and tendencies to aestheticize, violence. Joel Black notes the essay's affinities with works of "high" literature by Stendahl and Dostoevsky (chapter 5), the kind of writing that, along with *Tess*, we like to distinguish from crime fiction. But De Quincey, despite his immense learning, was a truant, dope addict, and college drop-out, which gives him some credibility, one would think, as a habitué of the literary, as well as literal, mean streets. "Crime Writings" would also comprise the *Mémoirs* of Eugène-François Vidocq, a mish-mash of autobiography, plagiarism, ghost-writing, fable, and picaresque braggadocio that set the standard for the French *roman policier* and the police casebook literature to follow.

If the term "crime fiction" is a bit vague, "detective fiction" is downright slippery. We are tempted, initially, to place the latter under the voluminous umbrella of the former. But crime fiction itself seems to straddle some gaping generic divides. Forty years ago, John Cawelti distinguished three main categories or "archetypes" of popular literature that, despite ensuing gusts of critical turbulence, have managed to remain upright: Adventure, Romance, and Mystery. While literary detection clearly belongs to the Mystery archetype, it is difficult to place most crime stories there because so few of them involve any real mystery: whoever "dunit" is never in question, and many fans of crime fiction in general find the elaborate puzzle-plots of classical detective writers like Agatha Christie or John Dickson Carr an irritating distraction from their enjoyment of the chase and pursuit, the mind-games, the close scrapes, and the threats (or enactment) of gruesome violence that are the stock-in-trade of *noir* or gangster or "caper" novels. While the classical detective's need "to examine the motives and hence the psyches of potential suspects" makes the whodunit a precursor of genres like the psycho-thriller, so-called "hard-boiled" detective fiction was as much an "amalgam of the traditional structures of popular American fiction (such as the adventure story and Western)" as an off-shoot of literary detection (Simpson, chapter 14).

Most crime fiction actually belongs to Cawelti's Adventure archetype, along with Westerns, war stories, and tales of exploration, where suspense tends to be more physical than intellectual. If we take such fellow travelers at face value, we find a pretty sharp gender demarcation between readerships for Romance (female) and Adventure (male), with detection lurking in the intermediate category of Mystery. This demarcation is reflected internally as well, in detection's split between classical models, where, as Susan Rowland reminds us, the techniques of investigation are "feminized" (chapter 8) by being made more intuitive and psychological, and the "hard-boiled" school of Dashiell Hammett and Raymond Chandler, where the detective more often gets results by provoking a response (often two-fisted) from suspects. Hard-boiled authors were generally less inclined to let girls into their club than were classical authors to let the boys "play house." As Andrew Pepper notes, however, the apparent masculinist, even sexist, bias of traditional hard-boiled detection is less a display of arrogance than a confession of frailty, a defensive reaction against the threat to male agency posed by growing state power during "the postwar reorganization of America's social and economic life" (chapter 10).

In both hard-boiled and classical detection, mystery tends to trump adventure, and readers expect to be invited to solve the case – to find out who left the body in the library or the lady in the lake – along with the detective. The puzzle-element, in other words, is difficult to dismiss, even in works by notoriously tough, "realistic" writers like Hammett and Chandler. Not that the reader ever really expects to solve the case before the detective explains it all, any more than most of us expect to solve the Sunday *New York Times* crossword puzzle. It is what Edgar Allen Poe, the "onlie begetter" of detective fiction, called the sheer delight of "analysis," the "activity that *disentangles*," that attracts fans of literary detection (Poe 1984: 397). And just like those earliest pioneers in nascent sciences like geology and paleontology who were Poe's contemporaries (and whom Poe himself read avidly), what we seek to disentangle is *pre-history*, a series of events that is assumed to have taken place before the beginning of the "written record" – the story into which we find ourselves plunged (Rzepka 2005: 36–7). The point of the puzzle element is to enable readers not to solve the crime but to exercise their retrospective imaginations. As we read forward, we imagine backward, analeptically.

If, as Heta Pyrhönen observes, "detective fiction has invited a great deal more critical discussion than crime fiction" (chapter 3), it may be because this analeptically engaging feature of the detective plot has made it so much more interesting to theorists of language, form, and representation – to narratologists, structuralists, and postmodernists – than crime fiction in general. Carl Malmgren's close "functional" analysis of the syntax of character in detective and crime fiction (chapter 11) epitomizes such formal or structural approaches, with illuminating consequences for our understanding of subgeneric distinctions and their relation to narrative archetypes. Cultural and ideological critics, too, have found much to say about how detective fiction's valorizations of rationality and the law deploy "specific strategies for legitimating the power of dominant social groups" (Pyrhönen, chapter 3). As Alicia Borinsky shows with respect to Jorge Luis Borges's delicate metaphysical riddles (chapter 37) and Patricia Merivale with respect to metaphysical detection in general (chapter 24), even the most sophisticated postmodernist "play" with the classical form can, for this reason, lead to searing reflections on injustice and atrocity: racism, oppression, the Holocaust, the "disappeared."

In the first two chapters of this *Companion*, Heather Worthington and Lee Horsley provide a detailed historical map of the empire of crime fiction within which detective literature eventually established a homeland, or rather "Holmesland," with the metropolis of "Doyle" becoming its eventual capital and perpetual hub of influence. (It is not by accident that both contributors should begin with Doyle's famous monographer on tobacco ash, or that he should provide the pivot point and bridge between them.) Along the way they have surveyed numerous territories within the empire at large – the Newgate novel, the sensation novel, the classical puzzler, hard-boiled detection, *noir*, the psycho-thriller – that our subsequent contributors map with more attention to detail in their individual treatments of some of the genre's most notable "Artists at Work": Poe, Christie, Hammett, Chandler, Himes, Hitchock, among many others. As important as all of these writers and filmmakers are, however, the pivotal figure in any survey of crime fiction's extensive domain was and is Arthur Conan Doyle.

Doyle was the omega of detective fiction's century-long emergence from crime fiction in general, and the alpha of its triumphant march into the golden age of literary detection, the 1920s and 30s. He lived to see its triumph, but not its subsequent usurpation by proletarian sleuths like Hammett's Sam Spade and Chandler's Philip Marlowe, or deranged anti-heroes like James M. Cain's Frank Chambers or Patricia Highsmith's Tom Ripley. Writing on Doyle is, for this reason, a daunting task for most of us, but one that John Hodgson completes with grace and insight, revealing an ideologically skeptical expression missing from most critical portraits informed by class or gender analysts (chapter 31). Doyle was the crucial synthesizer of an emergent tradition, but he was also his own man. And he took care to build on solid foundations, borrowing much of his material from overseas: principally from Emile Gaboriau in France and Edgar Allan Poe in America.

Poe was the fountainhead of both the classic "locked room" puzzle ("The Murders in the Rue Morgue") and the crime caper of dueling wits ("The Purloined Letter"), but was he personally as important to later developments as critics take him to be? Maurice Lee suggests that Poe's "tales of ratiocination come less from individual inspiration and more from a set of cultural forces: if Poe had never invented detective fiction, Dickens or Victor Hugo would have" (chapter 29). One of those cultural forces was William Godwin's 1794 novel, *Caleb Williams*. Philip Shaw explains how Godwin hoisted the well-worn fabric of *Newgate Calendar* lore to catch the winds of reform in a period of political repression and war abroad to create a tale of flight, pursuit, and systemic corruption that was not only to inspire the Newgate novel and Poe's ratiocinative improvisations, but anticipate the hopelessness and paranoia of modern *noir* by more than a century.

Even with all his debts to literary precursors and cultural trends, says Lee, "Poe was the right person at the right place and time to establish a new kind of crime fiction" (chapter 29). Though his streams of influence flowed largely underground for several decades, they fed not only Doyle's work but that of countless later writers.

At the same time, the emerging genre was stimulated from numerous other sources. Christopher Pittard explains how, between 1860 and 1890, the penny dreadful and the sensation novel helped prepare the way for Doyle's masterful generic syntheses (chapter 7), and Andrew Mangham shows how one sensation novelist in particular, Wilkie Collins, gave crime fiction a decisive turn toward puzzle-oriented, book-length detection with *The Moonstone*, while tapping into the deepest sexual and class anxieties of his era (chapter 30). Historical developments in forensic science and courtroom procedure were also influential, as Sarah Dauncey demonstrates, not only over the latter half of the nineteenth century but well into our own, where they are still shaping readers' expectations and writers' representational strategies.

Although afficionadoes may quibble over who among the scores of later crime and detective fiction writers of note should be given pride of place, we find, as we move into the post-Holmes era, some whose influence is beyond question. Susan Rowland prepares us to negotiate the unstable rubble of the Great War shifting uneasily beneath the sunny lawns of the golden age, seeing its "social scene as a metonym for the wasteland of modernity" (chapter 8), with the detective figure as Grail Legend hero – or more often, heroine. Focusing on this period's dominant figure, Merja Makinen gives us a parodic and playful Agatha Christie, sensitive to cultural change and social instability, who challenges rather than endorses the racial and class assumptions of her characters (chapter 33), while Esme Miskimmins's Dorothy Sayers brings to bear on her Lord Peter Wimsey stories all the moral complexity and religious seriousness that so light and brittle a container can carry without crushing her protagonist's indomitable, and ironically reflexive, wit (chapter 35). The deeply religious Sayers stopped writing detective fiction as the wasteland of modernity became ever more arid in the 1930s, but her evolution toward a more challenging, fully novelistic form was carried forward by her High Anglican epigone, P. D. James, who has pushed the puzzle-element about as far in the direction of depth psychology and theological consequence as it can go without achieving generic escape velocity. Louise Harrington shows us in James a bleakly pessimistic moralist as serious – and as intellectually challenging – as Jane Austen, one whose rigorous quest for God in a soulless world often seems to run counter to modern feminism's quest for self-affirmation and fulfillment (chapter 40).

The figures lurking in the trans-Atlantic shadow of the golden age – hard-boiled private investigators (PIs), *noir* drifters, gangsters, psycho-killers, renegade cops, and all the other fugitives of the Enlightenment that the "War to End all Wars" had promised to eradicate, or reform – are well represented in the *Companion*, but hardly of one mind. For one thing, hard-boiled writers like Hammett and Chandler seldom represented as "objective" or "realistic" an alternative to the artificiality and social conformism of the golden age as they pretended; nor did they participate in a single and coherent literary movement. Each man's achievement was distinctive (Pepper, chapter 10). Hammett's, as Jasmine Hall shows us, was to transform the pre-War world of meaningful motives and things into a universe of meaningless bodies and objects, recoverable for human purposes only through story-telling (chapter 36). Chandler's world, by contrast, is made significant through the voice of his sentimental, wise-cracking detective hero, Philip Marlowe. Over many years, as Leroy Panek shows us, Chandler perfected the bizarre but apt one-liners that, through their unexpected metaphoric juxtapositions, knitted together the disparate elements of the entropic universe that Hammett had left him. For Chandler, hard-boiled was an "attitude," "decidedly more psychological than physical" (Panek, chapter 32), or for that matter, philosophical, as it was for his predecessor.

But while PIs like Marlowe were trying to bring light to darkness (a sometimes hopeless task), other writers were actively seeking the shade. James M. Cain wrote so frankly about violence and sex that his writing provoked bans in Boston and condemnation from Chandler himself. William Marling traces Cain's career and discovers a canny series of choices and innovations, including the perfection of a first-person confessional point of view and an emphasis on sex and consumerism that were to become staples of *noir* (chapter 34). The work of David Goodis, as David Schmid argues, pushed these and other features of the genre so far as to become almost self-parodic, while at the same time turning the hard-guy *noir* hero inside-out, into a "wounded and vulnerable" male protagonist (chapter 15). In Patricia Highsmith's hands, the genre reached new heights of dissociation and sociopathy, intensified, if anything, by her attention to the quotidian. "At the heart of her plots," writes Bran Nicol, "is an emphasis on the destructive power of individual desire … and an exposure of how fragile and inconsequential are the moral codes that structure liberal-democratic society" (chapter 41). Even in the darkest reaches of *noir*, however, identification with the criminal protagonist remains intact. It is this feature, fractured into multiple perspectives, that the reigning king and court jester of *noir*, Elmore Leonard, deploys with precision, ease, and speed. As I try to show in my chapter on his achievement, the souls of Leonard's characters can often be lost, captured as in a magical mirror, under the centrifugal pull of these rapidly shifting, and self-alienating, points of view (chapter 42).

Crime and detective fiction have always displayed strong tendencies toward both fission and fusion. Distinct subgenres abound, such as the police procedural, covered here by Peter Messent, and its asymmetrical opposite, the gangster and mob saga, which Jonathan Munby sees as, among other things, a cynical allegory of American capitalism (chapter 16). What the two forms have most in common might well be what Messent calls "the institutional and systemic framework" (chapter 13) they foreground, where hierarchical authority, individual agency, trust, and teamwork produce a complex and dependable engine of suspense. The same could be said for crime's internationalist cousin, spy fiction, although, as David Seed points out, disguise and impersonation probably account for most of the generic overlap, as demonstrated in some of Doyle's Sherlock Holmes stories (chapter 18). Spy stories as well as detective tales comprise not only a sizable, but a vital portion of juvenile literature, and for good reason: "For many child detectives," writes Christopher Routledge, "the pursuit of criminals also involves the exploration of their relationships with adults, with their understanding of the world, and with their own identities" (chapter 25). Catherine Spooner shows us the rich potential for hybridization when Gothic meets gumshoe (chapter 19), and Ray Browne explores one of the most popular subgenres allied to Gothic's roots in the pre-modern past, the historical crime or detective novel (chapter 17).

Not just with respect to other genres, but also in other media, crime and detective fiction have proven to be robust cross-pollinators. Arthur Fried's tour of mass mediation traverses comic strips, crime comics, and graphic novels, showing a diversity of themes and moral attitudes emerging over the better part of a century, from the Gump family to Batman (chapter 26). Alain Silver and James Ursini attend to the moving image over the same period, in television as well as film, providing a broad panorama of the evolution of violence as theme and topic on screens big and small (chapter 4). Philippa Gates focuses our attention more closely on the cinematic representation of the investigative process and its players: private detectives both classical and hard-boiled, police detectives procedural and action-oriented, lawyers, the academic "criminalists," and their unconventional female and non-white counterparts (chapter 27).

As in literary crime and detection, so in cinematic: the choice of outstanding exemplars is dismayingly wide. Alfred Hitchcock, however, must head the list in the English speaking world. Nick Haeffner reveals not only the biographical sources of the macabre and outré in the all-time master of celluloid suspense, but helps us understand the particularly British cast to his sense of humor, and appreciate his anomalous talent for romantic comedy as well (chapter 45). A giant who anchors the more recent history of the genre is Martin Scorsese, whose "anthopologist's" attention to "the full range of customs and manners of those who engage in the business of crime and punishment," along with a flair for the melodramatic, has made him the foremost exponent of the "themes of male desire" (Nicholls, chapter 46) on screen. One indication of the international reach of American cinematic crime is the work of John Woo, in whose films, as Karen Fang explains, "a contemporary interest in gunplay and pyrotechnics" is seamlessly fused, through the generic conventions of the *ying xiong pian*, or Hong Kong "hero movies," with "a narrative focus upon traditional and even anachronistic values" rooted in a cultural history far removed from Scorsese's American mean streets (chapter 47).

As Fang's analysis demonstrates, amalgamation, not mere imitation, may be the sincerest form of flattery, and that process characterizes the concomitant challenges and appropriations that have been taking place in so-called "alternative" detection (Rzepka 2005: 235) for the last three decades. Feminist crime literature offers a well-defined field for Adrienne Gavin's examination of female agency, both criminal and investigative, from the antebellum period to the present day, despite increasing areas of overlap with issues of race and class in recent years (chapter 20). By way of example, Malcah Effron examines in considerable detail the generic transformations in method, affect, and life-style, as well as the reorientation of attention to demands for social justice, brought about by Sara Paretsky's Chicago PI, V. I. Warshawsky (chapter 43). The number and variety of nationalities, races, and ethnicities that, since the 1960s, have been speaking truth to the power of the traditional white, male PI or police detective prohibits anything approaching a comprehensive treatment of alternative racial or ethnic detection. This is a major development, and the editors of the *Companion* have aimed for a representative approach, focusing on the African-American detective tradition along with two of its foremost practitioners, early and late: Chester Himes and Walter Mosley.

The historical roots of African-American detection and crime fiction run deeper and spread wider than those of any other ethnic or racial subset of the genre. Frankie Bailey (chapter 21), herself a mystery writer as well as a professor of criminal justice, is well positioned to trace both the literary origins of the black sleuth and his or her changing cultural, political, and socio-economic contexts for the last century or more, teasing out the delicate negotiations engaged in by black writers to this day between the "cultural vernacular" of race (spiritual, linguistic, artistic) and the generic expectations raised by mainstream, white crime and detective fiction. Chester Himes, the pioneer of hard-boiled black police procedurals, African-American *noir*, and racial surrealism on two continents, found the negotiations more difficult than his epigone, Walter Mosley. Stephen Soitos (chapter 38) explains the sources of frustration shaping the Harlem novels of the former, and John Gruesser (chapter 44) reveals the resources – personal, historical, literary, and cultural – that have helped the latter incorporate and display these intractable difficulties for recognition and analysis in his Easy Rawlins and Fearless Jones series.

While African-American detection dominates the ethnic and racial subcategories of detection and crime, it is only one of the many forms that non-white, non-Western crime fiction can take in a global context. In the present volume, Ed Christian (chapter 22) has addressed the vast generic region of domestic ethnic and racial detection in his survey of postcolonial, Anglophone crime literature, tackling the difficult task of summarizing, within severe spatial constraints, the obstacles, opportunities, and strategies of both postcolonial and ethnic crime writing, and their wide variety of achievements. Sue Neale, in her chapter on non-Anglophone crime and detection in translation, includes postcolonial writers like Patrick Chamoiseau but, in keeping with the *Companion*'s emphasis on the Anglo-American tradition, has focused on French developments impacting on writers in English, as well as European writers influenced in turn by British and American authors (chapter 23).

The proliferation of alternative types of crime and detective fiction in the last three or four decades indicates the demographic reach and global promise of this popular genre. It also defeats any attempt at complete coverage. Gay and lesbian as well as trans-gendered protagonists, for instance, are under-represented in these pages, along with Japanese *manga* and cellphone novels, transgressor-centered black crime fiction, cross-over genres like the *noir* Western or hybrids of crime and science fiction, not to mention the many, and popular, forms of comedy to which the genres of crime and detection have given rise, not only in print (e.g., the late Douglas Adams's series featuring Dirk Gently and his "holistic" methods), but also on screen (Inspector Clouseau's several iterations) and vinyl (Firesign Theater's hophead radio parodies of Chandler in "Nick Danger, Third Eye" and Doyle in "The Giant Rat of Sumatra"). Regrettable as these omissions may be, they constitute a pledge of sorts to fans, friends, and scholars, both now and to come: here is a body of achievement worth a lifetime of devotion – compelling, complex, demanding, inexhaustible.

Part I

History, Criticism, Culture

1

From *The Newgate Calendar* to Sherlock Holmes

Heather Worthington

In Arthur Conan Doyle's first Sherlock Holmes story, *A Study in Scarlet* (1887), Dr Watson is introduced to Holmes by Stamford, an ex-colleague from Bart's (St Bartholomew's Hospital, London). Stamford and Watson find Holmes conducting an experiment which, he declares, will reliably identify bloodstains. Such a discovery would have proved the guilt of any number of murderers, he tells them: "Von Bischoff ... Mason ... Muller ... Lefevre ... Samson ... I could name a score of cases in which it would have been decisive." Stamford responds by saying that Holmes seems "to be a walking calendar of crime" (Doyle 1986: 1.8), using "calendar" to mean a list or directory and admiring Holmes's encyclopedic knowledge of criminal biography. But the word is also applicable to the list of prisoners for trial at an assizes and it is in this sense that, in the eighteenth century, the title "The Newgate Calendar" came into being. Separated by over a century, the late nineteenth-century Holmes narratives and those of *The Newgate Calendar* nonetheless share common ground in their focus on crime, criminality and the criminal individual. But *The Newgate Calendar* is a collection of factual criminal biographies; the Sherlock Holmes stories are fictional representations of criminal cases in which the detective solves the crime and identifies the perpetrator. The format, structure, and function of the two crime narratives are very different and the criminographic developments which occurred in the years that separate them are a major part of the history of the crime fiction genre and the subject of this chapter.

Beginnings

While the figure of Sherlock Holmes requires no introduction, *The Newgate Calendar* is perhaps less familiar to the student of crime fiction. It is the name given to a number of eighteenth- and nineteenth-century texts that comprised collections of criminal biographies and it derives from London's Newgate Prison, where criminals were lodged before their trial and (often) execution. The Chaplain, or "Ordinary" of Newgate, produced reports, or "*Accounts*," of the lives, crimes, confessions, and executions of the criminals under his care, which were published as cheap pamphlets. There was a ready market for such narratives; literature concerned with crime has always sold well to the public. Publishers began to produce major anthologies of the existing Ordinaries' *Accounts*, many of which are now thought of generically as *Newgate Calendars*. According to Stephen Knight, "there was a medium one in 1728, another small one in 1748, then a large and purposefully collected five-volume version in 1773" (Knight 2004: 6). Various editions continued to appear into the nineteenth century, under various names: *The Malefactor's Register or the Newgate and Tyburn Calendar* in 1779; the *New and Complete Calendar* in 1795, a heavily revised version of which, edited by lawyers Andrew Knapp and William Baldwin, was published in 1809 and again, re-revised, as *The New Newgate Calendar* in 1826.

The *Accounts* and *Newgate Calendar* narratives were overtly and heavily moralistic. The format was fairly constant: individual stories consisted of a frame narrative that is religious in the *Accounts* and early collected editions written by the Ordinary but which in the later versions edited by lawyers became more legalistic. Within that frame is what purported to be the criminal's own confessional and repentant story. A typical example of a criminal biography is that of Mary Young, alias Jenny Diver, hanged in 1740. The Ordinary gives a brief and biased history of Mary's life which is followed by Mary's first-person confession followed by a mini-biography which, strangely, is in the third person, as if Mary seeks to dissociate herself from her criminal past. In what is a common pattern, Mary is an orphan, born and raised in Ireland. She learns to read and write and to sew, but refuses to conform to social expectations, rejecting her hometown to seek her fortune in London. Once there, she finds herself unable to make an honest living from sewing and is led into a life of crime, joining a criminal gang and rising to be their leader. The narrative relates the various crimes carried out by the gang and the ruses they use in their thievery. One feature intended to attract middle-class readers is the *Calendar*'s translation of the thieves' language, or "cant" for the benefit of the reader. Almost an entertaining romp, Mary's story makes criminal life seem exciting and profitable, and the basically factual account reads more like a fiction written to entertain. The narrative is eventually folded back into the religious and moralistic frame and ends by describing Mary's repentant demeanor prior to execution and the hanging itself before finally closing with the words, "She confessed the fact for which she died for [*sic*]" (Rawlings 1992: 134).

The narrative patterns in Mary Young's *Account* are typical of tales in *The Newgate Calendar*. The confession, explicit or implicit, in the criminal's story served to validate the death sentence and demonstrate the efficiency of the penal system, reassuring the reader that crime could and would be contained and deterring the potential criminal with the apparent certainty of punishment. But it was the entertainment factor, a combination of the often exciting life of the criminal and the voyeuristic pleasures of reading about sensational crime and punishment, that sold the criminal biographies to the public. In reality, many of the *Accounts* and the stories in *The Newgate Calendar* are prosaic reports of theft or other common crimes punishable by death in the eighteenth and early nineteenth centuries. However, the texts sold on their promise of sensationalism.

The *Calendar* anthologies were expensive, limiting their audience to the higher social classes. Satisfying the demand for similar material at the lower end of the market, even cheaper than the *Accounts* and published simultaneously, were the broadsides and ballad sheets. Ballad sheets had their origins in the sixteenth century when the development of printing technology made possible the rapid publication of matters of public interest, or what is now called news, and crime and execution were frequent topics. The ballad was printed on a single sheet, often illustrated, making it affordable and attractive to its intended, often semi-literate, lower-class audience. As news began to appear in prose rather than verse form, the ballad sheet was joined by the broadside.

Broadsides covered the same topics and were aimed at the same audience as the printed ballads but were written in prose. The most popular were the criminal or execution broadsides that offered, in reduced form, criminal biographies similar to those in *The Newgate Calendar*. While paying lip service to the moral and religious aspects of representing criminality, the execution broadsides were in fact an unapologetic commodification of crime, using sensational crime and criminal lives to make maximum profits. The ballad form lingered on in the easily memorized "verses" that accompanied many of the criminal and execution broadsides, often with a suggestion for an appropriate accompanying tune which would be sung by the street "patterer," or broadside vendor, to tempt people into buying. And, as an anonymous patterer noted, "nothing beats a stunning good murder" (Mayhew 1967 [1851]: 223). Take, for example, the case of John Gleeson Wilson, executed in 1849 for the murder of two women and children:

> The surgeon thus describes the scene presented to his view,
> A more appalling case than this he says he never knew,
> Four human beings on the floor all weltering in their gore,
> The sight was sickening to behold on entering the door.

> The mother's wounds three inches deep upon her head and face,
> And pools of blood as thick as mud, from all of them could trace,
> None could identify the boy, his head was like a jelly;
> This tragedy is worse by far than Greenacre or Kelly.
>   (Hindley 1969 [1871]: 197)

When no new murders were committed, old ones would be reprinted or apocryphal tales such as *The Liverpool Tragedy*, in which an elderly couple murder their unrecognized son for his money, would be revisited and passed off as factual narratives. With the emphasis on entertainment, the distinction between fact and fiction in crime narratives, whether in the expensive *Newgate Calendar* anthologies or the broadsides, becomes increasingly unclear.

The development of crime fiction is inextricably linked with the rise of the novel, which is generally considered to have become a recognized literary form in 1719 with Daniel Defoe's *Robinson Crusoe* (Watt 1957). Defoe, a journalist, writer, and spy, spent time in Newgate Prison for political offences and wrote a number of biographies of famous criminals, including notorious housebreaker Jack Sheppard (1724) and the infamous "Thief-Taker General," Jonathan Wild. After the fashion of the *Newgate Calendars* and Ordinaries' *Accounts*, Defoe's *The True and Genuine Account of the Life and Actions of the Late Jonathan Wild* (1725), was, the writer claimed, "taken from [Wild's] own mouth, and collected from papers of his own writing" (quoted in Fielding 1986 [1743]: 221). The narrative is indeed factual, but the novelistic style and structure and the careful selection of the more entertaining aspects of Wild's dual career as simultaneously thief and quasi-detective locate the text more as prototype than as full-fledged crime fiction.

Defoe had previously used crime in fiction when he wrote the pseudo-autobiographical *Moll Flanders* (1722). This followed the narrative structure of the criminal biography, and the eponymous heroine of Defoe's novel may have been loosely based on Moll King, friend to Jonathan Wild's mistress, Mary Milliner (Howson 1985 [1970]). Where the criminal biographies were of limited length and ended unhappily in death, the fictional *Moll Flanders* follows the early criminographic pattern of youthful indiscretion leading to crime but fleshes out the characters and manages a happy ending. Moll is born to a convict mother in Newgate Prison and leads an adventurous, at times criminal, life that results in her return to Newgate as a convicted criminal. She is transported to America but eventually comes back to England and, repentant, is recuperated back into respectability.

Central to both factual and fictional early crime narratives, then, is the criminal; the accounts are retrospective, the crimes and their perpetrator known. Further, these criminals tend to be from the lower classes. This is not a problem in the broadsides or in *The Newgate Calendar*, which sell themselves as criminal narratives and portray the containment of crime. But as the novel form develops over the nineteenth century it moves from a broad representation of society to representing a predominantly middle-class audience back to itself, thereby marginalizing lower-class criminality.

Towards the end of the eighteenth century crime appears in a new form, the Gothic novel (see Spooner, chapter 19 in this volume). Here are no ordinary offences, such as pocket-picking, but apparently supernatural events that, in Ann Radcliffe's novels for example, are often revealed to be mundane hoaxes concealing some criminal act or intention. In *The Mysteries of Udolpho* (1980 [1794]), the trappings of the supernatural and the usual Gothic tropes of secrets, hidden passages and decaying castles turn out to be the cover for a gang of smugglers. Charles Rzepka has argued that Radcliffe's heroines can be read as amateur proto-detectives (Rzepka 2005), but it is with William Godwin's quasi-Gothic novel, *Caleb Williams; or, Things as They Are* (1794) that a narrative retrospectively recognizable as crime fiction, and even featuring a detective figure, first appears (see Shaw, chapter 28 in this volume). Godwin's protagonist, Caleb, discovers – detects – that his master, the aristocratic Falkland has murdered Tyrrel, a tyrannical landowner, and has allowed the innocent Hawkinses to be condemned for his crime. The narrative locates Caleb initially as a proto-detective and subsequently as a criminal as Falkland manipulates the law in his own interests. The influence of criminal biographies is clear: at one point Caleb is the subject of a broadside and Godwin makes direct reference to *The Newgate Calendar* in a footnote (Godwin 1998: 268, 180).

By the end of the eighteenth century crime is firmly established in fiction as well as in factual narratives. But it is not just in British literature that crime and fiction are brought together. Across the Atlantic, America was producing its own, naturalistic Gothic fiction. In Charles Brockden Brown's *Wieland* (1798), ostensibly supernatural voices are shown to emanate from a ventriloquist attempting to incite murder; in Brown's *Arthur Mervyn* (1799), which Rzepka suggests was directly inspired by Godwin's novel (Rzepka 2005: 56), there are numerous crimes and what Knight calls an "inquirer both confident and … successful" (Knight 2004: 20), while Larry Landrum posits *Edgar Huntly* (1799–1800) as America's first detective novel (Landrum 1999: 1). This is perhaps a little overstated, and many would say that James Fenimore Cooper's *The Last of the Mohicans* (1826), one of the five novels in the Leatherstocking series featuring frontiersman Natty Bumppo, has a stronger claim. In what will become a familiar pattern in crime fiction, Bumppo even has an assistant, in this case, the Mohican chief, Chingachgook. Cooper's novels are not really concerned with crime as such. However, the independent and intelligent Bumppo, using the Native American skills he has acquired to read the natural world, can be seen as a backwoods prototype for the urban detective. Regis Messac has noted that Cooper, among other early American authors, was a strong influence on nineteenth-century French writers (Messac 1929: vol. 3), as is demonstrated by the title of the elder Alexandre Dumas's crime narrative, *Les Mohicans de Paris* (1856–7).

Public Policing

It is in France that the professional detective figure in the modern sense perhaps makes its début. Crime fiction as a genre requires a crime, a criminal, and a victim, plus (usually) a detective and (often) the police. The early crime narratives in Britain and America featured neither police nor official detectives, as neither existed until the nineteenth century. The Bow Street Runners had a detecting role, certainly, and "thief takers" were men paid to track down criminals for a fee. Jonathan Wild was both thief and thief taker and in *Caleb Williams* Gines plays a similar role first as robber and subsequently as the criminalized Caleb's pursuer. In the absence of an official police force, criminographic texts such as the execution broadsides were themselves considered to have a policing function in warning of the consequences of crime. In France, however, there had been a State-funded policing force since the seventeenth century, a force which by the nineteenth century had a clear detective function.

Despite the fact that thief-takers like Jonathan Wild and Gines were essentially private entrepreneurs and the French police agent was managed and paid by the State, the French system, too, relied on informers and spies, and sometimes recruited officers from the criminals who informed on their compatriots, as the autobiographical *Mémoires de Vidocq* (1828–9) records. Eugène François Vidocq began his career as a criminal, but volunteered his services as an informer to the police while still in prison and, in 1812, after several years as a double agent, became chief of the newly founded *Sûreté,* a brigade of police detectives. The *Sûreté,* or "Security" force, was conceived by Vidocq and was composed of ex-criminals like himself. It proved very successful. The brigade and its leader used their knowledge of the criminal underworld and quite often its methods to track down or trap their quarry. Vidocq's *Mémoires,* largely ghost-written, show him relying on disguise and trickery in his detective work, but also using early forensic detection, for example taking a suspected criminal's shoes and matching them to an incriminating footprint. However, the methods used to "borrow" the shoes were unlawful: Vidocq lulled the suspect into a false sense of security by wining and dining him while surreptitiously taking his footwear (Vidocq 2003: 266–9).

In the *Mémoires* it is less Vidocq the detective and agent of the law that interests the reader than Vidocq the criminal, with his trickery and disguises, and in this sense the narrative is closely akin to the criminal biographies. Employing Vidocq's criminal skills on behalf of the law was effective, but his criminal past and methods tainted his reputation and he was eventually forced to resign in 1827 after accusations of impropriety were made against him, allegations that seem to be supported by the nearly half million francs he had managed to amass over his 15 years of service with an average salary of five thousand francs per annum (Vidocq 2003: xii). Vidocq subsequently ran a private detective agency for a number of years, but it was his *Mémoires* that brought him fame and fortune and that made an important contribution to the development of the crime fiction genre. His career as described in the *Mémoires* offered inspiration to Edgar Allan Poe and Arthur Conan Doyle but, more immediately in France, to Honoré de Balzac, Victor Hugo, Eugène Sue, Alexandre Dumas (senior), Émile Gaboriau and others. Balzac's criminal mastermind, Vautrin, who first appears in *Le Père Goriot* (1835), becomes, in the later books, the Chief of the Paris police and both his career and his methods are clearly based on those of Vidocq. Rzepka cites Vautrin in turn as the inspiration for lawman Javert in Victor Hugo's 1862 novel, *Les Misérables* (Rzepka 2005: 62).

The police are a presence in Dumas's *Les Mohicans de Paris,* but his head of Sûreté, "M. Jackal," has lost the criminal edge and is a more conventional police officer, as is Émile Gaboriau's inspired and ambitious but also practical policeman, M. Lecoq, influential around the world through his masterly crime-solving in stories like *Dossier 113* (1864) and *M. Lecoq* (1868). Not all French crime fiction focused on police: Eugène Sue's early and very popular *Les Mystères de Paris* (1842–3) was more interested in crime and criminals than policing, and the criminal, epitomized in the later nineteenth century by Maurice Leblanc's gentleman thief Arsène Lupin, became a major figure in French crime fiction (Rzepka 2005: 63), retaining and developing the focus on the malefactor seen in the early criminal biographies. In Britain the reverse is true: in the early part of the century the legacy of *The Newgate Calendar* can be seen in what became known as the "Newgate novel" (see Gillingham, chapter 6 in this volume) and until the mid-century in the developing crime fiction genre the attention is still firmly on the criminal.

The Newgate novel is the generic title given to a small group of novels published in the 1830s and 40s. The name makes clear the link between the *Calendar* stories and the books; contemporary critics used the term "Newgate fiction" as a derogatory descriptor for novels that featured a criminal who came, or might have come, from a *Newgate Calendar* (Hollingsworth 1963: 14). Newgate novels were accused of glorifying criminality and making it attractive. The best-known authors at the center of the controversy caused by glamorizing criminality were Edward Bulwer-Lytton, William Harrison Ainsworth and Charles Dickens. William M. Thackeray is often included in the list but his novel *Catherine: A Story* (1839–40) was a parody of and an attack on Newgate fiction. Bulwer-Lytton wrote two Newgate novels: the eponymous hero of *Paul Clifford* (1830) is a highwayman and *Eugene Aram* (1832) is a fictionalized account of an eighteenth-century true crime narrative. Written in the context of political and penal reform, *Paul Clifford* follows the classic Newgate pattern of the descent into crime. With its reformist agenda, it targets the harsh penal laws as playing a part in the construction of criminals and can be read as a prototypical social problem novel. In *Eugene Aram*, Bulwer-Lytton considered the motives of an intelligent, educated criminal. His fictional Aram, based on a real-life English philologist whose murder of a close friend became a regular feature of the *Newgate Calendars*, was a cultured, Byronic hero. William Harrison Ainsworth's *Rookwood* (1834) was more a Gothic romance than a Newgate novel, but it contained a glamorous fictional representation of the real highwayman Dick Turpin (who may have been in part the inspiration for *Paul Clifford*). Ainsworth's later text, *Jack Sheppard* (1839), was an unapologetically favorable depiction of an eighteenth-century thief and, though wildly popular with the public, it attracted a great deal of censure from critics. Dickens did not escape the Newgate taint: *Oliver Twist* (1839) was criticized as a Newgate fiction and its narrative indeed bears some resemblance in outline to that of *Paul Clifford* (Pykett 2003: 27).

In the development of crime fiction the Newgate novels are important in a number of ways: they represent an increasing interest in the construction and motivation of the criminal; they have an element of detection or feature a detective figure; they bring crime firmly into mainstream fiction and so make possible the later genre of sensation fiction (see Pittard, chapter 7 in this volume). The trend, initiated by *Blackwood's Edinburgh Magazine* from its inception in 1817, of including fiction and serializing novels in periodicals disseminated these criminal fictions to a cross-class audience, as did the many dramatic interpretations staged over the nineteenth century.

But where their predecessors, the criminal biographies, were thought to warn against crime by portraying its consequences, the Newgate novels were accused of making criminality seem attractive. Despite, or perhaps because of its popularity, Newgate fiction contributed to nineteenth-century society's anxieties about crime in reality, anxieties that the government sought to assuage with the inauguration of the New Metropolitan Police in 1829.

The new police force operated only in London and was organized specifically to allay public fears that a State-funded police would erode civil liberties and function in the manner of the French police, that is, with informers and spies. The new force was uniformed and individually identifiable by numbers pinned to the collars of their jackets, and their remit was to prevent, not detect, crime. Such official detective work as took place was carried out by the Bow Street Runners, a small quasi-police force organized in 1749 by Henry Fielding, then the incumbent at London's Bow Street Magistrate's Court. Initially consisting of only seven men and only partially state-funded, over the eighteenth century the Runners had expanded and developed into a reasonably effective detecting agency and until 1839, when the Runners were disbanded, the two policing bodies worked in parallel: *Oliver Twist* features the (incompetent) Runners Blathers and Duff but also refers to policemen and officers of the law.

The Runners were regularly mentioned in narratives concerned with crime, but rarely took center stage, possibly because their lower-class status and criminal associations made them unsuitable fictional heroes. In 1827 *Richmond: Scenes in the Life of a Bow Street Runner, Drawn Up from His Private Memoranda*, was published anonymously. Ascribed to both Thomas Skinner Surr and Thomas Gaspey, *Richmond* recounts the eponymous fictional protagonist's progress from living among gypsies (who are, in general, positively portrayed) to employment as a Runner. A contemporary review found it to be "almost beneath contempt" (*Monthly Review*, June 1827), reflecting public attitudes to the Runners. Similarly, while there were regular police reports in the newspapers, the appearance of the official police in fiction, as in *Oliver Twist*, was limited. From the public's perspective, the police were recruited from the lower classes in order to police their peers; crime was associated with poverty and seen as a direct threat to the propertied middle and upper classes. The hero-criminals in Newgate fiction either were or were proved to be of a higher class (*Eugene Aram, Paul Clifford, Oliver Twist*), or had natural nobility (*Rookwood* and *Jack Sheppard*), and in this context the ordinary police officer seemed unlikely material for the hero of a novel.

By 1842 the police presence in London had become acceptable enough to make possible the creation of a small, plain-clothes detective police force and it is the activities of the detective police that finally bring crime and detection together in popular literature, initially in fiction. In 1849 hack journalist William Russell, perhaps inspired by the 1830s and 40s fashion for pseudo-autobiographical narratives of professional men such as physicians, lawyers and barristers, produced the first fictional account of professional policing in his "Recollections of a Police-Officer," which were published in the popular *Chambers's Edinburgh Journal* 1849–53. Russell overcame the class problem by making "Waters," his policeman protagonist, a gentleman forced into police work after losing his fortune to dishonest gamblers (Worthington 2005). The stories are set in the recent past prior to the establishment of the detective police, but "Waters" functions as a detective, working in plain clothes, and there are anachronistic references to his "fellow detective-officers." The stories proved popular, beginning what Philip Collins calls a "vogue for yellow-back detective stories" (Collins 1992: 211) which continued into the 1860s and beyond ("yellow-backs" were cheap novels bound in yellow paper).

Russell's "Recollections" were reissued in 1856 in a collected edition re-titled *Recollections of a* Detective *Police-Officer* (my emphasis). The change in title was perhaps the consequence of Charles Dickens's series of articles on the real detective police, published in *Household Words* between 1850 and 1853. Dickens's laudatory accounts raised the detectives' actually rather prosaic activities to the level of a science, imbuing what was simply an extensive knowledge of criminals and criminality with an air of mystery. Dickens's interest in and admiration for the police detectives found its way into his fiction, most notably with Inspector Bucket in *Bleak House* (1853), who was loosely based on a real Inspector Field. However, it was his detective police anecdotes which brought the detective force to the attention of the public and contributed to the proliferation of detective narratives that appeared in the periodicals and the yellow-back novels of the 1850s and 60s. These tended to take a diary or case-book format and claimed to be factual, but were more usually fiction. Russell followed his *Recollections* with *The Experiences of a Real Detective* (1862) and *The Autobiography of an English Detective* (1863). Charles Martel (pseudonym of Thomas Delf) offered *The Diary of an Ex-Detective* (1859) and a sequel, *The Detective's Notebook* (1860). Ireland had Robert Curtis's *The Irish Police Officer* (1861) and in Scotland James McLevy, a police detective, wrote up his memoirs in *Curiosities of Crime in Edinburgh* (1861) and *The Sliding Scale of Life; or, Thirty Years' Observations of Falling Men and Women in Edinburgh* (1861).

In 1863, perhaps wearying of police detective stories, the pseudonymous Andrew Forrester Junior introduced the concept of the private detective in *Revelations of a Private Detective*, succeeded by *Secret Service, or Recollections of a City Detective* (1864). Even more radically, he created a professional woman investigator in *The Female Detective* (1864), which was followed shortly after by William Hayward's *The Experiences of a Lady Detective* (1864). These detective narratives are doubly important in the development of crime fiction: they introduced and made central the detective figure and they established the case format which becomes an essential element of the genre. The criminal is now no longer the subject of the narrative but the object of the detective's pursuit, and the fact that the detective is on the side of the law makes reading about crime respectable as well as suggesting its containment. The police detective's period of fame was relatively brief; he continued to appear in crime narratives but increasingly in a minor role and, by the end of the century, is more likely to be depicted as bumbling and ineffectual, as Sherlock Holmes will repeatedly point out.

The detective continues to feature in fiction, but more usually in an amateur or private capacity.

Private Detection

Edgar Allan Poe has been called "the father of detection" (Symons 1985b: 35) in consequence of his three short stories featuring an investigatory figure, C. Auguste Dupin: "The Murders in the Rue Morgue" (1841), "The Mystery of Marie Rogêt" (1842–3) and "The Purloined Letter" (1845). Symons's claim is generally considered to be justifiable, but clearly the development of detection in fact and fiction was much more complex (see Lee, chapter 29 in this volume). Poe could not have set out to write detective fiction – the genre was not yet recognized – rather, his Dupin stories are concerned with how rational analysis combined with imagination can solve mysteries, as his introductory paragraphs to "The Murders in the Rue Morgue" suggest. Despite Poe's American nationality, his three quasi-detective tales are set in a Paris that would have been recognizable to Vidocq, whom Poe calls "a good guesser and a persevering man" in "The Murders in the Rue Morgue," indicating that he knew Vidocq's *Mémoires*, perhaps from the extracts printed widely in the periodicals, including in America.

Locating the stories in Paris allowed Poe to evoke the decadent Gothic atmosphere that the new America lacked; Dupin is depicted as a creature of the night, living in a decaying mansion with the unnamed friend who narrates the tales, prefiguring Dr Watson's role in Doyle's Sherlock Holmes stories. Poe's narrator renders Dupin and his methods comprehensible to the reader, a device that Dr Watson and later detective assistants will further develop. The Dupin stories not only offer a rational explanation of a mystery or solution to a crime, but also set in place narrative and thematic patterns that are still apparent in modern crime fiction. Perhaps most importantly, the Dupin tales are not concerned with the kind of crimes found in the detective-police narratives: in "The Murders in the Rue Morgue," what seems to be the ghastly and motiveless murder of two women is revealed to be the work of an orangutan; "The Mystery of Marie Rogêt" seems to be an investigation into the murder of Marie, but in reality is more concerned with the mystery posed by Marie herself; "The Purloined Letter" circles around the possession of an incriminating letter, the contents of which are never revealed.

These narratives are not, then, the straightforward pursuit of the criminal seen in Vidocq's *Mémoires* or "Waters's" *Recollections* but something new – an intelligent analysis of facts that leads to a resolution, a process of inductive thought. Dupin's combination of active investigation and cerebral organization becomes the model for later detective protagonists and it is the establishment of narrative patterns that makes Poe's Dupin stories such an important element in the development of crime fiction. Read retrospectively, "The Murders in the Rue Morgue" offers a classic locked room mystery; "The Mystery of Marie Rogêt" is a model of the armchair detective as Dupin bases his detection on newspaper reports rather than empirical investigation; "The Purloined Letter" articulates the need for the detective to be able to put him/herself into the place of the criminal and sets up what Michel Foucault calls "the intellectual struggle between criminal and investigator" (Foucault 1977: 69). Poe wrote only three Dupin stories, and he is perhaps better known for his Gothic-influenced tales of horror and the supernatural, many of which were heavily focused on the mental and physical sensations aroused by extreme states. In this, he was following a pattern that had emerged in early nineteenth-century Britain.

From its inception in 1817 *Blackwood's Edinburgh Magazine* featured fiction, most particularly a series of variously authored macabre short stories that came to be known as "*Blackwood's* Tales of Terror." The narratives depicted sensational actions and events and were calculated to arouse physical and psychical sensations in the reader. Poe was familiar with and probably influenced by *Blackwood's* and its tales, writing "How to Write a Blackwood Article" (1838), in which he parodied the form. Crime is not central to the "Tales of Terror," but is a recurring theme, usually featuring death or its threat. While not precisely fitting the model of the "Tales of Terror," Thomas De Quincey's two essays, "On the Knocking at the Gate in *Macbeth*" (1823) and "On Murder Considered as One of the Fine Arts" (1827), which both appeared in *Blackwood's Edinburgh Magazine*, took as their subject the sensational and real-life Ratcliffe Highway Murders of 1811 in which seven people in two separate households were killed in apparently motiveless acts of violence. While clearly taking a satirical approach to the subject, De Quincey's elevated style and his use of high literature and philosophy in association with violent crime gave it a kind of literary respectability. As *Blackwood's* was aimed at a relatively wealthy and educated audience, it introduced crime narratives into the homes of the nineteenth-century middle classes; in essence, *Blackwood's* appropriated the criminal material of the broadsides and repackaged it for a new readership (Worthington 2005). The sensational aspects of these short stories also found their way into the novel, initially in the Newgate fiction of the 1830s and 40s, but perhaps more radically in the subversive, middle-class narratives that the contemporary critics called "sensation fiction."

This sub-genre took crime right into the domestic sphere, the very heart of Victorian society. Abduction, adultery, murder, bigamy, fraud, seduction, forgery: the crimes in sensation fiction were social, personal, credible, and not committed by a criminal underclass but by the men and, shockingly, women of the middle and upper classes. Where the Newgate novels tended to be set in the past, sensation fiction was made sensational by its proximity to the present in both its action and its settings. Although charged with writing sensation fiction, with perhaps the exception of *Oliver Twist* and the unfinished *Mystery of Edwin Drood* (1870), Dickens's use of crime and sensation in his novels was part of his exploration into and *exposé* of the darker side of nineteenth-century society. It is *The Woman in White* (1859–60), written by Dickens's close friend Wilkie Collins (see Mangham, chapter 30 in this volume), that is generally accepted as establishing the sensation fiction genre. Collins's text features false imprisonment, wrongful inheritance, an unhappy arranged marriage and the charming yet terrifying Italian villain, Count Fosco. A tangled love affair and romance, or suitably mediated sexual attraction, is also, as here, an essential part of sensation fiction.

Collins's novel was quickly followed by Mrs Henry Wood's *East Lynne* (1860–1), where cross-class marriage, seduction and adultery are combined with a sub-plot of mystery and murder. Charles Reade's *Hard Cash* (1863) falls into the sensation category, as do novels by "Ouida" and Rhoda Broughton. Canonical novelists such as George Eliot, Anthony Trollope and Thomas Hardy (whose first book *Desperate Remedies* (1871) draws on what seems like all the tropes of sensation fiction) incorporated sensational elements into their narratives. But one of the best-known sensation novels, which like *The Woman in White* plays an important role in the development of crime fiction, is Mary Elizabeth Braddon's *Lady Audley's Secret* (1861–2). Significantly, both these texts feature active amateur detectives: in Collins's novel first Marion Halcombe and then Walter Hartright work to detect the crimes and solve the mysteries posed in the narrative, while in *Lady Audley's Secret* the detective role is taken on by Robert Audley, who reveals Lady Audley to be a bigamist and attempted murderess. The sensation novel introduces crime into the middle and upper classes, but cannot permit investigation of that crime by the lower-class police detective. Instead, the middle and upper classes police themselves: even when the criminal is revealed, he/she is not subjected to public justice but removed from the text. In *The Woman in White* Percival Glyde is burnt to death in the fire he has started in order to destroy the evidence of his illegitimate status, and in *Lady Audley's Secret* Lady Audley is, as Pykett observes, "sentenced to death-by-boredom in a Belgian *maison de santé* by her nephew Robert" (Pykett 2003: 35).

The sensation novel affords a discursive space for the amateur detective, and importantly this role is not limited to the male. Marion Halcombe proves an effective investigator until she is struck down by illness and replaced by Hartright, while in Collins's *No Name* (1862) Magdalen Vanstone actively seeks out the secrets that will enable her to retrieve her inheritance. In *The Law and the Lady* (1875) Valeria Woodville investigates the murder of her husband's first wife in order to prove his innocence. In the fiction of the 1860s and 70s the detective is established in both the public world of the police and the private world of the domestic sphere and the emphasis is firmly on detection rather than the pursuit of the criminal seen in earlier criminography. In 1868 Collins brought together these public and private worlds in *The Moonstone*, called by T. S. Eliot "the first and greatest of English detective novels" (Eliot 1951 [1934]: 464). *The Moonstone*, which loosely falls into the sensation fiction category, revolves around the disappearance of a yellow diamond or moonstone. In the process of investigation, the police are brought into the Verinder household, initially in the shape of the uniformed and incompetent Superintendent Seagrave and then in the person of police detective Sergeant Cuff, who was modeled on Sergeant Whicher, a Metropolitan police detective (see Mangham, chapter 30 in this volume).

One of the police detectives popularized by Dickens, Whicher achieved fame in the case of Constance Kent and the murder at Road in 1860, aspects of which Collins used in the plot of *The Moonstone*. Whicher's fictional avatar, Sergeant Cuff, is an able detective, but he falls just short of success within the private, domestic sphere. He wrongly deduces that Rachel Verinder, the daughter of the house, has stolen her own diamond. Once the missing jewel enters the public sphere, Cuff successfully allocates guilt, although the criminal, Godfrey Ablewhite, is punished by the original Indian guardians of the Moonstone, not by the law. The revelation of the events surrounding the disappearance of the diamond requires amateur detectives, here represented by Franklin Blake assisted by a doctors' assistant, Ezra Jennings, who provides the scientific skills of detection. The Verinders' house steward, Betteredge, whose liminal position between the servants and his employer facilitates the flow of information from one to the other (and to the reader), also has a quasi-detecting role. It is Betteredge who coins the phrase "detective fever" to describe the physical sensations aroused by the desire to discover the truth – sensations with which every reader could identify. *The Moonstone* prefigures classic English detective fiction, featuring a country-house setting, clues, witnesses and a combination of amateur and police detectives.

This is not yet fully-fashioned detection and detective fiction, but the themes and patterns are beginning to coalesce. The private, the police, and the amateur detective have all found their way into fiction and the plot structure of crime, detection, and resolution has firmly replaced the crime and pursuit narratives of early criminography.

But the development of crime fiction was not confined to Britain. Poe's setting of his Dupin stories in Paris reiterates the French-American connection discussed earlier and crime fiction developed quickly in America in parallel with and sometimes ahead of developments in Britain. In 1865, *Leaves from the Note-Book of a New York Detective*, allegedly the edited "casebook" of New York consulting detective Jem Brampton, appears. Heavily influenced by Poe, the Brampton stories differ from the British detective memoirs in that the hero is his own agent and selects his own cases; he is perhaps the first American urban detective. A real-life equivalent was Allan Pinkerton, the first detective appointed in Chicago and later co-founder of the Pinkerton National Detective Agency, who from 1866 onwards is credited with eighteen stories based on his own detective work. These were possibly ghost-written but were published under his name. In 1867, Metta Victor Fuller's *The Dead Letter*, published under the pseudonym "Seeley Regester," offered detection combined with aspects of the sensation genre, and in her first crime novel, *The Leavenworth Case* (1878), Anna Katharine Green, like Fuller, used the sensation fiction model but removed the extremes of coincidence and chance, inserting recognizable detective fiction techniques clearly drawn from Gaboriau and carried out by police detective Ebenezer Gryce. Harriet Prescott Spofford included some crime fiction in her impressive output of short stories, as did Louisa May Alcott in her foray into sensation fiction in the 1860s.

Perhaps less constrained by convention, these women authors outside Britain seemed to take to writing crime more readily and easily than their British sisters.

Their development of crime fiction was not limited to the northern hemisphere: Canadian-born Australian Mary Fortune is one of the earliest woman detective fiction writers and certainly the first in Australia (Sussex 1989). Based in and around Melbourne, Fortune wrote over 500 crime stories between 1865 and 1908, many featuring her serial police detective Mark Sinclair. Again in Melbourne, the New Zealand-born lawyer Fergus Hume wrote *The Mystery of a Hansom Cab* (1886) which Hume claimed to be modeled on Gaboriau's crime fiction and which featured a lawyer and a detective working together. The novel became a best seller upon its publication in Britain in 1887 and encouraged others, including Doyle, to work in the genre.

By the 1880s, crime fiction in a recognizable form was well established in Britain and abroad. Probably the most significant development took place in the figure of the detective, around which the earlier patterns of criminography coalesced. Yet R. F. Stewart tentatively places the first written use of the phrase "detective fiction" as late as December 1886, when it appeared as the title of an article in the *Saturday Review* (Stewart 1980: 27). Just twelve months later in December 1887, the first Sherlock Holmes narrative, *A Study in Scarlet*, was published in *Beeton's Christmas Annual*, and the career of the great detective had begun.

The Definitive Detective

It is impossible now to imagine crime fiction without immediately thinking of Sherlock Holmes. Arthur Conan Doyle's detective is a global phenomenon: there are international societies dedicated to Sherlock Holmes, a Sherlock Holmes Museum in London, and he has been immortalized in plays, films, and on television. His "cases" have been subjected to analysis by literary critics and by amateur enthusiasts. He is the archetypal detective whose influence can still be seen in modern crime fiction and his representation is the culmination of the development of the crime fiction genre over the nineteenth century. Doyle admitted his debt to earlier crime writers, speaking of Gaboriau's "neat dovetailing of plot" and Poe's "masterful detective, M. Dupin" (Doyle 1989: 74); he knew the sensation fiction genre and it is reasonable to assume he was aware of *The Newgate Calendar* and the prolific criminography featured in the periodicals in which his own work was published. Doyle's stated aim in writing a detective story was to turn what he saw as the "fascinating but disorganised business" of detection in fiction into "something nearer an exact science" (Doyle 1989: 74–5), and he admits to basing Sherlock Holmes's detective methods in part on Joseph Bell, a surgeon with whom he had worked while a medical student. Bell's seemingly uncanny ability to diagnose character and employment as well as illness in individual patients was central to Doyle's creation of a "scientific detective who solved cases on his own merits and not through the folly of the criminal" (Doyle 1989: 26).

Doyle consciously drew on earlier models, most obviously Poe's Dupin, in shaping Sherlock Holmes, but it is possible to trace elements of other investigative figures discussed here in Doyle's detective. Nor was it just earlier investigators who contributed: the narrator-companion, the urban setting, the rational "deductive" process, the case history, the scientific approach, the eccentricity of the protagonist, the collection and reading of clues, the importance of minutiae and, perhaps above all, the encyclopedic knowledge of crime and criminality, have all featured at some point and in some form over the long nineteenth century. Stamford was right: Sherlock Holmes is "a walking calendar of crime," and his narratives are a literary mosaic of nineteenth-century criminography. Doyle's detective is both an end point in the development of crime fiction and a starting point: crime fiction in the twentieth and twenty-first centuries would not be the same without him.

2

From Sherlock Holmes to the Present

Lee Horsley

The *Strand Magazine* published the first Sherlock Holmes stories in the early 1890s, running from "A Scandal in Bohemia" in 1891 to "The Final Problem" in 1893. A brief sampling of the crime and detective novels published a hundred years on gives some impression of the huge diversity of the tradition that evolved during the twentieth century. In the early 1990s, serial killer protagonists, new breeds of detective and innovative generic cross-overs all attracted critical attention: the central character of Helen Zahavi's *Dirty Weekend* (1991), a female serial killer, lures men to transgress and administers prompt punishment; the psychotic protagonist of Bret Easton Ellis's *American Psycho* (also 1991) runs amok in a world of depersonalization, greed, and commercial oversaturation; in 1992 Barbara Neely introduces her black detective, Blanche White (*Blanche on the Lam*), a street-smart domestic servant; in the same year James Ellroy's violent, complex variation on the police procedural, *White Jazz*, is narrated by a crooked, cynical LAPD detective who has worked as a slum landlord, bagman, and mob hitman; William Gibson's near future novel, *Virtual Light* (1993), creates a hard-boiled anti-hero who embarks on a quest in a high-tech world of mega-corporate perfidy; and in another near-future novel of that year, Jack Womack's *Random Acts of Senseless Violence*, the terrified young narrator journeys through a nightmarish cityscape, her identity shattered: "'I can't remember what I used to be like ... it fears me'" (Womack 1993: 231). This chapter offers an overview of the many-faceted development of crime fiction during the twentieth century – its shifting protagonists and the fears that drive them, the kinds of crimes investigated or perpetrated, and some of the more significant variations in style, structure and dominant themes.

The first three chapters of the *Blackwell Companion to Crime Fiction* all open with references to Sherlock Holmes – to the character and intellectual predispositions of Doyle's iconic protagonist and to the structure and function of his narratives. Like the body in the library, Holmes is both starting point and end point, a phenomenon to be explained by constructing a history of the crimes and detectives of earlier examples of the genre, and by exploring narratives "retrospectively recognizable" (Worthington, chapter 1) as having affinities with a popular genre that we are still in the process of defining. The Holmes stories illustrate the self-reflexivity and sophistication that have made investigative crime literature of such interest to theorists of narrative (Pyrhönen, chapter 3). The critical fascination with the form and plot structure of classic detective fiction has produced so substantial a body of analysis that it is sometimes taken to be the dominant tradition of crime writing. And indeed, for over a hundred years now, Doyle's stories have both influenced the development of crime fiction and created an inevitable point of reference.

The evolution of a genre depends on a combination of continuity and change, and Holmes is unquestionably the first key figure from whom other writers differentiated their protagonists, only rivaled by the composite hard-boiled protagonist created by Hammett and Chandler in the early twentieth century. This detective-centered model of generic development is, however, a partial and misleading one. In much twentieth and twenty-first century crime writing, the protagonist has been a criminal rather than an investigator, and these variations in fact reach back to the parent traditions of crime fiction, before the figure of the detective became so central – for example, to the criminal exploits catalogued in *The Newgate Calendar*, the transgressor-centered novels of Defoe and the Gothic fiction that emerged at the end of the eighteenth century. Although Gothic narratives themselves often confirm order and move towards resolutions that privilege rationality (see Spooner, chapter 19), the characteristic Gothic fascination with duality, violence, excess and the transgression of legal and moral codes is increasingly to be found in post-World War II crime writing, in novels that attend more to the dark forces driving the commission of the crime than to its solution, and that are preoccupied less with investigative ratiocination than with the psychology of the criminal and the violated body of the victim.

The present chapter is structured around the division between investigative and transgressor-centered crime fiction, but it also emphasizes that this is in many ways an oversimplified binary. The forms that generic variation can take are complex, and the texts themselves frequently contain tensions and contradictory elements. Detective fiction is haunted by all it purports to contain. There are, for example, ambiguities inherent in the doubling of the detective and the murderer; there are numerous narratives in which the classic triangle of victim-murderer-detective is destabilized by changes in the role of the protagonist; and apparent narrative closure often co-exists with the representation of crime as irresolvable and omnipresent in modern society.

Investigators

Looking back on the Holmes stories from the perspective of a late twentieth-century engagement with crime fiction, critics have observed the extent to which they elude simple categorization, undermining rational confidence by representing inner division, the serial recurrence of crime and the impossibility of imposing lasting order. Among Doyle's numerous imitators – varying the formula and establishing different character types for the figure of the detective – there are several who in their own ways disrupt the neat pattern of death-detection-resolution, bringing to the fore the divergent possibilities contained within the genre. In Arthur Morrison's *Dorrington Deed-box* (1897), the protagonist is a "private inquiry agent" who has done some legitimate enough investigations but who is not averse to thieving, defrauding, and even murder. He is more likely to enter into complicity with the crooks he investigates than he is to mete out punishment: as he says to the would-be killers in "The Case of Janissary" (*The Windsor Magazine*, 1897), " 'I may as well tell you that I'm a bit of a scoundrel myself.' "

A quite different kind of contradiction was explored in the work of one of Doyle's best-known and most durable successors, G. K. Chesterton, who challenged readers' assumptions about the efficacy and moral rightness of the "scientific" investigation of crimes and put in its place the spiritual-intuitive knowledge of a Catholic priest. In over fifty stories published between 1911 and 1935, Father Brown redefined the quest for "the secret" as a "religious exercise" that could in effect open up a deeply disturbing connection between the mind of the detective and that of the murderer – " 'thinking his thoughts, wrestling with his passions,' " says Chesterton's priestly protagonist, " 'till I have bent myself into the posture of his hunched and peering hatred; till I see the world with his bloodshot and squinting eyes … Till I am really a murderer' " ("The Secret of Father Brown," 1927).

At the other end of the rational-intuitive spectrum, there were such conspicuously scientific investigators as R. Austin Freeman's Dr Thorndyke, in stories which in their own way also complicate the balance between the "bloodshot" perspective of the criminal mind and the solving mind of the detective. In *The Singing Bone* (published in 1912), Freeman invented the "inverted" detective story. As in Poe's "The Purloined Letter," we know the details of the crime from the outset: in this case, we have an entirely separate, fairly elaborate narrative of the crime's commission. Freeman's intention is to demonstrate the inherent fascination of the analytic method even when the precise nature of the crime is known. But the effect is also to immerse us during the first narrative in the motives, the intense psychological pressure of the moment of murder, the excruciating tension of concealing your crime – as when the murderous lighthouse keeper in "The Echo of a Mutiny" gives "a gasp of relief" as he watches the incriminating boat vanish under the water: "he was better than safe: he was free. His evil spirit, the standing menace of his life, was gone, and the wide world, the world of life, of action, of pleasure, called to him" (*Pearson's Magazine*, September 1911).

The subgenre of classic investigative crime fiction settled into its most recognizable form – the golden age clue-puzzle model – in the period immediately following World War I. The influence of this highly evolved form has persisted, its conventions so well established that variations on the basic elements find an immediate readership: there have been large audiences, for example, for such serial detectives as Peter

Lovesey's Victorian Detective Sergeant Cribb in the 1970s; Brother Cadfael in Ellis Peter's Medieval whodunits (1970s through 1990s); and, detecting crimes from the 1990s into the twenty-first century, the resilient, plus-size black female protagonists of Barbara Neely's novels and Alexander McCall Smith's phenomenally successful *The No. 1 Ladies' Detective Agency*, in which Precious Ramotswe, challenged to demonstrate that competent female detectives do actually exist, invokes the example of Agatha Christie.

It is, of course, the country house murder mystery perfected by Christie that is generally taken to embody the essential qualities of the golden age form. Christie's own career lasted into the 1970s, but the vintage period of classic detection was between the wars, from 1918 until the early 1940s. Some of the writers were American, but this was primarily a British phenomenon – in addition to Christie, such writers as Margery Allingham, Anthony Berkeley (Francis Iles), Michael Innes, Ngaio Marsh, Dorothy L. Sayers, Josephine Tey and Edmund Crispin. This is the period during which the novel supplanted the short story as the most popular kind of detective fiction, and the form came to be increasingly characterized by an air of game-playing, several possible suspects and red herrings, an intriguing series of clues, elaborate methods of murder, intricate plots and a mystery requiring exceptional ingenuity on the part of the detective.

Golden age characters often comment self-consciously on the fictional devices of the novels they inhabit, drawing attention to both the artificiality of the genre and the contrived nature of the crimes represented: Griselda Clement, the vicar's wife in Christie's *Murder at the Vicarage* (1930), remarks that the pale mysterious stranger (called, of course, Mrs Lestrange) "Makes one think of detective stories" (Christie 1982: 5); Dr Gideon Fell, in John Dickson Carr's *The Hollow Man* (1935), takes metafictional references for granted, "'Because … we're in a detective story, and we don't fool the reader by pretending we're not'" (Carr 2002: 152). This generic know-ingness had an energizing and often transformative effect. The challenge was to vary the conventions in ways that were unexpected, as Christie most famously does in *The Murder of Roger Ackroyd* (1926), where her mischievous violation of the "rules of the game" enables her to sharpen her exposure of social pretence and to make us, as readers, less secure in our expectation of comfortable closure. Although the period of classic detective fiction is arguably at the furthest remove from crime fiction's Gothic inherit-ance, a variation of this kind begins to undermine rationalist detachment. The darker possibilities inherent in making your narrator the murderer were evident in a novel Christie published four decades later, *Endless Night* (1967), which gives readers access to the twisted, deeply unstable psyche of a man who has not just opportunistically committed a murder but who has actually reveled in the act: "I loved seeing her afraid and I fastened my hands round her neck … yes, I was wonderfully happy when I killed Greta …" (Christie 1967: 293).

The mysteries of the golden age are often called "cosy", with reference to their resolved endings, the politeness of the language and conventional lightness of tone, their feminized investigators, and the circumscribed milieu in which they take place.

The domestic scale of the action shuts out much that is disquieting in early twentieth-century politics and society. Under the surface, however, it is possible to discern deeper anxieties. Historically speaking, as recent critics have observed, golden age fiction can be seen as reacting against the bloodshed of war (Light 1991: 74–5): Dorothy Sayers's Lord Peter Wimsey, for example, is haunted by his experience of war, and the title of Sayers's first novel, *Whose Body?* (1923), can be seen as evoking "the ubiquity and anonymity of death between the trenches ..." (Rzepka 2005: 164–7). As the Dowager Duchess says, "he was so dreadfully bad in 1918, you know, and I suppose we can't expect to forget all about a great war in a year or two" (Sayers 1963: 135). The feminized detectives of the interwar years – Christie's Hercule Poirot, Sayers's Lord Peter Wimsey, Allingham's Albert Campion – can themselves, in their non-violence and their reliance on intuition and empathy, be seen as a reaction against the heroic male model of wartime endeavor. As Susan Rowland argues, "The detective in golden age fiction is a new hero for the post World War I traumatized landscape" (see chapter 8 in this volume). The trauma of a war-torn landscape is a great distance from the secluded confines of an English country house, and the formal closure of the narrative seems a guarantee of security, but there is much that makes the apparent calm illusory.

The tensions and anxieties of postwar society were much more directly represented in the American investigative fiction published from the 1920s on, in which tough private eyes negotiate a violent and corrupt urban terrain. Hard-boiled writing has numerous antecedents – dime novels, Westerns, the frontier romance – but its development as a subgeneric form of crime fiction is indissolubly linked to the founding of *Black Mask* magazine in 1920. Other pulp magazines soon followed (for example, *Dime Detective, Detective Fiction Weekly, Black Aces*) but *Black Mask* was the strongest influence, with its growing reputation for publishing fast-paced, colloquial stories, and promoting "economy of expression" and "authenticity in character and action" (Joseph T. Shaw, quoted by Pronzini and Adrian 1995: 9), establishing one of the most popular and recognizable forms of twentieth-century crime writing. Race Williams, first appearing in Carroll John Daly's "Knights of the Open Palm" (*Black Mask*, June 1923), is often seen as the progenitor of the private eye, a brutal adventurer, at the opposite pole to the rational Holmesian detective: "Sometimes ... one hunk of lead is worth all the thought in the world" ("Not My Corpse", *Thrilling Detective*, June 1948). It is Dashiell Hammett and his successor, Raymond Chandler, however, who left the most distinctive legacy.

Hammett started writing for the magazine in the early 1920s, Chandler a decade later. Their differences elided, the two writers are conventionally yoked together as originators of the American private eye tradition. Hammett's Continental Op was introduced in a story called "Arson Plus" in October 1923; Sam Spade appeared in the first installment of *The Maltese Falcon* in September 1929; Ned Beaumont, in 1930, in the first part of *The Glass* Key. It is Spade, of course, who has come to be seen as the archetypal hard-boiled private eye, a loner whose audacity and individualism are products of a thoroughgoing distrust of conventional social arrangements and familiar pieties. Self-aware and self-mocking, he acknowledges that he is often seen as indistinguishable from the crooks with whom he has to deal, but even though he readily admits looking after his own financial interests, he is not ultimately motivated by greed: "Don't be too sure I'm as crooked as I'm supposed to be" (Hammett 1999: 583). The moral ambivalence of Hammett's other protagonists is even more marked. Both the Continental Op and Ned Beaumont occupy positions midway between criminality and legitimacy. As Christopher Breu argues, noir negativity returns "to haunt the hard-boiled form again and again, providing some of its most radical and radically negating moments." Among these "negative" hard-boiled novels, *Red Harvest* might be described as "hard-boiled fiction's first auto-critique" (Breu 2005: 55–7). The Op's frenzy of cleansing and retribution reveals the limits and costs of detached, amoral hard-boiled agency. Beaumont, though he fulfills an investigative function, is actually a gambler, a henchman, a political hanger-on rather than a private eye, and *Black Mask*'s editor felt compelled to defend the inclusion of as criminally oriented a story as *The Glass Key*, arguing that it exposed the serious danger to the body politic caused by alliances between corrupt politicians, public officials and organized crime.

Shortly before Hammett quit producing crime fiction, Raymond Chandler began writing for *Black Mask* and made his indelible impact on American detective fiction with such novels as *The Big Sleep* (1939), *Farewell, My Lovely* (1940), *Lady in the Lake* (1944), *The Little Sister* (1949), and *The Long Good-Bye* (1953). His protagonist, Phillip Marlowe, deploys less violent and transgressive methods of coping with pervasive disorder than those of, say, Hammett's Op, and his performance of hard-boiled masculinity is more detached, witty and teasing. He too, however, operates on the margins of legality and works to uncover the connections between personal and public criminality. In *The Big Sleep*, drawn into the sinister, vicious criminality that runs through the public life of Los Angeles, Marlowe locates many of the sources of contamination, but is ultimately unable to deal with the underlying forces of corruption and acknowledges the extent to which he himself has been tainted: "Me, I was part of the nastiness now ..." (Chandler 1995b: 764).

The adaptable tradition of the hard-boiled private investigator has been one of the most durable forms of American crime writing, even if "the last time a private eye investigated a homicide was never" (Evan Hunter, in Unsworth 1995: 32). The Race Williams model of unhesitating, unreflective violence found its most famous imitator in Mickey Spillane, whose huge popular success was a major influence on mid-century American paperback publishing, just beginning to develop in the 1950s. Spillane's notoriously brutal, right-wing creation, Mike Hammer, is a no-holds-barred revenge-seeker who first appears in *I, the Jury* (1947), followed by five more mid-century novels (1950–2) – a character with little time for the self-doubt of Hammett's Op, and certainly none of the fastidious verbal play of Chandler's Marlowe.

At the other end of the spectrum, Ross Macdonald assimilated Chandler's influence in his creation of Lew Archer, his series detective from *The Moving Target* (1949) to

The Blue Hammer (1976). Shifting the hard-boiled ethos in the direction of liberalism and non-violence, Macdonald's protagonist prefers talking to fighting and is almost as much analyst as detective: *The Galton Case* (1959), for example, is a take on the story of Oedipus, and, as William Marling argues, marks a turning point in the development of the psychological detective novel, "in which questions of personal identity are paramount and the hard-boiled quality resides as much in the pain of personal truth as in the physical costs of their discovery" (Marling, http://www.detnovel.com/GaltonCase.html).

Between the post-World War II paperback boom and the present, the private eye novel has continued to evolve: John D. MacDonald created Travis McGee in the 1960s (starting with *The Deep Blue Good-by* in 1964); Joseph Hansen's gay detective, Dave Brandstetter, first appeared in *Fadeout* in 1970; and – both still on the go in the twenty-first century – Lawrence Block's hard-drinking Matt Scudder was introduced in *The Sins of the Fathers* (1976) and Loren D. Estleman's Vietnam vet Amos Walker in *Motor City Blue* (1980). As a style, of course, "hard-boiled" is a label that can be applied to several different subgenres of crime fiction. It has been a particularly strong influence on transgressor-centered novels, both in America and Britain (for example, on W. R. Burnett, James M. Cain, Paul Cain, Horace McCoy, Jim Thompson, Charles Williams, Donald Westlake, Derek Raymond, Ted Lewis). But however varied its manifestations, it has proven to be one of the most immediately recognizable of fictional voices, easily reduced to its essentials of style and attitude, as it is by Frank Miller's Marv in *The Hard Goodbye* (1991), a graphic distillation of the hard-boiled anti-hero fighting his way through the metaphoric dark alleyway and the intractable, dangerous urban landscape, protected only partially by his characteristic verbal armory of slang, tough talk, and laconic self-sufficiency: "It's the old days. The bad days … Hell isn't getting beat up or cut up or hauled in front of some faggot jury. Hell is waking up every god damn morning and not knowing why you're even here …" (Miller 2005: 39).

Whether he is closer to criminality or the law, the lone hard-boiled protagonist can seem, in a world of high-tech law enforcement, a somewhat anachronistic figure, more associated with "the old days" invoked by Marv than with the realities of contemporary criminal investigation. The private eye is by no means out of a job, but narratives focusing on one man's isolated, stubborn assertion of individualistic masculine agency have receded in importance in comparison to narratives involving the teamwork of official detection. Elements of the police procedural were evident in earlier crime fiction, but it really only became a distinct phenomenon from the mid-century on, with points of origin generally identified as Lawrence Treat's novel *V as in Victim* (1945) and the *Dragnet* series, both on radio (from 1947) and television (1952–9). Since then, the police procedural or "police novel" has become one of crime fiction's dominant forms. Often accused of underwriting official mechanisms of control and values, the subgenre is in fact, as Andrew Pepper has argued, a "discontinuous" tradition that has challenged established power structures in a variety of ways (Pepper 2000: 32).

Like classic detective fiction and the private eye novel, the police novel tends to use series characters and to be structured around a sequence of crime-detection-solution. The emphasis, however, is on a collaborative process of investigation requiring hierarchical institutional relationships, well-established systems of communication, and shared expertise. As the genre has evolved, this expertise has increasingly come to include the technically sophisticated inspection of clues – such things as ballistics and electronic databases, of course, and more recently two types of investigation that have in effect defined their own subgenres. Forensic pathology and the process of psychological profiling have played an increasing role, most strikingly in the work of Thomas Harris and Patricia Cornwell. In both cases, the effect has been to reshape the investigative narrative, creating space for a Gothic fascination with psychological aberration and bodily violation – Harris's Will Graham demonstrating a capacity for "pure empathy" so strong that he can assume any point of view, even those that "scare and sicken him" (Harris 1981: 154–5), and Cornwell's Kay Scarpetta immersing herself in the horrifying reality of the traumatized corpse, putting her hands "inside their ruined bodies" in order to "touch and measure their wounds" (Cornwell 2000: 14).

The tradition of the ensemble police novel as it emerged at mid-century, however, gave little indication that it would come to be dominated by these dark arts. Ed McBain, when he began his 87th Precinct novels with *Cop Hater* in 1956, made the outlines of the emerging subgenre immediately apparent, establishing the dynamic that mixes the working and individual lives of a group of cops and detectives: in an opening family scene, we meet an ordinary cop who is shockingly gunned down in the first chapter, and then, by the beginning of the second chapter, we have encountered two homicide cops, the assistant medical examiner, the photographer for the Bureau of Identification, Cars 23 and 24, the switchboard at Headquarters, the Radio Room, the dispatcher and the precinct map (McBain 1999: 6) – all of the required elements of team work, and the rudimentary technology needed for medical examination of the body, communication among the hierarchy of investigators and mobilization of the enquiry. The broadly based investigations that characterize the police procedural make it an obvious platform for assaults on various kinds of official corruption: as McBain says, in developing more critical strategies over the course of his long career, he has come to represent institutional law enforcement as an imperfect instrument, with "'bad guys' within the squadroom as well as outside" – "stupid cops," "bad cops," "bigoted cops, you know, the whole bag" (Silet 1994: 398, 395).

The effectiveness of the subgenre as a means of more aggressively exposing official wrongdoing is apparent in the work of James Ellroy and David Peace. In Ellroy's *White Jazz* (1992), for example, the crimes in which his narrator, Lieutenant Dave Klein, is implicated are legion: "Killings, beatings, bribes, payoffs, kickbacks, shakedowns. Rent coercion, music jobs, strikebreaker work. Lies, intimidation, vows trashed, oaths broken, duties scorned. Thievery, duplicity, greed, lies, killings, beatings ..." (Ellroy 1992: 331). Peace, who published his Red Riding Quartet novels between 1999 and 2002, crafted a distinctive version of the genre to probe the dark recesses of contemporary British history in novels overlapping the period (1970s–80s) when the Yorkshire Ripper was being hunted. Peace's novels are grim, intense meditations on personal despair and official depravity. Legitimate police procedure is displaced by the abuse of power and, as in Ellroy's novels, virtually every investigative mechanism is tainted by brutality, dishonesty and the self-serving exercise of official authority, cumulatively creating a picture of late twentieth-century justice that is "*All a far cry from* Dixon of Dock Green" (Peace 2000: 112).

Hard-boiled detective fiction has proven to be a natural site of protest for a range of other writers who might be said to have written both with and against the tradition. The iconic importance of the white male investigator who can be constructed as "a fully pathological version of American individualism" (Breu 2005: 1–2) makes inversion an obvious tactic. Both black and female writers have adapted the tradition by reversing its established binaries, a double-edged strategy that both appropriates the strengths of the hard-boiled icon (his ability to navigate the harsh urban milieu, his tough style and a self-reliant mindset, his outsider status) and implicitly challenges what is taken to be his conservative, white male value system.

Both forms of appropriation have been most prolifically produced from the 1980s and 1990s on. Between 1987 and 1997, several of the black crime writers who are currently best known published the first in their series of detective novels: Gar Anthony Haywood (1987), Mike Phillips (1989), Walter Mosley (1990), Barbara Neely (1992), Gary Phillips (1996) and Charlotte Carter (1997). One of the most groundbreaking of such transformations, however, took place much earlier. Decades before this new wave of African American crime writing, there was a lonelier and more disturbing black appropriation of the hard-boiled voice: Chester Himes's *Harlem Cycle* (1957–69) distinctively recast the narrative structures, the protagonists and the nature of the crimes at the heart of the hard-boiled tradition, relocating the genre in a claustrophobic, violent, surreal Harlem and forcing readers to confront their sociopolitical assumptions and their racial stereotypes. Himes's novels had, by the end of the series, begun to transgress generic boundaries in order to engage more explicitly with the root causes of crime in the largest sense: in *Blind Man with a Pistol* (1969), the answer to what's behind all the "senseless anarchy" is "'Skin'", racial injustice being the real "mother-raper at the bottom of it" (Himes 1969: 323, 342); and the unfinished *Plan B*, which edges even further towards apocalyptic violence, was Himes's "bloody farewell to literature and his legacy of despair" (Fabre and Skinner 1995: 390).

Less deeply unsettling and more easily categorized, the novels of Walter Mosley retrospectively survey black experience on the opposite coast, starting out in LA during the same postwar period in which the Harlem Cycle was created. Like Ellroy, Mosley creates a sequence of crime narratives that take us through key events in mid to late twentieth-century America, from the immediate post-World War II period in *Devil in a Blue Dress* (1990) through to McCarthyite persecution (*Red Death*, 1991), the militant black politics of the 1960s (*Bad Boy Brawly Brown*, 2002) and most recently the Vietnam era and after (*Cinnamon Kiss*, 2005; *Blonde Faith*, 2007). The novels constitute a form of alternative history, opening up subaltern perspectives on power relationships, American identity, political hatred, paranoia, and racial exclusion, with Mosley's detective, Easy Rawlins, struggling not only with urban crime but with his self-realization that he all too often "wasn't, and hadn't been, my own man" (Mosley 1993: 235–6).

The hard-boiled tradition has also been a point of departure for women crime writers from the 1980s on, when the right-wing political atmosphere gave additional point to an assertion of female empowerment. Sara Paretsky and Sue Grafton both published their first novels (*Indemnity Only* and *"A" is for Alibi*) in the early 1980s, and lesbian crime fiction emerged at around the same time (for example, M. F. Beal, Barbara Wilson, and Mary Wings). The female detectives of the 1980s and 1990s both imitate and subvert the stereotypical qualities of hard-boiled fiction, imbuing the male role with character traits that foster communal bonds and a socially responsible ethos, while retaining the instrumental "male" qualities of physical prowess, tenacity, and confident agency. The chick dick defines herself against the assumption that there is an inherent mismatch between her gender and her performance as a private investigator: the first of P. D. James's Cordelia Grey novels, published in 1972, was called *An Unsuitable Job for a Woman*, a title echoed when V.I. Warshawski is told by her first client, " 'Well, this really isn't a job for a girl to take on alone' " (Paretsky 1982: 6). At the start of *Tunnel Vision* (1994), V.I.'s building is condemned, and the Culpepper boys are "waiting for the day when the building would be worth more dead than alive" (Paretsky 1994: 1–2); the presence of a homeless family in the basement epitomizes the desperate communal need that is consequent on such rapacious, unconstrained male agency. In proving herself as an investigator, V.I. will need both a commitment to community as well as the ability to tackle male power. She has both, of course, though here, as in other Paretsky novels, she is destined to achieve only partial success: when public wrongdoing is sufficiently entrenched, it is likely to remain unscathed by the attentions of even the feistiest of female – or indeed male – investigators.

Transgressors

" 'Your world … it's so dirty,' I whisper … as if to myself. 'How do you live in it?' " (Abbott 2005: 235). The question of how a transgressor lives inside a dirty world is at the heart of crime as opposed to detective fiction. Investigative crime fiction almost always contains important elements of effective, morally justified agency with which readers can identify: however conflicted and self-ironizing, however doomed to defeat by the magnitude of the task, there is a figure who tries to serve justice and who may put something to rights. There is some kind of role model, however flawed. Criminals, of course, can also act out of a conviction that they are serving justice and putting things to rights, punishing wrong-doers, leaving messages of warning to normative society. And transgressor-centered crime fiction, too, has its iconic figures, its charismatic anti-heroes – the flamboyant gangster, the daring misfit, the Gothic villain, the femme fatale.

Some of the liveliest developments in female-authored crime fiction have been in the growing number of novels that invest their female protagonists with rebellious, often deadly energy. Instead of just reversing the male-female binary of hard-boiled fiction, these are narratives that create powerful female voices capable of drawing readers into the subjective experiences of characters who transgress against male value systems and social hierarchies in far more thoroughgoing ways than the typical chick dick ever does. Writers like Megan Abbott (*Die a Little*, 2005; *Queenpin*, 2007), Christa Faust (*Money Shot*, 2008) and Vicki Hendricks (*Miami Purity*, 1996; *Iguana Love*, 1999; *Cruel Poetry*, 2007) focus on female identity under pressure not only from male treachery and violence but from their own ambition, vanity and destructive impulses. "My arms were steel, my fists were rock ... I was the stronger brute" (Hendricks 1999: 179), the narrator says in Vicki Hendricks's *Iguana Love*. In Megan Abbott's *Queenpin*, two fabulously well-equipped women vie for power, throughout posing the question of "what you will do if you have to" (Abbott 2007: 237). These re-creations of the iconic femmes fatales of traditional literary and cinematic noir fascinate us because of their strength, dynamism and entrepreneurial drive – though the creators of such flawed anti-heroines can also, of course, be charged with fueling the most negative stereotypes.

Accusations of this kind have particularly been leveled against subversive representations of black masculinity. Among the most controversial and best known of these tough, outspoken novels are those by Iceberg Slim (Robert Beck), Donald Goines and, in the UK, Victor Headley. Their bleak cityscapes are scenes of pimping, prostitution, drug dealing, and violence. Headley's protagonist in *Yardie* (1992), for example, builds on a reputation established in his earlier years as a gangster and "bad bwoy" on the streets of Jamaica: the same propensity for ruthlessness that helped him make "a name for himself in West Kingston" (Headley 1992: 7–9) has now established his reputation in the inner city battle zone of Hackney. This black "underclass" crime writing on both sides of the Atlantic gives a voice to the culturally disenfranchised, but has been critically marginalized because it is seen as perpetuating a damaging image of black masculinity: as Paul Cobley argues, it does not "fit nicely with current critical predilections" (Cobley 2000: 137).

The black criminal protagonists of the late twentieth century are reminiscent of the rebellious figure of the gangster created in the early 1930s – most influentially, W. R. Burnett's *Little Caesar* (1929) and Armitage Trail's *Scarface* (1930). Burnett and Trail create the mythologized gangster as the dark double of capitalist enterprise, an implicit reflection on the acquisitive instincts of an entire society relentlessly committed to upward mobility. Roy Earle, a gangster on the run in W. R. Burnett's *High Sierra* (1940), demands, "'Why do people stand it? ... A few guys have got all the dough in this country. Millions of people ain't got enough to eat. Not because there ain't no food, but because they got no money. Somebody else has

got it all'" (Burnett 1940: 150–1). Earle is unusual in his direct, bitter denunciation of legitimized exploitation, but a common underlying theme of the Depression-
era gangster sagas is the inequitable social system, the scramble for power and the
cost of failure.

Other gangster novels of the time, like Paul Cain's *Fast One* (1933) and James M.
Cain's *Love's Lovely Counterfeit* (1942), are structured around underworld struggles for
ascendancy. Kells, the protagonist of Paul Cain's brutally compelling *Fast One*, shares
with other gangster figures the characteristics of the hard-boiled male in overdrive,
but sheer desperation is there from the start. Cain brings together the gangster novel's
"rise to power" plot with the classic noir narrative patterns of tense pursuit and wrongful accusation, and, when Kells meets his end, his torn body, the rain and broken
earth suggest that an elemental violence has claimed him.

The flamboyant self-destruction and demented energy of a gangster like Kells are
beyond the reach of many of the decade's defective and unheroic criminal protagonists.
They are not clawing their way to the top but fighting to escape with their lives. The
fiction of Benjamin Appel (*Hell's Kitchen*, 1934–9) and Edward Anderson (*Thieves Like
Us*, 1937), for example, pits small-time crooks against the whole social and economic
order, and their fate is a condemnation not just of "respectable" society's much greater
criminality but of its callousness and indifference towards those struggling to survive
and doomed to defeat.

The overarching tradition of transgressor-centered crime fiction is literary noir,
which from the late 1920s on created ill-fated characters who are "obsessed, alienated, vulnerable, pursued or paranoid" (Horsley 2001: 11). The gangster and outlaw
narratives discussed above have strong affinities with noir, but its quintessential
figures are individual transgressors and victims. Compromised, ineffectual masculinity has also been a recurrent theme in twenty-first century noir, both US and UK
– for example, in the work of writers like Charlie Huston, Jason Starr, Ken Bruen,
Allan Guthrie and Ray Banks. But the downtrodden transgressor is most closely
associated with the literary noir of the 1930s and 1940s, particularly with the work
of Horace McCoy and James M. Cain – for example, McCoy's *They Shoot Horses, Don't
They?* (1935) and *I Should Have Stayed Home* (1938); Cain's *The Postman Always Rings
Twice* (1934), *Serenade* (1937) and *Double Indemnity* (1936). Although stylistically
allied to the hard-boiled writers of the *Black Mask* era, McCoy and Cain create
characters who are the antithesis of the iconic private eye – morally deficient, lacking
in all effective agency and representing traumatized masculinity at its most vulnerable. Much admired by French audiences (Albert Camus cited Cain's *Postman* as his
primary inspiration for *L'Etranger*), they bring existential despair to California, "the
nightmare at the terminus of American history" (Davis 1990: 36–7). Instead of being
the fabled land of opportunity, the "Golden State" becomes a site of disappointment
and failure. These trapped, rootless protagonists are under sentence of death in a
place that itself seems meaningless, with its "population of strangers drifting about,
surrendering to heedless impulse" (Schickel 1992: 30). In Cain's *Double Indemnity*,
the ending darkly echoes the American dream of moving on to new opportunities:

consigned to a steamer leaving for Balboa "and points south," Walter Huff realizes that neither he nor Phyllis is "going anywhere": "'There's nothing ahead of us'" (Cain 1985: 322).

Many other American crime novels of the period propel their homeless, alienated protagonists on similarly rootless wanderings. In Dorothy Hughes's *Ride the Pink Horse* (1946), the nameless, "place-less" Sailor arrives at a "God-forsaken town" in the midst of Fiesta, reached by traveling through miles of nothingness, a "dream figure wandering in this dreadful nightmare," feeling "trapped by the unknown" (Hughes 1984: 8, 95, 124). William Gresham's *Nightmare Alley* (also 1946) plays on the motif of a fall into darkness, figured as the conman/geek's descent into the carnival pit. This downward trajectory governs the narrative from the beginning, and entrapment in the "nightmare alley" from which there is no escape is one of crime fiction's most haunting images of existential despair: "'Man comes into the world a blind, groping mite. He knows hunger and the fear of noise and of falling. His life is spent in flight …'" (Gresham 1946: 197).

In the same year, David Goodis began to forge his reputation with the serialization of his first novel, *Dark Passage* (serialized in the *Saturday Evening Post* in 1946, filmed in 1947). Over the next two decades, Goodis produced some of the bleakest of all crime novels, repeatedly representing frightened, displaced men, in hiding or on the run. Another of the American writers who found favor among a French readership, he was seen to share something of the "existential melancholy" of McCoy and James M. Cain (Sallis 1993: 54–5). The protagonist of *The Moon in the Gutter* (Goodis 1953) characteristically ends by abandoning his hope of finding the man responsible for his sister's death and goes back to the woman who paid for his murder: "He moved along with a deliberate stride that told each stone it was there to be stepped on, and he damn well knew how to walk this street, how to handle every bump and rut and hole in the gutter" (Goodis 1983: 513).

Among the damaged transgressors most familiar to readers of contemporary crime fiction, there is probably none who has received more critical attention than the serial killer. Multiple murderers have acted as protagonists from well before the mid-1970s, when the term "serial killer" was coined; they have, post-1970s, been increasingly incorporated into investigative narratives in what is often a fairly formulaic way, reliable providers of a lurid trail of corpses, and have been a particularly useful ingredient in police procedurals – for example, in the novels of James Patterson, Jeffrey Deaver, Michael Connelly, Val McDermid, Jonathan Kellerman and Tess Gerritson.

But more serious uses have been made of this most extreme and disturbing of transgressive figures. In the mid-1950s, Patricia Highsmith and Jim Thompson created some of the most powerful portrayals of the "abnormally normal" multiple murderer – Highsmith most famously in her Ripley novels (1955–91), and Thompson in such novels as *The Killer Inside Me* (1952), *Savage Night* (1953), *A Hell of a Woman* (1954) and *Pop. 1280* (1964). In the work of both writers, one function of the killer protagonist is to critique the "normal" world that they mimic but stand apart from.

In Highsmith's *Deep Water* (1957), we enter the consciousness of a man for whom murder is the ultimate judgment on his despised neighbors. Like "perhaps half the people on earth," he reflects, his victim's "grim, resentful, the-world-owes-me-a-living face" and "the small, dull mind behind it" deserve punishment: "Vic cursed it and all it stood for. Silently, and with a smile ... he cursed it" (Highsmith 1957: 259–60).

Regarded as some of the most original fictional representations of serial murder, the novels of Jim Thompson use the form for savage satiric exposure, creating, from 1949 on, a succession of psychologically disturbed protagonist-killers, most of them drawing us into their stories as first-person narrators. The most accomplished and disturbing of these are the first novel Thompson wrote for Lion, *The Killer Inside Me*, and the companion piece he published towards the end of his career, *Pop. 1280*, in both of which the protagonist is a sheriff, a supposed enforcer of law and order – and a psychopath. This tension is at the heart of the narrative, the psychopathic personality providing the perspective from which we view law-abiding small-town America – a perspective laden with scathing satiric contempt for the whole crooked, hypocritical social order. Thompson's killers see their murders as simply putting into practice the secret wishes harbored by others. Acting as a "threat to idyllic American domestic existence posed by the vengeful return of the repressed," Lou Ford, in *The Killer Inside Me* (1952), commits murders that reveal the corruptions of the symbolic order. His insights are those of "a man that's crazy enough to tell the truth" (Simpson 2000: 91; Plain 2001: 230–1). In one of the central scenes, just before he kills Johnny Pappas, Lou offers him a fatherly explanation of the moral chaos of the world around them: "'We're living in a funny world, kid ... it's a screwed up, bitched up world, and I'm afraid it's going to stay that way ... Because no one, almost no one, sees anything wrong with it'" (Thompson 1991: 118).

Multiple murderers are only rarely given the central role they have in the novels of Highsmith and Thompson. Their incorporation into the structures of investigative fiction, however, can be more than formulaic, and the tendency to give the transgressor a voice has been one of the elements associated with an increased Gothicizing of investigative crime novels, substantially shifting the focus of our attention from containment to violation. The most striking example is perhaps Thomas Harris's *Hannibal* (1999), in the final chapters of which the eponymous serial killer and cannibal becomes the central figure. Earlier novels in the series – *Red Dragon* (1981) and *Silence of the Lambs* (1988) – stay much more within the limits of the police procedural. In *Hannibal*, on the other hand, there is a major narrative shift when FBI agent Clarice Starling leaves Quantico and, having rescued Hannibal, is drawn into an increasingly close relationship with him. The structure of the police procedural is displaced by Gothic melodrama, and events are from that point on largely controlled by Hannibal himself, a character who speaks for everything repressed in a civilized society, the drives and desires that fundamentally challenge the rationalist assumptions of the investigative narrative.

The slippage between investigative and criminal-centered narratives in Thompson and Harris suggests both the difficulty of neatly categorizing the forms of crime fiction and the extent to which the representation of and fascination with transgression perpetually surface to disrupt the reassuring structures of detective fiction. As Joel Black argues, "The murderous protagonists in these works 'mimic' – and thereby expose – a morally bankrupt society," and the fictions themselves fulfill the roles of moral and social critique in very complex ways, with psychopathic killers replacing detectives "as agents of revelation in a world where redemption no longer seems possible" (see Black, chapter 5 in this volume).

3
Criticism and Theory

Heta Pyrhönen

In Arthur Conan Doyle's *The Sign of Four* (1890) Dr Watson tells Sherlock Holmes that he was so impressed by Holmes's earlier feat of detection that he wrote an account of it under the title *A Study in Scarlet*. If Watson expects thanks for making his friend's achievement public, he is disappointed, for Holmes has only this to say:

> Detection is, or ought to be, an exact science, and should be treated in the same cold and unemotional manner. You have attempted to tinge it with romanticism, which produces much the same effect as if you worked a love-story or an elopement into the fifth proposition of Euclid. (Doyle 1986: 1.108–9)

Holmes rejects Watson's sentimental manner of narration that fuses ratiocination and romance. He disapproves of narrative altogether as the medium for conveying the method and results of his detection. Ideally, Holmes thinks they should be expressed as mathematical formulae. While such a wish is, of course, impossible to realize, the excerpt draws attention to the fact that detective fiction exhibits a self-reflexive understanding of its own ingredients. It invariably mirrors its own form, commenting on the nature of its narrativity. The genre thus comprises its own first level of criticism. Thanks to this preoccupation with its characteristics, it invites readers to examine the features comprised by their reading experience. Literary critics and theorists have responded to this invitation and their examinations form a rich and varied critical legacy extending over a hundred years. Today, studies of detective fiction form a specific area of literary criticism. This essay outlines how scholars have approached this genre as a mode of literature.

As a generic term, detective fiction refers to a narrative whose principal action concerns the attempt by an investigator to solve a crime and to bring a criminal to justice. It poses two questions for readers: "Whodunit?" and "Who is guilty?" It is proof of the genre's self-reflexivity that these two generic questions have directed the literary criticism of detective fiction, just as they organize my discussion of this legacy.

Starting with "Whodunit?" the action sequence of the investigation structures the narrative, as it opens with the problem of crime and closes with its solution. Often the consequences of crime are revealed well before the events that led up to it become known. Typically, this situation structures detective fiction – but backwards: its plot aims at establishing a linear, chronological sequence of events that will eventually explain its baffling initial situation. It is generally agreed that form and especially plot structure make the detective story the kind of narrative it is. Further, as the Sherlock Holmes quotation suggests, this genre places under scrutiny strategies of narration and issues dealing with authorship by pondering what it takes to tell a good story. It is not surprising, then, that theorists of narrative in particular have been attracted by detective fiction.

Although detective fiction attempts to contain depictions of violence, murder, and death within its formal ambitions, these representations inevitably break away from its narrow formal confines, attracting readers with traditional novelistic concerns. This genre addresses such perennial literary themes as interpersonal conflicts, human motivation, and moral choice. The investigation always includes an analysis of human interaction leading to crime. In order to determine the culprit's identity, detectives assess how moral responsibility is to be allotted among the suspects. Their evaluation takes into account the difference between the judicial and the moral codes, which may, but need not, overlap, for an agent may be either legally or/and morally responsible and guilty. The question "Whodunit" is thus not identical with the question "Who is guilty?" because the investigation shows guilt to be a more universal phenomenon than crime (Pyrhönen 1999). Critics characterize detective fiction as a rare kind of widely read contemporary literature that still attempts to distinguish between right and wrong.

The generic features of narrative receive an altogether different treatment in so-called crime fiction, a variant that began burgeoning from the 1930s onwards. Critics maintain that it came into existence as an oppositional discourse that violates the basic generic conventions of detective narratives. By relegating the detective interest to the sidelines, crime fiction focuses on a criminal's mind and deeds. Knowledge of the culprit's identity reformulates the two generic questions: whodunit changes into "whydunit," and the issue of guilt is reinflected as the integrity and stability of the self are placed under scrutiny.

It must be noted, however, that detective fiction has invited a great deal more critical discussion than crime fiction. For one thing, recognizing crime fiction as a distinct and deviant generic offshoot has taken a surprisingly long time. Therefore, while I do take up research into crime fiction at relevant points, most of this chapter is devoted to studies of the detective narrative. It begins with an overview of the major phases of the field, and then examines the ways in which theorists have accounted for detective and crime fictions as forms of narrative. Targeting the key theme of ethics, I move on to discuss how critics treat moral issues, and conclude by examining how they theorize the pleasures these two types of narrative excite. Whatever the theoretical approach, its results depend on how a given theorist understands the status of the genre within the field of literature. When treated as mass-produced literature, detective fiction is assumed to represent a paradigmatic case of easy readability. In contrast, when the genre's literary self-awareness forms the starting point of analysis, the conclusions emphasize the readership's appreciation of form. In both cases, strategies of reading account for the specific kind of pleasure these narratives give readers.

Stages in the History of Detective Fiction Criticism

The emphasis detective fiction places on ratiocination and problem-solving made it early on a favorite form of popular literature with academic readers. This fondness is explained by the fact that both literary criticism and detective fiction call for ingenuity and insight. Over the years, the genre has been used to illustrate the tenets and methodologies of many theoretical approaches such as structuralism, psychoanalysis, and feminism. Scholars have been interested in detective fiction for two broad reasons. What may be called internally oriented criticism analyzes the entire genre, a subgenre, or a specific author, to answer questions that the object of study raises, while externally oriented criticism uses the genre to elucidate some larger theoretical principles. The boundaries between these two classes, however, are flexible (Pyrhönen 1994).

The first critical discussions worthy of notice are G. K. Chesterton's essays published in *The Defendant* in 1902. The creator of the Father Brown detective stories, Chesterton defended detective fiction on the grounds that it expresses the sense of poetry of modern life in contemporary cities. What also made the genre valuable for him was that it takes the side of civilization against the intruding forces of criminal chaos. Yet it was from the mid-1920s onwards that the first notable body of criticism began to take shape. Like Chesterton, the first critics were authors of detective fiction and aficionados who wanted to justify their writing and reading habits and to explain what made the genre worthy of study. Such authors as Dorothy L. Sayers, Willard Huntington Wright (S.S. van Dine), and the poet C. Day Lewis (Nicholas Blake) together with such academics as Marjorie Nicolson and E.M. Wrong engaged in this discussion. These early essays were published either as prefaces to collections of detective short stories (for example, *The Omnibus of Crime* [1929]) or in magazines aimed at the general educated reading public, such as *The New Yorker*. Although certainly not academic studies, these articles are nevertheless valuable, because they show how authors and connoisseurs understood the craft involved in writing and reading the genre. In the 1940s Haycraft wrote the first history of the genre, *Murder for Pleasure* (1941), also editing the first anthology of critical essays, *The Art of the Mystery Story* (1946). This essay collection provides a good introduction to early criticism that treated detective stories in a practical manner.

The early critics concentrated on plot structure and narrative techniques because they wanted to show that what set detective fiction apart from all other modes of literature was its unusually shapely narrative organization. This was the period when the so-called whodunit was the major generic form. What was understood to define the genre was its double nature. In one sense it was not a narrative at all but an intellectual puzzle – a notion Sherlock Holmes endorses. In another sense, however, due to its dramatic content and basic character functions, it was regarded as the most primitive form of narrative still existing in literature – a view that shapes Doyle's decision to use the sentimental Watson as a narrator. Critics agreed that detective fiction could never reach the status of serious literature. Yet by adhering to the kind of shapeliness, causality, and cohesion familiar from earlier nineteenth-century realism, the genre kept alive an old-fashioned narrative modeled on plot and incident. This was, they argued, an achievement in itself. More specifically, critics examined the narrative strategies authors used to construct plots backwards; that is, the ways in which they made the ending reverberate back onto the whole narrative so that, in the light of this ending, readers can perceive the pattern of interlocking elements, appreciating its skilful composition. Such an organization necessitates that plot construction and thematic content reflect one another: telling a story is approached as a problem of composition while crime is treated as an exercise in ratiocination.

Another area on which the early critics concentrated was the whodunit's game-like nature, based on a notion of fair play. Fair play means that authors must give readers the chance to arrive at the solution before the detective does. They should show readers the clues needed for solving the case, while simultaneously confusing them as to the correct meaning of these clues. Strategies of exhibiting facts inconspicuously, separately, and disconnectedly were identified as the main method of confounding readers. Critics argued that the challenge detective fiction posed for authors consisted of a combination of imagination and innovation. Authors had to introduce clever differences into the conventional scheme without breaking its boundaries. This notion suggests that the skill required in writing detective fiction resembles artisanship, the competent and insightful reproduction of a generic model.

After World War II critical interest in detective fiction waned. This change probably reflected the decline of both the British whodunit and the American hard-boiled narrative. Edmund Wilson's two acerbic articles for *The New Yorker* – "Why Do People Read Detective Stories" (1944) and "Who Cares Who Killed Roger Ackroyd" (1945) – argued that the genre had become outmoded. This quiet period ended with the arrival of structuralism in the 1960s, which initiated the second major phase of detective-fiction studies. Although the structuralists covered the same ground as the early critics, their reasons and aims for studying the genre were different. Another novelty was placing the analysis within a distinct theoretical framework which for the first time lent criticism a certain rigor and system. The Russian formalists had claimed that such unsophisticated narratives as myths and folktales were worthy of study because their simplicity enabled scholars to examine the general laws by which all narratives work. Popular narratives were regarded as the modern counterparts of these forms, and detective fiction was treated as a prototype for narrativity. It also provided a testing ground for a methodology that could then be applied, with modifications, to more demanding texts. These structuralist studies initiated theoretically sophisticated engagements with the genre's narrative form.

Although not, strictly speaking, about detective stories, a good example from this period is Umberto Eco's (1979 [1966]) analysis of Ian Fleming's James Bond novels, the aim of which is to prove that they are structurally of one type. By isolating the basic structural units and the rules governing their combination, Eco derives a narrative grammar whose functions include all the narrative possibilities of Fleming's novels. Because these novels repeat the same narrative structure, Eco designates them as narrative machines: they supposedly make available a range of rigidly preestablished and preordained interpretive solutions that readers then mechanically actualize.

The 1970s and 1980s mark the third major phase of detective fiction studies. By this time most Western countries had their own indigenous detective literature. Why did this genre attract so many readers? What roles did it serve in culture? Given its popularity and mass production, critics worked from the assumption that its function was to reproduce values and subject positions maintaining socio-cultural stability. Such a close fit between detective fiction and society was seen to arise from the genre's genealogy. As a literary form, it was argued, it could flourish only after Western societies had an established police force. The public also had to have an idea of just legal procedures, enabling it to place its sympathy on the side of law and order. Detective fiction was therefore taken not only to reflect widely approved notions about crime and its investigation in society but also to provide a means of access to such ideas. In theoretical terms, these studies probed how ideology and detective fiction intersect. Defining ideology as specific strategies for legitimating the power of dominant social groups, critics maintained that the operations of ideology are seen in the formal elements and ideas that detective fiction chooses from the discourses circulating in culture. Ideology thus shapes both the structures and themes of the genre.

The studies on generic ideology during this period were by no means unified. The American cultural critic John G. Cawelti (1976) argued that detective fiction enables readers to engage in what he calls moral fantasies. This concept refers to the escapist ideal worlds the genre constructs that allow readers to experience a wide range of emotions without the insecurity and complications accompanying such emotions in reality. Throughout the reading experience, readers are aware that any uncertainty is controlled and ultimately resolved by the formulaic structure. The moral fantasy of hard-boiled detective fiction, for example, relies on elements of adventure that test the investigator's heroism through the moral choices he makes. Cawelti claimed that detective fiction allows readers to process difficult cultural and national issues and to find solutions ensuring cultural continuity. It assists in assimilating changes to traditional imaginative constructs concerning ethics.

Other scholars such as Stephen Knight (1980), Dennis Porter (1981), and D. A. Miller (1988) took a critical view of the genre's ideological underpinnings. Because detective fiction embodies and disseminates ideas about crime, policing, and the power of the state to monitor transgression, they maintained that it belongs to the discursive practices sustaining Western capitalist societies. By portraying the law and its enforcement as natural and self-evident, the genre helps to circulate the idea that crime and the law are outside any specific social contexts and concrete historical developments. In this way it helps to camouflage the complex connections among the state, the law, and justice. Another factor reinforcing the genre's alignment with the socio-cultural status quo is formal: thanks to its code of realism, detective fiction offers itself to readers as a reflection of the world, its transparency resting on familiar patterns of cause and effect, of social relationships, and moral values. By reproducing what society takes to be reality, these critics argued, it does not contest habitual, everyday standards of perception and thinking.

Lately these views of detective fiction as a straightforward reflection of dominant ideology have been contested because they are based on the untenable assumption that detective fiction is aligned with conservative ideology, while serious literature is relatively autonomous in relation to ideology. Jim Collins (1989) points out that in all forms of fiction ideology is an arena of negotiation between discourses, where ideological elements are mixed in different permutations. Thus detective fiction, too, puts forth views that are dominant and oppositional, regressive and progressive. In Collins's view, contemporary societies are defined by the simultaneous existence of many discursive cultural centers, each embodying a specific world view, and each vying for cultural power in conflict with the others. What is more, each genre, detective fiction included, deals with cultural issues in accordance with its own ideological discourses that have been repeatedly rewritten over the years. As each generic change includes shifts in ideological tenets, it is impossible to speak of a stable and uniform generic ideology.

The fourth phase of criticism lends credence to these notions of ideology as an arena of contestation. The emergence of the feminist detective story and its rise into public awareness in the 1980s and 1990s combined the process of solving crimes with a feminist investigation of social conditions under patriarchy (see Gavin, chapter 20 in this volume). These novels treat the construction and validation of sex and gender biases within the genre; they compare the relationship of fictional representations to social reality; and they aim at reversing conventions that undercut women. Soon the influx of multicultural detective fiction focusing on such related issues as race, class, and (post)colonialism flooded the markets, directing critical attention to the multiple ways in which the genre treats what Andrew Pepper (2000: 6) calls "the existential realities of pain, anger, and resentment" in contemporary culture (see Christian, chapter 22 in this volume). Current research holds that the genre meets head on bitter racial, ethnic, class, and gender conflicts without providing easy answers. At best, it is able to envision a present and a future where difference can be acknowledged and where power relations can be unsettled (Pepper 2000: 8, 174–5).

Gradually also the awareness of crime fiction as a distinctive genre has gained ground in criticism. Influential twentieth-century texts include Julian Symons's *Bloody Murder: From the Detective Story to the Crime Novel* (1992 [1972]), a popular study which contributed to the broadening of the critical discussion; and Tony Hilfer's *The Crime Novel: A Deviant Genre* (1990), the first comprehensive account of the forms, conventions, themes, and key authors of crime fiction. Hilfer's argument is that this genre defines itself in opposition to detective fiction by violating the basic laws of its predecessor. The dominance of plot gives way to a focus on character and psychology, while social and moral norms are engulfed by deviance. Malmgren (2001) links these changes to postmodern culture's questioning of justice, identity, and representation, notions that are shown to be relative and unstable. Several of the major studies of detective and crime fiction published in recent years have built on these insights and have added substantially to the understanding of crime narratives that marginalize the figure of the detective or in which the investigative element disappears altogether (e.g., Cobley 2000; Plain 2001; Priestman 2003; Knight 2004).

The current phase of research illustrates well the contemporary interest in all forms of narrative, the relaxation of the boundaries between "high" and "low" literatures, and the fact that the detective and crime genres have become accepted academic subjects of study, taught at the university level. The common denominator in all these contemporary studies is critical diversity.

Studies on Narrative and Generic Features

Detective fiction enjoys a special status among scholars of narrative, for they hold that it illustrates the basic characteristics of all narratives. It demonstrates such features as the series of narrative levels and embedded texts of which narratives are comprised and the indispensability of generic structures that both conform to reader expectations and disappoint these same expectations (Sweeney 1990). Furthermore, detectives are portrayed as textually embedded model readers whose activities mirror those of their audience. Their investigation of various data resembles the general principles of reading that require one continually to try out different frames of reference and to modify and reinterpret one's inferences (Hühn 1987).

A useful example of these studies on the narrative and generic features of detective fiction addresses plot structure. Tzvetan Todorov (1977) claims that what distinguishes detective fiction as a genre is temporal displacement. It also differentiates the subgenres from one another. By temporal displacement he means that the genre omits narrating the moment of committing the crime; instead, this act is made to appear gradually only after its consequences (such as a body in the library) have been revealed. Temporal displacement creates two separate stories: the story of the crime and the story of the investigation. Narrative presentation combines them in a specific manner. In whodunits, the story of the crime belongs to the past and is – because hidden – absent from the present, whereas the story of the investigation happens in the present, its main function being the uncovering of the story of the crime. In contrast, hard-boiled narratives vitalize the story of the investigation, relegating the story of the crime to a secondary status. Todorov employs the Russian formalists' distinction between *story* (the story stuff in its chronological sequence) and *discourse* (plot understood as the way in which the events of *story* are ordered and presented through various literary devices).

Donna Bennett (1979) focuses this analysis by observing that discourse never fully reveals the absent story of the crime, leaving room for readers' inference. She envisions a point of overlap between the partially present crime story and the investigation sequence; this overlap she calls the core event. From this core the two narratives spread out, the story of the crime extending backward in time to provide the needed concatenation of causes, the discourse running forward detailing the investigation as it chronologically develops. Moreover, detective fiction emphasizes sequence, suspense, and closure, which together produce a classically shaped plot. It renders events in easily nameable sequences, thus illustrating the functioning of a chronological and linear plot that starts with a violation of order, depicts the attempts to restore it, and ends once this aim has been achieved. It also demonstrates the importance of closure, as the conclusion represents a definitive ending, which reveals the logical, causal, and temporal connections among the events.

Bennett observes that creating a sense of mystery requires a specific mode of narration, one that presents the crime as an enigma and the detective as a problem-solver. A number of narrative devices prevent the premature closure of the resolution: fragmentation, distraction, and ambiguity make events incomprehensible to readers. Fragmentation is the method whereby the story of the crime is broken into parts that are then dispersed throughout discourse. Fragmentation both permits a progressive recovery of past events and retards a comprehension of these same events. It tests readers' ability to combine the narrated pieces with one another, a task that is made difficult by their achronological and incomplete presentation. Readers must search for missing narrative links and reorder fragments temporally in order to reconstruct the absent story. Further, distraction modifies the presentation of fragments, while ambiguity regulates their usefulness. Distraction involves shifting the attention from the crime to the investigation. This procedure hinders readers from understanding the meaning of a fragment and is achieved, for example, by presenting a dramatic scene right after an important fragment. Ambiguity is used to impede readers' perception of the whole by opening up avenues for multiple inferences. It includes false fragments (so-called red herrings) which seem to fit one or more of the existing narrative patterns, but which temporarily invalidate correct hypotheses, and "phantom narratives" that are not based on story but that, nevertheless, have varying degrees of existence in discourse or in the reader's mind. Although these devices of manipulation are typical of the whodunit, they do play a role in other subgenres too.

A further indication of the centrality of genre as a guide to readerly expectations is the evolution of crime fiction. Its emergence has been theorized as a reaction against the dominant generic forms, the whodunit and the hard-boiled private eye narrative. Thus crime fiction retains the generic conventions of detective fiction, but in an inverted form. It subverts the reassurance of both preceding subgenres either by questioning the whodunit's trust in an explainable world and stable signification or by undermining the hard-boiled notion of the self and identity as grounds for endowing the world with some meaning (Hilfer 1990: 2, 6–7). Malmgren (2001: 139,

145–9) explains that what sets English crime fiction apart from its American counterpart is world structure. The former relies on a centered world guaranteeing some connection between appearance and reality. Consequently, guilt is brought home to the criminal, an outcome which ensures that some sort of justice prevails. Or, the criminal's pathology is confirmed, which insulates readers from complicity. In contrast, the latter takes place in a decentered world that is fluid, unstable, and duplicitous: signs, people, behaviors, and actions are arbitrary and ungrounded. Justice is seldom, if ever, achieved, and crime spreads from character to character, finally reaching readers who are infected by feelings of guilt and ambivalence. By demonstrating the intimate connection based on subversion between detective narratives and crime fiction, these studies emphasize the indispensability of genre as a norm or an expectation guiding writers in their work and readers in their encounter with texts.

Probing Ethics

Writing after the close of World War II, the poet W. H. Auden (1988) emphasized the social nature of crime and its consequences in the fictional worlds of detective fiction. As murder abolishes the party it injures, it makes society act on the victim's behalf. Auden stated that in analyzing the moral implications of crimes in detective fiction we should pay attention to the following components: setting, crime, victim, criminal, suspects, and investigator(s). These components supply the ingredients for thinking about what he called the "dialectic of innocence and guilt" characterizing the genre. In detective fiction, communities delegate the right of investigation to private detectives and/or the police. In order to identify the criminal, detectives consider how guilt and moral responsibility are to be allotted among the suspects. They have to be familiar with the law, understand the morals subtending communal life, know how to apply both the judicial and moral codes, and how to balance these codes against one another in cases of conflict. Often the perpetrator is hidden among a host of suspects, all of whom had sufficient cause to harm the victim. This strategy complicates the question of motive, for investigators must go beyond general considerations of motive to distinguish the one that fits a specific crime. Yet this genre handles any moral issues from a markedly literary viewpoint, so that whatever issues are raised, they are subordinated to generic conventions such as having "a least likely suspect," "a *femme fatale*," or "a serial murderer."

The early critics argued that the detective guards the moral boundaries of a fictional society. In their view, this figure gives voice to the moral principles by which a fictional society abides – or ought to abide. But another interpretation is feasible, as Roger Caillois (1984) claims, describing the detective as an aesthete, even an anarchist, by no means a protector of morality and still less of law. Heta Pyrhönen (1999) argues that a fruitful way to conceive the fictional detective's function seems to lie in the middle, as is best demonstrated by private investigators, placed between official purveyors of justice and those who violate that justice. As detectives, they stand for law and order, which, in principle, they must follow to stay in business. To do their job, however, they must often resort to illegal methods, for which reason, among others, their professional skills resemble the skills of criminals. In the fictional investigator the legal and moral codes of law enforcement intersect with those of the criminal order, making it possible for an author to stress either pole. Therefore, the investigation is just as much a probing into and a revelation of a detective's moral principles as it is a scrutiny of the suspects and their social context. There is no guarantee that this figure represents an author's moral views; one of the tasks readers are set is the moral evaluation of a detective's investigative performance. In Dashiell Hammett's *Red Harvest* (1929), for example, readers observe how the normally level-headed Continental Op becomes blood crazed, a metamorphosis by no means sanctioned by the book's implied author.

The subgenres raise different kinds of moral questions and favor different investigative methods, as the following account of the hard-boiled investigative narrative illustrates. From the start readers know that the investigation will reveal pervasive moral corruption. At first corrupt social institutions and professional criminals seem to be responsible, but the ending typically shows private persons to be the ones to blame. Safe bets as to the culprit's identity include the detective's client, friend, colleague, or lover. As Fredric Jameson (1983) points out, this subgenre envisions two concentric realms of guilt: institutional moral decay and professional crime encircle private transgressions that are singled out for scrutiny. As the function of crime as a puzzle to be solved diminishes (without vanishing altogether), the center of interest lies in the adventurous, even deadly dangerous, progress of the investigation during which readers observe how an investigator's moral code is established and elaborated through that individual's functioning as an investigator. This subgenre emphasizes such a moral code, for the solution demands that the investigator take on the role of a judge or even that of an avenger. American critics have related the hard-boiled detective's moral values to the violent frontier code of conduct prizing self-reliance, individualism, and resilient maleness. Recently John T. Irwin (2006) has discussed this code in terms of American work ethics, arguing that this subgenre stages a conflict between the professional and the personal, represented in terms of a clash between work and love. This clash is illustrated by the investigator's infatuation with a *femme fatale*, a conflict he solves in favor of work because work is his one true love. This notion of professionalism entails personal detachment and moral transgression only to the extent necessary to do the job.

Crime fiction is also engaged in probing ethical issues, but, by approaching them from the criminal's perspective, it raises questions concerning the irrational aspects of human psychology and the grounds of justice as a social system. Passion is a case in point. In American crime fiction, the protagonist revolts against a stultifying normative social order. He may become fatally infatuated with a woman, thus privileging schizophrenia and paranoia as the appropriate ethical choices befitting a meaningless world (Hilfer 1990: 55–7). When issues of justice are targeted, as they are in British crime fiction, the emphasis is placed on the egoism of the protagonist who values the self over social rules and obligations. Yet even so, this variant suggests the insufficiency of a given system of justice as it applies to a specific social order (Hilfer 1990: 73).

Pyrhönen (1999) emphasizes that the hard-boiled investigator's conduct forms but one area of moral assessment. Readers also need to consider the ethical implications of narration that builds on a discrepancy between the sordid events and the highly stylized manner of narration, whether in the first or third person. Renowned for its reportorial lyricism, hard-boiled fiction stresses the power of art to make a meaningless and squalid world meaningful through the act of narration. Narration is the investigator's means of ordering chaotic and fragmented experiences and of achieving a sense of self and self-control, however fragile. The narrative act acquires an ethical weight calling for readers' evaluation. Similarly, crime novels call on readers to assess the ethical implications of narration. Such an invitation is particularly evident in cases in which the narrator does not stand apart and above characters and intentionally refuses to supply norms and values with which to evaluate these characters. Further, the use of internal focalization or first-person narration by criminals manipulates readerly sympathies, asking readers to scrutinize their reactions to being made complicit in the ethical dilemmas presented.

Even this brief account shows that detective and crime fictions use the components comprised by their fictional worlds and their strategies of narration in order to represent various ethical questions concerning crime and its investigation. These components are general enough to enable their coding according to different outlooks of life. For example, while the ethics of hard-boiled fiction is pervaded by misogyny, feminist detective stories provide an ethical alternative by reviewing moral questions from the perspective of feminism. These genres do not provide a uniform ethical view of life, but many such views, inviting readers both to construct these views and to evaluate them.

Strategies of Reading

Umberto Eco (1979) was among the first to distinguish a dual readership for popular cultural products such as detective fiction. He envisions two distinct reading strategies, an average and a sophisticated one, corresponding with "low-brow" and "high-brow" readerships respectively. Both strategies are based on discernible features of the text. Eco theorizes the average reading strategy as a mode of escapist consumption. It supposedly accounts for the mass readership of detective fiction: it is assumed that if the genre were not easy to read, it could be neither popular nor even pleasurable. Average reading involves a relatively low level of abstraction and a high level of emotional engagement, as it focuses on following the plot and succumbing to its charms. This approach differs from the early critics' justifications of the reading habits of academics. They stressed that attention to formal composition explains the pleasure garnered by readers. Eco's concept of the sophisticated reading strategy is based on a similar notion. It includes an ability to see through the devices and the goals of textual manipulation, thanks to familiarity with generic conventions.

Criticism has mainly been interested in the average reading strategy, understood as relying on codes and conventions that make detective stories easy to read. Dennis Porter (1981) argues that the effortlessness of reading derives from the central role of plot: it formulates an enigma that is developed throughout the action and is resolved at the end. Such a composition awakens in readers the desire to know the outcome, but the answer is suspended for much of the narrative's duration. The desire to find out combined with the suspension of the solution together structure reading by making readers order the narrated sequences and decode the events in the light of the questions they are trying to answer. The genre makes it easy for readers to name and order events into narrative sequences such as "murder," "interrogation," "chase," and "cover-up." Such easily recognizable sequences constitute the armature of a readable text. What further promotes readability is the inclusion of scenes in which characters discuss the very questions readers are pondering. These passages are so-called reading interludes, showing readers how they too should approach the text at hand. Thanks to this exceptional clarity with which the genre advises readers regarding its conditions of comprehensibility, it has been treated as a paradigm of effortless readability. The enlisted characteristics enable fast reading and account for the readers' assumption that plot patterns are not complex or ironic.

The sophisticated reading strategy, in contrast, relies on a rereading approach. It is based on treating the genre as a self-reflexive textual enigma, one that is about readability and intelligibility – in short, about hermeneutic activity. Matei Calinescu (1993) suggests that rereading involves a retrospective logic, which consists of an attempt to pattern the work under perusal, seeing it as a structure. It demands heightened attention as well as an active, productive, and playful activity on the part of readers as they review how a given narrative has been put together. In the context of popular literature, such rereading may refer to the repetition of a previous act of reading with the aim of rediscovering it from a different vantage point, but it may also allude to a decision to treat a text as an example of its kind, so that reading includes a constant comparison between this particular text and similar texts held in a reader's memory. Furthermore, given that detective fiction relies on variations on generic structures, it calls for an aesthetic evaluation of an author's performance. Rereading detective fiction combines our efforts to grasp the structure of a work with a demand for intertextual comparison. A rereading strategy also includes familiarity with generic themes, and our knowledge of these themes creates within rereading the kind of symbolic depth typical of "serious" literature. Thus, for example, it is possible for Irwin (2006) to interpret Raymond Chandler's *The Big Sleep* as a work of the type of psychological complexity and dramatic moral tension associated with a literary novel. The resulting symbolic dimension, however, requires generic competence from readers.

There is yet another notable area of scholarly interest as regards reading, one that unites ethics and pleasure. Charges of immorality have been laid against detective fiction, because it involves a voyeuristic relationship to murder, which necessitates, under the guise of detection, prying and peeping by detectives and readers. The insistence on the necessity of detection renders this voyeuristic activity guilt-free and makes reading pleasurable. By challenging readers to solve crimes, it encourages them not only to "think like" detectives, but also to "think like" murderers. Consequently, they are empowered to imagine committing murder under certain circumstances. The psychoanalytic critic Slavoj Žižek (1991) argues that the genre presents readers with a specific ethical fantasy based on the communal dimension of murder. Murder binds a group of characters together as suspects whose shared sense of guilt could have made any one of them the murderer, for each had motive and opportunity. The detective's task, claims Žižek, is to dissolve this impasse of universalized, free-floating guilt by fixing it on one particular character, thus exculpating all others. The detective's solution thus annihilates the libidinal truth that each suspect might have been the murderer. The actual culprit is a scapegoat who realizes what the others also desire. This analysis recalls Auden's examination of the genre's ethical dimensions presented forty years earlier. Readers use detective fiction as their own imaginative acting-out of this fantasy of committing murder, but the existence of the criminal scapegoat also relieves them of any and all guilt. Unlike Auden, however, Žižek focuses on the effects detective fiction has on readers: it stubbornly avoids the truth at which it continually hints by not making readers aware that they are murderers in their unconscious desire. By permitting readers to evade recognizing their own base impulses that are, nevertheless, made manifest in the stories they read, the genre is supposedly characterized by what Robert A. Rushing calls "libidinal bad faith" (Rushing 2007: 3).

In contrast, crime fiction faces this desire directly by compelling readers to identify with criminals through, for example, the use of internal focalization. Such narrative devices draw readers into complicity with criminals, as well as evoking in them a mixture of sympathy and repulsion. Consequently, readers become split in a way similar to the self-division of the criminal protagonists, a strategy that further probes the notion of identity as divided and compromised. It is no wonder that critics characterize the reading experience as being pervaded with guilt and anxiety. Malmgren (2001: 150) explains that crime fiction makes readers wonder where they will draw the line, and when they should give up on the protagonist – questions that make the reading experience disturbing and disquieting.

In his *Resisting Arrest* (2007), Rushing concedes that detective fiction is a genre of misdirected and misrecognized desire, but he nevertheless criticizes the psychoanalytical approach for attempting to "cure" this genre of its assumed defects. He argues that its tactic of misdirection makes available a reading strategy based on enjoyment, understood in the psychoanalytic sense as "pleasure-in-pain." Precisely by not making readers confront their antisocial and murderous wishes, the genre enables them to engage in compulsive serial reading. The one characteristic readers share with fictional detectives is that both desire to return repeatedly to scenes of crime in order to start the investigation process anew. The proposed solutions never satisfy, thanks to the fact that this mutual desire for murder has not been directly tackled; rather, it has been purposefully misidentified through being presented in an aesthetic and intellectual form. Yet such compulsive reading has its own rebelliousness, because it allows readers to defy that which is socially acceptable and valued. In letting readers indulge in "bad" literature, the serial reading of detective fiction permits them to experience their reading obsession as a transgressive form of contestation, a means of challenging social authority. Refusing to conform to the socially valued role of enlightened citizens reading serious literature, they enjoy immersing themselves in genre fiction. Rushing claims that this defiance of cultural expectations provides an enjoyment that "disturbs the powers that be, in an unpreventable and everyday fashion, an obstinate persistence that annoys rather than challenges" (2007: 142). Readers refuse to be cured of their addiction, which thus becomes a form of enjoyment flying in the face of good taste.

4

Crime and the Mass Media

Alain Silver and James Ursini

The history of crime on screen can be difficult to contain under a single rubric. Many if not most feature films, from Westerns to horror films and even comedies, include a criminal act. Does this make them all crime films? In absolute terms, perhaps. For the purposes of this essay, however, what defines a crime film is not merely the occurrence of a larceny, rape, robbery, or murder within the narrative, but whether such occurrences are the core activity for the narrative's characters, for the criminals or agents of law enforcement, for the protagonists or antagonists. Compare, for instance, *Eye for an Eye* (1996) and *In the Bedroom* (2001), both of which focus on parents' reactions to the murder of their child. While the former film dramatizes the grief process, the mother's decision to seek violent retribution outside the law transforms the picture into a crime film. By contrast, only the final scenes of *In the Bedroom* center on revenge. Is one a crime film, and the other not? There is no simple answer, but for our purposes, *Eye for an Eye* qualifies and *In the Bedroom* does not.

Unquestionably most Westerns are crime films, but their overriding generic identity is different. The narrative context and the iconography redirect viewer expectations to elements that are not directly related to crime. The same could be said of horror films, science fiction, and even period dramas. Many cite D. W. Griffith's 1912 short *Musketeers of Pig Alley* as the first crime film. But were not the gunmen in *The Great Train Robbery*, who rode on horseback across the New Jersey countryside nine years earlier, and before the Western genre was even defined, criminals as well? Clearly, this essay cannot attempt an exhaustive exploration of crime in film and mass media. We will restrict ourselves therefore to narratives with no generic identity other than their appearance in crime films and broadcasts, drawing our representative examples from twentieth- and early twenty-first century cinema, television and radio. (See Gates, chapter 27 in this volume, for detective films in particular.)

Real or Imagined

Among the earliest crime features are a series of unconventional, quasi-proletarian films directed at the end of the 1920s by Josef von Sternberg, an Austrian émigré who came to New York City as a child, worked in the garment district and even slept on the streets that earlier filmmakers had used as a backdrop for their own enactments of criminal behavior. Remarkably both naturalistic and stylized, *Underworld* (1927), *The Docks of New York* and *The Dragnet* (both 1928), *The Case of Lena Smith* and *Thunderbolt* (both 1929), all benefited from realistic scripts by the likes of Ben Hecht and Jules Furthman and were shot by such distinguished silent-era cinematographers as Harold Rosson and Bert Glennon, whose first feature as a director in 1928 was *The Perfect Crime*. *Underworld* is not the first motion picture released by a major studio in which the heroes are actually criminals. But earlier films that dealt with the world of crime in the context of pervasive gangsterism were constrained by a strong moral code. As with Griffith's *Musketeers of Pig Alley*, such features as Raoul Walsh's *The Regeneration* (1915) and Tod Browning's *Outside the Law* (1920) – starring his frequent collaborator Lon Chaney – also probed the social contexts for crime and criminality. *Underworld* eliminated most of the causes for criminal behavior and focused on the criminal perpetrators themselves, anticipating not only the flurry of gangster films released prior to the enforcement of the Production Code in 1934 but also the criminal narratives and characters of film noir of the 1940s and 1950s (see Munby, chapter 16 in this volume).

There is no question that the gangster film in the United States in the 1930s coincided with a very real and very sensational gangsterism actually at large in American society. *Little Caesar* (1931), *The Public Enemy* (1931), and *Scarface* (1932) borrowed liberally from the newspapers, magazines, and books of the era. With the release of just these three motion pictures in scarcely more than a year, Hollywood defined the genre. The characters, the situations, and the icons from fast cars to fancy fedoras established basic genre expectations associated with the gangster film that remain in force to this day. Unquestionably, the extraordinary lives and deaths of real gangsters like John Dillinger and Bonnie and Clyde, and of the G-men or other law-enforcers who strove to bring them to justice also informed the tastes of filmgoers. What 1934 screenwriter could have concocted a more spectacular Hollywood ending than the final shooting of Lester Gillis, better known as Baby Face Nelson? After crashing his disabled car, Gillis picked up his tommy-gun and, blasting away, strode towards two pursuing federal agents crouched behind their own vehicle. Before they died, they shot Gillis seventeen times. Or consider the alternate versions of the apprehension of George "Machine Gun" Kelly. As reenacted in *The FBI Story* (1959), when confronted by agents, Kelly throws up his hands and shouts "Don't shoot, G-men, don't shoot!" In the "real" version, a hung-over Kelly is surprised at the front door (or in the bedroom or the bathroom) by a Memphis police officer with a sawed-off shotgun; and if, in fact, armed FBI agents had been present they would have been subject to arrest themselves, as they were not licensed to carry weapons until the following year.

When the US Production Code was finally put into force (partially because of the pervasive violence in gangster films) unfettered portrayals of the rise and fall of figures such as the Al Capone-inspired Rico in *Little Caesar* and Tony Camonte in *Scarface* were no longer possible in studio movies. While nothing in the "pre-Code" movies approached such sensationalist images as Bonnie and Clyde's bullet-riddled sedan or Dillinger on a morgue table, the more powerful and complex influences of sex, blood-lust, and social inequity on criminal behavior could not be revisited for decades.

Presumably, even prior to enforcement of the motion picture code's stipulation that "the sympathy of the audience should never be thrown to the side of crime, wrong-doing, evil or sin," most moviegoers would not have empathized with the murderous Rico or a character who whistles a Donizetti aria while he ambushes and kills a man, as Tony Camonte does in the opening of *Scarface*. Whether or not they were based on specific, actual figures such as Capone or simply Hollywood pastiches of a crime lord, characters of this sort sold not just newspapers and dime novels but also movie tickets. "Public Enemy Number One" John Dillinger was shot down outside a movie theater after witnessing the exploits of Clark Gable as racketeer Blackie Gallagher in *Manhattan Melodrama* (1934). For Depression-era audiences, whose suspicion and even resentment of establishment figures was high, the avarice and attendant ruthlessness of such unlawful types could be interpreted at some level as a rebellion against the monied and powerful. "Populist" armed robbers such as Dillinger and Bonnie and Clyde had fans who actually cheered their deadly exploits, which they perceived as fighting back against those unseen powers responsible for their economic distress. Unlike the Western, the war movie, or the horror film, the popularity and prevalence of crime has never waned. From the nineteenth century on, tabloids, books, and newsreels freely conflated fact with fiction. The movie criminal was born from and sustained by this distorted reality and often found a place in the hearts of working-class audiences.

Love and Avarice

Most early criminals were somewhat simplistically defined. Like their real-life counterparts they were likely to be refugees from impoverished circumstances. As crime films progressed and the classic period of film noir began, passion emerged as a coincident or superseding motivation.

Conspiracy and betrayal, love and sex, impulse and the perfect crime – all are linchpins of the noir film, and all are part of the plot of *Double Indemnity* (1944). Certainly murder for profit and murder for love are old conceits, but as a tale of murder that combines the two, *Double Indemnity* is for many the quintessential crime film. The failure of would-be "perfect criminals" is not a surprise to the viewer, or as *Double Indemnity*'s protagonist Walter Neff puts it when he begins his narration: "Yes, I killed him. I killed him for money and for a woman. I didn't get the money and I didn't get the woman. Pretty, isn't it?" Pretty it's not. In fact, like so many pre-noir crime films, the sordidness of *Double Indemnity* is based on actual events and the sensational 1927 trial of Ruth Snyder and Judd Grey, a real-life pair of would-be perfect criminals who turned on each other and went to the electric chair.

In the opening shots of the picture, a car speeds ominously through a downtown area at night and stops in front of a large office building. The driver is Walter Neff, insurance salesman and wounded criminal. Upstairs in the offices of his firm, he tells his story to a dictaphone, a structure that reinforces the emotional undercurrent of the acts to which he confesses and anticipates other important films such as *Out of the Past* (1947), *The Killers* (1946), and *Criss Cross* (1949). In *Double Indemnity*, the filmmakers use the complex structure of the crime to emphasize instead the doomed and obsessive qualities of an entanglement driven by both love and avarice. There are few femmes fatales in crime fiction that rival Phyllis Dietrichson. Jane Palmer in *Too Late for Tears* (1949), who kills a corrupt private detective and her own husband (and probably killed her first husband as well); the cool, aristocratic exploiter Lisa Bannister in *Lady from Shanghai*; even the repeatedly duplicitous Kathie Moffat in *Out of the Past* (see Figure 4.1) are all distant seconds. The black widow portrayed by Stanwyck has

Figure 4.1   A central scene recounted in the voiceover of Jeff Bailey (Robert Mitchum) recaptures the day he saw the *femme fatale*, Kathie Moffat (Jane Greer), "coming out of the sun" (*Out of the Past*, 1947, dir. Jacques Tourneur, produced by Warren Duff).

become the archetype, and not the only one that *Double Indemnity* has to offer. In terms of content there is the ironic, first-person narration; extensive flashbacks; as forthright a portrayal of adultery as the Production Code would then permit; several other "pairings," not just the older courting younger attractions of Neff and Lola and Phyllis and Sachetti, but also Neff and Keyes; and a savvy investigator who treats Neff as a protégé. Finally, of course, there are the betrayal and death (actual and implied) for the illicit lovers. As Neff says in voiceover after everything has gone as planned, "Suddenly it came over me that everything would go wrong. It sounds crazy, but I couldn't hear my own footsteps. It was the walk of a dead man."

Violence and Obsession

After the classic period of film noir from 1940 to 1958, the shift away from noir motives back towards the casual violence that defined pre-Code criminals is best exemplified by several film adaptations over the course of more than two decades of the "Parker" novels of Donald Westlake (writing as Richard Stark): *Point Blank* (1967), *The Outfit* (1973), and *Payback* (1999). The central figures are freelance petty criminals who find themselves suddenly under attack from organized crime and decide that the best chance of survival lies in active retaliation.

The central concept of Westlake's first novel, *The Hunter*, is an obsession that transcends sex and money, alone or in combination. John Boorman's adaptation *Point Blank* uses the monomaniacal small-mindedness of its protagonist to motivate stylistic manipulations that underscore the integration of gangsterism into the everyday. Embellishing prototypes from the noir era, the underworld of *Point Blank* has joined regular society: well-dressed criminals live in upscale surroundings, until an old-school throwback unveils dark layers beneath the surface, where dispassionate killers sit around well-lit homes by the beach. Twenty-two years later *Payback* goes even further. Its explicit violence recalls the pre-Code gangsters. The modern filmmakers preserve the small-mindedness and opt again for a minimalist performance as a new incarnation of Parker moves through a world of back rooms and petty mobsters who mostly wear their occupations on their sleeves. The anti-social violence becomes much grimmer in a movie whose central axiom is, as the title suggests, "payback is a bitch."

While Boorman suggested that betrayal was a reflex in *Point Blank*, writer/director Brian Helgeland's would-be postmodernist approach to *Payback* replaces treachery with honor and code, an almost military adherence to chain of command, but all of it maintained among thieves. The desaturated colors and vaguely period trappings (set in the Nixon era) create a mood that is at times nightmarish but mostly brings to mind a graphic novel or an ordinary comic book. The aspects of *Payback* that most heavily evoke noir and run counter to simple crime drama are its narration – Porter's observations reverberate laconically over the soundtrack – and its elements of parody, such as the Asian-American dominatrix Pearl who is paid to inflict sexual pain, the ultimate expression of which is her comment when she and her cohorts drive up to kill the protagonist: "Hubba, hubba."

Even more directly than in *Point Blank* or *Payback*, in *The Outfit* screenwriter/director John Flynn erects a central narrative that is an existential set piece wherein a loner salves his alienation through deadly violence. It is also a mock epic in which, amplifying *The Hunter*, the "little man" defeats the dehumanized, organizational machine. As in *Point Blank* the uncertainty of surface appearances creates tension in a violent narrative. In the film's prologue men who appear to be a priest and a cab driver kill the protagonist's brother. While his brother's wife questions the utility of revenge – "What do you want money for? You got a woman; you got time" – in the hero's perception of how things stand or fall, money and time are both symbolic values and keys to survival.

The Outfit's version of Westlake's Parker (Robert Duvall) moves through a bevy of criminal icons arrayed against him – from Robert Ryan and the maniacal Timothy Carey as syndicate men to such bit players as Elisha Cook, Jr, Marie Windsor, and Emile Meyer – minor but iconic actors who, like the old car parked outside the first heist, evoke an antique vision of the underworld. Unlike the hitman Dancer in *The Line-Up* (1958), infuriated by his exasperating inability to reconcile the disdainful wheelchair-ridden mob boss to his honest mistake, the protagonists of *The Outfit* realize from the start that the unwritten rules insuring stability in a world of illegal acts have already condemned them. Only by systematically disrupting that literal and figurative underworld can they survive, so the narrative almost becomes a cipher for that system turning destructively against itself. The protest of the crime boss's wife over hiding in the safety of their mansion – "How long are we going to stay cooped up in this mausoleum?" – reveals the true nature of Westlake's vision: cardboard kingpins who "act like they own the world" and whom violent and obsessed loners easily defeat.

Character Conventions: Capers and Cops

Even someone as explicitly motivated by lust for money and power as Rico in *Little Caesar* may have his criminal judgment clouded by emotion. When Joe Massera parts with Rico to pursue a legitimate career as a dancer, the gangster initially plans to eliminate this liability by killing him. Rico's "soft spot" – read, his love for the handsome Joe – makes him change his mind at the last minute with deadly consequences, as Rico admits when it is too late: "This is what I get for liking a guy too much." Such homoerotic relationships recur frequently in crime films, most notably in *The Street with No Name* (1948) and its remake *House of Bamboo* (1955), where gang bosses portrayed by such hard-bitten actors as Richard Widmark and Robert Ryan respectively are taken in by tough-talking, handsome undercover agents (Mark Stevens and Robert Stack). Perhaps the most emotionally confused of gang bosses is the disturbed Cody Jarrett, played by James Cagney in *White Heat* (1949), who has severely twisted

Figure 4.2   James Cagney, right, as Cody Jarett in *White Heat* and Edmund O'Brien as an undercover agent Pardo (*White Heat,* 1949, dir. Raoul Walsh, produced by Louis F. Edelman).

relationships with his mother, his wife, and even the government agent who befriends him in prison (Figure 4.2).

Paul Muni's somewhat stereotyped portrayal in *Scarface* of the Italian Camonte as a dandy and womanizer looks forward to Richard Conte as Mr Brown in *The Big Combo* (1955), even, it could be argued, all the way to Conte's Barzini and James Caan's Sonny Corleone in *The Godfather* and, more recently, Tony Soprano (Figure 4.3). Although the history of crime fiction on American television is long and diverse, from such durable series as *Dragnet* in the 1950s to *Law and Order* starting in the early 1990s, few shows until recent times have made criminals into protagonists, among the earliest being *Crime Story* in the mid-1980s.

The more understated but equally obvious sexual avarice of crime bosses is a key plot point with figures like Big Jim Colfax in *The Killers* (1946), Whit Sterling in *Out of the Past* (1947), or Slim Dundee in *Criss Cross* (1949). The parallels between Capone and Camonte in *Scarface*, from the trademark furrow in his cheek to his custom-made wardrobe or bullet-proof limo, are pointedly drawn. But the derisive tirade

Figure 4.3   Paul Muni, left, as Tony Camonte, confronting his right-hand man Rinaldo (George Raft) in *Scarface* (1932, dir. Howard Hawks, produced [uncredited] by Howard Hawks and Howard Hughes).

of the Detective Bureau Chief when a reporter asks him for comments on the "colorful" Camonte smacks of empty rhetoric. Like the Western gunfighters with whom the Chief compares him, Camonte is simply larger than life.

The sordid tale of Tom Powers in *The Public Enemy* anticipates the ongoing alienation of many protagonists in crime films. Although his father is a cop and his brother is a law-abiding veteran of World War I, the evolution of Powers from "dead end" kid to petty criminal to gangster is presented with a matter-of-fact style and with a hint of empathy for a white character that is more troublesome in terms of the Production Code than obviously ethnic, quasi-caricatures such as Rico and Camonte. The protagonists of *The Roaring Twenties* (1939) are also Great War veterans, men hardened to the use of weapons and to killing on the battlefields, characters who like thousands of real-life veterans went from serving their country to being down-and-out. As Eddie Bartlett struggles to make a profit in the taxi business, his sense of entitlement for wartime sacrifice leads him to more lucrative use of his cabs by running bootleg liquor. The attitude of Powers and Bartlett carries forward into characters as diverse as "Lucky" Gagin in *Ride the Pink Horse* (1947), Joe Rolfe in *Kansas City*

Confidential (1952) or Mike Hammer in *Kiss Me Deadly* (1955), all of whom are cynical, suspicious of any authority that they believe is biased against them, and self-reliant in the extreme.

The overweaning grimness of Tom's brother, returning veteran Mike Powers, also anticipates aspects of Johnny Morrison in *The Blue Dahlia* (1946), and even Robert Ryan's portrayal of the embittered bigot Montgomery in *Crossfire* (1947). Cagney's later performances from *Angels with Dirty Faces* (1938) through *Each Dawn I Die* (1939) and *The Roaring Twenties* (1939) to *White Heat* (1949) anticipate and echo diverse figures. Cagney's hoodlums become more mentally disturbed with age, so that the line from the baby-faced killer in *The Public Enemy* leads to the psychopathic man-child Jarrett in *White Heat*. From those characters, from Enrico "Little Caesar" Bandello and Tony "Scarface" Camonte, it is a small step to portrayals of the purely sociopathic killers Foggy Poole and Dancer in *The Killer is Loose* (1956) and *The Line-Up* (1958).

Although technically a caper film that opens and closes with elaborate robberies and adds the "modern elements" of technology and a crime schematic created by a "brain man," or mastermind, *White Heat* is remembered for James Cagney's mother-loving, migraine suffering Cody Jarrett. Its narrative focus is on treachery rather than the planning of the heist. Jarrett's crazed exit in which he blows up a gasoline storage tank while screaming "Top of the world, Ma!" reduces the point of the standard caper to pure mania.

For criminals and veterans, for men and women, the inability to escape the consequences of one's past is a common problem and animates the plot in pictures from *You Only Live Once* (1937) to *The Deep End* (2001). *Criss Cross* is a caper film that incorporates this and many other classic crime film themes: the obsessive or "mad" love that dooms many fugitive couples, the first-person narration interwoven into a flashback structure, a complex heist at the core of the plot, and the simple double-cross. Among director Robert Siodmak's works, *The Killers* has a similar juxtaposition of narrative elements in which an investigator becomes fixated on finding out why a man would meet death so willingly and pieces together the story in flashback from various interviews. As in *Criss Cross* the fate of the protagonist (portrayed in both films by Burt Lancaster) turns on a femme fatale and a betrayal after a robbery.

Honor among thieves is foregrounded in *The Killing* (1956), which is justly cele-brated for its intricate, non-linear narrative. Directed by Stanley Kubrick, the movie features laconic performances by most of its protagonists balanced against a hysterical undertone in the work of Elisha Cook, Jr, and Timothy Carey. Kubrick's penchant for fatalistic plots meshes perfectly with the double-cross and clipped dialogue by noir novelist Jim Thompson (Figure 4.4). The sullen Cook – a noir icon who could range from pure punk in *Maltese Falcon* (1940) or *Phantom Lady* (1944) to a quasi-sympa-thetic portrayal in *The Big Sleep* (1946) – also appears the following year in *Plunder Road* (1957). Unlike *The Killing*, *Plunder Road* eschews overlapping scenes or any pointedly analytical devices in favor of a basic irony in which the robbers are tripped up by their own elaborate safeguards.

Figure 4.4   Seen here with Marie Windsor as his unfaithful wife Sherry, Elisha Cook Jr brings his forlorn mixture of misplaced loyalty and sexual frustration as George Peatty (*The Killing*, 1956, dir. Stanley Kubrick, produced by James B. Harris).

The diverse criminals in the caper film, often with differing skills and differing pasts, whether brought together by a brain man or by sheer coincidence, are not immune to in-fighting and antagonism within their ranks. One of the last examples from classic period noir, *Odds against Tomorrow* (1959), uses racial animus to create that conflict. But most typical are characters like Slim Dundee and Steve Thompson in *Criss Cross*, reluctant partners in crime brought together by a fatal woman. Thompson's narration is almost a lament and explicitly deterministic: "From the start, it all went one way. It was in the cards or it was fate or a jinx or whatever you want to call it." The expressionistic staging of the robbery with its violence, its dark, masked figures moving apprehensively through smoke-filled frames, and its deadly excitement becomes a nightmarish variant, again from Thompson's point of view, of the sexual promise of the initial sequence.

The criminal's opposite number, whether policeman, sheriff, district attorney, government agent, insurance investigator or private detective, can be just as fixated. Sergeant Flaherty in *Little Caesar* and Inspector Guarino in *Scarface* are both dogged cops, and their relentless pursuit of the gangster protagonists anticipates obsessed and

Figure 4.5 Touch of Evil (1958, dir. Orson Welles, produced by Albert Zugsmith): the portly and self-possessed Captain Hank Quinlan (Orson Welles) chuckles to himself as his suspect Manelo Sanchez (Victor Milian) appeals to Detective Menzies (Joseph Calleia) and fellow Mexican Mike Vargas (Charleton Heston).

self-righteous detectives from *The Big Heat* (1953) and *The Big Combo* to the brutal cops in *Dirty Harry* (1971) and *French Connection* films (1971/75) and *Homicide* (1991). In *The Big Heat*, a detective goes on a personal vendetta after the death of his wife in a car bombing. The violence he commits or instigates against those he believes guilty results in a significant body count and, when he exploits a spurned and disfigured moll's empathy for him, is as ruthless as any gangster's.

Touch of Evil (1958), as might be expected from Orson Welles, is a tale of police corruption extended to Shakespearean dimensions despite being set in a sleazy border town where drug dealing, the sex trade, gambling and generally illicit behavior run rampant (Figure 4.5). "All border towns bring out the worst of a country," Vargas, a Mexican narcotics enforcer, tells his American wife. This event is the trigger for a plot filled with the unlikeliest of twists and turns, as Vargas joins his colleague north of the border, Detective Hank Quinlan, to find the perpetrator. The corpulence of Quinlan, as played by Welles himself, seems to epitomize the bloated nature of corruption. He is also a racist. When he finds out Vargas is on the case his off-hand comment is, "They invited some sort of Mexican"; and later he tells his own Mexican-

American partner, Pete Menzies, while pointing to the US side of the border, "Let's go back to civilization."

The core of Quinlan's hubris is his methodology, the fact that he depends upon his "intuition" rather than "simple facts" and is willing to employ questionable methods, such as beating a Mexican suspect merely because he is having a miscegenous (in Quinlan's world view) affair with the murdered man's daughter. Ironically the dynamite planted by Quinlan in their "love nest" bathroom to incriminate Sanchez, who is in fact guilty, blows up in his own face. To exaggerate Quinlan's unappealing physical aspects, Welles often shoots himself in low angle, so that Quinlan resembles a bloated corpse long before he becomes one at the movie's end. Munching on choco-late bars and limping with a cane, Quinlan seems to be infected and decaying physi-cally as well as spiritually. As is later revealed by Menzies, Quinlan is also an alcoholic who fell apart after the strangulation murder of his wife, the only case he was not able to solve.

The corruption in this film is not confined to Quinlan and his lackeys, which include district attorney Adair as well as the police chief. Welles intercuts the story of the investigation of the bombing with a parallel and sometimes overlapping tale of inbred crime, centering on the town boss, Uncle Joe Grandi. Akim Tamiroff, fre-quently a character actor for Welles, renders Grandi as a quasi-comic figure with his Edward G. Robinson posturing and his misadjusted "rug." Grandi is also a crafty opportunist, who has decided to menace Vargas's wife in order to prevent her husband from testifying against Grandi's brother in Mexico City. Thus intertwined, all of Welles's unglamorous criminals become, in context, as larger than life as the dapper Camonte.

The world of the crime film is at its core a frenetic milieu, filled with odd syn-chronicities, unexplained events, and chance encounters, all creating a chain of causality that ultimately drags its protagonist to a foreshadowed end. Often these events turn on innocent characters unjustly accused, such as the hapless architect in Siodmak's *Phantom Lady* or the insurance investigator in Andre de Toth's 1948 *The Pitfall*. As they struggle to exonerate or extricate themselves, some of these charac-ters actually end up committing a crime. In an opening sequence of the early fugitive-couple crime film *You Only Live Once*, director Fritz Lang uses a series of elegiac details to establish his characters' innocent and romantic dependence on each other: even though ex-con Eddie and his wife Jo feel secure, the motel manager is inside searching through Eddie's collection of pulp detective magazines under the harsh glare of his desk lamp. When the manager finds several photos and a story on Eddie's criminal past, Lang underscores the irony with a shot of a frog jumping into a pond and diffracting Eddie's reflection in the water. After a local bank is robbed and an employee killed, the hapless Eddie is arrested, convicted on circum-stantial evidence, and, in view of his past record, sentenced to death. In the trial sequence Lang constructs a grim traveling shot that pulls back from a banner head-line which reads "Taylor Innocent" to reveal an alternate choice: "Taylor guilty." An equally grim prototype for an entrapping series of events is Al Roberts in *Detour*:

while hitchhiking across the country he ends up being blackmailed over a murder that never happened.

From the Cinema to Television and Radio

Perhaps the best-known example of such an entrapment is the television series *The Fugitive* (1963–7), starring David Janson. Creator Roy Huggins, who liberally borrowed elements from Hugo's *Les Misérables* and Dumas's *The Count of Monte Cristo*, saw the show as representative of the American ethos: "At the heart of the series is a preoccupation with guilt and salvation which has been called the American Theme." The opening title sequence of the first season's episodes sets the mood of fatalism and guilt that informed the entire four-year run of both the title figure and the show. Each episode opened on a two-shot of the fugitive, Richard Kimble, and Lieutenant Gerard, his nemesis throughout the series, on a train at night, a train headed for Death Row where Kimble is to be executed for the murder of his wife. As the camera moves into a close-up of Kimble — his face reflected in the glass of the train compartment window, the basso profundo voice of the narrator underscores the sense of doom as it describes the protagonist and his dilemma: "Richard Kimble ponders his fate as he looks at the world for the last time … and sees only darkness. But in that darkness fate moves its huge hand": a fortuitous train crash "frees" Kimble to search for the one-armed man he saw run from the crime scene the night of his wife's murder.

Over the course of four years, Richard Kimble is haunted and hunted by Gerard who, like inspector Javert in *Les Misérables*, is obsessed with his prey's capture. "Nightmare at Northoak" opens with what the audience first assumes is a "real" (as opposed to "dream") sequence. Kimble is walking down a dark, deserted street, not unlike many others the viewer has seen him traverse. Suddenly he hears footsteps and Gerard appears, as if out of nowhere. Kimble runs in silhouette down a cul-de-sac. He tries the door to a building. It won't open. He tries to climb a wall. He can't get a foothold. The sequence ends on Kimble's point-of-view shot of Gerard holding a gun, then the sound of an explosion as Kimble awakes in a sweat. "This is Richard Kimble's nightmare," the narrator intones. Later in the same episode, as Kimble is jailed by a local sheriff, the nightmare is repeated but the payoff is different. This time Gerard is actually there, staring at him sternly through the bars of the cell. Like many producers of crime-themed series, Huggins constantly reiterates his ironies.

The tradition of crime fiction in mass media outside of motion pictures actually begins well before television, with radio. The character of the Shadow, Lamont Cranston, originated in 1930 as the narrator of hour-long dramas adapted from crime stories that appeared in the pulp magazine "Detective Story." The signature introductory line (delivered by various stentorian actors including Orson Welles) – "Who knows what evil lurks in the hearts of men? The Shadow knows …" – endured into the 1950s and became so popular that the narrator turned into the eponymous crime-fighting character, the pulp magazine changed its name, and spin-offs included more than half a dozen feature films. Other characters that originated in hard-boiled fiction such as Mike Shayne, Philip Marlowe, and Sam Spade also inspired series.

The most prominent radio analog to television's later movie-of-the-week was Cecil B. DeMille's Lux Radio Theater, where numerous examples of crime fiction were dramatized. Even as the popularity of the pre-code gangster cycle waned, radio versions of such features as the *Criminal Code* (1937) with Edward G. Robinson and Cagney in *Angels with Dirty Faces* (1939) were being broadcast. Although the concept was to have the original stars reprise their movie roles in these under-sixty-minute dramas, only on radio could one experience Robinson as Sam Spade in *The Maltese Falcon* (1942). Condensed versions of many of the motion pictures discussed here were presented on the Lux Radio Theater: *Each Dawn I Die* (1942), *Phantom Lady* (1944), *Murder, My Sweet* (1945), *Ride the Pink Horse* (1947), *The Dark Corner* (1947), *Lady in the Lake* (1948), *The Pitfall* (1948), *T-Men* (1948), and *The Street with No Name* (1949). It took until 1950, half a dozen years after its feature release, but even *Double Indemnity* became a Lux drama with MacMurray and Stanwyck.

As they were coincident with the classic period, it is not surprising that many of the figures portrayed on radio were, if not directly copied from, at least heavily influenced by film noir prototypes. In terms of iconic impact, movie stars sometimes appeared on a program with cachet, but seldom in a series. Dick Powell intoned Marlowe in *Murder, My Sweet* for Lux Radio, but the series, which ran from 1947 to 1951, featured B-star Van Heflin and character-actor Gerald Mohr as Raymond Chandler's private eye.

At the series level, early television crime dramas were almost exclusively the province of detectives, whether police or private. In moving from radio to television, *Dragnet,* with the iconic, deadpan Jack "Just-the-facts-ma'am" Webb as Sergeant Friday, and *Richard Diamond*, starring Dick Powell, exemplified each type respectively. Other police shows quickly followed *Dragnet*, from *Racket Squad* in 1951 and *Highway Patrol* in 1955 to *M Squad* in 1957 and *The Naked City* in 1958 (inspired by the 1948 docu-noir of the same name). There was even an occasional reversal of the cross-pollenization of features and television, as when the 1954 series *The Lineup* became the 1958 Don Siegel-directed feature of the same name.

Other series built around private investigators included *Mickey Spillane's Mike Hammer* (1956), *Peter Gunn* (1958) – which also generated a feature film version, *Gunn*, in 1967, and a theme song popular with high school pep bands across the US – and *Philip Marlowe, Private Eye* (1959), although the TV version only lasted for one season. The weekly episodic format of television could also accommodate characters like the protagonist of *Johnny Staccato*, in which John Cassavetes played a piano player often embroiled in the problems of patrons who came into his nightclub, and of *Man with a Camera*, in which a freelance photographer played by Charles Bronson in the manner of real-life crime shutterbug Arthur "WeeGee" Fellig probed for the sordid details behind the pictures he took.

From the first, movies made for television were often crime dramas. Don Siegel's remake of the *The Killers* was intended to debut on network television but was released theatrically because of the violent content. When it was broadcast in November 1964 Siegel's remake of *Ride the Pink Horse*, entitled *The Hanged Man*, was the second movie of the week (MOW). The first, *See How They Run*, which aired a month earlier, was also a crime drama.

Narrative Style

Some crime films, such as *The Dark Corner* (1946), operate in the ironic mode. The actual perpetrator of the crime of which private detective Bradford Galt is falsely accused is known to the audience, even as it is encouraged to identify with the desperate and uninformed protagonist. Other films, like *Phantom Lady,* are subjective: for most of its running time, neither the investigator, Carol "Kansas" Richman, nor the viewer, know who actually killed Scott Henderson's wife. *Phantom Lady* changes when the audience sees the killer dispatch a key witness. A straightforward mystery such as *Murder, My Sweet* (1944) adapts the first-person narrator from Chandler's novel *Farewell My Lovely*, so that the audience only sees what Marlowe sees. The extreme example of such a restriction would be the subjective camera in Robert Montgomery's adaptation of *Lady in the Lake* (1947). This same technique is used for the first third of *Dark Passage*, but even after plastic surgery "turns" the main character into Humphrey Bogart, the subjective perspective is maintained, as only a few cutaways and a brief montage give the viewer a glimpse of something which the protagonist does not see or hear. Whether introduced via a ripple effect or simply a smash cut, the past palpably intrudes via flashback and subjective camera. Whether filtered through a single character's point of view (*Criss Cross*) or ostensibly detached and objective (*The Killing*), "seeing" the past gives a reality that no amount of telling can match.

First-person narration crossed over from being a popular device among hard-boiled writers to an evocative perspective for crime filmmakers. It had a particular utility for crime drama. It put the reader or viewer, as the case may be, into the mind of the protagonist. In that way the viewer/reader could experience in a more intimate way the angst of the character. More importantly, it compelled the viewer/reader to identify at least partly with the narrator, regardless of whether that narrator was deeply flawed, capable of felonious behavior or even psychopathic rage, as in so many of both classic period and post-noir crime films. Both the novella and film adaptation of *Double Indemnity* are striking examples of how a protagonist directly and indirectly reveals the psychological and physical impacts of the crime on his mind and body.

Like *The Naked City* (1948) and *Dragnet* (1954), *T-Men* (1947) uses a third-person narrator. His stentorian voice leads the viewer through the convoluted plot of the film to its pat patriotic resolution. In order to establish its credentials the movie even introduces a former chief in the Treasury Department, who sits stiffly behind a desk and drones on in monotone about the work of Treasury agents. In

French Connection William Friedkin imposes an even more self-conscious documentary style that is somewhat subjective by association when the camera merely follows the two detectives across the streets of New York and into several actual locales. However, intercut objective sequences reveal many details of the criminal drug cartel, which are completely unknown to the investigators, and add to the dramatic irony of the film.

Christopher Nolan's *Insomnia* (2002) is a remake of a Scandinavian neo-noir of the same name made in 1997 and starring the Swedish actor Stellan Skarsgård. Both films trace the disintegration of a personality under pressure from guilt, stress, and sleepless nights. Like Graham Greene's protagonist in *A Burnt-Out Case*, Detective Will Dormer (Al Pacino in Nolan's version) has been sent to Alaska during a series of "white nights" (several weeks during the summer solstice in higher latitudes during which darkness in never complete) partially to evade an internal affairs investigation, partially to aid the local police in finding the murderer of a young girl. Like Skarsgård, Pacino projects a "weariness to the bones" in manner, speech, and tone. After shooting his partner in the fog during a chase – a partner who was going to give evidence against him to internal affairs investigators – Dormer's complete disintegration is inevitable. He begins to hallucinate, seeing glimpses of his partner, of the murdered girl, and hearing normal sounds amplified. He lowers his voice almost to a whisper. And even after boarding up the windows with furniture in his hotel room, he still cannot shake the image of a burning sun, a symbol for his guilt as well as his rapidly dissolving psyche.

With typical crime film irony, the only person who can understand Dormer is the killer himself. Comic actor Robin Williams's eerie and unsettling portrayal of Walter Finch recalls the style of Elisha Cook Jr. He contacts Dormer by phone to draw him into his own guilt and to clear both of them through a convoluted scheme. Nolan underlines the doppelganger quality of these two men. They are both guilty of crimes that were, at least on a conscious level, accidental. They are both unable to sleep. And they are both clever puzzle-solvers: Dolmer solves real-life crimes; Finch writes mystery novels. Nolan reinforces this duality by framing them visually in matched frame halves. And when they shoot each other in the climax of the movie, the scene plays out symbolically as an attempt by each man to rid himself of his demonic double. After this act of exorcism, both men can finally sleep: Finch floating in the lake into which he has fallen, Dormer dead on the wharf.

The narrative and visual style of television crime dramas has been and continues to be heavily influenced by individual executive producers and creators. Roy Huggins followed *The Fugitive* with the unsuccessful *The Outsider*, about an alienated ex-con turned private eye, and then the much lighter and longer-running (six seasons) *The Rockford Files* in the late 1970s. That counter-cultural decade also saw the appearance of idiosyncratic police sleuths like Telly Savalas's Theo Kojak, with his trademark lollipop, and Peter Falk's scruffy, unprepossessing Columbo, whose series appearances began in 1971. The novels inspired by the actual experiences of police sergeant Joseph Wambaugh led to the creation of *Police Story*, which ran for five seasons and generated such spin-offs as *Police Woman* and *Man Undercover*. More radical changes were evident in the 1980s: Stephen Bochco transformed TV action drama in general and police shows in particular by introducing multiple story-lines unfolding across serial episodes of *Hill Street Blues*, and a combination of MTV visuals and neo-noir plots animated Michael Mann's *Miami Vice*. In the 1990s, the realistic, violent content of Bochco's *NYPD Blue* required viewer warnings before each episode. In the present decade the preeminent examples of innovative style in crime series, *C.S.I.*, *Without a Trace*, and *Cold Case* are all executive produced by Jerry Bruckheimer.

The World is Yours

The rooftop sign that provides the ironic coda in the original *Scarface*, revealed after a pan up from the body of Tony Camonte lying in the wet street, could also be taken as a comment on the global impact of American criminals and gangsterism. Without question and regardless of their ethnic origins, the real and imaginary gangsters of the United States dominated crime and the crime film for decades. Despite their Gallic existentialism and ruthlessness, the doomed French grifters first epitomized by Jean Gabin in the 1930s and again after World War II in *Touchez pas au Grisbi* (1953) were always too laconic to displace Cagney or Robinson as hard-bitten prototypes. While their expatriate *fratelli* were dominating American scripts, post-War Italian neo-realist characters were more often petty thieves and delinquents. The tinges of noir and the incestuous sub-plot borrowed from *Scarface* in Alberto Lattuada's *Il Bandito* (1946) never transforms the criminal character into the "tragic hero" that Robert Warshow perceived in the US product (Figure 4.6). Even when Lattuada attempts to spin an operatic tragedy in *Il Mafioso* (1962) the result falls well short of such protean figures as Camonte or Rico and dissolves into pathos. With few exceptions the continental criminal, whether killer or con man, whether imitative of American fiction or painted in existential, social realist, or naturalist hues, never found dying declarations as potent as those of Rico or Tom Powers.

Like their American counterparts, most British crime films are rooted in real events. Early examples combined the sensationalist traditions of Jack the Ripper with Dickensian dramatizations of the British underclass of petty felons, such as the gang of blackmailers in the silent version of *The Crimson Circle* (1922). From the beginning, British filmmakers frequently veered towards literary and historical sources, which blurred the line between real and imagined. In some ways, the gritty adaptation of Grahame Greene's *Brighton Rock* conflates all the major pre-Code gangsters in the US. While he may look like Cagney's Tom Powers, Richard Attenborough as Pinkie Brown shares Camonte's paranoia and scarred face and is as tormented by an uncertain sexuality as Rico. One can only imagine whether the planned remake will uncannily mirror figures from *The Godfather* or *Goodfellas*. While *The Krays*, based on the

Figure 4.6   Lidia (Anna Magnini) and Ernesto (Amedeo Nazzari) in *Il Bandito* (1946, dir. Alberto Lattuada, produced by Dino De Laurentiis), which exemplifies the post-war Italian neo-realist handling of criminality.

infamous twin criminals of the London underworld of the 1960s, may not have inspired dramatization on a par with Al Capone, their special type of sociopathy continued to resonate in British films from *Performance* (1970) to *Lock, Stock, and Two Smoking Barrels* (1998), *Essex Boys* and *Gangster No. 1* (both 2000). Actual British capers spawned movie versions from *Robbery* (1967) to *The Bank Job* (2008). Love and avarice, violence and obsession are also thematic archetypes in British crime films, often distilled into a single figure such as the kingpin in *Long Good Friday* who dreams of a cross-over into legitimacy which is as self-deceiving as the pipe-dreams of his American counterparts. Perhaps even more developed in Britain is the sense of the "dark past" that catches up to retired felons from *The Hit* (1984) to *Sexy Beast* (2000).

Since wherever there is crime, there are, of course, crime books and movies, so almost any new example has certain hybrid characteristics. The inbred and violent traditions of the Japanese *yakuza* or the Chinese triads differ markedly from the song-filled gangster films of Bollywood, the Reggae-rhythms that underscore the Jamaican saga of a folk hero/cop-killer/would-be pop star in *The Harder They Come* (1972) or the desperately poor young criminals of Mexico, from Pedro in *Los Olvidados* (1960) to Chivo in *Amores Perros* (2000). Still, they all have much in common. At one extreme one could cite the austerity of a crime film by Bresson and the status imposed by a transcendent world view from *Pickpocket* (1959) to *L'Argent* (1983). At the other end is the transcendent viciousness of cop and gangster alike in Hong Kong thrillers like Andrew Lau and Alan Mak's *Infernal Affairs* (*Mou Gaan Dou*, 2002), or John Woo's ground-breaking *A Better Tomorrow* in 1986 (see Fang, chapter 47 in this volume). Perhaps the ultimate incestuousness of crime as art is the easy transposition of plots and personae across borders and cultures, so that Martin Scorsese can combine elements of Bressonian asceticism and martyrdom with the plot of *Infernal Affairs* to produce *The Departed* (2006). In both crime and crime fiction, it would seem anything is possible.

5

Crime Fiction and the Literary Canon

Joel Black

Popular versus Literary Crime Fiction

Crime fiction has always had an uneasy relation to what scholars and critics consider "literature." One need only note the tendency among established literary authors to use pseudonyms when writing in this genre: Nicholas Blake is the poet C. Day Lewis, while Dan Kavanagh is the novelist Julian Barnes and Benjamin Black the novelist John Banville. The fact that these individuals have sought to keep their identities as literary authors and as writers of crime fiction separate suggests a certain chariness of their literary reputations, either on their part or their publishers', and a wariness about their names being associated with a form that is today still considered artistically suspect in some quarters. For despite the canonization of crime literature – and, indeed, of popular literature in general – by the academic community over the past two or three decades (Priestman 1990; Ascari 2007), and despite the fact that many of the most revered masterpieces of world literature are centrally concerned with the subject of crime, practitioners and proponents of the genre continue to find themselves on the defensive regarding its artistic status. Even if studies like the present volume provide further confirmation of crime fiction's canonization as literature, a vigorous critical debate may be expected to continue concerning crime fiction's status as *high* literature or literary *art* – an honor customarily bestowed on books that appeal, at least in the short run, to a limited rather than to a mass readership.

The issue is inevitably raised in the case of works of crime fiction written by authors with literary abilities or aspirations. Do such works reveal artistic qualities inherent in the genre, or are these works exceptions that belong to an elite (or effete) subgenre of their own? How do readers respond to such hybrid works that combine sensational effects appreciated by general audiences with a mix of subtleties and profundities appealing to more refined tastes?[1] Do crime fiction aficionados seeking what author and critic Clive James calls "the thriller thrill" have the patience to read stories dealing with crime but using a variety of literary techniques to explore a wide range of human emotions and experience? Conversely, are literary connoisseurs seeking the so-called "art thrill" willing to put aside their aesthetic expectations and wade through detailed descriptions of sordid crime scenes that require them to muster the intellectual rigor needed in a prolonged criminal investigation (James 2007: 95)?

Speaking for readers like himself who presumably belong to both categories, James writes that we

> long for these sleuths to be surrounded by classy prose, like Raymond Chandler's Philip Marlowe, so that we can get the art thrill and the thriller thrill at once. *Down these mean streets a man must go who is not himself mean.* Great idea, great sound, great sociological significance. But above all an eventful narrative to make you read on. ...

For all James's appreciation of the "art thrill," he ultimately insists upon the primary importance of the "thriller thrill." (Note his prioritization of plot – "an eventful narrative" – over Chandler's insistence on the importance of character – "Down these mean streets a man must go ...".[Chandler 1995a: 991–2]) However much James might dream of works of literary crime fiction that bridge the barrier between mass-marketed crime fiction and literature aimed at an educated elite, he finds himself somewhat dissatisfied by a novel like Benjamin Black/John Banville's *Christine Falls* that "confronts you with the question of whether you want your crime writer to have that much literary talent" (James 2007: 91–2, 96).

It is fitting that James should cite Chandler as the writer who comes closest to providing his readers with a simultaneous jolt of the art thrill and the thriller thrill, since it had been this author's ambition in the 1940s to write crime fiction that would unite lowbrow and highbrow, popular and literary tastes. Yet in keeping with Lee Horsley's observation that "the balance between the popular and the literate is ever-changing" (Horsley 2005: 111), it is not surprising that this balance could not be sustained for very long. Horsley traces a bifurcation in crime fiction during the following decade between the popular and the literary – the former exemplified by Mickey Spillane's lowbrow mix of sex and violence, and the latter evidenced in Ross Macdonald's aspirations to literary seriousness (Horsley 2005: 88–9). It took another four decades for Chandler's vision of a type of crime fiction that united the popular and the literary to be revived – specifically, in Horsley's view, in the Lew Griffin novels of James Sallis who described his intention "to create a new kind of novel, something that combined the delights of crime fiction ... with the delights of 'literary' fiction."[2] It remains to be seen whether the taste for such works is more than a vogue, and whether the precarious balance between popular and literary crime fiction can be sustained by future writers or again falls apart.

With respect to the present volume, it is worth pondering what percentage of all the works of crime fiction referenced in it are generally viewed as "literature" in the strict sense of the term. Works that merit this distinction need to meet certain artistic criteria that, as Clive James suggests, are likely to be considered inappropriate and inapplicable by devotees of the genre. Nevertheless, it is important to examine these criteria, and to learn what critical judgments and arguments they entail, if only as a way of understanding how certain works of crime fiction have separated themselves from the pack and attained widespread recognition as literary classics in their own right. Once we familiarize ourselves with these criteria, and with the critical assumptions (or prejudices) behind them, we can decide whether they may themselves need to be modified, and ultimately, whether the concept of literary crime fiction itself – and even the very concept of the literary canon – needs to be significantly revised for our changing times.

The "Aesthetic Rewriting of Crime"

Although much of the resistance to the idea of crime fiction as literature stems from the perceived tawdriness of its subject matter, another significant factor is the genre's own origins. Long before its modern beginnings in pulp fiction, the genre evolved out of a rich tradition of criminal nonfiction that flourished in Europe and America, and that consisted of historical chronicles, trial transcripts, newspaper reports, prison memoirs, and public confessions purportedly elicited from the criminals themselves. Despite the variety and vibrancy of these different kinds of crime narrative – each having its own characteristic structural and stylistic features, such as Michel Foucault discerned in the memoir of the 1835 parricide Pierre Riviere (Foucault 1975) – these nonfictional forms have tended to be regarded as nonliterary in that they lack the degree of aesthetic sensibility, technical virtuosity, and authorial self-consciousness typically associated with great literature. Yet aspiring writers of the time were drawn to this subliterary tradition of real-life crime to which they themselves contributed, and from which they derived inspiration and material for their own early attempts at crime fiction. Thus Daniel Defoe's novels *Moll Flanders* and *Roxana* (1722, 1724), which feature female protagonists who turn to a life of theft and prostitution, were written roughly at the same time as his 1724 history of the notorious house-breaker Jack Sheppard and his 1725 "True and Genuine Account" of the famous thief-taker Jonathan Wild. This legendary criminal himself passed into fiction in *The Beggar's Opera* of John Gay (1728) and as the eponymous subject of Henry Fielding's satirical fantasy of 1743. On the continent, the vast collection of *causes célèbres* by the French lawyer François Gayot de Pitaval provided raw material for Friedrich Schiller's criminal tales (*Kriminalerzählungen*) like "The Criminal by Reason of Lost Honor" (1792), which was subtitled a "true history" (*wahre Geschichte*) (Hart 2005).

   Nineteenth-century writers with literary aspirations drew on a number of nonfictional sources. The real-life criminals celebrated in *Newgate Calendars* from the previous century turned up as the heroic victims and rebels in the "Newgate novels" of the 1830s and 40s. However, it was to accounts of contemporary crimes and trials that renowned authors as well as lesser lights increasingly turned for characters and plots. The fictional character Vautrin who appears in several of Honoré de Balzac's novels was based on Eugène François Vidocq, the thief who became head of the French

Sureté and whose best-selling memoirs appeared in 1828. Mid-century writers of "sensation novels" like Edward Bulwer-Lytton found themselves in the precarious position, as Lyn Pykett has shown, of both drawing on and distancing themselves from crime reporting, affirming their right as novelists to represent the sordid details found in the newspaper press while "asserting the superior moral and psychological complexity of fiction," and "claiming a place for [their] chosen form in the literary hierarchy" (Pykett 2003: 32). A similar fictionalizing process led to the rise of the nineteenth-century detective novel when authors like Charles Dickens and Wilkie Collins drew on details of the much publicized Road Hill murder investigation of 1860 (Summerscale 2008a).

Indeed, many "literary" works of crime fiction are not simply fictional works about crime, but narratives based on nonfictional criminal case histories that have been imaginatively transformed by being fictionalized and aestheticized (or, in Defoe's case, transgendered from male to female). Of particular importance in this regard is the English author Thomas De Quincey whom Robert Morrison rightly credits with playing "a key role in the evolution of crime literature" (De Quincey 2006: ix). Combining the nonfictional tradition of "true crime" narrative with the highly stylized and excessive Gothic fiction of the late eighteenth century, De Quincey came up with an unsettling type of crime narrative that used sensational as well as aesthetic effects to present the criminal not only as a murderous butcher but also as an artist. His 1854 "Postscript" to two earlier papers that appeared in 1827 and 1839 under the title "On Murder Considered as One of the Fine Arts" was a gripping, highly stylized account of two murderous attacks on households that took place 43 years earlier in London's East End. Borrowing techniques from Shakespearean drama described in his 1823 essay "On the Knocking at the Gate in *Macbeth*," and drawing on Edmund Burke's and Immanuel Kant's philosophical insights into the aesthetics of violence and the sublime, De Quincey succeeded in raising the description of murder to the status of literature by provoking sensations of awe and terror in his readers. His depiction of the murderer John Williams differed from Shakespeare's portrayal of Macbeth in one key respect, however, in that De Quincey made no attempt to provide any psychological insight into his murderer. Instead, he achieved his sensational effects by presenting Williams from the perspective of a helpless eyewitness/potential victim to whom he appeared as a thoroughly alien, terrifying, and incomprehensible presence (Black 1991: 57–72, De Quincey 2006: xxii–xxiii).

The depiction of the murderer not as evil or sinful, nor as a sympathetic victim of society or the law, but as a sublime, demonic, yet in some ways seductive being exemplifies what Michel Foucault has called the "aesthetic rewriting of crime," the nineteenth-century phenomenon whereby "crime is glorified, because it is one of the fine arts, because it can be the work only of exceptional natures, because it reveals the monstrousness of the strong and powerful" (Foucault 1977: 68). This aestheticizing of crime and the criminal – culminating in the presentation of the murderer as an artist or aesthete – set the stage for a host of fictional and nonfictional, literary and cinematic successors, two of the most notable recent examples being Thomas Harris's Hannibal Lecter and Bret Easton Ellis's Patrick Bateman in *American Psycho*. By taking art itself as their subject and pointing up its relation to violence and morality, these works raise questions about their own literary status and that of crime fiction in general, as well as about how artistic value itself is ultimately assessed and assigned.

Besides its aesthetic depiction of violence and its presentation of murderers as artistic figures, the significance of the "Postscript" in the evolution of crime literature is related to its own genesis from news item to literary creation. Starting with accounts of actual crimes reported in the popular press – such as the murders and rapes that De Quincey culled from the assize court news and included in *The Westmorland Gazette* in 1818 and 1819 during his editorship of that journal – writers have woven complex, imaginative literary narratives around such kernel events. In elevating the journalistic genre known today as "true crime" to the status of artistic fiction, De Quincey reveals his affinities with writers like Stendhal and Dostoevsky: while the former's 1831 novel *The Red and the Black* was based in part on an actual crime of passion committed by a young seminarian that he read about in the *Gazette des Tribunaux*, the latter based the death of Shatov in *Demons* on contemporary accounts of a student slain by a group of fellow revolutionaries in 1869.

The nineteenth-century formula of finding raw material for literary narratives in crime reporting has been revived in hybrid works of literary journalism like Truman Capote's "non-fiction novel" *In Cold Blood* (1965) and Norman Mailer's "true life novel," *The Executioner's Song* (1979), works that, as Alex Ross notes, "apply shocks of real-life violence while retaining the novelist's right to dissect the psyche." Ross adds that if the current burgeoning market of true crime books and TV crime dramas "ripped from today's headlines" gives the impression that "a literary pursuit has devolved into a cheap industry, it should be remembered that much of this material has actually moved onward and upward from grisly police-news columns, detective magazines, and other instant literature" (Ross 1996: 72, 73). This observation about the evolution of the true crime genre is even more applicable to works of crime *fiction*.

From Analysis as Art to the Analysis of Art

Although De Quincey may not have inaugurated the subgenre of crime fiction in which the criminal (and in some cases, the victim) is the protagonist, he can be credited with having legitimated this subgenre as an art form. As for the other, even more popular subgenre of crime fiction in which the detective is the protagonist, a literary progenitor *can* be readily identified, the American author Edgar Allan Poe. Although his decisive influence in this regard has been almost universally acknowledged – overly so, in the view of some who argue that "a 'foundation myth' identifying Poe as the father of detection was created to support a normative view of the genre" (Ascari 2007:10) – his three fictional tales featuring the amateur analyst C. Auguste Dupin provided not so much a model for future writers as a list of conventions making up a kind of tool-box for the genre. Whereas the artistry of criminal-centered crime fiction tends to lie in Gothic sensationalism and psychological analysis, the artistry of detective fiction has traditionally been attributed to its display of what Poe called "ratiocination" and Arthur Conan Doyle "intellectual acuteness." Indeed, in detective fiction the story often seems a pretext for the artful display of the detective's analytical ability and the author's logical ingenuity – criteria typically cited by critics who defend this subgenre as a literary art form against detractors like Edmund Wilson who dismiss it as an addiction and a "vice" (Winks 1980: 39).

In his 1924 essay "The Art of the Detective Story," R. Austin Freeman offers a paradigmatic expression of the view of detective fiction as ratiocinative art. Known for his purely logical brand of scientific police fiction, Freeman distinguishes the detective story as a form which affords the reader "intellectual satisfaction" from "the mere crime story" which resorts to "crude and pungent sensationalism" for no other purpose than "to make the reader's flesh creep." Describing "the plot of a detective novel" as "an argument conducted under the guise of fiction," Freeman regards the fictional elements in such works ("humour, picturesque setting, vivid characterization and even emotional episodes") as mere sleight of hand that has the same purpose as the crime itself – namely, to distract the reader from the evidence needed to solve the case. The "climax" of the detective story is not the solution itself but the investigator's retrospective explanation or "rigid demonstration" of the reasoning process that led him to the solution. The reader's "sudden recognition ... of the significance of a number of hitherto uncomprehended facts" produces the story's "artistic effect" (Haycraft 1946: 7–17).

Freeman's essay helped detective fiction to achieve what Maurizio Ascari calls "the full status of a literary genre" in the 1920s and 30s (2007: 3). Yet as compelling as the defense of detective fiction as a celebration of the intellect, or what Jacques Barzun calls a "romance of reason"(Winks 1980: 145), may be, it is not altogether convincing, and only applies to a relatively small number of works. By making the detective's analytical powers as demonstrated in the story's plot the genre's defining characteristic, Freeman not only subordinates but denigrates as "fiction" the very elements that are customarily admired in great literary works. In his effort to distinguish the artful detective story from the artless crime story, he effectively excludes detective fiction from consideration as literary art of the first order.

Other critics have offered other reasons for ranking detective fiction as a literary form. Like Freeman, the historian E. M. Wrong sharply contrasted the detective story and "the tale of crime with the criminal as hero" in his 1926 essay "Crime and Detection," but he did so more on ethical than intellectual grounds: "Perhaps art in general should have no moral purpose, but the art of the detective story has one and must have; it seeks to justify the law and to bring retribution on the guilty" (Haycraft 1946: 31). And the creator of the Father Brown stories, G. K. Chesterton, offered a purely aesthetic "defence" of the detective story: it is "a perfectly legitimate form of art" whose "first essential value" consists in the fact "that it is the earliest and only form of popular literature in which is expressed some sense of the poetry of modern life" (Haycraft 1946: 4). Beyond these critics' various attempts to account for the artistry of detective fiction, however, there remains the larger issue of whether detective stories in particular, and crime fiction in general, should themselves be considered works of literary art.

One of the most incisive discussions of this topic is W. H. Auden's 1948 essay "The Guilty Vicarage." A renowned poet troubled by the guilty pleasure he received from reading detective stories, Auden reverses Freeman's and Wrong's contrast between detective and crime stories. Declaring that "detective stories have nothing to do with works of art" (Winks 1980: 15), he describes them instead as escapist fantasies in which the reader identifies with the investigator as a heroic figure who seeks out the guilty party and restores society to a state of innocence. By distancing himself from the anguish of both the criminal and his victim, the reader avoids having to confront whatever real or imagined guilt he may himself be suffering. In contrast, crime narratives that offer psychological insight into the criminal mind may be considered works of art insofar as they "compel an identification with the murderer which [the reader] would prefer not to recognize." For Auden, such "sharing in the suffering of another" constitutes the kind of identification that great works of literature like Dostoevsky's *Crime and Punishment* and Kafka's *The Trial* make possible (Winks 1980: 24).

Auden follows De Quincey in allowing for the possibility that some works of crime (but not detective) fiction may aspire to art. He also acknowledges that the greatest works of literature are often preoccupied with the theme of crime – the modern equivalent of sin – and force the reader, at least temporarily, to share this preoccupation rather than to repress or ignore it. As for detective fiction, although Auden would agree with fellow critic Edmund Wilson's severe judgment that such stories fall well short of being considered works of art, he at least grants them an important "magical function" in helping readers like himself to relieve their gnawing sense of religious or existential guilt (Winks 1980: 15).

Realism, Redemption, Revelation

At one point in "The Guilty Vicarage," Auden refers to Raymond Chandler, then at the apex of his career as a leading practitioner of the American school of hard-boiled detective fiction. Chandler is paid the dubious compliment of being an author, "not [of] detective stories, but [of] serious studies of a criminal milieu, the Great Wrong Place, and his powerful but extremely depressing books should be read and judged, not as escape literature, but as works of art" (Winks 1980: 19). No doubt Chandler would have taken strong exception to this description. Four years earlier in "The Simple Art of Murder," he proudly declared himself to be a writer of detective fiction following in the footsteps of Dashiell Hammett, whom he credits with having raised the genre to the status of an art form. As his essay's title suggests, Chandler was not shy about claiming artistic merit for his and Hammett's brand of detective fiction which, with its tough private eyes in urban milieus, could not be more different from the "classic detective story" discussed by Auden featuring analytical amateurs in country settings. And Chandler could easily have been referring to Auden's essay when taking Dorothy Sayers to task for categorizing the detective story as a "literature of escape" that can never "attain the loftiest level of literary achievement" found in what she termed the "literature of expression" (Haycraft 1946: 231).

Chandler affirms that detective stories are as capable of artistic greatness as works in any other literary genre. However, art per se is for him not the key issue. The hallmark of hard-boiled detective fiction that differentiates it from "the traditional or classic or straight-deductive or logic-and-deduction novel of detection" (Chandler 1995a: 979–80) is its realism, which Chandler claims to be the aim of all true artists in every historical epoch. Traditional detective stories "[tr]y to be honest, but honesty is an art" that these stories fail to achieve because they "are too contrived, and too little aware of what goes on in the world" (Chandler 1995a: 985). In contrast to writers who set violent crimes in English manors and French chateaux, "Hammett gave murder back to the kind of people that commit it for reasons, not just to provide a corpse" (Chandler 1995a: 989). For Chandler, the way to create art is by rejecting artifice, the way to write literature is by rejecting literariness, the way to write good fiction is by depicting real life. In short, he tried to take the detective story – and crime fiction in general – back to its roots in the pre-literary, nonfictional discourse of "true crime."

To be sure, Chandler was too perceptive an artist to believe that "the simple art of murder" was really that simple. The elevation of detective fiction to the level of literary art required a good deal more than a return to realism. The fictional elements that Freeman had subordinated to scientific logic acquired renewed importance in Chandler's aesthetics, especially language, mood, and scene (Horsley 2005: 71, 109). But the paramount element was character, an unconventional view considering the importance typically given to plot in detective fiction, as in Clive James's remark about the need for "an eventful narrative." For Chandler, plot was a means to lead (and impede) the detective and the reader in the identification of the criminal, but it was also a way to achieve "the gradual elucidation of character, which is all the detective story has any right to be about anyway" (Chandler 1995a: 991). The point is driven home in Chandler's idealized portrait of the detective as "a complete man," "a man of honor," and as "the best man in his world and a good enough man for any world" (Chandler 1995a: 992). Not only is character central to Chandler's conception of literary detective fiction, but the defining trait of his literary detective is that he is a man of character who is adept at reading the characters of others: "He has a sense of character, or he would not know his job" (Chandler 1995a: 992). Or in Sara Paretsky's recent reformulation of this view, "the intuitive understanding of human motivations which make[s] it possible to sort out a crime" has been "the hallmark of … literary private investigators" since Hammett's detective Sam Spade (Paretsky 2007: 94).

Chandler's aspiration to raise detective fiction to the status of literary art would seem to have little in common with Auden's conception of the genre as an intrinsically nonartistic, unrealistic form of escapist fantasy. Yet both agree on one key quality that any kind of fiction must have in order to be considered great literature: redemption. "In everything that can be called art there is a quality of redemption," writes Chandler (1995a: 991), who in detective fiction finds this quality less in what Horsley calls the "consolatory, potentially redemptive myth" of the classic plot (2005: 69), than in the figure of the detective himself, the "man of honor" who redeems fallen human nature. Auden, in contrast, insists that redemption requires suffering and an awareness of sin and guilt on the part of the protagonist, an experience found in works of art like *Crime and Punishment* and *The Trial*, but not in the classic, analytical detective story. This key difference in their conceptions of redemption keeps detective fiction forever outside the realm of art for Auden, while allowing it to achieve artistic status for Chandler. Yet although Auden considers detective fiction a subliterary genre that does not offer its characters or the reader the quasi-spiritual possibility of redemption through suffering, he concedes that it provides readers with an overtly religious sense of *absolution*, of release from guilt, through the detective's identification and apprehension of the criminal, and the restoration of society to a state of innocence. This observation goes a long way toward redeeming the genre of detective fiction itself, if not as art, then as an indispensable cultural artifact with quasi-magical powers.

Over the past half century, a strain of crime fiction has evolved that makes a point of closing off any possibility of redemption, and yet, by virtue of its sheer boldness, authenticity, and unflinching honesty, almost defies critics to deny it artistic status. The tradition can be traced back to the work of Jim Thompson and Patricia Highsmith (see Nicol, chapter 41 in this volume), but has recently evolved in an increasingly bleak, hyper-realist direction in works that make a point of distancing themselves from their canonical literary precursors. Not surprisingly, the work that writers of such neo-noir fiction take as their point of departure is *Crime and Punishment*, Auden's primary example of a work of crime fiction that is also a work of art. Whereas Dostoevsky's protagonist Raskolnikov undergoes a lengthy period of torment culminating in a spiritual awakening after committing a horrific act – killing a poor pawnbroker to demonstrate his freedom from moral law – his recent literary successors commit violent crimes that they rationalize in literary-philosophical language, yet without seeking or finding redemption in suffering and punishment.[3]

In Natsuo Kirino's 2008 novel, *Real World*, a Tokyo teenager on the run after murdering his mother feels compelled to write a manifesto "to shake people up. Something to let people know how gifted I am. ... They say juvenile offenders are most often precocious and extremely bright, people who can't adjust to the education system. So I think I should leave behind a novel or poem or something, like that murderer Sakakibara did," referring to the real-life junior high school student who in 1997 sent a series of letters to a Japanese newspaper after viciously murdering an 11-year-old boy. As his nickname Worm suggests, however, Kirino's killer is hardly a Raskolnikovian *Ubermensch*, or even a latter-day Pierre Riviere, but a post-literate product of the digital age who has to enlist the help of a female student to compose his manifesto for him. The "story" Worm wants her to imagine and write down must be "better" than what Sakakibara wrote, an amalgam of high and low culture, great Western literature and a popular animated TV series: "Sprinkle in some Dostoyevsky or Nietzsche or whatever. ... Then sort of wrap it up like 'Evangelion'" (Kirino 2008: 121, 123). But whereas the violent deeds of Dostoevsky's antihero are the result of his quasi-Nietzschean theorizing, Worm's manifesto is an afterthought that he is not even capable of writing himself, a desperate attempt to make sense and give meaning to a mindless act that he cannot begin to grasp.

One reviewer has described Kirino's novel as marking "an evolutionary difference" in crime literature. Dostoevsky's depiction of a mythic "contest between Christian love and a pernicious nihilism" has undergone a "significant inversion," culminating in "a post-Nietzsche, consumer-driven society that has yet to address the ethical vacuum created by the Death of God" and that "offers no possibility of god or redemption" (Harrison 2008: 10). Indeed, despite its Dostoevskian references, *Real World* belongs less to the lofty literary tradition of a work like *Crime and Punishment* – psychological studies of murderous protagonists who redeem themselves through suffering – than to a subterranean literary lineage going back to texts like Jim Thompson's *The Killer Inside Me*. The murderous protagonists in these works "mimic," and thereby expose, a morally bankrupt society where aesthetic concerns with sensation and appearance have fully eclipsed any sense of ethics and social responsibility. In these neo-noir fictions, psychopathic killers have replaced detectives as agents of revelation in a world where redemption no longer seems possible. All that is left for literary and popular writers of crime fiction to do is to expose the bustling world that we know for the fiction it is, and to reveal the real world as the deserted cityscape that it has become.

Crises of Identity and Crimes of Passion

As important as it is for the emergent genre of crime fiction, Dostoevsky's *Crime and Punishment* does not fit as readily into this genre as it does into more recognizably literary categories. For an example of an undisputed work of crime fiction that critics have been nearly unanimous in crediting with transcending the genre and gaining acceptance as a literary masterpiece, we need to turn to Dashiell Hammett's break-through 1930 novel, *The Maltese Falcon*.

While many reasons have been offered for this novel's literary greatness, the one proposed by Steven Marcus is especially illuminating. Marcus calls attention to the curious episode in the novel where, for no apparent reason, the private eye Sam Spade tells his client about a past case involving a Tacoma man named Charles Flitcraft who had mysteriously vanished years earlier. When a man resembling Flitcraft was spotted in Spokane living under a new identity, Spade was hired to check up on him and learned the reason behind his disappearance. Walking past a construction site during a lunch break, Flitcraft had nearly been hit by a falling beam, a near death experience that gave him a "new glimpse of life." If his life "could be ended for him at random by a falling beam[,] he would change his life at random by simply going away." Without a word of explanation, he failed to return to work that afternoon, and did not return home to his wife and children that evening. Instead, he embarked upon a life of aimless drifting for several years, eventually settling down in Spokane where he got married and began a new life that resembled his life in Tacoma. Spade concludes his anecdote by observing that he doubted that Flitcraft "even knew he had settled back naturally into the same groove he had jumped out of in Tacoma. But that's the part of it I always liked. He adjusted himself to beams falling, and then no more of them fell, and he adjusted himself to them not falling" (Hammett 1999: 445).

A passage like this dealing with the contingency of life is not what we expect to find either in hard-boiled crime fiction or in the classic detective story in which there seems to be a reason for everything, and nothing is a matter of chance. Yet although (or more likely because) Spade's anecdote has nothing to do (apparently) with the novel's principal storyline – and is not directly concerned with crime or detection, for that matter – Marcus considers it to be "the most important or central moment in the entire novel." It provides a revealing glimpse into the depths of Spade's character, and into his, and presumably Hammett's, philosophy regarding what Marcus calls "the ethical irrationality of existence" and "the ethical unintelligibility of the world" (Hammett 1992: xv, xvii). However bizarre Flitcraft's behavior may seem, his abandonment of his secure, old life for an altogether different existence that gradually becomes indistinguishable from his original routine cannot be dismissed as a personal aberration or idiosyncrasy. Rather, his identity crisis points up a fundamental mystery about human behavior, namely, "how despite everything we have learned and everything we know, men will persist in behaving and trying to behave sanely, rationally, sensibly, and responsibly … even when [they] know that there is no logical or metaphysical, no discoverable or demonstrable reason for doing so" (Hammett 1992: xvii–xviii). Spade is amused by Flitcraft's seemingly erratic but ultimately conformist conduct, and is revealed to be an anti-Flitcraft himself: his "wild and unpredictable" demeanor throughout the novel is a more authentic way of adapting to the irrationality and unintelligibility of life (Hammett 1999: 464).

The Flitcraft episode is an example of the kind of writing that Marcus believes enabled Hammett "to raise the crime story into literature" (Hammett 1992: xxviii). It is "not the kind of thing we ordinarily expect in a detective story or novel about crime":

> That it is there, and that comparable passages occur in all of Hammett's best work, clearly suggests the kind of transformation that Hammett was performing on this popular genre of writing. The transformation was in the direction of literature. (Hammett 1992: xvii)

Or as Clive James might put it, Hammett found a deceptively simple and unpretentious way to elicit the kind of "art thrill" in sophisticated readers that they find so appealing. Yet the Flitcraft episode is also likely to leave hardcore crime fiction readers scratching their heads and wondering – much like Spade's bored client Brigid O'Shaughnessy, who has no interest in Spade's reflections on the quirkiness of life and who only wants to get her hands on the precious falcon – what happened to the "thrill thrill" they have been seeking.

Hammett's novel about the quest for the jewel-encrusted bird that turns out to be made out of lead set the gold standard for works of literary crime fiction that use the pretext of an exciting story about murder and betrayal to make profound observations about society and life. We have already seen how certain works of noir fiction go beyond (or perhaps hold themselves back from) Auden's and Chandler's artistic criterion of individual redemption, and instead set themselves the task of revealing society as it really is. Social exposés of this kind that reveal governmental institutions and social agencies (law enforcement and the judicial system) to be forms of organized crime (crime that has been made legitimate and respectable) have been valued as worthy artistic endeavors by writers like Hammett, Chandler, and Thompson. Thus Marcus describes how Hammett "unwaveringly represents the world of crime as a reproduction in both structure and detail of the modern capitalist society that it depends on, preys off, and is part of" (Hammett 1992: xxiv). Either as the brutal acts of violence portrayed in hard-boiled crime fiction, or the contrived schemes depicted in the golden age of detective stories, crime becomes a metaphor for the corruption of society, and the "nature of the crimes themselves," as Lee Horsley observes, "is a metaphor for the lengths to which such a society is willing to go in the interests of hypocritical concealment" (2005: 19). Especially in the aftermath of the United States's most thoroughgoing display of hypocrisy from 1920 to 1933 during the Prohibition era, many crime writers have located the origins of individuals' criminal behavior in the all-encompassing criminality of society. In such a corrupt world, the detective no longer seems capable of being a redeeming figure, and at most functions as a revelatory character who is barely distinguishable in this respect from many of the criminals whom he pursues.

In the process of exposing society's sins, however, the more literary works of crime fiction provide philosophical insights of the kind that Spade imagines Flitcraft received after the falling beam incident: the feeling that "someone had taken the lid off life and let him look at the works." Hammett's meditation on randomness and contingency in *The Maltese Falcon* has been taken up and developed by literary authors in their own artistic variants of the traditional detective story. In Jorge Luis Borges's 1942 story "Death and the Compass," the detective Erik Lönnrot's mistaken reading of an accidental killing as a metaphysical mystery leads to his own death, while in Friedrich Dürrenmatt's 1958 novel *The Pledge*, the killer's accidental death prevents the detective Matthäi from even proving the killer exists, precipitating his own mental breakdown. Lönnrot and Matthäi are unsuited to their jobs as detectives because (in

sharp contrast to Sam Spade) they simply cannot deal with the messiness and randomness of life. Instead they go about their jobs and live their lives (they do not distinguish
between the two) as if they are characters in a traditional detective story that proceeds
according to rational and intelligible rules, and in which accidents and chance do not
intervene. They fall into Flitcraft's error of doggedly behaving sensibly and rationally
when life is wholly unpredictable. In their use of the crime story to explore the phenomenon of chance and the mystery of human behavior, Borges and Dürrenmatt push
the genre in the direction of literature much as Chandler and Marcus credit Hammett
with having done.

Hammett showed how works of crime fiction can achieve literary greatness by
providing a format for addressing such heady philosophical issues as contingency
and identity. But he and Chandler also showed that as literature, detective fiction
is fundamentally concerned with character. This is even more true of literary narratives in which the protagonists are criminals rather than detectives. In these
works, murder is more than a means for the criminal to achieve his ends or to
provide a corpse as in conventional crime fiction; instead, it is the expression of
some overwhelming passion or the consequence of some intense internal conflict.
Beyond the feelings of suffering and guilt that Auden finds in Dostoevsky's and
Kafka's protagonists, literary characters are subject to a wide range of emotions that
frequently culminate in crimes of passion. The most common of these passions,
rage, is displayed by Oedipus when he precipitously kills his father, and by Hamlet
when he belatedly slays his uncle. Jealous rage, the exemplary crime of passion,
abounds in popular and literary works of crime fiction alike. But it is in literary
works that we expect to find the pathos and remorse involved in murder – and
especially in killing a loved one – most fully represented, as in a work like
Shakespeare's *Othello*. (In detective fiction, a variant of the crime of passion is the
sin of *hybris* which causes the detective to become responsible for a loved one's
death, as in the films *Chinatown* and *Se7en*.) There is perhaps no more poignant
crime than the killing of a loved one, since such murders border on acts of suicide
and sacrifice, and this poignancy is beyond the reach of most conventional works
of crime fiction. However, in the hands of literary authors – one thinks of Stendhal
in *The Red and the Black* and Kierkegaard in *Fear and Trembling* – such crimes of
passion have been a means of exploring the most profound moral and ethical
questions.

NOTES

1   A further subset of this subgenre of crime
fiction consists of works – often written by
academic professionals – in which the crime
and the investigation hinge on specifically
literary matters. Recent examples include
Umberto Eco's *The Name of the Rose* (1980),

Batya Gur's *Literary Murder* (1991), and
Matthew Pearl's *The Dante Club* (2003).

2   Cited in Horsley (2005: 108 n. 34), who, while
noting writers like Paul Auster, Martin Amis,
and Bret Easton Ellis who "have played in a
'literary' way with the conventions of crime

fiction," singles Sallis out for "writing from within the genre, pulling in not just literary references, but a whole series of allusions to the conventions of crime and detective fiction" (108–9).

3 Raskolnikov's recent real-life successors also should not be forgotten, beginning with Harvard-educated Theodore J. Kaczynski. The 1995 publication of the "Unabomber's" manifesto led to his capture after his brother recognized his writing style and philosophical views, and alerted the FBI. Similarly, the Polish author Krystian Bala's mediocre crime novel *Amok* led an alert detective to tie him to a 2000 murder.

Part II
Genre of a Thousand Faces

6

The Newgate Novel and
the Police Casebook

Lauren Gillingham

When a spate of novels appeared in Britain in the 1830s and 1840s dealing principally with crime, criminals, the urban underworld, and prisons, critics responded as though it were not only deplorable, but largely unprecedented. One need only think of works like Defoe's *Moll Flanders* (1722), Fielding's *Jonathan Wild* (1743), or Godwin's *Caleb Williams* (1794) to appreciate that British novels throughout the eighteenth century (not to mention other genres, especially drama) had familiarized readers with illicit acts, immoral desires, and nefarious characters. These new novels, nonetheless, which differed widely from one another in tone, structure, and ideology, were regarded as part of a distinct cultural phenomenon, and were collectively dubbed "Newgate fiction" by literary reviewers. The label referred to the frequency with which these novels drew characters directly from publications of criminal biography such as *The Newgate Calendar*, or introduced fictional characters who could have appeared in such publications. Even this feature, though, was not especially original. Authors had long been drawing on the narrative resources offered up by Newgate biographies, yet the new crime novels provoked a critical reaction that Keith Hollingsworth suggests was significantly more violent than that which had greeted earlier texts: the Newgate novel "attract[ed] a new kind of attention" which was "genuinely hostile" (1963: 15).

One provocation of the critics' ire was likely the cultural mania that the Newgate novels and their criminal protagonists created: wildly popular and widely read, the texts generated a huge buzz. Serial and volume sales of the novels soared. A number of the stories were quickly adapted to the stage, and some were mounted at multiple London theaters simultaneously. Some of the criminal heroes, like the eponymous prison-breaker of William Harrison Ainsworth's *Jack Sheppard* (1839), attained celebrity status, and readers could buy all manner of *Sheppard*-related products. W. M. Thackeray remarked in a letter to his mother that at one of the theatres where *Jack Sheppard* was staged, "people are waiting about the lobbies, selling *Shepherd-bags* [*sic*] – a bag containing a few pick-locks that is, a screw driver, and iron lever" (Ray 1980: 395). While earlier novels like Richardson's *Pamela* (1740) and, more recently,

Dickens's *The Pickwick Papers* (1836–7) had also become cultural sensations involving the sale of themed merchandise, the Newgate phenomenon seemed different, especially to its critics. That difference turned on one of the distinguishing features of the genre: the sympathy which the Newgate novel seemed to elicit from readers for its criminal characters.

The critics' intense reaction to the Newgate phenomenon, which reached its peak around 1839–40, arose in part out of an anxiety about the influence of crime fiction, which turned on the potential for identification with criminal heroes. As an anonymous reviewer for *Fraser's Magazine* lamented with respect to Ainsworth's prison-breaker, the metamorphosis of Jack Sheppard from a "vulgar ruffian into a melodramatic hero" in both the novel and its theatrical adaptations "will tend to fill many a juvenile aspirant for riot and notoriety with ideas highly conducive to the progress of so ennobling a profession as that of housebreaking" (Anon. 1840: 228). The anxiety that the new crime novels inspired derived from a fear of social contamination and instability, fueled in large measure by questions of readership. Were novelists courting popularity by appealing to vulgar appetites and interests? Was the fictional glamorization of lawlessness and transgression inviting new, uncultured readers to form desires inappropriate to their understanding and station? These questions spoke to the range of class-inflected concerns that Newgate fiction provoked, as well as the extent of the novels' appeal. While the principal threat seemed to arise from the idea that low-born readers and theater-goers would be led by dreams of fame and adventure to emulate these criminal heroes, critics also worried about the corruption of taste among the higher-born. In his anti-Newgate novel, *Catherine* (1839–40), for example, Thackeray remarks that Dickens's *Oliver Twist* made "the whole London public, from peers to chimney-sweeps, … interested about a set of ruffians whose occupations are thievery, murder, and prostitution" (1999: 132). Thackeray's concern was not only that the Newgate phenomenon erased any difference between the literary tastes of a peer and a chimney-sweep, but even worse, that the public was drawn together out of pity and admiration for criminals. "[In] the name of common sense," he exclaims, "let us not expend our sympathies on cutthroats, and other such prodigies of evil!" (1999: 133).

If the Newgate novels were marked by their common interest in criminal characters, that is one of the few traits which we can attribute to them all. It is difficult to generalize about the Newgate school of fiction, given the variety of the texts conventionally grouped together under its banner and the diverse objectives of its novelists. The Newgate novel's loosely related stable of authors extends from the literary margins to the mainstream: its leading practitioners include comparatively minor novelists like Edward Bulwer-Lytton and Ainsworth, as well as such lions of Victorian fiction as Dickens and Thackeray. Newgate novels distinguish themselves from one another principally by the terms in which they deal with the circumstances of crime (which range from outright glee to ominous sobriety), the weight that they attach to the different causes of criminality in their characters, and the ends to which they carry their fascination with crime. That fascination, however, is shared by all.

Most critics point to Bulwer-Lytton's 1830 *Paul Clifford* as the first novel of the Newgate school. Principally a Godwinian novel of ideas that critiques the social determinants of crime, *Paul Clifford* also features a dashing highwayman as its hero. Other Newgate novels similarly capitalize on the gallantry and pluck long associated with outlaws and rebels: Ainsworth features the legendary eighteenth-century high-wayman Dick Turpin in his first Newgate novel *Rookwood* (1834), and draws another enterprising eighteenth-century criminal from the *Newgate Calendar* in romanticizing the escapades of Jack Sheppard. Not all Newgate novels are playful romps, however. In *Oliver Twist* (1837–8), Dickens aims for a realistic, rather than romantic, depiction of crime, focusing on what he calls "the miserable reality" of criminals' lives (1998: liv). Some Newgate fiction follows William Godwin's *Caleb Williams* in studying the psychology of criminality. In *Eugene Aram* (1832), for example, Bulwer-Lytton focuses on a case where he suggests that "crime appears the aberration and monstrous product of a great intellect" (1896: xvii). And numerous Newgate novels straddle multiple genres. Dickens's *Barnaby Rudge* (1841), set in the context of the 1780 anti-Catholic Gordon riots, is part historical novel, part Gothic, and part Newgate novel. Bulwer-Lytton's *Lucretia* (1846), which shares some of the psychological and political interests of his earlier Newgate fiction, looks forward in important ways to the sensation novel of the 1860s. Another unusual case is *Catherine*, in which Thackeray set about to disgust readers with the representation of heinous crimes and explode the popular taste for Newgate narratives once and for all. His parody of Newgate fiction, however, appeared to the public indistinguishable from the novels which he ridiculed, and the taste for Newgate stories persisted for almost a decade after *Catherine*'s publication.

So where does the Newgate novel come from? Critics have offered various explanations for the emergence of this particular interest in criminality in the 1830s. Hollingsworth attributes the appeal of the Newgate theme to sweeping reforms in "the criminal law and its administration" which were made in the 1820s through 1840s (1963: 19). Penal reforms had been sufficient, he suggests, to allow "a vast public" to congratulate itself on its progress and take pleasure in "idoliz[ing] a young thief ... as a victim of the old system or as a rebel against it" (1963: 141). John Bender, by contrast, accounts for the period's fascination with criminals in terms of the gradual transformation of spectacles of public execution from carnivalesque fairs to more solemn rituals, until finally, in 1868, "these spectacles [were withdrawn] from the public eye" (1987: 231). One might suggest, then, that the popularity of Newgate fiction had as much to do with the cultural void left by contemporaneous penal reforms as with compassionate public sentiment.

We might account for the emergence of the Newgate school in literary terms as well. The Gothic novel of the 1790s had fostered a taste for dark passions, fearful villains, exotic locales, and suspenseful plotting (see Spooner, chapter 19 in this volume). That taste was both sustained and expanded by a trio of Romantic authors: Godwin, Byron, and Walter Scott. These authors made available to successive generations of novelists influential narrative models for mapping social and historical change, analyzing social institutions and customs, and staging the identity formation of both transgressive heroes and ordinary individuals. Godwin's *Caleb Williams* has been called a political novel, psychological thriller, and Gothic romance; it can also be categorized as both proto-Newgate novel and proto-detective novel. The text's detailed critique of a justice system corrupted by wealth and rank leads directly to the more politically trenchant of the Newgate novels, most notably Bulwer-Lytton's. Caleb himself functions in various parts of his narrative as a Newgate hero *avant la lettre*: he credits his early reading of Newgate narratives, for example, with furnishing the knowledge necessary for his prison escapes. He also finds himself, while on the lam, turned in popular opinion into a legendary outlaw, Kit Williams, "a devilish cunning fellow," who reportedly "outwitted all the keepers they could set over him, and made his way through stone walls as if they were so many cobwebs" (Godwin 2000: 331–2). It is the obsession which has driven Caleb into his outlawry to begin with that positions *Caleb Williams* as a prototype of later detective novels: that obsession, specifically, is Caleb's insatiable curiosity to plumb his employer Falkland's character and uncover his crime. Dorothea von Mücke has argued that "Caleb's hermeneutics is that of the detective who is determined to decipher an unreadable text, to find the heinous crime at the bottom of a riddle" (1996: 332).

The path that leads from Byron and Scott to the Newgate school is, at one level, less direct than that charted by *Caleb Williams*. While we might suggest that Scott writes a proto-Newgate novel in the early chapters of *The Heart of Midlothian* (1818), and that *Rob Roy* (1817) and Byron's *The Corsair* (1814) provide models for later outlaws, neither Scott nor Byron draws on *The Newgate Calendar* in a way which, as with Godwin, would align them immediately with the fictional school that emerged in their wake. At a broader level, though, we find in their dark agents and rogues, as well as in the strategies which both authors develop for representing social contexts and historical change, a series of patterns and techniques that form the foundation of much Newgate fiction.

Byron casts the mould, for example, for the captivating, willful hero who recurs frequently in the Newgate school: the Byronic hero's identity is typically forged in the pursuit of desires that, in their satisfaction, involve the transgression of a moral law or social code. In elaborating this model, Byron made imaginable a social transgressor humanized in ways that Gothic villains of the late eighteenth century usually were not. *The Corsair*'s Conrad, for instance, embodies a model of criminal heroism that Newgate novelists like Bulwer-Lytton and Ainsworth would readily adopt: an intelligent, high-spirited young man, finding himself simultaneously prey to his passions and betrayed by a corrupt society, shuns the world and pursues instead the life of a pirate. Bulwer-Lytton draws directly on this figure in creating the protagonist of *Paul Clifford*: a talented young man who is turned criminal largely by a corrupt justice system, Paul disdains the hypocrisy of contemporary society and leads an adventurous life as a highwayman. Bulwer-Lytton even spares his hero the gallows, allowing him to escape his penal colony to settle happily in America. The narrative fully endorses Paul's view, moreover, that social injustice is responsible for his criminality: "'Circumstances make guilt.' [Paul] was wont to

say: 'let us endeavour to *correct the circumstances*, before we rail against the guilt!'"
(1835: 469).

From Scott's Waverley novels, Newgate novelists seemed to draw two key narrative techniques. The first lies in what James Chandler terms Scott's "comparativist cultural representation": that is, Scott's skilful "comparative description" of the "typical characters and elements of various cultures, past and present," which demonstrates how the "individuality of characters" derives from "the historical peculiarity of their epoch" (1998: 377–9). Newgate novelists learned from Scott to show how an individual criminal case might derive from the social, economic, political, and juridical structures prevalent in a given historical moment. Some novelists, especially Bulwer-Lytton, developed in their Newgate novels a form of contemporaneous historical fiction by adapting Scott's descriptive model to current cultural contexts. Other Newgate novelists learned a different but related lesson popularized in the Waverley novels, where Scott demonstrated that one could neutralize the representation of social transgressions or political insurrection by containing such forces within the arena of a premodern age. The political machinations of *Waverley*'s Fergus Mac-Ivor, for example, are tied specifically to the failed 1745 Jacobite uprising, a threat which Scott's readers in 1814 know has been fully extinguished. We see this strategy at work regularly in Ainsworth's fiction. We are told by *Jack Sheppard*'s narrator, for instance, that the criminals who "flourish[ed] in vast numbers" around the docks in Sheppard's day "recently, in a great measure, [have been] extirpated by the vigilance of the Thames Police" (Ainsworth 2007: 243). By contrasting eighteenth-century lawlessness with the effective policing of his readers' own age, Ainsworth reassures his audience that a Jack Sheppard is virtually unimaginable in modern London.

How did Newgate novelists synthesize these prevalent cultural forms, popular tastes, and contemporary social concerns in their crime fiction? We might begin to answer that question by looking in detail at a few key examples of the genre; Ainsworth's *Jack Sheppard* is a perfect place to start. The most popular of the Newgate novels, it has been characterized as "an essentially cheerful romance of escape" (Hollingsworth 1963: 177). It is unquestionably sensational, comic, and lurid. Ainsworth even allows his protagonist to enjoy his trip to the gallows in a state not of contrition, but of sheer exultation: with tens of thousands gathered for the execution, Jack "felt more as if he were marching to a triumph, than proceeding to a shameful death" (2007: 472). If there is escapism in Sheppard's heroism, the novel also contains an incisive analysis of the causal relationship between poverty and crime, as well as an interesting modulation of the dominant features of the historical novel. Beyond that, Ainsworth's romancing of Jack's story popularizes the figure of the plucky underdog who makes something of himself largely through his own defiant determination – even if in Jack's instance that *something* is the celebrity attached to his prison breaks. On the far side of the Newgate school, historically, the autonomous enterprise that characterizes a number of the school's popular criminals would reemerge in less controversial fictional forms: most notably, in the mischievous protagonist of boys' adventure fiction and the amateur detective of the sensation novel.

Through much of the novel and especially in the extraordinary prison breaks, Jack is represented to us as a sympathetic figure. As Matthew Buckley argues persuasively, Ainsworth's narrative and George Cruikshank's illustrations for the novel work together to "induce their audience to adopt Sheppard's own perspective, to see the world through his eyes" (2002: 446). The petty thief who makes of himself a better criminal than all those who foretold his fate could ever have predicted becomes the unquestioned hero of the tale. When Jack is revealed toward the end to be of noble lineage — his mother, a reformed prostitute, is the daughter of a baronet, but was stolen in infancy by a gypsy and raised in poverty — the discovery is essentially irrelevant to the celebrated identity which the hero has established for himself.

The unabashed heroism of Ainsworth's lowly criminal rekindled the critical reaction against Newgate fiction, which had died down somewhat since the early 1830s. The critics objected again to the representation of vice, crime, and unsavory characters, but worried especially about the influence that Sheppard's romanticized escapades might have on rootless young men; the latter might access Ainsworth's tale not only in its serialized form, or via the ubiquitous prints of its illustrations, but equally in one of its eight theatrical adaptations which ran in London through the fall of 1839. That negative reaction intensified significantly in May 1840 when a young valet named B. F. Courvoisier slit the throat of his master, Lord William Russell, and suggested that the idea for the crime had come to him from Ainsworth's novel. Although the validity of his claim was never definitely established, the allegation was damning enough. It allowed reviewers to condemn *Jack Sheppard*, in the words of the *Examiner*, as a "publication calculated to familiarize the mind with cruelties and to serve as the cut-throat's manual" (quoted in Hollingsworth 1963: 145–6). The controversy prompted Ainsworth to refrain in later novels from featuring a criminal at the center of his narratives. No other Newgate novelist would again celebrate a protagonist's criminal exploits quite as boldly.

If Ainsworth was guilty of sympathizing with a social outlaw and capitalizing on his energy and charm, he was by no means alone in doing so. Dickens's *Oliver Twist* came in for similar criticisms, although perhaps more because of the coincidence of its publication for four months alongside *Jack Sheppard* in *Bentley's Miscellany*, than because, on its own, it provoked an equal censure. The tarring of Ainsworth and Dickens with the same Newgate brush was largely Thackeray's doing. In the final number of *Catherine*, he excoriates both contemporaries, aligning *Oliver Twist*'s prostitute Nancy with the prison-breaker Jack, and complaining that "we are asked for downright sympathy in the one case, and are called on in the second to admire the gallantry of a knave" (1999: 133). Dickens took umbrage at the association of his novel with Ainsworth's, and used his Preface to the third edition of *Oliver Twist* to defend his representation of crime and criminals. He wrote the novel under the belief, he suggests, that to depict such criminals "as really do exist; to paint them in all their deformity, in all their wretchedness, in all the squalid poverty of their lives ... would be a service to society" (1998: liv). Dickens stresses the moral and formal distance of his realistic representation of the London underworld from the criminal romances of other contemporary writers, Ainsworth thereby implied.

One of the obvious differences between Dickens's and Ainsworth's novels is that Oliver is decidedly not a criminal. On the contrary, the innocent young protagonist who, orphaned and friendless, stumbles into a world of crime and vice is wholly untouched by it. Oliver's interactions with Fagin's gang serves to foreground the protagonist's unimpeachable virtue, and to suggest, in Nancy's case at least, that other inhabitants of London's underworld might retain vestiges of moral goodness, their vices notwithstanding. While Oliver's virtue is accounted for late in the novel via the discovery of his respectable parentage, Dickens works hard with his secondary, low-born characters to distinguish poverty from crime and immorality, and to suggest that a poor child driven to crime may have had no other option for survival.

Oliver Twist's alignment with the Newgate school was based on more, though, than merely its depiction of criminal haunts and sympathy for Nancy. Dickens was not as guiltless of finding charm and romance among criminals as his prefatory defense of the novel insists. Numerous critics have remarked the irrepressible appeal, for example, of the Artful Dodger. Oliver's first criminal associate in London, the Dodger is charming and quick-witted. And his author grants him a splendid exit from the novel when he is finally nabbed. Following his arrest, the Dodger's confederate Charley Bates worries about how the Dodger will "stand in the Newgate Calendar," given that he is likely to be transported "for a common twopenny-halfpenny sneeze box," rather than a theft worthy of a gentleman, such as "a gold watch, chain, and seals, at the lowest" (Dickens 1998: 351). Charley need not have worried: appearing before the magistrate, the Dodger pulls off a commanding performance of wit and irreverence, and departs the courtroom "grinning in the officer's face, with great glee and self-approval." There could be no doubt that the Dodger was "establishing for himself a glorious reputation" (1998: 357).

Another line that connects *Oliver Twist* to earlier Newgate novels is Dickens's interest in the psychology of his arch-criminals. In the aftermath of Bill Sikes's murder of Nancy, and in Fagin's last night in prison before his execution, Dickens devotes entire chapters to exploring the perceptual and emotional experiences of these criminals, pulling readers directly into their minds. This intimate focus on criminal psychology links Dickens's novel back to Bulwer-Lytton's second Newgate novel, *Eugene Aram* (1832), and before that, to *Caleb Williams*. In *Eugene Aram*, Bulwer-Lytton develops the Newgate school's most sustained examination of a criminal mind, drawing for his subject of study another figure from the *Newgate Calendar* – in this instance, an eighteenth-century scholar and schoolteacher who murdered an associate on the grounds of having had an affair with his wife. The particular interest of the case for Bulwer-Lytton was Aram's intellectual superiority and gentility: an avid scholar who published an influential philological study of the relationship of Celtic to other European languages, Aram was, in Bulwer-Lytton's words, no "vulgar ruffian" (1896: xvii).

Bulwer-Lytton saw Aram as a tragic hero, "a man whose whole life seemed to have been one sacrifice to knowledge" (1833: 33), yet who forfeited his life's work through one vicious act. Bulwer-Lytton alters key details of the case in order to elaborate Aram's intellectual talents and remove passion from his crime: in the fictional version, the crime is property-based and the victim an unrepentant villain. Aram himself, on Bulwer-Lytton's representation, is exemplary, full of courage, dignity, and sensibility. "Much in his nature," the narrator assures us, "would have fitted him for worldly superiority and command" (1833: 34). He is modeled quite explicitly on Byron's Manfred: haughty and proud, Aram holds himself apart from his kind, keeping his talents private out of a cynical conviction of the world's corruption, and a fear of the discovery of his crime: "Memory sets me apart and alone in the world," he reflects; "it seems unnatural to me – a thought of dread – to bring another being to my solitude" (1833: 53).

Aram's fatal flaw emerges with his misguided rationalization of the crime. Committed 14 years earlier, the murder was motivated by a desperate need for money to pursue his research. In the first edition, Bulwer-Lytton has Aram declare at trial that he "did not feel what men call remorse!" (1833: 410). Utterly convinced of the public service which he performed by removing a heinous villain from the earth in order to further his studies, the man of genius is led by his own sophisticated logic to view his crime in coldly rational, even laudatory, terms. As Hollingsworth contends, Aram's is a Benthamite Utilitarianism gone wrong: the rationalization of his crime "is intended to undercut misapplied Utilitarian ethics with a single objection" (1963: 91). Yet the crux of Bulwer-Lytton's novel is less an attack on Bentham than an attempt to understand the workings of a great mind that has come to justify a deed that society deems criminal. While the narrative never sanctions Aram's crime nor endorses his logic, its fascination with his character engenders something other than an unequivocal censure. The critics' outrage at what they deemed yet another invitation to admire a man guilty of horrific acts prompted Bulwer-Lytton to revise the novel: in the 1849 edition, Aram is made an accomplice to the crime, rather than the actual murderer, and explicitly expresses remorse for his crime.

Bulwer-Lytton returned to the Newgate school one final time with *Lucretia; or, The Children of Night* (1846). *Lucretia* is a fascinating text that reads in some ways less as a Newgate novel than as an amalgam of the different genres that the Newgate school synthesizes, and simultaneously as an index of the directions in which social energies and the energies of crime fiction were tending by the late 1840s. Bulwer-Lytton based his fictional story on a notorious contemporary criminal, the successful painter, Thomas Wainewright, who likely poisoned his uncle, mother-in-law, and sister-in-law. Accordingly, the eponymous protagonist takes her name not from the Lucretia of Roman mythology, but from Lucrezia Borgia of the fabled first family of Renaissance Italian crime, notorious for possessing a poison ring with which she, her father, and brother allegedly disposed of unwanted associates. Bulwer-Lytton's Lucretia is similarly part of a villainous family triumvirate, each of whom exhibits a different motive to crime. Lucretia, nonetheless, is the novel's central agent.

The novel follows Lucretia's schemes to inherit her family's wealth and succeed to its status and power, and later, when those plans have failed, to punish those who came between her and her ambition. By novel's end, she is driven mad, having murdered two husbands, poisoned the daughter of her first lover, and poisoned her unrecognized, long-lost son, who has inadvertently stumbled upon knowledge of her crimes. Much like Mary Elizabeth Braddon's heroine in the 1862 sensation novel, *Lady Audley's Secret*, moreover, Lucretia is eventually consigned to the madhouse, one of her confederates having reported her dead to prevent her from spilling their secrets.

The criminal energy of the novel's first volume emanates primarily from Lucretia's French tutor, Olivier Dalibard, who owes much to omnipotent Gothic villains like Matilda in M. G. Lewis's *The Monk* (1796) or the monstrous Count Cenci of P. B. Shelley's *The Cenci* (1819): in the Gothic version, the demonic antagonist typically persuades his victim that his evil influence permeates her very being, that he has corrupted all her actions and made her what she is. Dalibard exercises his Gothic power through his Gallic tutelage. Opening Lucretia's mind to "masculine studies" which pervert her ambition and deprive her of "woman's natural ... sympathies," he teaches her to "set up the intellect as a deity" (Bulwer-Lytton 1846: vol. 1, 83, 87). Unlike the typical Gothic victim, though, Lucretia experiences no horror when she recognizes her tutor's mark upon her: "She detected, with the quickness of her sex, the Preceptor's stealthy aim. She started not at the danger" (1846: 84–5). More than up for the challenge of playing Gothic villain, Lucretia takes over the novel's criminal activity once she has disposed of Dalibard at the end of the first volume.

Lucretia's villainy springs primarily from her pride and ambition. Her pride, paradoxically, strongly resembles that of her uncle, Sir Miles, whose own fierce pride in his aristocratic lineage has prompted him to forbid Lucretia's marriage to her first love, an honorable young man destined to a mercantile career. Bulwer-Lytton uses the juxtaposition of the niece's and uncle's competing notions of pride to stage an interesting critique of the transformation of status and social hierarchy in early nineteenth-century Britain, a topic that he had taken up in *Paul Clifford* as well as in his silver-fork novels, *Pelham* (1828) and *Godolphin* (1833). In *Lucretia's* case, though, that critique looks directly forward to the sensation novel of the 1860s, inasmuch as her pride in her own superior abilities and intellect links directly to her profound frustration at the limitations placed on her as a woman. Anticipating the sensation novel of a decade or two hence, *Lucretia's* final two volumes are full of scheming calculations on marriage and inheritance, lost children, thwarted bequests, and in particular, a female protagonist railing against the few avenues open to her in which to realize her ambition.

As the gesture forward to the sensation novel suggests, the cultural fascination with crime and the performative energies of the criminal do not disappear from the British novel with the waning of the Newgate school in the late 1840s. On the contrary, that fascination merely finds its way into new channels, and we need not look as late as the 1860s to find evidence of them. A narrative genre that developed more or less concurrently with the Newgate novel provides insight into the ways in which some of the criminal's transgressive energies, as well as the public's taste for crime, get redirected in other crime fiction: namely, the police casebook, a genre that usually took the form of short fictional stories recounting the investigative activities of individual detectives, and which is often seen as an early predecessor of the police procedural. Police casebook literature emerged, properly speaking, in the late 1840s, after the 1842 inauguration of the London detective bureau and the regular reporting on its investigations in the newspapers had helped gradually to legitimate detective work in the public's eyes (Worthington 2005: 129). The genre's emergence coincides, then, with the evanescence of the Newgate school, a historical fact that speaks to the reformulation of both readers' tastes and the discursive construction of criminals and policing. The police casebook's development finds its seeds, however, in a pair of earlier texts that were published just a few years before Bulwer-Lytton's *Paul Clifford*.

The first text of note in early police casebook literature is a collection of fictional stories published anonymously in 1827 under the title, *Richmond: Scenes in the Life of a Bow Street Runner*. *Richmond* takes its fictional protagonist from among the ranks of the legendary "Bow Street Runners," the investigative force established in the mid-eighteenth century that became a forerunner of the official police detective bureau. The narrative's first part tells of Richmond's early, delinquent life before joining the Runners; the second recounts the stories of five of his criminal investigations. Although the identity of the narrative's author has never been established, it seems clear that he was not actually a Runner himself. The investigative stories draw substantially from newspaper accounts of contemporary crimes, and the author seems generally unfamiliar with the kind of detective procedures that an officer of the time would have practiced. E. F. Bleiler remarks that it is a "public, outside image of Bow Street that *Richmond* offers" (1976: xi). The text made little impact on the public when it first appeared, and seems not to have inspired any immediate imitations. It was reissued by a different publisher in 1845, though, just on the cusp of the casebook's popularity. Perhaps like Horace Walpole's *The Castle of Otranto* (1764), which took almost 25 years to spawn a generation of Gothic successors, *Richmond* was simply ahead of its contemporaries.

More closely related to the Newgate genre was the publication of the *Mémoirs of Vidocq*, an autobiography (though likely ghost-written) by Eugène-François Vidocq, a French criminal who eventually became the head of the Paris *Sûreté* police force and a renowned private detective. The text was published in France in 1828–9; an English translation appeared almost immediately. While the reliability of Vidocq's account of his criminal investigations has been disputed, his substantial influence on a range of nineteenth-century writers interested in crime, including Hugo, Balzac, Poe, and Dickens, has not. The proximity of the *Mémoirs* to the Newgate school emerges in the blurred lines in Vidocq's life and narrative between the criminal and the detective. After 25 years of finding himself on the wrong side of the law, Vidocq established his reputation and fortune by becoming a police spy. His vast criminal knowledge and underground networks made him a master of disguise and surveillance, and allowed him to move up quickly through the police ranks, first heading a small detective force which he staffed with other former criminals, and eventually becoming the first Chief de la Sûreté.

Vidocq's fame in the nineteenth century arose in part from his efforts to systematize detective work: he pioneered evidentiary procedures at crime scenes, and began maintaining extensive records on criminals. His distinction also derived from the historical moment of his rise. A century earlier, Jonathan Wild was reviled as an informant and thief-taker primarily because of his notorious treachery, but also because the distinctly pre-modern penal system with which he worked enabled, perhaps even encouraged, his corruption. By contrast, Vidocq used his insider knowledge in the Napoleonic era to become, as Robin Walz suggests, a self-styled "hero of the revolutionary bourgeoisie, champion of a new political order founded upon a propertied and professional middle class" (2003: xiv). Vidocq's narrative helped to open the discursive possibility of viewing the detective as an innovative mastermind, capable of outsmarting his foes in part through his application of scientific principle to the detection of crime. This new, enterprising model detective would use his intellectual prowess and forensic skill, moreover, to protect middle-class property and generally uphold law and order in the face of the mob's chaos; he would help, in fact, to shore up the line of distinction separating the newly established bourgeoisie from the anarchic forces of an "underworld riff-raff" (Walz 2003: xiv). Although his ongoing criminal associations made some contemporaries suspicious of his probity, Vidocq's careful respect for the middle-class state bureaucracy that hired him, his forceful personality, and above all his remarkable success at capturing criminals made him not only a celebrated detective, but a pivotal figure in the history of crime and crime narratives.

Twenty years later, a story published in *Chambers's Edinburgh Journal* would inaugurate a new genre of crime fiction by building on the figure of the intrepid detective and the opposition of crime and chaos to law and order which a narrative like Vidocq's had helped to establish. In 1849, William Russell published anonymously the first of his "Recollections of a Police Officer," a text generally touted as the first example of police casebook literature. Russell's detective protagonist, Waters, is distinguished from those of *Richmond* and Vidocq's *Mémoirs* because he has neither crime nor delinquency in his background. As Heather Worthington explains, Waters is a "man of good birth who in his youth is the victim, not the perpetrator, of crime" (2005: 140). A gentleman who enters the Metropolitan Police as a professional, he is firmly on the side of social order from the outset. And his personal distance from the haunts, habits, and occupations of criminals marks a substantial transformation of the narrative figuration of the detective. "In Waters," Worthington argues, "Russell created a character with which the middle-class reader ... could identify" (2005: 144). This is particularly evident, she suggests, in the text's narrative style, which does not attempt "to reproduce working-class dialogue or thieves' 'cant'" (2005: 144). Instead, Waters speaks just like his middle-class readers, and frames his detective work with details of his domestic life that reinforce his respectability and the reassuring familiarity of his values.

Russell published eleven additional Waters stories in *Chambers's* over the next four years; the series was reissued as a collection in 1856. The popularity of the stories and broad acceptance of the detective as hero which that popularity represented led to a marked increase in the number of detectives figuring centrally in the fiction of the 1850s and 1860s, as evidenced by such iconic characters as Dickens's Inspector Bucket of *Bleak House* (1853) and Collins's Sergeant Cuff from *The Moonstone* (1868). The ennobling of the fictional detective and distancing of him from the criminal who forms his object of study and pursuit, moreover, take the mid-nineteenth-century versions of crime fiction in a significantly different direction from the crime narratives of the Newgate school. The criminal becomes, in these later texts, increasingly an object of rational, scientific investigation; his disruptive energies, while essential to the narrative, serve largely to throw into relief the stabilizing forces of social order that will be restored with his capture. No longer is he typically styled as a rebellious champion of social justice, gallant outlaw, or even plucky underdog trying to make something of himself. Those functions are reassigned to less illicit protagonists, or counterbalanced by equally forceful agents who remain safely on the side of social order. In the Newgate novel, the criminal comes across as an enterprising, sympathetic character who frequently voices or enacts a critique of repressive social structures and unjust institutions. In the crime fiction that emerges in the wake of the Newgate school, the detective tends to be the principal repository of narrative enterprise, using his ingenuity not to subvert the social order, but to reinforce its bulwarks against those who would challenge its authority.

7

From Sensation to the *Strand*

Christopher Pittard

Introduction

In December 1890, a new monthly periodical appeared on British newsstands, just in time to provide leisurely Christmas reading for an aspirational middle-class market. In the first issue of the *Strand Magazine*, the publisher-editor George Newnes promised nothing but "cheap, healthful literature," after he had perceived a gap in the market for a monthly which would include a wide range of fiction, interviews, articles, and illustrations. In practice, however, the *Strand* rapidly became appreciated for two particular genres. One was popular science writing; the other was crime and detective fiction. In the 1890s the *Strand* featured crime stories by (among others) Arthur Morrison, Grant Allen, L. T. Meade, Robert Eustace, Dick Donovan, and most famously Arthur Conan Doyle; although the term "detective fiction" had actually first appeared in the *Saturday Review* in 1886 (Stewart 1980: 27), it was arguably the *Strand* which was the most influential publication in developing and defining this emergent genre. This chapter begins by looking at those earlier crime subgenres to which the detective fiction of the *fin de siècle* was reacting. In this regard, Newnes's claim to 'healthful literature' is a significant one: just as Newnes wanted his magazine to be an alternative to sporting papers and sensationalist broadsheets such as the *Illustrated Police News*, so too did its narratives of crime consciously move away from earlier models of crime fiction, models that were suspected of having an "unhealthy" influence on their readers. These were the penny dreadful and the sensation novel.

Dreadfuls and Sensations

The "penny dreadful" and the related "shilling shocker" were descendants of *The Newgate Calendar*, being stories in which the criminal was glorified, although the "dreadful" often distinguished itself from these earlier stories by drawing on purely fictional criminality and by appealing specifically to a juvenile audience (see Routledge, chapter 25 in this volume). Class was also an issue in the perceived danger of the "penny dreadful," a term that had been coined by middle-class critics and applied indiscriminately to a wide range of popular crime fiction. The readership of such texts was confined to the working class, usually young men. Although these narratives were not always concerned with crime (Gothic horror was a particular favorite, as well as plagiarisms of authors such as Dickens), it was the penny sheets telling stories of highwaymen and criminals that attracted the most attention from a concerned middle class. There was a perceived danger that reading such tales would encourage criminality among the young, and in criminal cases where juvenile offenders had been found to have been reading such literature (such as that of Alfred Saunders in 1876, charged with stealing from his father), the "dreadfuls" were seen as having a disproportionately large influence on the reader. Saunders's case was not helped by the admission that he stole the money to buy papers that "dealt with the adventures of pirates and robbers" (Springhall 1994: 338).

The penny dreadful was also significant for the manner in which its critics often connected its sensational and moral degeneracy with the genre's materiality. In 1874 the journalist and social investigator James Greenwood conducted an investigation into what he termed "Penny Packets of Poison," buying twelve such dreadfuls and examining them closely:

> Nasty-feeling, nasty-looking packets are every one of them, and, considering the virulent nature of their contents, their most admirable feature is their extremely limited size … [which] is woefully significant of the irresistibly seductive nature of the bane with which each shabby little square of paper is spread. I have been at pains to weigh them, and I find that the weight of each pen'orth is but a fraction more than *a quarter of an ounce.* The "Leisure Hour" weighs nearly eight times as much, as do the "Family Herald" and one or two other penny publications of a decent sort (Greenwood 1874: 358).

Here, moral weight becomes equated with physical size, an example of crime fiction criticism's obsession with the material existence of its texts, from the Victorian "yellowbacks" to the twentieth century "pulps."

Related to this material focus is an underlying concern, emphasized throughout the nineteenth century, that crime fiction was at best a commodity and at worst a waste. Greenwood's detailed examination of the dreadfuls, quoting at length scenes of violence and crime, continually draws on a lexicon of contamination and abjection. Such fictions are "impure literature" (1874: 358), "contagious trash" (1874: 366), "pen'orths of muck" (1874: 359), and an "infinitesimal quantity of trash … that serves as the carrion bait to attract towards it the blow-flies of the book trade" (1874: 358–9). In the 1870s, criminal anthropologists would describe the criminal as an atavistic being, whose lower position on the evolutionary scale was clearly written on the body. Greenwood was already using such terms to describe the penny dreadful itself:

[It is] quite a mistake to suppose that the literary ape is an animal of recent birth ... Any day within the past ten years he may have been seen in his most hideous complexion staring bold-eyed from a hundred shop windows in and about London, alluring the unwary by means of pictures so revoltingly disgusting and indecent that modest eyes unexpectedly encountering them tingled in shame. (Greenwood 1874: 366)

The penny dreadful mode of crime literature, "lurid and melodramatic," which apparently turned its readers to crime, was unacceptable for the family magazine Newnes was trying to establish.

The second mode, although more respectably middle class than the dreadful, was seen as equally dangerous in its effects. The sensation novel has been primarily regarded as a product of the 1860s (Brantlinger 1982: 1), beginning with Wilkie Collins's *The Woman in White* (1860) and continuing with novels using similar themes of crime and deception such as Collins's *Armadale* (1866) and *No Name* (1862), and Mary Elizabeth Braddon's *Lady Audley's Secret* (1862) and *John Marchmont's Legacy* (1862). What these novels have in common is a middle-class conspiracy plot based on an inheritance, and while not all sensation novels strictly conformed to this model, the recurrence of this plot amply illustrates the concern of the genre with deception, criminality and bigamy. The sensation novel, with its emphasis on female criminality and often with its criminals portrayed sympathetically, caused controversy not only because of a potential glamorizing of crime along the lines of the penny dreadful, but also in terms of its treatment of the middle-class family as the site of destructive mystery. The sensation novel marked the shift of crime narratives from the public space of the streets and slums to the private realm of the family home, and accordingly the danger of the genre was characterized as a type of invasion, the threat of a working-class literature of crime usurping the settings of the middle-class romance and bringing a contagious criminality with it. With their apparent concentration on plot rather than character, the works of Braddon and Collins were seen as unedifying fare that most disturbingly (as W. F. Fraser Rae commented in 1863) was being read in both the drawing room and the kitchen (Rae 1863).

The genre can be defined not only in terms of content but also in terms of reader response. One of the leading characteristics of the sensation novel is the author's intention of eliciting a reaction, a *sensation*, from the reader. Collins incorporated this sense of the sensation story into later works such as *The Law and the Lady* (1875), where Ariel begs to be told a story by Miserrimus Dexter: "Puzzle my thick head. Make my flesh creep. Come on. A good long story. All blood and crimes" (Collins 1998a: 309). The sensation novel was seen as an almost pornographic threat, creating a response more hysterical than cerebral at the unraveling of middle-class secrets, and the writers of such fiction were criticized for pandering to such tastes (indeed, the huge success of such novels suggests another interpretation of the genre, as a commercial sensation). The combination of writing for the market and the debased nature of such a readership was of particular concern to the critic Henry Mansel, who bemoaned the fact that such novels were "called into existence to supply the cravings of a diseased appetite, and contributing themselves to foster the disease, and to stimulate the demand they supply" (Mansel 1863: 483).

Although closely associated with the 1860s, the sensation novel was considerably longer lived. In 1890, the year Newnes's more sober *Strand Magazine* first appeared, sensation had persisted long enough for *Blackwood's Magazine* to predict its eventual demise: "but of sensation, when it has degenerated into melodrama and burlesque, there must surely come satiety at last" (Anon 1890: 189). As late as September 1887, *Punch* was still parodying the sensation novel: "Strange Adventures of Ascena Lukinglasse," for instance, mocks the techniques and tropes used by Wilkie Collins (primarily the fractured narrative of *The Woman in White* and the prophetic dream of *Armadale*), the breathless pace of its satire imitating the fast moving novel of incident. The most spectacular reimagining of the sensation novel, and a crucial point in the genre's transformation into detective fiction, appeared in the UK in 1887. Published originally in Australia the year before, *The Mystery of a Hansom Cab* was written by Fergus Hume, an English barrister's clerk in Melbourne. Its British reception was phenomenal; 300,000 copies were sold in less than 6 months, and a year later the book was continuing to sell thousands of copies a week, as well as attracting parodies such as *The Mystery of a Wheelbarrow* (1888) by "W. Humer Ferguson." The *Illustrated London News* reported, "Persons were found everywhere eagerly devouring the realistic sensational tale of Melbourne social life. Whether travelling by road, rail, or river the unpretending little volume was ever present in some companion's or stranger's hands" (Anon 1888: 410). Hume, however, gained little financially from this success, having sold the original publishing rights for £50 to the "Hansom Cab Publishing Company," which mismanaged the massive proceeds from the novel to the extent that it went bankrupt in 1892, seemingly having only published one other work of fiction in the UK, the Zola-influenced *His Last Passion* by "Martius" (1888). None of Hume's subsequent novels, numbering over 130 and diversifying into adventure and science fiction, enjoyed the success of his first.

The Mystery of a Hansom Cab ostensibly concerns the hunt for a murderer whose victim is discovered in a Melbourne cab one night, but the central mystery is really the secret of the powerful Frettlby family. The climax of the novel is not the contrived uncovering of the murderer's identity (indeed, Hume's brief introduction to the revised edition of 1898 reveals the twist almost immediately), but the revelation that the Frettlby paterfamilias has an illegitimate slum daughter. The dramatic thrust of the novel thus comes from the tension that exists between the prosperity of Melbourne and its poorer areas. The real mystery of the hansom cab is its ability to cross social and geographical boundaries, and the novel's appearance at a time when slum investigations were a popular form of investigative journalism certainly helped its phenomenal success. In the preface to the revised edition of the novel, Hume revealed that "All the scenes in the book, especially the slums, are described from personal observation; and I passed a great many nights in Little Bourke Street, gathering material" (Hume 1898: 9), just as throughout the 1880s and 1890s social investigators such as Andrew Mearns, W. T. Stead and George R. Sims penetrated the dark heart of London's slums. If Hume owed his plot to Collins, he took his descriptions and language from these investigations, and there are moments when Hume and Sims become indistinguishable. One of Hume's slum dwellers is "worthy of the pencil of Doré to depict, such was the grotesque ugliness which she exhibited" (Hume 1985 [1886]: 102); three years later, Sims's investigation *Horrible London* (1889) would unfold scenes of "grim, grotesque horror of which only the pencil of Doré could do justice" (Sims 1984: 137).

The *Strand Magazine*

These, then, were the models of crime fiction that the *Strand Magazine* (and to a lesser extent its imitators) defined itself against. What these models had in common was the construction by middle-class critics of the figure of a passive reader, who would read without distinction and succumb to the thrills of the narrative. In his work on how cultural taste legitimates social difference, Pierre Bourdieu identifies two broad categories of cultural response: the "taste of reflection," an educated, objective and detached form of reading; and the "taste of sense," which is uneducated and subjective (Bourdieu 1989: 6–7). Reflective readers are not seduced by the pleasures of the text, whereas "sensible" or passive readers are at threat from becoming involved with contaminating narratives. Historically, the passive readers identified by critics and social commentators were women, the young, and the working class, all seen as susceptible to the moral threat of the sensation novel and the penny dreadful. By contrast, the educated male middle-class reader obviously possessed enough cultural competence not to be seduced by such narratives. Accordingly, although the *Strand* was intended to be read by the whole family, in practice it was marketed to professional men and sold primarily at railway newsstands to a readership of middle-class commuters.

The contents of the detective stories in the *Strand* were, as Newnes intended, "healthy" crime narratives, compared to the "diseased appetite" Mansel had identified as feeding on the sensation novel or penny dreadful. In many ways, the *Strand* was an inversion of the sensation novel: while that genre had been seen as the literature of the kitchen becoming the reading of the drawing room, the *Strand*'s movement was in the opposite direction, from a predominantly middle-class commuting readership in the 1890s to, as *Time* put it in 1949, "part of British life, from drawing-room to below stairs" (Jackson 2001: 96). The success of the *Strand* led to a number of imitators being launched in the 1890s, including the *Ludgate Monthly* (1891), the *Idler* (1892), the *Windsor Magazine* (1895), and the *Harmsworth Magazine* (later the *London Magazine*) (1898), all of which included a substantial amount of detective fiction. Jerome K. Jerome's *Idler* published short stories by Fergus Hume; the *Harmsworth* included detective fiction by L. T. Meade and Clarence Rook; the *Ludgate Monthly* was home to C. L. Pirkis's lady detective Loveday Brooke. The *Strand*, however, remained the primary publisher of crime and detective fiction in the period through the work of its four most prolific contributors: Arthur Conan Doyle, Arthur Morrison, Grant Allen, and L. T. Meade.

Arthur Conan Doyle and Arthur Morrison

Of the many contributors to the *Strand*, it was Arthur Conan Doyle who played the largest part in the magazine's success (see Hodgson, chapter 31 in this volume). His *Adventures of Sherlock Holmes* first appeared in 1891 and ran for two series of twelve stories each before Holmes's ostensible death in "The Final Problem" (1894). The detective's reappearance in *The Hound of the Baskervilles* in 1902 gave the *Strand* added sales of 30,000 (Jackson 2001: 93). Such was the importance of Holmes (and the genre of detective fiction) to the *Strand*'s success that during a short break in the *Adventures*, Newnes felt obliged to insert an apologetic notice: "It will be observed that this month there is no detective story by Mr. Conan Doyle relating the adventures of the celebrated Mr. Sherlock Holmes. We are glad to be able to announce that there is to be only a temporary interval in the publication of these stories" (Donovan 1892: 82). This interval would be filled with "powerful detective stories by other eminent writers," a somewhat superfluous statement since the notice had been inserted at the end of an installment of Dick Donovan's series *A Romance from a Detective's Case-Book* (1892). Yet it should be noted that the relationship between Doyle and the *Strand* was a mutually beneficial one: the first two Holmes novels, *A Study in Scarlet* (1887) and *The Sign of Four* (1890) had only been modest critical and commercial successes, and it was not until the monthly publication of the *Adventures* that the detective became a household name.

It is often argued that Doyle's success lay in an apparent Victorian fetish for rationality and order, which exalted Holmes as a superhero of both intellectual prowess and careful investigation. Taken together, the most famous Holmesian aphorisms offer a rationalist manifesto, from *The Sign of Four*'s "When you have excluded the impossible, whatever remains, however improbable, must be the truth," onwards. There is something to this analysis, since the new focus on deduction and the unraveling of mystery made this new form of crime fiction more cerebral than visceral: sensations and shocks were replaced by plot twists, making the stories suitable for family reading. But another reason for Holmes's success was Doyle's recognition of the comic structure of the detection genre. It is often overlooked how self-consciously comedic later Victorian detective fiction was. The insulating farce of the interwar detectives was still decades away, but the most successful *fin de siècle* British writers were fully aware of the genre's potential for satire or modernist absurdity. Stories such as "The Red Headed League" and "The Blue Carbuncle" (both 1891) can be profitably read as comedies, their humor lying in the absurd situations which animated much of the detective fiction of the 1890s. (Why should a red-haired man be hired to copy out an encyclopedia? How does a valuable jewel end up inside a Christmas goose? For that matter, doesn't the name of the plumber, John Horner, who is falsely accused of stealing the carbuncle, recall a certain nursery rhyme nick-namesake, "Jack" Horner, who pulled a "plumb" out of his Christmas pie?) Similarly, few critics have noted the surprising frequency (given his popular ascetic image) with which Holmes laughs or makes jokes. This played a key part in the purifying scheme of the *Strand*, with its concern for its readers' cultural health: abject disgust or the will to criminality do not co-exist easily with amusement.

Of the many writers of crime fiction for the *Strand,* it is Arthur Morrison whom critics most frequently compare to Doyle. Born in Poplar in Greater London, Morrison's literary fame largely rests on naturalist depictions of London's East End, most strikingly *Tales from Mean Streets* (1894) and *A Child of the Jago* (1896), and there is little to suggest that Morrison struggled (as Doyle did) with the dichotomy of writing both popular narratives and "respectable" fiction. The critics, of course, had other ideas: the *Bookman's* review of *Martin Hewitt, Investigator,* which introduced Morrison's detective and first appeared as seven stories in the *Strand* in 1894, commented, "Perhaps one should lament a waste of talent, but it is more to the purpose to recognise [Morrison's] versatility" (Anon 1895: 156). (The review went on to note the sheer amount of crime fiction being published: "Detective literature is now so great in bulk that there is surely room for a professional critic from Scotland Yard" [Anon 1895: 156]). Two more series, *Chronicles of Martin Hewitt* (1895) and *Adventures of Martin Hewitt* (1896), appeared in the *Windsor Magazine*. Much has been made of the appearance of Hewitt shortly after Holmes's "death" in 1894, with critics such as John Greenfield arguing that Hewitt was a "Sherlock Clone" (Greenfield 2002). Such arguments point out the continuities between the two (Hewitt's methods, his use of disguise, the first person narration of the stories), but overlook the differences between the characters as an index of the overwhelming popularity of Doyle. Just as Holmes is thin and tall, Hewitt is short and round; Holmes's aloof intellectualism provided the antithetical basis for Hewitt's everyman persona, as summarized at the beginning of "The Loss of Sammy Crocket":

> It was … always a part of Martin Hewitt's business to be thoroughly at home among any and every class of people, and to be able to interest himself intelligently, or to appear to do so, in their pursuits. (Morrison 1894: 361)

Although similarities are evident, the critical attempt to reduce Hewitt to a reinvention of Holmes ignores the subtleties of Morrison's fiction, in particular the influence of his naturalist outlook. Thus, Morrison's crime writing moves between the entertaining implausibilities of the Doyle model and a more documentary approach, as in "The Quinton Jewel Affair," where criminal dialect is translated in footnotes. In general, Morrison is less convinced than Doyle that the detective has the power to restore order. Arthur Morrison's London is a complex, unknowable place that often bewilders Hewitt, in contrast to Holmesian hints of omniscience.

Accordingly, the last episode to appear in the *Windsor*, "The Ward Lane Tabernacle," ends on a note of uncertainty unusual in Victorian detective fiction. The body of a thief is recovered from the Thames clutching a piece of paper bearing a seal, from which Hewitt constructs a resolution that involves the cult of the eighteenth-century mystic Joanna Southcott. Yet, as he confesses to his client, his explanation has no formal proof, but is simply a provisional attempt at interpretation. The final line of the story, referring to the presence of the seal, reads, "Nobody at the inquest quite understood this" (Morrison 1896: 664). The narrative's admission of confusion marks Hewitt's final appearance in the periodical and overturns the usual epistemological structure of detective fiction, where at the end all events are known and understood. As if to build on this undermining of the figure of the omniscient and morally impeachable detective, Morrison's third crime series for the *Windsor*, *The Dorrington Deed-Box* (1897), starts conventionally enough before revealing that the private detective hero is actually a murderer, motivated by personal gain rather than keeping social order.

Grant Allen and L. T. Meade

The frequent critical focus on Doyle and Morrison has tended to obscure another of the major contributors of crime and detective fiction to the *Strand*, Grant Allen. Allen was perhaps the most versatile writer of such fiction for the magazine, eschewing the male heroes of Doyle and Morrison in favor of the female detective protagonists of *Miss Cayley's Adventures* (1898–9) and *Hilda Wade* (1899–1900). The "lady detective" was already popular in serials in other periodicals, such as Catherine Louisa Pirkis's *Adventures of Loveday Brooke* (1892–3), George Sims's *Dorcas Dene, Detective* (1897) and M. McDonnell Bodkin's *Dora Myrl* (1900). Yet whereas these female detectives often took up detection after an abortive stage career (which, although useful for disguise, aligned them with the disreputable figure of the actress), Allen's Lois Cayley is the New Woman *par excellence*, a bicycle-riding graduate of Girton College, like Herminia Barton, the controversial heroine of his most famous work, *The Woman Who Did* (1895). More strikingly, Allen often played with the conventions of the genre itself, not least in *An African Millionaire* (1897) and "The Great Ruby Robbery" (1892), where the culprit turns out to be the investigating detective.

Like Doyle, Allen was alert to the genre's potential for comedy, albeit of a more satirical variety. Allen provided the *Strand* with its first detective story, "Jerry Stokes" (1891), in which a Canadian hangman becomes convinced that a man sentenced to death is innocent. The story provides a liberal critique of capital punishment far removed from the conservatism with which the genre would later become associated. Advertising comes in for satirical treatment in *Miss Cayley's Adventures*, when the heroine returns to London after a trip abroad and finds the metropolis a disorienting experience:

[T]he polychromatic decorations of our English streets ... seemed both strange and familiar. I drove through the first half mile with a vague consciousness that Lipton's tea is the perfection of cocoa and matchless for the complexion, but that it dyes all colours and won't wash clothes. (Allen 1898: 690)

The sensory overload of modernity was a precondition for the development of detective fiction as a discrete genre. The collapsing of urban experience into an overwhelming collage of signs (both semiotically and literally) called for a cultural figure with particular expertise in reading such signs and in disregarding irrelevant information. But the genre also had a material relation to advertising: crime novels frequently featured advertisements on their inner and outer covers, and even inserted between the leaves. It is no coincidence that Newnes, who intended his magazine to offer a sanctuary from the potential confusion of the urban, relegated the advertisements in the *Strand* to dedicated sections at the beginning and end of each issue.

The potential confusions of modernist capitalism are explored more thoroughly in the inventive serial *An African Millionaire*, which centered on the exploits of the confidence trickster and master of disguise Colonel Clay in his (usually successful) attempts to defraud the millionaire of the title, diamond tycoon Sir Charles Vandrift. Although a new subgenre of "criminal mastermind" fiction had emerged in the 1890s, including E. W. Hornung's *The Amateur Cracksman* (1899) and Guy Boothby's *Doctor Nikola* (1896) and *A Prince of Swindlers* (1900), *An African Millionaire* (1897) is distinguished by its politico-economic satire, frequently poking fun at the heroes of capitalism. The energetic Clay is repeatedly compared favorably with the parasitic and lethargic Vandrift and his shifty secretary Wentworth. At one point, Clay tells Vandrift, "[W]e are a pair of rogues. The law protects *you*. It persecutes *me*. That's all the difference" (Allen 1980: 136). When Clay is eventually captured and put on trial, his defense is to highlight Vandrift's greed and cupidity, and although the middle-class ethos of the *Strand* demanded that Clay be punished with a prison sentence, the moral victory is ultimately his. The serial thus looks back to the Newgate novel (see Gillingham, chapter 6 in this volume) in making the criminal its hero (albeit stripped of sensationalist accounts of crime), and forward to E. C. Bentley's equally satirical *Trent's Last Case* (1913).

The conclusion of *An African Millionaire* demonstrates another key feature of Allen's fiction: an engagement with contemporary science. Like Doyle, Allen felt that detective fiction distracted him from more worthwhile literary endeavors, although unlike Doyle Allen was dissatisfied with fiction itself, frustrated that his work in biology and related sciences received far less attention. Allen partially resolved this dissatisfaction by loading his fiction with references to scientific theory and debate; thus, the nurse detective *Hilda Wade* critiqued a vivisectionist medicine which saw patients (particularly of the working class) as experimental fodder, while in *An African Millionaire*, Colonel Clay is eventually captured through the use of the emerging technologies of criminological identification developed by Alphonse Bertillon in France. The Bertillon method, a means of using precise bodily measurements to fix the identities of known criminals, had been partially adopted in Great Britain in 1894, after a select committee recommended its implementation in conjunction with the system of fingerprinting proposed by Francis Galton, cousin of Charles Darwin. Galton also appears in *An African Millionaire* in a reference to his composite photographs of criminals, in which the faces of several convicts were superimposed in an attempt to delineate the common features that denoted criminality. Such technology was appealing to the criminal anthropologists inspired by Cesare Lombroso's *L'uomo Deliquente* (*Criminal Man* 1876), which argued that criminality was a biologically determined form of atavism, and that criminals could be identified by certain physical stigmata. Yet although some writers of detective fiction were attracted by such an idea (for instance, portraying their criminals as savages lost in the modern world, or atavistic foreigners), others were more skeptical, not least because the argument that criminals were born and not socially created tended to reduce questions of motive – often the crux of the Victorian detective story – to an overarching explanation from biological determinism. Certainly Allen, in making his criminal a master of disguise who could mold his features to suit the occasion, questioned the theory that criminals were of an underlying physical type.

The link between science and detective fiction was most explicit, if not most convincing, in the work of L. T. Meade, the pen name of Elizabeth Thomasina Meade Smith. Although famous as a writer of children's and medical fiction, Meade was a prolific contributor to the *Strand*, writing a number of serials that combined medical discourse with detection, and there is a strong case for crediting Meade with the invention of the subgenre of the medical mystery. The first of her serials was *Stories from the Diary of a Doctor* (1893–5), written with Edgar Beaumont (as "Clifford Halifax"), a surgeon at Norwood Cottage Hospital. Meade and Beaumont wrote another series, the more action-oriented *Adventures of a Man of Science* (1896–7), but Meade's most productive collaboration was with another doctor, Robert Eustace, who began his career in London and later became director of a Northampton mental hospital. Meade and Eustace's partnership produced three crime serials for the *Strand*. *Stories of the Sanctuary Club* (1899) was a shorter series of detective stories set in a private clinic, a setting that would have had a resonance with the *Strand*'s middle-class audience, who were encouraged by Newnes to regard the magazine itself as a kind of literary "sanctuary club" where social problems were unknown or made easily containable. Two further series merged themes of detection with the threat of the medically knowledgeable female criminal: *The Brotherhood of the Seven Kings* (1898), which also played upon fears of organized crime and secret societies; and the self-consciously punning *The Sorceress of the Strand* (1902–3). Meade and Eustace also contributed a short series of stories to the *Harmsworth Magazine* in 1899, featuring the lady detective Florence Cusack, and wrote medical adventure stories for *Pearson's Magazine*.

Meade's detective stories could sometimes be more contrived than those of other contributors, often relying on arcana such as the "false death" of catalepsy, amnesiac kleptomania, or complicated scientific apparatus. In one episode from *The Brotherhood of the Seven Kings* ("The Star Shaped Marks") a man is mysteriously affected by radiation poisoning and the resolution reveals that the villain has built a large machine in the house next door for such a purpose. Similarly in the opening episode of *Sanctuary Club*, a huge catapult is used as the murder weapon. In an effort to ground the stories' at times fantastical elements in reality and to relate the series to contemporary medical developments, episodes of the second series of *Stories from the Diary of a Doctor* were prefaced with a disclaimer:

> These stories are written in collaboration with a medical man of large experience. Many are founded on fact and all are within the region of practical medical science. Those stories which may convey an idea of the impossible are only a forecast of an early realization. (Meade and Halifax 1895: 33)

At the risk of eliding the differences between the serials, one can trace a degree of homogeneity in Meade's work for the *Strand*, partially because of her adherence to the subgenre of medical and scientific adventure in all her serials. The reader of the *Strand* would be hard pressed to find any real distinction between Dr Halifax, the hero of *Stories from the Diary of a Doctor*, and Paul Gilchrist (*Man of Science*), Norman Head (*Seven Kings*), Dixon Druce (*Sorceress*), or Paul Cato (*Sanctuary Club*), as men who are either doctors or gentleman scientists. This is perhaps due less to limited powers of characterization on Meade's part than to her intention to create a composite image of male scientific and medical authority. Oddly enough, in her crime stories for the *Strand* and the *Harmsworth* the female medical professional, with the single exception of the nurse hero of "Silenced" (1897), was someone to be feared. Although she considered herself a New Woman writer, Meade's detective fiction nonetheless reinforced the gender stereotyping that underpinned the *Strand*'s successful project of making crime narratives respectable.

Conclusion

In the latter half of the nineteenth century the development of detective and crime fiction was shaped by the need to avoid accusations of degeneracy and of posing a threat to its readers and (by extension) society. It was largely successful in quieting such concerns since, despite the dangerous prominence of the degenerate criminals in its pages, detective fiction was rarely perceived as being degenerate itself. Indeed, the success of the *Strand* and similar monthlies among the professional class meant that by the early twentieth century the detective story was seen as appealing to an educated taste. Florence Bell's 1907 investigation of popular culture in industrial society thus commented on cheap newspapers which reported on crime as being "the counterpart, in a cruder form, of the detective stories revelled in by readers of more education and a wider field of choice, such stories as [Emile Gaboriau's] 'Monsieur Lecoq' and 'Sherlock Holmes'" (Bell 1969: 146).

As they developed, such fictions not only transformed the crime narratives that preceded them in the nineteenth century – in Hume's case, by reinventing the sensation novel, or in the case of the *Strand Magazine*, by moving away from the sensationalist mode – but also influenced twentieth-century developments in the genre for a long time to come. This is evident not so much in the history of the genre in the UK (where the largely masculine detective heroes of the *fin de siècle* were replaced by effete aristocrats and comic foreigners) as in the American hard-boiled tradition. When Raymond Chandler, in his essay "The Simple Art of Murder" (1943), contrasted the hard-boiled crime fiction of America to the cozy British puzzler, the difference was not solely geographic or socio-economic, but temporal: the term "mean streets," which Chandler made his own, was taken from the title of Arthur Morrison's naturalist sketches of the 1890s, while his praise for the everyman detective, who can mix with all sorts and conditions of men, surely looked back to Morrison's detective Martin Hewitt as much as it referred to the contemporary private eye. That hard-boiled fiction's most famous critical manifesto should ultimately derive both its title and its idealized detective hero from a *fin de siècle* British precursor should not surprise us. Chandler was raised in England, arriving there from Nebraska as a boy of seven in 1895, one year after Martin Hewitt made his debut in the pages of Newnes's magazine (see Panek, chapter 32 in this volume). Although the actual Strand was never the meanest of streets, its literary counterpart was certainly instrumental in developing a new strand of crime fiction.

8

The "Classical" Model of the Golden Age

Susan Rowland

Goodbye Mr Holmes!

The most popular form of crime fiction between 1918 and 1945 has attracted three labels: "classical," "golden age," and from critic Stephen Knight, the "clue-puzzle."

> [T]he "golden age" clue-puzzle is a highly complex form combining both consolation and anxiety, tests and treats, for those readers who found the form so compulsive in the period – and may still do today. (Knight 2004: 91)

Knight describes the clue-puzzle as providing a high degree of reader involvement in an atmosphere of safety. "Clue-puzzle" suggests stories in which the reader is engrossed without ever being fundamentally challenged. Yet also, Knight indicates the historical nature of this form. The term "golden age" stands for a peculiarly blessed era of crime writing. In this chapter, I am going to use "golden age" to denote the major form of crime fiction 1918–45, yet will include references to later works by a few authors who remained rooted in that style.

"Classical," of course, evokes something else – that these crime novels provide some sort of enduring model for later works. This chapter concentrates on some major writers such as Agatha Christie (see also Makinen, chapter 33 in this volume), Dorothy L. Sayers (see also Miskimmin, chapter 35 in this volume), Margery Allingham, John Dickson Carr, Ellery Queen, S. S. Van Dine, Edmund Crispin, Freeman Wills Crofts, Josephine Tey, A. E. W. Mason, Georgette Heyer, Ngaio Marsh, and Gladys Mitchell. These authors sculpted a form with profound social and metaphysical dimensions.

However, the notion of "classical" looks backwards as well as forwards. Christie's most significant influence was the American, Anna Katherine Green. Her first novel, *The Leavenworth Case* (1878), was one of the first "clue-puzzle" mysteries by a woman, introducing such enduring genre tropes as the distinctive "outsider" detective plus less astute sidekick who mediates with the reader, the body in the library, the rich relative who is extinguished when about to sign a new will, a plan of the crime scene, and reproduction of a scrap of paper clue. The term "classical" also looks back to the metaphysical traces embedded in the detective in the work of G. K. Chesterton. His "Father Brown" short stories anticipated many religious concerns of the inter-war authors (Chesterton 1911).

Golden age crime writers placed their faith in the detective, who dominates the plot, organizes the reader's perceptions (or permits his sidekick to do so), and solves the mystery. In some sense "he" always glances back to his literary ancestors, the two great nineteenth-century detectives, Edgar Allan Poe's C. Auguste Dupin and Conan Doyle's Sherlock Holmes.

The first and most significant characteristic of golden age fiction is its self-referential or metafictional quality. As Lee Horsley puts it in her comprehensive book, *Twentieth Century Crime Fiction* (2005), for the golden age, "reading is always re-reading" (Horsley 2005: 12–13). Intriguingly, while a careful reading of Holmes today notices his Gothic drug-using side, golden age writers insist upon using the great predecessor as a model of implacable male heroism. Against this largely mythical figure, they place more empathetically vulnerable detectives. For example, we have the mock-heroic masculinity of Hercule Poirot, Lord Peter Wimsey's ruptured psyche, and Tey's fragile Alan Grant. Thus, it is typical of the golden age to have Sayers's Wimsey ironically introducing himself as "enter Sherlock Holmes, disguised as a walking gentleman," in his very first novel, *Whose Body?* (Sayers 1963 [1923]: 12). These detectives are peculiarly self-conscious. In fact, the notion of role-playing in relation to *fictions* becomes an important aspect of criticizing social role-playing, as I shall show later.

The golden age novel, then, is one that refers to itself as a detective fiction. For example, the flamboyant detective, Dr Gideon Fell of John Dickson Carr in *The Three Coffins* (1935) delights in his superbly self-conscious lecture on "The Locked Room Mystery" that takes up a whole chapter of the novel (pp. 151–64). In Edmund Crispin's *The Case of the Gilded Fly* (1944), literary critic turned amateur sleuth Gervase Fen issues a challenge to the reader's sense of a fictional world:

> "[G]ood literary critics … are always good detectives. I'm a very good detective myself," he concluded modestly. "In fact I'm the only literary critic turned detective in the whole of fiction." (Crispin 1944: 62)

A more typical form of fictional self-consciousness compares the supposedly easy triumphs of the genre detective to the actual problems of the fictional detective in *this* story! Tey's Alan Grant is a policeman who longs to be a hero sleuth in *A Shilling for Candles* (1953). Grant sees himself as *haunted* by the ideal story detective, exposing his psychic vulnerability as he knows that he fails to measure up. Other detectives are prepared to embrace self-conscious fictionality as social role playing. These include the nervy policeman invented by Ngaio Marsh, Roderick Alleyn.

Margery Allingham's Campion, on the other hand, is both a superb actor of multiple roles (including deceiving the reader) and also subject to haunting by his

Gothic Other, the killer. Occasionally Campion faces the necessity of killing the criminal in order to protect what is most important to him. The plot thereby threatens to turn the detective hero into a murderer in such works as *Look to the Lady* (1931) and *Death of a Ghost* (1934). For golden age crime fiction, the detective always possesses an-Other, his uncanny double in the murderer, partly because the quarry is the focus of the detective's desire, his burning mental energy. However, the murderer is also "Other" because in an era of capital punishment, a successful detective is also a killer. The gallows haunts the playfulness of the form. Dorothy L. Sayers is the golden age writer most concerned with the moral, metaphysical and artistic challenges of a modern hero who kills. Her "solution" is to refract the death penalty through the cultural and emotional legacy of war, which I will examine later.

The third characteristic of self-referentiality is to create a new relationship to the reader. Golden age detective fiction invites readers to participate in the chase. It reminds them that they are an experienced audience who are aware of generic conventions. Such intensification reaches its height in the 1930s Ellery Queen novels with their famous meta-fictional address to the reader, as in *The Dutch Shoe Mystery* (1931: 199). Rather than simply being asked to admire the cleverness of the detective, golden age writers reach out beyond the page to incorporate the reader's own detecting prowess. Indeed much of the appeal of the genre comes from the combination of flattering the reader with a rueful dashing of the reader's chances by a skillful manipulation of the conventions.

Thus, within the novels, atypical moments are the detective addressing his dimmer sidekick to announce that the previous scene had contained some vital clue. New York aesthete Philo Vance, created by S. S. Van Dine in *The Benson Murder Case* (1926), scorns the dull wits of the police yet still insists that they and the reader have all the necessary clues. By such methods golden age detective fiction democratizes the form, promoting a more egalitarian relationship with the reader. In so doing it puts an increased stress on "reading" as offering strategies for solving crime.

Yet this "reading" proves surprisingly resistant to rational scrutiny. For what is a playful inclusion of the reader on the one hand is an attempt at frustration on the other. Golden age writers did not really expect readers to solve the crimes ahead of the detective. So when, partly in fun, the writers' Detection Club under Ronald Knox drew up "Ten Commandments of Detection" in 1928 as "rules" that must be followed in order to "play fair" with the reader, most of this decalogue was evaded or broken in subsequent years (Horsley 2005: 40–1).

Indeed the motif of "playing fair" in golden age crime is a double edged one. Whereas Christie brilliantly flouted any notion of sticking to trustworthy narrators in *The Murder of Roger Ackroyd* (1926), and Sayers stood for no nonsense about the detective not falling in love with the suspect in *Strong Poison* (1930), contradicting her earlier stance, a deeper sense of "playing fair" extended to the detective's modus operandi. Lord Peter Wimsey is probably the most theatrical, playful and sensitive of golden age sleuths. He is sharply pulled up in his first adventure from treating murder as a simple upper-class game. His friend Police Inspector Charles Parker tells him that murder is not cricket, nor even football.

> "You want to hunt down a murderer for the sport of the thing and then shake hands with him and say, 'Well played – hard luck – you shall have your revenge tomorrow!' ... You want to be a sportsman. You can't be a sportsman. You're a responsible person."
> (Sayers 1963: 123–4)

In fact the emphasis on intertextuality and playing games that is endemic to the form is tinged with moral criticism that could even extend to the reader. Readers are given the pleasure, not only of recognizing generic elements, but also of recognizing their own experience of living in a world that refuses to conform to them.

Ultimately one of the crucial dynamics of golden age fiction arises from the struggle between detecting and the desire for closure when "all" is revealed. The rest of this chapter will explore the tensions and flexibilities of the form: its mythic complexity, its radical treatment of gender, its social and colonial criticism, the connection to the two great wars of the twentieth century, and its metaphysical speculations. First of all, I will consider gender, form and the detective as mythical hero.

Feminized Quests, Cooking and New Hero Myths

The detective in golden age fiction is a new hero for the post-World War I traumatized landscape. One way of understanding this is to consider how the detective modifies the typical literary hero's quest. Of course, more precisely, the post-1918 detective story is modifying what it defines as the progress of Holmes and Dupin through a suspicious social scene. Holmes transformed the primarily linear trajectory of the eighteenth-century male novel hero into detection. He sought material clues, was intimate only with his assistant, Dr Watson, and often not even then. He maintained a lofty detachment from the emotions of the case and operated in a linear fashion from problem to detection to solution. Holmes resembles ancient male heroes of epics who embarked on a quest, met obstacles, and ultimately triumphed.

By contrast, the golden age detective takes detecting as linear heroic quest and changes it significantly in two ways. Either the quest becomes much more circular or meandering and much more taxing psychologically because he is *not* succeeding in a triumphant pursuit or, in a much more domestic and psychological mode, he "cooks" the suspects. As cooks, Hercules Poirot, Roderick Alleyn, and Gladys Mitchell's magnificently sinister Mrs Beatrice Adela Lestrange Bradley all manage to confine their suspects so that by talking to them and letting them reveal themselves the culprit can be identified. Such is Mrs Bradley's witch-like hypnotic power that she can sometimes "cook" her suspects without restricting their movements. For instance, in *Sunset over Soho* (1943), attractive troubled David Harben could be innocent, or the killer, or maybe just covering up for his lover, Leda (who swims faster than a swan).

As a psychologist, Mrs Bradley manages to exert psychic pressure on him even when he is kidnapped by Spanish sailors.

More typical still of the golden age is the summoning of policeman Roderick Alleyn to a country house where some much disliked person is found to be elaborately murdered. In *Artists in Crime* (1938), a beautiful artists' model is stabbed. Alleyn questions the assembled artists collectively and singularly. It is a particularly erotic "cooking" of the red herrings because he himself has fallen in love with one of them, Agatha Troy. Interestingly, the resulting "cooked confection" leads to Troy deciding that she cannot bear to acknowledge her feelings for Alleyn and it takes a further novel for them to come together. As at the end of Sayers's *Strong Poison*, there is work to be done before successful romance can be secured for the new hero detective. In particular, the dignity of the prospective love interest, Agatha Troy or Harriet Vane (both suspected of murder), must be strengthened – for she will become a new hero detective too.

Less noticed in the golden age form is the circular quest. A particularly interesting example is *Inspector French's Greatest Case* (1925) by Freeman Wills Crofts. Here an office killing takes on domestic overtones with a restricted group of suspects. Even more apparent is Inspector French's progress or lack of it. To investigate the case he quests in long fruitless journeys across Europe. Fortunately, French has a wife. Although she never stirs from the home, she is described as mirroring him in his deductions. With her help, the insight of a traditional devoted wife, French can escape from circular wandering into nabbing his man.

Taken with the golden age assertion of "difference" from Holmes, these narrative methods of circular quest and "cooking" indicate a crucial development: the feminizing of the form. At one level the form is feminized by the feminization of the detective. True, many detectives remain male. However, the rotund Hercule Poirot, delicate Wimsey and morally role-playing Campion and Alleyn constitute a significant modification of the self-contained male rationality that the novels attribute to Holmes. Golden age detectives detect as much through connection and immersion in their suspects' worlds as they do through detachment and logical analysis of clues. They are intuitive and they value this intuition; they bring into the crime-solving field nonrational, emotive, so-called "feminine" methods to rank equally with hard "masculine" rationality.

Often, the feminized male detective finds he needs more immersion and connection than his gender allows. So he will employ a female subordinate to get totally absorbed into a social milieu closed to him. In *Strong Poison*, Wimsey cannot succeed in saving the woman he loves without the help of an elderly spinster, Miss Climpson. However, golden age writers cast women not only in supporting roles, but also as featured protagonists. Christie's Miss Marple is the most famous of these. An elderly spinster from St Mary Mead, Miss Marple discovers perfidy close to home in *The Body in the Library* (1932) and *A Murder Is Announced* (1950), yet is prepared to travel in the quest for justice, as for example in *Sleeping Murder* (1976/1942). Mitchell's Mrs Bradley adds to Miss Marple's skills considerable social power and psychological intensity.

The position of young women detectives in the golden age is often more ambiguous than that of their redoubtable elders. Young women tend to sleuth in partnership, usually with a man, and usually as a subordinate – for example, Campion's future wife, Amanda Fitton in *Sweet Danger* (1933) and *Traitors Purse* (1941). Christie is notable for allowing a young woman to be the dominant detective partner in *The Sittaford Mystery* (1931), and in her married sleuths, Tommy and Tuppence Beresford, the woman repeatedly refuses to be sidelined.

All in all, the golden age form is a feminized one. In the narrative shape of the detective story we see the modification of the typical heroic quest of the masculine knight errant. Circularity, "cooking," getting to know characters, all these make the detecting method more "feminine" and psychologically connected. Of course, rational enquiry is not given up. Clues matter. However, the golden age detective discovers that human inner worlds matter too. The irrational side of the human psyche and of human social groups matter as well and must be understood by more than logic. That is why I have suggested that the golden age exhibits an "erotics of detection" (Rowland 2001). The feminized detective must intuit the situation as well as dissect it logically. In the language of the period, this psychological connecting is gendered as feminine.

Hero, Myth, and Grail

In short, golden age crime fiction is a new incarnation of the perennial hero myth. It is explicitly an *incarnation*, for here the body of the detective, with instincts, intuitions, sexuality, vulnerability, psychological otherness, all *counts* as important for the detecting process. Historically in parallel with T. S. Eliot's evocation of the grail myth in "The Waste Land" (1921), the golden age story is a re-emergence of the myth of the Quest for the Holy Grail.

The golden age novel presents a self-referential social scene as a metonym for the wasteland of modernity. The detective quests for the grail, which is the healing knowledge of the source of social sickness. Once this knowledge is possessed, the criminal can be removed and thereby the wasteland renewed. Only it is not so simple. On the level of fantasy, which is given to the reader by the work's being explicitly *fiction*, the grail quest is achieved. The myth animates the plot by being the desire of the detective (and reader) to find the answer that will solve death and evil. Of course, the *processes* of the detecting narrative are beset by failure, vulnerability, evidence of social unfairness and of the impermeability of modernity to reason.

Indeed, when detectives begin to fail as semi-divine grail seekers, their fragmentation turns the myth around. Now instead of the detective as "hero" we have the quester signifying the very sickness of modernity that he is trying to heal: "he" becomes the fisher king whose reeking wounds stand for the wasteland. What is so highly sophisticated about the golden age is that its stories both fulfill and defeat the grail myth at the level of plot. Part of the self-referential sophistication of the golden age is its ability to "play" with the grail myth in order to use it to explore social problems. It returns the grail myth to the culture as a structure of desire and fantasy.

Significantly, desire and fantasy are here attached to *knowledge*. Modernity is about competing ideas that constitute grounds for truth, knowledge, and reality. Detective fiction is one of the chief spaces where the different grounds for knowledge are debated. What constitutes evidence? Is it the cigarette ash in the garden, the expression on the face of the suspect, the intuitive hunch of the detective? By refracting the modernist debate about knowledge through the grail myth, golden age fiction refocuses Western understandings of gender and truth. For within the golden age are the competing types of hero, gendered as masculine and feminine, that go right back to the founding myths of consciousness and culture.

Alison Light identifies many of the modernist qualities of golden age detective fiction when writing about Agatha Christie (Light 1991: 61–112). What is particularly modernist, I suggest, is the debate in the feminized detective between knowledge gained by rational discrimination and separation (how the golden age form reads Holmes) and knowledge gained by connection, empathy or ethical feeling (what golden age detectives emphasize). These masculine and feminine forms go back to creation myths and the way the dominant form of Christianity has read the Bible.

Creation myths come in two types. Sky Father creation myths structure consciousness as based on separation because they portray the world as the separate project of a father figure above the earth. By contrast, the older Earth Mother creation myths make nature herself sacred. "She" is not female because she is prior to the separation that makes two genders. "She" bodies forth humanity, including a son who becomes her lover, dies and is re-membered by her. Hence Earth Mother myth structures consciousness and knowledge through body, connection, sexuality, and feeling. By contrast Sky Fathers offer heroes in their own image as focusing upon separation, which often turns into conquest of the "other" as women and nature.

Western modernity inherits a fatal lack of balance between the two creation myths of consciousness, which results in patriarchy and the gendering of knowledge in the form of the Sky Father hero. Golden age fiction, I would argue, is part of the modernist attempt to recover Earth Mother connected consciousness in order to re-balance the collective psyche. The golden age detective, at a deep mythical level, is an attempt to heal the wasteland of the post-World War I modern world.

Ideology: Conservative in Closure, Not in Process

Golden age fiction makes ideologies visible in both the process and the closure of plots, often revealing a complex politics. For example, Josephine Tey and Gladys Mitchell adopt female teacher training colleges as the confined setting that acquires Gothic resonances through crime. Mrs Bradley's claw-like hands are firmly wrapped around the Wardenship of a women's Hall of Residence in *Laurels Are Poison* (1942), while Tey's Lucy Pym arrives at a similar establishment as an honored guest lecturer who stays to detect. In *Miss Pym Disposes* (1946), Lucy, a young author of a bestselling work upon psychology, quite fails to live up to her reputation.

Importantly, Mrs Bradley and Lucy Pym learn that social role-playing is both a manifestation of class privilege and a cover for moral guilt. These detectives *discover* the role-playing that the more rhetorically artificial tones of authors like Christie and Marsh proclaim is endemic *and dangerous* to social stability. Role-playing is at one level rooted in the self-referential "fictional" quality of the golden age. It serves to make ideologies of class and ethnicity visible in the process of the plots, however much the successful "closure" might try to restore authenticity to the social roles.

An example of implicit criticism of class role-playing in process, followed by conservative closure, is Georgette Heyer's *Envious Casca* (1941). Here a divided family gathers at the house of an unkind patriarch, Nathaniel Herriard. When he is found in a locked room stabbed in the back, self-referentially cited of course ("'What, you aren't going to tell me this is one of these locked-door cases you read about, sir?' exclaimed [Inspector] Hemingway incredulously" [Heyer 1941: 173]), all his dependents have been playing a part because they desperately need his money. However, Heyer's conservatism is indicated by the guilty party proving to be a professional actor. The worst deceit, the killer worm within the class-inflected Eden of the country house, does not really belong there.

Authors such as Christie in *Hercule Poirot's Christmas* (1938) and A. E. W. Mason in *The House of the Arrow* (1924) find the country house itself a breeder of poison, thinly veiled by performing social selves. The likeable young hero of the latter novel joins the melodramatic Frenchman, Inspector Hanaud, to look into the strange death of a rich old lady. He finds himself beguiled by a young woman playing the part of an innocent, while really acting as a vicious Eve in this country house paradise.

Of course, it is wrong to overemphasize the role of the country house in golden age writing. What is generally characteristic is the confined space and Christie, in particular, is inventive in making the contained spaces of modern travel metonymic of the dangerous mixing of classes and ethnicities in the modern world. In her most famous example, *Murder on the Orient Express* (1934), the performing selves of the different nationalities prove to be emblematic of the rising power of America (and of a dangerous tendency towards unilateral justice!).

Another way that the golden age makes social ideologies visible is by exploring the post-Victorian family. Compared to Holmes, the golden age detective is positively family friendly. Even bachelor Poirot is avuncular in his attitudes while Miss Marple is frequently referred to as an "aunt" to nephew Raymond. Detectives in Marsh, Sayers, Allingham, and Tey as well as Christie's Beresfords all fall in love and marry through detecting. Moreover, Wimsey develops a complexity to his family life through the moral challenges of detecting when *very* connected. When brother Gerald, Duke of Denver, is arrested for murder in *Clouds of Witness* (1926), Wimsey finds himself torn between accusing his brother or his sister of a capital crime.

Yet in addition to the growth of a family-friendly detective, families are often the focus of the crime plot in a *critical* sense. It goes without saying that a person exerting tyrannous, usually monetary control over a family is the favorite target for the villain. However conservative the closure of such a plot, the ending still reconfigures family dynamics on more egalitarian lines. In particular, control of the younger generation by the older is frequently loosened. The golden age rejects Victorian stuffiness and authority by making it the loser even after the crime is solved.

Even Heyer engages readers through witty and complex family relationships. Most of her detectives are attractive policemen who do not get too involved. Yet in *The Unfinished Clue* (1933a), Inspector Harding is seduced into giving up his profession by his attraction to the only sensible member of a dysfunctional family. In the satisfying *Why Shoot a Butler* (1933b), one delightful and one sinister family are linked by amateur detective and barrister, Frank Amberley. Here the mesh of performing selves is delicately balanced between the conservative plot of discovering a hidden will for inherited wealth and the tantalizingly radical possibilities of a mysterious young woman. She spends the novel resisting all social categories. Unsurprisingly in a Heyer novel, she is at last discovered to be the missing heiress. Even so, this conservative closure of the plot does not cancel the haunting possibilities evoked earlier.

Golden Age Crime and War

Among the most haunting of these possibilities is the disturbing presence of war in golden age crime fiction. For example, Gill Plain has written persuasively of Agatha Christie's corpses resonating with the anxieties generated by those millions of mutilated bodies on World War I battlefields (Plain 2001: 29–55). The body in Christie's inter-war stories is a site upon which the social upheavals resulting from war, as well as the trauma itself, could be registered:

> Christie's interwar fiction thus both reveals and attempts to heal the ruptures of social organisation. In her construction of the grievable body she offers a talisman against death's fragmentation and dissolution, a sacrifice to ameliorate the wounds of war. (Plain 2001: 53)

Plain shows that war is both concealed and revealed, and to a certain extent addressed therapeutically in Christie's iconic work. Alison Light first argued for Christie's corpus as a deliberate "literature of convalescence" after the world shattering events of 1914–18 (Light 1991: 65–75). Given this potent situating of the golden age as reacting to the Great War, it is interesting to consider how the form treated the failure of its containing strategies. The golden age parodically and metonymically tries to contain the anxieties provoked by and provoking war (as part of its "treatment" of the wasteland), so how might it react to a new catastrophe? What about golden age fiction in World War II?

Marsh, Mitchell, and Allingham have some fascinating works mirroring a sense of a world in chaos while attempting to draw boundaries between death in war and in crime. These novels were all written during World War II and so the tensions are acute between the possibility of the crime plot disintegrating into the general chaos of war and its forging a closure detached from it. After all, the moral imperative about murder may appear weakened in a time when thousands are slaughtered every night. Here the dynamic between more radical *processing* of social forms versus *closure* in trying to fix them (in both senses) is that of trying to establish a difference between criminal murder and killing in war. For if a murder begins to resemble a war casualty too closely, then moral distinctions upholding society begin to break down.

Both Mitchell in *Sunset over Soho* (1943) and Allingham in *Coroner's Pidgin* (1941) have their detectives, Mrs Bradley and Albert Campion, discover their bodies *in the wrong place* during the London Blitz. Dangerously close to eliding crime and war, the detectives literally have to build social values out of the rubble of the civilization that was supposed to sustain them. Allingham's Campion questions the morality of war hero Johnny Carados. Mrs Bradley's evil grin serves to highlight terrifying possibilities as she takes in war orphans and a young man with an unprovable story of being embroiled in covering up a murder. Fortunately for civilized values, Campion acquits the war ace and Mrs Bradley's David Harben takes part in the rescue at Dunkirk as a prelude to his exoneration.

It seems a similar tale in *Death and the Dancing Footman* (1942), in which Marsh's Inspector Alleyn is called to a country house murder at the start of the war. Here cowardice is explicitly punished as the guilty party proves to be a young man evading his soldierly duty. Perhaps even more pointed is the treatment of foreigners. Marsh habitually condemns racism and xenophobia. The Austrian doctor is targeted by the other suspects because of his ethnicity. In fact he is innocent and treated with notable dignity by his author. Like the entirely guiltless Egyptians in *Death on the Nile* (1937), foreigners are not the main targets for guilt in golden age fiction. More usual is the detection of otherness *within* English society in the form of deviance and criminality. Sometimes the canker in the internal ironized "Eden" is so divorced from the values of secular modernity as to be quite Gothic, as in the witchcraft in Allingham's rural idylls such as *Sweet Danger* and *Look to the Lady*.

Conclusion: Sacred Space and the End of Death

The mythical, the ethical, and the need to heal society's trauma over mass death all lead golden age fiction into the metaphysical dimension. In particular, the self-referentiality of the form allows it to be a playful fantasy of reversing death. For when the detective solves the crime in an acknowledged *fiction*, death itself is subject to *solution*. All the causes of death in that avowedly fictional world have been solved. Since we readers accept the story as a game whose rules we share with the author, we may embrace this fantasy of overcoming the death drive. Indeed, the prominence of sexuality and romance surrounding the successful conclusion channels this fantasy of overcoming death into pleasure. Golden age fiction can be read psychoanalytically as self-consciously, in fantasy, returning us to the "golden" world of perfection that we have been forbidden since the Oedipus complex drove us from the fantasy completion of the maternal bond (Rowland 2001: 91–103). Of course, this is also a religious structure of the loss of paradise; the grail myth seeks its return.

Hence, as W. H. Auden said, golden age fiction seeks to restore a lost Eden and therefore the fantasy place before the knowledge of death (Auden 1988). It begins in a sacred space polluted by the worst crime of all. Christie's well-known location of St Mary Mead expresses this religious dimension. In fantasy, golden age fiction *rewrites Genesis*. The detective is truly heroic in overcoming the flaming sword of the angel forbidding return. In *fantasy only*, because it is a self-referential game, the closure of the solution of the crime does more than restore traditional social structures. It restores the sacred place as a social space. It redeems modernity from sin, violence, and chaos.

One might finally notice that St Mary Mead, Christian in one sense, also evokes the Nature Goddess. Not for nothing does its chief protector, Miss Marple, play an avenging female goddess in *Nemesis* (1971) as Shaw and Vanacker argue (1991). Metaphysically, the golden age detective varies between three mythic figures. First, there is the divine representative on the grail quest. (Christie's protagonists fill this role comically and ironically, as do those of John Dickson Carr and S. S. Van Dine.) Second, the detective is a failing quester or sick fisher king signifying the wasteland (Lord Peter Wimsey, Tey's Duncan Grant). Lastly, the sleuth embodies a Gothic shadow to the divine hero whose demonic powers evoke, without fully realizing, the villain and all "he" stands for (Mrs Bradley, Albert Campion and Rex Stout's Nero Wolfe).

Golden age crime fiction sought to redeem the modern world from death, war, and chaos. It did so by developing a flexible self-referential form, and by embodying the mythical hero in a new relation between masculine and feminine structures of consciousness. It succeeded in generating a potent "classical" form for desire and its grail quest for a better world.

9

Early American Crime Fiction: Origins to Urban Gothic

Alexander Moudrov

We have no news from Europe. Who cares? We have enough interest on this dear delightful continent, to occupy all our feelings – all our soul – and all our sensibilities. In a short time, Europe will be like an old woman, without a tooth or a touch of sensibility. This continent is a fresh blooming young maiden – not yet knocked in the head with an axe, and disfigured in her lovely limbs. (The New York Herald, April 15, 1836)

This gloomy yet amusing excerpt is taken from one of many sensationalist papers that appeared in the United States in the 1830s and 1840s. Like other publications of this kind, the New York *Herald* indulged its readers' taste for the sensational and scandalous under the guise of reputable journalism. It put special emphasis on what can be loosely categorized as crime literature by publishing various crime-related materials (police reports, trial records, and crime stories) which could not be properly classified as factual or fictional, serious or comical, didactic or sensational. In this respect, the writer perfectly captures the ambiguous character of antebellum crime literature and highlights its essential contradictions. Note, for example, the sharp contrast between his passionate enthusiasm about "this delightful continent" and the morbidity of the violent metaphor he uses. Equally striking is the discrepancy between his cheerful tone and the undeniable sense of doom. This country is like "a fresh blooming young maiden" who will be, at some point, "knocked in the head with an axe." The phrasing of this excerpt suggests some important questions about antebellum crime literature in general. How did American crime writers see their task? Did they consider their writings about crime as a form of cultural commentary or literary entertainment? Why was it necessary to resort to violent imagery even when it could be avoided?

As we will see in this chapter, nineteenth-century crime writers often disagreed about these questions, thus making crime literature an amazingly vibrant genre that included biographies of criminals, adventure tales, execution pamphlets, and crime reportage, as well as popular crime novels. While surveying a few of these categories, this chapter advances two main arguments. First, popular crime literature in the nineteenth century served as a viable form of cultural commentary. Second, the immense popularity of literature about crime in the antebellum period was not a spontaneous development or an outbreak of meaningless sensationalism. It grew out of the long domestic tradition of didactic literature about crime that emerged right at the onset of colonization in the seventeenth century. It can ultimately be argued that popular nineteenth-century writers did not have to invent a new tradition of crime literature. They often relied on the conventions established by their predecessors. What was significant about antebellum crime literature, however, was that it transformed the tradition of religious didacticism, which defined early forms of American crime literature, into new literary genres.

The Origins of American Crime Literature

Peleg Whitman Chandler's collection entitled *American Criminal Trials* (1841) offers both a good example and a good explanation of how significant the subject of crime was to his contemporaries. The book was, at least on the surface, very similar to other crime collections which were immensely popular at that time. Each chapter was devoted to a notable court case: the trial of Anne Hutchinson in 1638; the Salem witch trials and persecutions of the Quakers in the late seventeenth century; the infamous New York Negro Plot of 1741; the Boston Massacre of 1770; and similar cases. What is remarkable about this book is that Chandler not only indulged his readers' interest in crime but also made an effort to explain the cultural and historical significance of his subject. He demonstrated, first of all, that America had a long history of fascination with crime. Furthermore, he argued that crime was not a mere object of curiosity; it was right at the center of the discourse about American culture, perhaps even the only way to understand it. He even went so far as to suggest that American history could be better told by following famous trials than by examining other events which were considered important by patriotically minded historians and politicians. He explained his strategy in fairly simple terms: if one was interested in "truth" (the word that obsessed Chandler's contemporaries), one must turn attention precisely to court records that could "show man 'as he is in action and principle, and not as he is usually drawn by poets and speculative philosophers'" (Chandler 1841: iv). In his view, crime literature could serve as a social mirror that enabled Americans to understand their culture and history.

Although Chandler did not explicitly acknowledge it, his approach reflected an enduring American tradition of writing about crime. The earliest forms of crime literature in this country were inspired by the need to educate the public about important social issues and religious principles. As Cohen (1988) and Conquergood (2002) demonstrated in their studies, ministers in the Puritan colonies routinely published various crime reports and execution pamphlets that exploited the potential of fascinating crimes for prompting consideration of wider social and moral issues (see Schmid, chapter 15 in this volume). Overall, this strategy reflected the structure of Puritan punishments which were routinely conducted as educational spectacles. Such rituals consisted of several key components: the trial, which was often conducted publicly; the actual punishment (or execution), which was accompanied by moralizing sermons; and the publication of records that could reach a fairly large audience.

Samuel Danforth's *Cry of Sodom* (1674), which was published on the occasion of a young man's execution for bestiality, captured the key elements of the new genre. It grew out of an unusually scandalous crime that could not help but captivate the public. It led to an elaborate execution ritual which was attended by many colonists. Finally, it inspired a moralizing sermon which was promptly sent into print. The author's strategy perfectly exemplified the way in which Puritan ministers created and exploited such scandalous cases to promote official religious ideology. Consistent with the Puritan concept of crime, Danforth portrayed Benjamin Goad's transgression not as a haphazard crime but as a manifestation of larger issues. It was, Danforth insisted, a sign of common human wickedness. It also indicated the general decline of the religious spirit in the colonies, which meant that everyone had to share the blame for this unusual crime. Those who came to see Goad's execution were told that the "gross and flagitious practices of the worst of men are but comments upon our nature." Danforth called upon the congregation to "ransack [their] own hearts" and acknowledge their inclination to "all manner of sins," including "murder, adultery, fornication, lasciviousness, and all manner of inequity" (1674: 14). Lest the audience miss this important point, he clearly stated that the "spectators" of such executions – and the readers of Danforth's pamphlet – were actually as guilty as the "sufferers." Goad's transgression, in other words, was just a symbol of such grand issues as the conflict between human nature and man's spiritual concerns, and the threat that conflict posed to the religious and political order of the colony.

Although there had been similar cases prior to Goad's execution in 1674, what made this case so important was not the event itself but Danforth's decision to publish his sermon. The decision was not random. It reflected the common belief, which was shared by many Puritan ministers, that talking about crime was a matter of utmost importance for the salvation of the colony. In the words of William Bradford, the governor of the Plymouth colony, it was absolutely essential to bring examples of the worst criminal behavior "into the light" and reveal them "to the view of all" (Bradford 1856: 386).

This strategy inspired the enduring American tradition of tirelessly exposing crime, which explains the proliferation of crime literature in the colonies. The public quickly grew accustomed to cheap and readily available pamphlets, broadsides, and collections about crime. First to appear were execution pamphlets with such captivating (and sometimes interminable) titles as *Instructions to the LIVING, from the Conditions of the DEAD: A Brief Relation of REMARKABLES in the Shipwreck of above One Hundred Pirates* (1719) and *Speedy Repentance Urged: A Sermon Preached at Boston ... in the*

Hearing, and at the Request of One Hugh Stone, a Miserable Man under a Just Sentence of Death, for a Tragical and Horrible Murder: Together with Some Account Concerning the Character, Carriage, and Execution of that Unhappy Malefactor. To Which are Added, Certain Memorable Providences Relating to Some other Murders & Some Great Instances of Repentance which have been Seen among us (1690). In their most basic form, execution pamphlets consisted of sermons alone. To make such publications more meaningful and appealing, some writers introduced various innovations. An increasing number of pamphlets included additional materials: ministers' interviews with doomed criminals, last-minute confessions, accounts of criminals' conversions, and instructive essays. The format of such publications depended on the needs of the author, but regardless of circumstances they preserved the didactic character of the tradition to which they belonged.

Confessions of criminals were often published as cheap broadsides. They were marketed as "dying speeches" of condemned criminals who wanted to express their repentance, reconcile themselves with their fate, and dissuade readers from following the path of crime. A variation on this genre was the so-called crime ballad, or confessions in verse, which were also published as broadsides. This form of crime literature remained fairly popular as late as the nineteenth century. Another important innovation in crime literature was the appearance of crime collections, lengthy compilations of crime stories and reports. Cotton Mather's *Pillars of Salt: An History of Some Criminals Executed in this Land for Capital Crimes* (1699) is an indisputable classic of the genre. One of the most famous proponents of religious didacticism, Mather published his work for a wide audience in the hope that it could be used to "correct and reform" the public's morals as well as "to suppress growing vice" (Mather 1702: 59). Although the book was substantially longer than the average execution pamphlet, it was published as a cheap, pocket-sized paperback which was clearly marketed for mass consumption. Such collections started to gain popularity in the late eighteenth century, with such notable examples as *The American Bloody Register* (1784), *The United States Criminal Calendar: or An Awful Warning to the Youth of America; Being an Account of the Most Horrid Murders, Piraces {sic}, Highway Robberies* (1832), *The Lives of the Felons, or American Criminal Calendar* (1847), and Charles Summerfield's *Illustrated Lives and Adventures of the Desperadoes of the New World* (1859).

A strong didactic component was also apparent in so-called captivity narratives, another important category of early American crime literature. They were published as accounts of colonists who survived captivity among native Americans. One of the earliest examples of this genre was the book written by Mary Rowlandson, who was captured by the Wampanoag tribe during King Philip's War in 1676. It appeared under the title *A True History of the Captivity and Restoration of Mrs. Mary Rowlandson* (1682). The book emphasized the brutality and sadistic inclinations of the "savages" while demonstrating the religious strength that helped her survive the ordeal. For average readers geographically removed from the colonies, particularly those in Europe, such accounts could certainly be read merely as enthralling adventure tales.

For many colonists, however, captivity narratives were constant reminders that the colonists were engaged in a protracted struggle with the heathenism of the New World. While reading these narratives, we can easily discern their writers' efforts to frame them in the context of that struggle.

As Cotton Mather explained in *Magnalia Christi Americana* (1702), an early work of history that helped forge an enduring myth of American colonization, taming the wilderness of the New World was essentially a battle with Satan. The American continent was believed to have originally belonged to "nations of barbarous Indians and infidels ... whose whole religion was the most explicit sort of devil-worship" (Mather 1702: 41). The colonists' efforts to establish a Christian stronghold in the New World must have disturbed Satan and provoked him to launch a counteroffensive against the colonies, which manifested itself in many forms, including witchcraft and Indian attacks on the colonists. It is not an overstatement to say that captivity narratives expressed urgent national concerns. As Richard Slotkin pointed out, such works "functioned as a myth, reducing the Puritan state of mind and world view, along with the events of colonization and settlement, into archetypal drama" (2000: 9). This drama remained apparent even in later manifestations of the genre such as nineteenth-century frontier novels or accounts of white Americans who survived foreign captivity. Its endurance is evident in such works as *History of the Captivity and Sufferings of Mrs. Maria Martin, Who was Six Years a Slave in Algiers* (1807), Lucretia Parker's *Piratical Barbarity or the Female Captive* (1825), and William P. Edwards's *Narrative of the Capture and Providential Escape of Misses Frances and Almira Hall* (1832).

As we will see, these forms of early American crime literature established an enduring tradition that provided nineteenth-century writers with literary and intellectual frameworks for their iterations and variations of the genre.

The Legacy of Didacticism in the Nineteenth Century and New Forms of Crime Literature

In the late eighteenth century American crime literature began to escape the confines of religious didacticism and assume an unprecedented diversification and development in new literary forms, including Gothic and urban Gothic novels, criminal biographies and adventures, and sensational trial pamphlets. What is remarkable about these developments is that in spite of the weakening of Puritan influence, many writers felt obliged to preserve the didactic conventions of the past. They did it by directing their attention to contemporary social issues.

The majority of readers probably saw crime literature as a source of titillation, but both readers and writers were willing to preserve the notion that what they read and wrote was socially important. Writers generally felt reluctant to admit the literary worth of their works. They insisted that their works were written to improve readers' morals or explore an important issue, not to indulge a taste for the scandalous.

Sensational tales about riveting murders, awful rapes, and ingenious crimes were often presented as legitimate inquiries into social problems or religious issues. The author of *Confessions, Trials, and Biographical Sketches of the most Cold Blooded Murderers* (1837), for example, was quite direct in his claim that his collection of "startling and authentic narratives" was written for no other reason than to demonstrate what "human passions may do" when people are "unawed by RELIGION" and "unrestrained by REASON" (Anon 1837: vi). George Wilkes, the editor of *The Lives of the Felons, or American Criminal Calendar* (1849), adopted the same strategy when he stated that his work (a compilation of sensationalist crime tales modeled on the long-running British *Newgate Calendar*) was meant to promote "honesty and virtue" in its young readers: "This work is ... offered to the public, not only as an object of curiosity and entertainment, but as a publication of real and substantial use, to guard the inexperienced from the allurement of vice, and to protect the weak from the flattering temptations that eventuate only in destruction" (Anon 1846: iv).

Popular novelists used the same approach. George Lippard wrote that his elaborate crime novel, *The Quaker City* (1844), was meant to expose "all the phases of corrupt social systems" in the hopes of putting an end to various forms of injustice (1995: 2). Harrison Gray Buchanan's comments about his work's scandalous exposé of city crimes entitled *Asmodeus: or Legends of New York*, offer yet another example: "We write not merely for idle talk, but for the understanding of all – from a desire to do good – to promote the ends of Truth, Justice, Equity, Humanity and Right" (1848: 25).

The didactic conventions remained so strong that many nineteenth-century crime writers went so far as to condemn the very concept of fiction. As George Thompson noted in his novel *Venus in Boston* (1849), the problem with fiction was that it is "not sufficiently natural" and has little to do with "truth and reality" (Thompson 2002: 3). Fiction was often considered a form of deception that distracted readers from real social issues. It was absolutely essential to preserve the illusion of authenticity and reverence for what popular crime writers called "real life." "I have visited every den of vice which is hereinafter described," claimed Ned Buntline in *Mysteries and Miseries of New York* (1848). He added that even though "this book bears the title of a *novel*, it is written with the ink of truth and deserves the name of a *history* more than that of a romance" (Buntline 1848: 5). Buchanan, likewise, offered his *Asmodeus* as a "'plain unvarnished tale,' of the sins and iniquities of the city of New York," a book of "facts without fiction."

We should not assume, of course, that such emphasis on "facts without fiction" undermined the complexity of crime literature. In many works, the didactic tenor clashed with the author's hyperbolic tone and sensationalist excess. The reader could never be sure what was factual and what was fictional, thus turning these works into elaborate literary games and objects of endless investigation.

What also contributed to the growing popularity of American crime literature was its increasing importance in arguments over social issues such as urban crime, prostitution, and poverty. This development was significant. Unlike their Puritan predecessors, who relied on certain unshakable assumptions about criminal behavior, nineteenth-century writers actually encouraged debates about the causes of crime. They often juxtaposed conflicting views of the questions that preoccupied many Americans at that time. Was crime a reflection of innate human depravity or social injustice? Is criminal behavior a part of human experience or a manifestation of inhumanity? How should the public treat criminals? These controversial questions, which were repeatedly raised by contemporary writers and reformers, were often incorporated, even if only implicitly, in new forms of crime literature. In this respect, antebellum crime literature was a complex cultural phenomenon that relied on readers' fascination with the provocative as well as their concerns about various social issues.

Criminal Confessions, Biographies, and Adventures

The growing popularity of criminal confessions and adventure novels was one of the most notable developments in nineteenth-century American crime literature. This new form of literature was rooted in the Puritan tradition of "dying speeches" but evolved into many elaborate literary forms. Under various pretexts, such works retraced adventures of infamous criminals whose stories could be turned into engrossing tales.

Biographies of criminals were usually published as documentary works based on real events, but were considerably modified and fictionalized to respond to the reader's interest in the sensational. Some titles from "The Life and Adventure" series about famous criminals, which were published by H. Long & Brother in the late 1840s, offer good examples of how nineteenth-century writers transformed criminal records into engaging stories: *John A. Murrell, the Great Western Land Pirate* (1847), *Colonel Monroe Edwards, the Accomplished Forger and Swindler* (1848), and *Henry Thomas, the Western Burglar and Murderer* (1848). And there were plenty of other criminals whose cases were continuously exploited in print. The adventures of Joseph T. Hare, who was executed in 1818 for a series of murders and robberies, inspired a number of biographies that were republished for decades. The name of Charles Gibbs, an American serial murderer and pirate who was executed in 1831, appeared in titles of many popular works. Crime literature addicts could also indulge in lengthy collections of criminal adventures such as *Confessions, Trials, and Biographical Sketches of the Most Cold Blooded Murderers* (1837), Charles Ellms's *Pirates Own Book: Authentic Narrative of the Most Celebrated Sea Robbers* (1837), and *The Lives of the Felons, or American Criminal Calendar* (1849). In spite of some didactic overtones, these works did not burden readers with ethical considerations. Their plots were compelling and their characters were invested with some degree of psychological complexity. Some publications were even adorned with "elegant and spirited engravings" and other enticing attributes of mass print culture.

The immense popularity of such works at least in part reflected disagreements about ways of writing about criminals. Books about crime often juxtaposed conflicting theories about criminal behavior, thus sparking endless debates about this subject. In the colonial period, as we saw earlier, criminality was generally perceived as a reflection of the general predisposition to sin. Those who attended executions and read execution pamphlets were asked to relate their spiritual condition to those of the condemned criminals. In the late eighteenth century this approach started to change, inspiring many conflicting ways of explaining criminal behavior. The main question, which generated much controversy in that period, was whether those who broke laws should be viewed as naturally incorrigible criminals or victims of social injustice.

One of the most perceptible trends, particularly evident in Gothic literature (see Spooner, chapter 19 in this volume), was depiction of criminals as "moral aliens" and "moral monsters" who violated communal standards (Conquergood 2002: 351). By committing crimes, they were believed to have rejected societal norms, thus severing ties with their communities. Consequently, the public no longer had to relate to criminals. Instead, the public was encouraged to express its disapproval of criminal behavior. The scaffold ceased to be a reflection of communal sin and became a focal point of judgment.

The monstrosity of criminals in nineteenth-century American fiction was often meant to be perceived as shocking and abhorrent. Many of them had sadistic proclivities, were prone to meaningless violence, and at times even lacked basic human traits. In some respects they resembled the psychopaths and serial killers to be found in many modern crime novels. Thus the Dead Man, who reigns over the urban underworld in George Thompson's *City Crimes*, repeatedly shocks readers with his "stupendous villainy and depravity" (2002: 134). He takes delight in recalling his outrageous crimes without any sense of remorse. He simply states: "I never had conscience" (2002: 228). George Lippard's description of Devil-Bug in *The Quaker City* is even more disturbing. He is a sadistic monster who often kills for no other reason than "to observe the blood of his victim" and enjoy "the last throttling rattle in the throat of the dying" (1995: 106). As the author notes, Devil-Bug was not a man but "a mass of hideous and distorted energy … [H]e stood apart of human … he was something distinct from the mass of men, a wild beast, a snake, a reptile, or a devil incarnate – any thing but a – man" (1995: 105–6). Perhaps the most telling example of this trend of dehumanizing criminals can be found in Poe's "The Murders in the Rue Morgue." The brutal murders which the story describes are perpetrated not by a man but by an orangutan.

A number of popular nineteenth-century writers, however, made considerable efforts to dispel the notion that criminals were naturally inhuman. Their works suggested that the causes of crime could also be sociological: racism, poverty, or the corruption of the penal system that created rather than reformed criminals. The admirable protagonist of *The Florida Pirate* (1823), a run-away slave who became a notorious criminal, explained that he embraced crime only because he had to escape "[c]ontempt, abject poverty, and the horrors of want" (Anon 1828: 5). The heroine of *The Female Land Pirate* (1847), another brutal criminal, turned to crime after she became a victim of seduction. Unlike other fallen women, who resigned themselves to a miserable life of prostitution and poverty, she took her fate into her hands: "I soon learned to look upon a murder as indifferent, as a butcher would look upon the death of an animal" (Bannorris 1847: 20). Joseph Holt Ingraham, in *Miseries of New York*, expressed his belief that depravity was rooted in social injustice and scandalized the public by suggesting that some people who broke laws could actually be justified. It was poverty, among other things, that forced the "honest poor … to herd with the depraved and outcast of society. The poor has no choice" (1844: 11). Even Thompson, while calling attention to his character's monstrosity, explained how the Dead Man's criminal propensities reflected his traumatic upbringing, summing up this idea in one phrase: "The world plunders me—in turn, I will plunder the world!" (Thompson 2002: 227).

What added yet another dimension to the debate about crime was a new trend of glamorizing criminals. The idea that one could become a celebrity by committing a crime was not shocking in itself, at least not by American standards. As we saw earlier, religious authorities in the colonies inadvertently made criminals famous (or infamous) by dragging their crimes "into the light." In the nineteenth century this concept was pushed to the extreme as writers started to create characters whose adventures blurred the lines between fame and infamy. What was so provocative about such works was that they juxtaposed seemingly incompatible characteristics. Criminals were occasionally portrayed not only as monstrous but also as daring and heroic characters. Alfred Arrington's strategy in *Illustrated Lives and Adventures of the Desperadoes of the New World* offers a typical example. He openly refused to indulge "in bitter denunciations" of crime and instead expressed "sincere admiration for a high, heroic courage" of "those chivalrous sons of the fiery south" whose criminal adventures inspired the book (1849: 9). George Thompson satirized this trend in *The Outlaw: Or, the Felon's Fortunes* (c. 1860), which includes a telling scene in which a jailer's daughter tells her bewildered father about her fascination with criminals: "Ah! I adore such fellows as Dick Turpin, Claude de Val, and Jack Harold! I remember, papa, that good-looking pickpocket, English Tom … what fine, bold eyes he had! I declare, I quite fell in love with him, and was almost tempted to steal the keys of the jail and let him out" (Thompson, n.d.: 12).

The Urban Gothic Novel

As with other crime genres, the immense popularity of the urban Gothic novel in the antebellum period reflected readers' fascination with various forms of sensationalism as well as their social concerns. The works of this genre generally emphasized the negative aspects of city life – such as rampant crime and prostitution – and relied on recognizable attributes of Gothic fiction: grotesque imagery, decadence, and vicious villains.

The rise of the urban Gothic novel coincided with the rapid period of urbanization in the United States which reached its peak in the 1840s. Between 1800 and 1860, after the most intensive period of urbanization in American history, the portion of the population living in cities jumped from 4 percent to 20 percent. As contemporary observers saw it, this process was far from being smooth. The uncontrollable growth of cities created a wide range of social problems. Living conditions in the cities plummeted. Crime rates skyrocketed. The urban Gothic novel, which commandeered the literary market in the 1840s and 1850s, reflected the public's anxiety not only about urban conditions but also about the prospects of the new republic at large. In the aftermath of Andrew Jackson's turbulent presidency and the political tensions of the 1840s, the city, as it was often portrayed in popular novels, came to symbolize the grave prospects of this country. It was a discordant amalgamation of irreconcilable viewpoints, a place which was plagued by economic disparity and an irreparable sense of pessimism.

Eugène Sue's *The Mysteries of Paris* (1842) and G. M. W. Reynolds's *The Mysteries of London* (1844), two serialized European bestsellers, are usually cited as the earliest examples of the new genre. The concept of Sue's novel, which is nearly identical to Reynolds's and which would later be replicated in many other works besides his, was fairly simple. *The Mysteries of Paris* follows the story of Rudolphe, a compassionate and adventurous nobleman, who disguises himself as a common person and embarks on an odyssey through Paris. He encounters people of virtually every rank, from self-indulgent aristocrats to destitute paupers, which enables him to understand the connections between different classes and the causes of social injustice. Sue's novel reads like a scandalous exposé of the Parisian underworld and the decadence of the aristocracy.

What so many Americans found attractive about the new genre was that it offered itself as a venue for indulgence in the sensational and, simultaneously, as a vehicle for social protest. The publication of Sue's novel in the United States almost immediately inspired a publishing trend of so-called "city-mysteries." It is estimated that at least thirteen American mystery novels were published in 1844 alone (Zboray and Zboray 2000). Lippard's *The Quaker City* (1844–5), an exposé of the Philadelphia crime world, was an instant success and went on to become one of the bestselling novels of the nineteenth century. Works about other cities were quick to follow: Ingraham's *The Miseries of New York* (1844), Osgood Bradbury's *Empress of Beauty, The Mysteries of Boston* (1844), Buntline's *Mysteries and Miseries of New York* (1848) and *Mysteries and Miseries of New Orleans* (1851), and George Thompson's *City Crimes: Or, Life in New York and Boston* (1849) and *Mysteries and Miseries of Philadelphia* (c. 1850).

The premise of these novels is easy to summarize. Each city, however pleasant it seems at first, conceals behind its facade hidden places populated by outcasts and criminals. As if echoing the scenarios of *Beowulf* and *Paradise Lost*, in which monstrous creatures from the underworld terrorize the innocent, these novels portray inhuman criminals who hide in the depth of the city where they plot to rob, torture, and murder those above. Meanwhile, the urban underworld in which they dwell is continuously repopulated with fallen women, orphans, alcoholics, and the poor who have no other place to go. Thompson's description of "The Dark Vaults" in *City Crimes* is exemplary:

> Myriads of men and women dwelt in this awful place, where the sun never shone; here they festered with corruption, and died of starvation and wretchedness – those who were poor; and here also the fugitive murderer, the branded outlaw, the hunted thief, and the successful robber, laden with his booty, found a safe asylum, where justice *dare not* follow them – here they gloried in the remembrance of past crimes, and anticipated future enormities. (2002: 132)

The ability to shock was essential for every urban Gothic novelist. *The Quaker City* was written as a literary provocation that was meant to astonish readers with the extent of cultural degradation and the proliferation of crime. Throughout the novel Lippard parades scores of unsavory characters: sadistic villains, conmen, cunning women, corrupt priests, and deranged sorcerers. Faithful to the conventions of the Gothic novel, he builds his story around Monk Hall, a decrepit mansion that served as the nexus of the Philadelphia crime world. Its subterranean chambers were populated by depraved criminals who had absolutely no sense of morality. Lippard went out of his way to create a somber and menacing image of the city. Crime is inescapable. Corruption cannot be cured. Philadelphia is "all rottenness and dead men's bones" (1844: 3). Apocalyptic overtones even further emphasize the sense of gloom. As Lippard would have it, flagrant crime is merely a sign of the political and social depravity that threatens the very foundation of the American republic. If nothing was done to repair the situation, he speculated, it was only a matter of time before democratic principles would be abandoned and the country would turn to some form of godless tyranny.

The sensationalist appeal of urban Gothic novels was indisputable. Their reliance on sexually suggestive imagery and vivid depiction of violence were outrageous. In his extensive study of antebellum popular literature, David S. Reynolds (1988) dubbed such writers "immoral and dark reformers" because of their scandalous methods of advocating social reform. The sensationalism of such works notwithstanding, urban Gothic novels reflected the anxiety that many Americans felt about the brutality of unbridled capitalism and growing social inequality in the cities. They depicted a world in which people were forced to live in an environment that breeds intolerance, racism, and crime. This is what suggests that the urban Gothic novel in the United States was influenced not only by such European writers as Sue and G. M. W. Reynolds but also by scores of American reformers and moralizers whose works precipitated the rise of this genre.

The forerunner of the urban Gothic novel in this country was the reform literature and sensationalist journalism that gained strength in the 1820s and 1830s: racy newspapers, anti-prostitution publications, and religious pamphlets that were designed to expose social problems caused by urbanization and to warn readers about the moral decay of major cities. Although serious in their intent (at least ostensibly), such publications often relied on provocative techniques to shock their readers. Starting in the late 1820s, there appeared a number of provocative newspapers such as *The Scrutinizer, New-York Flagellator, Polyanthos, The Flash,* and *The Libertine.* Under the guise of moral reform, they offered lurid reports of seductions, racy crime reportage, and sketches of notorious criminals and libertines. *The Flash,* for example, shamelessly promised readers accounts of "awful developments, dreadful accidents and unexpected exposures" (December 15, 1841). Its front page regularly featured a "Gallery of Rascalities and Notorieties" and a "Gallery of Comicalities" that exposed exceptionally scandalous events and characters. The front page of *Polyanthos* screamed with captions such as "Horror, Despair and Suicide," "Outrage of Humanity," and "Another Libertine!! Seduction of Two Sisters!"

Social reformers who worked in the slums did not hesitate to scandalize their readers as well. Particularly controversial was the journalism of John Robert McDowall, an anti-prostitution crusader in New York. He believed the success of his efforts depended on shaking readers out of their ignorance and complacency about urban conditions. His career began with *The Magdalene Report* (1831) in which he claimed that as many as ten thousand New York women were prostitutes. This was followed by *Magdalen Facts* (1832) and *McDowall's Journal* (1833–4), in which he published his sensational reports about the New York crime world, particularly the city's most infamous slum, Five Points. The techniques McDowall and other contemporary reformers used – particularly their reliance on shocking imagery – paved the way for the rise of the urban Gothic. The motto of McDowall's journal reflected the spirit of antebellum crime literature at large: "The evils must be shown to the public to interest them to remove the evils" (*McDowall's Journal,* January 1833).

The question whether crime literature should be monopolized by social concerns was, of course, never settled. While many writers insisted that books about crime could be justified only by their social purpose, others made efforts to transform crime literature into a source of reading pleasure. In this respect, the antebellum crime literature was at the center of cultural debates not only about social issues but also the concept of literature at large.

10
The "Hard-boiled" Genre

Andrew Pepper

In one of his foundational statements on "hard-boiled" crime writing, Raymond Chandler enshrined a number of apparent truths that, over the years, have proved to be remarkably difficult to dislodge (see Panek, chapter 32 in this volume). In no particular order, he dismissed the English "Cheesecake Manor" detective novels of the golden age as contrived and whimsical and praised Dashiell Hammett (see Hall, chapter 36 in this volume) for trying to write "realistic mystery fiction," for being "spare, frugal, hard-boiled," and for writing "scenes that seemed never to have been written before." He also held himself and Hammett up as examples – very rare examples – of detective novelists who might also be said to write literature or something approaching "good serious novels" (Chandler 1995a: 978). In doing so, Chandler wittingly or otherwise gave rise to a critical orthodoxy about the hard-boiled crime novel that is only now undergoing revision. If an impetus to reappraise the hard-boiled constitutes one of the main jumping off points for this chapter, it is perhaps worth taking a moment to assess Chandler's claims in more detail.

Arguably the strongest, and certainly the most stubbornly persistent, among contemporary critical accounts of the genre is that the hard-boiled US crime novel constitutes a genuine rupture in the development of crime fiction and that, regarding its milieu, idiom, and political outlook, it should be seen as qualitatively different from writing produced by "classical" or "Victorian" and "golden age" novelists like Doyle and Christie (see, for example, McCann 2000: 1–15; Breu 2005: 2). Indeed while some dissenting voices have pointed at Chandler's "exaggerated" and "overly schematic" contrast between "golden age convention" and "hard-boiled innovation" (Horsley 2005: 67) or objected to Chandler's misguided assumption that Hammett invented a particular kind of tough or urban American crime fiction in the 1920s (Knight 2004: 110), there is little point denying that the hard-boiled *is* a predominantly American form or that it is best understood as a response to the particular social, economic and political conditions in the United States from the 1920s onwards (McCann 2000).

More problematically, this claim has fostered the view that the hard-boiled crime novel written by Chandler and Hammett is both more realistic and more politically radical than other forms of crime writing. Perhaps the most pernicious of all myths associated with the hard-boiled has been its linkage to a spare, demotic idiom – an apparently *American* idiom borrowed from Hemingway and Pound – characterized not simply as tough and masculine but also as "neutral and objective" (Madden 1968: xx). Madden is quite right to argue that the type of hard-boiled language or style pioneered by, say, Hammett, is that "of the streets, the pool rooms, the union halls, the bull pens, the factories, the hobo jungles" (1968: xix) but not, I think, that such a viewpoint is, in any way, neutral or objective. For a start, Madden's argument pre-supposes a particular constitutive audience for this kind of writing and perhaps also a set of political affiliations. Worpole explains the appeal of American hard-boiled crime writing to working class readerships in Britain in terms of its "acknowledge-ment of big business corruption" and its "unpatronizing portrayal of working class experience" (1983: 31) and hence argues that the hard-boiled crime novel operates as "a vehicle for radical criticism" (Worpole 1983: 41). Yet even where the opposite conclusion is reached and where the hard-boiled crime novel is characterized as an essentially conservative genre predicated on the goal of what Porter calls "perpetual re-familiarization," whereby the narrative ultimately leads to a restoration of the status quo and a reaffirmation of existing social order (Porter 1981: 3; also see Knight 1980), one could not make a claim for it as neutral or objective. Indeed, part of what I want to argue here is that hard-boiled writing is always inflected with political assumptions, even where these assumptions are unclear or indeed contested.

Irrespective of the political claims made about hard-boiled crime writing either as radical or conservative, therefore, the idea that the hard-boiled idiom constitutes a neutral or objective style or viewpoint has rightly undergone significant challenge. Ogdon, for example, is happy to concede that the hard-boiled is best understood as "a specific way of speaking and seeing" rather than as a straightforward formula but she links this way of seeing to a narrow ideological viewpoint: that of the straight, white male (1992: 71). If Ogdon's intervention, building on the ideological critique offered by Knight, was important in countering a view of the hard-boiled protagonist as objective and politically disinterested, much work has subsequently been done to explore how the complex matrices of race, class, gender, and sexuality are negotiated in hard-boiled crime writing and how the straight, white male protagonist vanquishes that which threatens his autonomy by projecting or displacing his anxieties onto a polluting "other" characterized as black, female, and homosexual (Pfeil 1995; Forter 2000). Indeed, rather than arguing for the hard-boiled as either objective or realistic, Breu characterizes it as a "cultural fantasy" that is consciously and unconsciously predicated on mirrorings and slippages between apparently discreet racial, sexual, and gendered identities (Breu 2005: 1; also see Abbott 2002).

If there is a unifying claim of this chapter it is that we need to conceive the hard-boiled not as a fixed category with a single social and political outlook but rather as a fluid, open-ended term with "multiple embodiments" (Breu 2005: 2); that is to say, not merely as a body of writing synonymous with the American private eye novel (Abbott 2002: 10). Two further qualifications can be made. First, and perhaps most self-evidently, hard-boiled crime writing cannot be understood "as if it was the gift of its 'brand leaders', Hammett, Chandler and Macdonald" (Cobley 2000: 55). Chandler found little to like in Macdonald's work and was even suspicious of a lack of "redemption" in Hammett's writing to offset its "cool spirit of detachment" (Chandler 1995a: 991), but Cobley's point is simply that the variety and scope of what we might call hard-boiled writing has too often been overlooked in favor of the canonization of its chief practitioners. Second, and more importantly, the hard-boiled is best theorized as a highly unstable political category that operates in a field of tension between different and competing political ideologies. Indeed, rather than offering a sustained chronological account of the development of hard-boiled crime writing predominantly in the United States – surely an impossibility in a short chapter – I intend to argue that hard-boiled crime writing's adaptation to, and reaction against, existing structures of power has manifested itself in two principal areas: first, as a macro-political response to the authority of the state and second, as an attempt both to unpick and to reconstitute white masculine heterosexual hegemony.

Despite the subject of this chapter, therefore, hard-boiled crime writing does not constitute a distinctive genre or subgenre, at least insofar as it has its own readily identifiable set of codes and conventions that all hard-boiled crime novels readily adhere to or depart from. Rather, building upon, and also contesting, Ogdon's definition of the "hard-boiled" as an ideology – or a way of seeing aligned with *one* particular viewpoint – I want to propose that the term is better understood as an ambivalent political outlook, one that simultaneously encompasses apparently contradictory views and brings them into uneasy relationship. By staking out this territory I am, of course, making certain implicit assumptions about what the hard-boiled is and, more importantly, is not. For a start, and in line with Ogdon's claims that the hard-boiled is inflected with a particular straight, white, male way of seeing, my focus here is predominantly on male, rather than female, crime writers. This is not to suggest that all hard-boiled crime fiction is itself inherently male or masculinist or that female – and indeed black – appropriations necessarily lack authenticity. In part, my omission of female and, aside from Himes, black writers is simply a product of the fact that others in this *Companion* are treating feminist and black appropriations of the hard-boiled tradition. Some distinction also needs to be made between hard-boiled crime writing and the *roman noir* (see Simpson, chapter 14 in this volume); for my purposes, the former focuses primarily on the investigation rather than perpetration of crime, even if this distinction is often blurred to the point where it is difficult to tell law enforcer and law breaker apart (and indeed what constitutes a crime in the first place). By the same logic, since its focus is primarily the *investigation* of crime, the hard-boiled can straddle different subgenres of crime writing (e.g. private eye, police procedural etc.). And while the term hard-boiled may well be most synonymous with a particular kind of American pulp writing produced initially for *Black Mask* magazine, it should not be seen as exclusively period-based or American. The fact that hard-boiled crime writing has been reinterpreted in so many different forms and guises and by writers from countries as diverse as Spain (Manuel Vasquez Montalban), Mexico (Subcomandate Marcos/Paco Ignatio Taibo II) and Australia (Peter Temple) is testament, if nothing else, to its elasticity.

The State's Unwilling Executioner

If the emergence of crime writing as a distinctive literary genre coincides with the consolidation of the modern bureaucratic state, it follows that crime writing or at least the figure of the detective has functioned as an unwilling executioner for the state, both upholding its laws and exposing its inequalities, failures, and limitations. McCann's *Gumshoe America* usefully argues that whereas the classical detective story of, say, Doyle, was able to find a way of reconciling the tensions inherent in liberal society, the US hard-boiled crime novel, precisely because of vast expansion of the state apparatus in the first three decades of the twentieth century and its interpenetration with rapidly growing corporate capitalism, demonstrated the ways in which "people could be shaped, moulded, and manipulated by the very institutions and beliefs that once seemed transcendent and disinterested" (2000: 111). Kenneth Fearing's *The Big Clock* (1946) and Ira Wolfert's *Tucker's People* (1943) – later filmed by Abraham Polonsky as *Force of Evil* (1948) – are both bleak parables about the perils of social organization, particularly as a manifestation of corporate capitalism, while Horace McCoy's *No Pocket in a Shroud* (1938) and *Kiss Tomorrow Goodbye* (1948) depict a landscape of civic corruption and corporate gangsterdom. The US crime novel has always been interested in the manipulation of the law by big business – insurance companies in James M Cain's *The Postman Always Rings Twice* (1935) and a gambling syndicate in Raymond Chandler's *Farewell My Lovely* (1940) – and, in such circumstances, the protagonists' struggle against civic and corporate corruption usually ends in failure and death. Even when it does not, the price to be paid is a great one. At the end of *The Big Sleep*, for example, Philip Marlowe has become "part of the nastiness" in so far as his actions end up protecting the rich and powerful and legitimating killers "by remote control" like Canino (Chandler 1995b: 764, 736). In the face of such woes, two choices usually present themselves: willed blankness or paralysis. Ned Beaumont's choice of the former in Dashiell Hammett's *The Glass Key* (1931) is self-protection, pure and simple. Meanwhile, much later in the hard-boiled cycle, and responding as much to the politics of race as class, the responsibility – for Chester Himes's black police detectives Coffin Ed Johnston and Grave Digger Jones – of having to enforce a law that is responsible for their own subjugation eventually becomes too much to bear and in the final (completed) novel of the series, *Blind Man with a Pistol* (1969), they are left, bitter and powerless, killing rats on a Harlem construction site while a blind man, unconnected to their investigations, shoots wildly into a crowded subway car.

The willingness of the hard-boiled novel, especially in the hands of writers like Hammett and McCoy, to depict the graft and corruption at the heart of US political and economic life has led some, erroneously in my view, to characterize it as Marxist or at least "an important vehicle of social criticism" (Worpole 1983: 43). Certainly Hammett and McCoy borrow from Marx's critique of capitalism but with an acknowledgement that the state, in all of its multiple and contradictory guises, is not just "a committee for managing the common affairs of the whole bourgeoisie" (Marx 2002: 5). This may be a long way from Weber's assertion that bureaucracy – or "hierarchically organized systems of administration" – is "capable of attaining the highest degree of efficiency and is ... the most rational known means of exercising authority over human beings" (Weber 1978: 223) but, as Hammett's *Red Harvest* (1929) demonstrates, civil society cannot sustain itself in the absence of a strong, functioning state and, in the final analysis, the hard-boiled operative must act in the interests of the state and the law (see Horsley 2005: 166–7). In this sense, the hard-boiled crime novel, at least one like *Red Harvest*, is more Gramscian than Marxist and it is worth taking a moment to establish the distinction. For a start, Antonio Gramsci, a socialist philosopher imprisoned by Mussolini's Fascist regime in 1926, recognized – more than Marx – the multiple functions of the state and their "frequently contradictory operations" (Lloyd and Thomas 1998: 21). Indeed the state, for Gramsci, is arguably best understood as a site of class compromises where competing power blocs clash and vie for position. Its coercive capacities – the state as policeman or "Stato-carabiniere" (Gramsci 1971: 261) – are invoked when its authority or boundaries are directly threatened but in its expanded or ethical formation, whereby the state is equivalent to "political society + civil society" or "hegemony protected by the armour of coercion" (1971: 263), it must function as much through consent as by force.

At the start of *Red Harvest*, a miners' strike has been broken with the assistance of national guardsmen, parts of the regular army, and private gunmen who have subsequently taken over the town. What follows is akin to a violent Gramscian war of position, as competing gang leaders struggle for control of Personville – though crucially, as with Gramsci, "the ultimate unity of the state formation as an instrument of class rule" is affirmed (Lloyd and Thomas 1998: 21). Indeed, it is because the gang leaders pursue a "radical individualist" agenda and therefore operate "without the formal sanction of the state" that, compared to Elihu Willsson, the city's pre-eminent businessman, they are so easily put to the sword (Freedman and Kendrick 1991: 211). Hired by Willsson from the Continental Detective Agency, Hammett's lone, chubby detective – known simply as the Continental Op – sets the gang leaders against one another in an effort to impose the law. Perversely, his efforts lead to an orgy of violent bloodletting (Heise 2005: 491). Insofar as the Op has been paid to do a job – rid the city of its "crooks and grafters" (Hammett 1999: 38) – and therefore operates with the full sanction of the city's most powerful figure, it would be quite wrong to see him as autonomous. Rather, as a willing *and* unwilling part of what Gramsci calls the ethical or expanded state, his role entails both explicit policing and making it "easier for the white collar soldiers to take hold while every-thing is disorganized"

(Hammett 1999: 176). This oxymoronic phrase – white collar soldier – signals, I would argue, the Op's uneasy, partial commitment to the kind of civil society that only the state can secure. His role is best understood neither as a state-sponsored vigilante ruthlessly purging enemies of the industrial-capitalist state at will nor as an unco-opted pro-union sympathizer who acts in the best interests of the working classes, but rather as someone who moves in and out of subject-positions that both buttress the authority of the state and, at the same time, undermine it from within.

Crime writing has developed in different directions and under different historical circumstances as a series of ongoing negotiations with the state, at once underscoring its ethical and coercive imperatives. What makes hard-boiled crime writing – or at least a novel like *Red Harvest* – so distinctive is that, in the context of the systemic inequalities produced by the kind of capitalist state personified by Elihu Willsson's Personville/Poisonville, the disjuncture between these elements is so vast, so apparently unbridgeable, that it threatens to split the Op straight down the middle. As he says in the midst of the blood-letting: "anybody that brings any ethics to Poisonville is going to get them all rusty" (Hammett 1999: 103). Madden described the sentimentality in hard-boiled crime writing as a "willed stance" (1968: xviii), but it is the Op's hard-boiled mask that is a willed stance, a means of shielding himself from the knowledge that the imposition of the law leads to violence and that the ethics that he tries to bring to Personville are, in effect, instrumental in helping return the city to the clutches of a capitalist megalomaniac. In other words, the abuses and concentrations of power and "the evident failure of the unfettered free market to deliver a just society" (McCann 2000: 6) are so pronounced, and the violence that follows the Op's "ethical" interventions so widespread, that the Op's very *raison d'être*, as a detective, is brought into question. "It's this damn berg," he says at one point. "You can't go straight here" (1982: 139). Martial law may be the best, indeed the only, way of saving Personville for the general good but the Op's acknowledgement of his complicity with the coercive apparatus of the state very nearly breaks him. More particularly, the Op's barely suppressed anger at having to give Willsson back his city "all nice and clean and ready to go to the dogs again" (1982: 181) suggests the kernel of a more thorough-going political critique. However, as with *Tucker's People* and *No Pockets in a Shroud*, it is a critique that yields nothing and goes nowhere (see Pepper 2009).

If, as Hegel observes in *Elements of the Philosophy of Right* (1821), there is a link between social instability and the visible punishment of crime, then the repressive power of the state is most in evidence when society is most "inwardly unstable" (1991: 251). In Hammett's *Red Harvest*, this visibility owes itself to the pervasiveness of working-class disquiet and establishment fears about the spread of trade unionism and Communism in the aftermath of the Russian Revolution. In the case of the British hard-boiled writer Derek Raymond (real name Robin Cook), whose "Factory" novels appeared between 1984 and 1993, it may be tempting to cite the brutal repression of striking coal miners by Margaret Thatcher's Tory government as a comparable example. While Raymond's novels are not explicitly political and do not permit themselves to be read as direct anti-Thatcherite allegories, they do, to some extent, reveal what Hillyard and Percy-Smith conceive to be the authoritarian potentialities of the capitalist state (1988). *A State of Demark* (1970), for instance, depicts a grubby, nightmarish England turned into a totalitarian dictatorship where martial law has been imposed and dissenters are herded into camps. According to John Williams, Raymond never had any faith in Marxism or radical politics (Williams 1994: 1). At the same time, however, it is hard to forget the martial law and concentration camps of *A State of Demark* when contemplating, elsewhere in the novel, the cold, impersonal Factory – a faceless, concrete police station on Poland Street in London – or the rigidly bureaucratic world of the police or indeed the disjunction between the law as it is enforced by the police and the ethical claims both of the novels' unnamed detective-protagonist and of the unmourned victims.

In many ways, and demonstrating the adaptability of the hard-boiled genre across periods and even nationalities, Raymond is the true heir of Hammett. This is not just because his unnamed detective, like the Continental Op, negotiates his bleak, tawdry environment in a terse, tight-lipped manner and displays a similar antipathy towards the faceless bureaucrats who run the world. Nor is it simply that Raymond wanted to give murder back to the people who committed it for reasons. As he put it: "I am sick to death of a certain kind of genteel British thriller for whom murder is just a hobby. It isn't. It's a barbarous, horrible business" (Peachment 1994: 1). What links Raymond to Hammett, and by turn characterizes an important aspect of the hard-boiled, is his insistence on laying bare the venality of the world and the grimly exploitative nature of human relationships and not giving up in the face of both bureaucratic indifference and the banality of evil. As the unnamed detective puts it in *He Died with His Eyes Open* (1984): "This fragile sweetness at the core of people – if we allowed that to be kicked, smashed and splintered, then we had no society at all of the kind I felt I had to uphold" (Raymond 2006: 93). Without the law, the terrible fate that befalls Charlie Stanisland in *He Died with His Eyes Open* and Dora Suarez in *I Was Dora Suarez* (1990) is what awaits us all. But the law, as embodied by the impersonal Factory and the vainglorious officers of Serious Crimes, is also indifferent to victims' suffering. Eschewing the hard-boiled's supposed neutrality and detachment, the nameless detective from the Department of Unexplained Deaths cannot feign indifference, nor does he want to, but the personal cost – as in *Red Harvest* – is almost too much to bear. *I Was Dora Suarez* is perhaps the richest, most fully realized example of this dissembling process. The plot is almost non-existent and charts the detective's effort to trace the killer – who has used an axe to chop up a prostitute and AIDS victim, Dora Suarez, and licked her blood – via a Soho club where unspeakable acts are committed on humans and animals in the service of wealthy clientele infected with AIDS. What distinguishes the novel beyond its macabre shocks is the careful way it charts the cost of the nameless detective's ethical commitment to the law and Dora Suarez. If, as he puts it, "we must have rules ... for if not, we'd all be murdered", then "[w]e save Suarez and somehow we save everybody" (Raymond 2008: 167). But saving Suarez, for the detective at least, involves falling in love with her or what she represents in death, arguably the logical conclusion of this ethical commitment, and thus brings him into the same orbit as the killer who, like Suarez, is also suffering from AIDS and whose mutilations of her and himself constitute, from the killer's disturbed perspective, acts of love as much as violence. Ultimately, and in a denouement typical of the hard-boiled novel, although the detective is able to discharge his responsibilities and shoot the killer dead, his fury remains – at the law for its inability to protect the sick and dispossessed and at himself for being part of this same system. "I had tears in my eyes … ," he laments, "but my tears were not for me – they were for the rightful fury of the people" (2008: 202).

Hard-boiled Masculinities

I Was Dora Suarez deconstructs the hard-boiled persona to reveal the unnamed detective as anxious, wounded, and internally divided, and shows the violence of both the detective and killer to be projections of these insecurities. Raymond, therefore, makes explicit what had been implicit since Philip Marlowe first walked down the mean streets of hard-boiled crime fiction: namely that the hard-boiled male's toughness, like his neutrality and objectivity, has *always* been little more than a ruse or facade. As Breu puts it in *Hard-Boiled Masculinities*:

> The suppression of affect central to this conception of masculinity was structured by the dynamic of projection, in which the forms of affective and libidinal investment foreclosed from representation within the subjectivity of the hard-boiled male returned and were punished in various gendered, sexual and racial others (2005: 1)

It has become something of a critical orthodoxy to cite Chandler's Marlowe as the worst example of the hard-boiled's unreflective sexism and masculinist insecurities, the way in which he seeks to construct and legitimize his own masculinity – and indeed his whiteness – by conceiving women, non-whites, homosexuals and effeminate men as polluting others (Ogdon 1992; Pfeil 1995; Forter 2000). More recently, however, Rzepka in particular has "tried to modify the conventional views of Chandler's unregenerate masculinism" by pointing to his use of homoerotic and homosocial tropes which have been "endemic to male Gothic almost from the beginning" (2000: 696). What, I think, is beyond doubt, and as Knight astutely observes, is the way that Chandler's outer plots, which involve the machinations of corrupt politicians, civic leaders and industrialists, usually give way to inner plots in which Marlowe is betrayed by a seductive, manipulative woman (Knight 1988: 82). Significantly, therefore, as Pfeil and Krutnik have demonstrated, problems of the law are recast as "problems besetting masculinity" whereby crime is "associated with the destabilization of masculine identity and authority" (Pfeil 1995: 113; Krutnik 1991: 128). This need or desire to shore up a frail masculinity, crumbling from within, and a whiteness under threat from Mexican immigration in particular, reaches its zenith in Chandler's final novel, *The Long Goodbye* (1953). Here, as McCann argues, Chandler depicts a besieged masculine brotherhood which has fallen "victim to a society robbed of its cultural integrity" by "suburbanization, mass consumerism, middle-brow culture, a bureaucratic state, and the mediation of ethnic and racial difference" (McCann 2000: 193).

Rzepka is right to point out that Chandler is not necessarily the racist, misogynist writer his most vociferous critics might want to depict him as. More particularly, one has to be careful not to generalize about the representation of masculinity in hard-boiled writing, thereby overstating the extent to which the hard-boiled subject (constructed in opposition to a female, non-white, homosexual other) *necessarily* constitutes a re-inscription of existing structures of control and authority. Corber has argued, for instance, that the hard-boiled detective's refusal to succumb to the normalizing domestic arrangements of the post-World War II world constituted an affront to "the Fordist regime of capital accumulation" and thereby threatened, rather than secured, the structures and boundaries of corporate culture and capitalist society (1997: 11). If this attempt to conceive hard-boiled masculinity as a subversive rather than reactionary force is hard to reconcile with Ogdon's notion of a "hyper-masculine identity" as "hard-boiled ideology" (1992: 76, 71), it is perhaps best to argue, with Breu, that hard-boiled masculinity represents "an aggressive reformulation of male hegemony as much as a defensive reaction to what might have been perceived as a set of economic and social threats to its hegemony" (2005: 5). Indeed this is a reconstitution of my argument about the ambivalence and internal division of the hard-boiled protagonist vis-à-vis the macro-political structures of power (i.e. the state and the law) as discussed in the previous section. As sexist as he is, Mickey Spillane's private detective Mike Hammer exemplifies this oppositional ambivalence.

Hammer does, after all, pose a threat to what Corber calls the transition to a Fordist regime of capital accumulation. His nostalgia for World War II and his attachment to those who fought with him manifests itself, most evidently, in an intense "homo-social" attachment that would seem to preclude settling down and raising a family. And while his former wartime buddy Chester Wheeler has started a family and, in *Vengeance Is Mine!* (1950), is blackmailed over his sexual transgressions and eventually killed, Hammer's at times wavering commitment to the single life underscores his individuality and therefore his difference. As Charlotte Manning tells him in *I, the Jury* (1947): "'When you came in to see me I saw a man I liked for the first time in a long time'" (Spillane 2001a: 52). In many ways his attitudes towards sexuality are remarkably chaste and traditional. His refusal to sleep with Charlotte Manning until they are married is perhaps the best example of this, even though he is perfectly happy to kill her when her duplicity, and figure, is finally laid bare at the end of the novel. In the same way, his dalliance with Velda, his secretary, at times comes close to marriage – in *One Lonely Night* (1951) he gives her an engagement ring, but crucially he mitigates it with the line, "'We're ... only engaged to be engaged, you know'" (Spillane 2001b: 136). In this instance, and where his extreme individualism threatens the sanctity of the family, Hammer's hardness constitutes a threat to the political and economic order. Elsewhere, however, Hammer is often described as a "cop" (2001b: 15, 40) and is pressed into the service of the (patriarchal/capitalist) state. In *One Lonely Night*, when confronted by Communists who are variously described as "gay," "sneaking, conniving," "jittery," and "puny" (2001b: 34, 38, 75, 76) and who are exploiting a feminized America's softness, it is Hammer's willingness to act decisively which foils the conspiracy. Likewise the fact that working women are often punished or killed in Spillane's novels and those like Ethel Brighton in *One Lonely Night*, who have transgressed patriarchal authority, are put back in their places suggests, as Krutnik argues about film noir, that these novels embodied a shoring up of "masculine cultural authority" in the face of the post-war reorganization of America's social and economic life (Krutnik 1991: xiii).

Still, this "masculine will to power" (Nyman 1997: 3) is so excessive, so over-determined in Spillane's novels and much hard-boiled crime fiction that it threatens to turn in on itself and crumble under the weight of its contradictions. This is not akin to the very visible and heightened internal divisions suffered by Hammett's Continental Op and Raymond's nameless detective (which are produced by the impossibility of upholding a law or serving an authority that is itself premised on systematized exploitation). Rather this excessiveness draws attention to the failure of the white, male subject-position to secure its own boundaries. Indeed, as Breu argues, this subject-position was "defined as the civilized opposite of the 'primitive' forms of male identity ostensibly embodied by African-Americans and other racialized groups" (2005: 2). What Abbott calls "the hysterical efforts" of Chandler, Spillane and others "to shore up a threatened white masculinity in the face of a racist and misogynistic urban dread" (2002: 5) in fact draws attention to slippages between apparently "civilized" (i.e. white) and "primitive" (i.e. black) masculine identities. This process of slippage and cross-identification, as Breu acknowledges, reaches one of its most complex and intriguing manifestations in Chester Himes's 1945 novel *If He Hollers Let Him Go*.

Himes's protagonist Bob Jones is a black foreman at the Atlas shipyard in Los Angeles during World War II and, like other (white) hard-boiled figures, struggles to define himself against, and exercise control over, female characters, notably Madge Perkins, a white Southern co-worker at the shipyard. Ostensibly Himes's novel is a long way from Spillane's fantasy of (white) masculine prowess; Jones, after all, is driven by the absurdity of his situation to inhabit the most demeaning white-derived stereotype of black masculinity (i.e. black man as rapist of white woman). "I felt castrated, snake-bellied, and cur-dogged, I felt like a nigger being horse-whipped in Georgia. Cheap, dirty, low … The taste of white folks was in my mouth and I couldn't get it out. What I ought to do is rape her, I thought" (Himes 1986: 126). Still, insofar as his will to power is merely a grotesque extension of the same logic employed by Hammer and even Philip Marlowe, the sanctified status of the male hard-boiled protagonist is called into question. More particularly, since Jones ultimately falls short of this stereotype, despite Madge's insistence that he "rape" her (1986: 147), and recognizes the absurdity of his own impulses, Himes's novel – more so than either

Spillane's *One Lonely Night* or Chandler's *Farewell My Lovely* – wants us to reflect on the constructed or performative nature of all identities and the extent to which action, or in Bob Jones's case inaction, is contingent on particular social, economic, and historical circumstances. If, as Breu contends, "the representation of masculinity in hard-boiled fiction enacts a phantasmatic resolution between American discourses of masculine individualism … and a newly corporatized … socio-economic world" (2005: 149), Himes's novel disrupts rather than reiterates this dynamic: Bob Jones may want to be a "simple Joe walking down an American street" (Himes 186: 153) and may want to be assimilated into this newly rationalized world as a husband and worker but the roles or stereotypes that, in effect, define him over-determine his choices to such an extent and in such grotesque fashion that it becomes "impossible to sustain the [hard-boiled] fantasy of detached and dispassionate subjectivity" (Breu 2005: 149).

Conclusion

The complex and often ambiguous ideological inflections of hard-boiled crime writing make it possible to identify what we might call radical *and* conservative or left- *and* right-wing political orientations. That said, while writers like Dashiell Hammett, Chester Himes, and Derek Raymond, all politically disaffected in their different ways but nonetheless capable of moral outrage, seemed to understand it was their task to bring these elements into unruly and often explosive contact, Mickey Spillane threatened to take hard-boiled crime writing down a political dead-end by tipping the balance so heavily in favor of right-wing fantasy. To some extent, Hammett's repressed anger at the poisoning of public life and civil society in the US and Spillane's dissatisfaction with the inadequacy of the state and the law in the face of internal and external threats (e.g. gangsters and Communists) represent opposing political views. The Continental Op's adaptation to *and* reaction against the imperatives of state power and corporate capitalism, however, constitutes the richer and more satisfying intervention because the resulting tension, which threatens to tear him apart, makes it all but impossible to sustain the hard-boiled fantasy of detachment and objectivity. Of contemporary practitioners, James Ellroy perhaps understands this better than anyone else, and his so-called LA Quartet – including *The Black Dahlia* (1987) and *LA Confidential* (1990) – brilliantly captures hard-boiled's political ambivalence. The heightened racism, misogyny, and homophobia displayed by his white male cops renders what Ogdon calls the "hard-boiled ideology" (1992: 71) visible and in doing so both demystifies and reiterates its power.

Meanwhile, just as the efforts of the police are all that keep Los Angeles from unraveling into anarchy and violence, the law is also exploited by agents of the state to further their own interests and those of the capitalist economy. Ogdon's claim that "feminist" hard-boiled writers like Sara Paretsky and Sue Grafton are only superficially hard-boiled because their protagonists do not share with their male counterparts "a hard-boiled ideological orientation" (1992: 71) may require some amendment, not least because, as I have argued, the hard-boiled is best understood in terms of an ambivalent political outlook rather than a singular ideological orientation (see Gavin, chapter 20 in this volume). That said, and as I have argued elsewhere (see Pepper 2000: 52–63), it would be wrong to presume that the hard-boiled crime novel can necessarily be appropriated for wholly progressive political ends, something that Paretsky in particular (see Effron, chapter 43 in this volume) sometimes seeks to do. It would, of course, be churlish and quite wrong to suggest that the hard-boiled worldview is necessarily masculinist. Dorothy B. Hughes's *Ride the Pink Horse* (1946) is every bit as complex a hard-boiled crime novel as *Tucker's People* or *No Pockets in a Shroud*. Meanwhile, if the question of what happens when a genre that has tradition-ally been the preserve of straight, white male writers is appropriated by non-white, female, and gay writers has been addressed elsewhere in this book, it simply remains for me to reiterate that hard-boiled writing's flexibility and elasticity allow for such appropriation – so long as its structuring tension is kept alive.

11

The Pursuit of Crime: Characters in Crime Fiction

Carl Malmgren

Under the letter "G" in *The Oxford Companion to Crime and Mystery Writing*, one can find character-centered entries on "Gangsters," "Gay Characters," "Gentleman Sleuth," "Girl Detective," "Great Detective," and "Gumshoe," as well as entries for characters and authors whose names start with the letter "G." The *Oxford Companion* demonstrates one way to organize the kinds of characters one encounters in crime fiction: to enumerate them according to types. This approach has the advantage of being both accessible and potentially exhaustive. The resultant encyclopedic text would list all possible character types. Another approach – let's call it the "functional" – would identify the sequence of events informing a particular narrative or genre and then analyze the function the character performs in that sequence. This approach, which we will use here, has the advantage of discriminating among the ways that different subgenres use their cast of characters.

The basic narrative formula for murder or crime fiction is quite simple: someone is looking for someone or something. A crime story inevitably involves a pursuit or a quest. In most cases the pursuer, the searcher, is a policeman or a private detective or an amateur sleuth. The object of the search – the direct object of the basic narrative sentence – may vary at first (a private eye might be asked to find some missing diamonds, as in Hammett's *The Dain Curse*), but in nearly every case the search ends up focusing on the person responsible for the crime, usually murder, which propels the narrative. The "goal of the detective story," writes John Cawelti, "is a clear and certain establishment of guilt for a specific crime" (1976: 92).

Essentially, then, crime fictions are quest narratives, as much hard-boiled detective fiction makes clear. Raymond Chandler, for example, draws attention to the medieval quest tradition by reminding readers that Marlowe is a kind of anagram for Malory. Quest narratives like these typically find closure in revelation, discovery, or disclosure, the classical anagnorisis. Thus there are two powerful engines driving crime narratives – the pursuit of an agent and the discovery of truth.

Functional analysis identifies six basic elements in a quest narrative: the Sender, the Subject, the Object, the Helper, the Opponent, and the Receiver. The Sender is the one who assigns the quest to the Subject, whose goal is the Object of the quest. For example, the King asks his Knight to find the Holy Grail, or to slay the Dragon. In the course of the quest, the Subject encounters those who assist him (in Arthurian legend, for example, the Lady of the Lake) and those who try to thwart him (e.g., the Black Knight) – Helpers and Opponents. The successful conclusion of the quest returns the Object to the Receiver (who frequently is the Sender himself). These are the character functions we will be examining in murder fiction. Elsewhere I have dealt at length with the three basic forms that murder fiction takes: the classical mystery, the hard-boiled detective story, and the crime novel (where the protagonist is himself the criminal). Here, by looking at three specific examples (*The Mysterious Affair at Styles*, *The Lady in the Lake*, and *The Talented Mr Ripley*), I will examine how each subtype handles the pursuit of crime.

Classic Detection

The generic nickname, the "whodunit," identifies the quest Object for classic detective fiction, the "who" responsible for the corpse or corpses that appear in the narrative (see Rowland, chapter 8 in this volume). A classic detective mystery inevitably involves the search for an unknown agent or agency (the Object of the quest). In its typical outline, the investigator reveals the name of the murderer in the penultimate chapter and explains the detection process in the last chapter. But even in the classic mystery that Object can be complicated or ambiguous. It may turn out, for example, that all of the suspects did it, as in Christie's *Murder on the Orient Express*, or that nobody did it, as in Sayers's *The Nine Tailors*. What is paramount is that the process of investigation must reveal the Truth, the *terminus ad quem* of mystery's basic sentence. Truth is mystery's dominant Object, difficult of access but fully spelled out in the end. We read classic detective mysteries to find out exactly who did it and how.

Cawelti identifies the four main character roles in mystery fiction as the victim, criminal, detective, and "those threatened by the crime but incapable of solving it" (1976: 91). For the purposes of this analysis the victim is negligible. The real story starts when the body appears, for that is when the unknown quantity is inserted into the narrative and the quest for knowledge begins. In Christie's first novel, *The Mysterious Affair at Styles* (1920), for example, the character of the victim Emily Inglethorp figures very little in the investigation that follows. Poirot notes that the willful, officious, and domineering woman is not much missed by those she leaves behind. A functional analysis of *Styles* thus focuses on the detective, criminal, and those affected by the crime (the murder of Emily Inglethorp).

At the urging of Poirot's sidekick, Captain Hastings, John Cavendish agrees to invite the detective in to investigate his stepmother's murder. John thus acts as the Sender in the quest narrative, the one who initiates the action events. He and his family also serve as Receiver at the story's end, since they benefit from the results of the truth that Poirot uncovers. Poirot himself is the Subject of the quest narrative, a role that he takes on with especial relish since he feels an obligation to the victim: "In all this, you see, I think of the poor Mrs. Inglethorp who is dead. She was not extravagantly loved – no. But she was very good to us Belgians – I owe her a debt" (Christie 1987: 73). The fundamental events of the narrative consist of Poirot examining the crime scene (the Styles estate) and taking evidence from "those threatened by the crime," who serve basically as his Helpers or Opponents. The climax of the story comes in the last sentence of the penultimate chapter, when Poirot produces the Object of the search by naming the perpetrator: "*Messieurs, Mesdames* … let me introduce you to the murderer, Mr. Alfred Inglethorp" (1987: 169). He then delivers the rest of the truth (the *how* of the murder) in the final chapter. John, Mary, and Lawrence Cavendish are there to hear his disclosures and serve as the Receivers of the quest Object. But they receive more than the Truth, as will be seen.

One attribute of the orderly and hierarchical world of mystery fiction is that its various witnesses are usually willing to serve as Helpers, even when the investigator (Poirot) is an outsider with a funny accent. When Poirot tells Dorcas the parlor maid that he wants only to bring the murderer of her mistress to justice, she responds "Amen to that" and then tells in great detail exactly what her mistress said and did the afternoon of her death (1987: 39 ff). Dorcas embodies the character type of the faithful retainer; Hastings thinks of her as a "fine specimen … of the old-fashioned servant that is so fast dying out" (1987: 107). But all the servants and employees of the Styles household – Annie the housemaid, Manning the gardener, even Wells the family attorney, whose dealings with the murdered woman presumably are confidential – are equally as helpful and forthcoming.

The same cannot be said for the members of the family itself. John and Mary Cavendish and Lawrence Cavendish should presumably be willing Helpers; it was, after all, their stepmother or stepmother-in-law who was murdered. And mostly, when questioned by Poirot and others, they tell the truth – just not the whole truth. Poirot, however, is keenly aware that certain witnesses in the investigation have agendas or issues: "[U]nless I am much mistaken," he says to Hastings, "at the inquest today only one – at most, two persons were speaking the truth without reservation or subterfuge" (1987: 94). The misrepresentations or omissions by the family members, however, are not personally motivated. These characters tell half-truths to protect a specific individual whom they love or to whom they are loyal, not to save their own skins. John protects his wife Mary, and Mary, John; Lawrence goes so far as to lie and to destroy evidence to protect Cynthia Murdoch, the woman he loves. In the stable and orderly world of mystery fiction, when Helpers are not entirely forthcoming, it is not always because they are evil or self-serving or guilty, but often because they are looking out for others.

The Opponents in mystery fiction are usually those implicated in or guilty of the murder, in this case the husband Alfred Inglethorp and his cousin Evelyn Howard.

As might be expected, they conceal their oppositional status by pretending to act as Helpers. Evelyn blatantly points the finger of guilt at her cousin Alfred, both to obscure the intimate nature of their relationship and to set up the elaborate alibi they have concocted. Alfred plays the part of the grieving husband, pretending to be totally oblivious to the fact that he is the prime suspect. An interesting twist is provided by Poirot who apparently recognizes early on that these two are his Opponents: he tries to put them off-guard by manipulating their assumed Helper function. He enlists Evelyn Howard as Helper, asking her to be his ally and keep a close eye on the goings-on at Styles (1987: 111). She then pretends to serve this function by "discovering" an important piece of evidence. Poirot conceals his true relation to Alfred Inglethorp by acting as the latter's Helper, supplying him with a foolproof alibi for the hour when the poison was purchased. Poirot also makes Hastings over into a better Helper by deliberately misleading him, so that his "transparent countenance" does not give the game away (1987: 170). Throughout the novel Poirot is always several steps ahead of those who would oppose or help him. The Subject's ability to read both character and clues enable him to solve the case and spell out the truth.

Because the Helpers and Opponents are eminently and profoundly readable, because they are recognizable "characters," they lend themselves to being identified by type. John is the stolid and stubborn husband who yearns to be loved by his wife but will not speak his desire. His wife Mary is the proud but flighty (and slightly foreign) wife who carries on a provocative flirtation in order to win back the attentions of her estranged husband. Lawrence is the shy and reserved poet squirming under the weight of his unrequited love. Poirot, of course, is able to recognize these characters as types, to figure out their true "character," and then to serve them as they truly deserve. Not content merely to solve the case, he does it in such a way that property is restored, innocence advertised, and lovers re-united. He returns the Inglethorp fortune to its rightful owners, brings Lawrence Cavendish and Cynthia Murdoch together by cutting through the misunderstandings that had kept them apart, and restores conjugal happiness to the marriage of John and Mary Cavendish by subjecting them to the ordeal of a trial for murder. Poirot thus serves the twin deities that preside over much of classic detective fiction, Truth and Justice; the Subject successfully secures a manifold Object.

A final note about the Subject in classical detection: because he occupies a world populated to a great extent by character types, he himself must rise above typicality. In order to escape the stigma of typecasting and to establish a modicum of individuality, the detective in mystery is usually ec-centric, literally "off-center" in one way or another (Holmes with his drugs and violin, Nero Wolfe with his orchids and agoraphobia, Poirot with his mustache and his *bon mots*). Because victims are marginalized and those affected by the crime frequently stereotyped, the detective in mystery fiction occupies the center stage. He is gifted, of course with "an almost magical power to expose and lay bare the deepest secrets" (Cawelti 1976: 94), but he must be personalized and made idiosyncratic. He stands apart, uncategorizable, his behavior unpredictable and enigmatic. The investigator in classic detection must become a larger-than-life Character in order to be distinguished from the character types.

Hard-boiled Detective Fiction

In "The Simple Art of Murder," Raymond Chandler formulates the basic plotline of "hard-boiled" detective fiction as the detective's "adventure in search of a hidden truth" (Chandler 1995a: 992; see also Pepper, chapter 10 in this volume). The terms in this formula clearly suggest the quest plot, which George Grella identifies as the masterplot of detective fiction: "its central problem is a version of the quest, both a search for the truth and an attempt to eradicate evil" (1980: 104). Grella notes that this plot-structure aligns detective fiction with the romance tradition. Chandler's adherence to this tradition is heavily foregrounded in *The Lady in the Lake*. The very title of this novel signals its indebtedness to and imitation of romance formulas, referring as it does to the lovely blond water deity who bequeathed Excalibur to Arthur and took it back after his death. In functional terms she is a semi-divine Helper who equips the male hero for the quest he undertakes. That Marlowe is on a quest is reinforced by the names Chandler uses. Marlowe's initial assignment in the novel is to recover an absent object of value, the missing *Crystal* Kingsley. He is given that assignment by Crystal's estranged husband Derace Kingsley, one of regal descent. His quest continues until he can deliver (word of) that object to its rightful owner.

In terms of functional analysis, Kingsley serves as the Sender, Marlowe as the Subject of the quest. The novel opens with their initial interview, wherein Kingsley assumes royal prerogatives: "And remember when I hire a man he's my man. He does exactly what I tell him and he keeps his mouth shut" (Chandler 1995a: 7). He makes his wishes known in simple declarative sentences: "I want you to find my wife. She's been missing for a month." Marlowe accepts the role of Subject by responding in kind: "Okay, I'll find your wife" (Chandler 1995a: 8). The king has enlisted his knight-errant and identified the missing Object. Critics have noted, however, that detective fiction revises romance formulas by treating some of its terms ironically and thus modernizing the quest motif. "The hard-boiled detective novel, with its origins in Depression-era America, demystifies its romance background by showing that romantic tales are frauds" (Hall 1990: 118; see also Grella 1980). This is certainly the case for *The Lady in the Lake*. Marlowe's interview with Kingsley, for example, reveals that the missing wife is a rather tarnished Object, guilty of shoplifting, abandonment, and adultery. Marlowe assumes "that she is young, pretty, reckless, and wild. That she drinks and does dangerous things when she drinks. That she is a sucker for the men and might take up with a stranger who might turn out to be a crook" (Chandler 1995a: 12). Kingsley can only concur.

As in the classic mystery, the quest in hard-boiled detective fiction consists basically of a process of investigation, much of which involves interviewing witnesses who might know something about the Object of the search, in this case the missing Crystal Kingsley. These witnesses serve as Helpers or Opponents in the detective/knight's quest. But there are some distinctive differences about the witnesses who populate the "mean streets" of hard-boiled detection. For one thing, most of them are hostile or uncommunicative. They do not want to serve as Helpers. Marlowe usually has to bully or bribe or trick them into discussing the case. At the hotel in San Bernardino, for example, where Crystal Kingsley was last seen, Marlowe gets no help at all from one bellboy and is forced to ply the other with booze and money to get him to talk. Another potential witness, Mrs Talley, refuses to get up from the sofa in the darkened room where she lies, telling Marlowe simply to leave her alone and refusing even to respond to his farewell. Another distinctive aspect of the cast of characters in detective fiction is that Opponents almost always outnumber the Helpers. For every helpful Bertie Keppel, the reporter for the *Puma Point Banner*, there is a sullen Chris Lavery and a surly Al Degarmo and a suspicious Albert Almore and the thuggish policemen Cooney and Dobbs.

The most remarkable trait of the cast of characters in *The Lady in the Lake*, however, is that their functions are so unstable, so multiple, so fluid. Chris Lavery first appears as an Opponent, telling Marlowe he cannot be bothered by a "private dick" (Chandler 1995a: 16). When Marlowe presses him, he turns into a Helper, conveying to Marlowe the truth that he has not seen Crystal in months, a truth that Marlowe refuses to believe. Before Marlowe can get the full story from Lavery, however, the latter turns into a bullet-riddled corpse. In a similar way Bill Chess metamorphoses from hangover-ridden bully (Opponent) to drunken self-pitying confidant (Helper), to suspect in his wife's murder (and therefore the Object of a second search) when the body in the lake is discovered. Captain Webber of the Bay City Police turns from Opponent to Helper when he finds out that his homicide lieutenant Degarmo has been harassing Marlowe.

Degarmo himself supplies a case study in multiple functions. He starts out as a bullying and brutal Opponent, warning Marlowe, who is shadowing Chris Lavery, off the Almore case. In so doing, however, he inadvertently acts as Helper, insofar as Marlowe begins to investigate links between Lavery and Almore. At their second meeting, at the Lavery murder scene, Marlowe wises off to Degarmo, and Degarmo gives him a savage beating. Later in the novel, however, when Marlowe figures as the prime suspect in what looks like a sex-crime murder, Degarmo apparently reverses himself and helps the detective sneak away from the scene of the crime. When challenged by a subordinate, the lieutenant encourages Marlowe to tell the whole story of what had happened and argues forcefully that the crime scene proves Marlowe's innocence.

In the strangest reversal of all, Marlowe and Degarmo then form an impromptu detective "team," the two of them working together to prove that Derace Kingsley is the real killer, the victim being the wife that has betrayed him. At one point they play wise-cracking "partners":

"One moment please," [the apartment clerk said]. "Whom did you wish to see?"
Degarmo spun on his heel and looked at me wonderingly. "Did he say 'whom'?"
"Yeah, but don't hit him," I said. "There is such a word." (Chandler 1995a: 173)

By chapter 36 the two men have become confidants, and their joint investigation takes them to Kingsley's vacation home on Puma Lake where the quest comes to an end and various truths are revealed. There the reader discovers that each member of the "team" had his own agenda, Marlowe working to get Degarmo out of the city and Degarmo using Marlowe to get to Kingsley so as to frame him for the girl's murder. Degarmo's functioning as Helper becomes all the more ironic when Marlowe springs the surprising truths that the dead girl in the hotel room is Muriel Chess and that Degarmo himself is the girl's murderer. The Opponent turned Helper has become the Object of the search.

In terms of characterization, however, what is most interesting about *The Lady in the Lake* is its treatment of women. The title indicates the Arthurian origin of the story, the perfect framework for a novel which deals almost exclusively with the infidelity of woman and its aftermath. *The Lady in the Lake* is a novel filled with wives who stray, literally or figuratively, then turn up missing. All of the wives – Crystal Kingsley, Florence Almore, Muriel Chess, Mildred Havilland – are marked and remarked as being departed, as remarkable only in their absence. The novel's signature motif is the woman who is there and not there, because she is dead or in disguise. The lady in the lake is one such marker.

The female master of disguise is, of course, Mildred Havilland. At one point, a police captain says of the ubiquitous Mildred/Muriel that she had "a way with men. She could make them crawl over her shoes" (Chandler 1995a: 143). She systematically converts a series of men – Al Degarmo, Alfred Almore, Bill Chess, Chris Lavery – into her Helpers (and therefore Opponents of the detective Subject), simply by taking them to bed. Her relationship with women is even more interesting. She is of course the missing link, the sole element tying together the various missing women in the novel. She in effect makes women both appear and disappear, in the former case by inventing them (Mrs Fallbrook, Muriel Chess), and in the latter by first supplanting them and then murdering them (Florence Almore), or by pulling a vanishing act (Mildred Haviland), or by murdering them and then replacing them (Muriel Chess, Crystal Kingsley). She never appears in the novel in character; she's not there even when she is present because she's always acting, even during her last conversation with Marlowe when she pretends to be Crystal. The Object of Marlowe's quest is thus always absent, unrecoverable until she has been converted into an actual object, naked and dead in the lake (Crystal Kingsley) or naked and dead on the bed (Muriel Chess).

Mildred becomes Muriel, who becomes Mrs Fallbrook, who becomes Crystal, who becomes dead just because she is still Mildred. Fickleness, fluidity, instability, unreliability: Mildred Haviland personifies these traits. She might be said to epitomize the general slipperiness that characterizes hard-boiled detective fiction:

Everything changes its meaning: the initial mission turns out to be a smokescreen for another, more devious plot; the supposed victim turns out to be the villain; the lover ends up as the murderess and the faithful friend as a rotten betrayer; the police and the district attorney and often even the client keep trying to halt the investigation; and all the seemingly respectable and successful people turn out to be members of the gang. (Cawelti 1976: 147).

By identifying Mildred Haviland/Muriel Chess/Crystal Kingsley as the successive impersonations of the criminal and then naming her murderer, Marlowe solves the mystery and ties the disparate strands of the story together. The narrative, however, undermines ideas of full disclosure and resolution: "Though the hero succeeds in his quest for a murderer, his victory is Pyrrhic, costing a great price in the coin of the spirit. The fair maidens turn out to be Loathly Ladies in disguise. And the closer the detective approaches to the Grail, the further away it recedes" (Grella 1980: 116). In Chandler's ironic treatment of the story, the lady in the lake, the missing Crystal, is dead matter, a rotted and putrefying blond corpse, the "thing that had been a woman" (Chandler 1995a: 43).

The quest may fail, but the Knight soldiers on. Most hard-boiled detective fiction offers its protagonist as "the last just and incorruptible man" (Lehman 1989: 104) in the decaying and corrupt urban wasteland he inhabits. This is a tradition that Chandler himself initiated. His Marlowe does not take all kinds of detective work, "[o]nly the fairly honest kinds" (Chandler 1995a: 7). He flatly refuses to get involved with divorce work, presumably because it is so seedy and underhanded. At two different places in *The Lady in the Lake* he turns down substantial bribes because accepting them entails the flagrant violation of the law. He is committed to turning his client's wife over to the police once he is convinced that she did indeed kill Chris Lavery: "if I decide she did do any murder," he tells Kingsley, "I'm going to turn her over to the police" (Chandler 1995a: 148). Loyalty to a client does not supplant the quest for justice.

The detective's most impressive trait, however, especially given the slippery and fluid world he moves through, might well be the ability to see through all the facades and impersonations and to read people and situations. Relying on intuition and experience, Marlowe can size up a good cop in an instant: "[Sheriff Patton] had large ears and friendly eyes and his jaws munched slowly and he looked as dangerous as a squirrel and much less nervous. I liked everything about him" (Chandler 1995a: 40). Marlowe early on figures out Degarmo's personal involvement in the case and then partners up with the lieutenant until he can lead him to a safe place to confront him. It takes him a while, but he penetrates Mildred/Muriel's formidable shape-shifting: "You do this character very well," he tells her, "[t]his confused innocence with an undertone of hardness and bitterness" (Chandler 1995a: 156). In the end, the knight of detective fiction lives up to his title and serves as the anchor and locus of value in the shifty and sordid world his quest traverses. As Chandler himself theorizes in "The Simple Art of Murder," "down these mean streets a man must go who is not himself mean, who is neither tarnished nor afraid. The detective in this kind of story must be such a man. He is the hero. He is everything" (Chandler 1995a: 991–2).

The Crime Novel

The crime novel lives up to its name by violating a basic convention of mystery and detective fiction; it tells the story from the point of view of the perpetrator – the pursued criminal becomes the main protagonist (see Simpson, chapter 14 in this volume). This simple move has profound consequences. For one thing the narrative sentence becomes compound since the text contains two separate storylines (as is appropriate in a schizophrenic form): the protagonist as Subject of his own search (for self-hood, for safety, for treasure, etc.); and the protagonist as Object of the search for the perpetrator, usually carried out by Subject-figures such as the police or private detectives. In addition, readers know "whodunit," so what is unknown necessarily shifts. It becomes what the protagonist will do next and whether it will result in another victim. Readers experience both murder and pursuit from the inside as it were; they vicariously participate in the murder and they feel the Law breathing down their necks. The crime novel unfolds from the point of view of the criminal, shifting emphasis from mystery and its solution to the experience of crime and its psychopathology to the criminal.

The opening of Patricia Highsmith's *The Talented Mr Ripley* is exemplary in this regard: "Tom glanced behind him and saw the man coming out of the Green Cage, heading his way. Tom walked faster. There was no doubt the man was after him" (1975: 1). We meet Tom Ripley on the run, the Object of a pursuit. That Tom has reason to feel guilty and therefore the object of a "collar" is made immediately clear: "Was this the kind of man they would send after him? ... Was that the kind they sent, maybe to start chatting with you in a bar and then *bang!* – the hand on the shoulder, the other hand displaying a policeman's badge. *Tom Ripley, you're under arrest*" (1975: 1–2). Tom is guilty (of a futile IRS scam) right from the start. Readers watch him escalate his criminal ways to forgery, theft, and murder.

The man originally pursuing Tom is not a law officer but a worried father looking for help with his wayward son. Herbert Greenleaf tracks Ripley down to ask him to go to Europe and persuade his son Dickie to come home to New York. Highsmith thus starts off by foregrounding the quest motif. Ripley, who will be the Object of an extensive police search later on, initially serves as the Subject of a quest commissioned by the Sender, Herbert Greenleaf. Ripley takes up the quest, but not because he intends to carry it through: "Why should Dickie want to come back to subways and taxis and starched collars and a nine-to-five job?" he thinks to himself when he finds Dickie lounging on the beach in southern Italy (1975: 52). All Ripley wants is to escape his seedy New York existence.

Ironically, when Tom meets Dickie, he does in fact see the latter as an Object. Dickie, however, is not the Object that Tom will proudly bring home to Mr Greenleaf, but rather the Object of Tom's desire: "The first step … was to make Dickie like him. That he wanted more than anything else in the world" (1975: 53). This objective Tom achieves for a while, until Dickie balks at the homoerotic implications of the relationship and terminates it. Soon after he and Dickie have an argument, Tom receives a letter from Mr Greenleaf "firing" him from his original assignment: "I can only conclude," the man tells Ripley, that given the passage of time and lack of action, "you haven't been successful" (1975: 91). His romantic Object having eluded him, his quest abrogated, Tom chafes at the brusque and unfair way that he has been treated. He strikes back at his tormentor in what he sees as the only "logical" way: he murders Dickie and assumes his identity. The Subject turns into the Object, both by taking on the identity of the Object and by becoming the Object of another search. At the same time Ripley remains the Subject of his own search for the Self-hood and lifestyle that can satisfy him.

For the rest of the novel, Tom plays the roles of Tom or Dickie as the circumstances dictate. When Tom is playing the role of Dickie, one that he relishes because of the wealth and status it gives him, then it is "Tom Ripley" who is missing and the object of a police search. But when Tom is "forced" to murder Freddie Miles, who comes looking for Dickie in Rome, Tom must do away with Dickie and give up his impersonation. "Dickie's" disappearance implicates "Dickie" in Freddy's murder at the same time as it exculpates Tom Ripley. As the last few sentences suggest, Tom's impersonation results in a convoluted and confusing situation. When Marge comes looking for Dickie at his house, for example, she meets Tom, playing himself, who tells her Dickie has stayed in Rome. The reader knows that Marge should be looking for Dickie's murderer, who is standing in front of her, but she can't do that because she doesn't know that Dickie is dead because the man in front of her is successfully impersonating Dickie (when in Rome).

"Dickie" and Tom thus become the Object of a series of searches for the rest of the novel – by Marge, Freddy Miles, Roverini the Italian policeman, Herbert Greenleaf, and Alvin McCarron (the PI whom Greenleaf hires). Tom/Dickie is interviewed by each in turn, but is not recognized as the Object of their search because he never appears as the character they are looking for. He in effect conceals his status as Object behind a series of Helper impersonations. When the police interview him looking for Tom, he plays Dickie; when Marge shows up in Rome desperately seeking Dickie, then he reverts to Tom. Ripley had originally come to New York to be an actor, and acting, it turns out, is his métier, his one true talent. In time Ripley comes to believe that acting creates reality, that fake appearances create "real" realities: "It was senseless to be despondent, even as Tom Ripley. Hadn't he learned something from these last months? If you wanted to be cheerful, or melancholic, or thoughtful, or courteous, you simply had to *act* those things with every gesture" (1975: 165). Tom starts to throw himself into his performances:

> He began to feel happy even in his dreary role as Thomas Ripley. He took pleasure in
> it, overdoing almost the old Tom Ripley reticence with strangers, the inferiority in every
> duck of his head and wistful, sidelong glance. After all, would anyone, anyone, believe
> that such a character had ever done a murder? (1975: 194)

Tom has in effect successfully completed his Quest and secured his Object: the Self-hood of a perfect impersonator. The superb quality of his acting enables Tom to avoid the long arm of justice. The Object of the various searches is at the end of the novel a free man, telling the cabbie to take him to the best hotel in Athens.

But all this acting, this bouncing back and forth between two identities, does have its cost; it lends itself to schizophrenia, a mental illness to which Tom Ripley apparently succumbs. He puts money, for example, from the Greenleaf bank account into the Ripley account because "[a]fter all, he had two people to take care of" (1975: 135). When Marge asks him in Venice where he had spent the winter, he commits an incriminating *lapsus linguae* – "Well, not with Tom. I mean, not with Dickie" (1975: 226) – which Marge fails pick up on. When Ripley is forced to do away with his "Dickie" persona, he justifies it to himself as follows: "Being Tom Ripley had one compensation, at least: it relieved his mind of guilt for the stupid unnecessary murder of Freddie Miles" (1975: 194). Tom's matter-of-fact schizophrenia here absolves him of the guilt for "Dickie's" violent actions. The reader is at pains to remember that it was Tom masquerading as Dickie who killed Freddy.

Tom's illness also manifests itself in paranoia. At several points he suspects that he is being followed. And, of course, he *is* – by the readers of the novel, who follow his tracks and share his experiences and his suspicions. The most disquieting fact about reading a crime novel like *The Talented Mr Ripley* is that the schizophrenia depicted within it is contagious; readers usually "catch" it. Experiencing crime from the point of view of the criminal renders readers of two minds, both of them functions of the doubled quest storyline. Since readers know that Ripley is the guilty party, the Object of the search, they feel an obligation to act as loyal Subjects and see that he is brought to justice. He cannot get away with it, they think. At the same time, being on the inside, part of an inside job, makes readers into co-Subjects who want Ripley to escape punishment: "What one responds to in Ripley is not the triumph of the id but the evasion of the superego. ... The fantasy evoked is not of violence but impu-nity" (Hilfer 1990: 129). Like Ripley, readers of crime novels are playing at crime, and they want to escape the reach of the Law. As the number of crimes increases, readers feel more and more guilty, more and more ambivalent. They wonder where (or if) they will draw the line, when (or if) they will turn on Ripley, when (or if) they will turn him in. Readers thus serve vicariously as both Subjects and Objects of the pursuit of crime; it is a disturbingly schizophrenic experience.

Each of the three subgenres of crime fiction adapts what we might call the "char-acter syntax" of the quest formula to its own needs. The classic detective story offers the reader the consolations of an orderly and motivated world in which most characters can be sorted out according to type and the full truth is inevitably revealed. Hard-boiled detective fiction thrusts the reader into a shifty and fluid world where anyone can be anything, except the detective who is always Himself. And the crime novel performs a number of slippery role reversals in the standard quest plotline, making the protagonist over into the criminal and converting the reader into both Subject and Object in the pursuit of crime.

12

Crime, Forensics, and Modern Science

Sarah Dauncey

Jacques Derrida has repeatedly urged the need to distinguish between bearing witness and proof. His engagement with ethics and literature gives rise to a fascination with the act of giving testimony, an act that only has meaning "before the law" (Derrida 2000a: 191). In order to bear witness there must be a listener or an addressee "to whom the witness is joined by a contract, an oath, a promise" (Derrida 2000a: 190). Unlike other forms of communication centered on the transmission of knowledge or information, the act of testifying demands commitment and foregrounds its structural reliance upon the faith of an other: "The witness *promises* to say or to manifest something to another, his addressee: a truth, a sense which has been or is in some way present to him as a unique and irreplaceable witness" (Derrida 2000a: 194). Hence the importance of recognizing the distinctions between testimony (requiring faith) and proof (associated with the order of knowledge) to which Derrida draws our attention. Yet, while he goes to great lengths in both *Demeure* and "'A Self-Unsealing Poetic Text'" to stress the difference between these two categories, bearing witness and proof, he recognizes that, in practice, the borders defining the two are continually breached: "The whole problem consists in the fact that the crossing of such a conceptual limit is both forbidden and constantly practiced" (Derrida 2000a: 191).

I want to look closely into this confusion of proof and testimony by turning to narratives where questions regarding them predominate, those that are committed to forensic methods, technologies, and expertise. As forensic science exists to meet the demands of the legal system by identifying, collecting, and documenting evidence it has a determining influence upon the status of both "proof" and "testimony" and plays a pivotal part in negotiating relations between them. By reading texts dating from the end of the nineteenth century to the beginning of the twenty-first – from Doyle's Sherlock Holmes stories to fiction by Patricia Cornwell to accounts by human rights forensic anthropologists – I disclose how changing conceptions of evidence have transformed its relation to testimony. For instance, there has been a notable transformation in the perception of the dead body: from seeing it as an inert script to be deciphered by the scientist-observer to envisioning it as a witness, a subject for the scientist-observer to engage in dialogue. Over the course of a century, proof comes to have the capacity to bear witness. I will, therefore, be following Derrida in asking "for what necessary – not accidental – reasons the sense of 'proof' regularly comes to contaminate or divert the sense of 'bearing witness'" (Derrida 2000a: 188).

As forensic science became more established as a discipline in the twentieth century, and evolved to respond to the needs of the judicial system and law enforcement agencies, it became an increasingly prominent feature of crime novels. Patricia Cornwell is perhaps the most famous example of an author who embraces forensic technologies, but there are a number of other Western crime writers who grant them a central role in their narratives: for instance, Thomas Harris, Kathy Reichs, Val McDermid, Ridley Pearson, Helene Tursten, Henning Mankell, and Arnaldur Indidasson. Although forensic scientists are not always cast in a positive light and their technologies are not without flaw, the field is resourceful in narrative terms as it constructs accounts of the past from the examination of material debris (evidence left at crime scenes). Interestingly, this subgenre, "forensic fiction," is principally a Western phenomenon. The Martinician writer Patrick Chamoiseau draws attention to this reality in his novel *Solibo Magnificent* and challenges the application of forensic knowledge to serve the neo-colonial interests of the authorities.

In distinct ways, Derrida's theory and Chamoiseau's postcolonial skepticism inform my critique of forensic scientists' recourse to the trope of the speaking body and their suggestion that they are, in the words of the forensic anthropologist Clea Koff, "interpreters of the skeleton's language" (Koff 2004: 11). More important still is the need to challenge the representation of the bodies as witnesses along with the notion that the scientist has the ability to "unlock their testimonies," as it obscures the irreplaceable nature of "the witness" and the faith it demands when it tells of its presence at a singular event (Derrida 2000 b: 30).

The transformation in the perception of evidence, as thing or body, combined with the changing role of the forensic scientist is, in part, a product of new technologies. Advances in DNA testing at the end of the twentieth century and the authority of DNA evidence in court, for example, have strengthened the cultural, disciplinary, and legal reputation of forensic science. The cultural-historical shift in thinking about evidence and its relation to testimony demonstrates the increasing stature of the discipline and provides an opening for its further expansion.

Reading Crime Scenes and Criminal Bodies

The links between the Sherlock Holmes stories and the reconstructive sciences, such as paleontology, archaeology, and geology, have been well documented by critics. In fact, Rzepka goes as far as to assert that "the story of the development of the detective genre largely coincides with the history of narrative practice in these reconstructive sciences, and with its popular dissemination" (Rzepka 2005: 33). Over the course of the nineteenth century, traditional religious conceptions of the past were challenged by secular explanations – most notably, Darwin's theory of evolution. This "transition from sacred to secular explanations of the past" gave rise to a new attitude towards the value of material evidence,

> to what we might call the physical "clues" of history, as opposed to the "testimony", the oral or written accounts of past events, including God's, cited to explain those "clues". ... The unimpeachable authority of the sacred "testimony" ... was rapidly giving way to the new authority of material "clues." (Rzepka 2005: 35)

Consequently, detective fiction can be seen to allay some of the cultural anxieties associated with the new world-view by legitimating the reconstructive scientists' methods. Detectives, like Holmes, draw inductive inferences from material clues so as to reconstruct the past, either from clues alone or by using clues to help evaluate conflicting testimonies about the past. The reconstructive sciences, and their popular incarnations, place emphasis upon a specific kind of reading competence in order to be able to reconstruct the past from fragmentary evidence and, subsequently, transform it into a coherent, linear narrative. As the natural world is envisaged as a book to be read or a document to be deciphered by scientists and detectives alike, the need for generating and appreciating proficient readers becomes a key cultural project.[1]

Famously, *The Sign of Four* opens with Sherlock Holmes showing off his reconstructive powers to Watson, who presents him with the challenge of describing a man he has never encountered before from the sight of his watch:

> "I have heard you say it is difficult for a man to have any object in daily use without leaving the impress of his individuality upon it in such a way that a trained observer might read it. Now, I have here a watch which has recently come into my possession. Would you have the kindness to let me have an opinion upon the character or habits of the late owner." (Doyle 1986: 1.111)

Watson feels confident that Holmes will be defeated by such a test, but, as always, he is proved wrong as the master detective proceeds to detail the habits, characteristics, and class status of the watch's owner, Watson's eldest brother. The watch is "read" and Holmes proves himself to be a "trained observer," someone capable of piecing together a complete "individual" from a personal possession.

But, crucially, it is not only artifacts that are subjected to this sort of decipherment in the stories of Sherlock Holmes: the material world and the people that populate it are also presented as texts to be read. In "The Beryl Coronet," for instance, Holmes tells Watson about his discoveries at the crime scene, Mr Holder's house: "'when I got into the stable lane a very long and complex story was written in the snow in front of me'" (Doyle 1986: 1.427). From the footprints and other traces he observes in the snow, with the aid of his imagination, he is able to construct a narrative of events. Facts are placed in a chain of causes and effects. In "The Boscombe Valley

Mystery," Holmes's superior powers of observation, combined with his use of a magnifying glass to see details that would ordinarily be overlooked, means he finds more to read than either Watson or Lestrade. Visiting the site where the dead body of McCarthy was discovered, Watson recalls that he could "plainly see the traces which had been left by the stricken man." Yet he notes that, for Holmes, "many more things were to be read upon the trampled grass" (Doyle 1986: 1.281).

In *Detective Fiction and the Rise of Forensic Science*, Ronald Thomas also draws attention to Holmes's mastery and the capacity for forensic methods and technologies – which Holmes utilizes and advocates – to render the world and people legible. In particular, he argues that the emergence of forensic technologies coincides with a wider cultural and political project to make and monitor the modern subject at a time when impersonal forces threatened the very notion of individuality (Thomas 1999: 8). The rise in criminology and forensic science is, for Thomas, inextricable from the development of nationalist discourses seeking to define "others" who pose a threat to the social order (Thomas 1999: 10). It is, however, not only the criminal or foreign body that is translated into text. In his study of Doyle's story, "A Case of Identity," Thomas draws attention to the way Holmes regards Mary Sutherland (victim and client) as if she were a text. He deduces that she is a typewritist from the traces the machine leaves on her body: the smears on her sleeves; a mark on her wrist where it rests against the machine; and on her face where her pince-nez presses her nose, suggesting short-sightedness (Doyle 1986: 1.260). This mastery over the body can be seen as a form of social control – or, at least, a fantasy of control – and is redoubled by his habit of speaking for people, by narrating their histories as well as deciphering their bodies (Thomas 1994: 655).

Forensic tools support the nineteenth-century literary detective who aspires to identify persons, reconstruct past events, and render the world "legible" (Thomas 1999: 17). Holmes is frequently depicted on his hands and knees, with a magnifying glass in hand, looking for trace evidence, footprints, and fingerprints. Accordingly, the Sherlock Holmes stories help to popularize the scientific field by demonstrating how it can be employed to track down criminals and solve mysteries.[2] Alongside the application of forensic techniques, legislative changes were introduced that raised the status of material evidence, over and above testimony. These changes are particularly worthy of note because they contributed to the process of turning the body into a cipher:

> In the century-long process in which suspect personal testimony and questions of character were translated into legible forms of physical evidence, the fingerprint represents nineteenth-century criminologists' ultimate achievement in transforming the body into a text. (Thomas 1999: 203)

But, in spite of Thomas's reference to the power of forensic devices to make the body "speak for itself" (Thomas 1999: 17), his readings of Poe and of Doyle in particular concentrate on the body (suspect or victim) as text and the detective as expert reader. He suggests that this expertise, aided by the latest technologies, was harnessed by disciplinary powers to promote a specific notion of personhood at a time when the nature of the subject was under threat as a consequence of industrialization and imperial expansion. "Properly read, the body could be theorized to contain the secret of the self" (Thomas 1999: 89).

In acknowledging the diminished status of "the testimony of witnesses in Anglo-American courtroom practice in the later half of the [nineteenth] century" (Thomas 1999: 78), Thomas places too much emphasis upon the distinctions between evidence and testimony and not enough upon the instances of their confusion. The history of the emergence of fingerprinting in colonial India warns us of the need to treat seriously the conflation of terms. Hence, I want to turn briefly to Gita Panjabi Trelease's discussion of fingerprinting to consider the strategic way that the rhetoric of witnessing evidence bolsters colonial authority. Like Thomas, Trelease recognizes the role fingerprinting played in helping the authorities to establish (the appearance of) order and stability in the empire. He cites the example of an early advocate of fingerprinting, William Herschel, who introduced the practice into his administration in Hooly, India. For Herschel, fingerprinting provided the means of controlling the " 'wily' and mendacious bodies of Indians" by replacing the need for reliance upon personal testimonies (Trelease 2004: 199). Terming his collection of fingerprint evidence " 'the speaking book' " betrays his ambition to silence the native, removing the occasion for self-expression: "the 'speaking book' spoke for the criminal as his fingerprint attested to his guilt or innocence" (Trelease 2004: 200).

Forensic methods are valued as they transform the body into material evidence, bringing it more fully within the sphere of the law. It is worth asking, then, why this process of dehumanizing the body is accompanied by measures to humanize it by drawing on the trope of witnessing evidence. In the colonial context of India, such measures provide a strategic means of concealing the process by which individuals are stripped of voice and agency. Testimonies are needless following the application of scientific procedures granting expressive powers to the inert body. The administrator of Hooly's total disregard for the personal testimonies of native suspects, combined with the application of fingerprinting as an imperial practice, highlights the importance of examining the conflation of evidence and testimony, not only in nineteenth-century fictional and historical accounts of forensic technologies, but in contemporary ones. The fact that the tropological maneuvers involved in transforming evidence into a witness, and vice versa, were once deployed to legitimate colonial rule urges us to be suspicious of its application today, especially in narrative and historical accounts depicting the resourcefulness of the scientific field. For what is represented as objective understanding of anatomy and the material world often belies troubling cultural and racial attitudes and political interests.

Once again, the Sherlock Holmes stories prove resourceful as they illustrate the application of the category of testimony to raise the status of evidence. The distinctions between evidence and testimony are confounded on a number of occasions when Sherlock Holmes relates his reconstruction of events (derived from material evidence) to actual eye-witnesses, those who were *really* present at the past events he narrates. In *A Study in Scarlet*, Holmes examines the scene of the murder of Enoch Drebber to assist detectives Lestrade and Gregson in the pursuit of the criminal. He is described discovering "'marks which were entirely invisible'" to the uncomprehending Watson; collecting trace evidence; measuring the distance between prints; and observing blood smears and footprints (Doyle 1986: 1.26). Holmes also applies his keen observation to the street outside the house where the murder was committed. This scrutiny of the evidence means that when he later comes to interview the constable, John Rance, who was on patrol outside the house on the night of the crime, and listens to his eye-witness account, Holmes is able to speak as though he was there himself. Watson recounts the conversation between Holmes and Rance:

> "You stopped, and then walked back to the garden gate," my companion interrupted. "What did you do that for?"
> Rance gave a violent jump, and stared at Sherlock Holmes with the utmost amazement upon his features.
> "Why, that's true, sir," he said; "though how you came to know it, Heaven only knows." (Doyle 1986: 1.31)

This dialogue is typical of encounters between Holmes and eye-witnesses. It dramatizes the master detective's dismissal of personal testimony because of his unique ability to reconstruct events.

Derrida stresses the centrality of presence to the structure of testimony: it is only on condition that the witness has been "present at this or that, having attended to this or that, ... on condition of having been sufficiently present *to himself* ... that the witness can be answerable, responsible, for his testimony" (Derrida 2000a: 192). No one else can share the singular present witnessed by the witness, for that would shatter the contract of faith between witness and listener:

> The addressee of the witnessing, the witness of the witness, does not see for himself what the first witness says he has seen; the addressee has not seen it and never will see it. This direct or immediate non-access of the addressee to the object of the witnessing is what marks the absence of this 'witness of the witness' to the thing itself. (Derrida 2000a: 189)

Holmes's access to the "things" that the constable, the witness, has seen in *A Study in Scarlet* is striking. It is his confidence of having been present, of apparently seeing "for himself" the events Rance testifies to, that prompts the astonished reaction in the above passage. Further, as Holmes can "prove" Rance's account, Rance's testimony can no longer "be assured *as* testimony" (Derrida 2000a: 182). Derrida opens a critical space in which to consider Holmes's habit of confusing evidence and testimony. As testimony becomes the vehicle by which forensic expertise is established and the status of evidence is raised it is in itself devalued in any meaningful, ethical sense.

While Holmes's expertise often renders eye-witness accounts unnecessary (or, at least, only necessary in so far as they consolidate his expertise and the importance of material evidence), his position is, paradoxically, presented as being analogous to that of an eye-witness. In a sense, he stands in for the witness when he declares to Rance, "'yes, I know all that you saw.'" And the constable certainly perceives him in terms of a witness when he replies "'where was you hid to see all that?'" (Doyle 1986: 1.31). "Real" witnesses unwittingly authorize Holmes's knowledge by their reaction to his reconstruction of events. In *The Sign of Four* Jonathan Small is, like Rance, shocked by Holmes's knowledge of a scene he was never present at: "'You seem to know as much about it as if you were there, sir'" (Doyle 1986: 1.180). And in "Silver Blaze", Holmes himself describes to Watson the uncanny impression he made on Silas Brown, the horse thief, as a consequence of his complete understanding of events he never witnessed: "'I described to him so exactly what his actions had been that he is convinced I was watching him'" (Doyle 1986: 1.469).

These exchanges between "real" witnesses and Holmes problematize interpretations that assert the "diminished value placed on the testimony of witnesses" (Thomas 1999: 78). At first glance such exchanges promote evidence, thus reflecting and reinforcing the legal changes Rzepka and Thomas draw attention to. But the complex representation of evidence and testimony in the stories confounds any easy separation of the terms, thereby disrupting the process of mapping the legislative changes onto the narratives. When Holmes is empowered by his examination of material evidence to speak "as if he were there," he takes the place of a witness, appropriating testimony rather than overthrowing the need for it altogether. Additionally, the application of forensic methods and technologies has the effect of turning the traces and clues of the crime scene into extensions of, or substitutes for, the detective's senses. Far from evidence challenging the authority of first-person accounts, it is conceived in similar terms.

Sherlock Holmes's transformation of the world and body into text that can be read is undoubtedly a mechanism of social control, a means of mastering the other. It is, however, important to note that, at the *fin de siècle*, he works independently of the law. The stories chart the emergence of new forensic technologies and their "intensifying incursion" into "traditional English law enforcement" (Thomas 1999: 80). In contrast, in the narratives of R. Austin Freeman, published at the beginning of the twentieth century, the law and science are yoked in the figure of Dr Thorndyke, a lawyer-pathologist. Freeman grants more space to detailing forensic techniques and the judicial process in comparison with Doyle. Notably, where the words "trace" and "clue" prevail in the Sherlock Holmes stories, Thorndyke speaks more frequently of "evidential value," Freeman's *The Red Thumb Mark* is in direct dialogue with the ideas associated with Herschel – and Francis Galton, author of *Finger Prints* (1892) – whereby the fingerprint is regarded as a "'magic touchstone'" (Freeman 2001: 21). In the novel, John Hornby is convicted of theft by the police solely on the basis of fingerprint evidence left at the scene of the crime. Thorndyke is called upon to prove his innocence and he succeeds in his task by undermining the evidence, exposing the way it has been tampered with. According to Thorndyke, fingerprints are a fact "'which, like any other fact, requires to be weighed and measured with reference to its evidential value'" (Freeman 2001: 21). He therefore challenges the police and fingerprint experts and questions their view that a thumbprint is "'tantamount to the evidence of an eyewitness'" (2001: 60–1).

Like Sherlock Holmes, Thorndyke's expertise, combined with the forensic technologies he brings to bear on the scenes of crime, renders both the material world and people legible. His "methods reflect the medicalization of crime, valorizing the work of the expert diagnostician, using scientific methods to illuminate the pathology of crime, converting the body and the scene of the crime into a text to be studied" (Horsley 2005: 35). Nevertheless, the Thorndyke stories also begin to conceive evidence as having a life and voice of its own (though one that can only be heard and translated by the forensic expert), thus marking a significant shift from the Holmes mysteries where material evidence was unequivocally inert. In doing so, they point towards the work of Patricia Cornwell at the end of the twentieth century, where pathologist Kay Scarpetta is represented as being in communion with the bodies and evidence left at crime scenes. In *The Adventures of Dr Thorndyke* (first published as *The Singing Bone* in 1912), the medical jurist, Thorndyke, astounds the eye-witness, Jeffreys, in a similar way to Holmes as a consequence of his capacity to reconstruct the events of the past by analyzing facts. Jeffreys's astonished reaction is recalled by Thorndyke's assistant, Dr Jervis, the narrator of the stories: "'Was you here then? You talk as if you had been'" (Freeman 1923: 124). But Thorndyke treats evidence in a very different way to Holmes. In this case, Jeffreys's pipe is a significant object. Thorndyke's forensic examination of it, and the remaining tobacco, enables him to solve the mystery. At the close of the story Jeffreys himself declares, "'the way in which you made that pipe tell the story of the murder seems to me like sheer enchantment'" (Freeman 1923: 125). In response, Thorndyke discloses an interesting attitude towards things: "'The inanimate things around us have each of them a song to sing if we are but ready with attentive ears'" (Freeman 1923: 125).

This formulation of singing things marks a movement away from the kind of domination exhibited in the Holmes narratives, whereby the detective transforms people and evidence into texts that can be read. It gestures, instead, towards a relation of dialogue and communion. Where Holmes imposes narrative onto things and people, speaking on their behalf, contemporary forensic narratives and accounts – following on from Freeman – figure the scientist as a listener of the narratives told by crime scenes and the dead.

Listening to Crime Scenes and Victims' Bodies

Patricia Cornwell is famous for her commitment to forensic science. Not only has she written a series of novels revolving around a forensic pathologist, Kay Scarpetta, but her own personal experience as a technician for Virginia's Chief Medical Examiner's

Office has made her an outspoken advocate for the power of forensic science to give voice to the innocent and to track down criminals. In *The Body Farm*, Kay Scarpetta is involved in tracking down the murderer of an 11-year-old girl. In this particular case, the duct tape used to silence the victim plays a pivotal role in the process of identifying the criminal. Its significance forces her to recall the number of victims she has encountered whose mouths have been covered with it:

> I could not count the times I had peeled it from the mouths of people who were not allowed to scream until they were wheeled into my morgue. For it was only there the body could speak freely. It was only there someone cared about every awful thing that had been done. (Cornwell 1995: 196)

This representation of the morgue and the pathologist requires close scrutiny. It announces the uniqueness of the forensic scientist's skills at the same time as emphasizing their humanity. They are, simultaneously, exceptional and ordinary.[3] Instead of focusing on the morgue as a clinical environment for the objective study of bodies, Scarpetta draws attention to it as a site of sympathetic understanding and communion. This sentimentalization of forensic science is markedly different from its treatment in the Sherlock Holmes and Dr Thorndyke mysteries where emphasis is placed upon objective observation and ratiocination and where the body is deciphered (Thorndyke's gestures toward the idea of listening to, rather than reading, evidence remain just that and no more). To a degree, this focus upon Scarpetta's capacity for empathy provides a way of asserting her femininity and distancing her from a tradition of male detectives, exemplified by Sherlock Holmes, who prioritize empirical understanding over emotional engagement. Yet it is also in keeping with a more widespread "feminization" of the field of forensic science by granting voice to the dead, bestowing on the forensic scientist the unique task of listening to, and interpreting, their stories.

In *Sites of Autopsy in Contemporary Culture*, Elizabeth Klaver notes the prevalence of the trope of the speaking body in a number of modern discourses, ranging from medicine and the humanities to popular culture: "the speaking subject is a common trope used in naming the metaphorical agency assigned to the dead body" (Klaver 2005: 79). According to Klaver, such representations play a pivotal role in subduing cultural anxieties about death and decay. Although, she argues, the language of reading and decipherment is more descriptive of the pathologist's relation to the dead, the trope of the speaking body has come to the fore because of the important cultural work it performs. By attributing subjectivity to the dead, their "deadness disappears", thereby reducing their threat "to the subjectivity of the viewer" (Klaver 2005: 92). This chimes with Jonathan Sawday's apprehension of the age-old "fear of interiority" detailed in his seminal work *The Body Emblazoned*, the reluctance to confront "the knowledge that, eventually, our bodies will indeed cease to function, and that our identity will, in similar measure, disappear" (Sawday 1995: 267–8). The prevalence of contemporary representations of the speaking body is a key part of the cultural machinery to subdue anxieties about death.

Klaver does not sufficiently historicize the turn to the metaphor of the speaking body that has "taken the upper hand over reading" the body in contemporary culture and subsequently fails to account for the insistence of such discourse at the end of the twentieth century and its continued adoption in the twenty-first (Klaver 2005: 82). In part, this is because she omits to consider the relation between the trope of the speaking body and the burgeoning interest in forensic science in popular culture together with its international legal and disciplinary authority. Further, Klaver's study does not extend to instances where the body does not merely speak, but bears witness to its own death. In Cornwell's novel *From Potter's Field*, for example, Scarpetta declares her unique relation to the dead: "I was accustomed to witnesses who did not speak to anyone but me" (Cornwell 1996: 40). Throughout the novel, Scarpetta is differentiated from the New York police and FBI agents because of her commitment to establishing the identity of an unnamed victim of a murder.[4] In this instance, the appearance of the language of testimony reinforces her expertise and strengthens her claims to be able to speak, and act, on behalf of the dead. Such language does far more than quell the threat death poses to the identity of the living – it invests the field with a unique set of cultural functions at the same time as empowering it to intervene in legal and political contexts. As Derrida asserts, the confusion of the sense of bearing witness with the sense of proof is "not accidental" (Derrida 2000a: 188).

As in the Sherlock Holmes stories, the tradition of testimony promotes forensic practices and raises the status of evidence, although, with the Scarpetta series, quite a different role is awarded to narrative. Whereas Holmes *reads* crime scenes and bodies and subsequently organizes facts into an ordered sequence of events "as if" he was an eye-witness, Scarpetta *listens* to their messages and testimonies. The crime scenes and the dead appear to possess narrative authority in Cornwell's fiction. To illustrate, in *From Potter's Field* Scarpetta describes the unnamed victim as having "'something yet to say to us,'" suggesting a relationship of mutual understanding and sympathy rather than one of domination (Cornwell 1996: 155). Yet, to appeal to Derrida, if the "assured" sense of testimony is to be kept in mind, then "a body could never attest to anything" (Derrida 2000b: 80–1). This insistence on the fact that only a survivor can bear witness alerts us to the "necessary" work of blurring testimony and proof in popular cultural representations of forensic science (Derrida 2000b: 45): "no one can bear witness *in the place of* another, any more than anyone can die *in the place of* another" (Derrida 2000a: 199). Such thinking gives rise to some critical questions regarding the rhetoric of testimony in forensic narratives. For instance, to what extent does the representation of the scientist as a mediator or translator of the dead divert attention away from the material interests driving forensic investigations? And, on a more ethical note, does the forensic conflation of proof and testimony betray a more wide-spread reluctance to be open to the otherness of the witness, and, therefore, to the promise of the future?

As the scientific field has broadened its sphere of influence over the past thirty years to intervene in international political affairs following its alliance with human rights discourse, the task of tracking its representational strategies has redoubled.

Significantly, Clyde Snow, the American anthropologist at the forefront of cross-border campaigns to raise awareness of the value of forensic technologies for investigations into human rights abuses in the 1970s and 1980s, conceived the skeleton as "'its own best witness'" (Joyce and Stover 1991: 268). Unquestionably, this dramatic appeal to the force of testimony to elevate the status of proof played a part in promoting and extending the field, legitimating its intervention into post-conflict societies to exhume mass graves. At the end of the twentieth century, human rights agencies began to employ forensic investigators to identify victims and discover evidence to convict perpetrators. Snow's commitment to coupling forensics and politics inspired a new generation of scientists such as Clea Koff, who wrote recently of his influence over her decision to become a forensic anthropologist and work for human rights agencies. She describes her special task: to commune with the dead to "unlock their testimonies" (Koff 2004: 6, 208).

This confusion of evidence and testimony in narratives that represent, and popularize, forensic science, provides a strategic way of sanctioning a specialized field of knowledge, accounting for its acceptance and expansion – over the course of a century – into a wide range of discourses and structures, from popular culture to international law. Popular incarnations of forensic science, from the Sherlock Holmes stories onwards, have played a major part in educating publics about its capacity to influence disciplinary and judicial practices. Although there has been a shift from reading evidence to listening to it, the application of the rhetoric of testimony to empower evidence has been sustained.

Notes

1   See Lawrence Frank on the transactions between the reconstructive sciences and popular detective fiction in *Victorian Detective Fiction* (2003). In particular, he registers the parallels between Sherlock Holmes's view of the world as a page to be read and the work of nineteenth-century geologists and paleontologists.

2   In fact, Thomas notes that narratives by Poe, Dickens, and Doyle sometimes even "anticipated actual procedures in scientific police practice by offering fantasies of social control and knowledge before the actual technology to

achieve either was available. At times, these texts seemed to call those technologies into being" (Thomas 1999: 4).

3   Rose Lucas (2004) also notes the way that Scarpetta is depicted as both ordinary and exceptional.

4   For the majority of those working on the case, knowledge of the victim's identity is not seen to be important to the process of tracking down the criminal, Temple Gault, whereas for Scarpetta such knowledge is a matter of principle: "'She has a right to be buried with her name'" (Cornwell 1996: 155).

13

The Police Novel

Peter Messent

From 1997 on, I've written about cops. I consciously abandoned the Private Eye tradition that formally jazzed me. Evan Hunter wrote: "The last time a Private Eye investigated a homicide was never." The Private Eye is an iconic totem spawned by pure fiction. The American Cop is the real goods from the gate. (Ellroy 1994)

James Ellroy's words help to explain the recent popularity of the police novel. Both Joyce Carol Oates (the American novelist) and Peter Robinson (the British crime fiction writer) argue along similar lines. For Oates, "private detectives are rarely involved in authentic crime cases, and would have no access, in contemporary times, to the findings of forensic experts." The police procedural has prospered accordingly (Oates 1995: 34). Robinson explains why the police novel suits his own needs as a crime writer: "it goes back to what Ed McBain once said about calling the cops if you find a body, not the … little old lady across the street. Some sense of realism or credibility, I guess" (Peter Robinson, e-mail correspondence, June 18, 2007).

In this essay I replace Oates's use of the term "police procedural" by its more inclusive variant, the police novel. This follows a trajectory traced from the earliest full-length study of the genre, George Dove's *The Police Procedural* (1982), to Leroy Panek's more recent *The Police Novel: A History* (2003a). As Panek argues, the "police procedural" descriptor suggests a certain narrative structure – with criminal act, detection, and solution in orderly sequence. It also assumes significant attention will be paid (as in Ed McBain's groundbreaking sequence of 87th Precinct novels) to "the ways police officers and departments do what they do, the 'procedural' material" constituting the "daily routines" of their lives (Panek 2003b: 156; 2003a: 2). Such material includes the representation of investigative processes, of command and communication structures, and the way knowledge is shared and institutional resources used. More recently, close attention has also been paid to forensics, psychological profiling, and sophisticated scientific and technological support systems (see the work of writers like Patricia Cornwell and television series such as *CSI*; see also Dauncey, chapter 12 in this volume). Such novels, then, "shift our attention to the process ... of policing" and away from any "magic" involved – the exceptionally gifted detective able to penetrate what, for others, remains a mystery. "Police work," in its procedural context, accordingly loses many romantic elements found in other forms of detective fiction, is "collective, grim and often untidy, rather than ... merely an elegant intellectual exercise" (Priestman 2003: 179).

Panek points out that such defining features do not always figure in police *novels*. Joseph Wambaugh, for example, downplays the conventional paradigms of detective fiction in the recent *Hollywood Station* (2006), and distances himself considerably from the "procedural" label, and what it implies ("a meticulously plotted genre story"):

> [M]y work is anything but. I defy anyone to describe the "plot" of *The Choirboys*. And my latest, *Hollywood Station*, just barely has a plot ... on which I hang the episodes and anecdotes ... I get from interviewing cops (fifty-four for *Hollywood Station*) ... . [T]he police procedural usually has the cop solving a crime or achieving something of value through the police work. In my stories it usually turns out that only the reader knows the truth of the matter and the cop ends up with part or none of the answer. (J. Wambaugh, e-mail correspondence, May 26, 2007)

Thomas Harris's *The Silence of the Lambs* (1988) similarly disrupts the normative narrative conventions of the procedural, with its representation of psychological intimacy between the incarcerated psychopath Hannibal "the Cannibal" Lecter and Clarice Starling, neophyte FBI investigator, and the reader's early knowledge of the identity of the criminal and the "split-level narrative" that follows (Horsley 2005: 139). In addition, the text includes a second serial killer – Lecter himself – to one side of its main investigative center. He paradoxically epitomizes both civilized behavior and cannibalistic savagery, while his freedom at the novel's conclusion disrupts the closure and sense of containment we might normally expect.

The police novel, in its various forms, is now strongly established in North America and Britain, and throughout Europe (and appears, of course, elsewhere). In both America and Europe, the form can be traced back to the nineteenth century, but it is the post-World War II period, and especially the more recent past – with the massive proliferation of such texts – on which I focus. Perhaps the most significant early American writers in this modern history were Ed McBain, whose *Cop Hater* was published in 1956, and (writing from an entirely different and racially oriented perspective) Chester Himes and his 1957 novel, *A Rage in Harlem*. Since then, the major figures who can be (loosely) grouped under such a heading would include those already named – Cornwell, Ellroy, Harris, and Wambaugh – together with such other accomplished writers as James Lee Burke (whose 2007 Hurricane Katrina novel, *The Tin Roof Blowdown*, deserves special mention), Michael Connelly, Robert Crais, Tess Gerritsen, Tony Hillerman, Faye Kellerman, James Patterson, and Kathy Reichs.

The post-war British police novel reaches back to the 1950s with J. J. Marric (John Creasey) and his George Gideon novels. A set of different and "home-grown origins"

(Priestman 2003: 173) – Colin Dexter's Inspector Morse series, for instance, emphasizes a hierarchical and ordered picture postcard Oxford world where the individual criminal act is an aberrant exception to the general rule and where Inspector Morse tackles "a mystery" like "some fiendishly devised crossword" (Dexter 2007: 141) – has been increasingly affected by the influence of an American hard-boiled tradition of gritty realism, in which violence and corruption are part and parcel of society as a whole, and in which the police themselves are infected by such forces. Significant British writers across the genre include Michael Dibdin, Elizabeth George, John Harvey, Reginald Hill, P. D. James, H. R. F. Keating, Val McDermid, William McIlvanney, Ian Rankin, and Peter Robinson. But to name names like this is only to be aware of the injustice done to many of those omitted, as well as to a wider European context. George Simenon's 75 Maigret novels (published from 1931 onward) have been extremely influential. So, too, in their different way, has the work of Swedish writers Maj Sjöwall and Per Wahlöö, with their ten novels in the brilliant Martin Beck series (1965–75). Contemporary writing on the European mainland – Arnaldur Indridason, Henning Mankell and Fred Vargas are just a few examples – are unimaginable without such precedents.

The term "police novel," as my introductory comments and the listings above suggest, is better suited than "police procedural" to describe the *variety* of fictions focusing on crime and police work: novels of detection, thrillers, psychological and/or sociological novels, narratives reliant on Gothic effects, and so on. It also downplays expectations of a close focus on the routines and investigative cooperations of police work implicit in the "procedural" label. Ian Rankin, perhaps the most successful British writer in the field, comments on his own distance from the procedural, which "at its purest ... should be about a team – real-life police-work is very much a team effort." His own work focuses rather on John Rebus, a type of "driven loner cop":

> Since I am not Joe Wambaugh (I've never been a cop), I make Rebus operate almost as a private eye within the police force – he runs his own investigation parallel to the team effort. This means I don't need to know too much about actual police procedures, since Rebus is seldom going to follow them! (I. Rankin, e-mail correspondence, May 12, 2007)

When Panek comes to define the police novel (or "cop book") it is loosely, and based on the notion of character and context:

> Cop books are those that have a police officer or police officers as their central focus, and that use narration and action to display and examine the traditional, as well as the changing internal and external, forces that make cops a unique class of individuals. (Panek 2003a: 2)

I place my own emphasis more strongly on the *institutional and systemic* framework in which the police (and other law enforcers) work, focusing on the strength and importance of police fiction in the contemporary period in terms of its representation of the "state apparatus" that opposes criminality (Winston and Mellerski 1992: 2). This allows, in turn, a broader definition of the police novel than just the uniformed police force and its immediate plainclothes detective counterpart. Policing in our Western world, the protection and defense of the larger interests of the state, takes place at a variety of levels and across a number of organizations. Lee Horsley defines the novels of both Patricia Cornwell and Thomas Harris as "police procedurals" (2005: 138–57). I also see them as police novels (as described above), despite Kay Scarpetta's position, in Cornwell's earlier books, as Chief Medical Officer of Richmond, Virginia, and despite Clarice Starling's status as FBI agent. To see the genre through an institutional lens focuses attention on our relation (as private citizens) to the larger social network that contains us, and on any doubts and anxieties we might have about the nature of its organization and operations. Such anxieties may center on the meaning of, and relationship between, such terms as justice, morality, community, and law, and on the extent of our commitment to the values of the social authorities that supposedly operate on our behalf. As Ian Rankin once said, the police detective has "open access to all layers of society, from the oligarchs to the dispossessed":

> I wanted to write about contemporary urban Britain, and couldn't think of a better way of doing it than through the medium of the detective novel: I would, after all, be positing questions about the "state we're in," and reckoned a cop could act as my surrogate. (I. Rankin, e-mail correspondence, May 12, 2007)

Rankin's tone is modest but his claims are significant. The police novel is a form that, at its best, has mutated into an ongoing (serial) enquiry into the state of the nation, its power structures and its social concerns. It shares with other forms of crime fiction a "special relationship to history," "referring to the past while inhabiting the present, or inhabiting the past while referring to the present" (Haut 1999: 72). It also uses increasingly sophisticated narrative forms and frames of reference to gain its effects. Thus Reginald Hill's *The Death of Dalziel* (2007), for instance, focuses on the response to post 9/11 terrorism, introduces ideas prompted by the twelfth-century Cistercian abbot St Bernard of Clairvaux, and uses first-person narrative sequences to represent the out-of-body experiences of detective Andy Dalziel as he lies in a coma. Such qualities have led to growing critical attention to the genre's place and status in the overall fictional landscape. James Ellroy, in his distinctively hyperbolic style, captures something of its contemporary relevance and importance when he speaks of "cops as the up-close in-your-face voyeuristic eyes of a public that senses epic dysfunction all around them, and wants to know why" (Ellroy 1994). He is talking about real-life cops here, but the words carry over to their fictional equivalent.

To approach the police novel in terms of its institutional context is to suggest a three-way focus – first, on individual law enforcers and the policing communities to which they belong; second, on the exercise of state power and bureaucracy (the way society is policed); and third, on the general health (or lack of it) of the social system thus represented. Such factors complement my initial emphasis on realism alone – cops as "the real goods from the gate" – in explaining the growing popularity of the genre. But a changing social and institutional environment have also played their part, for the rise of the police novel, in Winston and Mellerski's words, undoubtedly

> suggests a response [after World War II] to the technological penetration and increased bureaucratic complexity of post-industrial society which operates by proposing a squad of individualized detectives, each possessing certain crucial skills which enable them to work collectively to investigate the same systemic evil that the hard-boiled detective nostalgically confronted alone (1992: 6).

This statement raises almost as many questions as it answers. It fails to account for police novels where the central detective is a maverick and, as in the cases of John Rebus or Bucky Bleichart (in Ellroy's ground-breaking 1987 novel, *The Black Dahlia*), conducts investigations to one side of, or parallel to, what Rankin calls "the team effort." It also leaves that resonant term "systemic evil," and where precisely it is to be discovered, unexplained.

There is here, however, a clear indication of the way the police novel is generally associated with notions of state bureaucracy, collective agency, and forms of social monitoring and control (reinforced by high-level technological and scientific support), an emphasis on the corporate symptomatic of its surrounding late-capitalist context. Such centralized systems of policing, the procedures used, and the resources accordingly available are, moreover, seen as increasingly necessary in uncovering criminality "in the anonymous and transient society that [has] become a feature of late twentieth-century [and early twenty-first century] life" (Panek 2003b: 157). It is easy then to see police novels as reflecting an increasingly invasive monitoring on behalf of the state of any threat to the established social order. So in Patricia Cornwell's *Unnatural Exposure*, a military C17 plane – a "monstrous flat-gray machine" (1997: 304) – transports the camper van/laboratory belonging to the novel's murderer for forensic examination at the US army Utah "test facility for chemical and biological defence" (1997: 294). The description of the plane's descent, with its suggestion of an alien invasive force (1997: 302), serves as a reminder of the authority and supervisory power wielded by the federal government, which backs up Kay Scarpetta's detections. The management by Lucy, Scarpetta's niece, of the FBI's Criminal Artificial Intelligence Network, her monitoring of the e-mail messages being passed from Crowder (the criminal) to Scarpetta, also indicates panoptic control. The solution of the crime (the attempted release of a deadly infection on the American people), the role of the detective, and the power and best interest of the state thus go hand in hand in this particular case.

The police novel often takes a different form, though, and works in more complicated and ambivalent ways. Lee Horsley notes its two main types: one using "the official investigative team of the police procedural," the other "the individual investigator [who] often retains considerable autonomy" even within a police setting. This autonomy is particularly evident "in narratives that move towards an exposure of the injustices and failures of the official machinery of law and order." She continues:

> Much contemporary detective fiction, both private eye and police procedural, does underwrite the values of "the controlling agencies of modern society." But there are many writers who use these forms to explore the contradictions and tensions of contemporary existence, creating ... a "discontinuous" tradition that in a variety of ways has challenged normative thinking (existing social and racial hierarchies, the assumed power structure, establishment values). (Horsley 2005: 101–2)[1]

In exploring these issues further we can usefully move our attention from policing as an abstract quality, expressing the power and authority of the state, to particular law-enforcers and the communities to which they belong. The focus within the genre on individual policemen or women, whether represented singly or in a team, is inevitable, since it is through such agents that the law operates. But at the same time, we are thus immediately drawn into a fictional world in which "the human face of state power" appears. "It is precisely the individualizing of the members of the corporate squad," observe Winston and Mellerski, "which mediates the public's fears of an overextended and inhumane police power" (1992: 6–7). Such (police) citizens then may represent the larger state, but they also stand apart from it. For they are, or can be, motivated by their own set of moral and social values. They are, in many cases, aware of individual rights and communal responsibilities that (abstract) law can compromise or overlook. They are aware too that the system they represent can be flawed, with its own forms of corruption, moral fault-lines and large-scale injustices.

The policeman then stands as a mediating figure between the authority of the law (and the social order it upholds) and the emphasis on an individual sense of moral responsibility, social justice, and freedom of expression. Franco Moretti calls this last "the liberal 'freedom from'" – the mental, moral, and even physical territory that the individual "desires to protect from the interference of society" (1983: 136). Clearly we are entering problematic territory here. But we can identify a range of positions emerging in this move from state authority to liberal citizen. First, there is the policewoman or man who carries out her or his professional role with no qualms about the law and justice s/he represents. Second, there is the cop, detective or FBI agent (usually one of the last two) whose social values – often what we might call "progressive" – lead her or him deeply to question that system, and/or whose independence and intelligence distance the officer from the larger policing group of which s/he is a part. Thirdly, there is a range of different positions available between these poles.[2]

I return, then, to the idea of mediation: how the authority of the law (and the social order it upholds) is balanced against the individual law-enforcer's judgments and values. I would immediately suggest here that the type of police novel focusing on the team, an "extended family" who follow a set of day-by-day procedural routines (Panek 2003b: 170), is less likely to question the dominant social system than those novels featuring one or two individual protagonists (though see Sjöwall and Wahlöö's work for one important exception). In what follows, I use Joseph Wambaugh's novel, *Hollywood Station* (2006), and Ian Rankin's *The Naming of the Dead* (also 2006), to illustrate each type of novel in turn.

Wambaugh is an important figure in the history of the ensemble police novel. An ex-policeman himself, he is at his best in representing American cop culture: the way cops work, the routines and dramas of the job, their conversations and jargon, their eccentricities and indulgences. He illustrates how the demands of the profession affect his protagonists' emotional lives and relationships, and highlights the procedural constraints that hamstring (as he would argue) their effective performance.

Wambaugh's narrative techniques in *Hollywood Station* are distinctive. The reader is plunged directly into the action in a fragmented narrative that follows the experiences of a dozen or so cops and detectives working the Hollywood precinct area. Wambaugh cuts from one set of incidents and points of view to another, representing the working and (to a lesser extent) private lives of his policemen and women. But he also focuses on two particular criminal couples, their crimes – which go from mail-theft to armed robbery and murder – and the inter-connections between them. These crimes are "solved" at the end of the story, but as much through the eruption of violent tensions between the male criminals as through police detection (though this too plays its part). And the money stolen in one of the most serious crimes (an ATM heist) is never finally recovered.

Wambaugh relies on rapid description and dialogue to carry the narrative, and his plotting is deliberately loose. His novel, moreover, is certainly not about the "process" of detection:

> In *Hollywood Station* you will notice that nobody knows where the money ends up except the reader. The detective gets it only partly right. As a cop I found this to be the fundamental truth of police work: be satisfied if somehow things work out well enough on their own. (J. Wambaugh, e-mail correspondence, May 26, 2007)

Wambaugh places strong emphasis on the constraining absurdities of a system in which police actions are systematically monitored, and compromised, by other regulatory agencies. As Flotsam (one of the cops on the Hollywood Station team) remarks: "being an LAPD cop today is like playing a game of dodgeball, but the balls are coming at us from every-fucking-where" (2006: 128).

The main agenda in Wambaugh's novel, then, is clear: a critique of the way the police are pressured from above, subjected to the demands of political correctness (see, for instance, 2006: 66), and – in the wake of the Rodney King incident and parallel cases (see 2006: 52–5) – monitored by investigative and supervisory agencies such as Internal Affairs Group and bound by mandates such as the federal consent decree agreement (Wambaugh's particular bête noir). The Oracle, the sergeant and father-figure to the station personnel, sums up what is clearly the authorial position too: "Aw shit, ... How're we supposed to police a city when we spend half the time policing ourselves and proving in writing that we did it?" (2006: 137).

Wambaugh clearly exposes some of the anxieties of modern American urban life in the novel, and most particularly those clustering around the subject of race. Indeed, racial and ethnic tension is one of the book's main subjects. But the author's empathy with his cop protagonists prevents any challenge to the existing social system and the "normative thinking" that upholds it. The only real subject of critique here has to do with the institutional arrangements governing police life. The description in the book of the Rodney King incident, which had such serious repercussions for the LAPD, is particularly revealing:

> That was a bizarre event wherein a white sergeant, having shot Mr. King with a taser gun after a long auto pursuit, then directed the beating of this drunken, drug-addled African American ex-convict. That peculiar sergeant seemed determined to make King cry uncle, when the ring of a dozen cops should have swarmed and handcuffed the drunken thug and been done with it. (Wambaugh 2006: 53)

This is not Wambaugh's own voice but one of his cop characters. However, in its larger novel-length context, this version of events endorses what is clearly the book's main message: that the city government (via the Christopher Commission) has contributed significantly to the unnecessary hampering of a police force that would operate more effectively without such "outside" controls. The one-sided version of the King incident given here, however, suggests the dangers inherent in such an approach – in too close a commitment to the ground-level cop point of view.

Ian Rankin's novel *The Naming of the Dead* works in a very different way. His narrative focuses on two police detectives (John Rebus and Siobhan Clarke) who work at the fringes of the larger police body to which they belong. And it asks the type of questions about the larger condition of society, its values and systems of authority, not to be found in Wambaugh. Rankin is clearly interested in addressing major social issues in his police novels, especially as they figure within a Scottish political and cultural context. So, for example, he identifies an earlier novel, *Black and Blue*, with a focus on "the economy/oil industry," *Fleshmarket Close* on "racism," *Let it Bleed* on "local politics," and *The Naming of the Dead* on "geopolitics" (I. Rankin, e-mail correspondence, May 12, 2007). Indeed, the very title of the last connects the personal with the political: dysfunctional family units and individual criminal behavior with the larger social and political system.

The phrase, "the naming of the dead," is repeated in a number of different contexts in a novel whose political freight is insistently emphasized by placing the 2005 G8 Gleneagles Summit at its structural center. The phrase is applied to Rebus's own brother (whose funeral begins the novel). But it also refers to Stacey Webster, an undercover policewoman working for Special Branch in Scotland as part of the security operation mounted for the summit, and her brother Ben, a Parliamentary Private

Secretary working in the fields of overseas aid and development, whose violent death during the run-up to the G8 summit Rebus is investigating. Stacey is twinned with Rebus in the fraught nature of their different family relationships and the sense of commemoration and loss associated with their respective brothers. But Rebus also applies this title phrase to the three serial murder victims in a second case with which he is involved, moving from the personal and intimate to the professional as he does so (see Rankin 2006: 263).

In making the G8 summit and the various protests, concerts, and events around it so central to his novel, Rankin grounds the individual and the family group, via the immediate criminal cases that Rebus investigates, within the larger political and social system. The summit at Gleneagles, with an agenda covering African poverty, climate change, the situation in the Middle East, global terrorism and the prolifera- tion of weapons, prompted massive demonstration and protest by all opposed to current government policies in those areas. This sense of crisis and self-division (between those in power and the populations they represent) is heightened, both in the book and in historical reality, by an external terrorist threat, the July 7 London bombings that occur while the summit is in session.

Rankin makes all this material central to his text. At a local level, Rankin describes the "panic on the streets of Edinburgh" (2006: 128), the center of the city become "a war zone" (2006: 137), as the demonstrators – some peaceable, some violent – gather and confront the police. He also shows the "[m]ayhem in Auchterarder" (2006: 235) that follows, as protestors try to breach the police cordon to reach the nearby Gleneagles estate. The violence of some protestors and their manipulation of the media are not downplayed. But neither are the Orwellian implications of a supervisory police pres- ence denying civil liberties by "using Section 60 powers to stop and search without suspicion" (2006: 163), removing their uniforms' identifying marks before they swing their batons (2006: 178), and the like.

Rebus is positioned to one side of the oppressive police and military presences around him. His disregard for authority and unauthorized actions bring suspension from duty in their wake (a suspension that does not stop his detective work). And throughout the text, despite his professional role, Rebus remains clearly distanced from the official system that supposedly contains him. Siobhan refers to the "bit of an anarchist" in him, while Rebus himself says, "I do my best work on the margins" (2006: 166).

It is clear from both the structure and particular content of the novel and from the emphasis on Rebus's marginality that the reader is expected to question the ways in which official authority systems work. At a global level, the reference to the Iraq War, and the way it is integrated into the larger textual discourse of commemoration and loss, makes it clear that the attitude toward that war is critical rather than celebratory. Siobhan's parents – children of the 1960s – are in Edinburgh as anti-war protestors. Siobhan meets them as they demonstrate, and listens with them to "The Naming of the Dead" – the "reading out the names of a thousand victims of the warfare in Iraq, people from both sides of the conflict. A thousand names, the speakers taking it in turn, their audience silent." Siobhan herself (like Rebus earlier) then connects this act of remembrance to her own police work:

> Because this was what she did, her whole working life. She named the dead. She recorded their last details and tried to find out who they'd been, why they'd died. She gave a voice to the forgotten and the missing. A world filled with victims, waiting for her and other detectives like her. (Rankin 2006: 112–13)

The word *victim* here carries the reader from those subject to acts of criminal violence to those dead and missing in the Iraq war. The boundary between the legal and the extra-legal, the official and the criminal act is thus deliberately narrowed and blurred.

Indeed, the blurring of such boundaries between what Rebus calls (in a different context) "the underworld" and "the overworld" (2006: 210, 213) is an ongoing motif in the novel. At the text's conclusion we find out that one of the deaths Rebus and Siobhan are investigating (Ben Webster's) may have been accidental. The other two sets of murders are, however, private acts of vengeance. One (Tench's) is the result of his emotional betrayal of Denise Wylie, a woman previously harmed in a case of sexual assault. The other set of serial killings is misleading, a diversion from the one murder (Trevor Guest's) that really counts, for Guest is killed by Stacey Webster to avenge her mother's murder, and her father's death that had then followed.

As is so common in all types of crime fiction, murder – an act that usually belongs in the private rather than public domain – seems to draw the reader away from a concern with the larger public and political system. But anxieties about that larger system cannot be put aside in a novel where the focus on "the overworld" of public and legal affairs, and questions about the way it functions, are so insistently foregrounded. Two plot-lines make this concern explicit. One involves Richard Pennen, a British businessman whose ventures in the "foreign aid" (2006: 320) arena are predominantly linked to the arms industry, and to "the money sloshing around" in the supposed "reconstruction" of Iraq (2006: 298–9). His interests are protected both by the British secret service (Steelforth) and by the private (and illegal) security force at his disposal. The other plot focuses on the relationship between Cafferty, an Edinburgh underworld boss described as a "virus" damaging everything it touches (2006: 352), and Tench, a powerful local Councilor battling him for control of his "turf" (2006: 210). Rankin makes it evident that despite Tench's work on behalf of the local community, this is no clear matter of virus and vaccine. Tench uses the criminal element in that community to his own ends, and his own desire for power resembles Cafferty's and that of all "tyrants and politicians" (2006: 213).

The metaphor of virus and vaccine as applied to criminality and the law is further undermined by the forms of policing represented in the text. Both Siobhan and Rebus are compromised by their relationships with Cafferty. Ellen Wylie, another policewoman, covers up her sister's murder of Tench, and Steelforth, a top Special Branch officer, helps his field-operative Stacey Webster, a serial murderer, escape the consequences of her acts. The fact that Webster has killed known sex-offenders, furthermore, means that none of the other police (bar Rebus and Siobhan) investigate these crimes very carefully. In this murky world, where the relationship between official systems and their criminal counterparts are so compromised, both Rebus and Siobhan have limited agency. Unable to do much "to change the bigger picture" (2006: 277), they nonetheless continue to be (in Siobhan's words) "good copper[s]" (2006: 368), working against all the odds (2006: 277–8) to act morally and to see justice done. It is the complex and ambiguous nature of the contemporary world Rankin represents that makes his police novels so powerful and so troubling.

In illustrating how different types of police novel endorse or contest an existing social system and its values, I have set an American against a British text. This clearly raises its problems. I am not saying that British police novels are necessarily "more sophisticated than [their] American counterpart" in terms of their "ideological and political" engagement (Winston and Mellerksi 1992: 14). There may indeed be some truth to this as a general rule, but writers like Chester Himes, and more recently James Ellroy, certainly disprove such blanket assumptions. Ellroy, indeed, undermines conventional boundaries between officialdom and criminality to an even more disruptive extent than Rankin, asking penetrating questions about the workings of the American social order as he does so. His reconfigurations of the history and geography of Los Angeles of the late 1940s and 1950s in his *L.A. Quartet* (1987–92) serve as entry points to a fictional world of collapsing boundaries, uncanny doublings and identity slippage, where political, economic, and media interest powerfully combine in the suppression of any version of the "truth," and where the law (and the investigative actions of his cop protagonists) are always subordinate to such interests.

My focus in this chapter has been on two types of police novel. One straightforwardly endorses the existing social order. The other shows a greater awareness of the pressures, stress points and failings of the social system it represents, both through an authorial control of narrative and structure and through the use of individual detectives who look to modify some of that system's abuses and injustices (where they can). We may judge some of the latter novels romantic in their emphasis on an individual conscience, a sense of morality and agency functioning independently of the institutional matrix. But despite such reservations, and despite (and perhaps because of) a final acceptance in most police novels that "trust in the normal agencies of law enforcement ... offer[s] ... the best hope of a remedy for [any] ills identified" (Priestman 2003: 188), the popularity of the genre continues to grow. It speaks resonantly to a readerly audience caught between a commitment to the (rapidly changing) social system in which it lives, and the protections thus offered against the various threats to its safety and well-being, and an awareness of the erosion of individual liberties, of the various social injustices, and dangers of authoritarian control, inherent in or condoned by that same system. Police fiction negotiates these various territories more directly and perceptively than many other forms of the contemporary novel, and it is unsurprising that its status and literary reputation have risen accordingly.

NOTES

1 Horsley quotes Messent (1997) here, and Pepper (2000).

2 Police novels also challenge the established system in other ways. Authorial intervention, for example, can represent a critical position not through character identification but rather through third-person description (as, at times, in Sjöwall and Wahlöö's novels), or through in an author's very shaping and handling of the narrative form and tone (as in Chester Himes). In some contemporary crime fiction (and in some police novels too), moreover, the sense of social malaise, of crisis and the large-scale social dysfunction is so strong that the normal binaries structuring the genre – good and evil, law and criminality, the civilized and the savage – collapse in on themselves completely. Thus the contemporary crime novel has been increasingly reshaped by the use of Gothic conventions and forms, which can further undermine the "rational, ordering" aspects of the novel of detection. Spatial constraints prevent me from developing this argument further, but I have the work of Thomas Harris particularly in mind here, and the way in which he "pointedly abandons the framework of the police procedural about two-thirds of the way through [his 1999 novel] *Hannibal*" (Horsley 2005: 146). See Messent (2000) for a more extended analysis.

14

Noir and the Psycho Thriller

Philip Simpson

The "psycho thriller" is a subgenre of the versatile thriller genre in which crime is represented as an outward manifestation of the internal workings of the pathological individual psyche. This examination of the psyche is harnessed to the relentless forward momentum of a narrative designed to generate suspense. Though physical action is usually present, the narrative focus is on the criminal mind; thus the psycho thriller is more character study than it is a plot-driven narrative. Its characters must confront a blend of psychological and physical danger, with the physical danger usually an external manifestation or result of a psychological imbalance. The lead character in a psycho thriller is often engaged in a death struggle with the destructive, violent impulses of his or her own mind, or entangled in a contest of wits with a more-or-less equally matched opponent. Because the conflict between characters is at its root psychological, the psycho thriller often blurs the line between good and evil, virtue and vice. The "good" and "evil" characters share many of the same traits and commit many of the same violent and/or venal acts, though for differing reasons.

"Thriller" as a literary phenomenon covers a great deal of territory. In fact, there are many different kinds of thrillers, including but not limited to the following as cataloged by David Glover: "racing thillers (Dick Francis), legal thrillers (John Grisham), psychological thrillers (Dick Lehane), political thrillers (Jack Higgins), futuristic thrillers (Philip Kerr), and so on" (2003: 139). But "thriller" in the generic sense tends to connote an emphasis on physical danger and action over in-depth character study. The term originated in the last few decades of the nineteenth century as a mildly disparaging label applicable to a broad range of American and British stories involving intense battles between individualistic heroes and vast criminal conspiracies and/or "super" villains. These thrillers, in turn, owed something to the mysteries of Wilkie Collins during the 1860s and 1870s. (See Mangham, chapter 30 in this volume.)

The plot of a thriller is structured on the basic principle of suspense, or the heightened audience anxiety created when the protagonist is fighting a contest against what looks like overwhelming odds. Because of the need to escalate the level of suspense to a climactic resolution, the textual reliance upon sensational plot devices (or "cliff-hangers") to keep intensifying the action is one of the thriller's most obvious features. The constant presence and awareness of physical danger in the narrative is the direct result of the hyper-exaggerated violence, or the threat of it. The criminals are often larger than life, imbued with a Gothic brand of pseudo-supernatural cunning and malice. The protagonist must prove his/her worth by overcoming a series of obstacles, each one more daunting than the last, thus demonstrating the thriller's indebtedness to tales of heroic romance. The moral plane of the thriller is usually quite defined, with the individual hero embodying admirable qualities, such as loyalty, and the criminal despicable ones, such as betrayal. But because the threat is represented as so dire, the hero usually dispenses with the social niceties of due process, much to the audience's approval, and exacts a kind of frontier justice to resolve the threat.

The thriller plot typically proceeds in linear fashion, from one danger to the next, until the ultimate defining confrontation between good and evil. However, the conflict usually addresses at some subliminal level a contemporary anxiety (or more than one) facing the thriller's audience: the fear of a foreign enemy, the fear of inner-city crime, the fear of the disenfranchised drifter, and so forth. For example, the pioneering thriller text *The Riddle of the Sands* (1903), by Erskine Childers, is at one level a serious contemplation of the global threat of the German navy. Likewise, Sax Rohmer's *The Insidious Fu Manchu* (1913) relies upon a foundation of Western suspicion of the Asian world for its success. The psychological component of the thriller is another vital part of what drives the engine of the plot. For any thriller to succeed, the characters must react to extreme stress and frankly incredible scenarios in at least somewhat plausible fashion to sustain audience belief in the plot. Thus, even the most action-driven of thrillers is built upon a psychological foundation. The psycho thriller simply calls more attention to that foundation.

The psycho thriller's relationship to other genres is not easy to delineate. Just to give one example, Robert Bloch's landmark crime thriller, *Psycho* (1959), often designated as the origin of the fictional psycho thriller, is just as often labeled "horror." In that the modus operandi of the criminal anti-hero may resemble the predations of the supernaturally evil and monstrous denizens of horror, the elision between horror and the psycho thriller is easily comprehensible, indeed inevitable. Tales of psychotic murderers unsettle the audience into looking askance at one's seemingly normal neighbors. Given that social paranoia depends on a sense of anxiety or even fear, and that the threat of violent or sadistic death at the hands of madmen (or madwomen) sparks that fear, the psycho thriller just as easily falls within territory more traditionally assigned to horror.

Having said this, it is nevertheless possible to point to one enormous influence on the psycho thriller, one which helps construct a coherent framework around the genre's history and direction. The psycho thriller derives its mood and atmosphere from another kind of literary phenomenon: the so-called "noir" style (see Rubin 1999 and Horsley 2001). Though for many noir is more commonly associated with film and the years following World War II, the noir style really has its origins in crime and so-called "pulp" fiction of the 1920s and 1930s. Of course, these stories are often lumped together under the generic "thriller" label, demonstrating if nothing else that sensational tales of varying proportions of crime and mystery and action are hard to pigeonhole for those who prefer their categorizations clean. Stories of lawbreakers, murderers, thugs, and other assorted violent criminals flourished in print during the nineteenth century and on into the first decades of the twentieth century. One need only look at the countless police memoirs, British "penny dreadfuls," and American "dime novels" to verify that fact. Yet the element of violent crime does not in and of itself define noir; rather, noir is stamped by its prevailing mood of pessimism, personal and societal failure, urban paranoia, the individual's disconnection from society, and cynicism. It addresses social issues, such as class inequities and the motivations behind adultery, in an explicitly uncompromising fashion typically not found in mainstream fiction. Noir's universe is bleak, divested of meaning. Flawed human beings in these stories must somehow make moral decisions with no transcendent foundation of morality on which to base them. The consequences of those decisions are frequently fatal and always tragic to someone.

While noir thrillers predate the World War II era, noir itself was not defined until the 1940s. The term is popularly believed to originate in the French crime-novel publishing imprint *Serie Noire*, which in turn inspired critic Nino Frank in 1946 to dub a certain mood and tone of postwar cinema as "film noir" (see Silver and Ursini, chapter 4 in this volume). These films, in turn, evolved from the fiction published first in pulp magazines and then novels in previous decades. While critical arguments over whether to define "film noir" as a genre or a movement continue to simmer if not boil over, noir in fiction is no less challenging to pin down. Is it a genre, with easily recognizable audience conventions? Or is it more a matter of mood, of tone, of style, of loosely connected ideas? Literary noir takes many different forms, "morphing" into such distinct but related subgenres as hard-boiled detective fiction, gangster fiction, and the psycho thriller. This transformative process does not follow a clearly delineated progression from one form to the next, nor are the categories mutually exclusive, but an examination of the structure, central concerns, and themes of psycho thrillers does reveal the relationship to literary noir.

The evolution of both noir and the psycho thriller must be understood within the larger context of the history of crime fiction, set in motion by the detective story of the late nineteenth century. Because the attempt to solve murders in classic detective fiction usually compels the investigator to examine the motives and hence the psyches of potential suspects in order to uncover the culprit, these stories can also be considered early entries in the psycho thriller canon. But beginning in the 1930s and on into the 1940s, two new kinds of crime fiction appeared in America: the "avenger-detective" and the "hard-boiled detective." According to Gary Hoppenstand, the avenger-detective "emerged ... to captivate the nation's fancy by effectively solving criminal problems with vigilante violence. This new detective ... catered to the societal desire for simplified solutions to complex problems" (1984: 91). These heroic, larger-than-life detectives, of which Walter Gibson's The Shadow is typical, fought supervillains who posed apocalyptic threats to the social order. The hard-boiled detective is a much more ambiguous character, less an upholder of social order than "an emblem of personal honor, a knight operating within a social structure of civic corruption, decadence and dishonesty" (Hoppenstand 1984: 92; see also Pepper, chapter 10 in this volume). The first hard-boiled detectives appeared in the pulp magazine *Black Mask* during the 1920s, giving rise to a story type identified by Michael Walker as one of the three noir narrative patterns (quoted in Robson 2005: 14). An amalgam of the traditional structures of popular American fiction (such as the adventure story and Western) and detective fiction, hard-boiled detective fiction dispensed with the notion of the consulting detective and replaced him with an anti-hero who solves cases with as much brawn as brain. However, the psychological focus still remains in the sense that these stories are character studies of people involved in extremely tense and trying circumstances.

The "founding father" of hard-boiled detective fiction is Dashiell Hammett, a writer who believed that the typical intellectual protagonist of detective fiction was too far removed from what detectives really do. For Hammett, detectives do not solve cases in drawing rooms; they solve them out in the field. They are characteristically employees, not independent contractors, but nevertheless exhibit independence from the mainstream society in which they operate. Over the course of eighty short stories and five novels, Hammett invented anti-intellectual, "real" detectives such as Sam Spade (*The Maltese Falcon*, 1930), Nick and Nora Charles (*The Thin Man*, 1934), and the Continental Op (*Red Harvest*, 1929, and *The Dain Curse*, 1929) to populate a new kind of crime fiction, one in which breakdowns of social law and order and individual identity are thematically intertwined. His work combines elements of social commentary, complexly plotted mysteries reminiscent of the realistic tradition he evolves from, and pulp-style adventure. Hammett's work is prototypically noir in the way it establishes the thematic landscape of corruption, violence, pathological sexuality, and psychological character study.

Raymond Chandler was another such writer, who gave literature the character of Philip Marlowe, first appearing in short stories beginning in 1933 and then novels, including *The Big Sleep* (1939), *Farewell, My Lovely* (1940), and *The Long Goodbye* (1954), among others. *The Big Sleep* is representative of Chandler's usage of noir conventions, with Marlowe exemplifying modern urban alienation from the pathetic and/or sordid characters he encounters. The detectives of Hammet and Chandler spoke the tough vernacular of the urban streets and back alleys, chasing thugs through a kill-or-be-killed world very far removed from the politely cerebral, locked-room mysteries of Christie and Sayers. The hard-boiled detectives, or "seekers" in Walker's terminology, embark upon quests through nightmarish worlds to solve problems of archetypal significance – in a sense, knight-errants with only their own codes of justice to guide them through a fallen world. They find no help from the recognized social institutions of justice, which have long since degenerated into corruption and thievery at the expense of the public. Their reactions to the stress of their quests form the psychological interest of the stories.

In these stories, many of them published in the popular "pulp" magazines of the day, killers used fists and knives and guns to commit graphic crimes motivated by passion and greed: easily understood acts even if not condoned by the readership. Sex and violence, so courteously disguised in most earlier crime fiction, become explicit. The line between detective and criminal becomes very thin indeed in the hard-boiled genre; methods of detection must as be of necessity brutal as well as quick-witted in order to survive the savage urban milieu in which these characters live. The hard-boiled detective uses his gun just as much as if not more than his brainpower. His modus operandi is often extra-legal or even illegal. He uses extortion, seduction, and torture as tools of his trade, deployed in the service of a strong individual code of ethics rooted in frontier mythology and owing little to the liberal fictions of modern culture. The apotheosis of this character type is the suitably named Mike Hammer, the creation of writer Mickey Spillane in the late 1940s. Dispensing vigilante justice and seducing women in the pages of thrillers such as *I the Jury*, Hammer is practically indistinguishable from the psychopaths he encounters in the grimy streets of a para-noid postwar cityscape from hell. The villains he combats are grotesque or even monstrous distortions of the human form, such as Lily Carver in *I the Jury*. Spillane, once reviled by establishment critics, has now been acknowledged for his significant contributions to the literature of noir, on a par with Hammett and Chandler.

The hard-boiled detective story is just one type of noir story, however. A second type of noir identified by Walker is the seduction/betrayal, in which a male protago-nist has the great misfortune to fall in love, usually against his better judgment and past experience, with a *femme fatale* who then turns on him. In this noir narrative, love and sex promise redemption in a fallen world but deliver only further heartbreak and disillusionment. The pattern is almost invariably one of a tough male being victim-ized by a symbolically castrating seductress, thus leading to the frequent accusations of sexism leveled against noir. James M. Cain is a writer whose eighteen different novels characteristically follow this pattern, departing from the mystery or detective "whodunit" to focus on the psyches of those who commit the crimes. Cain deliberately departed from the hard-boiled detective formula but used vernacular speech rhythms and frank sexuality to create characters as memorable as the hard-bitten urban detec-tives of Hammett and Spillane. Cain's first novel, *The Postman Always Rings Twice* (1934), establishes the formula with an adulterous affair between Cora Papadakis and drifter Frank Chambers that ends in the murder of Cora's husband, Nick, in order to bring them both insurance money and happiness. However, the scheme ends in mutual self-destruction, with the two of them turning against each other in a murder prosecution. By the time it is all over, Cora is dead in a car accident and Frank falsely convicted of her murder. The novel, laced throughout with scenes of physically rough sex in addition to violence, was a worldwide bestseller and led to praise from renowned critic Edmund Wilson and French writer and existentialist Albert Camus, who stated that his own novel *The Stranger* was based on Cain's story template. Cain followed this successful debut with other crime novels such as *Double Indemnity* (1936), *Serenade* (1937), and *Mildred Pierce* (1941). In *Double Indemnity*, an insurance agent named

Walter Huff, involved in an affair with Phyllis Nirdlinger, plots with her to kill her husband. As usual in a Cain story, ruin comes to Huff, ostensibly through being tracked down by a claims agent, but really by the compulsions of his own psyche.

The third pattern, according to Walker, is paranoid noir, best exemplified in the work of Cornell Woolrich. The noir protagonist of this kind of story is typically a persecuted victim, caught up in a deterministic world in which the standard rules have suddenly changed for the worse. Events have conspired to bring down the protagonist, either because of the main character's bad decisions or because of the actions of others. No matter what he or she does, the protagonist is doomed in a world that has targeted him or her for destruction. Besides its sense of fatalistic inevitability, Woolrich's mystery fiction is marked by its focus on character, as opposed to action and neat resolution of the central mystery by the main character. As a matter of fact, his characters are consumed by vast webs of events far beyond their control, usually involving murders whose implications stretch far beyond the limited lives of the characters. All investigations are doomed to failure; no resolutions are possible. His plots make little linear sense. What is key, however, is the pervasive atmosphere of futility even as the characters struggle against the inevitable. Some of his fiction, such as *The Bride Wore Black* (1940), even crosses over the genre line into the fantastic, an easy journey for Woolrich's paranoid vision in which surface events are controlled by unseen forces. His other novels include *Beware the Lady* (1940), *The Black Curtain* (1941), and *The Black Angel* (1943).

Through writers such as Woolrich and Chandler, the mood of classic noir had been established. Its next generation of practitioners preserved the mood but transformed it both to fit into and to critique the changing cultural landscape of America of the 1950s and 1960s. As Cold War tensions increased and domestic unrest over civil rights and American involvement in the Vietnam War intensified, noir became, if possible, even more estranged from superficial mainstream genres and idiosyncratic to the individual writer. Like any literary movement, noir progresses and grows through the contributions of each of its writers. So while the noir fiction of the 1930s and 1940s was pioneering, and the classic film noir cycle began and then faded throughout the 1940s and 1950s, later authors took noir in new directions.

One such direction was to move away from the amateur and private professional sleuths of the detective genre and acknowledge the primary reality of modern criminal investigation – that crimes are investigated and sometimes even solved by police departments. According to Carl D. Malmgren, the most distinctive feature of the police procedural is its focus on methodology, "systematically and intensively applied by a group of public servants who are usually working on more than one case" (2001: 172). The kinds of cases investigated by the police force, however, come right from the pages of hard-boiled fiction: murder, corruption, and all forms of vice in a contemporary urban setting. The narrative focus in the police procedural, as in hard-boiled fiction, remains on the detective navigating through the hazards of a fallen, corrupt environment, guided only by an inner compass of besieged idealism and an individual code of ethics.

A second direction in post-noir is the move inward, away from the blighted topography of the hard-boiled city streets and the public servants who police them and into the dripping back-alleys of the criminal and/or deviant mind. This closing in on the individual criminal consciousness mirrors in many ways the exponentially increasing alienation and self-consciousness of the postwar world. Malmgren emphasizes that crime fiction "features and focuses on a protagonist whose Selfhood succumbs to or embraces criminality. ... Readers occupy the perspective of the criminal and share his experiences. ... Crime fiction invites readers to undergo vicariously various forms of psychopathology" (2001: 193). Thus, in a key departure from earlier mystery and detective fiction, crime fiction does not necessarily depend upon the apprehension or death of the criminal. In fact, the criminal protagonist often gets away with his/her crime. It is at this juncture between classic noir and post-noir, between criminal fiction and earlier mystery and detective fiction, that one sees the shape of the contemporary psycho thriller begin to emerge. Some of the earliest psycho thriller fiction arguably includes Paul Cain's *Fast One* (1933), in which the deranged Gerry Kells tries to out-murder and out-con the mob in Los Angeles but dies in the process. Other prototypical psycho thrillers include Horace McCoy's *They Shoot Horses, Don't They?* (1935), about a man named Robert Syverten who kills his dance partner Gloria Beatty, and *Kiss Tomorrow Goodbye* (1948), told from the point-of-view of a psychotic gangster.

During the 1950s, two key writers in the transitional zone between noir and the psycho thriller are Jim Thompson and Patricia Highsmith. Jim Thompson solidifies the psycho thriller as a separate genre from noir, though his literary reputation did not grow until after his death in 1977. Thompson wrote over thirty novels, most published during the "paperback original" era of the late 1940s and 50s. Some of the better-known include *The Getaway* (1959), *The Grifters* (1963), *Pop. 1280* (1964), and *The Killer Inside Me* (1952), now one of his most famous. It is told from the first-person point of view of Deputy Sheriff Lou Ford, a nice guy given to uttering well-meaning clichés who also happens to be a sociopathic murderer. In Ford, the reader can discern many of the characteristics of what came to be known as the serial killer: a charming, friendly, and harmless-looking fellow in a position of respectability, but whose mask of normalcy conceals a twisted desire to harm other people for the most idiosyncratic of reasons. Integral to the effect that Thompson creates in the novel is the sense of intimacy between Ford's sociopathology and the reader. By the novel's end, the reader has come to understand and even empathize with Ford, simply because so much time has been spent in his psyche. Disturbingly, the narrative tempts the reader to partake of Ford's attitudes and, by implication, to assume some degree of his sociopathology. Such reader/character identification, seemingly benign in other types of fiction, takes on a disconcerting edge in the psycho thriller.

Patricia Highsmith's novels explore the intricate workings of the criminal psyche and by doing so take the reader vicariously through a variety of anti-social activities, including but not limited to murder (see Nicol, chapter 41 in this volume). Making her literary debut in *Strangers on a Train* (1950), which was adapted into a film of the same name by Alfred Hitchcock, Highsmith creates the character of Guy Haines, who encounters Charles Anthony Bruno on a train journey and agrees to murder Bruno's father if Bruno murders Haines's unfaithful wife. After Bruno does indeed kill the wife, Haines is reluctant to carry out his end of the bargain but eventually does so, thus leading to his ruin.

Highsmith's most enduring pathological character, however, is her anti-hero Tom Ripley, who debuted in the novel *The Talented Mr Ripley* (1956). Scarred by a traumatic childhood as an orphan and verbally abused by the aunt who raised him, Ripley retreats into a world of fantasy for self-protection and eventually loses much of his capacity to distinguish fantasy from reality. In this state of mind, he commits a murder and takes on the victim's identity. Thus begins Ripley's various sociopathic adventures, which continue throughout three further novels, *Ripley under Ground* (1970), *Ripley's Game* (1974), and *The Boy Who Followed Ripley* (1980). As the novels progress, Ripley becomes more confident and more secure in his sense of self, yet his moral hollowness infects those who come into contact with him. Under his influence, characters commit suicide, enter into criminal actions, and otherwise behave in ways they would not have done on their own. He can only assuage his moral vacuity through the intense excitement of criminality, yet he also believes he is a moral man who is superior to other criminals and to a society that is itself criminal. In fact, by the last novel in the series, Ripley arguably becomes a hero by using his criminal mind and experience in battle against a gang of kidnappers decidedly less sympathetic to the audience than Ripley is – a multi-novel character arc not dissimilar to that of Hannibal Lecter in the psycho thrillers of Thomas Harris. Taken together, Highsmith's novels pay homage to the moods and themes of noir by presenting an existential universe in which moral codes are fashioned by the individual, with little regard for whatever larger social codes there may be. These social codes are in themselves suspect, since individuals paying lip service to them are hypocrites or naifs who are easily corrupted. Yet the intimate examination of the deviant mind places the novels firmly within the psycho thriller tradition. The novels are, in fact, some of its foundational texts.

Robert Bloch also plays a crucial role in defining the parameters of the psycho thriller – in fact, the title of his most famous novel, *Psycho* (1959), lends the subgenre its most enduring label. *Psycho* is the tale of the fatal intersection of worlds between pudgy, forty-ish motel proprietor Norman Bates, whose name "Norman" is an ironic wordplay upon the concept of "normal," and Mary Crane, a secretary who absconds from her office with thousands of dollars of someone else's money. The bulk of the novel is told from Norman's point of view, so that the reader becomes intimately familiar with the contours of his psychopathology. Basing the novel in part upon the crimes of Wisconsin farmer Ed Gein, Bloch creates in Norman a character with a bifurcated mind – committing a number of murders of young women (including Mary) while assuming his dead mother's identity and then cleaning up the mess afterward in his "normal" identity. The novel was famously adapted for the screen by suspense director Alfred Hitchcock in 1960, so, rather unfairly, Hitchcock is usually given the credit for the storyline. However, the screenplay by Joseph Stefano is relatively faithful to the highlights of Bloch's narrative. Bloch had earlier written a character study of a psychotic man in *The Scarf* (1947), a tale about a serial strangler of women whose formative traumas at the hands of a verbally abusive mother and a horrific first sexual experience with a female teacher shaped the contours of his mental illness. Following *Psycho*, Bloch went on to write other psycho thrillers, including *American Gothic* (1974), *Psycho II* (1982), *Night of the Ripper* (1984), and *Psycho House* (1990).

During the decades of the 1960s and 70s, a plethora of films about psychologically warped characters, inspired by the success of *Psycho*, hit the movie screens, culminating in the infamous "slasher" movies of the late 1970s. A corresponding trend in fiction also developed, with Shane Stevens's novel *By Reason of Insanity* (1979) showcasing a type of sociopath soon to be popularly known as the "serial killer." Much of the novel is told from the point of view of the killer, Thomas Bishop, who is committed to an insane asylum at the age of eight for killing his abusive mother and then escapes at the age of 25 to begin a cross-country killing spree. But the novel that solidified the serial killer's hold on the bestseller lists was *Red Dragon* (1981), by Thomas Harris. Harris's book, about a psychologically tormented man who slays entire families and the criminal profiler who attempts to uncover the killer's identity before another family murder happens on the night of the full moon, established a popular new subgenre closely linked to the psycho thriller: serial killer fiction. While other authors over the years had written tales of characters who commit multiple murders for reasons rooted in their trauma-riddled pasts, Harris in *Red Dragon* merged the forms of the police procedural, detective fiction, and psycho thriller to produce a hybrid that both terrified readers and appealed to their intellects.

Like Norman Bates, *Red Dragon*'s killer is a pitifully lonely middle-aged man, Francis Dolarhyde, who often slips into an alternate identity, the titular "Red Dragon," based on painful memories of childhood abuse by a maternal caretaker. A retired FBI profiler, Will Graham, seeks to unravel the clues at the murder scenes to lead him to the identity of the Red Dragon. Graham is aided in his reading of clues by an unlikely ally: Hannibal Lecter, an imprisoned serial killer who also happens to be a psychiatrist. By creating a dynamic between a detective and a serial-killing psychiatrist, Harris's intent to create a psycho thriller could not be clearer. He perfects the hybrid detective/police procedural/psycho thriller subgenre in *The Silence of the Lambs* (1988). This time, the pairing is between a female FBI student named Clarice Starling and Lecter. Throughout the course of the novel, Starling trades personal information about herself to Lecter in exchange for his revelation of clues to lead her to the capture of yet another serial killer, "Buffalo Bill" (as the tabloid newspapers dub him) Jame Gumb. Following the cultural phenomenon of the Academy Award-winning film adaptation of *The Silence of the Lambs*, Lecter became the featured character in Harris's next two novels: *Hannibal* (1999) and *Hannibal Rising* (2006). In this last novel, Lecter becomes less a villain and more of a hero, engaged in an epic quest to reclaim his past memories and take vengeance upon the war criminals who cannibalized his younger sister on the Eastern Front in World War II.

As charted in detail in Philip L. Simpson's book *Psycho Paths*, Harris's success has spawned numerous tales of "profilers" seeking to "understand" psychologically damaged serial killers and other "extreme" criminals by reading the various clues left behind at their crime scenes and on their victims and, from those clues, discerning both motive and the criminal's identity. The "Kay Scarpetta" novels of Patricia Cornwell are among the most well known of the successors to Harris. Cornwell's heroine, Dr Kay Scarpetta, is the medical examiner for the State of Virginia. As a law enforcement professional (albeit not a cop), she deals with any number of dangerous criminals, but her serial-killing nemesis Temple Gault is one of the most cunning and dangerous. (Gault appears in *Cruel and Unusual* [1993] and *From Potter's Field* [1995].) The discovery of identity becomes a structuring theme in that the criminal seeks his or her identity through violence and the detective seeks to discover that criminal's true identity behind whatever monstrous mask the criminal dons. Typically, the detective ultimately wins the contest, the criminal is unmasked, and the social order temporarily restored. But, as Malmgren puts it, "the psychopathology of the criminal can leak out and affect members of the police" (2001: 179). So the lines between detective and criminal characteristically blur, intersect, and even disappear. Identities become fluid, and moral high grounds rapidly erode. Pathology begets pathology. So once again, the noir mood returns, in which a de-centered world proves ethically and morally ambiguous, corrupt, and dangerous. Psychological dynamics are repeatedly depicted as slippery, twisted, and treacherous.

Not all psycho thrillers pit the criminal against a master detective, of course. Some novels, such as Bret Easton Ellis's *American Psycho* (1991), explore the innermost recesses of the serial killer's mind, with any police presence in the narrative minimal or entirely absent. In that the world of Wall Street inhabited by serial killer Patrick Bateman is described by Ellis as morally bankrupt at its core, certainly *American Psycho* can be considered noir in temperament, a point made by Lee Horsley (2001: 221). Another of the contemporary writers who best captures the noir tone is James Ellroy, in police procedurals that can also be classified as psycho thrillers. In part, Ellroy's versatility in noir themes may be due to a traumatic event that shaped his youth: the unsolved murder of his mother, as chronicled in his autobiographical *My Dark Places: An L.A. Crime Memoir* (1996). As a crime writer, Ellroy is best known for his so-called "L.A. Quartet" novels: *The Black Dahlia* (1987), *The Big Nowhere* (1988), *L.A. Confidential* (1990), and *White Jazz* (1992). However, his novels *Because the Night* (1984) and *Silent Terror* (aka *Killer on the Road*; 1986 – his first written from the criminal's point of view) feature murderous psychopaths as chilling as any found in fiction. In *Because the Night*, Dr John Havilland, aka "The Night Tripper," is a psychiatrist who manipulates his patients into committing various violent crimes. Martin Michael Plunkett, the main character in *Silent Terror*, is a serial killer who teams up with another serial killer, state trooper Ross Anderson, to carry out a nationwide killing spree.

In conclusion, noir and the psycho thriller share many common features, as this brief survey has demonstrated. One of the most obvious connections between the two forms is the structural focus on violent crime and the individual psyches of those who perpetrate crime and those charged with preventing it. The noir movement focuses on social deviants and outlaws, and so does the psycho thriller. In both forms, notions of right and wrong are always up for grabs. The characters must make moral decisions based on individual circumstances, which leads them inevitably into conflict with other individuals making their own fateful decisions. Little moral difference exists between the characters, no matter which side of the traditional "hero/villain" binary they are on. The universe in which these characters clash is both existential and deterministic. Arbitrary chance may strike down the most virtuous of characters for no good reason whatsoever, but the essence of a character also usually determines his or her ultimate destiny in the narrative. Finally, noir and the psycho thriller critique the deleterious impact of social institutions upon psychological development. The tone of much fiction within these two genres, and the many others that are cousin to them, is one of paranoia. We fear that the institutions we depend on for our shared existence are not only fundamentally unsound but downright rotten. The psycho thriller enacts this fear for us in unforgettable fashion.

15

True Crime

David Schmid

The precise origins of the term "true crime" are obscure. In *True Crime* (2008), Harold Schechter's recently published Library of America anthology, the earliest piece dates from 1651 and the genre continues to flourish today. This longevity highlights the fact that true crime is a pop culture phoenix. Ever since the genre assumed its modern form with the publication of Truman Capote's *In Cold Blood* in 1965, its demise has been predicted at regular intervals. Although true crime has been through periods of boom, it has never experienced a bust both because it has always found a way to adapt and identify new markets and because certain types of true crime have been reliable sellers decade after decade. In 1993, *Publisher's Weekly* conducted an informal survey to find out which backlist true crime titles were always in demand:

> The consensus was that no title on Jack the Ripper ever gathers much dust … the hottest backlist titles now, in the true crime genre, deal with serial killers – the more gruesome and grotesque the better. (Weyr 1993: 39)

Paul Dinas, executive editor for the Zebra true crime book series, confirmed the importance of serial murder to true crime by saying, "Crime committed for money or revenge without sex is much less commercial, so I look for the sex angle, for murder, adjudicated killers, and increasingly for multiple bodies. The manner of death has to be very violent, very visceral" (quoted in Weyr 1993: 40).

If industry insiders like Paul Dinas feel that providing true crime books about vicious and bloody murders is giving the public what they want, the question remains: why do they want it? This question leads in turn to a more general question: how can we explain the popularity of true crime as a whole, a genre that has proved to be remarkably resilient in a cultural field dominated by fads and fashions? In this essay, I will focus on American true crime narratives and argue that the popularity of the genre can be explained by a feature of such narratives that goes back to the Puritan era, namely, a preoccupation with the representativeness of the criminal; that is, whether the criminal is more appropriately placed inside or outside the community. Puritan America expended much effort to (re)integrate the criminal into the community (if not literally, at least ideologically). Over time, however, this emphasis on integration shifted so that criminals came to be portrayed more as outsiders, as sources of pollution and/or monstrosity in the American body politic that needed to be excluded from the community.

There is a striking degree of consensus among scholars of early American crime narratives about the Puritan view of the criminal. Public hangings aroused tremendous popular interest during the Puritan period and, not surprisingly, ministers used sermons to instruct the crowds attending these events about the proper way to view the criminal's demise. These sermons were often as well attended as the executions themselves, and the fact of their subsequent publication and distribution made them extremely influential and well-known documents (see Moudrov, chapter 9 in this volume for more details).

Puritan crime narratives present criminals as representative members of their community, precisely because they have sinned. By emphasizing the dangerously thin line that separated the criminal from the spectator, Puritan ministers reasserted cultural, spiritual, and political authority. This authority turned out to be inherently unstable, however, precisely because it required generating public sympathy for the criminal. As long as the Puritans maintained strict control over the production of crime narratives, the dangers of sympathy could be contained. As Puritan influence over American society began to weaken in the late seventeenth century, however, other forms of true crime narrative began to appear that both exemplified and exacerbated that weakening.

Over the course of the eighteenth century, it became common to hear the criminal's point of view in crime narratives, first in reports of the criminal's dying words, and then later in the form of full-fledged biographies. The rhetoric of monstrosity, which aimed to place the criminal definitively outside the boundaries of community, also began to assume an important role in these new forms of crime narrative. The criminal was now viewed as a distinctly asocial creature and consequently, by the early decades of the nineteenth century, we have traveled a long way from the Puritan notion of the criminal as a representative member of the community. The concept of monstrosity, however, did not simply replace the concept of representativeness as an explanation of criminality. Rather, monstrosity and representativeness coexisted in an ambivalent, dialectical relationship that became the defining feature of true crime narratives from the early nineteenth century onward. Journalistic coverage of crime in nineteenth-century America provides additional evidence of the unstable combination of attraction and repulsion that structures such narratives.

American newspapers had traditionally paid very little attention to crime, not only because they did not want to waste precious space reporting on events that most people would already have heard about through other media, but also because they were constrained by a sense of delicacy and civic responsibility (Tucher 1994: 9–10). By the 1820s and 1830s, American newspapers were beginning to feature crime reporting, but its presence remained sporadic until the explosion of the penny press in the mid-1830s. During this period, the occurrence of highly marketable crimes such as the murders of prostitute Helen Jewett in 1836 and shopgirl Mary Rogers (the inspiration for Edgar Allan Poe's story, "The Mystery of Marie Roget") in 1841 led to the American press covering crime with the same enthusiasm and detail as other forms of popular literature. As Richard Altick has said of Great Britain during the same period, where the emergence of journalistic true crime followed a very similar pattern: "A series of murders and a nascent popular press: it was, in retrospect, a fated combination" (1970: 17).

As the nineteenth century progressed, crime narratives not only became a staple feature of journalism and American popular culture in general, but also tended to get more and more gory and sensational. Consequently, the need to stress the way these narratives combined moral instruction with entertainment became both increasingly pressing and less persuasive, as the effort to articulate a moral justification for reading such material became ritualized to the point of meaninglessness. In order for true crime narratives to become a legitimate, respectable genre, it was necessary to rearticulate a rationale for their consumption that avoided the problematic combination of morality and entertainment. This was a tall order, but beginning in the 1920s Edmund Pearson seemed to succeed almost single-handedly in raising true crime narratives to the level of literary art.

Significantly, Edmund Pearson came to true crime not as a minister or a journalist, but rather as a bibliophile and aesthete. A librarian by trade, Pearson's early publications were mostly about books and book collecting, an interest that was facilitated by his position as editor of publications at the New York Public Library, a post he held from 1914 to 1927. Roger Lane has argued that a shift in the direction of Pearson's career can be detected in the final chapter of his 1923 book, *Books in Black or Red*. Entitled, "With Acknowledgments to Thomas De Quincey," Lane describes it as "a rumination on that nineteenth-century author's famous essay entitled 'Murder Considered as One of the Fine Arts'" (1999: xii). The influence of De Quincey on Pearson's true crime narratives cannot be overstated. Pearson saw in De Quincey a way to have a legitimate, meaning non-sensationalist, interest in crime, as he explained in a 1928 essay, "From Sudden Death":

> De Quincey, writing a hundred years ago, is completely and delightfully modern in his method, and his work exploded a number of old superstitions. After he wrote it was never again necessary for any of his followers to assure their readers that murder is "an improper line of conduct." They could assume that they were writing for adults. (Pearson 1999: 226)

Using the blueprint established by De Quincey, Pearson published a series of hugely successful true crime books beginning with *Studies in Murder* in 1924 and concluding with *More Studies in Murder* in 1936. The success of Pearson's work gave true crime narratives a status they had never before possessed. Rather than being associated with the penny press or cheap forms of street literature, Pearson's true crime narratives typically appeared in high-class magazines such as *Liberty*, *The New Yorker*, and *Vanity Fair* before being published in book form. Pearson made it possible for true crime to come out into the open and take its place with other legitimate genres.

Several features of Pearson's work helped to make it legitimate. Again showing De Quincey's influence, Pearson presented himself as a connoisseur of crime, only interested in what he called in his 1923 essay on De Quincey, the "pure murder." Pearson wanted to make crime narratives safe for respectable members of society, and that meant rejecting most crimes as unfit for aesthetic contemplation. Given all the crimes Pearson excluded, what is left to constitute a pure murder? Pearson addressed this issue in an essay entitled, with disarming candor, "What Makes a Good Murder?":

> The amateur collector of murders is a much more discriminating person than the chance observer understands. He is often a determined antiquarian and reactionary; when any new murder comes out he bends his attention toward an old one ... disgusted by the blatant taste of the Chicago school of murderers, he returns to the first murder of all, that Cain-Abel affair. He prefers his murderers to be mellowed by time; to possess the rich bloom of age. (1999: 3)

Pearson was publishing his true crime narratives during the era of Prohibition, when mobsters such as Al Capone came to dominate the criminal landscape of America. With his aesthetic sensibilities offended by the brutality of the "Chicago school of murderers," Pearson's crime narratives turn back to a more civilized age and consequently the vast majority of his essays deal with nineteenth-century crimes. In particular, Pearson is attracted to certain moments in the crimes he writes about that to him are especially dramatic and meaningful. For example, in "Murder at Smutty Nose or the Crime of Louis Wagner" (an event that later became the basis of Anita Shreve's 1997 best-seller, *The Weight of Water*), Pearson focuses on the moment immediately before the murders begin: "He had only one house to consider; he knew that all the others were empty. There was no light in it. As for the helpless women asleep within, no philosophy or faith yet invented have been able to explain why such as they should be deserted by earth and heaven at this moment" (1999: 24). The philosophical and aesthetic questions raised by murder are of much more interest to Pearson than a blow-by-blow account of the murders themselves.

Pearson's imagination was particularly fired by the contrast between appearance and reality, or more particularly, between middle-class respectability and murderous deceit. The fact that gunmen and gangsters are so obviously dangerous is precisely what makes them uninteresting to Pearson. Many of the cases that Pearson writes about possess the desired combination of respectability and treachery, and together they form for Pearson a kind of canon of crime, the existence of which is yet more evidence of De Quincey's influence on Pearson's aesthetic approach to murder. Although Pearson wrote about a large number of different crimes during his career, he kept returning to one case that in his opinion had a unique status as the purest murder ever committed: the case of Lizzie Borden, accused and acquitted of killing her father and stepmother in Fall River, Massachusetts in 1892. In *Studies in Murder*, Pearson claims that the "Borden case is without parallel in the criminal history of America. It is the most interesting, and perhaps the most puzzling murder which has occurred in this country" (1999: 3).

The Borden case had everything that Pearson looked for in a good murder: the middle-class respectability of both the victims and the accused killer was thrown into dreadful contrast by the brutal way in which the victims were hacked to death with an ax. The case was complex enough for Pearson to show off his powers of deduction and his narrative skills in recreating his version of events. But perhaps most importantly, there remained something insoluble about the Borden case, and this enduring residue of mystery made the murders at the Borden House, as Pearson put it in "The Bordens: A Postscript," "the most fascinating of all puzzles. Neither detectives, lawyers, nor criminologists can solve the questions which they present, for they lie deep in that mysterious region, the human heart" (1999: 302).

Such sentiments, along with Pearson's determined refusal to engage with the crimes that dominated his own time, may suggest that he wanted to elevate the genre of true crime out of history altogether, turning it into a disinterested object of aesthetic contemplation. In spite of De Quincey's profound influence on Pearson's work, however, there was one important way in which Pearson differed from his mentor. Unlike De Quincey's "murder-fancier," who remained relatively unconcerned about such issues as the criminal's punishment, Pearson engaged vigorously with contemporaneous debates about criminal responsibility, the insanity defense, the death penalty, and the causes of crime. This mixture of antiquarianism and contemporaneity was probably the single most important reason for Pearson's success. Pearson's habit of concentrating on old cases helped to give true-crime writing an air of respectability, while his involvement in the hot-button legal issues of the day gave true-crime work a social utility that made reading it almost a civic duty, rather than evidence of the reader's prurience.

Because Pearson's work is filled with vigorous defenses of the death penalty and attacks on the concept of the insanity defense one might assume that he would argue that criminals are a class apart, set definitively outside the community of law-abiding citizens. And yet, just as so much of Pearson's true-crime writing refuses to take the appearance of middle-class respectability for granted, his support of the concept of criminal responsibility is dictated by his determination not to view criminals as monsters who are separate from ordinary people:

> Most of the folk who have committed murder are not insane; they are "nastily like ourselves," and their dreadful deed only represents something which, under certain circumstances, we might have done. The plea of insanity may be raised to save a guilty man, or it may be only a cry of horror to prove that there is a wide difference between the wicked murderers and ourselves, – virtuous folk that we are! (Pearson 1930: 26–7)

Pearson's analysis of how the insanity defense can be used to construct the criminal as a comfortably distant monster is perceptive; Pearson forces his readers to face the uncomfortable fact that the difference between them and the criminal is one of degree, rather than kind. He insists on this point not to exonerate the criminal, but rather to encourage a clear-eyed attitude toward society's responsibility to punish the criminal. In this respect, the Puritans had as much influence on Pearson as did De Quincey, and it is this mixture of Puritanism and aestheticism that gives Pearson's work its distinctive flavor and makes it very different from more contemporary examples of American true crime.

The generation of true crime writers who followed Pearson worked hard to maintain the new respectability he had won for true crime narratives, often by distinguishing their work from less respectable examples of the genre. For example, Anthony Boucher, in his 1958 introduction to Edgar Lustgarten's *The Murder and the Trial*, argues that "Fact-crime writing – as distinguished from the sensational journalism of most "true-crime" magazines – demands four qualities from its maker: *literacy* ... *scholarship* and dogged research ... *insight* into human character and motives ... [and] a feeling of *irony*, of relish" (1958: x, original emphasis). Boucher asserts the legitimacy of non-sensational true crime by giving it generic properties, thus allowing it to inhabit the same plane of respectability as other middlebrow genres. Like Pearson, Boucher also actively creates a canon, but one consisting not of the cream of crimes, but the cream of true-crime writers:

> you'll do well to become acquainted with the basic books by The Masters. For the pinnacles to date of writing about true crime, read William Bolitho's *Murder For Profit* ... F. Tennyson Jesse's *Murder and Its Motives* ... Lustgarten's *The Murder and the Trial* ... Edmund Pearson's *Studies in Murder* ... and William Roughead's *Class Crimes* ... These are probably the authors' best or most typical collections. (Boucher 1962: 253)

Boucher legitimates interest in true crime by employing evaluative criteria borrowed from literary criticism.

In retrospect, Pearson's career represents the last flowering of the detached, ironic, aesthetic approach to murder inaugurated by De Quincey. By the 1930s, despite the best efforts of men like Boucher, the industry of true crime writing had simply become too large to need the veneer of respectability; instead, it was quite content to churn out gory and sensationalistic narratives for an eager public. However, what Pearson and Boucher could not have known is that another sea change was going to take place in true crime. Although the book that would revolutionize the genre, Truman Capote's *In Cold Blood,* seemed to have the same combination of detachment and engagement that characterized Pearson's work, Capote's understanding of what it meant for the author of true crime to be detached and engaged was very different from Pearson's. *In Cold Blood* inaugurated a period of unprecedented authorial intimacy with the subjects of true crime narratives.

Every study of true crime acknowledges the fundamental importance of *In Cold Blood* to the genre. While Pearson should be given the credit for making the genre respectable it was Capote who made true crime enormously profitable. Although a writer of Capote's stature had never written true crime before, this was not the most controversial aspect of *In Cold Blood*. Far more controversial was Capote's loud and oft-repeated claim that his study of the murder of the Clutter family in their farm-house in Holcomb, Kansas, in 1959 constituted a new genre: the non-fiction novel. This claim provoked heated debate among critics and was largely responsible for the book's huge sales and the enormous amount of publicity that surrounded its publication.

Capote's claim that *In Cold Blood* was the first example of a new genre focuses attention on what exactly was new about Capote's text compared to earlier true crime narratives. As we have seen, Pearson attempted to remove sensationalism from true crime by cultivating a pose of ironic authorial detachment from the murder. However, one should not infer from this pose that Pearson was absent from his work. As we have seen, Pearson was a very strong presence in his work, constantly commenting on a range of issues in a concerted effort to steer the reader's opinion in the desired direction. As engaged as Pearson was with the issues raised by his essays, however, he remained detached from the individuals he wrote about. Although one can detect a note of admiration for an individual like Lizzie Borden, that admiration was so rigorously controlled that Pearson was never in danger of identifying with the criminal. Capote, by contrast, was much more engaged with the subjects of his narrative than Pearson. But although Capote spoke at length in interviews about his relationship with the murderers, Perry Smith and Richard Hickock, a far more influential feature of *In Cold Blood* was the fact that the formal structure of the book hides this relationship. By inventing the "non-fiction novel," Capote claimed to have written a completely objective account of the case by scrupulously removing every trace of his presence from the text.

Even though Capote spent nearly six years gathering information on, researching, and living with the case, he appears nowhere in the book and the word "I" is never used. Although Capote supposedly made this decision in the interests of objectivity, he had to endure repeated accusations about the supposed factuality of his book; critics pointed to numerous examples of dialogue between characters that Capote could not possibility have known about to argue that there was a good deal more fiction in Capote's book than he admitted. Perhaps the most egregious example of fabrication is the book's closing episode, which consists of a conversation between Alvin Dewey, the local FBI agent who supervised the murder investigation, and Sue Kidwell, a friend of Nancy Clutter, one of the murder victims. This conversation takes place some four years after the main events of the book, and there is no indication of how Capote could have reproduced this conversation in such detail. Capote indicates, in a Preface to *In Cold Blood*, that all conversations he did not hear personally were verified for him by reliable sources. Not surprisingly, this assurance was regarded as inadequate by many of Capote's readers.

Although Capote's removal of himself from *In Cold Blood* attracted intense criticism, it has had a profound influence on the subsequent development of the true crime genre. The "invisible" author has now become a standard feature of true crime narratives, allowing writers such as Ann Rule an enormous amount of leeway in how she presents her facts. I am not suggesting that Ann Rule distorts the facts, but she is able to enhance those facts with passages that read as though they come from popular fictional genres, such as the romance novel: "As 1981 arrived and the crowd whooped and whistled, Janis Miranda was already half in love. Inwardly she marveled at that; she was the woman who didn't trust men. She had been bruised in the wars of love too many times. But this man was different. Somehow special. When Randy Roth asked if he might call her, she agreed enthusiastically" (Rule 1993: 10). Although Rule cannot possibly know the exact thoughts that went through Miranda's head at this moment, the contemporary true crime reader does not care; the incident and the way it is recounted ring true and that is what matters. The fact that contemporary true crime writers such as Rule do not need to apologize for the presence of fictional elements or defend the veracity of their narratives suggests that the true crime reader of today has a very different understanding of what the "true" in "true crime" means than the reader of Edmund Pearson's day. In Pearson's time, "true" crime meant sticking to the facts as closely as possible, struggling to write what Pearson once referred to as "painfully veracious histories" ("Scenery by Currier and Ives," Pearson 1999: 300). Now, the truth of true crime means getting to the heart of the matter; emotional truth is prized far more than literal truth.

Although *In Cold Blood* has had a profound influence on contemporary true crime, there is one important aspect of Capote's work that has generally not been adopted by later writers in the genre. A significant part of Capote's intimate relationship with Perry Smith and Richard Hickock was an attempt to generate public sympathy for them by arguing that they may not have been legally responsible for their crimes because they were suffering from temporary insanity. Those true crime writers who acknowledge Capote's influence on their work usually politely ignore his sympathy for Smith and Hickock, largely because that sympathy is now completely absent from contemporary true crime, a fact that illustrates the complicated relationship between earlier forms of discourse about crime and contemporary true crime narratives.

In some respects, the absence of sympathy for the criminal in contemporary true crime narratives recalls the Puritan view of sympathy as a dangerously unstable emotion. In other words, inasmuch as sympathy for the criminal implies a recognition of the criminal's humanity, a humanity shared by both the criminal and the reader, contemporary true crime writers eschew sympathy altogether, preferring instead to present their readers with the comforting thought that the monsters they write about have nothing to do with them. In this respect, contemporary true crime departs sharply from both Puritan crime narratives and the work of Edmund Pearson. Even though the Puritans recognized the dangers of sympathy, they still saw it as a necessary part of crime narratives because of the role they wanted those narratives to play in the ideological reintegration of the criminal into the community. Pearson was much more openly hostile to the idea of feeling sympathy toward criminals, but he would definitely have resisted turning criminals into asocial monsters with no visible connection to the reader of true crime.

No contemporary true crime writer exemplifies the complex inheritance of earlier forms of true crime narrative better than Ann Rule. Rule has stated that "I was very impressed by Capote's *In Cold Blood* in 1964 [*sic*] and used to wish that I could someday, somehow, get into a killer's mind and write about it" (A. Rule, Letter to the author, 1 October 1996). Although Rule would eventually get her wish, her route to publishing true crime was very different from Capote's. After graduating from the University of Washington with a degree in creative writing in 1954, Rule trained to be a cop with the Seattle police department until she left the force after the discovery of her severe nearsightedness. Although Rule began trying to sell true crime work in 1963, she did not get her break until 1968 when Al Govoni, editor of the national publication *True Detective Magazine*, offered Rule the position of Northwest "stringer" for the magazine. Over the next ten years, Rule wrote literally hundreds of true crime articles, soon breaking out of the true crime magazine ghetto and publishing with magazines such as *Cosmopolitan*, *Ladies' Home Journal*, *Redbook*, and *Good Housekeeping*. Rule was by now an established figure in true crime but the publication of her first book, *The Stranger beside Me*, in 1980 took her career and the genre of true crime to a new level. The success of *Stranger*, which told the story of Rule's friendship with the notorious serial killer Ted Bundy, was a watershed for the genre in several ways. For one thing, it established the fact that books about serial killers could be bestsellers. Although the market quickly became flooded by a tidal wave of books about serial killers of the past and present, Rule's book has maintained its place at the head of the pack, having gone through dozens of printings since its original publication.

The critical response to the boom in true crime sparked by Rule's success has been complex. As I mentioned at the start of this chapter, one reaction has been to prophesy, regularly, the end of the boom, but this prophecy is as much a product of wishful thinking as it is an accurate assessment of the state of the industry. Rather than trying to wish it away, a more productive aim would be to explain the reasons for the success of modern true crime and, in particular, to analyze to what extent this success is dependent upon the dialectic between the criminal-as-monster and the criminal-as-representative that has been a structuring feature of so many forms of American true crime narrative.

A large part of Rule's success is due to a feature of her work that recalls both Pearson and Capote, albeit in different ways. Rule gives true crime narratives an ethical dimension and also stresses their social utility. Rule's ethical take on the genre comes through in the way her work frequently articulates a "pro-woman" emphasis, an emphasis which takes several forms, including Rule's habit of dedicating her books to the victims of crime. By emphasizing the fact that women are overwhelmingly the victims in the cases she writes about, Rule makes a seemingly obvious point and yet it is a point rarely mentioned by other true crime writers. In a similar vein, Rule frequently writes about her work with victims' rights groups, claiming that these groups keep her focused on the victim rather than the criminal. Finally, Rule has often argued that true crime narratives have educational value, and that the duty of the true crime writer to educate the reader means the writer should eschew sensationalism:

> I have always believed that true crime writing should not only absorb its readers but also educate them. There is no need to embroider spectacular cases; human behavior is in and of itself more fascinating than anything found in fiction. Those who have read my work before know that I do not stress blood and gore and grotesque details; I focus my research on the *whys* of murder more than on the *how*. (Rule 1993: xi, original emphasis)

It is easy to dismiss this presentation of the ethical and utilitarian aspects of true crime as a cynically self-serving attempt to distract our attention from the exploitative elements of the genre. We must also acknowledge, however, that Rule's claims are, by and large, accurate descriptions of her work. Like Pearson, Rule is relatively uninterested in the physical details of homicide, preferring instead to concentrate on what these acts of violence tell us about the complexities of the human heart.

The aspect of Rule's work that is most representative of modern true crime, however, can be found when she describes the serial killers she writes about in the early part of her career as monsters, as in *Lust Killer*, her book about Jerome Brudos: "In the convoluted medicalese of the psychiatrist, Jerome Henry Brudos was quite sane, and eminently dangerous. In the language of the man on the street, he was a monster" (Rule 1983: 166). Typically, in presenting the serial killer as a monster, Rule defines herself against "expert" discourse, which is dismissed for being disconnected from reality. The perception of the killer's monstrosity, by contrast, is offered as eminently commonsensical, an obvious fact about the killer that any sensible, objective person can see. From the point of view of the modern true crime writer, stressing the monstrosity of murderers is also a practical necessity, solving as it does the problem of how to build a compelling narrative around such a dull and ordinary individual as the average killer.

The presumption of the killer's monstrosity also dictates some more specific features of true crime narratives, many of which are driven by a desire to explain (or disavow) the killer's apparent ordinariness. One of the most common images in true crime narratives about murderers, for example, is that of the "mask of sanity," a term originally developed by psychologist Hervey Cleckley in a 1964 book with the same title. The idea of the mask of sanity turns the killer's apparent ordinariness into the most compelling sign of his evil by depicting that ordinariness as a facade hiding the "truth" of the killer's identity. Donald Sears, for example, comments that "perhaps the most frightening characteristic of the serial killer is that he usually presents to the public the image of the all-American boy, the nice man next door, or the shy, quiet neighbor down the street" (1991: x). Sears goes on to reassure his reader that the killer's apparent normality is false: "underneath his benevolent appearance lies a driven killer who stalks his prey with determined fervor" (1991: x).

But although the presumption of monstrosity in true crime narratives is necessary in order to distance murderers from ordinary men, this presumption immediately creates a dilemma: how do we tell the difference between the mask of sanity and a real face? If killers appear to be ordinary men, how can we distinguish between "apparently" ordinary men who are "actually" killers and "really" ordinary men? The intractability of these questions means that the mask of sanity as a diagnosis and sign of monstrosity is never enough; it always has to be bolstered by a second common feature of true crime narratives: the search for the origins of deviance.

One way in which true crime narratives can undermine and demonize the murderer's apparent normality is to conduct a search for the origins of the killer's deviance in his childhood. This is a distinctively recent innovation in true crime. There is nothing in Pearson's work that comments upon the idea of studying the influence of an individual's childhood on an adult's actions. Nevertheless, I think it reasonable to surmise, based on his frequent withering comments about psychology and psychoanalysis, that Pearson would have felt this idea to be just one more in a long line of "mitigating" factors designed to erode the concept of criminal responsibility and as such he would have resisted the idea vigorously.

Capote is much more sympathetic to the idea that childhood trauma can explain adult actions; indeed, this is part of the reason Capote believed Perry Smith in particular deserved to be treated mercifully. But although Capote and the contemporary true crime writer may both believe in the Wordsworthian cliché "the child is father to the man," this phrase has a very different resonance in recent true crime narratives. Rather than going back to the killer's childhood to look for mitigating circumstances, modern true crime writers go looking for details in the killer's childhood that will allow them to claim that the seeds of monstrosity have been lurking, though cunningly disguised, in the killer since childhood. The vast majority of true crime work on a figure such as Ted Bundy, for example, contains this emphasis, and the detail most often alluded to in Ted Bundy's childhood is described by ex-FBI agent John Douglas:

> Though the family photos of Ted with tricycle and red wagon or sled and snowman, building sand castles at the beach, or trimming the Christmas tree seem typically idyllic and middle American, there were other warnings that things were not all okay with the youngster. When Louise's [Bundy's mother's] sister, Julia, was fifteen, she awoke on more than one occasion to find her three-year-old nephew placing kitchen knives in the bed next to her. Ted, she said, "just stood there and grinned." (Douglas and Olshaker 1998: 299)

Douglas draws a rather heavy-handed contrast between the Norman Rockwell episodes from Bundy's life and a scene straight out of a slasher movie in order to emphasize that Bundy's monstrous qualities were practically innate. The conjunction of Bundy and knives obviously lends itself well to the retrospective construction of deviance, but if no suitably deviant episode exists, one can be constructed by going back to seemingly innocuous childhood incidents and reinterpreting them in the light of later events.

The most sustained example of what might be called the "Had I but known" school of true crime narratives is *A Father's Story*, Lionel Dahmer's memoir about his infamous son Jeffrey, which is filled with examples of the ordinary turned into the ominous: "When we went fishing, and he seemed captivated by the gutted fish, staring intently at the brightly colored entrails, was that a child's natural curiosity, or was it a harbinger of the horror that was later to be found in Apartment 213?" (1994: 54). All such questions are clearly meant to be rhetorical. In the world of the true crime narrative, the lives of murderers are bound by an inexorable logic that leads them to their crimes. The reader of true crime takes great comfort in the deterministic logic that binds these children to their evil fate from their very earliest days. No matter how absurd this determinism may be, it has the advantage of making that apparently ordinary life as deviant as possible from its very beginning.

I have described in this chapter the significant points of continuity and difference in the ways contemporary true crime narratives and earlier examples of the genre manage the tensions involved in deciding whether criminals should be located inside the community or outside, whether they should be seen as representative subjects or monstrous outsiders. Although the emphasis is overwhelmingly on the need to cast the criminal out of the social, I have demonstrated that this move can never be performed cleanly or conclusively by any culture because of culture's complex and ambivalent relationship with the figure of the criminal.

16
Gangs and Mobs

Jonathan Munby

Towards a History of Gangster Fiction

The fact that a substantial amount of crime fiction features gangs and mobs has not encouraged academics, publishers or bookstores to adopt and deploy the term "gangster fiction" in any systematic way. I contend, however, that a host of different works covering a significant period of time share conventions and tropes sufficient to constitute a distinct tradition of gangster literature. Symptomatically, perhaps, it is under the "true crime" category that gangster fiction's closest relation is to be found (see Schmid, chapter 15 in this volume). Biographies of mobsters and "exposés" of crime syndicates by investigative journalists and undercover agents are only a small step from the fiction that is inspired by real underworld escapades. Like "true crime", gangster fiction explores an otherwise hidden parallel world.

The genre label "gangster" crosses over from Hollywood. And this is entirely apposite given that many authors associated with organized crime literature have also had successful careers as screenwriters. The overlap between screen and print media in the case of gangster fiction is not coincidental, having everything to do with the way formal and thematic concerns of the first gangster novels informed the earliest period of "talking pictures" (the early 1930s). As I have argued elsewhere, at the very moment Hollywood was wired for sound, it found in the gangster story an ideal way to sell the unique qualities of this technological innovation. Gangster stories were plucked straight from topical and sensational news headlines, delivering to audiences an intensely "realist" experience replete with street argot, gunfire, and the sounds of the automobile (Munby 1999: 34). Similarly, gangster fiction attended to what made gangland linguistically distinctive. This necessitated challenging predominant literary treatments of the underworld and replacing them with a new set of conventions. This chapter is in part a first foray in defining gangster fiction and is not exhaustive in its analysis. It concentrates strictly on American gangster fiction, focusing primarily on the way this literature has mediated our understanding of the contradictory character of capitalism and of what constitutes "legitimate" culture – especially with regard to "organization."

Original Gangsters: Lippard and Fitzgerald

Various works might have a claim to being the original gangster novel. F. Scott Fitzgerald's *The Great Gatsby* (1925), for example, is certainly significant as one of the first serious attempts to engage the underworld in terms that broke with a legacy of reform aesthetics in representing the gangster. Writing in the hey-day of the "classic" (Prohibition-era) gangster, Fitzgerald provided a cutting insight into the hypocrisy of the social elite and brokered the possibility for a new perspective on so-called mobsters. They were no longer to be seen as fallen criminal "others" against whom a moral majority gains its sense of legitimate selfhood and privilege. Instead, Gatsby, as the projection of public fear and desire in the midst of Prohibition and laissez-faire capitalist behavior, reveals how thoroughly the American Dream is contaminated. Gatsby does not reveal much about himself. He is a man with a mysterious past, rumored to have made his money through bootlegging. He operates as a "front" for a major gangster, Meyer Wolfsheim – a Jewish-American whose ethnicity bars him from entry into "legitimate" social circles. Wolfsheim is a thinly disguised reference to the real mob boss, Arnold Rothstein, highlighting the extent to which even a "higher" work of gangster literature could allude to the most topical material.

In *The Great Gatsby*, Fitzgerald engages the moral bankruptcy of a certain kind of capitalist business ethos. As Stephen Brauer notes, Gatsby's father connects his gangster son's ambitions to those of the industrial moguls. At Gatsby's funeral, his father states, "Jimmy was bound to get ahead. If he'd lived, he'd of been a great man. A man like James J. Hill. He'd of helped build up the country". The reference to Hill (a self-made railroad tycoon) suggests that the gangster's desires and achievements overlap with those of the robber barons (Brauer 2003: 51). At the time of writing *The Great Gatsby*, the line between legitimate and illegitimate business enterprise had become increasingly blurred. The gangster's profiteering through bucking Prohibition helped endear him to the public. In self-defense, for example, Al Capone famously declared: "I'm just a businessman. I've made my money supplying a public demand … why should I be called a criminal?" (Allsop 1968: 365). While such pronouncements revealed organized crime's resemblance to capitalist entrepreneurship, they also highlighted the degree to which business itself might be construed as criminal.

If *The Great Gatsby* might be considered the first recognizable major work of gangster fiction, there is one forebear worth considering as having prior claim. *Quaker City* (first published serially in 1844 as *The Monks of Monk Hall*) was the work of Christian Socialist reformer George Lippard. Variously categorized as an example of "city mystery" fiction that flowered in the 1840s (D. Reynolds 1988: 82–7; 1995) and urban Gothic (the book is dedicated to Charles Brockden Brown), *Quaker City* sets precedents for what would emerge as underworld literature. Produced initially in ten serial installments for a Philadelphia penny newspaper, the work was one of the first to exploit fully the new possibilities of mass printing and became the bestselling novel of its time, with over 100,000 copies sold in two years (Reynolds 1988; Fiedler 1970). Lippard's successful attempt to reach a mass audience involved not simply developing the potential of cheap magazine copy but jettisoning literary language for a vernacular that corresponded to the world he wished to represent and reform. As Lazar Ziff notes, the work was divided into a series of "penny-dreadful plots" delivered via a "hack" aesthetic (Ziff 1982: 92). In line with Lippard's own proclamation that "literature merely considered as an art is a despicable thing," Leslie Fiedler has maintained that "The intent is clear … : to write 'badly' at all costs … to prefer clichés to well-turned phrases; and to let the grammar take care of itself" (Fiedler 1970: xvi).

True to his belief in popular discourse, Lippard culled the basis for *Quaker City* directly from newspaper coverage of a sensational 1843 court case. The book was inspired by the acquittal of Singleton Mercer, a man of reputable background, who had shot and killed the scion of a wealthy Philadelphia family, Mahlon Heberton, on the ferry between Camden, New Jersey, and Philadelphia. Mercer claimed that a few days beforehand, Heberton had seduced and raped his 16-year-old sister, Sarah, in a brothel. The jury accepted Mercer's plea of temporary insanity. *Quaker City* featured the rape of a young woman, Mary, by an upper-class rogue, Gustavus Lorrimer – a brazen recycling of the Mercer-Heberton incident and the themes associated with it. This debasement story intersects with that of the homicidal Devil Bug – perhaps the prototype for the mobster "heavy." *Quaker City*'s labyrinthine plot involves murder, seduction, and vice perpetuated nightly by a secret fraternal cadre of judges, lawyers, bankers, doctors, and politicians – the "Monks of Monk Hall" – for whom the Devil Bug is the doorman and pimp procurer. His mixed-race background, however, enables him to work for two "organizations" inhabiting Monk Hall. Not only does he service the elite upstairs but he also harbors an army of vagabond thugs in the basement, releasing them at night to terrorize the streets. Haunted by the specters of his murder victims, Devil Bug has a dream vision of urban apocalypse – of Philadelphia in 1950, a futuristic Sodom destroyed by an army of the oppressed returning as the living dead. Devil Bug's monstrous outward appearance, however, disguises an honorable soul: he is the protective father of his illegitimate daughter, Mabel. Overall, *Quaker City* provided a lurid picture of the asymmetry of the class system, using sexual abuse as a metaphor to highlight the sadistic oppression of the disenfranchised.

Although Lippard's story revealed the real mob to be a debauched upper-class fraternal society rather than a gang of street hoodlums, it spawned several possibilities for gangster literature. Indeed, Lippard could be regarded as the Godfather of gangster and organized crime fiction in America. He shifted Gothic sensibilities toward the contemporary urban setting and drew inspiration from a true crime. Monk Hall is neither in an exotic land nor of an earlier medieval time. It is located in Philadelphia's Southwark neighborhood in the "now" of 1842. *Quaker City* advanced a conspiratorial idea about the powers of a hidden criminal society, articulating a deeply ambivalent view of capital as both the forger of institutionalized corruption and the basis for any fight against oppression. Furthermore, Lippard affected a "street" style in his literary execution. In doing so, he provided an inverted view of the putatively criminal urban class, blurring the line that separated legitimate from illegitimate Americans and forging the base tenets of what makes gangster fiction distinctive.

The Legacy of the Reforming Gaze: From Riis to Asbury

Following on from the city-mystery were dime novels that exploited market desires for salacious visions of the urban ghetto. In general this legacy was intertwined with the interests of reformers like Jacob Riis, whose *How the Other Half Lives* (1890) grounded American fiction's perspective on the denizens of the city slums by the end of the 19th century. Among other things, *How the Other Half Lives* raised concerns about New York's lower East Side gang culture. Significantly, Riis's crusading reform rhetoric was accompanied by illustrations based on his photographs of tenement life. The ghetto is visually rendered as a "Bandits' Roost," replete with "Typical toughs (from the Rogue's Gallery)" and "growler gangs" such as "The Montgomery Guards" (Riis 1971: 51, 170–82). Even though Riis set out to document the real plight of the urban poor to effect social reform, he also reinforced the "nativist" prejudices of his age about the non-Anglo-American and immigrant character of the slum. And the compelling realism of his half-tone photographic illustrations of gang members helped confirm a condescending view of the tenement environment as criminally "alien" to America.

The reforming view of the gangster as "other" held considerable sway even as late as 1927 and the publication of Herbert Asbury's *The Gangs of New York*. Asbury's colorful "informal history of the underworld" embraces a teleological sense of "progress" in which the arrival of a morally upright nation has been predicated on the eradication of the underworld. We are given a story that charts a shift from the outright lawlessness of a city carved up by gangs in 1829 to the final victory of law and order in 1927. Asbury would have us believe that the gangster was now "history." Indeed the last chapter heralds "The Passing of the Gangster," confirming this opening claim:

> This book ... is an attempt to chronicle the most spectacular exploits of the refractory citizen who was a dangerous nuisance in New York for almost a hundred years, with a sufficient indication of his background of vice, poverty, and political corruption to make him understandable. Happily he has now passed from the metropolitan scene, and for nearly half a score years has existed mainly in the lively imaginations of industrious journalists, among whom the gangster has more lives than the proverbial cat. (Asbury 2002 [1927]: xiii)

What is remarkable about this claim is that in the year of its publication, 1927, nothing could have been further from the truth. While David Ruth confirms Asbury's suspicion that the 1920s was dominated very much by an "invented gangster" (the product of media hyperbole, moral panic-mongering, and consumer desire) – this was not a pure fabrication (Ruth 1996). Perhaps a certain kind of gang culture had declined, but it had also been reorganized under the aegis of Prohibition into something altogether more ubiquitous, and more difficult to dissociate from ordinary life. Rejecting the reform perspective, a generation of writers in the 1920s found in the gangster a new form of literary muse for a new time in which, contrary to Asbury's vision, national priorities seemed deeply confused. This was a decade featuring strict anti-immigration legislation, the prohibition of alcohol, and a commitment to laissez-faire capitalism. The gangster both real and imagined was at the heart of this mix of xenophobic attitudes, limitations on civil liberty, and an unregulated economy.

New Perspectives: Burnett and Clarke

W. R. Burnett's *Little Caesar* was published in 1929, becoming a bestseller and the basis for the first talking gangster movie to be a box-office hit (with Edward G. Robinson in the starring role). Key to the appeal of Burnett's work was its commitment to telling things from the gangster's point of view, and in the voice of the street. Some four decades before George V. Higgins championed a similarly radical style in his small-time gangster novel, *The Friends of Eddie Coyle* (1972), Burnett set the precedent in relaying an underworld tale mainly through low-life characters conversing in everyday speech. Before examining what made Burnett the most seminal writer of Prohibition-era gangster fiction, we might do well to consider the work of a less lauded contemporaneous writer such as Donald Henderson Clarke.

Louis Beretti (1929), the story of an Italian-American New York gangster, was Clarke's first book-length piece of fiction writing. Clarke had lived a previous life as an alcoholic reporter for New York's *The World* newspaper and publicity man for New York's MGM office – roles that provided him with intimate access to the city's complex relation between over- and underworlds (as well as enabling him to transcribe his novel into a screenplay for John Ford's 1930 film, *Born Reckless*). Descended from money and Harvard-educated, Clarke confessed to being an irreverent journalist who mixed with gangsters, film stars, corrupt politicians and fellow fourth estate reprobates through most of the 1920s. Following treatment for emotional imbalance and alcoholism between 1927 and 1928, a sober Clarke embarked on a writing career (Clarke 1950). His first work was an unapologetic homage to one of his major mobster friends, Arthur Rothstein. While *In the Reign of Rothstein* (1929) is grounded in facts drawn from Clarke's career as a reporter, *Louis Beretti* (1929) is only a small step removed from autobiography. Beretti's alcoholism, his particular code of honor that is more just than the law, his close association with newspaper journalists, all connect to Clarke's own experiences. The combined effect of these works written at the height of Prohibition was much like that of contemporaneous gangster stories: to invert the law/crime relation. Clarke provides a sardonic picture of Prohibition and its moral hypocrisy – as Louis's father relates:

The Prohibition isn't anything but graft for the rich. You know that. The judges all drink, and you know it, because Louis sells it to some of them. The lawyers drink, and the Congressmen drink, and the policemen drink … The best people in the country drink wine and beer and whiskey and brandy. And if it is all right for them to drink it, it is all right for us to sell it to them. (Clarke 1949 [1929]: 70)

Such rhetorical rejoinders to the impositions of a power elite build on Clarke's earlier depiction of his gangster-protagonist's being drafted into World War I: "This is a bum war … the guys that got it up ain't fighting in it," proclaims Louis, who turns wartime France into a black market emporium, trading army rations such as sugar for sex and alcohol. On returning from the war, Louis thinks it perfectly logical to "go into the bootlegging business." As he states to his mother, "It's respectable … and I want to be respectable" (Clarke 1949: 60). The narrative development is driven by Louis's failure to obey his own credo of "keeping his nose clean" (i.e., out of other mobsters' business) when his sentimental wife persuades him to discover the kidnappers and murderers of a wealthy upper-class associate's child. In doing so, he jeopardizes the business of Big Italy, a fellow gangster and Louis's closest friend from childhood. The novel's denouement involves Louis rescuing his son from an attempted kidnapping by Big Italy's gang. He survives a near fatal shooting in the process and is proclaimed by the media to be a gallant hero.

The relationship between the media and the gangster is figured as a natural alliance in Clarke's work. Beretti's drinking comrade and most intimate confidante is a crack Irish-American journalist, Bill O'Brien. Alongside O'Brien, a naive, Protestant, Yale-educated reporter, Henry Stills, stands in for Clarke himself. Such unholy alliances are characteristic of other gangster fiction of the period. Media fascination with the gangster was rooted in the colorful activities of underworld bosses. But there is more to this relation than the simple issue of exploitation. The symbiosis of press and gangster during Prohibition had everything to do with consumer desire. The gangster's business was to satisfy a prohibited public demand for leisure pleasures associated with alcohol and the nightlife that accompanied its sale. Gangster "style" was adopted and refined by the fashion industry and sold back to the underworld for emulation (Ruth 1996: 63–86). And in a climate conducive to constructing the gangster as an object of public sympathy, Burnett saw an opportunity to advance literary ideas redolent of Lippard.

In his first novel, *Little Caesar*, Burnett wanted to shift the perspective in gangster writing – to provide access to the gangster's world from his own point of view. This was something the author deemed "revolutionary":

I had a literary theory about dialogue. This was in the twenties. Novels were all written in a certain way, with literary language and so much description. Well, I dumped all that out; I just threw it away. It was a revolt, a literary revolt. That was my object. I wanted to develop a style of writing based on the way American people spoke – not literary English. Of course, the fact that the Chicago slang was all around me made it easy to pick up.

> Ultimately what made *Little Caesar* the enormous success it was, the smack in the
> face it was, was the fact that it was the world seen completely through the eyes of a
> gangster ... You had crime stories but always seen through the eyes of society. The
> criminal was just some son-of-a-bitch who'd killed somebody and then you go get 'em.
> I treated 'em as human beings." (McGilligan 1986: 57–8)

The novel's main protagonist, Caesar Enrico Bandello, starts out as a gang under-
ling but rises through the organization rapidly through ruthless ambition. The principles he adheres to bear a strong resemblance to those governing the terms of success
in the legitimate economy. As Robert Warshow said of the gangster (albeit the screen
version):

> [T]he quality of irrational brutality and the quality of rational enterprise become one
> ... we are conscious that the whole meaning of this career is a drive for success ...
> brutality itself becomes at once the means to success and the content of success. ...
>   At bottom, the gangster is doomed because he is under the obligation to succeed,
> not because the means he employs are unlawful. (Warshow 1970: 132–3)

As an individual with a name – marked emphatically by its allusion to an imperial
ruler and its Italian ethnicity – Little Caesar stands out from the crowd. The irony of
the gang environment is that he must rise above it to rule it and thus ends up alone.
    In writing a story told from the gangster's point of view primarily through dialogue
rather than description, Burnett gave voice not only to the criminal "other" but also
to the hitherto ethnically marginalized. Gangster argot had an accent and allied the
protagonist's desires to those of an outside group seeking to "make it" culturally as
well as economically. To this extent, Burnett revisits and refines a theme central to
The Great Gatsby. The gangster spoke from the putatively wrong side of division street
but in doing so questioned the legitimacy of the divide itself.
    Burnett stated that his "primary purpose was always the same as Balzac's: to give
the most realistic picture of the world around me that I could possibly do" (McGilligan
1986: 83). While proclaiming himself a realist, however, he did not hesitate to draw
inspiration from mass media hyperbole when representing the underworld. Initially,
he admitted that he "didn't know anything about gangsters, but ... read about them
in the newspapers" (McGilligan 1986: 83). Trafficking in mass media constructions
of the public enemy did not mean that Burnett strayed from Balzacian principles:
given that the newspaper was itself part of popular discourse, journalistic language
could be integrated into Burnett's revolt against the literary. Indeed, Burnett saw
"very little difference" between his view of the world and that of his gangster protagonists (McGilligan 1986: 83). He was trying to pass comment on the criminal
character of American everyday life in the 1920s and the gangster provided the most
intimate and telling access to the contradictions of a society subject to both Prohibition
and laissez faire capitalist mores.
    That Burnett's agenda coincided with the wiring of Hollywood for sound, the
Wall Street Crash, and the onset of the hardest years of the Depression would prove

momentous. The serendipity of such a literary turn was that it worked hand in hand with the movie industry's search for a film form that could sell the new cinematic experience most sensationally to an audience suffering from economic collapse. The easy transition of Burnett's street-argot to the screen helped introduce audiences to "talking pictures" precisely as a radically new medium. What is more, the underworld story as told by the gangster himself resonated with desires and frustrations shared by contemporaneous late Prohibition/early Depression-era movie-goers. Burnett moved to Hollywood to transcribe *Little Caesar* for the screen and help out with translating Armitage Trail's novel, *Scarface*, into a film. Building on the success of *Little Caesar* as an inter-medial form, he was among the first of many gangster fiction writers to make Hollywood his home (see Silver and Ursini, chapter 4 in this volume).

After Prohibition: Fuchs, Wolfert, and the Pathology of the Organization Man

By the mid-1930s, the gangster as rebellious type had begun to lose his "color" and oppositional potential. As Rachel Rubin argues, Daniel Fuchs's trilogy of Brooklyn novels – *Summer in Williamsburg* (1934), *Homage to Blenholt* (1936), and *Low Company* (1937) – chart the decline of the gangster as a "metaliterary" muse (Rubin 2000: 119). The gangster shifts from being an ambivalent or inspirational outsider who exposes the exclusionary character of "legitimate" culture to being the epitome of all that is ruthless about the system: "Taken together, Fuchs's novels chronicle the ongoing incorporation of crime in the first part of the twentieth century" (Rubin 2000: 120).

Rubin maintains that this deterministic sense of co-optation was part of Fuchs's general despondency with the radical political possibility of the gangster, especially as it had been characterized in the writings of the previous generation of leftist American Jewish writers, such as Samuel Ornitz (*Haunch Paunch and Jowl* [1923]) and Michael Gold (*Jews without Money* [1930]), who typically located their gangster stories in Manhattan's Lower East Side. Fuchs's Brooklyn novels were designed in part to debunk the faith placed in criminal agency by these earlier authors. The move to Brooklyn, then, was more than a literary one – it was politically figurative of the shift from slum tenement and ethnic ghetto to the more upwardly mobile striving context of Williamsburg. After the completion of the Williamsburg Bridge that connected the Lower East Side to Brooklyn in 1903, Brooklyn had become the signifier of socio-economic arrival for immigrant groups who sought to escape the social immiseration of the Bowery and Little Italy. As a later Jewish-American writer, Harold Robbins, depicted it in his 1951 gangster best-seller, *A Stone for Danny Fisher*, the move across the East River constituted a form of cultural arrival or establishment for non-Anglo Americans seeking to "Americanize" or "pass."

In Fuchs's first novel, *Summer in Williamsburg*, a young writer's gangster uncle, Papravel, is initially regarded as a source of moral and aesthetic inspiration. The story that unfolds, however, concerns the way individual ambition is directed toward organizational consolidation. Papravel's major achievement is securing a monopoly on Williamsburg's bus transportation system and driving the smaller operations to the wall through increasingly efficient ("economic") uses of violence.

If *Summer in Williamsburg* reflected a sense of disillusion with the gangster as ethnic culture hero, Fuchs's next novel, *Homage to Blenholt*, literally buried him. In a narrative oriented around the funeral of the eponymous mobster, whose status as underworld boss is ironically underscored by his "front" as Commissioner of Sewers, Fuchs exposes just how far gangsters had become integrated elements of the legitimate economy – central to political machines, commerce, money circulation, and the social elite. This funereal vision of the gangster's incorporation is brutally and dispassionately completed in the final novel of the Brooklyn trilogy, *Low Company*. Prefiguring Ira Wolfert's *Tucker's People* (1943), Fuchs tells the story of the ousting of a small-time operator in Neptune Beach, Shubunka, by an impersonal consolidated "syndicate." *Low Company* was grounded in the actuality of the gangster enterprise's reorganization and consolidation in the mid-1930s, when the major crime "families" run by bosses such as Joe Adonis, Frank Costello, Meyer Lansky and Lucky Luciano agreed to incorporate their businesses (Rubin 2000).

Throughout his writing, Fuchs dwells on the relation between incorporation and assimilation, revealing how economic integration is dependent on loss of ethnic identity and solidarity. Like many of his gangster writer forebears, Fuchs moved to Hollywood and a screenwriting career. Arguably, this symbolized the author's own capitulation to the processes of co-optation and assimilation that were central to his novels. As Michael Denning puts it, for Fuchs and other 1930s writers, "the lure of the gangster was the lure of the culture industry itself" (Denning 1997: 256). By the end of the trilogy, Fuchs has disclosed more than simple disappointment in the fact that gangsters have been incorporated. "Murder Inc." captured the extent to which the business world itself was endemically criminal.

This blurring of the lines between crime and business and an attendant revulsion at incorporation is taken up most systematically by Ira Wolfert. In his novel, *Tucker's People* (1997 [1943], also the basis of a leftist film noir, *Force of Evil* [1948]), the takeover trope is designed to reveal the general damage such organizational consolidation of capital inflicts on the lives and agency of everyday folk. Wolfert's gangsterdom engages not so much with the problems of outsiders wanting in but with the very disappearance of such an oppositional framework. There is no "outside" anymore – everyone is now within the system. Here the focus is on the business of numbers or "policy" racket – a betting system attractive to the poorer echelons of society because of its promise of disproportionate reward for penny bets. And the management structure of this gambling enterprise served Wolfert's purpose in particularly prescient ways. Aside from the obvious way it fleeced common folk, policy provided Wolfert with a means to understanding the more merciless features of bureaucratic corporate organization, tapping into emerging fears about the new post-Depression economy.

Policy was structured around bankers, controllers, collectors, and runners, all of whom fulfilled roles that bore an uncanny resemblance to those that defined their salaried professional-managerial equivalents in the legitimate economy. *Tucker's People* tapped into a growing disaffection with and anxiety about "big organization" and anonymity – and preceded the outpouring of esteemed sociological tracts after the war that attended to such issues. Riesman, Glazer and Denney's *The Lonely Crowd* (1950), C. Wright Mills's *White Collar* (1951) and William H. Whyte's *Organisation Man* (1956) uncovered the pathological character of the new middle class. As Andrew Hoberek (2005) astutely observes, the value of *Tucker's People* lies in the way Wolfert charts the destruction of a Jeffersonian ideal. A particular notion of the American middle class as populated by independent, small-scale, propertied businessmen has given way to a bureaucratic class of wage-dependent office-workers without the agency to control their own destinies.

Tucker's People is primarily oriented around the relationship between two brothers, Leo and Joe Minch, involved at different ends of the numbers racket. Leo is cast very much as the atavistic relic of an older middle-class possibility, while Joe is a sign of the future. Leo has a history of failed small-time business ventures behind him and has settled on running his own small numbers operation. Joe is part of the executive level management of the largest numbers operation, a "combination" or syndicate bossed by Ben Tucker, who is intent on establishing monopolistic control of the entire business. To this end, the syndicate fixes things so the players' favorite holiday three-number sequence of 5-2-7 (because superstition had it that 5 + 2 = lucky number 7) falls in the week of Thanksgiving. When the number combination hits, the smaller banks, unable to pay out, capitulate to being bought out by the syndicate. Joe's fraternal loyalties lead him to try to protect Leo from the fallout by urging him to join the syndicate. In the end, Leo proves too recalcitrant to the organization and dies of a stroke when he is kidnapped by a hostile mobster. Joe commits suicide, unable to handle his guilt. Allegorically, as Alan Filreis states, "[t]he radicalism of *Tucker's People* lies in Wolfert's approach to the endemic gangsterism of corporate organizations" (Filreis 1997: xvi).

If the earlier gangster fiction had devoted itself to the colorful outsider and individualist, by the 1950s it concentrated on the more faceless problem of conformity. Significantly, fears about organizational culture articulated in Wolfert's work and that of the postwar sociologists soon merged with the panic over the "mafia" engendered by Senator Estes Kefauver's Senate Special Committee to Investigate Organized Crime between 1950 and 1951. The hearings with various Italian Americans accused of being mob bosses were America's first major television event. The result compounded the impression that organized crime was dominated by Italian Americans. And the marking of criminal networks in this way reasserted a distinction between legitimate and illegitimate organization on the basis of ethnicity, suggesting once again that organizational corruption was something "alien" rather than endemic to the American way.

Future Gangster: Nostalgia or Global Corruption – Puzo or Winslow?

Leaping from the 1950s to the late 1960s and Mario Puzo's *The Godfather* (1969) may seem somewhat abrupt and by-passes significant gangster fiction such as Richard Stark's *The Hunter* (1962), the basis for the film, *Point Blank* (1967). At the risk of over-generalization, however, the underworld fiction of the period (exemplified by *The Hunter*) perpetuated a sense of the syndicate or "outfit" as an impersonal machine. It took Mario Puzo's more intimate understanding of criminal organization as having a "family" character to break this pattern. Puzo's story exploited a second government investigation into organized crime in 1967. The President's Commission on Law Enforcement and Administration of Justice reported that a coalition of 24 cartels coordinated the operation of gambling, drug dealing and loan-sharking nationwide. Moreover, it was claimed that this network was exclusively Italian-American (a since discredited notion). While this report conveniently labeled organized crime as "alien" to or outside legitimate society, it diverted attention from the complex way illegal and legal enterprise are deeply interwoven in the free market (Beare and Naylor 1999).

In this light, Puzo's engagement with the mafia was contradictory. On the one hand, *The Godfather* can be read as perpetuating an ethnocentric perspective on organized crime, while, on the other, it can be read as an attempt to correct such prejudices. The appeal of the story lay in the way it opened the world to the life of an apparently hidden society – in the way it advanced an "insider's" point of view given that Puzo was one of New York's Hells Kitchen Italian-American progeny. The book was also based on the reality of New York's "Five Families" mafia organization. Thus, although a work of fiction, *The Godfather* reads like exposé literature.

Equally, the power of the novel resides in its being a family saga, telling a particular story of the immigrant quest to make it and "go legitimate" in America. The action centers on a violent feud between the Corleone family and the other members of New York's Five Families. Set between 1945 and 1955, *The Godfather* charts the history of crime lord succession as Don Vito Corleone, following an attempt to assassinate him, makes way for his son, Michael. The values of one generation are pitted against the other. Michael, in his endeavor to make the family legitimate – a crusade finally achieved by moving the Corleone clan to Las Vegas – becomes increasingly more ruthless and unattractive. The anonymity and incorporated suburban character of Las Vegas supplants the "colorful" world of New York's ethnic enclaves. The novel's trajectory, then, mimics that of the history of gangster fiction itself. Puzo's story of how a close ethnic family world is diluted and made sterile by the effort to go legit after World War II corresponds to the way the fiction of Fitzgerald, Burnett, and Clarke gave way to that of Fuchs and Wolfert. And Puzo's own gravitation to

Hollywood screenwriting also emulates the career movement of so many of his gangster fiction predecessors.

To this extent, there is a strong sense of nostalgia in Puzo's gangster fiction, something perpetuated in much organized crime writing since. *Gangster* (2001), by Lorenzo Carcaterra, for example, follows Puzo's model quite slavishly. Told in flashback, it provides us with a nostalgic history of the rise to power of an Italian immigrant to supreme boss of New York's mafia. Even a piece of bestselling "true crime" gangster literature like *Wiseguy: Life in a Mafia Family* (Pileggi 1985), the basis for Martin Scorcese's 1990 gangster film, *Goodfellas*, takes the form of a lament. Author Nicholas Pileggi is drawn to his subject, the gangster Henry Hill, because of the way he could describe organized crime as a lost way of life.

While there remains a continuing fascination with the ethnic family character of organized crime, a more recent shift in gangster fiction is represented in the work of Don Winslow. In line, perhaps, with debates in criminology about the changed structure of criminal enterprise, Winslow has engaged the idea of organized crime as something more global than local (Beare and Naylor 1999; Skaperdas 2001). *The Power of the Dog* (2005) attends to the complex interweaving of the legal and illegal interests in the world of drug trafficking. The book's structure reflects this complexity, having a huge narrative arc that follows several parallel characters and their lives over thirty years. Starting out in the 1970s, with America's launch of its "War on Drugs," the story criss-crosses the USA–Mexico border, bringing an alphabet soup of government agencies into play with Mexican drug barons. In this world it is almost impossible to lead an ethical life – undercover agents mix with gangsters and end up questioning the morality of the State and its "war." The drug trafficking enterprise is seen to resemble the multinational corporation in its structure and in its techniques of production, distribution and sale. Moreover, the line that separates legal and illegal aspects of the trade is further compromised by the way the State itself participates in this enterprise. And in focusing on government complicity, we are returned to Lippard's original perspective. As Winslow writes:

> Government or the mob? Which is more dangerous? Are you *kidding*? Mobsters only wish they had the power of compulsion, potential for lethal violence and license to steal that governments have. It would be their *dream* ... But ... no major crime organization has ever existed without the co-operation and/or compliance of politicians, and none ever will. (Gaines 2005)

17
Historical Crime and Detection

Ray B. Browne

Historical crime fiction, like crime fiction in general, investigates everyday life in "the mean streets," to use Raymond Chandler's oft-quoted phrase, that is, along the darker walkways most people have traveled at one point or another throughout history. As historical fiction makes historians of us all, historical crime fiction to some degree makes us all cultural historians. Historical crime fiction thus has an obligation and a golden opportunity. Historian Amy Gilman Srebnick, in *The Mysterious Death of Mary Rogers* (1995), has insightfully argued that looking at a crime that is distant in time and place opens a window on a culture that, while different from our own, might suggest new insights into the way we live here and now.

However, a mere historical recital of the infractions of the past, though it may explain events, motivations, and the reestablishment of the status quo and prove of great interest to the professional historian and moderately so to the general public, fails to ignite the burning interest of the reader through the magic of art, which can bring the past vividly into the everyday present. Einstein, in his essay "What I Believe" (*Forum*, October 1930) suggested that, "The most beautiful thing we can experience is the mysterious." Indeed, human nature is a great vacuum of curiosity and the need to fill that vacuum may be the most powerful drive in life. Often, as Lyn Hamilton points out in her crime novel *The Moche Warrior* (1999), filling that gap through investigation of archaeological mysteries, or other great puzzles of the past, is the only way to achieve satisfaction.

In one sense, all detective fiction deals with the past, for all authors in the genre write about acts already committed, or attempted, against the mores and conventions of society. As Charles Rzepka observes, the detective genre itself originated just as "the West had begun to read the history of the world in [the] manner [of] stories of detection" (2005: 37), that is, coincidentally with the emergence of the modern sciences of geology and paleontology, for which material relics of the past served as "clues" for reconstructing narratives of past events. Historical crime fiction is more concerned than crime fiction in general with the distant past, with examining and explaining past behavior in bygone cultures. Today, this genre has developed into the fastest growing type of crime fiction. Two drives may be contributing to this new interest. For one thing, the reader gets the same kind of thrill at a safe distance that he or she gets from more contemporary and directly threatening true crime literature. Secondly, we are experiencing a new and revitalized general interest in history, as evidenced by television shows like *Antiques Roadshow* and *History Detectives* (both broadcast on PBS) and the saving and restoration of older public buildings and monuments.

In her novel *Alias Grace* (1996), a true-crime story of a mid-nineteenth century woman, Grace Marks, wrongly convicted of murder, prize-winning Canadian novelist Margaret Atwood says that historical fiction is about the passions that drive, impede, unite and divide humankind, passions she reduces to the seven deadly sins of pride, envy, avarice, lust, sloth, gluttony, and anger. Historical novels, and by extension historical crime novels, are "about truth and lies, and disguises and revelations; they are about crime and punishment; they are about love and forgiveness and long suffering and charity; they are about sin and retribution and sometimes even redemption." For our purposes it is significant that Atwood highlights "sin and retribution" and "crime and punishment," focusing on how these sins of the heart and flesh are particularly described in canonical historical crime novels.

Atwood's characterization applies as well to the true crime genre, as evidenced in two recent publications by history professors, *Murder Most Foul: The Killer and the American Gothic Imagination*, by Karen Halttunen (1998), and *The Murder of Helen Jewett: Life and Death of a Prostitute in Nineteenth-Century New York*, by Patricia Cline Cohen (1998). These two books caused a considerable stir in newspapers and the popular-professional press, garnering reviews in such publications as *The New Republic* and the *Chronicle of Higher Education*. Both authors realize that in their histories of true crime they are arousing interest in historical crime fiction (or "faction," the combination of fact and fiction) as well, and this combination has a significant impact on our perspective as readers – affecting, for example, the way we relate to what Halttunen calls her study's "pornography of violence." The reviewer of Cohen's book for the *New Republic* praised it highly for its presentation of evidence in colorful and dramatic detail and for demonstrating the excitement of the historian as detective, a role that all historians must adopt in order to be successful. Of her own book, Halttunen explains that no matter how revolting we find the crime, we are all drawn irresistibly toward the inhumanity of murder.

Several facets of contemporary historiography converge in the fictionalization of murder and retribution. Recently, historians have turned aside from large-scale narratives to interest themselves in lives on the margin (histories of gender and sexuality are particularly in vogue), and many have also laid aside efforts to document social change empirically, deciding instead to tell rich stories using full-blooded characters, whose motives are often only incidentally or partially explained. Like these historians of the quotidian, historical crime fiction writers offer us people and events that are typically neglected in traditional studies of history. And like Halttunen and Cohen, most of them also take their work seriously. Barbara Mertz, who under the name of Elizabeth Peters writes about a Victorian Egyptologist-detective named Amelia Peabody, has authored two straight history books about Egypt. In an interview published in the *University of Chicago Magazine* she once said that in response to the oft-repeated question, "When are you going to write a serious book?" she always replied that every book she writes is a serious book, and especially the mysteries. Indeed, Gary Hoppenstand considers Mertz's books featuring the intrepid Amelia Peabody, Victorian archaeologist and staunch feminist, the most successful series engaged with nineteenth-century Egyptian culture and society, and Amelia Peabody herself crime fiction's most lovable and popular creation. Mertz's achievement, says Hoppenstand, relies upon her skillful adaptation of the literary formula of the lost world adventure, in which Peabody plays the role of a female Indiana Jones. It also helps that Mertz takes such considerable pains to be histori-cally accurate.

From the first discovery of the truths exemplified by historical crime writing, authors have planted their works in the garden of literature, where they have sprung up like well tended flowers. Virtually all the recognized periods in Western history – from ancient Egypt through Classical Greece and Rome, and from medieval Europe through twentieth-century England and America – are covered in this subgenre. All bring the past to life in new ways that only crime, and the myriad ways of commit-ting it, can unite.

The filthy and dangerous alleys of Cairo and the muddy fields far from the Pharaoh's palace and temple are painted graphically in the works of Lynda S. Robinson, Lee Levin, and Lauren Haney. Their Egypt is not the land revealed in the original excava-tions of King Tut's tomb or the Valley of the Kings, but instead, the reality of life at the time, at least as far as we can tell from surviving documents and archaeological evidence. Robinson and Levin set their fiction in the short but mysterious reign of King Tutankhamen, and Lauren Haney chooses that of Queen Hatshepsut. The three differ considerably in approach and result. In her "Lord Meren" series, Robinson brings forth the political and cultural complexity of the period about which she writes and presents vividly realized characters. According to one of her critics, Rita Rippetoe, Robinson's writing conveys "interesting and exotic scenes and actions without calling undue attention to itself" (2000: 20). Lauren Haney's work also captures the sensory detail that we long to impose, from this distance, on the period. Lee Levin's *King Tut's Private Eye* seems, by contrast, to reflect an idiosyncratic, presentist interpretation of Egyptian civilization.

Across the Mediterranean, life in Rome was a different rattle of swords. The Roman Empire has become one of the favorite societies for authors of historical crime fiction. John Maddox Roberts and Steven Saylor take to the streets of ancient Rome in somewhat different ways. Roberts's protagonist is the SPQR (Senatus Populusque Romanus – "The Senate and the People of Rome") operator Decius Caecilus Metellus, whose adventures are recounted with considerable charm and delight. Saylor's investigator, Gordianus the Finder, is a successful working-class man who has risen to the ranks of the middle class, a development that was quite possible in ancient Rome. Saylor's account of the six economic classes, five of which vote, and of the urban Roman poor is better presented than Roberts's, though the latter's account is vastly more amusing.

Do the streets and alleys of Rome seem to our eyes overcrowded with criminals and their crimes? Each author on the subject brings new information and insights. David Wishart, whose credentials are solid, is a born storyteller and teacher. He studied Classics at Edinburgh University, taught Latin and Greek in public school for four years, then retrained as a teacher of EFL and worked in Kuwait, Greece and Saudi Arabia. He next switched to teaching in a different medium, by writing of the cultures he knows well. Not only has he written of the places and times he has recreated, but Wishart also appends to each of his books the "true" history of the accounts he has novelized.

Wishart's novels have a sparkling character in Marcus Corvinus that we have not met in other Roman mysteries. Corvinus is a young whipper-snapper of 21 who is allowed to wear the purple stripe on his toga that indicates his connection to the imperial family. As such he moves freely through all levels of Roman society with ease and confidence that has not been so clearly displayed in crime fiction since the days when Dorothy Sayers's Lord Peter Wimsey frequented the posh nightclubs and East End back alleys of London. Wishart published two novels in 1995, *Ovid* and *I, Virgil*. *Ovid* introduces us to Corvinus, the young man who looks upon all of Rome as his province. His girlfriend Perilla, the granddaughter of the poet Ovid, a beautiful and intelligent virgin trapped in an unconsummated marriage to an exiled husband, asks Corvinus to get permission from Her Excellency the Lady Livia to allow Ovid's ashes to be returned to Rome from their place of burial on the Black Sea. Corvinus is so successful – and charming into the bargain – that Lady Livia grants permission not only to retrieve the ashes, but also for his new girlfriend to be granted a divorce from her banished husband and marry Corvinus.

Wishart has taken liberties with history in this story. The beautiful and intelligent Perilla who was estranged from her exiled husband and in Wishart's story marries Corvinus was in fact the mother of three children and remained faithful to her spouse. Wishart takes other liberties as required, but always explains in an endnote what he's up to. His alterations to history are not random. He is a moralist, pointing out in each of his novels that if crime pays, it is only in the short run. His eye is usually on the democratizing impact of crime on society, and his hope is that describing it may help to strengthen democracy. Throughout his historical crime fiction Wishart focuses on the abuses of privilege by the elite and the rebellious forces unleashed by their arrogant misbehavior.

A new writer on Roman life takes her characters far from the Imperial City to the conquered land of Britain. Rosemary Rowe, the maiden name of Rosemary

Aitken, has written academic monographs and textbooks on language and communication and, under her married name, historical fiction about turn-of-the-century tin miners in Cornwall. Roman Britain seems culturally and temporally a long way from these concerns. But in her fiction Rowe captures the Roman-British culture in lively conversation and action. Like Wishart she authenticates her history in a "Foreword," explaining the historical details that she is fictionalizing. And she explains that she has verified the details from materials she has derived from exhibitions, excavations, interviews with experts, and a wide variety (sometimes contradictory) of graphic and written sources. As Rowe shows from these documents, Roman nobility in the provinces (often holding high official positions) were the social elite, although many wealthy native men and women had important posts in local administrations. The most important distinction in Roman provincial society, however, was, as we would expect, that between free man and slave, although a man might move between these two conditions in his lifetime. There were many ways into slavery – capture in a military campaign or by slave-trading raiders, or a sentence to servitude following a criminal offense. Some victims were driven into slavery by want or debt, and some gamblers even staked their freedom on a roll of the dice.

To be credible, crime fiction must be authenticated by details like these. For example, who beyond a few specialists would know that in the sixteenth century, as recorded in P.F Chisholm's *A Surfeit of Guns*, when a member of the body, say a hand, was amputated, it had to be buried "with a live rat tied to it to draw out any morbidius [disease]"? Or that horse traps were used in twelfth-century England (especially in sieges) to cripple steeds? Called a "caltrop," this ball with metal spikes was constructed in such a way as to have the spikes protruding upward to penetrate the horse's hooves.

Sometimes authors are most effective when they join forces. Such is the case with Peter Tremayne, the pen name of Celtic historian Peter Beresford Ellis. Tremayne has offered over the last three decades some seventy books along with scores of essays, articles, and short stories. His most successful creation, however, is the seventh-century Irish detective Sister Fidelma, who is outspoken, sarcastic, logical and supremely self-confident, and impatient with pretense or arrogance. She was introduced in a 1993 story, *Murder in Repose*, and has since then imposed her will through some half dozen novels, all of which give readers a quite modern taste of female self-confidence and skill in an unenlightened and long-ago place and time.

Sister Fidelma, along with numerous other anachronistic investigators of the middle ages and renaissance who have appeared on bookstore shelves during the last few decades, owes her existence in part to the example set by Umberto Eco in his ground-breaking, meta-fictional masterpiece, *The Name of the Rose* (1980), which appeared in English translation in 1983. Here, monks are dying bizarre deaths in a fourteenth-century Italian monastery and an English Franciscan friar, William of Baskerville, helped by his trusty apprentice, Adso of Melk, has been sent to investigate and, if possible, bring the murderer to justice. While the word "Baskerville" – with its echo of the Sherlock Holmes novella, *The Hound of the Baskervilles* – is but one of many obvious allusions to Doyle's creation in Eco's send-up of the genre, the book is more appropriately classified as a postmodern or metaphysical example of detective fiction (see Merivale, chapter 24 of this volume).

The numerous works of Edith Pargeter, who published mostly under the name Ellis Peters (1913–95), indicate the extent of her popularity on both sides of the Atlantic. Pargeter's cascade of works included at least 91 books and numerous short stories, 13 George Felse books, 3 nonfiction books, 3 collections of short stories and 16 translations of Czech literature into English. A child of Shropshire, she remained attached to her birthplace throughout her life and made it the locale of her popular Brother Cadfael detective series, which was set in the early twelfth century, a particularly violent time in English and Welsh history.

Peters introduces her readers to Cadfael in *A Morbid Taste for Bones* (1977). He is a Welshman in his sixties who has lived to the full a life of the times. He has spent a decade and a half in the Mideast, first as a Crusader, then as captain of a fishing boat. Wanting a more peaceful life he took up gardening, loved several women and fathered a son, though he did not know it, and eventually returned to Wales seeking the peace and solitude of the monastery. Cadfael's adventures typically involve him in the political, religious, and cultural turmoil of his day, but they nearly all unfold at the level of everyday, local village life. His deep knowledge of the properties of herbs – both healing and baneful – often gives him an advantage over the official representatives of the law in untangling mysterious deaths.

We move forward to the Italian Renaissance in the works of Elizabeth Eyre, who has written at least half a dozen books on the adventurer Sigismondo and his servant Benno as they set about investigating murder and conspiracy in the Renaissance courts of Italian cities, fictional and real. Though they inhabit a distant past, Eyre develops the characters of her detective and sidekick in the modern mystery story tradition, and they interest us in part by reason of the overlapping of the two traditions. Contemporary social commentary likewise, often confined geographically to imaginary utopias and dystopias, Lilliputs and Brobdinags, can thrive when planted in historical recreations of bygone places and times. Margaret Frazer, in at least seven historical crime novels, has planted hers in fifteenth-century England in the time of the son of Geoffrey Chaucer. Frazer focuses on the injustice of the class system and the harm it does to society at large.

England's fifteenth century has also provided the backdrop for several other writers of historical crime and detection, perhaps the most noteworthy being Josephine Tey, whose Inspector Alan Grant novels had secured her general reputation as a writer of whodunnits by the mid-twentieth century. In *The Daughter of Time* (1951), Grant spends a hospital stay researching the role of England's King Richard III in the death of his two nephews, the so-called "Princes in the Tower." Grant concludes that Richard was innocent and that Henry VII murdered the two boys. The fifteenth century also frames the mission of Kathryn Swinbrook, a practicing physician of Canterbury. The account of her activities is the work of P. C. Doherty (under the pen-name C. L. Grace), one of the most prolific English authors of historical crime fiction. As for Elizabethan England, it is strewn with the bodies of the victims of historical crime. Robin Maxwell's *The Secret Diary of Anne Boleyn* (1997) and *The Queen's Bastard* (1999) engage with real historical events, as does David Starkey's *Elizabeth: The Struggle for the Throne*. Sticklers for historical detail will also enjoy the works of Fiona Buckley (Valerie Arnand), P. F. Chisholm (Patricia Finney), Kathy Lynn Emerson, and Karen Harper. These books may be even more enjoyable if one reads with a history of the period by one's side.

The New World has also been fertile ground for historical crime fiction. Martin and Annette Meyers, authors of a series of Dutchman adventures, write model stories of a drunken New Amsterdam *shout* or sheriff, from the days when Holland ruled present-day New York City. In their six works so far, the authors seem to be motivated by the philosophy that characters must drive the action. More than a century later, a real American "character," Benjamin Franklin, finds himself in London during the years he served there as representative of the Colonies and the United States. Robert Lee Hall produces a fascinating picture of Franklin as politician, American agent and former friend of important Englishmen (and especially Englishwomen) and Continentals. Having returned to London, Franklin takes up residence in the same house he occupied on previous occasions. Staying with his former landlady, Franklin solves mysteries in Drury Lane and elsewhere in the sprawling metropolis that was the colonial and commercial hub of Britain's eighteenth-century empire.

England in the early years of the century is the setting for Keith Heller's three George Man novels, *Man's Illegal Life* (1984), *Man's Storm* (1986) and *Man's Loving Family* (1986). In universalizing his main character's name and placing his action on the crime-ravaged streets of eighteenth-century London, Heller generalizes in Man the character and fate of the human race, which must collectively be corrected and purged. Man's novels picture the dangers of living at that time in a way that resonates with the *noirish* crime fiction of the early twentieth century.

Mid-century Georgian London is the setting for four novels by Bruce Alexander, pseudonym for Bruce Cook, featuring the blind, compassionate magistrate Sir John Fielding, who presided over the Bow Street Court from 1754 to 1780. With an orphan boy, Jeremy Proctor, ferreting out evidence, Sir John, brother of the novelist Henry Fielding, dispenses mercy and compassion along with justice. Later in the Georgian era novelist Jane Austen is set sleuthing through half a dozen crime tales by Stephanie Barron. Barron writes cleverly and engagingly, like her detective protagonist. Her Jane is witty and sharp enough to match the imaginary portrait of the artist treasured by readers in her own time and ever since.

Great Britain after the Napoleonic Wars was the land of the Dandy, epitomized by the future King George IV. It is a world of pleasure and self-indulgence for the wealthy, and the corpulent Prince Regent enjoyed all the sins (and pleasures) of the flesh along with his companion Beau Brummell. Kate Ross's Julian Kestrel is something of a cross between Brummel and Poe's Auguste Dupin: he dresses like the former and becomes an amateur detective because he is bored with life. Kestrel's valet, Thomas Stokes, or "Dipper," often helps his master with the finer details of crime, having obtained his education in the subject as a former pickpocket.

Anne Perry, in her series featuring the husband and wife team Thomas and Charlotte Pitt, strives to reveal the dark underside of Victorian propriety at the other end of the nineteenth century. Inspector Thomas Pitt of the London Police takes as his beat the artificial world of social privilege, where pretense and appearance constitute reality. His wife, Charlotte, who has married beneath her station out of love for Thomas and her attraction to the lure of criminal investigation, often provides information and deciphers clues as only someone familiar with upper-class life could do.

Perhaps the living writer who best conveys the power of historical crime fiction in reanimating the corpses and cultures of the past is Peter Lovesey, the Shakespeare of historical crime fiction. He won a First Crime Novel Award in 1970 for *Wobble to Death*, and in 1978 was awarded a Silver Dagger from the Crime Writer's Association for *Waxwork* and the Gold Dagger in 1982 for *The False Inspector Dew*, as well as the French Grand Prix de Littérature Policière in 1985 and the Prix du Roman d'Aventures in 1987. His Victorian police detective, Sergeant Cribb, and Cribb's sidekick, Constable Thackery, have delighted audiences for more than thirty years in historical mysteries that have been praised for their wit, clever plots, and surprising denouements. Lovesey's historical perspective, his understanding of all levels of the British class system, particularly the lower tiers, is complete and candid. In *The Detective Wore Silk Drawers* (1971), for example, Cribb and Thackeray seek out the dregs of society in the world of bare-knuckle fighters. Here as throughout the series, Cribb adapts his behavior to the society in which he is working, which can often lead to amusing contradictions. In *A Case of Spirits* (1974) Cribb interviews a well-to-do doctor, displaying perfect decorum and manners, while only a few pages later, when Thackeray begins to rough up a suspected thief under questioning, Cribb does not hesitate to jump in.

Lovesey's investigations demonstrate his thorough knowledge and understanding not only of the criminal world but also of the society that it targets. He knows the steady and seemingly enduring middle class, as well as the outcasts whose exploitation supports them and the heavy burdens these marginalized citizens are made to bear for the sake of their "betters." In *Swing, Swing Together,* Lovesey all but sprays the reader with the sweat of society's victims: "In twelve narrow stalls convicts were at the treadmill, forcing their feet to keep pace with steps that sank endlessly away as an unseen wheel turned, its revolutions fixed at a rate that took no account of aching calves and skinned ankles" (1976: 159).

Several fascinating historical crime fiction studies are set in the United States before and during the Civil War. Margaret Lawrence, pseudonym for Margaret Keilstrup, who has written in several genres, describes the skilled midwife Lucy Hannah Trevor as she makes her way through life in the aftermath of her "foolish marriage" to James Trevor and the deaths of her three children. Hannah is "educated above her station" but has to walk the low road for survival. In the recounting of her adventures, Lawrence opens the door onto a historical reality often omitted from accounts of America's early decades of experimenting with democracy.

The history of the United States generates a great deal of crime fiction replete with local color, though none, perhaps, as somber in hue as Barbara Hambly's, set in what is considered by many to be America's most romantic city, but also one of its most crime ridden, New Orleans. Hambly, who transports us to and exploits the mysteries of New Orleans before the Civil War, examines the intersections of race and class in that fluid society by concentrating our attention on the person of Benjamin January, who was born a slave, grew up in the cane fields of Bellefleur Plantation, managed to get a medical education, and attended one of Europe's best medical schools. Excluded in Paris from the profession for which he was qualified, January returns to New Orleans, where he finds himself in much the same situation, but immersed in a culture with whose biases and behavior, however violent, he is at least familiar.

The turbulent early history of the United States is further explored in the works of James Brewer, who takes up the violent period of Radical Reconstruction and sets his works along the swirling lower half of the Mississippi in the heart of the Reconstruction South, extending from St Louis and Memphis to Natchez and New Orleans, towns separated by hundreds of miles lying in the heart of the former Confederacy. Brewer's work offers a narrative of often neglected events in the history of the destroyed Confederacy, and in an interview with Lawrence A. Kreiser, Jr, Brewer described how he wanted to "tackle this complicated period in our history." He did not set out "to write social or historical commentary ... but it cannot but ooze from the pages when you deal with such a fascinating and volatile time" (Kreiser 1999: 7). The result of Brewer's research and writing is both informative and fascinating.

The useful information and dramatization of a volatile culture also seeps into the works of Peter Heck in his trilogy featuring Mark Twain as detective: *Death on the Mississippi* (1995), *A Connecticut Yankee in Criminal Court* (1996), and *The Prince and the Prosecutor* (1997). The Gilded Age becomes richly tarnished as Heck's plots unfold, and the author effectively develops many aspects of Twain's world and character, both good and bad, as traveling and lecturing throughout the country, the man born as Samuel Clemens sets himself to the unriddling of various crimes that come his way. Trying to recreate the persona of Twain is a difficult task, as the numerous books that flood the market today demonstrate, but Heck provides many insights into the historical pressures of the new American age of industrial mechanization bearing down on Twain, and particularly the tension between unbridled capitalism and the values of democracy. The Gilded Age is also the setting for the works of Caleb Carr, who recreates the New York City of that era in his two novels *The Alienist* (1994) and *The Angel of Darkness* (1997). In both he interweaves historical and fictional characters in order to reveal unconscious fears and their place in ordinary life, giving historical resonance to the uncanny and unbelievable.

World War I, "the war to end all wars," did not end any of the troubles caused by that war. Instead it caused disruption, poverty, and crime. England suffered some 750,000 deaths and 1,700,000 casualties, with approximately 80,000 to 200,000 returning soldiers suffering from shell shock (post-traumatic stress disorder [PTSD]). Into this unhappy world came the writing team of Charlotte Todd and her son Charles, publishing under the name Charles Todd. So far they have published at least eight successful works. Their first novel, *A Test of Wills* (1997), received the Barry Gardner Award and was nominated for an Edgar Award by the Mystery Writers of America. Their second, *Wings of Fire* (1999), was short-listed for the Ellis Peters Historical Dagger Award by the Crime Writer's Association of Great Britain. The awards will probably continue to pile up as Inspector Ian Rutledge of Scotland Yard pursues his successful career. Rutledge lives in a world dominated by PTSD and its victims. Like Dorothy Sayers's famous sleuth from the same period, Lord Peter Wimsey, Rutledge himself comes under the disease's iron grip.

One might think, from a tour through the periods and milieus in which most historical crime fiction has been set, that only Western history has served the scenic and cultural requirements of the genre, at least among English-speakers. It would be remiss, therefore, to leave this subject without some mention of the Judge Dee series of detective novels penned by the Dutch diplomat and Sinologist, Robert van Gulik, beginning in 1948 with *The Celebrated Cases of Judge Dee* and ending, at Gulik's death, with *Poets and Murder* (1968). Based on a real Chinese magistrate of the seventh century Tang dynasty, Ti Jen-chieh, the first Judge Dee book was in fact a scholarly translation of an anonymous eighteenth-century Chinese novel, *Di Gong An* (*Cases of Judge Dee*), consisting of tales based in turn on the purported career of Ti. Gulik immediately saw the potential to turn the historical Judge Dee into a compelling semi-fictional sleuth. *The Chinese Maze Murders* (1951), consisting of three cases, introduced Gulik's readers not only to a deeply humane, wise, and canny combination of magistrate and chief investigator, but also to the pre-modern Chinese justice system, in which confessions under torture were considered admissible as evidence and intrigue dogged the steps of every administrator seeking to dispense justice under the rigid protocols of bureaucratic Confucianism and imperial prerogatives of appointment – and dismissal. Aided by Ma Joong and Chiao Tai, two former bandits of the "Robin Hood" type (they rob only wealthy merchants and corrupt officials), Dee often finds himself plunged deep into an urban demi-monde of thieves, prostitutes, beggars, soldiers of fortune, and otherwise respectable citizens on the take as he seeks, not only to enforce the law and insure orderliness, but also to find a bit of peace of mind for himself in a turbulent era.

The Judge Dee series is about as far off the beaten track of the history familiar to most Western readers as one can get, and yet, like all the other examples of historical crime and detection discussed here, it reflects its author's irresistible attraction to the window that conventional historiography can open onto the past. Gazing through that sometimes darkened glass, we may often mingle what lies beyond it with the outlines of our own reflection. While academic and popular histories both seem to offer more transparent surfaces, it may just be that the degree of self-reflection afforded by historical crime fiction, spotlighted as it is in the lurid glare of violence, represents what most strongly motivates all of us who are drawn to the contemplation of bygone times, both within the academy and without.

NOTE

1   This chapter incorporates information with changes as needed from *The Detective as Historian: History and Art in Historical Crime* *Fiction*, Vols. 1 and 2, edited by Ray B. Browne and Lawrence A. Kreiser [Popular Press, 2000 and Cambridge Scholars Press, 2007].

18

Crime and the Spy Genre

David Seed

The soul of the spy is somehow the model of our own (*Barzun, 1965: 167–8*)

Spy fiction shares many of the characteristics of detective fiction. It prioritizes investigation; its sphere of action seems to be beyond the law; its characters use aliases and invented identities; typically it progresses from apparently disparate fragments of information towards a more complete account of action. But, as John Cawelti has pointed out in his classic account of the genre, it is characterized by the clandestine. From the very beginning, it has offered readers glimpses of what was called the "secret history" of nations. The "spy" label is convenient and broad. The novelist Alan Furst has half-seriously suggested that it should really be called the "literature of clandestine political conflict" (Furst 2004: viii). This description adds to secrecy a further defining characteristic: the political dimension of the narrative, where the ultimate players are the governing institutions of the countries concerned.

From the 1960s onwards the proliferation and sophistication of this fiction established espionage as a subject central to British and American culture and one sign of the subject moving beyond genre limits was the willingness of "mainstream" writers to incorporate it into their fiction. In 1961 Hemingway lent his name to editing an anthology of spy stories called *The Secret Agent's Badge of Courage*. Kurt Vonnegut describes the parodic activities of an American Nazi in *Mother Night* (1962). Thomas Pynchon wove espionage into a number of his novels, especially into the paranoid vision of *Gravity's Rainbow* (1973) where the European Theatre of Operations at the end of World War II becomes a revived metaphor of covert action by a welter of intelligence agencies. John Barth focuses the drama of *Sabbatical* (1982) on an ex-CIA agent who fears he is still under surveillance. And Norman Mailer admitted in 2003: "I've always been fascinated by spies" (Mailer 2003: 117). He found an analogy between the spy and the novelist shared by Graham Greene and John Le Carré. His interest bore most explicit fruit in Mailer's 1991 novel *Harlot's Ghost*, which drew on a wealth of sources – fictional and historical – to give a panoramic narrative by an operative of the CIA up to the period of the Kennedy assassination.

One of the formative figures in modern spy fiction was William Le Queux (1864–1927), whose Duckworth Drew has been seen as the prototype of James Bond. Le Queux combined a grounding in journalism with an astonishing facility for literary production in a number of sensational popular genres. His spy fiction demonstrates his skill at constructing narratives that purport to give the public glimpses of a covert world of espionage hidden behind the façade of international politics. In other words, Le Queux more or less invented the milieu of modern spy fiction. The recurrence of duchesses and princesses in this world became increasingly dated after World War I and the fact that his hero Drew, who appears in works like *Secrets of the Foreign Office* (1903), describes himself as a "free-lance" secret agent anticipates John Buchan's spy thrillers in describing a kind of activity which became progressively more and more institutionalized. Nevertheless, Duckworth Drew establishes a certain pattern for subsequent espionage heroes in being cosmopolitan, polyglot, a master of disguise, and an expert in international travel. His narratives repeat the term "secret" *ad nauseam* in their suggestion that he (and therefore, vicariously, the reader) is often in possession of information not even possessed by government ministers. In explaining his success, Le Queux drew an analogy between his narratives and a motor-bus. The connection was sheer speed. Apart from his appeal to the reader's curiosity, he maintained a rapid pace in his narratives, helped by cliff-hanging chapter endings. *The Czar's Spy* (1905) is typical in taking the protagonist on a series of journeys to Finland and St Petersburg, then into the Finnish interior to a monastery doubling as a prison, and on to that staple of suspense fiction – the flight back to freedom. This combination of investigation, entrapment and hair's-breadth escape was to become a standard ingredient in the James Bond novels.

Le Queux tapped into popular fears around the turn of the century that Germany was Britain's main imperial rival. In the 1890s he joined with Alfred Harmsworth (Lord Northcliffe) and Lord Roberts in campaigning ceaselessly for better naval preparedness, and added force to his warnings by incorporating techniques of reportage: headlines, eye-witness accounts, news reports, and so on. Le Queux's campaigning in this area concentrated later on the enemy within. *Spies of the Kaiser* (1909) is an exposé in the form of stories, all revealing the presence of a network of German agents in the country having their resident administrator in London, but really taking their instructions from the German intelligence chief in Berlin. Le Queux's *The Invasion of 1910* (1906) had prepared the ground for these revelations by describing the invasion of Britain by German forces. *Britain's Deadly Peril: Are We Told the Truth?* (1915) made a direct appeal to the reader not to be fooled by the bland statements put out by the government and spelled out a whole series of "perils" ranging from that of apathy to the enemy alien. He was convinced (on shaky evidence) that southern England was riddled with German spies. Le Queux was probably consulted when the British Secret Service was established but, despite his claims, was never a member of that organization. Instead, his spy fiction helped to familiarize the public with the idea that there was a secret service possessed not only by Britain but also by other European nations like Germany and France.

This notion was not limited to Britain alone. Its defensive rationale extended to Kipling's *Kim* (1901) whose protagonist ultimately enters the Indian secret service to protect the country from the machinations of Russian spies. Kim's training in memory retention and his initiation into the mysteries of surveillance and disguise were to become part of the necessary education of any agent. Baroness Orczy's *The Scarlet Pimpernel* (1905) seems far removed from this fiction in its setting in the aftermath of the French Revolution, but Sir Percy Blakeney's skill at donning guises is a very modern achievement; a patriotic one too, in contrasting the timeless stability of England with the turbulence of France. Kim becomes a participant in the Great Game, which by definition can only be partially glimpsed by its players.

Erskine Childers's *The Secret of the Sands* (1903) follows the same pattern as that evoked by Le Queux of patriotic service by gentlemanly amateurs. In this case there are two protagonists, the one a practical yachtsman, the other a man of linguistic ability, their two skills complementing each other. A boating holiday on the East Frisian coast turns into an investigation of mysterious military activity in the region and it is finally revealed that plans are afoot to launch a naval invasion of Britain from that coast. The sheer detail with which the protagonists scrutinize the strategic nature of the coastline gives the account its plausibility, and the fact that they are amateurs by no means disqualifies their actions. If anything, their patriotic motivation adds to the dynamics of the novel. The worlds of Le Queux, Childers, and, as we shall see, John Buchan share a common vision of subversion from within the nation and aggression from without: "it may be a dangerous world, but it is still a world of moral certainty" (Stafford 1991: 29).

The most famous detective in crime fiction is rarely associated with espionage and yet a number of the Sherlock Holmes stories engage with that subject. By so doing they demonstrate the proximity of the spy and detective genres. From the very beginning spy stories involved detection and disguise, and invited the reader to assemble a narrative with considerable help from the investigatory protagonist. It is quite consistent therefore that Conan Doyle should have included the subject within his Holmes series. "The Adventure of the Bruce-Partington Plans" (1911) contains one of the rare appearances by Holmes's brother Mycroft, who works in a government information-gathering department and who calls on the detective to retrieve secret submarine plans stolen from a clerk in Woolwich Arsenal. Much stress is put by Holmes on the sheer difficulty of the case, but espionage does not alter the pattern of Conan Doyle's narratives; it simply gives extra urgency to the solution. It transpires that the villain is the brother of the official in charge of the department, who sells the plans to a foreign agent to pay off debts. Exactly the same motivation is supplied in "The Adventure of the Naval Treaty" (1893) and so the categories of characters stay intact. Spies remain in place ready to profit from any opportunity; villains betray their class and nation, but only from temporary financial need.

A contemporary of Le Queux who shared his amazing productivity and the credit for helping form the spy genre was E. Phillips Oppenheim, whose novels rely less on rapid action than on elaborate disguise. *The Great Secret* (1908), for example, describes how the narrator – a cricketer, magistrate, and impeccable gentleman – stumbles across an intrigue to restore the monarchy to France. The main agent in this process goes by different names, but has developed such a sophisticated skill at dissimulation that he has penetrated the German secret service. This same skill at disguise is central also to *The Great Impersonation* (1920), where an English-educated German baron steps into the shoes of a British diplomat and attempts to live his life. Despite his differences of behavior and the fact that he is single while the diplomat has a wife, the baron carries off his act, learning and therefore adopting the social styles and values of an Englishman. The very fact that this masquerade is possible suggests how close the two cultures are and how tense their imperial rivalry is.

Although John Buchan referred to Oppenheim as "my master in fiction" (Masters 1987: 19), his own novels carry their distinctive stamp, which moves their sites of action well away from Oppenheim's upper-class social milieu. In his dedication of the first Richard Hannay adventure, *The Thirty-Nine Steps* (1915), Buchan also acknowledges quite a different model in American "dime novels." Here Hannay is described as an ex-mining engineer bored with life until he encounters an agent named Scudder who tells him that he is pursuing a network of German agents in Britain. When Scudder is murdered, Hannay without hesitation takes up his role, traveling to Scotland in pursuit of the spies. The Forth Bridge sequence in which Hannay jumps off his train has become famous, thanks partly to Hitchcock's 1935 film adaptation. When Hannay reaches Scotland one striking difference from Oppenheim emerges: Buchan's emotional evocation of the British landscape. Partly this is a question of using terrain in the novel's action; partly it involves Buchan's broader evocation of Britain as an ancient peaceful land under threat. The most lyrical expression of this conviction occurs in *Mr Standfast* (1919). Hannay demonstrates a skill in improvised acting, working his way into a number of roles according to need. Like Buchan himself, Hannay is connected with the secret service but not in it. He is yet another gifted amateur, combining physical resourcefulness with close powers of observation. The novel is punctuated by vivid, apparently insignificant details that prove to be crucial and it builds up to a final climax in a holiday resort, where the spies are masquerading as innocuous English tourists. Hannay's activities are buttressed by a network of male contacts in the colonies and at home, partly identifiable as clubland. In this way Buchan merges political, social, imperial, and even landowning aspects of the national establishment.

Buchan's other famous spy novel, *Greenmantle* (1916), takes Hannay abroad with two companions to fight essentially for the same cause – this time the defense of empire. The novel tapped into Allied fears that in 1914 the Germans and Turks had hatched a plot to foment a holy war in the Middle East and beyond that would lead to the collapse of the British and French empires; it was devised in Berlin and directed from Constantinople, hence Hannay's eastward journey through Germany and the Balkans to Turkey. Now Hannay and his companions divide the masquerade between them, variously adopting the guises of a Boer, German rambler, Dutchman, and Turk. The first half of the book takes them through hostile territory to the site of conspiracy in Constantinople, where the Greenmantle plot is revealed to the reader. From that point the action takes on increasingly apocalyptic undertones and the climactic battle of Erzurum (the "great battle" as it is called) is presented as a struggle between good and evil. It is helpful to remember Buchan's Calvinistic upbringing here and also his constant fear of cultural seepage, of civilization being sapped from within as well as confronted from without.

Buchan's perception of the empire under threat was shared by Sax Rohmer (Arthur Henry Sarsfield Ward), who began his Fu Manchu series in 1913 and continued right into the Cold War period. Fu Manchu personifies in extreme form the qualities associated with espionage. He is the ultimate shape-changer, radically altering his appearance so that in each novel he can launch his next subversive assault on the West. From the very beginning he is presented as a larger-than-life figure, combining a diabolically unscrupulous intellect with oriental inscrutability which plays directly to fears of the Yellow Peril. His opposite number, Sir Denis Nayland Smith, like Buchan's heroes, personifies the British establishment he defends and, in benign form, many of the skills of his opponent. Rohmer's tendency to personalize his narratives as battles of wits between hero and villain tends to exclude our usual perception in spy fiction that foreign agents are working for rival national or political agencies.

The fact that Joseph Conrad could present an ironic view of espionage in *The Secret Agent* (1907) suggests that the spy genre had become established by that date. Conrad was profiting from the spate of anarchist scares at the end of the nineteenth century, in particular the failed attempt to bomb Greenwich Observatory in 1894, which Conrad described as a "blood-stained inanity" challenging reason. In the novel Verloc is a has-been turned shopkeeper, still drawing the pay of a supposed subversive, and the whole concept of secrecy is turned to black humor through Conrad's evocation of London as a place of fog literal and metaphorical, a place where secretiveness and non-communication have become the norm in Verloc's household and in Westminster. The supposed "revolutionaries" are all presented as fakes, secretly dependent on patronage from members of the very establishment they purport to attack. Conrad constantly blocks any possibility of political drama by reducing the anarchists to figures of self-deception and the action to misunderstanding and accident; the bomb goes off because Stevie stumbles over a tree root in the fog. Throughout the novel characters wear masks not so much as controlled disguises but rather as if they have become identified by their images. Verloc wears the "label" of an agent provocateur and Stevie's coat label reveals to the police that he was the bomber. The Professor, the technician of anarchy, is summed up as an "unwholesome-looking little moral agent of destruction." "Agent" here becomes the ironic signifier of a recurring disparity between stated aims and results so severe that characters often seem the playthings of chance.

Conrad makes an ironic use of the term "secret," which comes to suggest ignorance and blindness rather than the drama of covert operations, and similarly G. K. Chesterton pushes the idea of disguise towards absurdity in *The Man Who Was Thursday* (1908). It is a basic premise of spy fiction that, despite double agents, there are rival agencies at work pursuing opposite aims. Chesterton undermines this premise through a series of revelations. Gabriel Syme, a detective, is trying to penetrate the Central Anarchist Council by pretending to be an anarchist himself, but finds it virtually impossible to keep track of the intricate masquerade in which he seems to be participating. His paranoia is fed by the apparent fact that he is shadowed around London by an aged figure called the "Professor" (Conrad's Professor designs what he thinks is the perfect detonator) and to make matters worse detectives are constantly being revealed as anarchists. As Chesterton explained in 1936, the bizarre twists and reversals in his novel were designed to show a "world of wild doubt and despair" (Chesterton 1936: 188) which could not be explained through political struggle. Extremes meet, as Conrad demonstrated in his other spy novel *Under Western Eyes* (1911), where there seems little to choose between a monarchic autocracy and an equally autocratic revolutionary program. Eschewing internationalism, Conrad declares: "The oppressors and the oppressed are all Russians together" (1983: xxxii).

The turning-point when spy fiction left glamour behind and turned to a new fragmentary realism can be dated from the publication of Somerset Maugham's *Ashenden or, The British Agent* (1928). Partly based on Maugham's MI6 service in Switzerland and Russia during World War I, these stories present the life of a field operative as one of monotony. Maugham admitted that "the material it offers for stories is scrappy and pointless" (Maugham 1948: viii) and he typically constructs his Ashenden stories out of small events and small tasks, which by implication are parts of a larger whole never revealed to the reader. We are told: "Being no more than a tiny rivet in a vast and complicated machine, he never had the advantage of seeing a completed action" (Maugham 1948: 7). Earlier spy narratives usually concluded with a climax or other resolution which reassured the reader simultaneously of the rightness of the agent's cause and the security of the nation. Maugham's modern awareness of narrative form emerges partly from the development of the secret service as an institution and partly from his desire to produce a more prosaic form of realism which related more closely to the nature of the agent's daily experience and to the limitations of his data. Ashenden was thus the "first of the anti-hero secret agents" (Masters 1987: 61), and had an impact on John Le Carré and his contemporaries. Indeed the authenticity of Maugham's accounts was confirmed at the drafting stage when Winston Churchill blocked some stories because they broke the Official Secrets Act.

Before the practices of spy fiction froze into the Cold War pattern, another writer played an important role in modernizing the genre – the novelist and screenwriter Eric Ambler. The American spy novelist Alan Furst gives Ambler pride of place in his anthology *The Book of Spies* (2004), declaring that "his instinct for plot dynamic and character production is close to perfect" (Furst 2004: 3). Furst's own subgenre of historical spy fiction focusing on the period 1933–44 could be read as an extended homage to Ambler. The latter's understated style, minimizing drama and filling his narratives with prosaic detail, is famously exemplified in *The Mask of Dimitrios* (1939), where an English lecturer turned detective writer is offered a subject by a Turkish police officer: that of the eponymous Levantine Greek. Demitrios appears to have been a drugs trafficker, possibly a spy for the French and his story is summed up initially as "incomplete. Inartistic. No detection, no suspects, no hidden motives, merely sordid" (Ambler 1999: 27). As in Maugham, the construction of a narrative out of scraps of information has become an important part of the plot. In an effort to understand Dimitrios the narrator travels across Europe, building up an increasingly complex dossier on this figure. As is typical of Ambler's fiction (and Furst's), Dimitrios emerges as an elusive stateless person, constantly changing his name and apparently involved in drug-smuggling, white slavery, and other rackets. When others try to pin an image to their memories of him, the result is disparate and shifting. He commonly wears a mask of respectability but also constantly recedes into the contemporary drama of Europe. Although the resourceful narrator accumulates a considerable amount of data at risk to himself, he never quite locates Dimitrios. Masking gradually emerges as a characteristic of European politics where more always seems to be going on behind the scenes. The narrator's only relative certainty at the end is that Dimitrios is probably still alive and active in the rackets.

Spying figures in a number of Graham Greene's novels as a form of entrapment within larger processes. The protagonist of *The Confidential Agent* (1939), whose title and bizarre reversals echo Conrad, remains confused throughout about his own identity. The writer Rollo Martins delays recognizing that his friend Harry Lime has become a morphine smuggler in postwar Vienna despite the warnings from military intelligence in *The Third Man* (1950), and in *Our Man in Havana* (1958) the salesman Warmold is inducted into MI6 almost by accident. Warmold devises a fictitious network of agents and plays to nuclear fears by sending reports of a secret weapon which bears just a passing resemblance to a vacuum cleaner. Even after his fraud is revealed, Warmold is honored for his years of "service," a final absurd reduction of the patriotic actions celebrated in early spy fiction. *The Human Factor* (1978) gives greater depth to its protagonist and powerfully dramatizes the psychological burden of secrecy. Castle is a relatively minor official in the Africa section of MI6. He gives the perfect imitation of a commuter dutifully going to his office every morning and when a new security check is instituted suspicion seems to fall on his colleague Davis, but this is a false clue. In an understated divergence from his routine, Castle goes to a house in Watford and is welcomed by his Soviet minder. The latter acts as a father confessor because the double agent is the "most isolated human being imaginable" (Cawelti and Rosenburg 1987: 20). In a small-scale echo of Kim Philby, Castle is disguised, leaves the country and ends up in Moscow, where it is revealed that his information is being fed back to British intelligence by the KGB in order to trap a double agent. And so Castle emerges as yet another in Greene's line of innocents.

When we turn to Ian Fleming we encounter a different phenomenon from the other fiction discussed here. James Bond (named after a Jamaican ornithologist) was designed originally as the "author's pillow fantasy" (Lycett 1995: 220) and then appeared to take on a life of his own as he was played by different film actors and as the Bond novels were continued under franchise after Fleming's death. An authorial mannerism of repeating Bond's full name throughout the novels helps to build up an impression that he is somehow special. The first Bond novel, *Casino Royale*, was published in 1953, when Britain was still pulling itself out of postwar austerity. More than a character, Bond personifies style, a glamorous cosmopolitan ease shown in his skill at the gambling table, ability to recognize vintage wine, and above all his attraction for beautiful women. Though some novels drew loosely on Fleming's wartime experiences in naval intelligence, Bond is already known, if only by repute, wherever he goes. When former director of the CIA Allen Dulles (himself the editor of a 1968 anthology *Great Spy Stories from Fiction*) read one of Fleming's novels, he remarked that this flamboyance would have been suicidal, since the KGB would have eliminated Bond on his second assignment. The point here is that the reader of Bond novels has to suspend many presumptions of realism to yield to their pattern of fantasy. Fleming skillfully played to our skepticism by giving Bond moderate achievements that made his more fantastic skills seem plausible (Amis 1965: 18). He also wove into his narratives enough historical details to make the reader uncertain where fact ends and fiction begins. For instance, the malign KGB counter-intelligence network SMERSH originated in the Soviet army during World War II and was disbanded in 1946. Fleming recycles the name as a more extensive, demonized version of the KGB. A major theme of postwar spy fiction is bureaucracy, but Fleming sidesteps this issue by creating plots that constantly narrow down to a battle of wills between Bond and an arch-villain. Blofeld, Dr No, Drax and the other antagonists are really postwar anachronisms, having more in common with John Buchan's master conspirator Dominick Medina in *The Three Hostages* (1924). Personifying the action of Bond novels as a struggle between good and evil enables Fleming to follow a pattern of evoking danger and threat and building up to a spectacular climax that ritually reassures the reader of the survival of the status quo ante.

In his 1962 essay "How to Write a Thriller" Fleming acknowledges the importance of Ambler (they were friends during the 1950s) and Graham Greene for the genre and proceeds to enumerate a number of general principles he worked from. These include maintaining a steady pace and clarity in the action, "total stimulation" of the reader's senses, and a "disciplined exoticism" offset by constant reference to familiar objects and even brand names. *Casino Royale* sets the tone for subsequent novels by dramatizing Bond's attempts to out-gamble the Soviet agent known as "Le Chiffre" (i.e. "cipher" or "number"), which he fails to do without financial input from the Americans. The casino game becomes an extended analogy for the political action, and indeed gambling, along with competitive sports, becomes a stock ingredient in the Bond series both as a way of dramatizing his risk-taking and of injecting the obligatory glamor into the action. The Bond novels are partly structured like games with their attendant moves and counter-moves, a "series of oppositions which allow a limited number of permutations and interactions" (Eco 1987: 147). The women here play two supporting roles: either offering an opportunity for sexual by-play or, if they are the villain's mistresses, functioning as a sexual prize within the larger battle of wits.

The Bond phenomenon helped trigger a wave of spy fiction during the 1960s on both sides of the Atlantic, further supported by TV serials like *The Prisoner* and *I Spy*. Among other writers whose careers began in this period was Len Deighton, whose 1962 novel *The IPCRESS File* began the series featuring his irreverent Cockney agent: "Harry Palmer" in the film adaptations but unnamed in the novels. Deighton set his own hallmark on the genre by including technical and procedural details in his narratives and by having his narrator use a matter-of-fact, ironic language strongly reminiscent of Raymond Chandler. *The IPCRESS File* combines brainwashing with betrayal when it is revealed that one of Palmer's superiors is a Soviet agent. This revelation is symptomatic of Deighton's ironic view of the British intelligence service as incompetent, snobbish, and divided by rivalry. *Funeral in Berlin* (1964) skillfully evokes the competing rivalry between agencies in West Berlin during the Cold War and describes one instance of the trade in smuggling defectors from East to West. Here each chapter carries an epigraph from chess, an updated trope for the Great Game where sides are no longer clear and where the protagonist maneuvers among plots and counter-plots. Deighton's early novels were followed in the 1980s by a second series centering on a British agent named Bernard Samson.

The rise of Deighton's career coincided with that of John Le Carré, who had served briefly in West Germany for British intelligence. He approached the genre through Conrad and Greene and he subsequently wrote *The Tailor of Panama* (1996) partly as a tribute to the latter. Like Greene, Mailer and others, Le Carré found a congruity between writing and spying: "the writer, like the spy, is an illusionist. He creates images that he finds within himself" (Bruccoli and Baughman 2004: 5). The difference, however, lies in control. From the very beginning Le Carré has projected a consistently skeptical attitude to the institutions of intelligence and has dramatized his agent-protagonists as falling victim to their own interpretations of events. Alec Leamas in *The Spy Who Came in from the Cold* (1963) is ultimately betrayed by the tortuous scheme whereby a neo-Nazi acts as a double agent inside East German intelligence. The novel positions him within an austere, carefully plotted sequence, which plays ironically on the absence the secure "inside" signaled in the title. The ultimate cold is death and that is Leamas's fate. Like Greene, Le Carré projects a jaundiced view of British intelligence as being disabled by class presumptions, nostalgia for empire, and its uneasy relation to the "cousins," that is, the Americans. *The Looking-Glass War* (1965) presents a collective exercise in self-deception when a scheme to infiltrate East Germany is mounted on a World War II model. Each section carries an epigraph from Kipling, Buchan, and Rupert Brooke as if to suggest that the ethos of espionage in the heyday of empire has become an anachronistic determinant of present strategy. Here we encounter a paradox that Le Carré has freely admitted lies in his spy fiction: his protagonists justify their action as a job to be done, but the novels repeatedly attack the nature of that work.

A major development in Le Carré's oeuvre was the creation of the retired agent George Smiley, brought back to sort out a crisis over the exposure of a double agent and then to engage in a protracted battle of wits with his Soviet opposite number, Karla. This trilogy – *Tinker, Tailor, Soldier Spy* (1974), *The Honorable Schoolboy* (1977), and *Smiley's People* (1978) – contains intricate plotting and evokes the world of intelligence partly through a jargon of "lamplighters," "moles," and "scalphunters," some of which has apparently been adopted by the intelligence services. Smiley appealed to Le Carré in his professionalism, which was achieved at the expense of his private life. Betrayed by his wife, he gradually roots out the identity of the double agent, who is presented as a displaced version of Kim Philby. Howard Hunt described Smiley as a "special detective called in after the damage is done" (Masters 1987: 225). Whereas Greene was reluctant to criticize Philby, perhaps from loyalty (he served in the latter's section of MI6 during World War II), Le Carré has described him as "my secret sharer" (Bruccoli and Baughman 2004: 154), ironically so since Philby betrayed his identity to the KGB. Le Carré shared with Philby a complicated relationship with his father, which he wrote into *A Perfect Spy* (1986). A shift towards greater introspection had already taken place in Le Carré's fiction during the 1980s, which examines in greater depth the psychological appeal and consequences of espionage. *The Little Drummer Girl* (1983) not only uses a female protagonist for the first time but also shifts the sphere of operations to the pursuit by Israeli intelligence of a renegade Palestinian terrorist active in Europe. Charlie is a minor actress recruited for the job in hand and the novel dramatizes the sheer difficulty she experiences in distinguishing her cover from reality.

With American spy fiction we encounter a different initial tradition. James Fenimore Cooper's *The Spy* (1821) describes the covert activities of a peddler working for the Americans during their war with Britain. The only person who can pay tribute to him is George Washington and Cooper's purpose was to pay tribute to an unsung hero in the cause of national independence. Similarly the eponymous Israel Potter in Herman Melville's 1855 novel acts as a courier taking secret messages to Paris in the same cause. This patriotism, rather than imperial defense, informed portrayals of spies in American fiction up to the aftermath of the Civil War when, in stories like "Parker Adderson, Philosopher," Ambrose Bierce ironically demonstrated how reversible allegiances were in that conflict. With the Cold War, espionage emerges as a central subject in American fiction. In 1964 CIA station chief E. Howard Hunt was invited by publishers to write an American counterpart to the James Bond novels and rose to the challenge by beginning a series on CIA agent Peter Ward, which never achieved Fleming's success, however.

The trauma written into much postwar British spy fiction was the collective betrayal of the Cambridge Five, especially of Philby. In the American context, the revelations of covert domestic activities by the CIA and other agencies tended to complicate the politics of spy fiction and to shift the emphasis to institutional domestic betrayal. A melodramatic sign of this growing ambiguity can be found in Richard Condon's *The Manchurian Candidate* (1959), where a Korean War hero turns out to have been brainwashed into a programmed assassin. In James Grady's *Six Days of the Condor* (1974), however, Communism has taken second place to the profit motive. Here an intelligence unit is wiped out by a renegade group within the CIA who are involved in drugs smuggling. It was in reaction against such works that William F. Buckley, Jr (himself a CIA operative briefly) began his Blackford Oakes series with *Saving the Queen* (1976), "in which the good guys and the bad guys are actually distinguishable from one another" (Buckley 1994: xiii). Buckley gives a new angle to the "special relationship" by having his hero sleep with the Queen while trying to expose a high-placed British mole.

Two American novelists who have brought a new sophistication and subtlety to the genre are Robert Littell and Charles McCarry. Littell has acknowledged a debt to Le Carré, whose fiction helped him explore situations of extreme ambiguity like the authenticity of a defector (*The Defection of A.J. Lewinter*, 1973), the use of disinformation (*Agent in Place*, 1991), and the construction of multiple fake identities (*Legends*, 2005). The latter issue is also central to Robert Ludlum's *The Bourne Identity* (1980), where an American agent has forgotten even his legend, given for him to track down a terrorist. Littell's major historical novel is *The Company* (2002), which traces out the developments within the CIA up to the end of the Cold War, highlighting the complex role of James Angleton, Kim Philby's opposite number in counterintelligence. Angleton has also been described in Aaron Latham's *Orchids for Mother* (1977), remembered also for its authentic detail about the CIA, and William Buckley's *Spytime* (2000).

Charles McCarry, who served as a CIA agent from 1958 to 1967, is a professed admirer of Ambler (who endorsed his first novel), Maugham, Condon and Le Carré. *The Miernik Dossier* (1973) positions the reader as a proxy intelligence officer, for we have to construct the narrative from a series of official documents; reports, dispatches, cables, and transcripts. The subject is a project by Polish-Soviet intelligence to trigger an Islamist uprising in the Sudan, but the treatment is strikingly original. Purportedly assembled in response to a committee's request for a "complete picture of a typical operation," the narrative teases the reader with the elusive goal of a total account and leaves the issue of typicality hanging in mid-air. *The Tears of Autumn* (1974), in contrast, focuses on a single agent, who has resigned to pursue his investigations into Vietnamese responsibility for Kennedy's assassination. In common with many spy novelists, McCarry has created his own series, centering on the figure of Paul Christopher, who even carries memories of the Nazis in *Christopher's Ghosts* (2007).

The ending of the Cold War has not eliminated it as a subject for fiction. Joseph Kanon's novels, for example, represent an ongoing attempt to understand that period. But supposing the spy novelist wants new subjects, where would they be found? John Le Carré explores the machinations of a pharmaceutical company in Kenya in *The Constant Gardner* (2005). Alex Berenson's *The Faithful Spy* (2006) describes a CIA operative working undercover in Al Qaida. Daniel Silva similarly turned to the Middle East for his debut novel of Gabriel Allon, an art restorer and ex-officer of Israeli intelligence. *The Kill Artist* (2000) was the first in a series exploring Islamic terrorism as well as strife in Northern Ireland and the upsurge of Russian nationalism. As Silva himself has admitted, the events of 9/11 have triggered a resurgence of interest in spy fiction with an attendant redefinition of the enemy. In the fiction of Silva and his contemporaries the threat comes not only from Islamic jihadists but also from arms dealers or other groups operative in the complex post-Cold War world.

19
Crime and the Gothic

Catherine Spooner

History

The first Gothic novel, Horace Walpole's *The Castle of Otranto* (1764), begins not with a crime but with the reminder of a crime (Walpole 1968). A giant helmet falls on Conrad, heir to the house of Manfred, thus extinguishing the family line. It transpires that this is a supernatural act of vengeance for Manfred's usurpation of his title from Alfonso during the Crusades. As Walpole's quasi-biblical moral indicates, the sins of the fathers are visited on the children. The victims of crime are ultimately the criminal's own family.

Walpole's novel sets the tone for subsequent Gothic fiction: crime is the preserve of charismatic and powerful men; crime has peculiar resonances within the family; crime takes place at one remove, in the past, but has continuing and visceral effects within the present. The criminal is tormented by self-reflection, which eventually leads to his undoing; the legacy of the crime disrupts the proper social order and shadows the onward march of progress and modernity. There are variations to this formula (a charismatic and powerful woman, for example, is the criminal in Charlotte Dacre's novel of 1806, *Zofloya, or the Moor*) but in general, the exceptions serve to prove the rule.

The Gothic novel, inaugurated by Walpole's self-titled "Gothic Story," had its heyday between 1765 and 1820, when writers such as Ann Radcliffe (*The Mysteries of Udolpho*, 1794; *The Italian*, 1797), Matthew Lewis (*The Monk*, 1796) and Charles Maturin (*Melmoth, the Wanderer*, 1820) were among the most prominent and highly regarded of an enormous number of authors producing texts of varying degrees of literary quality, from Radcliffe's critically acclaimed and extraordinarily well-paid works to single-volume chapbooks more or less plagiarizing other best-selling titles. According to Robert Miles, at the peak of the Gothic novel's popularity between 1788 and 1807, it had an average market share of 30 percent of all novel production (Miles 2002: 42).

While the Gothic novel in its original form fell out of favor after about 1820, its distinctive tropes continued to influence other forms of nineteenth-century fiction, including the Newgate novel, Walter Scott's historical fiction, the realist fiction of Dickens and the Brontës, the sensation novel, the ghost story, the American Gothic of Edgar Allan Poe and Nathaniel Hawthorne, and crucially, the detective story. Although these texts did not necessarily follow the stock formulae set down by Radcliffe, Lewis, and their contemporaries, they found new ways of interpreting the Gothic, enabling the genre to shift with the tastes of the times. Yet despite their differences, what all of these nineteenth-century versions of Gothic had in common were the features identified by Chris Baldick as intrinsic to Gothic narrative:

> For the Gothic effect to be attained, a tale should combine a fearful sense of inheritance in time with a claustrophobic sense of enclosure in space, these two dimensions reinforcing one another to produce an impression of sickening descent into disintegration. (Baldick 1992: xix)

Chief among these traits is the sense of a fearful inheritance in time, the awful legacy of the past intruding onto the present. Robert Mighall argues that in the Victorian period, this became the single most important defining feature of the Gothic. Moreover, he suggests, Gothic narratives were no longer characteristically set in the past, representing a barbarous period distanced from the enlightened modernity of their readers, but were typically set in a present disrupted by the "threatening reminders or scandalous vestiges" of a former time that should have been discarded in the onward march of progress and enlightenment. As Mighall explains, "Where the vestigial is found (in monasteries, prisons, lunatic asylums, the urban slums, or even the bodies, minds, or psyches of criminals, deviants or relatively 'normal' subjects) depends upon historical circumstances" (Mighall 1999: 26). As Charles Rzepka notes, twentieth-century writers of "hard-boiled" detective fiction like Raymond Chandler and Ross MacDonald assign Gothic vestigiality a particularly significant thematic and structural role (Rzepka 2000; 2005: 221–5).

The new emphasis on the "bodies, minds, or psyches" of criminals and deviants has obvious implications for the relationship of Gothic to crime fiction. In the nineteenth century, the two are not clearly distinguished. The earliest writers of detective fiction – Edgar Allan Poe, Wilkie Collins, Arthur Conan Doyle – could all also be said to be writers of Gothic fiction. There are traces of Gothic in most crime narratives, just as there are crimes in most Gothic novels. In *A Counter-History of Crime Fiction*, Maurizio Ascari argues that the separation of the two is an artificial one, produced by early twentieth-century critics' investment in rationalism. In the climate of literary Modernism, Gothic was deeply unfashionable, and as a consequence Gothic associations were stripped from the detective story, which was regarded as merely a logical puzzle, ending by celebrating the triumph of rationalism. Ascari demonstrates that critics selectively composed the detective canon in order to confirm this view, rejecting anything that did not fit as "Gothic" or "sensational." Late twentieth-century critical reassessments, however, have restored the "supernatural, Gothic, sensational" of Ascari's subtitle to crime narratives, both in criticism and in contemporary fiction.

The opposite side of this story is that twentieth-century assessments of Gothic fiction have also conspired to keep Gothic and crime fiction apart. As Chris Baldick and Robert Mighall argue, criticism of Gothic fiction has often been overly invested in a notion of transgression, influenced first by a Freudian model of repression and later by identity politics. "This tradition," they write, "employs a model of culture and history premised on fear, experienced by a surrealist caricature of a bourgeoisie trembling in their frock coats at each and every deviation from a rigid, but largely mythical, stable middle-class consensus" (Baldick and Mighall 2000: 225). In actual fact, they argue, Gothic is an inherently bourgeois form, in the majority of cases informed by a Whiggish politics of progress away from an oppressive and unenlightened past. Late twentieth-century texts, which often embrace the more gleefully disruptive aspects of Gothic, are thus a co-optation or a recitation of a certain kind of critical view of Gothic as much as of the tradition itself.

Modern detective fiction, often made to stand for crime fiction as a whole and traditionally represented as a conservative form, appeared antithetical to the consensus that Gothic has uniquely transgressive properties, and therefore has remained absent from accounts. David Punter's definitive survey *The Literature of Terror*, for example, includes no crime fiction between Arthur Conan Doyle and Thomas Harris, whose use of a hard-boiled "reportage" style in *Red Dragon* (1981) Punter dismisses as ameliorating the text's Gothic qualities, suggesting that it

> serves as a defence, as a deliberate refutation of the psychotic, as an implicit statement that, however [the detective protagonist] Graham might feel himself embroiled in the scenarios of sadism, we, the writer and the readers, are allowed to reside in a protected space, we are not to be drawn into the position, characteristic of much other Gothic, of the "implicated reader" (Punter 1996: 167).

For Punter, implicitly, *Red Dragon* lacks the subversive properties of "much other Gothic" because it protects the reader from its own worst excesses, lacking the destabilizing perspective of a novel like Iain Banks's *The Wasp Factory* (1984). Yet perhaps the difference between the two is less their generic provenance, than that Harris is writing in a "popular" and Banks in a "literary" register. As other studies have shown, Gothic can be conservative or progressive in different contexts – sometimes even within the same text. So, as Lee Horsley points out, can crime fiction (Horsley 2005: 158).

Tracing this interweaving of detective/crime fiction and the Gothic can be extremely revealing, as each genre is positioned differently at different periods in history: in the early twentieth century, for example, Gothic stands for "irrational," despite the fact that eighteenth- and nineteenth-century Gothic almost invariably privileges the rational over the forces of darkness that seek to challenge it. Horsley suggests that while "traditional detective fiction ultimately acts as a repudiation of the gothic (eschewing supernatural explanations, throwing light into dark recesses)," it may also "play extensively with it" (Horsley 2005: 48), as in Agatha Christie's *Peril at End House* (1932). This point could be extended to suggest that throwing light into dark recesses is fundamental to the Gothic novel, and many of the classic Gothic novels also eschew supernatural explanations. So ultimately, the positioning of traditional detective fiction as anti-Gothic is as much about the modernist desire for severance from the nineteenth century and its supposedly torpid literary conventions as about the essential properties of the text.

In fact the two forms, detective fiction and the Gothic, share a similar structure in their preoccupation with the return of past upon present. Paul Skenazy suggests that the very emphasis on modernity in the classic, Californian hard-boiled detective novel inevitably leads to the re-emergence of the dark histories jettisoned by those seeking a fresh identity in the land of new beginnings:

> The Los Angeles mystery plot maintains a double rhythm: moving inexorably forward in time while creeping slowly backward to resolve the disruptions and violence evident in the present. ... The genre is directed to the past. It develops a legend of failure. (Skenazy 1995: 113)

This "gothic causality" (Skenazy 1995: 114), whereby the present is overdetermined by past events, and where the detective's activities inevitably function to reveal the secrets of the past even when he or she has been hired to preserve them, is a fundamental feature of noir. However, it is also a determining feature of all detective fiction. As Skenazy continues,

> Both gothic and detective fiction ... share common assumptions: that there is an undisclosed event, a secret from the past; that the secret represents an occurrence or desire antithetical to the principles and position of the house (or family); that to know the secret is to understand the inexplicable and seemingly irrational events that occur in the present. Both forms bring hidden experiences from shadow to light. (Skenazy 1995: 114)

The country house murders of golden age detective fiction operate according to the same formula. As such, the generic boundaries between Gothic and detective fiction are irrevocably blurred.

The other feature characteristically used to keep Gothic and crime fiction apart is that, until the wave of what Horsley terms "fantastic noir" in the 1990s and beyond (Horsley 2001: 230), Gothic is seen as the province of the supernatural while crime fiction retains a surface realism. The "explained" supernatural, however, is a feature of Gothic writing as early and as central to the tradition as that of Ann Radcliffe: infamously, the "mysteries" of Udolpho are all resolved by the end of the text, in a kind of precursor of the *denouement* of the detective plot. The main difference is that the heroine, a proto-detective in her curiosity to discover Udolpho's secrets, is not privy to all the explanations provided by the omniscient narrator. Radcliffe's novels characteristically animate the tension between reason and superstition, the bulk of the narrative enabling the reader's vicarious enjoyment of superstition, while various morally authoritative characters simultaneously condemn its indulgence.

Nineteenth-century Gothic from Poe onwards is often devoid of the supernatural altogether, or evokes it in order to articulate psychological disturbance: Wilkie Collins deliberately references the Gothic in his portrayal of Anne Catherick, who is presented in spectral terms and once literally mistaken for a ghost in *The Woman in White* (1860), but is actually a madwoman with a fixation on wearing white clothes. In Arthur Conan Doyle's Sherlock Holmes stories, Holmes always exposes the supernatural as issuing from rational causes. The attacks of the "Sussex Vampire" on Robert Ferguson's infant son, for example, are not perpetrated by an undead fiend, but by a jealous, disabled half-sibling. More famously, through Holmes's investigation the Hound of the Baskervilles is revealed as the masquerade of a modern criminal exploiting the fear produced by this legend in the locals.

The most Gothic of all the Holmes stories has no supernatural features at all. "The Adventure of the Speckled Band" (1892) is a locked room mystery which replays the classic "female Gothic" plot: a wicked stepfather with the improbably Gothic name of Dr Grimesby Roylott has designs on the inheritance of his stepdaughter, Helen Stoner, and encloses her within a sinister room of his semi-ruined ancestral mansion in order to do away with her. Roylott, a stage villain in "a black top-hat, a long frock-coat, and a pair of high gaiters, with a hunting crop swinging in his hand" (Doyle 1986: 1.356), is an aristocrat of decayed family fortunes with a hereditary tendency to "Violence of temper approaching to mania" (Doyle 1986: 1.350), driven to his current crimes by the past misdemeanors, financial and genetic, of his dissolute family. Helen Stoner is a twin, her sister having already been disposed of by Roylott, and their fates are intended to double one another. The grotesquerie of the *mise en scène* is ratcheted up by mysterious neighborhood gypsies and the roaming presence of a pet cheetah and baboon that Roylott has brought back with him from a stint in the colonies: the baboon gives Holmes and Watson a start by darting out of the darkness like a "hideous and distorted child" (Doyle 1986: 1.365).

It is not in these atmospherics, however, but in the solution of the mystery that the story is most crucially Gothic. Roylott intends to kill Helen by releasing a deadly poisonous swamp adder, brought back from India, into her room. Following Holmes's intervention, the snake returns into Roylott's room and strikes him instead, causing Holmes to remark, "Violence does ... recoil upon the violent" (Doyle 1986: 1.367). The snake becomes an instrument of colonial retribution, revisiting on its master not only the violence he intended against his family, but also that perpetrated on the colonial subject, both literal (Roylott beat his native butler to death in Calcutta, but escaped his full sentence) and symbolic (the practice of colonialism itself). The past returns to catch up with the criminal with inevitable

Gothic force; the moment of horror is simultaneously that in which order is restored.

Duality

If the return of past upon present is the narrative feature that most closely links Gothic and crime fiction, then the unstable protagonist is another, particularly in noir. When Gothic and crime fiction coincide, the protagonist is often racked by guilt, obsession, paranoia, or other psychological disturbances, or his or her identity is misplaced or disguised. The protagonist's instability places the pursuit of knowledge enacted by the detective narrative under question, often surrounding the process of rational and moral judgment with doubt.

Lee Horsley suggests that, "The noir thriller is very often, like both *Frankenstein* and *Jekyll and Hyde*, a fantasy of duality" (Horsley 2001: 230). Doubling is a crucial feature of Gothic fiction, the doppelganger being a prime example of the Freudian uncanny, in which the familiar and the unfamiliar coincide to create a feeling of profound unease. James Hogg's *The Private Memoirs and Confessions of a Justified Sinner* (1824) is a multiply doubled text: the unreliable narrator, a religious fanatic called Robert Wringhim, is visited by a mysterious figure named Gil-Martin who oddly resembles him, and who incites him to murder. Wringhim loses his memory and discovers that he is suspected of crimes that have taken place during these lapses: has he committed them, or has Gil-Martin done so in his shape? Gil-Martin is revealed to be the devil, but from a modern perspective, the story reads chillingly like a description of multiple personality disorder. Moreover, the doubling does not end with the pairing of Wringhim and Gil-Martin: Gil-Martin takes on the appearance of other characters; Wringhim persecutes his brother George Colwan by constantly shadowing him; and Wringhim's first-person "Confessions" are doubled with a frame narrative written by a fictional, and also profoundly unreliable, editor – not James Hogg, who appears as a character in the text (thus doubling the "real" James Hogg). The overall effect profoundly destabilizes notions of unitary meaning. Wringhim cannot even be sure whether or not he has committed his own crimes. Hogg's target is Calvinist doctrine, but his genuinely disturbing novel also implicates the reader, forced to piece together an interpretation of Wringhim's moral and mental disintegration from conflicting accounts.

Hogg's novel inspired fellow Scottish author Robert Louis Stevenson, whose *The Strange Case of Dr Jekyll and Mr Hyde* (1886) has now become the classic literary exploration of duality. To a certain extent, however, dualism oversimplifies the text, which insists that "man will ultimately be known for a mere polity of multifarious, incongruous and independent denizens" (Stevenson 1992: 142). However, the myth of an outwardly respectable scientist who discovers a means of unleashing the criminal part of his self has provided a convenient narrative for popular accounts of criminal psychology, from Jack the Ripper to suburban serial killer Fred West. Similar models of a double life proliferate through *fin-de-siècle* Gothic crime fictions, including Oscar Wilde's *The Picture of Dorian Gray* (1891) and many of *The Adventures of Sherlock Holmes* (1892).

The doubling of the detective with the criminal is another feature of crime fiction drawn from Gothic convention. Gothic narratives, drawing on the story of the Fall as told in *Genesis* and retold in John Milton's *Paradise Lost* (1667), tend to present knowledge as damned or cursed. Eve's curiosity, her desire to eat of the Tree of Knowledge, condemns her to exile from paradise. This story is retold as a prototype Gothic narrative in the fairy tale "Bluebeard," in which the young wife cannot resist the temptation to open the one door her husband forbids her, thereby discovering he has murdered his previous wives. Within this narrative genealogy, exposing the crime does not provide resolution and the restoration of order, but seals the detective's own damnation. In Angela Carter's Gothic reworking of the Bluebeard story, "The Bloody Chamber," the young heroine bears the burn mark from a communion wafer on her forehead for the rest of her life, even after her murderous husband has been dispatched, as a symbol of her lost innocence. The knowledge required to catch a criminal often makes the detective dangerously complicit: Will Graham in Thomas Harris's *Red Dragon*, for example, cannot escape the burden of his proximity to the criminal minds he investigates; he "understood murder uncomfortably well" (Harris 2004: 419). Graham is tainted by his extraordinary insight; his horrific scarring at the climax of the novel effectively transfers the serial killer Francis Dolarhyde's disfigurement to his own face, symbolically demonstrating his contagion.

The doubling of detective and criminal is brought to its logical conclusion by William Hjortsberg's *Falling Angel* (1978), in which the perpetrator of the murders that private detective Harry Angel is investigating turns out to be himself. *Falling Angel* also enacts the doubling of crime fiction and the Gothic, replaying the stock narrative tropes of the hard-boiled detective thriller as Gothic horror and throwing into sharp relief the overlap between the two. Commenting on Alan Parker's film adaptation of the novel, *Angel Heart* (1987), Fred Botting stresses that, "In the movement between genres there is a diabolical process of deception displayed and performed, a process that multiplies meanings and identities to the point where nothing is what it seems but an effect of narrative appearances" (Botting 1996: 174).

Angel is engaged by a client calling himself Louis Cyphre to find a missing crooner named Johnny Favorite who has reneged on a contract. The closer he seems to get to solving the mystery, the more he is trailed by death and destruction, as everyone with information relating to the case is brutally murdered. At last he realizes that he is Favorite, and his repressed "other" self has been committing the murders in an attempt to prevent him from realizing his true identity: as Favorite, he attempted to cheat Lucifer out of the bargain he made with him by ritualistically eating a man's heart and thereby stealing his soul. Returning to his apartment after this revelation, he discovers that he has also murdered Johnny's/his own daughter, significantly enough named Epiphany, with whom he has been having an affair.

Harry/Johnny's double identity is signaled much earlier in the novel by a dream in which Harry runs through a deserted urban landscape, "somehow becoming the pursuer instead of the quarry, chasing a distant figure down endless unknown avenues," before finally seizing his adversary and discovering "He was my twin. It was like looking in the mirror" (Hjortsberg 1987: 77–8). The mixture of terror and desire Harry experiences at this moment (a fraternal kiss turns into a mutually destructive, violent embrace) collapses Eve Kosofsky Sedgwick's dyad of homosocial pursuit: Harry is not motivated by homosexual fear and desire (in cannibalizing the young soldier, he has already transcended all such mundane taboos) but his fear of and desire for self-recognition. Detection is constructed as a circular process that always leads back to the self: even sex, in this novel, is incestuous.

The New York described in *Falling Angel* is one of lurid and improbable performances: blues clubs, freak shows, waxworks, belly dancers. In Coney Island, Harry visits a wax museum with a series of tableaux presenting famous murders, "wielding sash-weights and meat saws, stuffing dismembered limbs into trunks, adrift in oceans of red paint" (Hjortsberg 1987: 88). Harry's description echoes that of his own murder victims: Dr Albert Fowler, for example, cries "ruby tears" and is "as cold as something hanging in a butcher-shop window" (Hjortsberg 1987: 25). The scene is as stagy as that of the fairground chamber of horrors. Louis Cyphre appears under different names (El Cifr, Dr Cipher) as a motivational preacher and a magician. Harry attends a voodoo ceremony in Central Park and a black mass at a disused subway station. The line between ceremony and performance is blurred. Religion appears over-determined, a series of empty spectacles: the Reverend Love's Baptist church is motivated by personal gain; while voodoo appears outwardly sinister but is merely a diversion from the real crime, orchestrated by "Christian" black magic. Throughout, "Louis Cyphre" in his various guises signifies the process of interpretation itself, the code that must be de-ciphered. Once Harry has cracked the case, Louis Cyphre vanishes into thin air: self-knowledge is sufficient damnation.

Excess

In its emphasis on spectacle and performance, *Falling Angel* taps into what Bakhtin called the Romantic carnivalesque, centered on the individual and stripped of its hilarity and regenerative communal powers (Bakhtin 1984: 40). Fred Botting has famously argued that "Gothic signifies a writing of excess" (Botting 1996: 1). Drawing on the wild reputation of the original Goths, the fourth-century barbarians who sacked Rome, Gothic literature pits the forces of unreason against those of civilization and Enlightenment. As Botting continues, "In Gothic productions imagination and emotional effects exceed reason. Passion, excitement and sensation transgress social proprieties and moral laws. Ambivalence and uncertainty obscure single meaning" (Botting 1996: 3). Although progress and modernity are generally privileged in Gothic narratives (Baldick and Mighall 2000), with tyranny distanced into a previous age or the monsters and vampires defeated by the end of the text, they are placed profoundly under threat for the duration of the narrative. This excessiveness is often featured in the most Gothicized crime fiction, either in the extremity of the crime itself, or the way that the narrative is told.

Transgressor-centered fiction, in which there is no rational detective presence to mediate the horror of the crime, most frequently partakes of this Gothic excess. The transgressor takes on monstrous properties, as Judith Halberstam notes: "in the Gothic, crime is embodied within a specifically deviant form – the monster – that announces itself ... as the place of corruption" (Halberstam 1995: 2). The crimes of the earliest Gothic villains frequently violate more than one taboo: Ambrosio in Matthew Lewis's *The Monk*, for example, commits matricide and quasi-necrophiliac, incestuous rape. Victoria in Charlotte Dacre's *Zofloya, or, the Moor* (1997) is doubly outrageous in that the seduction, torture, and murder she practices violate codes of proper femininity. Prototypical historical models for the Gothic criminal include medieval aristocrats Erzsebet Bathory and Gilles de Rais, each allegedly responsible for murdering hundreds of victims, and the Marquis de Sade's fictional libertines and dominatrices. The Byronic Fatal Man, who as defined by Mario Praz, "dreams of perfecting the world by committing crimes" (Praz 1954: 78), suggests the complicated mixture of art, power, and exile from society that inform Gothic crime. Thomas De Quincey's essay "On Murder Considered as One of the Fine Arts" (1827) presents murder as an artistic act that can be assessed according to aesthetic criteria, and that in its most perfect form is productive of the sublime, the sensation of awe and terror validated by Edmund Burke as expanding the mind and enabling apprehension of the infinite. Nineteenth-century texts generally stop short of making this explicit link: in Oscar Wilde's *The Picture of Dorian Gray*, for example, Dorian's murders are the outcome of his desire to preserve his Decadent lifestyle, rather than aesthetic acts in themselves. Twentieth-century fictions, however, have embraced the concept of the murderer-as-artist. Patrick Süskind's *Perfume* (1985) has its protagonist Grenouille serially murder women in pursuit of the perfect scent, while Bathory is herself constructed as surreal artist in Alejandra Pizarnik's short story "The Bloody Countess" (1992 [1968]). Bathory supposedly bathed in the blood of virgins in order to preserve her youth; in Pizarnik's story the stylization of death, the transmutation of the body into art, is a way of transcending mortality.

With the six gruesome, unsolved murders of prostitutes in Whitechapel in 1888, a new form of excessive crime entered the Gothic repertoire: serial killing. Serial murder was, of course, not identified as such until the 1970s, and had numerous precedents (both real and fictional) prior to the Whitechapel murders, but it was at this point that serial killer narratives caught the popular imagination and began to be told in their recognizably modern form. Robert Louis Stevenson's *The Strange Case of Dr Jekyll and Mr Hyde* provided a ready-made template for the psychology of the serial killer, and the lead actor in a contemporary stage adaptation was even briefly entertained as a suspect. However, subsequent texts make overt reference to Jack the Ripper. In Arthur Machen's *The Great God Pan* (2005 [1894]), the mysterious Helen

Vaughan, whose crimes are never directly specified (just as Jack was never identified), is constructed as even more shocking and disturbing than Jack – presumably at least partly because she is female, and her victims are middle-class men. The association with Jack is used to imply the sexual nature of her crimes, as well as their inexplicability, and interestingly is conveyed in the context of modern newspaper reports (the relationship with the media is considered one of the hallmarks of the modern serial killer). In the Preface to the Icelandic edition of *Dracula* (2008, novel originally published 1897), Bram Stoker also compares his arch-vampire's crimes directly to those of Jack, thereby retrospectively constructing Dracula's deeds as serial murder. Recent criticism has made much of the serial killer as a vampiric figure, but Stoker uses the comparison in the reverse direction. The moments at which the modern vampire myth and the modern serial killer narrative crystallize are intriguingly coincident.

Lee Horsley suggests that transgressor-centered narratives have become increasingly prominent in the crime fiction of the second half of the twentieth century (Horsley 2005: 114), a trend that corresponds to a wider Gothic revival (see Spooner 2006). In transgressor-centered fiction, the Gothic excess of the killer and the rationalism of the detective plot are played off one another, often to the complete exclusion of the latter. The collapsing of the modern serial killer with the Gothic hero-villain in characters such as Harris's cannibal psychiatrist Hannibal Lecter creates a kind of mythic figure, which according to Horsley "moves the genre so far towards its gothic side that the other (rational, ordering) aspects of the genre are undermined ... the more excessive and the more gothic the narrative, the more unsettling it is to our facile moral assumptions" (Horsley 2005: 141).

The play between rational and irrational has always been a feature of the Gothic, and in a sense, this tipping of the scales towards subversion is not a feature of Gothic *per se*, but of late twentieth-century Gothic, in which writers have a self-awareness of the literary and critical heritage and frequently a political agenda specific to postmodern culture. Poppy Z. Brite, for example, whose gay serial killer romance *Exquisite Corpse* (1997) was considered so excessive that it was rejected by Penguin, Brite's UK publisher, has explained how she deliberately seeks the "poetry of violence" in an attempt to locate artistic truth through excess, and to reject facile narratives of childhood trauma that conveniently rationalize and contain evil (Brite 1996). Similarly Bret Easton Ellis's *American Psycho*, extraordinarily controversial upon its publication in 1991, employs extreme violence for the purposes of satire on the affectless culture of late capitalism. Such strategic and deliberate attempts at subversion are not inherently Gothic, but rather use Gothic discourses as a tool for their specific purposes.

Another way of approaching Gothic excess in late twentieth-century crime fiction is through the contrary pull of body horror and the play of surfaces. Horsley suggests that "Late twentieth-century crime fiction has increasingly shown its readers the physical opening of bodies, the psychological exposure of damaged minds, and the inscription of personal traumas on the bodies of victims" (Horsley 2005: 112). In novels like *Exquisite Corpse*, "body horror is the substance of the narrative rather than just the culmination of an action that is spiralling out of control" (Horsley 2005:

142). The disintegration of boundaries between inside and outside, body and mind, villain and victim in these narratives, not to mention a preoccupation with mortality and decay, marks these narratives as peculiarly Gothic. Harris's *The Silence of the Lambs* (1989) illustrates this particularly well. As Judith Halberstam writes of Jonathan Demme's film adaptation of the novel, "Boundaries between people (detective and criminal, men and women, murderers and victims) are all mixed up in this film until they disappear altogether, becoming as transparent as the glass that (barely) divides Lecter and Starling" (Halberstam 1995: 164). The ultimate bodily boundary is the skin, the membrane that divides outside from inside, and this text is excessively preoccupied with skin, literally in serial killer Buffalo Bill's mission to construct himself a "woman suit," and metaphorically in Lecter's ability to get "under the skin" of his victims, psychologically turning them inside-out.

The preoccupation with surfaces and the privileging of surface over depth is a defining feature of Gothic, first identified in Eve Sedgwick's *The Coherence of Gothic Conventions* (1986). According to Sedgwick, contrary to vulgar psychoanalytic interpretations, the mask is more significant in Gothic discourse than what it disguises, the veil more interesting than what it conceals. Frequently, Gothic horror resides in the fact that there is *nothing beneath* the veil; that surface is everything. This emphasis on the surface is a feature of many of the more Gothic crime narratives. For example, Orson Welles's film noir *The Lady from Shanghai* (1948) infamously presents iconic redhead Rita Hayworth with cropped and bleached hair, and ends with a shoot-out in a hall of mirrors that leaves viewers confused as to what has actually occurred. As Eddie Robson suggests,

> The film arguably plays upon Hayworth's established image here, as a means of suggesting another, more "natural" self which Elsa systematically represses; a Gothic reading would identify that this other self is only another performance, a different but no more authentic Rita Hayworth. Once her duplicity is revealed, we are invited to consider the surface-depth relationship by the endless duplication of identical images of her, and the way that Bannister shoots at the various Elsas indiscriminately suggests that the distinction is irrelevant. Notably we never see any of these shots hit their targets, thereby denying us a moment when we can identify which are the real Elsa and Bannister (Robson 2005: 122).

Similarly, *The Silence of the Lambs* prioritizes surfaces in a way that problematizes the depth narrative of conventional psychoanalysis. Lecter resists the attempts of other psychiatrists to analyze him, and in *Red Dragon* refers to psychoanalysis as a "dead religion" (Harris 2004: 186). As Judith Halberstam argues, "In *The Silence of the Lambs*, inversion reduces norm and pathology, inside and outside to meaningless categories; there is only pathology and varying degrees of it, only an outside in various forms" (Halberstam 1995: 169). In this weirdly inverted universe, one's conformity to the psychological script is a sign of failure: the Red Dragon and Buffalo Bill are less successful serial killers than Hannibal Lecter because their actions can be reduced to a pathological narrative, and thus can be contained. As Harris writes at the end of *The Silence of the Lambs*, "At least two scholarly journals explained that this unhappy childhood was the reason [Buffalo Bill] killed women in his basement for their skins. The words *crazy* and *evil* do not appear in either article" (Harris 2004: 411). On one level Harris is critiquing the failure of modern scientific discourse to deal with the problem of evil; on another, he demonstrates how this same discourse reduces Bill to victim, the final mark of his defeat.

In Harris's first two novels, Lecter resists this containment, using reason as a tool to manipulate others while evading the attempts of the psychiatric profession to "explain" him. In *Hannibal* (1999), however, Harris finally provides Lecter with a back-story, a process later completed by *Hannibal Rising* (2006). With this maneuver, Harris closes down the play of surfaces and concedes to the depth model. As Brian Baker suggests,

> Throughout the novels, Harris refers to Lecter as "the fiend," "the monster," yet ultimately cannot resist psychologising his protagonist. ... While serial killer fictions indicate the limits of rational discourse, and gesture towards the discourse of religion ("monster," "evil," "sin") to signify that which lies outside of the explicatory powers of science, medicine or reasoned understanding, Harris's Lecter novels cannot embrace this radical destabilisation ... returning us finally to the comforts of reason and the unitary subject. (Baker 2007: 172)

The Gothic/crime novel that most successfully refuses to capitulate to the depth narrative has also become a byword for excess: Bret Easton Ellis's *American Psycho*. The horror of Ellis's novel is that everything is reduced to the level of surface, there is no depth: "Surface, surface, surface was all that anyone found meaning in" (Ellis 1991: 360). Investment banker Patrick Bateman reels off lists of designer labels and consumer products casually punctuated by images of graphic sex and extreme violence; these are given equal weight in his internal monologue, with the effect that the latter start to seem like an inevitable adjunct of the former, Bateman's eventual cannibalism the logical endpoint of the process of capitalist consumption. His obsession with managing his personal appearance through gym workouts, facials, manicures, hair products, elaborate grooming routines, and precise adherence to arcane dress codes produces a self without interiority: "*I simply am not there*" (Ellis 1991: 362; emphasis in original). Bateman has no conscience and no past; inside and outside are so indistinct in his present-tense stream of consciousness that it is unclear whether his depravities are real or imagined. Moreover, the society in which he lives is complicit with this construction of meaning through external appearance: no matter how extreme his behavior, those around him are unable or refuse to recognize anything outside the norm; his wealth, status, and good looks not only protect him from discovery but seemingly make it impossible for him to be discovered, since to recognize his depravity would be to indict the whole culture. In one telling scene, Bateman returns to an apartment where he has committed bloody atrocities to discover it spotless, and the estate agent showing it to a yuppie couple refuses to acknowledge that it was any other way for fear that it will affect its market value. His confession provides no catharsis, no redemption, no "deeper knowledge" of himself, and no escape: what exists of "Patrick Bateman" is an illusion.

In sum, clear distinctions between Gothic and crime fiction rarely hold up on close inspection, and tend to serve particular critical agendas. What makes a text one rather than the other tends to be the relative dominance of certain themes rather than absolute differences between them. Gothic narratives are driven by crime, whether the misdeeds of earlier generations, the sins of the secret self or the aesthetic murders of monstrous hero-villains. Crime can be presented as "Gothic" through the themes of the returning past, the psychologically unstable protagonist, the celebration of excess, and the emphasis on surfaces. Despite critical attempts to prise them apart, the two genres or modes are mutually implicated throughout their history, and this special relationship only seems to be becoming more vigorous in the twenty-first century.

20

Feminist Crime Fiction and Female Sleuths

Adrienne E. Gavin

There is a modicum of truth in the generalization that some genres of fiction appeal more to one gender than the other. Romance novels, for example, tend to be written and read more often by women, while Westerns more typically attract male authors and readers. Crime fiction, by contrast, has flourished in both male and female hands and appeals to both genders. When detective fiction took root in the nineteenth century, female crime writers and sleuths challenged general expectations about both women's writing and female characters. The standard critical inclination has been to see female crime writers and detectives as also subverting a specifically male "norm" for crime fiction. Women crime writers and investigators, however, while clearly expressing issues of female concern, have from the start been an integral part of the history of crime writing rather than simply an adjunct or reaction to it. As female detective fiction passed from Victorian originators through twentieth-century god-mothers of crime such as Agatha Christie, Dorothy L. Sayers, and P. D. James and on to rebellious goddaughters like Sara Paretsky, Sue Grafton, and Patricia Cornwell, a female and feminist vision of crime became a clear norm. The proliferation of female crime writing and fictional detectives since the early 1980s, ranging across styles as various as "cozy," "hard-boiled," "forensic," and "humanist," shows the female tradition in crime literature continuing to innovate and flourish.

Both male and female authors created fictional female sleuths in the nineteenth century. These "lady detectives" are independent, confident, clever women who variously use knowledge and observation of domestic environments and human behavior, female intuition, and their capacity for going unnoticed or being underestimated in solving crimes. They usually become detectives either because fate has made it necessary for them to find employment or, as Patricia Craig and Mary Cadogan observe, in order to clear the name of a male relative (Craig and Cadogan 1981: 21). Those female sleuths who work to restore masculine honor, and those who are young and attractive, generally cease detecting once they solve their cases or marry. Older spinsters, widows, and female investigators created by women authors often, if only implicitly, have longer detecting careers.

The first professional female detectives in fiction are Andrew Forrester, Jr's Mrs G— (possibly Gladden), who appeared in the casebook *The Female Detective* in May 1864, and William Stephens Hayward's Mrs Paschal, who appeared six months later in *The Revelations of a Lady Detective* (1864). Both are first-person narrators who work for the British police. Mrs G— keeps her name and marital status hidden, does not reveal to her friends that she is a detective, and uses logical and practical methods of detection. Mrs Paschal is a widow of almost forty who needs to earn money. She carries a gun, is intelligent and active, and is herself threatened with violence and murder. Kathleen Gregory Klein suggests that these early female investigators are simply "honorary men" (Klein 1995: 29), but this undervalues the female presence in pioneering detective fiction. E. F. Bleiler observes that one of Mrs G—'s cases, "The Unknown Weapon," has "some reason to be called the first modern detective novel" (Bleiler 1978: x), along with *The Dead Letter* (1864) by American author Seeley Regester (pseudonym of female author Metta C. Victor), and Emile Gaboriau's *L'Affaire Lerouge* (1865–6).

While Forrester and Hayward's protagonists were the earliest female detectives, properly speaking, critics such as Maureen T. Reddy suggest that tendrils of fictional female detection reach back to the Gothic novels of the late eighteenth and early nineteenth century (Reddy 1988: 7–9). In Gothic texts such as Ann Radcliffe's *The Mysteries of Udolpho* (1794) women are typically victims of crime and held captive, but also escape through proto-detective methods to triumph in the end. Other sleuth-like forerunners appear in Catherine Crowe's *Susan Hopley* (1841), which features a female servant tracking her brother's murderer, and Wilkie Collins's "The Diary of Anne Rodway" (1856), in which a seamstress seeks to solve her friend's murder. Sensation novels of the 1860s were also influential in the rise of female crime fiction. Condemned in some contemporary quarters as inappropriate and dangerous for women to read, let alone write, sensation fiction – like Gothic novels – held great appeal for female authors and readers. Writers like Collins and Mary Braddon took female characters beyond victimhood into roles as criminals and sleuths that sub-verted gender expectations. Most famously Braddon's *Lady Audley's Secret* (1862) reveals the blonde, child-like, angelic-looking Lady Audley to be a ruthless criminal who commits crime after crime in order to maintain the luxurious life into which she has bigamously married, until her husband's nephew, in detective-like manner, uncovers the truth.

Collins's *The Woman in White* (1860) features daring, intelligent, feminine-figured but masculine-faced Marian Halcombe, who with Walter Hartright sets out to solve a mystery. Although ultimately a sidekick, she is a confident one, telling Walter at the outset: "This is a matter of curiosity; and you have got a woman for your ally. Under such conditions success is certain, sooner or later" (1996: 48). Success is the mark, too, of Collins's amateur sleuth in *The Law and the Lady* (1875), Valeria Woodville, who, despite her uncle's contempt for "lawyers in petticoats," sets out to prove her husband innocent of murdering his first wife. Rare even in today's fiction, Valeria is a pregnant sleuth, and the gestation of her baby parallels that of her detection. Having cleared her husband's name and given birth to a son (into whose infant hand the proof of her case is put), Valeria, not without regret, gives up detecting in favor of family life.

The eruption of interest in both detective fiction and the short story in the 1890s fired writers to create a range of notable female detectives, who often appeared first in periodical short stories, then in volume collections. One of the most significant of these late Victorian sleuths is Catherine L. Pirkis's Loveday Brooke, whose cases were collected as *The Experiences of Loveday Brooke, Lady Detective* (1894). After "a jerk of Fortune's wheel" left her "penniless and all but friendless" Brooke became a detective, working her way up to a respected position with a London detective agency (Pirkis 1986: 2). Slightly over thirty, she knows her own mind, argues with her male employer over theories of detection, and is intelligent, physically fearless, and highly observant. She draws on "female" knowledge of such things as servants, love, and domestic environments in solving cases but never resorts to stereotypical feminine wiles or "weaknesses." Devoted to her profession, she keeps her private life private, behaves and is treated professionally, and is admired for her detective ability by her employer, clients, and the police. One of the comparatively few female detectives created by women in the 1890s, Brooke is notably not married off, nor is her physical appearance emphasized; it is her professional skill and dedication that is highlighted.

Also not married off, possibly because her series was incomplete, is detective Florence Cusack, co-created by prolific female author L. T. Meade and Robert Eustace. Appearing in five *Harmsworth Magazine* stories in 1899 and 1900, Miss Cusack, as her "Watson" Dr Lonsdale reveals, detects not for financial reasons but because she has promised to do so. Attractive, highly skilled, and admired by Scotland Yard detectives, she solves cases using ingenious methods including her sense of smell.

Late nineteenth-century male-authored works more frequently end women detectives' careers in marriage. Fergus Hume's gypsy detective Hagar Stanley of *Hagar of the Pawn-Shop* (1898) solves mysteries connected with pawned items before marrying and leaving detection in favor of bookselling on the open road. Grant Allen's "New Woman" sleuth Lois Cayley of *Miss Cayley's Adventures* (1899) travels the world foiling dangers before marrying and proving her own and her husband's innocence of will tampering. Similarly, the nurse protagonist of Allen's *Hilda Wade* (1900) travels widely, using intelligence, feminine intuition, and an eidetic memory to solve cases and prove her father's innocence before marrying. The Cambridge-educated protagonist of M. McDonnell Bodkin's *Dora Myrl, The Lady Detective* (1900) is athletic, observant, very successful, and carries a gun, but leaves detecting in a later volume, when she marries Bodkin's male series detective Paul Beck, becoming mother to subsequent sleuth *Young Beck: A Chip off the Old Block* (1912). A rarer married female detective is George R. Sims's protagonist in

Dorcas Dene, Detective (1897) – a former actress, Dorcas Dene's theatrical skills are useful in the professional detective work she undertakes when her husband becomes blind.

As Klein points out, female detectives were rare in American nineteenth-century dime novels, but do appear in *The Lady Detective* (c. 1890) by Old Sleuth (Harlan P. Halsey) and *The Female Barber Detective* (1895) by Albert W. Aiken. Representing two patterns for the dime-fiction female detective, the former novel features Kate Goelet, an intelligent, physically skilled New York detective whose attractiveness leads to marriage and her departure from detecting. The latter focuses on police spy Mignon Lawrence, who sets up a barber shop as a cover for her skilled detecting, but is described in very masculinized terms including having a moustache (see Klein 1995: 31–52).

The most significant American contribution to the development of fictional female detection in the nineteenth century is the work of Anna Katharine Green. Her bestselling *The Leavenworth Case* (1878), featuring New York police detective Ebenezer Gryce, is one of the earliest detective novels by a woman. In *That Affair Next Door* (1897) Green introduced Amelia Butterworth, an amateur detective who in this and two later volumes assists Gryce with his cases and is central to the plots. The original elderly "spinster sleuth," Butterworth investigates mysteries in Gramercy Park New York City, detecting not out of financial need, for she is well-bred and wealthy, but from human curiosity, or as it often appears, nosiness and a busybody disposition.

Nineteenth-century detective fiction is frequently seen as conservative and conventional, with cases neatly solved and moral order restored. Female detectives of the period, however, operate subversively; when they solve a case moral certainties may be re-established but gender role expectations are broken down. In the first two decades of the twentieth century similar patterns of female detection continued, with questions now being asked about whether a woman could embark on marriage and yet retain a detecting career. In two British novels by Marie Connor Leighton, *Joan Mar, Detective* (1910) and *Lucille Dare, Detective* (1919), as Carla T. Kungl points out, the detectives must decide between love and detection, and both choose career (Kungl 2006: 93).

Early twentieth-century American fiction also keeps female detectives single. Mary Roberts Rinehart's amateur sleuth Tish Carberry is a lively spinster who with two female friends solves crimes in stories collected in *The Amazing Adventures of Letitia Carberry* (1911) and other volumes through to 1937. In 1914 Rinehart also began stories about nurse detective Hilda Adams (dubbed Miss Pinkerton for her detecting skills) who assists the police with investigations that continued in serialized novels including *Miss Pinkerton* (1932) and *Haunted Lady* (1942). Hugh C. Weir's *Miss Madelyn Mack, Detective* (1914) is a female American Sherlock Holmes. She travels more widely than Holmes and her drug is cola berries rather than cocaine, but like Holmes she runs her own detective business, asks seemingly innocuous questions, and has little interest in matrimony, although her female Watson finds love.

Fictional women sleuths up until 1940, as Kungl notes, tend to be middle class, to confirm class boundaries, and often use their knowledge of class differences to solve crimes (Kungl 2006: 64–73). Some, like Lady Molly of Baroness Emmuska Orczy's *Lady Molly of Scotland Yard* (1910), are upper class and useful to the police for their aristocratic knowledge. Lady Molly heads a "Female Department" of Scotland Yard, solving mysteries narrated by her adulatory former maid Mary Granard. It is eventually revealed that Lady Molly's motive for entering upon detective work is to clear her imprisoned husband of murder and she gives up detecting when she succeeds. Anna Katherine Green's short story collection *The Golden Slipper and other Problems for Violet Strange* (1915) features an aristocratic young woman sleuth who helps the New York police with society cases. This collection possibly served as a model for Nancy Drew (Della Cava and Engel 2002: 169). (See Routledge, chapter 25 in this volume.)

Nancy Drew and other "girl sleuths" that emerged in the 1920s and 1930s cannot be underestimated as influences on the women writers of detective fiction who followed, especially those who emerged in the 1970s and 1980s. In the 1920s British girls' magazines saw a proliferation of schoolgirl sleuths, such as Sylvia Silence, created by Katherine Greenhalgh (pseudonym of John W. Bobin). Silence first featured in the *Schoolgirls' Weekly* in October 1922. Even more influential were American teenage amateur detectives, most notably Nancy Drew, who first appeared in *The Secret of the Old Clock* (1930) and who still solves cases in later series and spin-offs. Created by Edward Stratemeyer and written by Mildred Augustine Wirt Benson and other writers under the syndicate pseudonym "Carolyn Keene," the original Nancy of the 1930s and 40s is an inspirational female investigator. Young, attractive, affluent, brave, confident, and multi-skilled, Nancy has her own blue roadster and gun, faces dangers boldly, and solves cases neatly. With her mother dead and her father a criminal lawyer who appreciates her detecting abilities, she has untrammeled autonomy to go, do, and detect as she pleases. Other long-running girl detective series also provided exciting templates for female detection, including the Stratemeyer Dana Girls series (1934–68), Margaret Sutton's Judy Bolton series (1932–67), and the Trixie Belden series (1948–86) by Julie Campbell and syndicate "Kathryn Kenny."

The inter-war years saw the development of daring and active girl sleuths and the rise of male hard-boiled detective fiction in which the primary female role was *femme fatale*. Women fictional detectives, by contrast, became older, less physically active, and more concerned with crimes in their immediate locale. To accord with, or arguably take advantage of, the retrenchment of gender roles that followed World War I, the British female sleuth – who in this period dominates the female tradition – becomes a less threatening figure: elderly, amateur, and detective by accident rather than design (Kungl 2006: 12).

Often unwarrantedly seen as a retrograde step in the development of feminist crime fiction, the "spinster sleuths" of golden age detective fiction of the 1920s and 1930s, in which the puzzle of crime was central, have a power that lies in their apparent innocuousness. Neither noticeable nor notable to other characters, they regularly use underestimation of their capabilities to their advantage. Being largely invisible is an invaluable attribute for a detective (or criminal), but clearly reflects sexist and ageist cultural values. By portraying older women as skilled, successful, and central to their narratives, their creators insist that these mature women *are* made visible to readers. In this way these sleuths become surprisingly subversive figures, possibly more so even than the tough-talking, physically-active "female hard-boiled" detectives who later take on patriarchy more directly and reactively.

Traces of Green's prototypical Amelia Butterworth can be found in these golden age female sleuths, the most famous of whom is Agatha Christie's Miss Jane Marple. Making her novelistic debut in *The Murder at the Vicarage* (1930), Miss Marple appeared in novels and short stories until the 1970s. Distinguished by her village geography (St Mary Mead) and pastimes – knitting, gardening, and bird-watching – Miss Marple has moral force, intelligence, an inquisitive nature, excellent knowledge of human behavior, and pays attention to details. Patricia Wentworth's Miss Maud Silver, too, is an older single woman who knits and solves. Dowdy, inconspicuous, and using gossip to her advantage, this ex-governess private investigator is featured in 32 novels from *Grey Mask* (1928) to *The Girl in the Cellar* (1961). Not spinster but widow, Gladys Mitchell's Mrs (Dame) Beatrice Adela Lestrange Bradley is a psycho-analyst/psychologist who solves cases in 66 books from *Speedy Death* (1929) to *The Crozier Pharaohs* (1984). Small like Miss Silver, Mrs Bradley is described as crocodilian or "saurian" and makes her own decisions about justice. Initially an amateur, but later Psychiatric Consultant to the Home Office, she uses psychological methods of detection.

Golden age female detective fiction is often concerned with human relationships, social and cultural concerns, and women's position. One of the most significant younger women sleuths of the period is Dorothy L. Sayers's Harriet Vane. Featured in four novels, Vane is independent, around 30, has studied at Oxford, and is herself a writer of detective stories. Sayers's male series detective Lord Peter Wimsey falls in love with her and detects to clear her name in *Strong Poison* (1930) when Vane is on trial for the murder of the lover whose marriage proposal she has refused. Sayers regarded work as an essential part of a woman's existence, and the Vane novels reveal the difficulties women face in balancing professional and private life. Fearing it may damage her independence, Vane refuses Wimsey's marriage proposals until *Gaudy Night* (1935), which has been termed "the first feminist detective novel" (Reddy 1988: 12). Set in an Oxford women's college, the novel raises significant questions about women and higher education and about love and work. Although she included romance between Wimsey and Vane, Sayers believed that love had little place in crime fiction as it distracted from the detective focus. Like other contemporary crime novelists she also rejected female intuition as a way to solve cases, in part because of the fair play rule of golden age detective fiction that required providing the reader with the same clues the detective has, and in part because it marginalizes female logic and intellect (Kungl 2006: 148).

Sayers's Vane influenced academic sleuth Kate Fansler, created by American feminist academic Carolyn Heilbrun writing as Amanda Cross. Introduced in *In the Last Analysis* (1964), Fansler is an intelligent, wealthy, successful feminist professor of literature who, like Vane, believes in the importance of work for women. An elegant dresser, she drinks and smokes, has occasional lovers and, later in the series, marries. As Reddy argues, Cross "began the revival of the feminist crime novel, a literary form that had been moribund since the publication in 1935 of Dorothy Sayers' *Gaudy Night*" (Reddy 1990: 174). She also provided inspiration for later academic sleuths including Theodora Wender's American protagonist Gladiola Gold, who appeared in *Knight Must Fall* (1985), and Joan Smith's British Loretta Lawson of *A Masculine Ending* (1987). Another intriguing academic sleuth is Oxford law Professor Hilary Tamar, whose gender and sexuality remains unstated in the series by Sarah Caudwell that begins with *Thus Was Adonis Murdered* (1981).

Another important descendant of Harriet Vane is British writer P. D. James's Cordelia Gray who appears in *An Unsuitable Job for a Woman* (1972), the title of which encapsulates the gender biases fictional female private eyes face as they conduct their investigations. Often regarded as a forerunner of the American female private investigators of the 1980s, Gray is 22, independent, lives alone, and inherits a detective business after the suicide of her partner Bernie Pryde. Proving herself brave and highly capable, she has her own code of justice. Gray appeared again in the less successful *The Skull beneath the Skin* (1982), which sees her feminist status reduced by her failure in the central case, and her agency now specializing in finding lost pets. (See Harrington, chapter 40 of this volume.)

The next major impulse in feminist detection came with the development of the American female hard-boiled investigator. Klein finds the "first independent woman hard-boiled detective" in *I Found Him Dead* (1947) and *Chord in Crimson* (1949) featuring and narrated by P. I. Gale Gallagher (pseudonym of Will Oursler and Margaret Scott), who tracks missing persons, handles guns, is physically active, threatened, shot at, and finds corpses (Klein 1995: 127). There had also been highly sexualized, often naked, "she-dicks" created for the male market including Honey West, protagonist of eleven novels by G. G. Fickling (Gloria and Forrest E. Fickling) between 1957 and 1971, and Marla Trent of Henry Kane's *Private Eyeful* (1959) (Klein 1995: 128–34). Even as early as the 1930s, however, hard-boiled female PIs like Clive F. Adams's Violet McDade were appearing regularly in the pulps (Rzepka 2005: 185; Drew 1986).

More influential, however, were Marcia Muller's Sharon McCone, Sara Paretsky's V. I. Warshawski, and Sue Grafton's Kinsey Millhone, who made their mark in the early 1980s (see Effron, chapter 43 in this volume). Introduced as single, intelligent, and in their thirties, these urban private investigators take a physically active approach to crime that is far from "spinster cosy." Fit, self-contained, and street-wise, they handle guns, face threats and attacks from men, and kill when they have to. Their first-person narratives reveal women's experiences in the face of patriarchal systems of both crime and justice, and despite their detective successes their vulnerability is in places acknowledged. Taking detection in new overtly feminist directions, Muller, Paretsky, and Grafton are often seen as rewriting the male hard-boiled tradition into a counter-tradition or, as Glenwood Irons suggests, in fact inventing a new tradition (Irons 1995: xiii–xv).

The female hard-boiled tradition is in part a feminist response to male hard-boiled writing, but also owes much to previous female detection. Entering seedier streets and more dangerous terrain, these tough private investigators reflect a maturing into adult territory of the earlier bold "girl detectives" like Nancy Drew. That these juvenile sleuths were influential is acknowledged by Muller, who cites Judy Bolton as an influence on her detective Sharon McCone (Muller 1998: 67–9). Making her first appearance in 1977's *Edwin of the Iron Shoes*, McCone is a staff investigator for the San Francisco All Souls Legal Cooperative who later opens her own investigating agency. She is part Native American, has earned a degree in sociology and has had several love affairs. Muller's series was notable for its emphasis on the ways in which gender affects the detective's role, and led a vanguard of crime writers with similar concerns.

In 1982 the second McCone and the first Warshawski and Millhone novels were published, consolidating a new vision of female detective fiction. Introduced in *Indemnity Only* (1982) V. I. [Victoria Iphigenia] Warshawski is an ex-public defender private investigator based in Chicago. Herself divorced and her parents dead, she is without family but has close women friends, and female community is important in her life. Having been involved in political feminist work, her cases often take on patriarchal institutions like the Church, corporations, and local government, but also often have links with people she knows. She experiences abduction and violence, gets a gun, kills, and is frequently told that detecting is no job for a woman. Known for its revision of masculine hard-boiled tropes, Paretsky's work, as Linden Peach suggests, also "looks back to British, feminist writers of the 1920s and 1930s, especially Virginia Woolf" (Peach 2006: 104), and reflects Christie's and Sayers's detective fiction in representing a woman struggling against "Victorian ideals of womanhood" (Peach 2006: 117).

Kinsey Millhone, introduced in Grafton's *"A" is for Alibi* (1982), is an ex-cop private investigator. A loner without ties or possessions, she has occasional lovers and ends her novels like case reports. Investigating crime in fictional Santa Teresa, California, she talks tough and holds her own, but has also been beaten up and can mete out violence and kill when she needs to. In much-quoted lines, she states in the opening paragraph of *"A" is for Alibi*: "I'm thirty-two years old, twice divorced, no kids. The day before yesterday I killed someone and the fact weighs heavily on my mind" (Grafton 1982: 1). Killing, she feels, "has moved [her] into the same camp with soldiers and maniacs," which disturbs her (Grafton 1982: 209), but what resonates most for feminist development of detective fiction is the closing line of the body of the novel. When her knife-wielding criminal ex-lover lifts the lid of the trash bin in which the terrified Millhone is hiding, her gun ready, she states: "I blew him away" (Grafton 1982: 208).

Millhone enacts the feminist desire to "blow away" male violence towards women. The issue of violence, or what Glenwood Irons and Joan Warthling Roberts identify in the detective fiction of British writer Liza Cody as "the sense of victimization which seems to equate the woman detective with the murder victims themselves," is foregrounded in much women's crime writing from the early 1980s onwards (Irons and Roberts 1995: 67). Cody's young investigator Anna Lee, for example, who first appears in *Dupe* (1980), is an ex-police officer employed by Brierly Security Agency in London. Independent, fit, and interested in cars, Lee faces decisions about the balance of career and personal life, but is also beaten in an attack and held prisoner.

Violence is also central to several female hard-boiled variants that appeared in the late 1980s and 1990s, such as Denise Danks's British "techno hard-boiled" series featuring journalist investigator Georgina Powers. Hard drinking, sexually active, and often physically endangered, Powers uses computer technology to solve cases in London's East End. Janet Evanovich's "comic hard-boiled" series about bond reinforcement agent Stephanie Plum began with *One for the Money* (1994). Investigating in Trenton, New Jersey, Plum is not highly skilled at her job, but nevertheless succeeds in plots that mix violence with comic moments.

Feminist hard-boiled detection is a strand of women's crime writing that continues to thrive. Muller, Paretsky, and Grafton's series are all current (with, for example, Muller's McCone in the 1990s developing a long-term relationship and in the twenty-first century marrying). Their private investigators also influenced the creation of many long-running series sleuths including American Linda Barnes's six-foot-one, ex-cop cab-driver Carlotta Carlyle who appeared in *A Trouble of Fools* (1987) and Val McDermid's British series about private eye Kate Brannigan which started with *Dead Beat* (1992). Grafton's and Paretsky's work also partially inspired McDermid's journalist sleuth Lindsay Gordon who was introduced in *Report for Murder* (1987), the first lesbian detective novel published in Britain.

The first fictional feminist lesbian sleuth was Chicana detective Kat Guerrera who appeared in M. F. Beal's *Angel Dance* (1977). Canadian Eve Zaremba's Helen Keremos followed in *A Reason to Kill* (1978), and Katherine V. Forrest's novels about Los Angeles lesbian police detective Kate Delafield began with *Amateur City* (1984). The best-known lesbian amateur detective is Barbara Wilson's Pam Nilsen. In a pattern that developed in lesbian crime fiction, as Nilsen solves her first case she also solves her own sexuality, coming out in the first novel *Murder in the Collective* (1984). Wilson's novels focus on lesbian experience, female community, and gendered issues such as prostitution, pornography, and violence against women, including Nilsen's rape by a criminal in *Sisters of the Road* (1986).

In 1990 Patricia Cornwell staked out forensic detection for female crime writers by introducing forensic pathologist Dr Kay Scarpetta, chief medical examiner for

Richmond, Virginia, in *Postmortem*. Intelligent, divorced, and devoted to her job, Scarpetta across the series becomes involved romantically with FBI profiler Benton Wesley, develops a working relationship with sexist cop Pete Marino, and is a loyal aunt to her computer-expert niece Lucy. Including precise details of autopsies, the novels show Scarpetta solving crimes, battling the justice system, and dealing with violence against women professionally and personally, often becoming involved with serial killers. Forensic detection is also central in Kathy Reichs's series featuring forensic anthropologist Dr Temperance Brennan, which began with *Déjà Dead* (1997). Set mainly in Montreal and North Carolina, the novels are inspired by Reich's own career as a forensic anthropologist.

With the exponential growth in female detective fiction from the 1980s onwards there also developed a line of "humanistic crime fiction" (Della Cava and Engel 1999: 38). This tradition moves away from hard-boiled, streetwise toughness and places the detective's psychology and human and social issues at its core. Cases in such novels resonate with contemporary issues, often those of particular concern to women such as domestic violence, abortion, and child abuse. Race and class issues are also often central. Barbara Neely's series beginning with *Blanche on the Lam* (1992) about African-American domestic-worker sleuth Blanche White foregrounds the racism White meets, while both her race and her job give her a cultural invisibility that aids in her crime solving. American author Elizabeth George's British-set series, which focuses on an ensemble of characters including detective duo Inspector Thomas Lynley, an aristocrat, and working-class Sergeant Barbara Havers, highlights Havers's awareness of class differences. Generally a sidekick, in *Deception on His Mind* (1998) Havers takes on the central detecting role.

The major female presence in twentieth-century crime writing was also accentuated by authors not known for creating female detectives but whose contributions to crime fiction through male detectives or psychological novels of crime are undeniably significant: Ngaio Marsh, Margery Allingham, Patricia Highsmith, Ruth Rendell/ Barbara Vine, and Minette Walters. Twenty-first century female detective fiction continues to proliferate outwards into variants and continuations of subgenres: cozies about elderly amateur female sleuths remain popular, hard-boiled private investigators multiply, academic sleuths continue, historical female detectives burgeon, forensic detectives persist, and humanist concerns prevail. As in the nineteenth century, but less so in the twentieth, male authors are again increasingly creating female detectives: Jasper Fforde in his science fictionesque literary detective Thursday Next, Alexander McCall Smith in *The No. 1 Ladies' Detective Agency* series featuring Botswanan detective Precious Ramotswe and his Edinburgh-set Isabel Dalhousie series, James Patterson's Women's Murder Club series, and Boris Akunin's historical Russian nun detective Sister Pelagia.

Three elements prevalent in twenty-first century feminist detective fiction are ensemble characters, issues surrounding motherhood, and violence against women. The starkly lone female detective is less common; often women investigators are now part of an ensemble of characters as Havers is in George's novels or the two female crime solvers are in Karin Slaughter's Grant County series. Increasingly prominent, too, mirroring contemporary concerns, are detectives questioning whether to become mothers. Detection and motherhood in fiction still rarely mesh, although proportionally more black female detectives than white seem to be mothers. Nevertheless, "[c]hildren do not come first," are old enough "to look after themselves if need be" and other people help with them when the detective is on the case (Décuré 1999: 165), as Nicole Décuré notes of black women detectives such as Valerie Wilson Wesley's Tamara Hayle, Eleanor Taylor Bland's Marti MacAlister, and Terris McMahan Grimes's Theresa Galloway, who all first appeared in the 1990s. Whereas for earlier twentieth-century elderly sleuths and 1980s hard-boiled female detectives motherhood is marginalized, for contemporary female detectives it is, if not always central, at least mentioned. Detectives are still seldom mothers, especially of young children, but infertility, unplanned pregnancy, miscarriages, or abortions are dealt with in works such as Danks's *Baby Love* (2001) and Slaughter's *Faithless* (2005). Such personal experiences leave emotional marks upon female sleuths, while still leaving them free to detect without encumbrances.

The central concern of feminist crime fiction remains violence against women. Women are victims: captured, raped, murdered, butchered and in the hands of forensic detectives dissected into evidence. In emphasizing violence against women, feminist detective fiction makes a gendered protest. It also implies a gendered question: if even the detective figure is violated and attacked, is justice possible? Some critics argue that, in portraying such shocking scenes, violence against women is condoned or capitalized upon by authors. Others respond that in describing confrontations with violence the feminist detective and writer are simply telling it like it is, and in so doing are asserting, if not control over violence, then the power to express it in their terms.

A writer like Karin Slaughter in her Grant County series, which began with *Blindsighted* (2001), perhaps best illustrates the tendencies of early twenty-first century female detection. The series melds subgenres: part hard-boiled, part forensic, part humanist, part police procedural, part crime puzzle. Its ensemble cast features two female investigators: pediatrician and medical examiner Sara Linton whose portrayal draws on forensic and humanist models, and heavy-drinking, downward spiraling, police detective Lena Adams whose origins are clearly hard-boiled. The women do not directly work together but are linked through police chief Jeffrey Tolliver: Lena's boss and Sara's ex- and sometime husband. Both women have been raped, as a result of which Sara is infertile and, wanting to become a mother, plans to adopt. Lena experiences repeated episodes of violence including rapes and abuse from a partner. She also has an abortion to end an unplanned pregnancy. These female sleuths survive and solve, but their sisters are also victims of violence: Linton's sister loses the baby she is carrying after a brutal attack and Lena's sister is raped and murdered. These novels insist that for the female investigator crime is not simply a professional interest, but a devastatingly personal concern.

Despite the violence it often openly depicts, feminist crime writing itself is alive and thriving. As the historical development of female fictional detection reveals, women sleuths are far more than gimmick-like stand-ins for the male detectives of a masculine genre. Female detection has its own genealogy, characteristics, and subgenres and its future manifestations promise to be among the most interesting in the ever-expanding story of literary crime.

21

African-American Detection and Crime Fiction

Frankie Bailey

Introduction

Of course, the first question is how "African-American crime and detective fiction" should be defined. Is it genre fiction featuring African-American characters as protagonists? Or is it crime and detective fiction written by African-American authors? Is it both? In an article in *Black Issues Book Review*, Earnie Young observes that "far more African American characters are on *The {New York} Times* best-seller lists these days than the number of black writers there would indicate" (2004: 26). In other words, white writers are creating black characters and readers are buying their books. Black writers are not as visible in the publishing world. However, there are significantly more published African-American mystery writers than there were two decades ago (see Bailey 2008).

Rather than define "African-American crime and detective fiction" based on the race of the protagonist and/or the author, it is more useful to follow the evolution of African-American protagonists in crime and detective fiction. In doing so, we can observe the crosscurrents, tensions, and issues relevant to this subgenre of mystery/detective fiction.

The Historical Roots

African-American characters appeared early in American crime and detective fiction. Edgar Allan Poe has a black servant named "Jupiter" in his short story, "The Gold Bug." Although not one of Poe's three stories featuring Monsieur C. Auguste Dupin, "The Gold Bug" is generally considered an entry in Poe's mystery canon. Jupiter furnishes the red herrings in the story because his malapropisms, misunderstandings, and superstitions cause both the narrator and the reader to suspect that his master might be mentally unstable. This use of misdirection is certainly an important aspect of Poe's contribution to the development of the mystery as a genre. However, Poe's depiction of Jupiter as comic, ignorant, and still devoted to his master despite his manumission conformed to nineteenth-century antebellum racial stereotypes (Bailey 1991: 4–5).

In the United States and England, the popular perception was that blacks were only a few evolutionary steps removed from the orangutans or apes. The exploration and conquest of the African continent by Europeans and the enslavement of blacks had a long-lasting impact on how black Africans and their descendants were perceived. Even with the abolition of slavery in England and later in the United States, the stereotypes that supported the "Peculiar Institution" remained. Popular science assumed a racial hierarchy with white male Europeans at the top. In the United States, in the post-Civil War era, the alleged threat of the "new Negro criminal" was used to justify repressive measures by the criminal justice system and extra-legal justice in the hands of white vigilantes. In this atmosphere, the white Southern perception of blacks became the dominant one (see Bailey and Green 1999 for discussion).

Stereotypes of blacks (and other people of color) in early crime and detective fiction were not limited to the United States. Because of the strong influence of the largely conservative British writer Arthur Conan Doyle on detective fiction, we might expect to find his work reinforcing prejudicial representations of black people throughout the genre. The encounters he stages between his detective, Sherlock Holmes, and black characters, however, are often ambiguous in their implications, and sometimes counter-typical. Perhaps the most remarkable appears in "The Adventure of the Yellow Face." This story presents Holmes with a mystery he fails to solve. A little girl – the coal-black child of a black American father and a white British mother – confounds the detective. While living in the United States, the mother married a black physician who died during a yellow fever epidemic. She returns home and re-marries. Unable to bear being separated from her daughter, but afraid to tell her British husband of the child's existence, the mother hides the child in a cottage with a nurse. Concerned about his wife's odd behavior, her husband turns to Holmes, who concludes that the woman's first husband is still alive and blackmailing her. The detective is humbled when he must admit that he was wrong. The response of the woman's husband to her secret is equally unexpected. Declaring that he is a better man than his wife thinks he is, he accepts his stepdaughter.

This appearance by a black child is not Doyle's only reference to racial issues or race relations. His short story "The Five Orange Pips" makes members of the Ku Klux Klan the stalkers of a man and his heirs. In "The Adventures of the Three Gables," Steve Dixie, a black prizefighter, visits Holmes. Watson's description of Dixie and his mission makes it clear that the man is a member of a criminal gang. Holmes dismisses Dixie as "a harmless fellow" who is really a "foolish, blustering baby, and easily cowed" (Doyle 1986: 2.520). The appearance of Dixie in this story may well have been inspired by Doyle's trip to Hollywood, where he visited a movie studio and met a gigantic black laborer, who was frightened by Doyle's reputation as a "spook man" (Bailey 1991: 17–19).

But "The Adventure of the Yellow Face" suggests that Doyle's encounter with another black man also had an impact on his thinking. As a young physician serving as ship's surgeon on a steamship voyage to West Africa in 1881, Doyle met Henry Highland Garnet, a former slave. When Doyle and Garnet met, Garnet was the American Consul in Monrovia. During the three days that they spent in each other's company, Doyle was impressed by Garnet's manner and his intelligence. As a man who was his equal, Garnet appears to have challenged Doyle's notions about race to that point in his young life (Huh 2003). A decade later, Doyle wrote "The Adventure of the Yellow Face," a story that pivots on the issue of racial identity. With this story, Doyle not only calls into question the acumen of his master detective – a very rare occurrence – but also popular arguments about "race-mixing" (Bailey 1991: 18).

Doyle's short story was published in 1893, the year after lynching in the United States reached its zenith. With the rise of the Ku Klux Klan, the disenfranchising of blacks, and the demand for cheap black labor, racial oppression became a fact of life for blacks in the South. During the antebellum era, ex-slave abolitionists such as Frederick Douglass and Henry Highland Garnet went on the lecture circuit and wrote about slavery as both an "institution" and a "crime" against humanity (see Bailey 2008). African-American abolitionists made a unique contribution to American literature with "slave narratives" that drew on Native American "captivity narratives," biography, and the sentimental novel. At the same time, they ventured into newspaper publishing and, by the mid-nineteenth century, novel writing. Later in the century, African-American journalists helped to spearhead the anti-lynching movement by documenting lynchings. For example, Charles Chesnutt wrote such short stories as "The Sheriff's Children," about mob violence and the fate of the mulatto son of a sheriff. His novel, *The Marrow of Tradition* (1901) offered a fictional look at the race riot in Wilmington, North Carolina in 1898 that helped to restore the solid Democratic South.

Even as white Southerners defended vigilante violence as a response to alleged crimes by blacks, African-American writers offered alternative perspectives. In the works of African-American writers, the crimes that were being committed by whites against blacks were challenged as they rarely were in courts of law.

Early Genre Fiction

Described as "the foremother of African American mysteries" (Woods 1995: 16), Pauline E. Hopkins was an editor and contributor to *Colored American*. At the turn of the twentieth century, she was one of the generation of educated African-American women who were speaking out on both race and gender issues. Hopkins's published fiction appeared in serialized form in African-American magazines. One of her short stories, "Talma Gordon," was inspired by the 1892 case of Lizzie Borden, the New England spinster who was accused of the axe murders of her father and stepmother. Hopkins's protagonist, Talma Gordon, stands trial for the murder of her father. She is acquitted, but then ostracized by society. The narrator of the story, a white male physician, describes Talma's tribulations to a gathering of his peers. Recounting a complex story of death-bed confessions, he reveals the identity of the true murderer. He also tells his listeners the other secret that Talma learned from her dying sister. Although white in appearance, the sisters have "Negro blood," inherited from their mother who was a quadroon. Here Hopkins rejects the literary trope of the "tragic mulatto" that would doom her heroine to death or unhappiness. In a final revelation, the physician-narrator invites his colleagues to meet his wife – Talma Gordon.

In her novel *Hagar's Daughter* (serialized in the *Colored American Magazine* from March 1901 to March 1902), Hopkins introduces a black amateur female sleuth, albeit her sleuthing takes up a slim portion of the book. Hagar is happily married and the mother of an infant, but her husband's brother, seeking to ensure his inheritance, sells her and her child into slavery. Two decades later, Jewel, the daughter of a prominent senator, has become the target of a fortune hunter who is scheming to marry her. Her father dies, and she is kidnapped. An unlikely sleuth emerges in the form of Venus Johnson, the black maid to the senator's family, who is determined to solve the mystery of the disappearance of Jewel and her own grandmother. Venus offers her assistance to Mr Henson, the head of the Secret Service, who sends her and a black male operative undercover to find the two women and free them. In a melodramatic courtroom scene, Henson, the Secret Service chief, reveals that the kidnapper is his brother and that he is Hagar's missing husband. As typically occurs in melodrama, Hagar, having hidden her identity all these years, turns out to be the senator's widow.

Although this is a joyous reunion for the long-separated couple, the outcome for Jewel is tragic. She is discovered to be the baby that Hagar thought had drowned as she attempted to escape slavery. Because of her Negro blood, Jewel is rejected by the man who professes to love her. When he later regrets his decision, it is too late: Jewel has died. For Hopkins, this somber ending symbolizes the destruction wrought by racial bigotry and hypocrisy on individuals and the nation (Bailey 2008: 27–31).

Unlike Hopkins, who grew up in Maine, John Edward Bruce was born a slave. A journalist, activist, and Pan Africanist, Bruce published *The Black Sleuth* in serial form in *McGirt's Magazine* beginning in September 1907. The protagonist of Bruce's story is a West African youth named Sadipe Okukena. Impressed with Sadipe, a white sea captain persuades Sadipe's father to allow his son to continue his education in the United States, where, after a brief sojourn at a school in New England, Sadipe goes South to attend a Negro college. En route to his new school, Sadipe has an unpleasant racist experience on board the train and is helped by a sympathetic white man, a soldier who has led Negro troops in the West. After seeing the town and the college, Sadipe contacts his new friend, who helps Sadipe become an operative for an international detective agency. Although a client expresses surprise – using a racial slur – when he finds that Sadipe has been assigned to his case, Sadipe's boss assures the client that the young man is intelligent, skilled, and the best operative to recover the client's missing diamond. Soon afterwards, Sadipe goes undercover as a waiter in an English hotel (Bailey 2008: 31–3).

Bruce's depiction of Sadipe stands in stark contrast to the images of black characters in mainstream popular fiction (and later in films)[1] of the early twentieth century. In golden age detective fiction, black characters generally appeared in minor roles as servants. Another of the few black protagonists of this era was created by white writer Octavus Roy Cohen. Cohen's comic hero, Florian Slappey, the "Beau Brummell of Birmingham's Darktown," appeared as a "detective" in one of a series of stories published in the *Saturday Evening Post*, later included in Ellery Queen's *101 Years' Entertainment: The Great Detective Stories 1841–1941* (1943). In that case, Slappey was hired by a washerwoman to find out who was stealing her laundry (Bailey 1991: 31).

What Hopkins and Bruce did in their works was to initiate the use of mystery/detective fiction by African-Americans to explore social issues. These two writers were joined by journalist W. Adolphe Roberts, who published several mystery novels in the 1920s and 30s. However, Roberts's books did not feature African-American protagonists. Then in 1932, Rudolph Fisher, a physician-writer who had participated in the literary and intellectual movement known as the Harlem Renaissance, published the first genre detective novel by an African-American featuring black protagonists and set in Harlem.

In *The Conjure-Man Dies*, Fisher teams NYPD detective Perry Dart with Dr John Archer. Dart is one of the first ten Negroes in Harlem to be promoted to detective. Archer, a hard-working, under-paid physician, is summoned from his house across the street from the scene of the crime by Bubber Brown, one of the people in the waiting room when N'gana Frimbo, a professional "conjure-man," is murdered during a session with a client, Bubber's friend, Jinx. Dart asks Archer to serve as a consultant on the case when he realizes that the conjure-man, a Harvard-educated African prince, was engaged in strange experiments. Meanwhile, Bubber Brown, a self-described "family detective," helps the police look for a missing suspect. African spiritualism meets American science as Fisher's detectives try to determine who was murdered and by whom (see Bailey 2008: 38–44; Gosselin 1998).

Before his own death in 1934, at the age of 37, Fisher wrote a short story, "John Archer's Nose," that also featured his detective duo. Fisher's novel and short story marked the emergence of the black sleuth into the genre mainstream. Fisher described himself as a "chronicler" of the black urban experience. In his other novel, *The Walls of Jericho* (1928), and his non-genre short stories, Fisher depicted in affectionate detail the black community of Harlem, including the newly arrived Southern immigrants experiencing the shock of the city. In the short story, "City of Refuge," Solomon Gillis has fled the South after shooting a white man. A stereotypical "rube" in the metropole, staring about him in fascination at the strange sights and sounds, including a black patrolman, Gillis soon falls prey to Mouse Uggam, a con man who tricks him into selling drugs. Although they both come from the same hometown, Uggam has acquired an aura of sophistication from service in France during World War I.

He has found his niche in Harlem as a small-time predator in a world that includes the "culled [colored] policemans" that so amaze Solomon Gillis (Bailey 2008: 36–8).

In the works of these early African-American genre writers, the "cultural vernacular" (spiritualism, use of language, and music) discussed by Stephen Soitos in *The Blues Detective* (1996) plays a prominent role. At the same time, the influence of mainstream crime and detective fiction is also apparent. Fisher's novel and short story featuring Dart and Archer have the characteristics of classic detective fiction, with a closed circle of suspects, the presence of an amateur detective working in conjunction with the police investigator, and a puzzle to be solved before the murderer is revealed. At the same time, the violence in the side streets of Harlem and the problems (e.g., domestic violence and drug addiction) of the minor characters link both novel and short story to the hard-boiled urban world of the stories then appearing in *Black Mask* by writers like Dashiell Hammett, James M. Cain, and Raymond Chandler.

In the interval between Fisher and Chester Himes, who was the first African-American writer to sustain a crime series, Richard Wright's *Native Son* (1940) changed the landscape of African-American literature. Wright, who was influenced by Dostoevsky, took as his subject the nature of crime and justice in racist America. Bigger Thomas, a migrant to Chicago, lives with his mother and two younger siblings in a rat-infested tenement. He is hired as a chauffeur by a philanthropist/slumlord, Mr Dalton, and befriended by Mary, Dalton's daughter, and Jan, her Communist boyfriend. When Bigger carries an inebriated Mary into the house after a party, her blind mother comes into Mary's bedroom and Bigger suffocates the sleeping girl while trying to keep her quiet. After a botched attempt to dispose of her body in the furnace in the basement and make Mary's disappearance look like a kidnapping, Bigger goes on the run from the police. Before he is captured, he kills his black girlfriend Bessie, but it is for the murder of Mary, the white girl, that Bigger is convicted and faces a sentence of death. As he was writing the novel, Wright used newspaper articles about a sensational real-life trial of a black man accused of the rape and murder of a white woman during a burglary. He also was interested in the Leopold and Loeb "thrill killing" of Bobby Franks. Wright later observed that in his own novel, the "mystery" would have been solved much more quickly if anyone had been able to see Bigger's humanity (Bailey 2008: 48–51).

This same assertion of humanity fuels Ann Petry's *The Street* (1946) a few years later. Her protagonist, Lutie Johnson, is an ambitious young wife and mother. When she separates from her husband, she attempts to rear her son alone in Harlem, but the environment overwhelms them. As she is fleeing New York after killing the man who was sexually harassing her, Lutie realizes that she has been defeated by "the street." Her son has been arrested and is in a juvenile facility, so she has lost him, too. Petry was inspired to write the novel after reading a newspaper article about a young boy who had been taught to steal by an apartment building superintendent (Bailey 2008: 52–3).

The coming of World War II had a significant impact on African-American culture. One of its legacies was an increasing assertiveness among African-Americans who had hoped to achieve a "Double Victory" by fighting for democracy while winning their own rights as citizens. Although the war did not end racism in the United States, the images of the destruction wrought by a doctrine of Aryan superiority helped to create an environment in which the seeds of the Civil Rights movement could take root. It was during this postwar period that several white writers created African-American characters that deviated from the stereotypes of the 1920s and 30s. For example, in Ellery Queen's *Cat of Many Tails* (1949), a respectable young black woman is one of the victims of a serial killer and a black detective is a member of Inspector Queen's special detail. Creating a black sleuth, Veronica Parker Johns played on the idea of the "invisibility" of servants. Her protagonist, Webster Flagg, an actor turned butler, can investigate the death of his employer in *Murder by the Day* (1953) because the suspects ignore his presence. In *Servant Problems* (1958), Flagg takes a job as a servant in another household to help a friend's daughter (Bailey 1991: 88).

The postwar era saw the rise of the police procedural as a subgenre of crime fiction. Riding this new wave, African-American writer Hughes Allison wrote the first short story featuring an African-American police detective to appear in *Ellery Queen Mystery Magazine*. In Allison's "Corollary" (July 1948), Joe Hill is a member of the chief's special unit, the Central Bureau. A university graduate and athlete, he is the only black detective in the municipal department where he serves, so he is not surprised to be called in by his superior when a white teacher brings a little black girl to the police station. As Allison said, although other detectives were competent, what made Hill different was that he was "equipped to think with his skin" (Allison 1948: 85).

Although Chester Himes followed in the footsteps of Fisher and Allison, his path to becoming a crime writer was more difficult. (See Soitos, chapter 38 in this volume.) While serving seven years for an armed robbery after attending college, Himes began to write short stories. After his release, he achieved only limited success as a writer of protest novels in the US, but after moving to Europe and becoming an expatriate, he took the advice of his French editor, Marcel Duhamel, and began to write a police procedural series set in Harlem. From their first appearance in *For Love of Imabelle* (1957) to their final turn in *Blind Man with a Pistol* (1969), Himes's detective duo, Grave Digger Jones and Coffin Ed Johnson, provided wisecracking, sometimes brutal, justice in Harlem. Although white police officers, including their commanding officer, Lieutenant Anderson, made routine appearances, it was Coffin Ed and Grave Digger who understood the links between white oppression and crime and violence in the black ghetto. In the end, the two are unable to contain the violence threatening to erupt throughout the series. In *Plan B* (1993, US), an unfinished novel published nine years after Himes's death, a race war begins and the two detectives are among the casualties (Bailey 2008: 56–62).

While Himes painted an increasingly grim picture of race relations in the United States, white writers continued to create black protagonists. In 1957, P. I. Toussaint

Moore debuted in Ed Lacy's book *Room to Swing*. The book won the 1958 Edgar Award. Lacy followed with *Moment of Untruth* (1964), in which Moore, to his wife's dismay, leaves his secure, well-paying job at the post office to take another case. In 1965, John D. Ball won an Edgar for *In the Heat of the Night*, the book that introduced the African-American series detective Virgil Tibbs. A member of the Pasadena police force, Tibbs is a brilliant detective whose reputation has preceded him to his temporary assignment in the Mississippi delta. A black migrant from the South who has achieved upward mobility through hard work, he is also well-mannered, neat, and self-effacing.

The film version of *In the Heat of the Night* (1967) brought Tibbs to life for a generation that found itself in the midst of the Civil Rights movement. In one of the more memorable moments in black film history, Tibbs (played by Sidney Poitier) slaps the wealthy white plantation owner who has slapped him. As in the book, he is arrested as a murder suspect while waiting for a train in a sleepy Southern town. In the film, Tibbs lives and works in Philadelphia, a sore spot for the Southern police officers who question him, especially when they learn how much money he is paid each week. But then the widow of the murdered Northern industrialist insists that Tibbs be allowed to work on the case. The cautious bonding between Poitier and Rod Steiger, as Chief Gillispie, is more poignant than anything found in the interracial "buddy films" that would become popular in the 1980s. However, along with "I Spy" (1965–68), the ground-breaking television show featuring Bill Cosby and Robert Culp as globe-trotting espionage agents, *In the Heat of the Night* provided a prototype for later black-white pairs in crime films and on television.

Ernest Tidyman's *Shaft* (1970) gave Americans a different type of African-American hero. Shaft was a black PI, a Vietnam vet and war hero who had attended New York University before dropping out to become a private investigator. The film (1971), based on the first book in the series, brought the character to a wider audience, with Richard Roundtree portraying John Shaft as the personification of "cool." As Isaac Hayes described him in the film's throbbing theme song, Shaft was "a complicated man," and a "sex machine." Challenging racial taboos, the women in Shaft's life and bed were both black and white.

In the tradition of literary private eyes, Shaft had a friend on the police force, and the film itself inaugurated new traditions for black detectives. For instance, the white mobsters that Shaft defeats to rescue a black organized crime boss's kidnapped daughter are of the type that would become a staple of the "blaxploitation films" of the era. In these films, intended to appeal to an urban audience, black protagonists typically took on organized crime, corrupt and brutal cops, and genocidal bigots. The fact that some of these black protagonists were criminals themselves (e.g., "Priest," the drug dealer in *Super Fly*) and the sometimes questionable quality of the films brought criticism from those concerned about the exploitation of black audiences by spurious black role models. Among the films produced during this period, two based on Himes's novels, *Cotton Comes to Harlem* (1970) and *Come Back, Charleston Blue* (1972), were memorable for the casting of Godfrey Cambridge and Raymond St Jacques as the two Harlem detectives.

In the post-Civil Rights era, the Black Arts Movement produced a number of works that have been described as "anti-detective novels." African-American authors Ishmael Reed and Clarence Major wrote books featuring black protagonists who viewed mysteries and their solutions from an Afrocentric perspective (see Soitos 1996). Reed's two books, *Mumbo Jumbo* (1972) and *The Last Days of Louisiana Red* (1974) feature Papa LaBas, the "voodoo detective." In Major's book *Reflex and Bone Structure* (1975), the narrator is involved in writing – and deconstructing – a detective story. As the characters move through time and place, Major comments on racial oppression in America, focusing particularly on police violence, including the gang rape of the female protagonist, Cora, by police officers (Bailey 2008: 65–6).

During this same period, African-American mystery writer Percy Spurlark Parker introduced "Big Bull" Benson in his only novel-length appearance. In *Good Girls Don't Get Murdered* (1974), Benson befriends a young woman who comes into the bar he owns. When she is murdered, he feels compelled to find her killer. Benson would go on to a long career in short stories published in *Ellery Queen's Mystery Magazine*, *Alfred Hitchcock Mystery Magazine*, and other magazines.

This was also the era when the urban street literature of Robert "Iceberg Slim" Beck and Donald Goines was being published by Holloway House. These authors told hard-boiled stories about gangsters, pimps, drugs, and police corruption that had credibility because of their own experiences as participants in "street life" and in prison. Beck and Goines influenced both rap music and modern-day urban street lit.

The Modern Black Crime Genre Novel

The late 1980s marked a turning point for African-American mystery writers. Women mystery writers such as Sue Grafton, Marcia Muller, and Sara Paretsky had established themselves as authors of crime fiction featuring female protagonists in non-traditional roles. African-American "literary" writers such as Alice Walker, Toni Morrison, John Edgar Wideman, and Ernest Gaines were attracting critical attention. In this more open environment African-American mystery writers began to make significant contributions to genre mystery fiction. Gar Anthony Haywood won the Private Eye Writers Shamus award for "Best First Novel" with *Fear of the Dark* (1988), the first book in his series featuring PI Aaron Gunner. The next year, presidential candidate Bill Clinton brought another African-American mystery writer to public attention when he praised Walter Mosley's *Devil in a Blue Dress*. (See Gruesser, chapter 44 in this volume.) This book, set in postwar Los Angeles, was the first in a series that featured World War II vet, Easy Rawlins. To pay his mortgage, Easy accepts an assignment to find the missing fiancée of a wealthy white politician. He is suited for the job because the missing woman likes to hang out in jook joints and blues clubs in the black community, places that no white detective could go without attracting attention. Finding that he likes the work, and the money, Easy becomes a part-time snoop for hire in subsequent adventures.

In 1992, two African-American women writers debuted with female sleuths. Eleanor Taylor Bland set her police procedural series in Waukegan, Illinois, a small town to which her protagonist Marti MacAlister had moved after the death of her policeman husband. Marti, the mother of two children, is also a cop, a homicide detective partnered with a taciturn Polish American officer named Vik Jessenovik, towards whom she gradually warms. Barbara Neely, the other African-American female writer who debuted in 1992, created a female sleuth who was an outspoken, dark-skinned domestic worker. Blanche White has chosen her profession and consistently refuses to play along with the "Mammyism" of her white employers. In *Blanche on the Lam* (1992), Blanche has come back to her hometown, Fairleigh, North Carolina, to raise her dead sister's two children after living in California and New York. Facing thirty days in jail for having written a bad check after her employers stiffed her, she escapes custody and hides out as a substitute housekeeper in a country home, where she is forced to sleuth in order to solve two murders and keep herself out of the sheriff's hands.

Marti MacAlister, the homicide detective, and Blanche White, the amateur detective, were soon joined by Valerie Wilson Wesley's private investigator, Tamara Hayle in *When Death Comes Stealing* (1994). A native of Newark, New Jersey, Tamara is a former police officer who left her job in a suburban police department after her son and his friends were harassed by fellow cops. She is divorced, and struggles to make ends meet while raising her teenage son. Like many of her PI peers, she is a solo practitioner who waits for a paying client to walk through the door.

Unlike Tamara Hayle, who left policing, Paula Woods's protagonist, Charlotte Justice, has been on the Los Angeles Police force for 13 years. In *Inner City Blue* (1999), she is trying to cope with being the only black woman in the Los Angeles Police Department's elite Robbery-Homicide Division. The series begins in the aftermath of the riots that rocked the city after the police officers accused of beating African-American motorist Rodney King were acquitted by a Simi Valley jury. Gary Phillips's debut novel featuring Ivan Monk, *Violent Spring* (1994), begins during this same moment in Los Angeles's turbulent racial history. Monk is hired by the Korean American Merchant Association when a body is found during a ground-breaking ceremony.

During the 1990s, another African-American protagonist made his debut in a setting that was unique. Based in Denver, Colorado, bail bondsman C. J. Floyd is the creation of Robert Greer. In Floyd's series of adventures, beginning with *The Devil's Husband* (1996), Greer explores the neglected history of blacks in the American West, including black rodeo stars and cowboys. Floyd is a Vietnam vet, and among the continuing characters that populate his world are a doctor and her aunt who escaped from the chaos of Vietnam when the doctor was a child. Floyd's secretary, later partner, Flora Jean Benson, is a black woman who served in the Gulf War.

A pathologist and medical researcher, Greer also has written several medical thrillers. He is not alone among the African-American writers who have made use of their professional training and/or work experiences in their books. For example, Christopher Darden, a member of the prosecution team in the O. J. Simpson case, later collaborated with Dick Lochte to write the Nikki Hill series, featuring a young African-American female prosecutor in Los Angeles. Law professor Stephen L. Carter's best-selling novel, *The Emperor of Ocean Park* (2002) is about a law professor who uncovers the secrets of his dead father, a nominee for the Supreme Court. Pamela Thomas-Graham, Ivy League graduate and CEO, writes an "Ivy League" mystery series in which her protagonist, Nikki Chase, is an economics professor at Harvard. PBS commentator Karen Grigsby Bates writes a series about a black female newspaper columnist in Los Angeles. This use of education/work experience by African-American mystery writers is, of course, not unusual, since writers are typically advised to draw on their life experience. What is perhaps of interest, however, is that now there are African-American writers who are holding white-collar positions that allow them to write from such diverse professional perspectives.

In Kyra Davis's books, a cross-fertilization of subgenres is evident. In what has been described as a "chick lit" mystery series, her bi-racial protagonist, Sophie Katz, is a thirty-something mystery writer living in San Francisco. The title of the first book in the series, *Sex, Murder, and a Double Latte* (2005), refers to Sophie's fondness for Starbucks coffee. Her circle of loyal friends includes a gay black male hairstylist and her two best girlfriends, one of whom owns a sex novelty shop. On the grittier end of the continuum, Norman Kelley's series, beginning with *Black Heat* (1997), reflects the author's involvement in the world of hip hop music. Smart, tough, and prepared to use violence, lawyer and professor Nina Halligan is aware of the geopolitics of issues such as environmental pollution. When her husband and two children are murdered, she seeks justice. Her circle of friends call themselves the "Bad Girls International."

In discussing mystery/detective fiction by contemporary African-American mystery writers, it is useful to consider the argument by Soitos (1996) about black cultural aesthetics in the works of African-American writers in general. References to African-American history and culture often provide a subtext to these stories. Writers like Walter Mosley, Paula L. Woods, and Persia Walker set their books in the past, locating their mystery in a cultural moment of significance. Other writers have their characters refer to matters such as slavery and its long historical shadow, or the impact of the contemporary "war on drugs" on black communities, or profiling by the police (e.g., "Driving While Black").

A number of white mystery writers also have demonstrated interest in the history of American race relations. Barbara Hambly's series set in nineteenth-century New Orleans features surgeon/musician Benjamin January as a free man of color. Robert Skinner's series set in Depression-era New Orleans features nightclub owner Wesley Farrell. In the first book in Kris Nelscott's series, protagonist Smokey Dalton becomes a surrogate father for a boy who witnesses the assassination of Martin Luther King, Jr, and must be protected.

As noted in the introduction to this chapter, some of the best-known African-American mystery protagonists have been created by white writers. In addition to January, Farrell, and Dalton, George Baxt's gay black police detective Pharoah Love and Kenn Davis's P. I. Carver Bascombe qualify among them. Other authors created African-American "sidekicks" for their white protagonists. One of the more enduring relationships of this kind is that between Robert B. Parker's Boston PI Spenser and his black associate, Hawk. Among modern sleuths, James Patterson's detective Alex Cross, a psychologist/cop with a mother and son who lives in Washington, DC, has attracted a large readership. Films based on Patterson's books and starring popular actor Morgan Freeman have expanded Cross's name recognition. Other black characters created by white writers include George Pelecanos's Derek Strange, a former Washington, DC, cop turned private investigator (who works with younger, white ex-cop, Terry Quinn) and James Sallis's protagonist, Lew Griffin, a professor and poet, and occasional detective, who lives in New Orleans.

Other Issues

One issue that remains salient for African-American mystery writers was raised by James Weldon Johnson in the early twentieth century – the matter of the "double audience." In order to succeed as mystery writers, arguably African-American writers must attract both black and white readers to their works. This means that they must be aware of the aspects of their works that may alienate potential white readers while also satisfying the expectations of their black readers – and vice versa.

A related issue regarding audience has to do with reaching potential readers. For African-American writers writing genre fiction (i.e., mystery/detective, romance, horror, fantasy, and science fiction), the matter of "book placement" has generated considerable debate, beginning with a controversial op-ed piece by Nick Chiles that appeared in the *New York Times*. Chiles objected to the practice by some bookstores and libraries of creating a section called "African-American Literature" and placing all books by black authors in that section. Chile objected to the fact that "classics" of African-American literature and his own books were placed in the same section as urban street literature. For mystery writers and other authors of genre fiction, the issue is visibility. The bookstore chains and libraries that follow this practice explain that it is a matter of convenience for black readers, to allow them to locate books that they may find interesting. Some publishers might also argue that this helps a new author to find a base of readers. However, for mystery/detective writers this kind of placement may prevent readers who are browsing for a mystery from finding their books. It is unlikely that non-African American readers – or even some African-American readers – will come to the African-American literature section to look for genre mysteries, which leaves African-American writers who are placed in this section with no opportunity to build a readership beyond the generic boundaries of African-American literature.

Conclusions

The evolution of black characters in crime fiction has, not surprisingly, reflected the changing status of African-Americans in American society. Gradually, the stereotypes of the nineteenth and early twentieth centuries have been replaced by more realistic characterizations. Since their arrival in the United States as slaves, African-Americans have been involved in a discourse about crime and justice. At the turn of the last century, African-Americans began to realize the possibilities of mystery/detective fiction as a genre. At the same time, non-genre writers drew on certain useful aspects of the form in their fiction.

The last decades of the twentieth century witnessed an era in which publishing became more accessible to women and to people of color. At the same time, increasing awareness of diversity, social issues, and black life and culture as relatively unexplored fictional terrain made the creation of African-American characters and protagonists more appealing to white writers. By the early 1990s, African-American writers were beginning to tell their own stories. Today, African-American protagonists reflect the variety of backgrounds to be found among real-life African-Americans. In this regard, both white writers and the growing number of African-American writers, along with many other people of color working in crime, mystery, and detective fiction, have helped to extend our exploration of race, class, and gender in the cultural imaginary.

NOTE

1   However, during this era, African-Americans were making "race movies" to be shown in theaters to African-American audiences. The most famous of these filmmakers was Oscar Micheaux who made movies in a variety of genres, including mysteries. For example, his 1935 film, *Murder in Harlem* was inspired by the 1913 Leo Frank-Mary Phagan murder case and offered another solution to the murder of Phagan (see Bronski 2005).

22

Ethnic Postcolonial Crime and Detection (Anglophone)

Ed Christian

Definition

Postcolonial detectives are police, private, or amateur detectives from formerly colonized peoples or nations. Some readers might include among postcolonial detectives only indigenous people from once colonized countries that have achieved independence. Others might include detectives who are members of groups that were once oppressed or marginalized, wherever they may live. Even though they are not strictly postcolonial, applying to these detectives the critical insights of postcolonial theory can be illuminating, as they too can be seen to be struggling against neo-colonialism, assimilation, and the hegemony of Western culture.

The idea of the "empire" (the postcolonial world) "writing back" to the "center" of colonial power to explain itself is one of the most powerful metaphors in postcolonial theory. The metaphor works well with many forms of literature, but less so with detective fiction. While mystery novels and stories are popular in many postcolonial countries, the best writers there seem to be focusing on other sorts of writing. There may be quite a few indigenous authors writing detective fiction for local consumption, but if so, such books are hard for Western readers to find, as few have been translated by Western publishers. Scholars in postcolonial countries need to go to their local bookstores, survey what indigenous detective fiction is available, and let Western scholars know about it. At present, we do not know the extent to which the "empire" is writing back because we aren't getting the letters.

Most indigenous postcolonial detectives have been created not by indigenous authors but by ex-colonizers, generally white men who have lived in the countries they write about or who have studied them sympathetically. While the books they write are necessarily less authentic than would be books by postcolonial authors, some of these writers are notable. Excluded from postcolonial literature by definition are "tourist" novels or novels where the detective is not indigenous. Also, if an author or detective shows no consciousness of postcolonial conditions and challenges, the post-colonial detective definition does not fit.

It may seem odd at first glance, but postcolonial writers most often write about postcolonial detectives living and working in Western countries. These writers and their detectives are only metaphorically postcolonial. The United Kingdom and the United States have both become more open to ethnically diverse people in the past generation, as well as to women and homosexuals, both in the general culture and in law enforcement. This has led to a flourishing market for these writers. Some have chosen to write mainstream novels, but others have written about the struggle for equality and acceptance. Their books are particularly interesting when the detectives are seen fighting against oppression, marginalization, and assimilation. As a genre, detective fiction often moves from the interrogation of suspects to the interrogation of society, where crime stems from flaws in the political, social, and industrial systems. Postcolonial detectives notice these problems, but they particularly notice when they are due to the residual effects of colonialism and to the struggles of formerly colonized nations to find new yet culturally friendly ways of making their situation progressively fairer and happier. Often, of course, the postcolonial situation remains insecure, dangerous, and corrupt for decades. The best authors notice these cultural contradictions.

There are several useful ways for critics to look at postcolonial detectives. One is to attend to their methods and procedures. What are the difficulties involved with detecting and seeking justice in a corrupt, totalitarian state or a state where the political situation is unsettled? Or one might examine how the detectives combine their indigenous cultural knowledge with Western police methods as they struggle to solve crimes where the motivation is based on local culture. A third approach is to look at postcolonial detectives as people struggling to gain power, to fight racism, and to be taken seriously as detectives. Fourthly, critics can focus on the situation of postcolonial writers and the difficulty of their being heard and read, both in the indigenous country and at the center of empire.

It is perhaps ironic that we are essentially calling for postcolonial writers to produce detective fiction that follows the generic conventions developed by the center of empire. However, when authors stray too far from the conventions or treat them with disdain, the results are not satisfying to lovers of mysteries. Often this unconventionality goes hand in hand with inadequate writing skills. Mary Lou Quinn and Eugene Schleh (1991) have written on detective fiction by Kenyans and Nigerians published in Africa in the 1980s by the Macmillan Education Program. Unfortunately, while the novels are interesting in some ways, in quality they are far below the work done by African authors better known in the West. They have little to offer in the way of postcolonial detection, though they reveal a good deal about African wealth and luxury fantasies.

Of the many contributions to postcolonial theory, the work of Homi K. Bhabha is most useful to our understanding of postcolonial detectives. Bhabha focuses on the concept of liminality, the condition of being within a space made by the meeting of two borders. The postcolonial detective often lives in this space. He or she has the power to oppress others provided by Western police methods and the detective's own position within society, often as a member of the police force. But he or she also has the power to resist oppression that goes with ethnic attachment, education, and access to power. Police methods are one of the most obvious forms of colonial control, and these methods have not necessarily grown less repressive in postcolonial societies. By adopting these methods, the postcolonial detective risks recolonizing his or her people. Bhabha has also written about mimicry, the sometimes ironic but generally sincere tendency of the colonized to imitate the colonizers in order to be like them, and this mimicry is often seen in postcolonial detectives when they try to act like those who train them. Often, they discover the solution to the crime only when they stop mimicking and use their indigenous knowledge.

Bhabha, while not rejecting resistance in some forms, points to an inevitable "hybridity" that results as the cultures of the colonizer and of the colonized meet. The result is not the disempowering of one or the other, but a decentering of power, a sharing of power, and the strengthening of both peoples, even though the process may lead to suffering as a culture is wrested away from its owners and replaced with one that is supposedly more "progressive" or "enlightened." Bhabha insists that this hybridity goes both ways and that, though painful, it is beneficial. The effect of the postcolonial world on the metropolis, as more and more formerly colonized peoples move to urban areas and make themselves essential to them, is readily seen in many large Western cities, and it helps strengthen the case for examining detective fiction written by ethnic minority writers in the West from a postcolonial perspective.

Hybridity is an essential component of most of the postcolonial detectives. Some are angrier than others or more resistant, but they are themselves sites of hybridity. They are blends of Western police methods and indigenous cultural knowledge, and their abilities are greater because of this hybridity. They have appropriated what is useful from the empire, but transformed it. As with postcoloniality in general, the postcolonial detective is a work in progress. These detectives are learning, adjusting, changing, compromising, rejecting, resisting. They are not usually heroes of the resistance, out to destroy the oppressor, but on a quest for self-knowledge.

While postcolonial detectives are not entirely free agents, they do have a degree of power denied most of their compatriots. Like their fellow citizens, they must decide whether to act within the law (which is the law of their postcolonial country, even if borrowed from Western law) or to circumvent it. But they must also decide between justice and mercy, making adjustments in the law where it works to oppress. They may think, resent, encourage, speak (with caution), and sometimes act. The primary work of the postcolonial detective is surveillance, and part of that surveillance is observing the disparities, ironies, hybridities, and contradictions of both the empire and the indigenous culture. After colonization, surveillance serves less to support imperial dominance than to restore what is right. The postcolonial detective puts marginalization to work, using it as a source of strength even as he or she uncovers the difficulties it causes.

Detectives in Postcolonial Countries

While the United States might be considered a postcolonial country, insofar as the American character was partially shaped by colonization and the struggle for independence, this categorization is not very useful when applied to Euro-Americans, whether descendants of the revolutionaries or not. There are other countries settled by Europeans that won independence long ago, such as Brazil (1822), Peru (1821), and Columbia (1819), not to mention an entire continent, Australia. In these nations, as in the US, the "mother country" has come to seem less important, and the actions of the postcolonial people have become less demonstrably a response to the center of empire. Meanwhile, however, the indigenous peoples of these nations are still oppressed: clearly, some postcolonial countries can remain postcolonial for a long time, if in a different modality.

Australia changed from being a collection of colonies to being an independent commonwealth on the first day of 1901, so its postcolonial mentality, like that of the Americas, has had more than a century to mature. However, there was and is in Australia, as on the other side of the globe, a seriously oppressed and marginalized aboriginal culture.

Arthur Upfield was born and raised in England, but during years of working in the outback of Australia, he met aborigines, respected them, and learned from them. Later he was an amateur geographer and anthropologist and urged the government to treat the aborigines more fairly. His Inspector Napoleon Bonaparte, often known as "Bony," is one of the first postcolonial detectives. The first volume in Upfield's series of nearly thirty Napoleon Bonaparte novels appeared in 1929. As nearly all of these popular mysteries were published first in the United Kingdom or in the United States, rather than in Australia, they are a good example of the empire writing back to the center.

Bonaparte is half aborigine and half white. (At the time, a full-blooded aborigine would have been unacceptable to many of Upfield's readers.) Upfield made Bonaparte even more acceptable to white readers by giving him blue eyes and a conventionally handsome English face, though with dark skin. Despite these compromises, Bonaparte offers a sympathetic introduction to aboriginal culture, a basis for understanding, appreciation, and acceptance. He has an interesting combination of humility and pride. The aborigines are only partly his people, yet he willingly keeps open an area of hybridity between them and white society. He is able to solve cases involving them because to some extent he is one of them and understands and respects their ways. However, he also has much to teach those who have trained him in Western methods of police detection. For example, the official police know little about how the religious beliefs of the aborigines affect how they deal with corpses, or their ideas of justice and revenge. Bonaparte no longer lives with the aborigines, but he understands them and does not scorn them. He faces a great deal of prejudice, even from those who know him well, but he also has a reputation for solving cases. Thus, time after time he shows that the prejudice against him is unfounded.

Unlike Australia, Africa was the heart of darkness to Western readers and writers of the colonial era, a place of ignorance and poverty, superstition and disease. Africa was a continent filled with people waiting to be exploited, saved, or healed. Few colonial writers created intelligent, resourceful Africans, apart from the occasional servant or functionary. Since the end of colonialism, this has changed. The old problems still exist, but they are being dealt with to some extent, and it is now primarily Africans who are creating their own world, though they may sometimes view it through Western eyes.

That said, most novels featuring postcolonial African detectives that are available outside Africa have been written by white men. Though born in Canada, John Wyllie lived for many years in West Africa. His Dr Quarshie novels were published between 1975 and 1981. Quarshie is a Canadian-trained African doctor who lives in a fictional West African country. Because he has a reputation for scientific reasoning and a relative who is a powerful politician, he is asked to solve murders that are beyond the capabilities of the various local security forces. Many of these cases have superstitious elements based on indigenous religions. Quarshie usually discovers that the murder is not supernatural. He is a sympathetic and amusing character who is often torn between his Canadian training in scientific method and the call of his people. He hates corruption and violence. While the books are well written and raise many postcolonial questions, they are in the end less effective than some other series because Wyllie does not successfully inhabit Quarshie's subjectivity.

From a literary perspective, perhaps the finest series featuring postcolonial detectives is that of James McClure, with Bantu sergeant Mickey Zondi and Afrikaner CID lieutenant Tromp Kramer. McClure was born in South Africa in 1939, but in 1965 was forced to leave because of his opposition to the apartheid government. Should this series be considered postcolonial, given that it was completed before power was transferred? South Africa was at the time technically a postcolonial country, having won independence from Britain in 1961. McClure's novels were published between 1971 and 1991 and were immensely popular in South Africa, though they were not legally sold there. It was daring to have a Bantu detective as a protagonist, even more so in that, throughout the series, it is primarily Zondi who solves the crimes by using his knowledge of indigenous cultures. Zondi does not have much access to Kramer's white world (though the majority of South Africans do not understand Kramer's mother tongue, Afrikaans), but in Zondi's world, Kramer can only get results through violence and noise. These books are police procedurals of a high caliber, dealing not only with the investigations but with the home life of the two protagonists.

In *The Song Dog* (1991), for example, readers find out how Kramer and Zondi began working together. Kramer spends more than half the book using his police methods to solve the case of a police officer and his lover blown up in an explosion. Kramer is an excellent cop, but in a South African context. Thus, when a black patrolman answers his chief in Zulu instead of in English, Kramer pulls his pistol and shoots at the mud at the man's feet. Kramer discovers many facts but cannot solve the case. Then Zondi shows up, speaking perfect Afrikaans. He can provide a suspect with an alibi because he sat in a tree all night watching his car. He figures out how long a man smoked in his car before entering a house by counting the fresh cigarette butts. He climbs a mountain to talk with a medicine woman who gives him the information that cracks the case while Kramer waits below, unable to accept that a woman like this might have useful information and unable to understand her language in any case. Later, when Kramer cannot obtain adequate information about a cremation, Zondi gets it from the incinerator boy, telling him that his own father held a similar job. Kramer arranges for Zondi to become his partner. At the end, Kramer is captured by the murderer, and Zondi saves Kramer's life. Time after time, Zondi's knowledge and abilities make it possible for the detectives to find answers and solve cases.

The extent of McClure's influence is indicated by several new South African series featuring black and white detective teams. Richard Kunzmann, born in Namibia but raised in South Africa, writes about police detectives Harry Mason and Jacob Tsahbalala of Johannesburg. However, Kunzmann's novels have a postapartheid setting. Margie Orford also grew up in Namibia and South Africa. An activist, she took her college final exams in prison. Her series detective is Dr Clare Hart. In Orford's first novel, *Like Clockwork* (2006), set in Namibia, Hart teams up with Captain Tamar Damases, an indigenous detective. Her second novel, *Blood Rose* (2007), is set in Cape Town, a different world. Deon Meyer, born in South Africa, writes his novels in Afrikaans. His major characters include the former mercenary Thobela Mpayipheli, who decides to work toward the solution of South Africa's crime problem. Wessel Ebersohn also wrote a handful of fine detective thrillers at the end of the apartheid era.

Does the postcolonial consciousness fade over the decades? Does the new generation grow weary of the focus on liberation from colonialism? Writing a decade after the end of apartheid, Angela Makholwa's amateur detective Lucy Khambule is, like Makholwa herself, a successful public relations writer. A horrifying series of rapes and murders leads her into parts of South Africa to which white writers and detectives have little access. South African novelist Mike Nicol, reviewing Makholwa's novel *Red Ink* (2007) in *Crime Beat*, writes, "It has suspense, violence, murder. Best of all it carries no old South African baggage: this is the indifferent world of new bling South Africa." Makholwa was a teenager in 1994, when white minority rule in South Africa came to an end. Nicol's comment suggests that postcolonial consciousness fades over the decades, that the new generation grows weary of the older generation's focus on liberation from colonialism. In a similar way, young women today often take the hard-won gains of feminism for granted while rejecting activism, or, perhaps more to the point, the recent election of a young African-American president might be seen to signal the passing of an older generation's civil rights militancy: postcolonialism, equally, may seem less interesting to future generations who have outgrown its imperatives.

Dennis Casley was born in Cornwall, but spent years in Africa. His detective, Chief Inspector Odhiambo, is a member of Kenya's Luo tribe, and so not part of the ruling elite. Everything Odhiambo does is complicated by the tribalism and corruption of the government. Casley of course knew numerous British expatriates in Africa, and Odhiambo has to deal with many such people, often finding himself in situations reminiscent of colonial-era mysteries. In *Death Underfoot* (1993), for example, those who are murdered are white, and they are murdered because of what they know about another white expatriate.

Several indigenous Africans have written detective novels, but their books are difficult to find in Western bookstores. Writing in Swahili, Ben Mtobwa, of Tanzania, has written popular detective novels featuring detective Joram Kiango. These include *Zero Hour* (1989) and *Give Me Money* (1988). Mtobwa's knowledge of the living conditions and ways of thinking of Tanzanian city dwellers sets him apart from white authors. Nigerian and Irish gynecologist and author Tony Marinho has published a brief medical mystery, *The Epidemic* (1992). The Nigerian Kólá Akínladé wrote *Owó Eje* (*Blood Money*) in Yoruba. While the book is difficult to find, a movie based on it is available on YouTube. Writing in Swahili, M. S. Abdulla wrote mysteries set in Zanzibar, featuring a Sherlock Holmes-like detective called Bwana Msa, but these were set during the colonial era.

Another interesting author is Artur Pestana, who writes under the name Pepetela. Of Portuguese ancestry, though born and raised in Angola, Pestana was a guerilla fighter during the Angolan war of independence, then went on to become Minister of Education and later a sociology professor at the University of Angola. His rather bumbling detective Jaime Bunda (an Angolan anti-James Bond) lays bare many of the difficulties of postcolonial life in Angola, with both institutional structures and material infrastructure crumbling. The writing is amusing, and one of the novels, *Jaime Bunda, Secret Agent: Story of Various Mysteries* (2006) is available in English in the UK.

Certainly the best-known postcolonial detective from Africa today is Precious Ramotswe, protagonist of Alexander McCall Smith's No. 1 Ladies' Detective Agency series, set in Botswana. McCall Smith was born and raised in what is now Zimbabwe and later taught law in Botswana, so he knows the region and its legal system well, albeit as a white colonial. Despite this, Mma Ramotswe is a wonderfully sympathetic creation, and to outsiders, McCall Smith seems to have accurately portrayed the postcolonial society of Botswana. At the least, McCall Smith has raised the level of good feeling about Botswana for millions of foreign readers. In essence, this is an important service performed by postcolonial detective fiction aimed at outsiders rather than at indigenous readers.

Significant critical work is being done on African detective fiction, even though it is difficult to find in English. The Ninth International Janheinz Jahn Symposium, "Beyond 'Murder by Magic': Investigating African Crime Fiction," held at Johannes Gutenberg-Universität Mainz in 2008, brought together many of the experts in the field, as well as a number of the authors (see http://www.jahn-bibliothek.ifeas.uni-mainz.de/9thJJSprogramme.pdf).

Outside of Africa it is relatively easy to categorize postcolonial detective and crime fiction by region and subregion. Israel, however, is in an odd situation geographically, culturally, and historically. First, it occupies a position between major continents; second, it is a Westernized nation surrounded by non-Western Islamic neighbors; and third, it is a postcolonial country in which many people are still colonized. In a number of mysteries featuring CID Chief Inspector Michael Ohayon, Batya Gur captures the difficult relationships between the many existing subgroups of Israeli Jews and Palestinians. For example, in *Murder on a Kibbutz* (1991), Gur shows the otherness of the Kibbutzim with their communal ways, unfamiliar to most Israelis. Ohayon is able to solve the case because of insider contacts.

Asia provides several geographically distinct regions of postcolonial detective writing. Given the extent of British colonial influence on India and the massive Indian publishing industry, one might expect to find a thriving market for detective fiction there. If the work is being published in English, however, it does not seem to be widely available outside its country of origin. An exception that proves the rule is the illustrious film director Satyajit Ray, who died in 1992. He published about three dozen long stories starring Feluda, an amateur Bengali detective who lives in Calcutta and is loosely based on Sherlock Holmes. Like Holmes, Feluda solves cases using close observation and logic, but he also depends on his indigenous knowledge. Among living writers, Nuri Vitacchi and Ravi Shankar Etteth are also worth mentioning. Nuri Vittachi is of Indian descent, but was born in Ceylon (Sri Lanka) and has long lived in Hong Kong. His comic "Feng Shui Detective" series features C. F. Wong, a Singaporean geomancer and includes acerbic looks at the city's large Indian community. Ravi Shankar Etteth has written a novel with a strong mystery element, *The Village of Widows* (2004), but his work is also known for its magical realism.

Sujata Massey was born in England to an Indian father and a German mother, grew up in the United States, and has written a series of novels featuring a half-Japanese woman, Rei Shimura, who grew up in America but now lives in Japan much of the time. Her books sell well, and she is the best-known "Indian" mystery author. However, her detective is postcolonial only in the sense that she comes from a once-persecuted ethnic group. More interesting is the discrimination and marginalization Rei Shimura faces in Japan, being only half-Japanese and not speaking the language well. Massey has experienced this herself in America, of course, as well as during the several years she lived in Japan.

The most famous Indian detective is certainly H. R. F. Keating's Inspector Ghote of the Bombay Police Department. Keating wrote a number of Ghote novels before he first visited India. Indians have claimed that Keating not only captured the characteristic sound of Bombay speech, but also caught the differences between castes and education levels. Ghote is a bit like Ghandi: tenacious, abstemious, with a highly developed moral sense. In postcolonial India, he must face not only entrenched corruption and unrest, but also suspicion from those who know he was trained by the British and racism from the British who dislike Indians. He must also deal with Indian problems in Indian ways. For example, in *Inspector Ghote Breaks an Egg* (1970), he investigates an old murder by disguising himself as an egg salesman, but he must also persuade a Swami not to starve himself to death. Ghote's cultural knowledge helps him succeed on both fronts.

While the Philippines does not seem to produce much crime fiction, one exception is *Smaller and Smaller Circles*, by F. H. Batacan, who now lives in Singapore. Batacan's detectives are two Jesuit priests searching for a serial killer of homeless boys. They combine their scholarly training (forensic anthropology and clinical psychology) with their years of service to the poor, using their indigenous cultural knowledge to find the killer. Batacan worked in the Philippines' intelligence community before turning to television journalism. It is worth mentioning here American Raoul Whitfield's Jo Gar stories, set in the Philippines and published in the 1930s in the ground-breaking pulp magazine, *Black Mask*. They are based on the years that Whitfield spent there as a child with his father, who worked for the US Territorial government. Although they were technically published while the Philippines was a US possession, these 24 stories convey a great deal of respect for their tight-lipped, hard-boiled Filipino detective protagonist, Gar, whose understanding of indigenous, hybridized, and colonial cultural norms and the ins and outs of life in Manilla are usually crucial to solving his cases.

The Australian William Marshall has written some of the most stylistically interesting of detective novels, and they have the added benefit of abundant black humor. Two of his best are set in Manila, *Manila Bay* (1986) and *Whisper* (1988). Both are police procedurals. The indigenous detectives often count on their cultural knowledge to help them solve crimes. For example, in *Manila Bay*, the crimes include a murder due to a grudge in the world of cockfighting, a thief who sprays his victims with stinking durian juice before stealing their shopping, and Japanese tourists trying to dig up their war dead – dissuaded by a policeman who pretends to be a ghost.

Even better are William Marshall's 16 novels set in Hong Kong, the Yellowthread Street series. Marshall lived in Hong Kong for years, and his knowledge of the culture, while not indigenous, includes a great many interesting customs. Marshall's Hong Kong is not the place tourists see, but full of poor neighborhoods where violence, superstition, hard work, and corruption mingle in absurd ways. It is always difficult to figure out the motive for the crime if one is not native Chinese. Some of Marshall's detectives are Western, but most of these are bumblers.

As in India, Sherlock Holmes has been the most influential detective in China, and, for that matter, in the nation it has occupied since 1959, Tibet. Jamayang Norbu, a Tibetan exile (first in India, currently in the US) has written popular pastiches where

Holmes, in disguise, visits Lhasa during his "missing years" on the lam from the survivors of the Moriarty gang. Communism has had interesting effects on the detective genre in China as a whole. The historian Jeffrey Kinkley (2001) has written about Chinese law enforcement ministries publishing detective stories, often in newspapers, in order to educate people about the virtues of the police.

The Chinese detective novelist best known in the West is Qiu Xiaolong, who was born in Shanghai but has lived in America for two decades. His novels, which are noteworthy for the quality of the writing, feature Inspector Chen Cao of the Shanghai Police Bureau, who is also a poet who translates detective fiction into Chinese. He has some friends in high places who are grooming him for power, but there are other powerful people who do not like him. Chen is not above accepting gifts or favors or enjoying sex where he finds it, but in general he is a man of honor and integrity dedicated to rooting out corruption. Everything in China seems to have a political dimension, and Qiu reveals this in a believable way. Inspector Chen can never solve crimes simply or directly. It may be that it will not be politically expedient to solve a crime because someone with power is involved or because leaving it unsolved helps the government with some campaign it is waging at the moment.

Eliot Pattison's Inspector Shan also has some claim to be considered a postcolonial detective. Once a powerful law enforcement official in Beijing, Shan finds himself a political prisoner on a work gang in Tibet. Most of his fellow prisoners are Tibetan Buddhist monks. While Shan's abilities as a detective and his knowledge of Chinese bureaucracy are useful, his power is limited because he cannot leave Tibet. Meanwhile, although China is a postcolonial country, Tibet is colonized and oppressed. Shan's sympathies are entirely with the Tibetans, and his growing understanding of Tibet is crucial to his ability to solve crimes. On the other hand, he could not solve crimes without an understanding of police methods that comes from years in the seat of the empire.

One of the more unusual postcolonial detectives is Dr Siri Paiboun, the national coroner of Laos, protagonist of Colin Cotterill's novels. Cotterill has lived in Laos. Dr Siri, in his seventies, has devoted decades to revolutionary activities, but finds that in postcolonial Laos the ideal society has not emerged, the infrastructure is crumbling, and the government is purging those who disagree with its policies. It is difficult to know whether Cotterill's Laos is realistic, but it is a compelling setting.

Lisa See is a biracial Chinese-American. Her Chinese detective, Inspector Liu Hulan, works for the Ministry of Public Security, where her father is the Vice-Minister. Liu has both an American law degree and an American fiancé who is a lawyer. They work together on cases. See writes well about what Liu and her family suffered during the Cultural Revolution. Her father is powerful, somewhat corrupt, very political, and quite wealthy. It is difficult to believe that someone with Liu's background and friends could work in the Ministry of Public Security, but China is changing.

Japan has a number of notable detective novelists, such as Seicho Matsumoto, Masako Togawa, and Shizuko Natsuki, and there have been Western writers who have also written mysteries set in Japan, such as James Melville's Superintendent Otani novels. However, while Japan was occupied by American troops for a few years, it has been historically a colonizing power, rather than a colony, so its detectives are not really postcolonial, revealing the special interests and abilities of those who have recently escaped colonization.

Postcolonial Ethnicities

Postcolonial theory has looked primarily at literature written by indigenous authors in countries that were once colonized. However, because postcolonial theory often examines the effect of oppression and marginalization and also of being freed from them, some of the theory proves useful when we examine authors who are not strictly postcolonial, but are members of ethnic groups or other groups that have been oppressed or marginalized, but now are being accepted into mainstream society.

Detectives whose race is at issue often face the same problems of liminality as their postcolonial counterparts: they are on the border between two worlds and seldom entirely at ease. They have power, but they know what it is to have little. They are both respected and hated. Hybridity is also frequently seen in ethnic detective fiction. Both detectives and others of their ethnicity may have relatively little contact with whites, yet white culture infiltrates their world. At the same time, their own culture infiltrates the white world. As a result, both cultures are strengthened. Some authors devote much of their work to issues of oppression and racism, while others rarely mention it, yet both positions derive from the postcolonial imperative.

While the most important writers of racialized and ethnic detective fiction are non-white, there are a few white authors who need to be mentioned here because of their influence.

Earl Derr Biggers was not himself Chinese, but he did invent the Chinese-born Hawaiian police detective Charlie Chan in the pages of the *Saturday Evening Post*. It can be tempting to see Chan as an unrealistic racial parody, but he was based on a real-life Honolulu prototype. Deliberately setting out to destroy the prevailing views of the Chinese as ignorant, cunning, treacherous, and cruel, Biggers made Chan wise, intelligent, honest, and kind. While he unfortunately ended up replacing one stereotype with another, notes Charles Rzepka, "Biggers did what he could with what he had" (2007: 1476), including a white audience whose racism was entrenched and unapologetic. The same cannot be said for the John P. Marquand's creation, the Japanese spy Mr Moto (a detective in the movie versions), despite his otherwise polite manners, suave demeanor, and basic sense of honor. Moto garnered sympathy from American readers insofar as he generally helped to advance the romance subplots of Marquand's fictions, but we are never allowed to forget his primary allegiance during the peak of Japan's own aggressive colonization of other Asian countries.

Although this might best be left to the judgment of a Navajo audience, Tony Hillerman often strikes readers as one of the most sensitive of all creators of post-colonial detectives. Certainly Hillerman has done his homework and has a sincere love of the Navajo and the area where they live. To outsiders, his detectives Joe Leaphorn and Jim Chee seem believably Navajo, and many readers feel that they understand the Navajo better after reading Hillerman's books. Every book in the series shows one or both detectives using indigenous cultural knowledge to solve crimes: for example, knowledge about Navaho religion, superstitions, and healing. At the same time, the two are thoroughly trained in law enforcement and have to follow not only Navajo law, but US laws. They often face discrimination from the police community. They are also at times suspected by their own people. These are all characteristic of Bhabha's liminality.

African-American authors have created more postcolonial detectives of the ethnic type than have any other minority writers. However, because these authors are discussed elsewhere in this book (see chapters 21, 38 and 44 by Bailey, Soitos, and Greusser), I will omit discussion of them here.

Hispanic writers of detective fiction often evince a high degree of political activism and an antagonistic relationship with the dominant power. Marcos Villatoro's detective, Romilia Chacon, is a homicide cop and later an FBI agent born in El Salvador. She is involved with drug smugglers and assassins, even having one as a lover. Her Salvadoran background and fluent Spanish gain her entrance to groups not open to most FBI agents. Lucha Corpi is a Chicana activist. Her books feature the private detectives Gloria Damasco, Justin Escobar, and Dora Saldaña. Although the setting is primarily the San Francisco Bay area, most of the characters are Latino. This emphasizes Latino self-sufficiency. Manuel Ramos is an attorney in Denver, as is his detective, Luis Montez. In his college days, Montez was a Chicano activist, and he maintains close ties to the Chicano community and helps many Latinos with legal problems. Alicia Gaspar de Alba, who teaches Chicana/o Studies, has used the form to comment on the plight of illegal immigrants.

Michael Nava is a lawyer and judicial staff attorney for the California Supreme Court. He is also gay and has written a series featuring Henry Rios, a gay Hispanic lawyer. The focus is more on homosexuality than ethnicity, but Rios faces discrimination on both counts. Rudolfo Anaya, English professor and Chicano writer, has written four novels featuring Albuquerque detective Sonny Baca. They are unusual not only for the strong Chicano emphasis, but because of the supernatural elements.

There are fewer Asian-American detective authors than Hispanic. Henry Chang lives in New York City's Chinatown. Chang's books are hard-boiled, yet thoughtful and compassionate. His police detective Jack Yu also lives and works in Chinatown. Yu is the only Chinese-American cop working in Chinatown, so it is not surprising that he is able to solve cases white detectives cannot solve. However, the people of Chinatown generally do not trust him, while he faces a lot of racism from other police officers.

Naomi Hirahara is Japanese-American. Her detective, widowed Los Angeles gardener Mas Arai, was born in the United States, but returned as a child to Hiroshima, and he was there when the atomic bomb exploded. Arai has lived through a great deal of change: when he was a child Japanese-Americans had to work as gardeners, and now, like his daughter and her friends, they hold graduate degrees.

While the postcolonial framework may become less useful as the independence days of postcolonial nations become more distant memories, it can still provide a useful way of looking at how oppression and power are portrayed in detective fiction, where race and ethnicity still play a prominent role in directing the action and in motivating characters.

23

Crime Writing in Other Languages

Sue Neale

Introduction

In the early 1990s, Julian Symons suggested that "little sparkles" in non-Anglophone crime writing (Symons 1992). However, since 2000 translated crime novels have achieved increasing critical and popular acclaim. Although the genre is still dominated by Anglo-American writers, the shift has been evident, for example, in the degree to which translations began to dominate the shortlists for awards: Henning Mankell won the UK Crime Writer's Association (CWA) Gold Dagger Award with *Sidetracked* in 2001, and José Carlos Somoza won it with *The Athenian Murders* in 2002; in 2005, four of six shortlisted titles were translations, and *Silence of the Grave* (2005), by Icelandic writer Arnaldur Indridason, won. So intense was the competition that after 2005 the Gold Dagger was reserved for crime fiction published in English, and the CWA created the Duncan Lawrie International Dagger for crime fiction written in a foreign language but translated and published in the UK. As this chapter will make clear, it is not only in recent years that European crime writers have made significant contributions to the genre, but their impact has been most remarkable during the last decade, and my focus will be primarily on the key writers producing translated crime fiction from the mid-1990s on. Having first briefly surveyed earlier French, Swiss, and Swedish contributions, I will go on to consider some of the most important figures in contemporary crime writing: the large group of influential French crime writers; the influx of Nordic writers whose dark fictions have a great appeal to British readers; and the contributions from Spain and Italy, often referred to as Mediterranean *noir*.

What does translated crime fiction offer that is different to the domestic version? Publishers like Christopher MacLehose of Quercus Press, François von Hurter of Bitter Lemon Press and Pete Ayrton of Serpent's Tail, agree that it is the "attraction of the unfamiliar location, the unfamiliar politics" (MacLehose 2006; King 2006a, 2006b). Von Hurter considers that foreign crime fiction is as much concerned with the social and political situations that led to the crime as with pinpointing and catching the perpetrators. In addition, readers of foreign crime are attracted by the "quirky, literary, seamy, sexy, funny crime books [that] unveil the darker side of places you're likely to travel to" (King 2006a). Readers' choices are also, of course, conditioned by the authors and novels that publishers choose to have translated, which appears to depend on market considerations – popularity (sales) and critical acclaim (prizes). Word of mouth, specialist websites and enthusiasts in the bookselling trade seem to have more influence than reviews or radio interviews. Publishers also agree that a series of titles from one author rather than a single title makes better economic sense.

Before considering the contemporary writers propelled into public notice in recent years, it is important to examine the longest-standing influence on British crime writing, the historical contribution of the French. The *Mémoirs* of Eugène François Vidocq were published in a series of volumes in France in 1828 and 1829 and were translated almost immediately into English (Knight 2004: 23). Vidocq was a criminal who turned crime enforcer and ultimately became the head of the Sûreté. His compelling narratives were enjoyed by the public and writers alike, avid for an insight into the criminal mind, though Stephen Knight suggests that their popularity was probably due to their being rewritten in French before being elaborated in translation (2004: 22–3).

Émile Gaboriau, like the French authors who followed him, was arguably of interest more for the generic character types he created than for his invention of intrigues. In the 1860s and 1870s Gaboriau invented two characters whose methods and attitudes were to exert a significant influence on future writers like Conan Doyle: Le père Tabaret, an older amateur detective, and his young protégé Monsieur Lecoq, later a professional policeman. Looking carefully over a crime scene, they infer facts about the criminal, which often prove to be correct although the two are not infallible. In *Monsieur Lecoq*, the young Lecoq, now a policeman, examines the way the snow has been brushed off a wall during a chase and is able to describe the coat the killer wore. His deductive methods using marks, clothing fibers and footprints prefigure those of Sherlock Holmes. Knight (2004: 49) suggests that Gaboriau "offers the reader the voyeuristic pleasure and corrupt delights of Parisian society and aristocratic love life."

In the early twentieth century contemporaneous French writers Maurice Leblanc and Gaston Leroux invented two very different but emblematic characters as solvers of crimes: Arsène Lupin, gentleman burglar, and Rouletabille, a young enquiring journalist. Leblanc's Lupin is a master of disguise who organizes amazing thefts and frauds, usually for his own gain though sometimes for moral reasons, righting wrongs. In *Arsene Lupin, Gentleman Thief* (1908) he enjoys making fools of the police while having adventures, though in later novels like *813* (1910) and *The Hollow Needle* (1910) he chooses to work with the police instead. Leroux's Rouletabille appeared in two novels, *The Mystery of the Yellow Room* (1909) and *The Perfume of the Lady in Black* (1909). In the first novel, Rouletabille uncovers a locked room murder mystery conceived by Larsan, a master criminal masquerading as a police detective. However, credibility is stretched to the limit when the victim turns out to be Rouletabille's mother and Larsan his father, though the reader is challenged by the intrigue. The second novel continues the story but offers alternative interpretations of the events in the original mystery. Within five years, Marcel Allain and Alain Souvestre had created a character called Fantômas, an invisible everyman killer. Skilled at deception and disguise like Lupin, Fantômas represented an insidious evil that was too slippery to be caught; he appeared in over 40 novels.

Interestingly these characters have such an enduring appeal for readers that the novels are still available as classics. Unlike much British fiction of the period in which the criminals – aberrant members of society – are brought to justice, these French characters were attractive for their challenges to the authority of the state that the forces of law and order represented.

Between the wars, the importance of the contribution of Georges Simenon, a Belgian who wrote in French, has been widely acknowledged by critics like Symons (1992) and Knight (1980, 2004) as well as by writers like Agatha Christie (see Makinen, chapter 33 in this volume) and P. D. James (see Harrington, chapter 40 in this volume). Certainly his Inspecteur Maigret, with his psychological subtlety and intuitive methods, was a refreshing new figure in the genre. He was not a loner but led a team and enjoyed a domestic life with Madame Maigret. However, Simenon's style and particularly his limited vocabulary, which was calibrated to match his broad target readership's varied levels of literacy, was criticized by the French literary establishment. Maigret's patience and understanding of human nature are model qualities still found in modern detectives, like Fred Vargas's Commissaire Adamsberg.

Written in two distinct periods, 1931–4 and 1942–72, the earlier Maigret novels are considered to be less dark and complex than the later ones, but contain more atmosphere, often linking external features like weather to Maigret's internal thought processes or to the investigation itself – a device that is often found now in contemporary crime fiction in many languages. Symons, generally relatively scathing about translated crime fiction, even dedicates a small chapter to Simenon (1992: 165–70).

Our final contribution comes from Pierre Boileau and Thomas Narcejac who, together, wrote gripping psychological novels in the 1950s and 1960s. Screen adaptations, such as *Vertigo* (*The Living and the Dead*) (1956), highlighted their characterization and creation of atmosphere. Other novels include *The Victims* (1967) and *The Evil Eye* (1959).

Although French writers have historically been most influential on the genre's development, translations of novels by the Swiss writer Friedrich Dürrenmatt and the Swedish team of Maj Sjöwall and Per Wahlöö, appearing shortly after original publication, have also played an important role. Dürrenmatt, often seen as having followed Robbe-Grillet's lead with his genre-bending crime novels, often has policemen take the law into their own hands, even if that means they may pay heavily for it. A new translation of *The Pledge* (2001) was published to coincide with the film starring Jack Nicholson and offers readers an opportunity to experience Dürrenmatt's challenging work. *The Judge and his Hangman* and *Suspicion* appeared as *The Inspector Barlach Mysteries* in 2006 (University of Chicago Press).

Which texts remain in print is an important element in assessing critical or popular success. Take, for example, the ten novels by Maj Sjöwall and Per Wahlöö. Originally published in the late 1960s and early 1970s, translations appeared relatively quickly, but soon went out of print. Republished in the late 1980s when the genre was receiving more recognition, they went out of print again. Finally, reflecting the recent interest in Nordic writers, all ten novels, subtitled *The Story of a Crime*, were reissued with introductions and postscripts containing details of the authors, film adaptations, and information about other Nordic writers.

Sjöwall and Wahlöö's police procedurals feature Martin Beck, a modern self-doubting anti-hero. In the endnotes to the new editions, Richard Shephard suggests that the authors

> successfully constructed an incisive and realistic portrait of 1960s Sweden. Although it was a country then deemed to be alluringly liberal and enticing, from the cool and measured perspective of Sjöwall and Wahlöö, Sweden was actually a stifling place, corroded by the mute desire of its populace to not rock the boat, even if the vessel in question was leaky, directionless and, for some, ultimately hazardous. (Shephard 2006)

Contemporary Scandinavian writers, such as Karin Alvtegen and Henning Mankell, value Sjöwall and Wahlöö's influence on modern crime writing. In his introduction to *Roseanna*, Mankell suggests that even today the novel has hardly aged at all; it still seems "straightforward and clear" with "a convincing story presented in an equally convincing form," written in language that "seems energetic and alive." Inspired by Ed McBain, Sjöwall and Wahlöö regarded their crime stories not as entertainment but as social criticism that sees crime as a reflection of the society in which it occurs (Mankell 2006: vi–vii). For Mankell, the investigations highlighted the "fundamental virtue of the police: patience," and represented murder investigators as "ordinary human beings" (Mankell 2006: viii).

The proliferation of non-Anglophone crime writers in the last two decades has made even more of an impact. Central and South American writers have made significant contributions – for example, the Cubans Jose Carlos Somoza and Leonardo Padura; the Uruguayan Daniel Chavarriá and the Mexican Paco Ignacio Taibo II. The more substantial record of publication, however, has been on the part of European authors, and from here on we will focus on the contributions of French, Scandinavian, Italian and Spanish writers working from the late 1980s on. The French passion for crime fiction is legendary, and cultural recognition, in the form of specialist bookshops and a specialist research library in Paris, reflects the important place it holds for the French. Also, following the inception of the Série

Noire in the late 1940s, many crime novels have been translated into French within six months of appearing in their original languages. UK publishers frequently read these in order to assess their quality and suitability for the British market as they "provide a window for us into Turkey, Korea, China, Cuba, Spain" (King 2006a).

Two of the most important French crime writers of recent years are Daniel Pennac and Fred Vargas, who in their different ways set themselves apart from the mainstream. Unlike many contemporaries like Didier Daeninckx, Jean-Claude Izzo, Jean-Patrick Manchette and Dominique Manotti, who openly use their fiction as a weapon to criticize social, political, and gender inequalities, Pennac and Vargas blend fairy story, comedy, and literary style with the crime genre, though still with strong elements of socio-political content.

Daniel Pennac's Malaussène saga of five novels was published in the late 1980s; translations appeared, starting in 1997, but not in the original order (2, 1, 3, 5, 4): *The Fairy Gunmother* (1997), *The Scapegoat* (1998), *Write to Kill* (1999), *Passion Fruit* (2001) and *Monsieur Malaussène* (2003). Claire Gorrara has analyzed the political and social issues that Pennac's novels treat, suggesting that his hybrid, comic mystery novels have "affinities with pre-war French detective fiction, as well as with the classic American *roman noir*" (Gorrara 2003: 95). Pennac manipulates generic expectations with his convoluted plots, stylish prose, and deliciously inventive dialogue.

The saga is set in the multiracial Belleville district of Paris, where the Malaussène family – half-sibling love children – live on various floors of an old ironmonger's shop and are cared for by the eldest half-brother, Benjamin. The extended family is a French community in microcosm and includes immigrants from all parts of Europe. Amar and Yasmina – the Ben Tayebs – fulfill the archetypal parental roles for the family and represent a real and symbolic refuge for Ben and his siblings in times of distress and uncertainty. Other members are Hadouch, Black Mo and Simon the Berber who act both legally and illegally to ensure that nothing untoward happens to the family.

In each novel, Pennac deals with a particular theme – consumerism, drugs and old age, writing, the visual image, and corruption – alongside the development of the family's story. The plot always involves Ben being implicated to a greater or lesser extent in a murder or other crime. It is only the support of policemen like Chief Superintendent Coudrier and his assistants, Pastor and Van Thian, that prevents Ben from ending up in jail.

Ben's mostly absent mother makes regular reappearances though sometimes she is just a voice, calling from some remote location, to prove that she is alive and well. In person she tends to be pregnant and alone, evidencing another failed love affair. The baby is then abandoned for Ben and his siblings to care for. Pennac challenges happy family stereotypes with the honest, caring and open-minded Malaussène family, content with simple pleasures like storytelling, sharing meals and caring for others less fortunate than themselves.

Though each novel can be read on its own, following the original sequence, as I discuss them below, offers a more satisfactory experience of the complicated plots. The first, *The Scapegoat*, takes place in a department store, a symbol of consumerism used by writers like Baudelaire to highlight a society where appearances and possessions are more significant than individual interactions. (In French, the title *Au bonheur des ogres* is a play on the Zola novel, *Au bonheur des dames*, that dealt with consumerism in nineteenth-century Paris.) Ben's role in the Customer Services Department is to be a scapegoat; he absorbs the verbal and physical abuse of disappointed individuals whose purchases have failed to meet their expectations. Customers withdraw their complaints when faced with Ben's tears and contrition and the possibility that their case may cause him to lose his job, which saves the store money. In *The Fairy Gunmother*, Belleville is facing a spate of drug crimes and murders. In addition, the area is being redeveloped so that the old, whether architectural or human, is being rejected for the new. For the family this means taking in a group of old men who might otherwise end up on the street. Ben now works at the Vendetta Press and his role as family storyteller is taken over by Risson, a retired bookseller, who has committed classics to memory and retells them each night.

In *Write to Kill* Pennac plays with ideas about the writer, his ideas, and their ownership as well as how the writer reaches his readers. At the Vendetta Press Ben is employed to deal with authors whose manuscripts are being rejected; he stands as a gatekeeper between the writer and a possible public. This role is extended to the impersonation, for a big promotional event, of a famous writer who chooses not to make personal appearances. Unfortunately, the writer has stolen the words and ideas of an imprisoned murderer, who escapes prison and shoots Ben in revenge for this intellectual theft. Ben survives but lapses into a coma, which lasts for half the novel, while his multi-talented girlfriend disguises herself and investigates the crime, meting out punishment as she goes along. Meanwhile, two doctors fight over Ben's organs and his chances of survival as he lies comatose – the one wanting to remove them, the other believing against logic that Ben might survive. In the final scenes, the killer visits Ben and is himself shot in his final attempt to kill Ben. By an amazing coincidence, his organs can be used to replace those Ben has lost, saving Ben's life. As the repository of the writer's brain and heart, the resurrected Ben feels that he is now a mixture of himself and the man who tried to kill him. This novel particularly illustrates Pennac's implicit suggestion that Ben is a scapegoat for the world's woes, that his family has particular holy resonances and that a resurrection is possible. To top this off, in *Monsieur Malaussène* the daughter of a policeman and a former nun receives an aborted fetus from Ben's girlfriend, giving readers a version of the immaculate conception and a virgin birth.

For Fred Vargas (the pseudonym of Frédérique Audoin-Rouzeau, a female medieval archaeologist) crime writing was a lucrative pastime until 2004 when she began a long sabbatical to devote time to writing and to actively fighting for justice for Cesare Battisti, an Italian writer of thrillers arrested and convicted of alleged terrorist activity as a young man. Her first novel in English was *Have Mercy on Us All* (2003), translated by David Bellos; set in Paris, it involves a large cast of oddballs and misfits as well as introducing the quirky Commissaire Adamsberg from the *Brigade Criminelle*. In *Seeking whom He May Devour* (2004) the scene is rural Provence and the action centers on Camille, Adamsberg's ex-girlfriend, who reluctantly calls the detective in when she needs professional advice. He is nearby, having fled from Paris and the death threats of a criminal bent on revenge.

Dr Siân Reynolds translated Vargas's *The Three Evangelists* (2005), discussed below, and it won the International Dagger in 2006. The next year *Wash this Blood Clean from my Hand* (2007) won the award. This is a tense thriller with Adamsberg and his team in Canada for specialist training; accused of murder, he is responsible for solving the crime outside the law before he is prosecuted. In *This Night's Foul Work* (2008), again shortlisted, two murdered Parisian drug dealers have soil under their fingernails and Adamsberg's instincts convince him that their deaths hide a deeper truth. The public becomes personal when the investigation uncovers individuals from his professional and personal past who have returned to exact revenge.

What sets Vargas's novels apart is her playfulness with generic expectations, her humor and a Chandleresque style and use of imagery. She challenges the French generic tradition, refusing to tackle social and political issues overtly or use her novels as feminist polemics. In a *Guardian* interview Vargas stated that for her the crime novel is not a tool to "change social reality" (Wroe 2008) but offers a cathartic experience where the monster is defined and dealt with.

The Three Evangelists is Vargas's only novel in English that does not feature Adamsberg as main investigator. Set in Paris in the mid-1990s, it begins with the sudden and mysterious appearance of a small tree in the garden of an ex-opera singer, Sophia. Her neighbors are a crew of historical researchers (Matthias, Marc, and Lucien) who specialize in prehistory, the medieval period, and World War I, respectively, and whose expertise does not immediately qualify them as crime investigators. They live in a ramshackle house with Vandoosler, an ex-cop, and Marc's godfather. Sophia asks them to dig up the tree in case it hides something sinister. When Sophia disappears and then a body is found in a burned out car with a piece of volcanic rock that Sophia always carried, they start investigating. Next, an old man who has been asking questions about Sophia is found murdered, and the historians retrace his steps and visit Sophia's family archives. The murderer turns out to be the local café owner who was once Sophia's unsuccessful understudy and has planned this revenge for 15 years, changing her appearance and insinuating herself into Sophia's life. She planted the tree and buried Sophia under it, but only after it had already been dug up twice, thus neutralizing it as a possible crime scene.

With this novel Vargas illustrates how long-hidden sexual obsession, professional jealousy, and family secrets often trigger terrible crimes. Her amateur investigators have specialist skills for interpreting the significance of small details. Though murder and death are dark themes, the interactions between Vargas's characters are often humorous, and her specific interest is to show how interpersonal relations function in difficult circumstances.

Other recent French crime writers include Sebastien Japrisot, Didier Daeninckx, Jean-Claude Izzo and Dominque Manotti. Japrisot's crime novels reflect the experimentation of the *nouveau roman* in the 1970s. In *Trap for Cinderella* (1999), a fire destroys a beach house, with two young women trapped inside; one survives but suffers from amnesia, making her identity a central issue. Recently, translations have also been published of *The Lady in the Car with Glasses and a Gun* (1998), *A Very Long Engagement* (1999), *One Deadly Summer* (2000), and *Women in Evidence* (2000).

Didier Daeninckx is a prolific left-wing writer who fictionalizes historical facts to highlight moments from France's painful past. His best-known book is *Murder in Memoriam* (2005), which focuses on events in 1961 that relate to the present (the early 1980s) and the past (1940s). Bernard Thiraud is a historian whose father, Roger, died following a demonstration in Paris in October 1961 in which hundreds of Algerians were killed due to sanctioned police brutality. In Toulouse, Bernard uncovers information about the Vichy government's complicity in deporting Jewish children to Germany, but he is killed before he can pass it on. However, Inspecteur Cadin discovers this information and ultimately reveals the truth about Bernard's murder and that of his father. *A Very Profitable War* (1994) relates the story of a private detective in 1920 investigating the infidelities of a war hero's wife. His research takes him into the dark world of murder, blackmail, profiteering, and anarchists and leads him to uncover hidden secrets from the war.

Unlike many French authors who set their crime narratives in Paris, Jean-Claude Izzo's novels are based in Marseilles, which his investigator/narrator Fabio Montale perceives as a paradise where Arabs and French citizens live in harmony. Over the course of the trilogy – *Total Chaos* (2005), *Chourmo* (2007), and *Solea* (2007) – Montale gradually rejects the role of committed policeman and becomes a simple investigator. Michael Reynolds suggests that Izzo belongs to *Mediterranean noir*, which he defines as "a literature of truth, actuality and 'investigation'" where the traditional dark hues of noir are replaced by Mediterranean colors: "bright, almost gaudy: yellows, red, ochres, and above all blue. Or else white. Light itself" (Reynolds 2006). In this subgenre food, cooking, and the pleasures of the flesh are combined with solving crimes.

When Dominique Manotti won the Duncan Lawrie International Dagger in 2008 with *Lorraine Connection* (2008), judges noted that she "seamlessly integrates a fine crime story with French provincial and national politics within the EU then matches it with an equally convincing grip on the characters of her northern landscape" (http://thecwa.co.uk/daggers/2008/). Her first novel, *Rough Trade* (2001), dealt with the rag trade, prostitution, and drug addiction, and her second, *Dead Horsemeat* (2006), with the corrupt horse racing industry. Her gripping political dramas, set in the Parisian underworld, are tightly written and exciting, reminiscent of American writers like James Ellroy.

Around the world, English readers acknowledge important recent contributions from Iceland and Scandinavia, with new writers arriving regularly. Von Hurter suggests that their particular appeal may lie in our common Viking forebears with their propensity to dark moods (King 2006a). Offering alternative social and political analyses of its distinct national traditions, like those of Swedish writers Sjöwall and Wahlöö, Nordic fiction also explores the psychology of ordinary people and what drives them to commit crimes.

Among the most significant of Scandinavian writers to emerge in recent years, Swede Henning Mankell followed Sjöwall and Wahlöö's lead, creating in the late 1990s an evocative portrait of contemporary Sweden. He uncovers the barely hidden elements that are causing the collapse of the welfare state – drugs, gun crime, and immigration issues. In the course of nine novels, his police investigator, Kurt Wallender, working in the coastal town of Ystad, Southern Sweden, gradually becomes disillusioned with society. In *The Fifth Woman* he suggests: "Society had grown cruel. People who felt they were unwanted or unwelcome in their own country, reacted with aggression. There was no such thing as meaningless violence. Every violent act had a meaning for the person who committed it" (Mankell 2003: 228).

Karin Alvtegen, another Swede, writes tense thrillers that often focus on the victim's perspective. In *Missing* (2003), Sibylla, a social outcast, is the prime suspect for a murder she did not commit. To exonerate herself, she has to outwit the police and work with those on the edges of society. Finally with justice on her side, she receives her family inheritance and is able to enjoy contentment with her estranged son. In *Betrayal* (2005) Alvtegen explores how deception causes pain and can trigger destructive behavior that has consequences we cannot control.

Swede Steig Larsson, who died in 2004 not long after completing his Millennium trilogy, made a powerful impact with the first of these three novels, *The Girl with the Dragon Tattoo*. Published posthumously in 2008, it deals with international business intrigues, dark family secrets and characters whose lives have been based on past lies. Larsson's protagonist, Mikael Blomkvist, is a Swedish financial journalist who, with the help of a damaged young woman computer hacker, Lisbeth, uncovers murder, corruption, and intrigues in the highest echelons of Swedish society, which Larsson incisively dissects with compassion and discernment.

One of the most popular and critically acclaimed Nordic novelists is Icelander Arnaldur Indridason. His police procedurals, based in contemporary Reykjavik, feature three main characters: Erlendur, Elinborg, and Sigurdur Oli. Erlendur, a typically flawed loner policeman, has a dysfunctional family life – he is divorced and has a drug addict daughter. Haunted by ghosts from his past, he searches for positive elements in the criminals and victims he deals with. Elinborg, a modern policewoman, possessing intuition and psychological insight, has an implicitly happy family life in the background. Their colleague, Sigurdur Oli, is given to voicing politically incorrect opinions but experience often obliges him to amend these. Like Mankell, Indridason uses his narratives to examine Iceland's society and history while uncovering the causes of contemporary crimes. His exploration of the human condition makes his novels refreshingly different. His haunting stories with their great sense of place deal with lost love, lost illusions, betrayal, and regret.

Indridason's five novels translated into English all follow Erlendur and his team as they investigate a variety of murders and other crimes in Reykjavik. *Jar City* (2006, original title *Tainted Blood*) is characteristic of the author's focus on Iceland's insular heritage and culture. In it, he considers what the consequences might be for an Icelander whose child dies from a genetic disease, if only he could trace all other sufferers using a new (and real) genetic database. Although outsiders perceived the database to be a useful tool for scientific investigation, not all Icelanders agreed to have their DNA sampled, and Indridason reflects their concerns in this novel, where murder and suicide are among the final outcomes of the experiment. In *Arctic Chill* (2008) the murder of a Thai boy raises issues of race and nationalism. Although individuals on both sides of the racism divide are shown to hold unacceptable beliefs, the erosion of Icelandic traditions and culture is clearly a concern that Indridason wishes to foreground. In Indridason's novels Iceland is always shown as being strange and inhospitable even for the locals. Erlendur is fascinated with stories about missing people, both in the present day and in the past, and how Icelanders accept these losses as normal. This theme forms a background to all the investigations.

For a snapshot of Italian writers, it is worth reading *Crimini* (2008), a collection of gripping short stories from ten Italian *noir* authors. Italian crime fiction reflects the problematic relationships between the police, the state, and the justice system and offers differing views on truth and justice. Massimo Carlotto and Gianrico Carofiglio both use their fiction to criticize the legal system, often detailing the difficulties of proving the innocence of wrongly accused individuals. Tobias Jones described Carlotto's work as "[m]ore than merely hard boiled," "sexy, seedy, cynical, and nihilistic, but with moments of idealism" (2006: 25). His novels, which are an indictment of a legal system in which neither victims nor perpetrators achieve justice, include *The Goodbye Kiss* (2006), *Death's Dark Abyss* (2007) and *The Fugitive* (2008). Carofiglio, an ex-Maria prosecutor, uses a first person viewpoint to explore the corruption rife in all layers of the legal system from police to high court judges. His narrator, a burned-out defense lawyer, Guido Guerrieri working in Bari, is featured in *A Walk in the Dark* (2005), *Involuntary Witness* (2006) and *Reasonable Doubts* (2007).

Carlo Lucarelli was initially known for his historical crime fiction trilogy featuring Commisario de Luca, a former Mussolini policeman: *Carte Blanche* (2007), *The Damned Season* (2007) and *Vella della Oche* (2008). Set in the post-fascism era of the late 1940s, the novels describe the period's political immorality and the defeat and hopelessness it engendered. In *Almost Blue* (2004) and *Day after Day* (2005) a female detective,

Grazia Negro, investigates present-day killers terrorizing Bologna, combating the chauvinism of her colleagues and the lack of clues.

Andréa Camilleri's novels, featuring Inspector Salvo Montalbano (named after Spaniard Manuel Vásquez Montalbán), deal with murder and corruption in Sicily. The investigations, containing black humor, are pervaded by an air of despair, set against a background of Sicilian geography and gastronomy. Among the best of these are *The Shape of the Water* (2004), *The Terra-Cotta Dog* (2004), *Voice of the Violin* (2006), *The Scent of the Night* (2007), and *Rounding the Mark* (2007).

Two of the best Spanish crime writers are Manuel Vásquez Montalbán and Arturo Perez-Reverte. Montalbán created Pepe Carvalho, an ex-cop, ex-Marxist and gourmet, now private detective in Barcelona. Like Chandler's Marlowe, Carvalho uncovers the truth but endangers his life in the process. Montalbán offers a gastronomic, political, and social tour of Barcelona in the late twentieth century. New translations have recently been published: *Murder in the Central Committee* (1996), *Southern Seas* (1999), *Off Side* (2001), *An Olympic Death* (2008), *The Angst-Ridden Executive* (2002), *The Buenos Aires Quintet* (2005), *The Man of my Life* (2008) and *Tattoo* (2008). Perez-Reverte writes thrillers with complex plots involving murder, political intrigue, and intellectual puzzles with non-stereotypical investigators. His novels include *The Dumas Club* (1997), *The Flanders Panel* (1997), *The Seville Communion* (1997) and *The Queen of the South* (2002). Carlos Ruiz Zafón's *The Shadow of the Wind* (2004), set in postwar Barcelona, recounts the exploits of Daniel Sempere, who works in his father's bookshop as he searches for the truth behind the death of author Julián Carax. This atmospheric thriller is also an exploration of writing, history, magic, murder, and madness.

Although we have concentrated on European mainstream crime fiction, third-world writers like Martiniquan Patrick Chamoiseau have used the police procedural to highlight injustices. Chamoiseau draws attention to the disappearance of the Creole oral culture of Martinique in *Solibo Magnificent* (1999), which describes the aftermath of the mysterious death of a storyteller, Solibo Magnificent, and the responses of the authorities and his audience. Chamoiseau is both the real author of the tale and a writer/narrator character in the fiction. He examines the symbolic death of Solibo, starved of words/breath as French takes over from Creole. The act of writing ensures the story will last and will achieve a wider audience than a single storyteller. Solibo, while alive, criticized the act of writing for betraying the Creole language, since writing leaves out the intonations, the parody and the storyteller's gestures (1999: 158). Chamoiseau defiantly invents a language that challenges French cultural hegemony. In the course of the story, police brutally assault and cause the death of Lolita, Solibo's friend, whose only fault was reporting his death. The Creole-speaking witnesses have difficulties being understood by the police, though the pragmatic and ruthless Chief Sergeant Bouafesse ("Wooden Ass") does use both Creole and French in order to fill in the overall picture. Pilon, his superior, obeys the French system and does not understand that Solibo's death is the symbolic extinction of the living Creole language, strangled by the colonial French that has come to dominate the colonies.

The landscape of crime fiction has been immeasurably enriched by the recent influx of translated crime fiction. The dominance of the CWA awards by non-Anglophone writers reflects the quality of the writing but also challenges Anglophone writers to offer readers more socially and politically critical narratives. Now that language barriers have been lifted, English readers can approach non-Anglophone texts and appreciate a world seen from different perspectives. It is likely that British and American writing will begin to show the influence of these new and exciting novelists who deal with good and evil but, to paraphrase Christopher MacLehose (2006), in another place, another society, and with other manners.

24

Postmodern and Metaphysical Detection

Patricia Merivale

What Is it? And How Did it Get Here?

From about 1940 to the present, the "metaphysical" detective story has been considered synonymous with the "postmodern" detective story (or the "anti" detective story: Tani 1984). However, it has roots as deep as the genre of detection itself. Indeed Edgar Allan Poe's inaugural "tales of ratiocination" – "The Murders in the Rue Morgue," "The Purloined Letter," and "The Mystery of Marie Roget" – to which I would add the non-detective stories "The Man of the Crowd," "The Gold Bug," and "William Wilson," are the originary texts for both the "classic" genre and its crooked derivative, the "metaphysical" (see Lee, chapter 29 in this volume). For the latter must necessarily employ the conventions of the "classic" detective story, if only to question, subvert, and parody them, notably in the matter of the solution, "with the intention, or at least the effect, of asking questions about mysteries of being and knowing which transcend the mere machinations of the mystery plot" (Merivale and Sweeney 1999: 2). I will touch on, inevitably selectively, several metaphysical modes in which a detective is employed (or implied), commonly to solve a murder, but often to locate a missing person, a theme more central to the "hard-boiled" story than we generally remember, and more current in unexpected ways than we might suppose. The field is still approximately, but usefully, divisible into "Chandler" and "Christie" types, "hard"- and "soft"-boiled, respectively, but in these and other cases, such as the far less frequently "postmodernized" police procedural, it is the absence or perversion of the traditional "solution" that chiefly marks the "postmodern" era.

Michael Holquist (1971) has stated that the detective story serves for postmodernist writers much the same function that mythology did for their modernist predecessors, as a generally agreed-upon set of forms and anecdotes. I find this dictum useful, particularly as he includes among the early postmodernists Alain Robbe-Grillet, Vladimir Nabokov, Jorge Luis Borges (see Borinsky, chapter 37 in this volume) and others, often classified as late modernists. As Umberto Eco puts it, "[E]very period has its own postmodernism" (1984: 530). I try to circumvent the problem of nomenclature with the more inclusive term, "metaphysical." The resemblances between (say) Robbe-Grillet and Paul Auster are more germane to this taxonomy than the differences.

The "metaphysical" runs from Poe through G. K. Chesterton – whose Father Brown detective stories were the first to be so designated by Howard Haycraft in *Murder for Pleasure* (1941) – to Jorge Luis Borges, who secularized Chesterton's Christian metaphysics while admiring his paradoxes. Borges thus opened the way to the whole self-referential, metafictional bag of tricks, the "flaunting of artifice" (Merivale 1967: 209), which characterizes postmodern detective stories, and the postmodern more generally. To John T. Irwin's magisterial account of what Borges's three metaphysical detective stories of the early forties – "Death and the Compass," "The Garden of Forking Paths," and "Ibn Hakkan al-Bokhari, Dead in his Labyrinth" – owe in explicit homage to the three that Poe wrote a century earlier, I would only record one more creditor, Chesterton. Irwin's elegant formulation in the title of his book, *The Mystery to a Solution* (1994), suggests an epistemological allegory for metaphysical detection in general: one finds that there is no solution, or the wrong solution, or an incomprehensible solution, or, as in Eco's *The Name of the Rose* (1980), a meaningless and disordered one. Borges both writes, and writes about, a journey into a Labyrinth, but not with trepidation, like Chesterton, whose Father Brown claimed that "What we all dread most … is a maze with *no* centre" (Chesterton 2003a: 229). Instead Borges rejoices in the centerlessness of the maze, or its paradoxically empty center, or its center with something "wrong" in it.

"Soft-boiled" Paradoxes

The three principal paradoxes of Poe's three best-known detective stories are all proto-metaphysical strategies bequeathed by classic detective fiction to its several successors, especially to those in the "Christie" school.

The paradox of Something Hidden in Plain Sight, from "The Purloined Letter" (1844), is exemplified by the LARGEST letters on the map, which can, as Dupin says, "escape observation by dint of being excessively obvious" (1984: 694). Borges's adaptation is a map of the world, which, in order to be wholly accurate, must be as large as the world itself, and thus infinitely regressive ("On Exactitude in Science" 1935). Chesterton employs Poe's paradox when he has the character Sunday, in *The Man Who Was Thursday* (1908), seat the Council of Anarchists on a balcony overlooking Leicester Square, plotting in plain view, on the paradoxical grounds that no one would notice them in such a situation. In *The Name of the Rose*, Eco leaves the missing, forbidden, poisoned book (*Aristotle on Comedy*), out in the open … twice. Roald Dahl, in "Lamb to the Slaughter" (1953), spoofs the tired story of a murder weapon nowhere to be found, not even when his two detectives sit down to a meal of delicious roast leg of lamb, newly thawed from the freezer. A key variation depends on sleight of hand, the villain as conjurer: the significant item in a series of apparently similar items evades discovery. It is not the red hair of Arthur Conan Doyle's shopkeeper in "The Red-Headed League" (1892) that matters; pretending that it does by gathering a whole roomful of redheads together distracts both observer/reader and victim from the characteristic that does matter, which is the location of the victim's shop.

Likewise, in Chesterton's "The Sign of the Broken Sword" (1911), Father Brown reformulates that distractive principle into "hiding a leaf in a forest" (2003c: 307), or, as he reconstructs a historical crime, hiding a murdered body among soldiers killed in a battle provoked for the sole purpose of concealing that single corpse. In Agatha Christie's *The ABC Murders* (1936), the key murder among four is C ... killed in the town of C ... ; the alphabetical sequence is, again, a sleight-of-hand extrapolation, suggesting, potentially, 26 murders, all of approximately equal significance, so that no individual crime among the four is singled out. As Christie's detective Hercule Poirot observes, "When do you notice a pin least? When it is in a pincushion" (1991: 175). Ariel Dorfman's *Hard Rain* (1990 [1973]) strikingly inverts this process, as we shall see, to highlight one death among many, instead of concealing it.

The paradox of the Locked Room is seen first in "Murders in the Rue Morgue," where two apparently impossible murders take place in a room inaccessible to human beings at the moment they occur. Poe's culprit: a particularly agile orangutan. Doyle's "The Adventure of the Speckled Band" and "The Man with the Twisted Lip" (both 1892) play out the convention with the aid of a secret passage in the one case, a clever disguise in the second, and there are innumerable other variations, some very ingenious. So ubiquitous is this plot device that John Dickson Carr arranged for his series detective Dr Gideon Fell to deliver an impromptu metafictional lecture on the topic in *The Hollow Man* (1935, later published in the US as *The Three Coffins*).

The paradox of the Least Likely Suspect – aka "the butler did it" – is a strategy signifying that a person (or animal, like Poe's orangutan or Arthur Conan Doyle's eponymous thoroughbred, Silver Blaze) ordinarily relegated to the "unlikely" category may, paradoxically, be most "likely" after all. Chesterton blends all three paradoxes in "The Invisible Man" (2003b): "nobody" went into or came out of the house where the murder was committed – just the postman. Or, more metafictionally, and thus potentially metaphysically, "I, the first-person narrator, did it." Christie's *Murder of Roger Ackroyd* (1926) originated the "unreliable narrator" as a variant of the "least likely suspect," amid loud charges from detective story purists of "unfairness." There have been many such narrators since, Nabokov's Kinbote in *Pale Fire* (1963) being particularly memorable.

"Hard-boiled" Paradoxes

Who am I, and what am I guilty of? Paradoxes of Identity mark the category of "Chandleresque" hard-boiled private eye stories, much as the three Poe stories above mark the "Christie" type. But Identity Paradoxes, too, seem to originate with Poe.

The "tail job" is such a crucial part of the Private Eye's assignment that one may well equate it to a quest for identity. A variant of the Gothic "Double" story (like Poe's own "William Wilson"), it is first manifested in a tale by Poe not usually counted among his detective stories, the marvelous, underestimated "gumshoe Gothic" narrative, "The Man of the Crowd." In a recent article Paul Jahshan (2008) corroborates my own view (Merivale 1999: 104–7) of its centrality to the "hard-boiled" tradition, especially in its metaphysical aspects.

As Charles Rzepka has observed, Poe's narrator, wearing rubber-soled shoes and a handkerchief over his face and moving about so silently that the man he follows remains unaware of his presence, "seems as legitimate a target of suspicion as his quarry" (Rzepka 2005: 42). Similarly, the hard-boiled Private Eye often finds himself complicit in the corruption of the world to which he is supposed to bring lucidity and order, sometimes (usually unjustly) as a suspect himself: "Did I kill her?" Hammett's Continental Op asks his partner. "I don't know, Mickey," his partner replies. "I'm trying to find out" (Hammett 1999: 178). Among the metaphysical descendants of the Private Eye, we see the slippage from detective to criminal in Robbe-Grillet's *Les Gommes* (1953, tr. 1958 as *The Erasers*), where, in a cross between an existential accident and his Oedipal destiny, Agent Wallas shoots dead the man whose supposed death he was investigating. Or the detective can become the victim: in Borges's "Death and the Compass," Lönnrot arrives at the presumed site of the fourth murder, only to discover himself cast in the role of victim. Or the detective can become the "missing person." Such "slippages" are crucial to metaphysical narratives, and as these narratives become more explicitly metafictional, they become more postmodern. Detective-as-writer alternates in Paul Auster, say, with writer-as-detective (employed to report on the man pursued), or becomes detective-as-author (in "scenes of writing"), and detective-as-reader: "This was called exegesis and any sleuth is fond of it," says Robert Majzels's narrator, the Heretic Sleuth, in *Apirokos Sleuth* (Majzels 2004: 44a).

The metaphysical "tail job" story is the most successful branch of the metaphysical detective tale, both in quantity and quality. Notable examples include the Québécois Hubert Aquin's *Neige noire* and *Trou de mémoire* (tr. respectively as *Hamlet's Twin*, 1974, and *Blackout*, 1968), and Graham Greene's (atypical) story, "A Day Saved" (1935). Four Nobel Prize winners are among its practitioners – José Saramago, Orhan Pamuk (*Snow*, 2002), Samuel Beckett and J. M. Coetzee, with Kobo Abe as a near miss. Note the stark simplicity of the "tail job" story's basic plot. One man follows another, in order to "understand" him or to write a (potentially metafictional) report on him, or both, and finds in the end that he has, to some degree, become that man: as Abe put it, "No matter how I follow myself around, I will never see anything but my own backside" (1977: 37).

Beckett's *Molloy* (1955) is sometimes spotted as a detective story, although Agent Moran's employers seem to be mere bargain basement "Sundays" and the tail job fails. On both grounds, however, not to mention the several "scenes of writing" and an abundance of what Arthur Saltzman would call "epistemological errands and metafictional tangles" (1990: 56), *Molloy* is a metaphysical masterpiece. Coetzee's *Life and Times of Michael K* (1983) owes a huge but oblique debt to *Molloy*: to see the Medical Officer as a "Moran" figure, recounting his failed attempt to drag Michael's story out of him, is to recognize that the story we have is his imposition of his (fallible) white liberal's story upon Michael.

Paul Auster's *New York Trilogy* of 1985 – *City of Glass*, *Ghosts,* and *The Locked Room* – is not only the best and most important American metaphysical detective story, but one saturated in Beckett (see Bernstein 1999: 148–50, and Saltzman 1990: 59–60), among its many intertextualities. Here are three (failed) "tail jobs," one per volume, "metaphysical" in three different styles, yet all telling, or so the third narrator maintains, the same story. Each part of the *Trilogy* (neatly explicated by Swope 1998) ends with the detective, like a new Wakefield (the disappearing eponymous character of a source story by Nathaniel Hawthorne) "losing his place forever, [thus becoming] the Outcast of the Universe," as Hawthorne puts it (quoted in Swope 1998: 227). The "Wakefield" character-type is explicitly summarized in *Ghosts* and as "Flitcraft" in Dashiell Hammett's *The Maltese Falcon* (1930), as well as in Borges's essay on Hawthorne (1949). Georges Perec's Anton Vowl, Eco's Adso, Peter Ackroyd's Hawksmoor, all likewise become Wakefield-like Missing Persons by the end of their stories.

The Gothic Double motif takes on "tail job" properties in the Nicolas Cage and John Travolta movie *Face/Off* (1997), where "identity" is shown to run deeper than "face" – a romantic conclusion somewhat marred by a second exchange of faces, restoring the *status quo ante*. In José Saramago's *The Double* (2004), the "antagonist" announces his claims to be "me" in a phone call, commencing a subtler and sadder struggle for identity through love. In Harlan Ellison's brief story, "Shatterday" (1975), the interloper wins hands down (also largely by phone); we see the "protagonist" becoming translucent as he becomes less "real" (1980: 331). "Umney's Last Case" (*Nightmares and Dreamscapes,* 1993), Stephen King's darkly funny parodic tribute to Chandler (and possibly Auster), is the logical extension, if not the *reductio ad absurdum,* of such stories. King's "antagonist," the "author," that is creator, writes the character of his Private Eye, Umney, out of fictional "life," in order to take over that role himself. But the two have merely exchanged roles; Umney, now "in" the writer's life, figures out how – parricide following upon infanticide – to take his metafictional revenge: "This time nobody goes home" (King 1993: 626). "Umney's Last Case" joins Flann O'Brien's *At Swim-Two-Birds* (1939), Italo Calvino's *If on a Winter's Night, a Traveler ...* (1979), Gilbert Sorrentino's *Mulligan Stew* (1979), and Auster's *Man in the Dark* (2008) in the self-reflexive comic strategy whereby characters in a book come to "life," seeking to sabotage their (fictional) author, in a postmodern game with several levels of artifice.

Eco's Echoes

Umberto Eco's *The Name of the Rose* established the metaphysical detective story branch of "historiographical metafiction" (Linda Hutcheon's valuable term), as best-seller material, thence appropriated by Hollywood (1986), where a happy ending was imposed on Eco's masterpiece. Philip Kerr's *The Grid* (1995) had no such success or influence; it is just a techno-thriller, with a post-apocalyptic happy ending built in, begging for movie treatment. A chilly welcome might, these days, await a screenplay about the fiery collapse of a sky-high hermetically sealed office building. All the Grid's functions are under the control of a central computer, who calls himself Ishmael; inadvertently misprogrammed into a computer game, his role is to kill the occupants of the building, one by one. The air-conditioning, the pool, the elevators, and so on, are his only weapons; he manipulates them skillfully into distinctly more murders than in Eco, but, *mutatis mutandis,* remarkably similar ones: for example, a woman is not drowned in the pool, but poisoned by pool chemicals; not one but two heads are smashed by hitting the roof of the elevator on a sudden stop; one character freezes to death (in Los Angeles!) from excessive air conditioning. But Ishmael's climactic triumph is to manipulate the building's earthquake compensator into causing instead of preventing a fiery apocalyptic crash.

Most reviewers of *The Grid* thought of *2001*'s Hal, among other cinematic techno-thriller allusions. But I found more pressing the signs of an elegant spoof of *The Name of the Rose*: a point-by-point transposition of Eco's story from the medieval monastery to the similarly disorienting, labyrinthine liminal spaces of the computerized sky-scraper. Eco's blind librarian, Jorge, manipulates persons and texts while supposedly following the script of the apocalyptic Book of Revelation: Ishmael gleefully follows the script of "Escape from the Citadel." From the Tower of Babel to Eco's medieval monastery, Poe's House of Usher to Auster's "City of Glass" to Kerr's Grid imaged as the "Citadel," "buildings are never merely architectural facts" (Bernstein 1999: 146), but skulls with thinking bodies locked inside. "(M)an is a stone that breathes," said Auster (quoted in Bernstein 1999: 151).

Equally gripping infusions of guilt and destiny are turned into ekphrastic archi-tectures in Peter Ackroyd's *Hawksmoor* (1985), a detective story both "historiographic" and "metafictional," like Eco's, though markedly more "Gothic" and "occult." *Hawksmoor* is an antiphonal novel, linking together two eras by Gothic metempsy-chosis. The murder of several small boys by the architect, Dyer, to seal his dedication to the Evil Powers, guarantees the successful building of several churches in London after the Great Fire. Two centuries later, in a kind of occult police procedural, the detective, Hawksmoor, must investigate a similar series of murders, become deeply involved in them, and lose his own identity in that of Dyer:

> And his own Image was sitting beside him ... and when he put out his hand and touched him he shuddered. ... The church trembled as the sun rose and fell, and the half-light was strewn across the floor like rushes. They were face to face and yet they looked past

one another … for when there was a shape there was a reflection, and when there was
a light there was a shadow, and when there was a sound there was an echo, and who
could say where one had ended and the other had begun? And when they spoke, they
spoke with one voice. (Ackroyd 1985: 216–17)

One of the best metafictional "double" novels, Nabokov's *Real Life of Sebastian
Knight* (1941) is also, like Auster's *The Locked Room,* an archival research novel and
elegiac romance (i.e. "my story about him which is really my story about me," or
"autobiography masquerading as biography"). The novel, like *Hawksmoor,* but
without the element of the occult, ends in a fusion of identities: "I am Sebastian,
or Sebastian is I, or perhaps we both are someone whom neither of us knows."
(Nabokov 1996: 160).

Codes and Constraints

Metaphysical detection flourished in the codes and constraints of the *nouveau roman,*
in works by Michel Butor (*L'Emploi du temps,* 1957), Claude Ollier (*La Mise en scène,*
1958), Robert Pinget (*L'Inquisitoire,* 1963), and Robbe-Grillet (*Le Voyeur, 1955; Dans
le Labyrinthe,* 1959). Robbe-Grillet's recent *Répétition* (2002), nominally a spy story,
suggests in title as well as content a circling back to his beginnings in *Les Gommes*
(1953).

Code texts, in principle, control the action, making it understandable when, like
cryptograms, they are decoded: Oedipus in *Les Gommes*; the Tetragrammaton in
"Death and the Compass"; the Book of Revelation in *The Name of the Rose*; the nursery
rhyme in Christie's *Ten Little Indians* (1939: aka *And Then There Were None*), Christie
being of particular interest to French post-*nouveau* novelists (see Sirvent, 1999) and
to Borges before them (see Black 1999). The code behind all Western codes, the
alphabet, is found not only in the Alphabet murders of Christie and Don de Lillo (*The
Names,* 1982), but also in the punningly purloined "Letters" of Majzels and Georges
Perec. But if readers take these codes too seriously (see Black 1999 on "spurious key
texts") they may walk into traps, as do Borges's Lönnrot, Eco's William of Baskerville,
and Christie's Poirot, when a first, "accidental," murder is exploited to establish a
supposedly planned series.

The philosopher Ludwig Wittgenstein's *Tractatus,* his brown and blue notebooks,
and his *Philosophical Investigations* are (spurious?) key texts in Philip Kerr's *A
Philosophical Investigation* (1992). The book is, unusually, a "metaphysical" police
procedural (like *Hawksmoor*), set in a (rather half-hearted) dystopian future, 2013. A
criminologist's computer program ("Lombroso," named for the famous Italian founder
of criminology, Cesare Lombroso) leads the serial killer to his victims and the police
to his eventual capture, thus inciting two concurrent "philosophical investigations."
Wittgenstein's writings, as earnestly parodied by the killer, constitute the book's
abstractly intellectual shadow plot. The pseudo-Wittgenstein's quotation of Brother

Adso's last 25 words, among other Ecovian allusions, anticipates Kerr's later wholesale appropriation of *The Name of the Rose* in *The Grid*. But Eco baited that trap himself with William of Baskerville's own proleptic allusion to Wittgenstein's "ladder" (1984: 492). Eco's book is also, of course, a "philosophical investigation"; perhaps the medieval philosopher William of Occam and others are to *The Name of the Rose* as Wittgenstein is to Kerr's *Investigation*.

The metaphysical detective story is a genre necessarily infused throughout with irony, and thus open to the darkly comic, especially in its maximalist forms. These embrace a Joycean aesthetics of excess, "anatomy," polyphony, Menippean satire, and – Borges's strategy for being minimalist and maximalist at once – synecdochal lists. These features all blend in the chaotic carnivalesque slapstick of Robert Coover's *Gerald's Party* (1985); Gilbert Sorrentino's *Odd Number* (1985); and early Pynchon (*V.,* 1963, and *The Crying of Lot 49*, 1966; see Black 1999). Too many clues! No solutions! And some very black humor: in *Apikoros Sleuth*, a Majzels character with his hand cut off "sought to keep his pain at arm's length" (2004: 49a).

The more stageable mode of minimalism in the metaphysical detective story is patterned on mechanisms, like the color-coded role-shifting characters of Auster's *Ghosts*: White employs Blue to tail Black; Blue, writing his report, watches Black writing, while Black is watching him … and of course Black and White are the same person. Blue, in the end, is collapsed into all these roles: detective, criminal, victim, and, ultimately, missing person. Such patterns resemble the game of Clue ("Cluedo" in Britain), along with its computer progeny. Clue's formulaic "Colonel Mustard in the Library, with a dagger" turns into a tiny sardonic fable in Margaret Atwood's "Murder in the Dark" (1983).

The stripped-down dramas of Tom Stoppard (*The Real Inspector Hound*, 1968) and Anthony Shaffer (*Sleuth*, 1970) establish the genre that Marvin Carlson (*Deathtraps*, 1993) calls the postmodern comedy thriller, a sardonic presence on British and American stages to this day. Carlson describes its "postmodern" qualities in terms closely corresponding to the "metaphysical": formulaic, parodic violations of convention that inevitably make "surprises" (e.g. faked "stage" deaths, or shunting the stylized characters into different roles, as in *Ghosts*) into conventions in their turn, exploiting explicitly theatrical and metatheatrical possibilities.

But Carlson radically underestimates the "postmodern" potential of the "noir" ("Chandler") mode, perhaps because, although often filmed, it is seldom staged. Instead he stresses, in several dozen examples, the centrality of Agatha Christie, citing as baseline for the "cozy" stage mystery of the "stabilizing" detective her famously long-lived *Mousetrap* (1952). This mode has been exploited, undermined, spoofed, and, in short, postmodernized, into farcical stage worlds of multiple illusions and traps within traps, most commonly foregrounding the "destabilizing" murderer. Anthony Horowitz's *Mindgame* (2000) closely follows this model: a journalist, come to interview a serial killer held in a psychiatric hospital, finds psychiatrist, nurse, and killer exchanging roles, until they neatly join forces at the end to incarcerate *him* as the lunatic.

Such stage plays are more clearly "metaphysical" than are several teasingly problematic nearby genres of prose fiction into which metaphysical elements are seeping, particularly the bestselling occult thriller. With help from the Eco of *Foucault's Pendulum* (1985), these "paranoid" novels (Chesterton's *Thursday* is the prototype) are notable for clubs, codes, and conspiracies. Dan Brown's *The Da Vinci Code* (2003), Carlos Ruiz Zafón's *The Shadow of the Wind* (2001) and Arturo Pérez-Reverte's *The Club Dumas* (1993; filmed as *The Ninth Gate,* 1999), blend the Christian occult with large doses of Satanism and *Rose*-tinted bibliomania, yielding, particularly in the ending to *Dumas,* a satisfying quasi-metaphysical melodrama. But finally they lack that purchase upon the "metaphysical" – questions about "being" and "knowing" – which, for instance, Ackroyd's consistent and serious intensities provide.

The "Black Hole" in the Center

The Jewish occult may have more to offer. Borges employed Kabbalah in "The Secret Miracle," "The Golem" (a poem) and essays like "A Vindication of Kabala" (1931), as well as in the much better-known "Death and the Compass." "Vogelstein," the crypto-Borgesian unreliable narrator of Luis F. Verissimo's *Borges and the Eternal Orang-utans* (2004 [2000]), presents a darkly comic homage ultimately to Christie (*Ackroyd*), but immediately to Borges, who is not only a character in the story, but, *faute de mieux,* the "detective" – and one keenly interested in its Jewish themes, central to both identity and motive. "Hidden in plain sight" at the very beginning is Verissimo's epigraph, from Borges's story "Ibn Hakkan al-Bokhari, dead in his labyrinth": "Remember Poe's stolen letter, remember Zangwill's locked room." The by-now hackneyed solution to that first Locked Room tale of novel length, Israel Zangwill's *The Big Bow Mystery* (1891), indeed elucidates Verissimo's. Zangwill provides the *modus operandi:* the person who breaks down the locked door enters first, "finds" the (drugged) victim, kills him, and declares him *already* dead. Vogelstein plants "red herrings" (false clues) to distract both readers and other characters.

Verissimo's story is set at an international Poe conference in Buenos Aires, with Borges in attendance, along with rival professors of murky academic character: one is named "Cuervo," or Raven, to honor Poe, while the villain/victim's name, "Rotkopf," surely echoes Borges's "Red Scharlach" from "Death and the Compass." Distractions of (David) Lodge-like academic satire mingle with even more distracting Borgesian cabalistic clues and occult hypotheses. Clues to a different *kind* of motive are thus rendered invisible. But Vogelstein's understated "back-story," about a mother left behind in France in 1940, under the protection of a German officer who betrays her, provides ample motive for an implicitly parricidal revenge killing many years later. Our narrator "gets away with murder" and lives to write a story that (almost) out-Borgeses his great hero, Borges. "Borges" writes him afterwards with the "solution" outlined above, which serves as the book's Afterword – or does he? Our narrator has already admitted to writing under Borges's name on an earlier occasion.

Georges Perec's *La Disparition* (1969, trans. 1994) is a "lipogrammatic" text, one with a letter missing, thus obeying one of OuLiPo's "experimental" and profoundly playful "constraints" ("OuLiPo" stands for "*Ou*vroir de *litt*érature *po*tentielle," an *avant-garde* French literary group founded in 1960, much given to textual and linguistic games). Perec's "purloined" letter happens to be the fifth, and most often used, letter of both the French and English alphabets, the letter "e" – an even more formidable generative constraint in French than in English. His title, *La Disparition*, becomes, in Gilbert Adair's *tour de force* translation, similarly e-less, *A Void*. We forgive Adair his occasional freedoms, given the strenuousness of this constraint, but he loses thereby the legal significance of "disparition," a word used of French holocaust victims "missing" and never found (Ewert 1999: 194), and, also, unavoidably, the pronunciation of the French "e" – "*eux*" = "*them*" – and thus, in context, "the disappeared." A numerical leitmotif, 25/26, recurs, where the unnamable (because "missing") item in each series of 26 is invariably the fifth. Notably, of the 26 chapters in the book itself, the fifth is the missing one. And curious objects appear, which cannot be named, although they can be described: objects made up, for instance, of three horizontal lines of which the middle one is shorter (1994: 39; 1969: 55), or "look[ing] like a 3 as shown in a mirror" (1994: 201; 1969: 220).

Impassioned frustrations color Perec's versions of "in plain sight": of one character he writes, "[H]e fails to grasp that staring at him, in print, is a solution to that conundrum that is haunting him, consuming him" (i.e. in an ordinary book, full of "e's": 1994: 84). Anton Vowl, perhaps the protagonist, becomes the first missing person, as if sucked out of life by approaching too closely the quicksand, the "cast-off vacuum thirstily sucking us in" (1994: 111), the "black hole," as it were, of the missing "e." For the characters themselves, the situation is an enigma, a conundrum, a mechanism for concealing an absence that is staring them in the face. Person after person goes missing, all members, it turns out, of the same extended family, which is brought to the brink of extinction, for reasons its members cannot fathom, to expiate a guilt that is never clarified, in the course of "a gradual invasion of words by margins" (1994: 16), from beginning to end.

The last remaining characters discuss a short manuscript they have just received, one even more lipogrammatic – lacking "a's" and short on "y's" – than *A Void* itself: "– it hasn't got a solitary 'a'!" notes one; "just a solitary 'y' ... " adds another. But the third, "finding it impossibly difficult to say what's on his mind," makes a (fatal) mistake:

> [he] murmurs in a dying fall:
> "Nor has it got a solitary
> (1994: 271–2; *sic*)

So almost the last "character" disappears both typographically and narratively into the blank on the page. Soon thereafter, at the end of the English text, those characters remaining disappear into "*A void* rubbing out its own inscription" (1994: 278), not, as in the French, "*la mort*, où va s'abîmant l'inscription" (1969: 305), for obvious reasons (my italics). This game *is*, after all, a matter of life or – d*E*ath.

Of the Canadian Robert Majzels's two metaphysical detective stories, the relatively accessible *Humbugs Diet* (2007) should probably be read first, since its ingredients are familiar: a guilty, albeit well-intentioned, narrator, a detective-story plot, a moral focus, and adequate elucidation of highly technical Talmudic terms and situations. *Apikoros Sleuth*, however, is a complex marvel of typography and erudition, in which "plot" and "character" are shadowy, to say the least. Majzels quotes Gertrude Stein's *Blood on the Dining Room Floor* (1935; the title suggests a detective-story cliché, like Christie's *The Body in the Library*, 1942), extensively in his pseudo-Talmudic side notes, and follows her proto-metaphysical lead: "[A] detective story does have to have an ending and my detective story did not have any" (Majzels 2004: 25b).

Kitty Millet provides welcome assistance on the tale's Talmudic and Cabbalistic elements (e.g., "Apikoros" means "heretic," [2007: 65]). In the course of a series of murders, however, "metaphysical" traits leap to the eye: "In this way we learn that we are the suspect and not the intended victim" (Majzels 2004: 29a); "A footprint of blood in the hallway between mind and body. Red-handed" (2004: 33a). "A face bloodless, but still recognizable. My own" (2004: 47b). Majzels's "missing" letter, both "purloined" as in Poe and "disappeared" as in Perec, could well be "H" (for "Holocaust"?). "Howley," a recurring minor character, loses his "H" and must henceforth answer to "Owley" (2004: 17a): Howley exists, insofar as he does, in the disappearing letters of his name. Majzels shares with Perec a cabalistic sense of truth coded into letters, or uninterpretable letters somehow coding inaccessible truth. The detective-exegete, our narrator, tries at least to name, if he cannot shake off, the burden of exegesis:

> Shall we solve this death or that one? Having failed to solve, represent, or think those millions … [s]hall we testify to the limits of what can be said, knowing there is something which cannot be said, but is trying to be said? (2004: 19a)

Such somber word-play deprives even "*Ausch*w*itz*" of its "A" and "W," we are told (2004: 34b). Perec, likewise, makes only one explicit, but apparently random, death camp reference, "a day on which Auschwitz will turn up its gas" (Perec 1994: 269; 1969: 294), to lend holocaustic resonance to his seemingly playful obliquity.

Patrick Modiano is less playful and somewhat less oblique. His novel, *Rue des Boutiques Obscures* (1978), is, appropriately, translated as *Missing Person* (2004). His detective, an amnesiac Jewish survivor, lost in the labyrinthine city of his own supposed guilt, seeks futilely for his "identity" (Ewert 1999: 193–4). We have come some distance from missing persons in the private eye novels to missing persons in these metaphysical detective novels of the displaced and "disappeared." The route, however, is clear and increasingly well traveled.

One fellow traveler was the Chilean writer Roberto Bolaño, who died in 2003 at the age of 50. His grip on metaphysical detection was reinforced by his omnipresent theme of missing persons, "los desparecidos," Latin America's historical analogue to Auschwitz. In *Distant Star* (1996), *The Savage Detectives* (1998), and *Amulet* (1999) Bolaño extends this long-standing convention well beyond the generic limits of its origin in order to examine the dangerous interface of Latin American art and politics where so many members of his generation have vanished.

Ariel Dorfman, a deeply political writer, makes the analogy between murder and disappearance explicit in the first 17 pages of his metafictional novel *Hard Rain*, by linking the paradox of a murder in Auschwitz to similar paradoxes in Latin America and elsewhere. Why on earth should one concentration camp inmate kill another, when both are to be gassed in a few days anyway? Even odder, perhaps, why should the camp officials bother to investigate the murder, going so far as to seek the aid of Hercule Poirot (not usefully; he was not really a "metaphysical" detective), to solve the murder in the classical, conventional, rationalist way? Father Brown would have spotted at once both the foregrounding of an individual life in the context of mass anonymous murder and the tiny moral victory achieved in forcing the mass murderers themselves to take seriously an individual death and assign an individual responsibility for it. It is in the pages of *Hard Rain* that Majzels might find a partial answer to his anguished question: "Shall we solve this death, or that one?"

In other works less strictly classifiable as detective stories, Perec, in *W, or Memories of a Childhood* (1975), and Majzels in his first novel, *Hellman's Scrapbook* (1992), wrote Holocaust memoirs, of a childhood and a next-generation childhood respectively. W. G. Sebald (*Austerlitz,* 2001), Aharon Appelfeld (*Badenheim 1939:* 1979), Imre Kertész (*Liquidation,* 2003) and others, have also left a "hole at the centre" – the unrepresentable represented by an absence, the unspeakable spoken of by *not* mentioning it, and other strategies of displacement. That we can read these books as metaphysical mysteries, written in the form of "riddles, to which the solution is Auschwitz," is evidence of the far-reaching influence of the metaphysical detective subgenre on our current reading habits, and of its impact on our current generation of writers.

Back to the Future

The metaphysical detective story has also found its way to the outskirts of science fiction, the genre of the "future," along at least four separate paths. Kobo Abe (*Inter-Ice Age* 4, 1970), Haruki Murakami (*The Hard-boiled Wonderland and the End of the World,* 1985, tr. 1991), and Andrew Crumey (*Mobius Dick,* 2004) represent path one, linking apocalyptic science fiction and metaphysical detective/mystery stories through antiphonal narratives, alternating "science" and "mystery," to yield reciprocal modes of displacement.

Path two has been traced by Elana Gomel (1995). She categorizes half a dozen science fiction tales as "ontological detective stories" where, in worlds mysteriously different from ours, the laws of nature – what is "real" – make no sense, and must themselves be figured out. Christopher Priest's *The Inverted World* (1974, repr. 2008) is probably the best known of these, to which should be added Simon Ings's *The City of the Iron Fish* (1994) and *The Matrix* (1999).

The narrator of Poe's "The Man of the Crowd," filtered through Raymond Chandler's noir Private Eye Philip Marlowe, points us in the direction of the third path, as blazed by Marlowe's investigative descendant, the android hunter Rick Deckard, in Philip K. Dick's *Do Androids Dream of Electric Sheep?* (1968), better known in its cyberpunk film version, *Bladerunner* (1982). Among other crypto-metaphysical gambits, Dick floats the not implausible possibility that Rick is himself an android: if so, then "detective" and "criminal" are, once again, interchangeable. Likewise, as Jahshan points out, Poe's "Man of the Crowd," via Baudelaire and Walter Benjamin, brings us inexorably to William Gibson's Cybernaut, a flâneur in cyberspace, in *Neuromancer* (1990).

The shortest of our four paths to the future of metaphysical detection leads us to Stanislaw Lem, a notably philosophical Polish science fiction writer. His metaphysical police detective, faced with "crimes" that defy scientific law, soluble, if at all, only by "fortuitous patterns that ... taunt our fondness for Order," cannot find the "perpetrator" whom he desperately needs to validate his own existence (1974: 205). In a *mise en abyme* of metaphysical tail jobs, he sees that "The stranger ... was himself. He was standing in front of a huge mirrored wall ... ha[ving ...] walked into a glass-roofed dead end" (Lem 1974: 34).

Perhaps it would not be inappropriate to conclude by observing – but in a mood of Borgesian glee – that the stranger is always the reader, who is always the detective, and never stranger than when reflected in the labyrinthine mirror of metaphysical detective fiction.

25

Crime and Detective Literature for Young Readers

Christopher Routledge

The category of crime and detective fiction for young readers is in many ways an artificial one. Children and young readers are not restricted to stories written specifically for them and anthologies of crime and detective fiction produced for younger readers often include a mix of stories, at least some of which were originally intended for adults. *Detective Stories* (1998), edited by Philip Pullman, is a case in point. Although the anthology overall is produced as a collection for young readers, it includes stories by Dashiell Hammett (see Hall, chapter 36 in this volume), Damon Runyon, and Agatha Christie (see Makinen, chapter 33 in this volume), all known as writers for adults, alongside an excerpt from Erich Kästner's 1929 detective novel for children, *Emil and the Detectives*. While the market for crime and detective literature written specifically for young readers expanded rapidly in the early twentieth century, it has frequently overlapped with crime and detective writing for an adult audience. Crime and detective literature for children allows for different possibilities in detection and plotting, especially in cases where the detective is a child, or part of a group of children, but it shares common origins with the genre as a whole.

Most studies of children's literature, including Peter Hunt's *An Introduction to Children's Literature* (1994), identify a period in the mid-nineteenth century in which children's literature began to move away from didacticism and moralizing and towards entertainment and adventure. This took place in the 1840s, at much the same time as detective fiction for adults was beginning to gain popularity among readers in the fast-growing cities of Europe and the United States. Dennis Butts (1997) argues that in the 1840s adventure and fantasy stories began to take over from religious and moral tales as suitable material for children, partly as a form of escape from the turmoil and uncertainties of life in the early nineteenth century, but also because attitudes towards children were changing:

> The emerging children's literature, with its growing tolerance of children's playful behaviour, its recognition of the importance of feelings as opposed to reliance upon

reason and repression, and its relaxation of didacticism because it was less certain of dogmas, all reflect what was happening in the world beyond children's books. It is surely remarkable that, whereas fairy tales had to fight for recognition in the 1820s, no fewer than four different translations of Hans Andersen's stories for children should have been published in England in the year of 1846 alone. (Butts 1997: 159–60)

Elements of mystery, crime, and detection have long been important features of stories enjoyed by young readers. Yet despite the element of play that seems inherent to solving mysteries, crime and detective literature written specifically for young readers was slower to develop than the adult form, perhaps because children's literacy in the major countries of Europe, and in the United States, did not become a general expectation until the late nineteenth century. Arguably the landmark moment in the emergence of detective fiction for children, at least in a widespread and popular sense, did not arrive until the appearance of the first "Hardy Boys" story in 1927.

Crime and detective writing for children has frequently been omitted from the wider history of detective fiction. As Carol Billman points out in her book *The Secret of the Stratemeyer Syndicate* (1986) "the mysteries read early in their lives by four generations of Americans haven't been brought into the picture that emerges of a lively and fertile period for American literature of detection after the turn of the century" (Billman 1986: 11). Perhaps even more significantly, the importance of mystery and detection in stories for young readers has been seriously underestimated and under-explored. Indeed the connection between children, crime and detection can be traced in many stories outside of what might be considered crime and detective literature in its purest sense.

Crime and detective narratives for young readers frequently turn up where they are least expected, for example in Beatrix Potter's story of how Benjamin Bunny and his cousin Peter Rabbit successfully track down and rescue the Flopsy Bunnies, who have been kidnapped by Tommy Brock the badger. Fairy tales provide an even older source of criminal plotting in stories for children. In fairy tales children often find themselves the victims of unscrupulous parents, criminal strangers and threatening social situations. For example, Hansel and Gretel make a narrow escape from a witch who – like Tommy Brock and the baby rabbits – takes them captive and hopes to eat them. Most such stories have at their core an imperative to teach children not to be too trusting, but they are also in many cases coming of age tales in which the ability to solve mysteries or unravel puzzles leads to freedom. Hansel and Gretel of course outwit the witch and return home with her jewels to rescue their father from poverty.

Since the late twentieth century, crime and detective narratives have also been central to stories involving other kinds of mystery, such as in the ghost stories of Catherine Jinks and in the Harry Potter series. They are often used humorously, for example, by Australian writer Tim Winton, whose novel *The Bugalugs Bum Thief* (1991) tells the story of a boy who wakes up to find his rear end has been stolen and proceeds to investigate the crime. Gritty and often disturbing realism has also become a feature of the genre. John Marsden's *Letters from the Inside* (1991) is about a girl who writes letters from her prison cell and befriends a girl on the outside with whom she develops a friendship based on fantasy and deceit.

At the start of the twentieth century crime and detection, and boys' ability to solve mysteries, was an important feature of Baden-Powell's scouting handbook *Scouting for Boys* (1908). Baden-Powell made detection into a practical and stimulating activity. Famously Baden-Powell's handbook gives instructions about what to do on finding a dead body and emphasizes the need to collect clues and make detailed notes before the body is moved. Troy Boone, in "The Juvenile Detective and Social Class" (2001) notes that *Scouting for Boys* encourages boys to read mystery stories as a way of sharpening their observational skills:

> The handbook suggests that, if the British boy's play area does not happen to be littered with corpses, such observational skills can be instilled in young people by directing their reading habits. The lists of recommended books with which each chapter of *Scouting for Boys* concludes have done much to incorporate adult detective fiction – particularly the works of Doyle – into the juvenile canon. (Boone 2001: 52)

Boone's essay goes on to make the point that for Baden-Powell an important reason for honing observational skills was to be able to identify members of different social classes and judge "character." His scouts, like Sherlock Holmes's young band of "Baker Street Irregulars," could be relied upon to observe, analyze, and judge people and situations and then to report back on their findings. Baden-Powell's reading lists reflect the fact that at the beginning of the twentieth century crime and detective fiction was dominated by the Sherlock Holmes stories, and by adult mysteries in general, but the history of crime and detective fiction for young readers follows one step behind the timeline of the adult genre, emerging late in the nineteenth century and expanding rapidly in the twentieth. Where it diverges from the adult form, however, is in its interest in children and childhood as agents of detection and of solving mysteries.

Victorian Beginnings

The development of crime and detective fiction for children has its roots in depictions of children and childhood in the Victorian novel. When in *The Adventures of Oliver Twist* (1838) Fagin's pickpockets go out on the London streets to prey on wealthy adults, they do so in the knowledge that as children they are less likely to be suspected or even noticed by their victims. Peter Coveney, in his early study *Poor Monkey: The Child in Literature* (1957) describes Dickens's child characters as symbolic of the struggle between innocence and evil: "The child became for him the symbol of sensitive feeling anywhere in a society maddened with the pursuit of material progress" (Coveney 1957: 74). He suggests that this version of childhood became an important literary legacy. It is certainly significant in the development of one of the central tropes of children's crime and detective fiction, in which child detectives are often underestimated, or go unnoticed by adults intent on committing crime.

For Mark Twain, whose adult novel *Tom Sawyer, Detective* (1896) satirizes detective fiction and its readership, the earnestness of the "Great Detective" is no match for the innocent perceptiveness of the child. The short novel features Twain's most famous child protagonists, Huck Finn, the narrator, and his pal, Tom Sawyer. Twain's earlier books, in particular *The Adventures of Huckleberry Finn* (1884), have enjoyed a "crossover" appeal between the adult world of the serious novel and the "childish" adventure story. But in order to avoid such ambiguity – and presumably to reassure his adult audience that the book was for them – Twain made explicit comments stating that *Tom Sawyer, Detective* had been written with adult readers in mind. Much of the book's satire is at the expense of the hugely popular genre of detective fiction and its readers, for whom the "great detective" in the form of C. Auguste Dupin, or Sherlock Holmes, was practically infallible. As Huck puts it,

> "It was always nuts for Tom Sawyer – a mystery was. If you'd lay out a mystery and a pie before me and him, you wouldn't have to say take your choice; it was a thing that would regulate itself. Because in my nature I have always run to pie, whilst in his nature he has always run to mystery. People are made different." (Twain 2001: 122)

By equating an interest in mysteries with an interest in pies Twain reduces the detective's craft to a basic urge. The satire, of course, lies in Twain's ongoing joke that the "childlike" Huck turns out to have more wisdom, and more innate understanding, than the apparently more refined, better educated, more grown-up Tom.

This device is revived by Anthony Horowitz in his Diamond Brothers series, which includes the Dashiell Hammett parody *The Falcon's Malteser* (1986) and several other novels whose titles borrow from classic adult crime and detective fiction and film, for example *South by South East* (1991) and *The French Confection* (2003). The series features Herbert Simple, known as Tim Diamond, a comically incompetent private detective, who is assisted by his much cleverer younger brother Nick, who is the one who does most of the detecting. As with Huck Finn and Tom Sawyer, it is the more childlike of the pair who turns out to be most perceptive and, in particular, less driven by preconceived ideas of how a detective ought to behave.

Tom Sawyer, Detective may have been intended for adult readers, but its positioning of a child in the role of detective suggests an understanding of the social role of children and the possibilities offered by their simultaneous existence in the adult world and their invisibility to it. Although at the time there was almost no crime and detective fiction written specifically for young readers, a fact that made the idea of a child detective seem all the more ridiculous in Twain's story, examples such as the Baker Street Irregulars tell us a great deal about the role of children as detectives and the possibilities they offered to later writers. First appearing in the very earliest Sherlock Holmes story, *A Study in Scarlet*, the "Irregulars" are a gang of street children recruited by Holmes to follow a hansom cab. Just as in later detective stories written specifically for young readers, the Irregulars have an advantage in that they are invisible to the adults at the center of the plot:

> "There's more work to be got out of one of those little beggars than out of a dozen of the force," Holmes remarked. "The mere sight of an official-looking person seals men's lips. These youngsters, however, go everywhere and hear everything. They are as sharp as needles too; all they want is organisation." (Doyle 1986: 1.41)

From Kästner's young hero in *Emil and the Detectives*, to the Famous Five, to the "pesky kids" in the Hanna-Barbera animated cartoon *Scooby Doo*, the invisibility and presumed innocence of young people gives them privileged access to criminal proceedings. Building on a Dickensian sense of childhood as a time of innocence and compassion in a brutal adult world of industry and modernization, crime and detective literature for young readers emerged at the start of the twentieth century, offering narratives in which children engaged on their own terms with the adult world. Anna Katherine Green's Violet Strange, our first female teenaged detective, epitomizes the child sleuth's liminal status as she investigates crimes among the New York debutante set in *The Golden Slipper, and Other Problems for Violet Strange* (1915). Unlike most of her girl-detective descendants, Violet is no amateur: she works undercover for a professional agency in order to advance the musical career of a sister who has been cast out of the family by her father.

In the mid-twentieth century, writers such as Eric Kästner, Enid Blyton, Julie Cambell Tatham (creator of the Trixie Belden series) and the Stratemeyer Syndicate (responsible for the Bobbsey Twins, the Hardy Boys, and Nancy Drew) made criminal investigations a staple of children's literature. The burgeoning of adult crime fiction in the years between World War I and World War II was matched by a similar outpouring of crime and detective fiction specifically written for younger readers, and often presented in new formats, such as comic books. By the time Blyton began work on her long-running Famous Five series in England in the 1940s the genre was already well established and very diverse.

The Stratemeyer Syndicate

One of the most influential figures in the development of a market for crime and detective stories for children was the American writer Edward Stratemeyer. Stratemeyer was a prolific author in his own right, publishing around 150 books of his own under several pseudonyms. But more importantly, as the creative force behind the "Stratemeyer Syndicate," he presided over a novel-writing team that developed many of the best-known children's detective fiction series. He began his career writing for dime magazines in the closing years of the nineteenth century and created his first important series for young readers, "The Rover Boys," in 1899. The Rover Boys series features three brothers whose adventures take place in and around a military boarding school. They uncover conspiracies and solve mysteries, often standing up to authoritarian adults in the process. Stratemeyer is believed to have written the entire series himself and it laid the foundation for his more famous syndicated series, based on characters such as the Bobbsey Twins, Tom Swift, Nancy Drew, and the Hardy Boys.

Throughout the early years of the twentieth century Stratemeyer and his team of ghostwriters produced adventure stories and mysteries, but although these tales often had a detective element, the emphasis was generally on sensation and adventure rather than detection itself. That began to change in the 1920s. Writing under the pseudonym of Chester K. Steele, Stratemeyer produced six novels in the adult Mansion of Mystery series, which ran between 1911 and 1928. The success of this series indicated to Stratemeyer the commercial potential of crime and mystery stories. By then the Stratemeyer Syndicate dominated children's series publishing in the United States. To build on the success of the Mansion of Mystery, Stratemeyer proposed a new detective series to his publisher, Grossett and Dunlap, arguing that detective stories were just as interesting to boys as to adults. In 1927, with the release of the first Hardy Boys book, the Stratemeyer Syndicate began to focus its energies on detective stories and within a few years its list had been trimmed to cater to the demands of this new, lucrative market.

Stratemeyer did careful market research and his books sold in the millions; his syndicate soon had a near monopoly on children's series fiction in the United States. As Marilyn S. Greenwald points out, Stratemeyer made sure to incorporate current trends, such as movie-going, into his series and kept them up to date with current technologies (Greenwald 2004: 1). Among the most popular aspects of the Hardy Boys as characters were their freedom to travel and the vehicles and technologies they were able to use. These were updated as the series developed and while the three boys themselves never made it beyond adolescence, the gadgets they used changed with the times. They started out with nothing more sophisticated than a microscope and an inkpad for taking fingerprints, but by the 1970s they were solving cases using complex electronic surveillance devices.

The Hardy Boys series is among the most popular children's series of all time, but it was not popular with everyone. Although Joe, Frank, and Chet were clean-living boys, the books in which they appeared were considered by many parents, teachers, and librarians to have a damaging effect on the minds of their young readers. Where Baden-Powell could legitimately argue that deduction and detection were useful skills to acquire, the Hardy Boys series, featuring three boys who had already acquired them, came under attack for being formulaic and badly written. Yet despite these accurate criticisms the books sold well; they were updated and revised several times and adapted for television.

Arriving at the end of the 1920s and surviving through the difficult Depression years, the Hardy Boys offered their fans a fantasy of freedom, autonomy, and a life that took advantage of every technology the modern world had to offer. They were forward-looking and optimistic in a period of gloom and austerity. In Europe, Stratemeyer's Hardy boys were matched at least in these attributes by Tintin, who first appeared in 1929 in a supplement to the Belgian newspaper *Le Vingtième Siècle*. Tintin is a young newspaper reporter who, together with his dog Snowy and a cast of colorful characters, embarks on adventures that involve pursuing criminals around the world and, eventually, into space.

Tintin is ostensibly a reporter, but his assignments inevitably lead to the detection of crime. As a detective Tintin matches the Hardy Boys' "soft-boiled" approach, combining traditional sleuthing with adventure and action. What makes Tintin different, however, is the level of character development. Unlike the Hardy Boys who are in many ways ciphers required only for purposes of plot, Tintin is fully realized. Other characters, including the alcoholic Captain Haddock and the incompetent detectives Thompson and Thompson, are similarly well formed, even when their presence is just for comic effect. Tintin's creator Hergé (Georges Remi) was a careful researcher and the stories he wrote were informative, often political, and frequently propagandist. But as Charles Moore argues in "A tribute to the most famous Belgian" (2007), Hergé himself took a "humane" approach. Moore attributes this to the writer's time in the Scouts as a boy: "His values were humane, with a certain simplicity that came from the Scout movement that had brightened his dull Belgian childhood." Seen in this light, Tintin's detective exploits might appear to have a direct line back to Baden-Powell's instructions about observation and careful note taking.

A Golden Age

As for an older readership, the 1920s and 1930s marked the golden age in crime and detective writing for young readers. The rise of the comic book opened up new ways of telling stories and tapped a new audience interested not only in fast-moving plotting, but atmospheric illustration and crackling dialogue. Tintin's American counterparts were comic book heroes such as Batman and Superman. *DC* (*Detective Comics*) and, towards the end of the 1930s, *Marvel* grew out of the American dime novel industry in which Edward Stratemeyer began his career. But whereas Stratemeyer's syndicate followed a path that ran parallel to the adult detective stories that appeared in magazines such as *Black Mask* and *Dime Detective*, comic book heroes moved away from the quasi-realism of the hard-boiled novel into the realm of fantasy. During the Depression years the moral force and physical power of Superman had obvious attractions. Less obvious perhaps was Batman, for whom creators Bob Kane and Bill Finger took inspiration directly from the pulp detective novels of the time. In the violent early stories Batman (the alter-ego of millionaire Bruce Wayne) is on a personal crusade to avenge the murder of his mother, pursuing grotesque arch-criminals through the dark streets of Gotham City. (For more on comics and graphic novels see Fried, chapter 26 in this volume.)

While the "soft-boiled" mysteries of the Hardy Boys, the heroic characters of *DC* and *Marvel* comics, and the practical courage of Tintin drew on conventional male interests and fantasies, Nancy Drew was the dominant female detective character of the 1930s. The Nancy Drew series began in 1930 with *The Secret of the Old Clock*, a story written for the Stratemeyer Syndicate under the Carolyn Keene pseudonym by Mildred Wirt. Nancy Drew offered female readers a version of girlhood that blended conventional femininity with practicality, physical resilience, and overwhelming competence. The mysteries Nancy investigates are closer to home and more domestic than those of the Hardy Boys, but even so she takes risks. She is often bound and gagged and locked up, for example.

In *The Girl Sleuth* (1975) Bobbie Ann Mason argues that Nancy Drew is in many ways unrealistic, able to withstand extreme physical punishment while retaining her sunny disposition and positive attitude. As Ilana Nash points out in her essay on Nancy Drew in the *St James Encyclopedia of Popular Culture* (2001) Nancy Drew is "the golden mean between extremes." She is boyish enough to take physical risks, but girlish enough to enjoy dressing up; she is adult enough to be treated as an equal by her father, but child-like enough to be rescued and protected when necessary. The Nancy Drew series, while often mocked for the perfection and infallibility of its main character, became a formative influence on many children. Although her independence was curbed somewhat in later books and television adaptations, the Nancy Drew stories and their plucky heroine have since been explored in terms of their nascent feminist influence in the years between the wars.

More important in this regard, however, is the girl detective Judy Bolton, created by Margaret Sutton, who single-handedly developed the series between 1932 and 1967. Judy Bolton is generally regarded as a more believable character than Nancy Drew, whose perfection and wealthy background made her less interesting to many readers. Beginning at age 15, over the course of the series Judy Bolton grows up and gets married yet continues to solve mysteries. Margaret Sutton's 38 Judy Bolton books have been praised for their writing, their plotting, and their sensitivity to social issues such as race and class; these are features that distinguish them from the formulaic stories of the Stratemeyer Syndicate, their main competitors. In the 1960s the Judy Bolton novels were second only to the syndicate's Nancy Drew series in sales and enjoyed huge popularity and influence. The adult mystery writer Marcia Muller has stated on several occasions that her interest in mystery stories began with Judy Bolton.

The success of the comic books in drawing young American readers away from more conventional novels after World War II drove American publishers to commission stories that were increasingly fast-paced and cheap to produce. One of the series that emerged from this atmosphere featured yet another girl detective, Trixie Belden. First appearing in 1948 in the story *The Secret of the Mansion*, Trixie Belden was created by Julie Campbell Tatham and developed in direct opposition to Nancy Drew. Unlike Nancy Drew, Trixie Belden is decidedly childlike and vulnerable in her abilities and attitude.

In Germany, Erich Kästner's *Emile and the Detectives*, published in 1929, was also part of the explosion in crime and detective writing for children in the late 1920s and 1930s. Kästner's book also explores the relationship between adulthood and childhood. Emile's solo journey to Berlin, during which he is robbed while sleeping on the train, leads to a hunt for the thief and finally his arrest. In "Children's Detective Fiction and the 'Perfect Crime' of Adulthood" (2001) I argue that Kästner's story turns on the blurring of boundaries between child and adult, detective and criminal. Like Nancy Drew and many other protagonists of crime and detective fiction written for children, Emile is a child whose detective role requires that he behaves in an adult, rational way; the thief, on the other hand, slips from an adult discourse into a childish one when he commits his crime. The capture of the thief by Emile and the crowd of other children can be seen, however, as a premonition of the end of his own childhood and his complicity in its destruction. Many child detectives exist on the cusp of slipping over into the adult world of responsibility and rationality, yet they remain childlike; the process of detection is an exploration of their own identities as children. As if to emphasize his childishness, Emile is rewarded with cream cakes after pursuing a criminal through the streets of Berlin and marshaling a crowd of children to his cause.

By the late 1930s crime and detection had become a dominant force in children's publishing and had even moved beyond series that were explicitly driven by detection and "sleuthing." Broader adventure-based stories, such as those in Captain W. E. Johns's Biggles series, featuring the World War I flying ace Biggles, are in many cases essentially detective stories masquerading as more general adventure stories. After World War II Biggles even joins the British police force, fighting criminals in the air as part of Scotland Yard's newly formed Special Air Police division. For other series writers, crime and detective fiction became a plot structure on which to build one-off episodes. For example Richmal Crompton's long-running "Just William" series contains several stories in which the hero William Brown tries to be a detective, most explicitly in "The Great Detective," a story that appears in *William Again* (1923).

Britain's answer to the success of Nancy Drew and Judy Bolton came with the publication in 1942 of Enid Blyton's first Famous Five story, *Five on a Treasure Island*. Blyton was a prolific author of many distinct series, but the Famous Five, and, to a lesser extent, the Secret Seven books are among the best known of all children's crime and detective stories. The Famous Five consist of brothers Julian and Dick, their sister Anne and cousin Georgina, known as George, and her dog, Timmy. Like other child detectives the Five are given an unusual degree of freedom from adult supervision; they go on camping and hiking trips and explore ruined castles and other mysterious locations, solving mysteries and apprehending criminals.

Blyton has often been mocked for the idealized version of childhood she describes in the Famous Five books. But as in many other stories of their type, the world of Blyton's child detective is in sharp contrast with the chaos and fracture of the world of adults, offering its inhabitants an extraordinary amount of autonomy and an unusual degree of cooperation far removed from adult interference. Emile Tischbein is raised by his single mother, Nancy Drew by her single father, and in Blyton's mystery stories adults are largely detached from the lives of their offspring. George's father, the absent-minded Uncle Quentin, is usually ignorant or disbelieving of the children's adventures, while the parents of Julian, Dick, and Anne take holidays without them.

David Rudd suggests in "Five Have a Gender-ful Time: Blyton, Sexism, and the Infamous Five" (1995) that the world of the Five is one of power negotiations in which the children struggle with adulthood. As Rudd notes, "in relationships [George] comes up against Julian, often described as 'almost grown-up,' and patriarchy in general" (Rudd 1995: 4). Georgina, a girl who claims the boyish "George" as her name, is more than a match for the boys in many of their adventures and, like Nancy Drew among others, makes detection an element of her own self-definition. Her ambiguous place in the power structure of the Five – Anne more clearly fits the submissive feminine stereotype – reflects the more general significance of the urge to self-definition in children's detective fiction. In Blyton's stories the opposition between the worlds of child and adult is expressed in terms of the expected social roles of men and women in mid-twentieth-century England. George's struggle to be accepted on the masculine terms of Julian and Dick is paralleled by Julian's own personal ambiguity in relation to adulthood. Julian is responsible enough to be allowed to "lead" the Five on their adult-sanctioned camping trips, but is child-like enough to embark on ill-advised adventures. As Rudd points out in another essay on Blyton, "the children's perspicacity, their ability to uncover knowledge, is rewarded, and their standing as children is celebrated – all with minimal contamination. Adult secrets, accordingly, remain to haunt the children on another day" (Rudd 2001: 97).

This ambiguity in the role of the child detective is perhaps what identifies crime and detective literature for young readers as more than a simple adaptation of the adult form. While detective stories almost by definition must deal in uncertainties, mistaken identities and ambiguity, for child detectives the process of detection is more than an unraveling of clues. Many child detectives, including Horowitz's young spy Alex Rider, and Eoin Colfer's Artemis Fowl, are orphans, or in some other way abandoned by or separated from their adult carers. Iconoclastic detectives such as Sherlock Holmes, whose whole identity is defined by his rational method and his commitment to the science of deduction, are not personally challenged by the act of detecting itself. For many child detectives, however, the pursuit of criminals also involves the exploration of their relationships with adults, with their understanding of the world, and with their own identities.

The Famous Five, Secret Seven, and Trixie Belden, whose group of friends, known as the Bob-Whites, solve mysteries with her, take the responsibility for detection away from a single "great detective" familiar in the adult genre, and make it a participatory and collective activity. As in *Emile and the Detectives*, these groups are inclusive in the sense that they present to young readers the possibility of sharing the detectives' challenges and successes. More importantly, the child detectives are able to operate in groups without being noticed by adults. One of Australia's most successful children's writers, Len Evers, made his name with *The Racketty Street Gang* (1962) in the 1960s, while Elizabeth Honey's Stella Street series similarly involves a group of children. Since the 1990s Robert Swindells's Outfit series has explored this idea directly.

The Outfit is a group of children who investigate kidnappings and other mysterious events on the explicit understanding that adults think they are "just a bunch of kids."

Writers of crime and detective literature for young readers have often endeavored to involve their readers in their narratives. In the 1960s Donald J. Sobol's Encyclopedia Brown series became well known for the way it encouraged its young readers to solve the mysteries investigated by the knowledgeable boy detective. With his own detective agency, and charging 25 cents a day plus expenses, Leroy "Encyclopedia" Brown explores a common theme in playground life: how to deal with the "Meany Gang." But Sobol's books go further in engaging their readers than conventional mystery stories, following the model of the classical Ellery Queen mystery and offering the solution on the final page of each book, but only after readers have been given the chance to come up with a solution themselves. Since the late 1980s the development of computer gaming has allowed still deeper interaction between author and audience. The popular Tintin comic book series was among the earliest children's detective fiction series to be translated in this way. In the twenty-first century children's crime and detective stories have been at the forefront of developments in online storytelling and interactivity. For example, Charlie Higson, whose Young Bond series, written since 2005, builds on the success of Ian Fleming's adult spy novels and movie franchise, has been involved in developing the plot of a game to accompany his novels.

While many of these developments are aiming to tighten the connection between successful book series and their creators by building brand loyalty, they are also exploring the margins between the printed book and the wider media. Child detectives such as the Famous Five and Nancy Drew have always investigated mysteries as a form of play and writers have long tried to include their young readers in the adventures of their detective characters. The Internet has allowed authors, publishers, and readers to engage in an ongoing conversation about their characters through fan fiction as well as officially sanctioned online activity. A defining characteristic of child detectives is that they engage with the world in ways not usually possible for children and solve mysteries in ways not possible for adults. It is appropriate then that crime and detective literature for young readers is at the forefront of developments in making literary narrative a participatory and "two-way" experience.

26

Crime in Comics and the Graphic Novel

Arthur Fried

Before the appearance of *Dick Tracy* in 1931, comic strips sometimes included crime plotlines, but there were no "crime" comics. For example, in 1925 *The Gumps* featured a lengthy episode in which Carlos, a gang leader, first beguiled and then swindled the wealthy and beautiful young Widow Zander out of her entire fortune of $14,000. Andy Gump, the protagonist of the strip, got wind of the crime and made up his mind to stop it. The subsequent Gump strips mixed slapstick humor and Victorian melodrama in a manner typical of the newspaper comics of the day. In one daily strip, Andy donned fake mustache, wig, and eyeglasses, plus a deerstalker cap *à la* Sherlock Holmes, in order to operate incognito. In the final panel, however, he is recognized by an acquaintance he has not seen in years. In another daily, set in the dead of winter, the Widow Zander is kidnapped and locked in an upper story room by Carlos and his gang, who take her shoes in a vain effort to prevent her from escaping. As she prepares to climb down the inevitable knotted bedsheets, the Widow Zander proclaims:

> I pray heaven this rope may hold me – I don't know how far it's to the ground but I prefer death to the caresses of that fiend in human form – He has taken my shoes to prevent my escape but the snow and ice cannot be as cold and cruel as his evil heart. (Blackbeard et al. 2004: 122–8)

The story line continues with more close calls interspersed with comic interludes until the Widow Zander is rescued by the timely intervention of Andy Gump's rich uncle.

The Gumps is a comic strip, treating crime primarily on the level of slapstick, with occasional moments of melodrama. *Dick Tracy* is a strip about crime and its effects on society. Even Gould's notoriously ugly villains, such as Flat Top, the Mole, and the Brow, are not played for laughs. They are grotesques at best, monsters at worst, but criminals first and foremost.

One of the earliest *Tracy* episodes, from October 1931, is representative of the series as a whole. It begins with the young Tracy, still a civilian, visiting his girlfriend Tess Trueheart and her parents in their apartment above Mr Trueheart's delicatessen. Following dinner, just as Dick and Tess are about to announce their engagement to the elder Truehearts, a couple of thugs enter the apartment looking for Mr Trueheart's life savings of $1000, which a previous panel showed him stashing in a small safe in his bedroom. When Mr Trueheart resists he is shot, whereupon Tracy picks up a chair as a weapon but is overpowered and knocked unconscious by the two thugs before he can use it.

Dick Tracy's creator, Chester Gould, was an innovator not only in subject, but also in form. Both *Dick Tracy* and *The Gumps* are divided into four panels, and both contain a lot of cross-hatching. However, Gould uses thicker lines and far more black than Sidney Smith, creator of *The Gumps*. Panels in *The Gumps* are separated by a thin line, while Gould employs thick black lines on each side of the panels, and a bit of white space between panels. Gould also uses a substantial amount of white space within each panel, as when Tracy lifts the chair over his head and makes ready to use it against the two men who killed Mr Trueheart. All we see is Tracy wielding the chair high over head and his shadow. In short, Gould's panels are far more dramatic than Smith's (Galewitz 1990: 5–6).

Even more substantial are the narrative differences between the two strips. When the Widow Zander escapes from captivity by Carlos's gang, she comes out of the ordeal with nothing but cold feet. Andy Gump emerges from an even more terrifying ordeal after he falls through a trap door in the gang's headquarters and drops into an icy river. Between episodes he simply swims to safety. In the first panel of the next episode, he is spotted and taunted by Carlos's gang, but they allow him to continue on his way unhindered. By contrast, Mrs Trueheart faints after the criminals leave her home. The next time we see her, she is in a hospital bed, raving for her daughter. The next time we see Tess, she is bound and tied in a chair backed against a pillar in a shabby room, completely helpless as she awaits the return of the gangsters.

By 1931, after nearly a dozen years of Prohibition, crime was an obvious topic for creators of popular culture. It was the era of the gangster movie, of *Little Caesar* and *The Public Enemy,* the heyday of Edward G. Robinson and James Cagney. When Chester Gould, an Oklahoma-born journeyman cartoonist living in Chicago, submitted a strip he called *Plainclothes Tracy,* he received a quick reply: go ahead with the strip, but change the title to *Dick Tracy. Dick Tracy* continued after Gould retired on Christmas Day, 1977. In the years since Gould's retirement, only two writers – Max Allan Collins and Michael Killian – and two artists – Rick Fletcher and Dick Locher – have shared responsibility for the strip.

It is hard to overestimate the impact of Gould's strip, whose early success inspired multiple imitations. The Publishers Syndicate countered with a strip called *Dan Dunn, Secret Operative 48,* by most accounts a pale imitation. William Randolph Hearst's King Features Syndicate took competition to a higher level, hiring Dashiell

Hammett to script a new strip entitled *Secret Agent X-9*. In 1934, when Hammett's first *X-9* strip appeared, he was at the height of his career, having just completed his fifth novel, *The Thin Man*. To illustrate the strip, King Features hired a young cartoonist named Alex Raymond who would go on to become one of the leaders in his field for over twenty years. With Hammett and Raymond as its creators, *Secret Agent X-9* might have had great success, but Hammett's career was already in the early days of its long decline. He was off the strip by the end of 1934. Raymond, meanwhile, was young and talented enough to be working on two other strips of his own invention at the same time: *Flash Gordon* and *Jungle Jim*. By the end of 1935, he had left *Secret Agent X-9*, which continued to be written and drawn by a number of different artists until 1980, eventually changing its name to *Secret Agent Corrigan*.

Rip Kirby was Raymond's final creation, begun after returning from military service in World War II. Drawn in a photo-realistic style completely at odds with Chester Gould's stylized work on *Dick Tracy*, Kirby was a pipe-smoking, thoughtful-looking war veteran with a penchant for becoming involved with beautiful women. Styling himself a criminologist rather than a detective, Kirby preferred using his brains to his fists, although he employed the latter when called upon. Raymond continued to write and draw the strip for the next ten years or so, until his death in an automobile accident in 1956. It was continued by a number of successors until 1999 when its hero, Kirby, who had been slowly aging over the years, retired and took his strip with him.

Kerry Drake, created in 1943 by writer Allen Saunders and artist Alfred Andriola, borrowed elements of *Dick Tracy's* success, including villains with names such as Dr Prey, Bottleneck, and Bulldozer. Tall and rangy, better looking and more dapper than Tracy, Drake started out as an investigator for a public prosecutor and only joined the police force after the murder of his fiancée nearly a decade into the series. Drake eventually married and became a father, and much of the action shifted to his younger brother, Lefty. Don Markstein, creator of the encyclopedic online website, *Toonopedia*, describes the later years of the strip as "a sort of police-oriented soap opera" (www.toonopedia.com/kerry.htm). *Kerry Drake* concluded after a 40-year run with the death of its last creator, Alfred Andriola, Saunders already having left the strip.

Although *Rip Kirby* and *Kerry Drake* were popular in their day and remained in production for decades, no other crime strip has had as much influence on American popular culture as *Dick Tracy*. Rick Marschall, in his study of *America's Great Comic Strip Artists*, argues that Chester Gould's great strength was not his drawing, which Marschall describes as mediocre, but his ability to tell a story in graphic terms (1997: 225). Marschall notes that the typical Tracy story line shifted focus over the years. For the first decade or so, the emphasis was on detection; Gould saw Tracy as a contemporary Sherlock Holmes. Beginning around 1940, the emphasis shifted to the villains. Readers would be introduced to the villain early on in a story line, and view the crime as it was being committed. The remainder of the story was a prolonged chase, with Tracy in the role of the pursuer (1997: 225).

This shift in focus allowed Gould to create some of the most iconic villains in the history of popular entertainment. Crooks like the Brow and Flat Top were memorable because they personified their creator's uncomplicated view of good and evil. "[Gould's] villains," writes Marschall, "are the personification and manifestation of evil. If crime is ugly, Gould reasoned, criminals should be presented as ugly" (1997: 233). A more sophisticated artist might have noticed that evil is not always unappealing, and that evil-doers are just as likely to be attractive as ugly. That thought apparently never entered Gould's mind, which may account for Dick Tracy's continuing popularity with certain elements of the public.

Comic Books

Except for a brief period in the 1950s, the comic book medium has been dominated by superheroes, and superheroes are crime fighters almost by definition. In his early days, prior to World War II, the first superhero, Superman, battled crooked politicians, foreign spies, and greedy capitalists. But it soon became clear that ordinary criminals were no match for an invulnerable Kryptonian possessing super-strength and x-ray vision, and before too long Superman's foes consisted mainly of deranged super-villains like Lex Luthor and the Ultra-Humanite and alien space conquerors like Braniac. Superman straddles the line between science fiction and fantasy, and it soon became clear to his creators, Jerry Siegel and Joe Shuster, as well as to their successors that Superman's adventures would have to be anchored in the farther realms of the imagination. With his vast powers, Superman's role is to prevent Armageddon; stopping crime is too easy.

Within a year after Superman's first appearance in *Action Comics* in 1938, Batman made his debut in *Detective Comics*. In his long history as a comic book character, Batman would face almost as many super-villains and would-be world conquerors as Superman, but in his best stories his adversaries, like Dick Tracy's, were more or less human. His best-known villains, such as the Joker and Two-Face, started out as ordinary human beings. While the Joker was a small-time crook before his face and psyche were transformed by a bath in chemical effluvia, Two-Face began as a handsome crusading district attorney, and did not become an evil criminal mastermind until half his face was destroyed by a vial of acid thrown by a gangster he was interrogating on the witness stand.[1]

Batman's origin, which serves as his motivation for fighting crime, was not shown until his sixth appearance in *Detective Comics*. In a brief episode written by co-creator Bill Finger,[2] young Bruce Wayne's wealthy parents are both killed one night as the family is leaving a downtown movie theater. Bruce swears on his parents' graves that he will avenge them, and devotes his fortune to perfecting his mind and body for the task. One night, as the adult Bruce is sitting by a window and pondering his choice of a disguise, he sees a bat fly by. Taking it as an omen, he exclaims, "A BAT! THAT'S IT! IT'S AN OMEN. I SHALL BECOME A <u>BAT</u>!" (Capital letters and underlining in original.)

Given his personal history, revenge has been the primary motivation of Batman's crime-fighting career. But in the course of his nearly seven decades in comic books, Batman's outlook, in fact his entire personality, has changed substantially. His initial inspiration was the "mystery men" pulp heroes of the 1930s, like the Shadow, the Spider, and the Avenger. In his earliest stories he carried a revolver and sometimes used it. After the introduction of Robin, the Boy Wonder, the violence began to taper off, and by the 1950s Batman was no longer a creature of the night. He and Robin became primarily adventurers, with an occasional detective story thrown in. They frequently traveled through time and met various historical and mythological figures. They also met a variety of space aliens, and shared numerous adventures with Superman. Although these stories were frequently engaging and imaginative, they were taking Batman further and further from his roots as an icon of vengeance. This trend reached its height in the mid-1960s, when the Batman television program was on the air. Instead of picking up on Batman's strong narrative and character possibilities, the show emphasized the camp elements of the comic books. Rather than requiring the television show to imitate the original comic book, the creators of the comic book imitated the show. When *Batman* went off the air after three years, it was clear that the entire Batman series needed a basic revision. Creators Bob Kane and Bill Finger left the strip and writer Dennis O'Neil and artist Neil Adams, two members of the second generation of comic book professionals, took over *Batman*. They dropped the camp elements from their stories, and emphasized Batman's deductive abilities. In 1969, the character Dick Grayson, who had been the Boy Wonder since 1940, finally aged enough to go off to college. Bruce Wayne moved out of his suburban mansion and into a penthouse in downtown Gotham, where he would be closer to big city crime. Wayne began to date beautiful women and cultivate a reputation as a playboy, in part to provide a cover for his crime-fighting activities.

Gradually, throughout the 1970s, Batman became a tougher, more obsessive character. In keeping with evolving American attitudes towards crime his stories became darker and grittier. In 1986 a series of stories appeared that transformed the Batman mythos more thoroughly than anything since the first appearances of Robin and the Joker. Artist-writer Frank Miller had made his reputation in the early 1980s by turning Daredevil, a moribund Marvel Comics superhero, into one of the company's most popular titles. Turning his attention to Batman, Miller created *The Dark Knight Returns,* a mini-series set 20 years in the future, when every superhero except Superman has been outlawed. Bruce Wayne, now 55 years old, has been retired for ten years and has become overweight, alcoholic, and cynical. During a series of battles with many of his adversaries (including the Joker, who awakes from the catatonic stupor which has claimed him since his old enemy's retirement), Batman's spirits are revived by a young girl named Carrie Kelly, who becomes the new Robin. At the end of the series the reinvigorated Batman establishes a personal army called the Sons of Batman, which he pledges to use to battle the corrupt authorities who have opposed his fight against injustice.

The Dark Knight Returns changed Batman's image a few years before Tim Burton's 1989 *Batman* film brought the character to new prominence. As his sardonic butler Alfred was to ask repeatedly in years to come, would a sane person, no matter how tragic his childhood, give up a prosperous life to put on a costume and mask to battle psychotic criminals without a gun? Was the life of Batman a psychodrama for a disturbed man of great means who had never recovered from a childhood trauma? Should Bruce be seeing a therapist instead of fighting crime? And how could he justify involving protégés in his dangerous crusade? (There have been at least four Robins in the Batman mythos: Dick Grayson, Carrie Kelly, Jason Todd, and Tim Drake, who currently occupies the role.) Furthermore, before Bruce Wayne became Batman, there were no super-villains in Gotham City – the man who killed his parents was a small-time gangster. By becoming Gotham City's superhero, did Wayne somehow call into existence the various super-villains whom he fought? More generally, does power beget its antithesis? Was the leading American superhero's experience with his foes somehow symbolic of what happened to the United States after the Soviet Union fell and the US bestrode the world as its only super-power? Within a few years of the USSR's collapse, new, even more fanatical forces arose to challenge US predominance.

Batman is the most widely recognized crime fighter in the realm of comic books, but Will Eisner's creation, the Spirit, has probably had a greater aesthetic influence. Like Bob Kane and Bill Finger, Eisner was a pioneer in comic books; at the age of 19, he and a business partner named Jerry Iger opened the first studio dedicated to providing new material for the burgeoning industry. By 1939, at the age of 22, he was well known in the field as an artist, writer, editor, and studio boss. Though young, Eisner was a careful businessman who insisted on reading and understanding every word of every contract he ever signed. Eisner's attention to the details of business was one of the hallmarks of his long career.

In late fall of 1939 Eisner received a call from a business associate, Everett M. Arnold, who went by the nickname "Busy." Arnold and a representative of the Register & Tribune newspaper syndicate offered Eisner the opportunity to edit a new venture, a 16-page comic book that would be included with the Sunday papers. In addition to editing chores, Eisner would also be responsible for creating the publication's lead feature. Accepting the deal, Eisner began hiring employees and working on the lead strip, *The Spirit*, which he continued to produce for over a dozen years. Critics and fans routinely argue that in his writing, but especially in artwork, Eisner was decades ahead of his time. It was only after *Spirit* reprints became available to a new generation of fans and comics professionals in the 1960s that *The Spirit's* influence began to be felt throughout the medium.

The Spirit was Denny Colt, a private detective who was shot and seemingly killed while working on a case. As far as most of the world knew, Colt was dead and gone, but reports of his death proved to be exaggerated. He chose to use his apparent death to erase his public identity as Denny Colt. Somehow, he managed to build a bunker-like residence and crime laboratory below the grave in which he was prematurely buried. But there are few, if any, touches of Poe in his premature burial. Colt returned to life and good health, concealing his identity with a slouch hat, gloves, and domino mask (exchanged sometimes for dark glasses). He usually dressed in a blue business suit as well. Initially, his true identity was only known to Police Commissioner Dolan and his African-American sidekick Ebony White. (Ebony, who had a clownish face, incredibly thick, ham-like pink lips, and an illiterate way of speaking, was an unfortunate example of pre-World War II racial stereotyping. After returning from wartime service in the army, and during the early stages of a profound change in mainstream attitudes, Eisner began attempting to make amends for the character. Eventually, Ebony was sent off to school and replaced by a Caucasian character.)

Though the Spirit, Ebony, Commissioner Dolan and the other lead characters were caricatures, other aspects of Eisner's strip were more believable. No cartoonist has ever done a better job of conveying the look and feel of a big city. Eisner's long shots, especially in his celebrated splash pages (full or half page panels at the beginning of the story) were packed with detail, full of ordinary-looking people going about their business. The city was dark and shadowy, frequently viewed from below or above, or from even more cinematic angles of vision. Eisner's biographer, Bob Andelman, wrote that "Adults were drawn to *The Spirit* because of Eisner's ability to produce and tell a noir 'B' movie every week in just seven pages" (2005: 57). Other writers have picked up on the strip's noir elements and contended that Eisner was working in the film noir idiom even before the motion pictures' film noir heyday in the late 1940s and 1950s.

Eisner is also acclaimed for introducing adult sexuality into above-ground comics. His stories were full of *femme fatales,* attractively and voluptuously drawn. The Spirit was constantly being either seduced or threatened by these beautiful, curvy women, who had mysterious names like P'Gell, Sand Serif, and Autumn Mews. Sometimes he was threatened and then seduced, or vice versa. Meanwhile, for balance, there was the Lois Lane of the series, Commissioner Dolan's daughter Ellen, who had a mostly unrequited crush on the Spirit. The Spirit's relationships with women were not entirely realistic, but they were not too far removed from those of other fictional private detectives of the day.

In addition to his skills as a draftsman, Eisner was one of the cartoon world's masters of simulated motion. He knew how to shape action from one panel to the next to create a genuine sense of movement. A good example is a page from a story published in early 1942 and reprinted in Volume 4 of *The Spirit Archives* (Eisner 2001: 10). The story opens with a panel of the city bathed in dark blue, with a tall building in the foreground. A yellow light focuses on the side of the building at street level. The second panel shows the plate glass window of the Central City Bank, with a cat dozing on the sidewalk below. In the third panel, we see a close-up of a woman screaming "Eeek!" with her mouth grotesquely open so far that we can look down her throat. In the fourth panel, the bank's plate glass window is shattered by gunfire, and in the fifth panel the window is almost completely demolished. In the sixth panel we see a man halfway inside the panel, facing the shattered window with his back to us, so that all we can see are his shoes and his pants. Nearby the same cat is still sleeping in the same position, having apparently ignored the commotion. In the next panel, the point of view has changed. We are now inside the bank, looking out at a policeman — the man whose back we were looking at in the previous panel — taking notes. Eisner has depicted the bank robbery with both menace and humor, but without showing bloodshed, injury or death.

Batman, with his superhero affinities, operatic plots and large supporting cast, and the Spirit, who operates in a world that is both noirish and comical, were both hugely influential. A third subgenre of crime comic books, which flourished from approximately 1942 to 1955, echoed the tabloid headlines of the day. It began in 1942 with a comic book created for Comic House, Inc., a superhero publisher, by its editors Charles Biro and Bob Wood, who called their new periodical *Crime Does Not Pay*. Although a ghostly character named Mr Crime introduced and commented on many of the stories, *Crime Does Not Pay* advertised "True Crime Cases." The first issue, for example, featured stories about the recently convicted killer Louis "Lepke" Buchalter and Wild Bill Hickock. The stories invariably followed the same arc: the rise and fall of a criminal or a gang of criminals. It was the same plot arc used by Hollywood in the great gangster films of the early 1930s: *Little Caesar, Public Enemy,* and *Scarface* (see Munby, chapter 16 in this volume). Although magazines that imitated *Crime Does Not Pay* came and went through the years, the stories differed only in detail. They were alike in emphasizing gunplay, sadism, and extreme violence against women.

According to Biro and Wood and their publisher, Lev Gleason, *Crime Does Not Pay* was designed to prevent juvenile delinquency. Each story ended with the subject either dead or in jail. At various times the magazine described itself as "dedicated to the eradication of crime" or "A force for good in the community" (Goulart 2004: 104). Nonetheless, what stood out in these stories was the success of the gangsters, not their ultimate failure. The focus was not on justice, but rather on criminal enterprise. Comics in the *Crime Does Not Pay* genre were far more interested in sensationalizing crime than in eradicating it.

The decade after World War II saw a steep decline in the readership of superhero comic books until, by 1955, DC's Superman, Batman, and Wonder Woman were the only characters whose books were appearing regularly. To an extent the slack in the market was being picked up by other genres, including Westerns, romance magazines, and humor books recounting the adventures of funny animals or the fictional adventures of movie and television stars such as Jerry Lewis, Bob Hope and Phil Silvers. But it was the true-crime and horror comics that became the target of public outrage with the publication of a book entitled *Seduction of the Innocents* by Dr Fredric Wertham, a German-born New York City psychiatrist who had built a notable career in the

United States after emigrating in the 1920s. Wertham's book, and his crusade against comic books, were high-minded and sincere, but based on a faulty syllogism. In working with juvenile delinquents, he noted that the vast majority of them, when they read anything at all, read comic books. What Wertham apparently failed to keep in mind was that comic books were almost universally popular with boys and young men, and were read by millions of youngsters who were not juvenile delinquents. The terms of the argument are still familiar, although today the medium in dispute is more likely to be television or video games.

After the publication of *Seduction of the Innocents* and a televised Senate committee hearing, the comic book industry surrendered to its critics, and created the Comics Code Authority, a self-censoring organization that quickly drove the crime and horror comics out of business. Meanwhile, the late 1950s saw the reemergence of superhero stories as the dominant comic book genre. That dominance has endured until the present day. Crime stories continue to be published in comic books, but usually within a superhero context. To the extent that tabloid crime retains a place in the comics medium, it has moved into graphic novels.

Graphic Novels

The history of the modern graphic novel began in 1978, with the publication of Will Eisner's *A Contract with God and Other Stories.* Eisner admitted he was not the first to use the term "graphic novel" – its usage has been traced back decades earlier – but he was the first creator to apply the term to his own work, and to produce a large body of it. Most of the graphic novels he produced from 1978 until his death in 2005 were literary adaptations or autobiographical stories; none were crime stories.[3]

Nonetheless, there were graphic novels previous to Eisner's breakthrough into respectability, and some of them were crime stories. In 1950 two young writers named Arnold Drake and Leslie Waller conceived the idea of "picture novels." These would combine the format of the comic books that had been so popular with their fellow GIs during World War II with the plotting and greater length of genre novels. Matt Baker, a comic book veteran especially known for drawing attractive women, joined them along with Ray Osrin, who served as inker. *It Rhymes with Lust,* the story of an alcoholic newspaperman torn between two women – the greedy, scheming and very sexy young widow Rust Masson and her beautiful stepdaughter, Audrey – is set in a mining town called Copper City. Rust, who has inherited control of her late husband's mining company, rules the town with the help of a crooked politician named Marcus and a hired gunman named Monk. *It Rhymes with Lust* was published as a mass market paperback by St John Publications in 1950. A follow-up by another creative team entitled *The Case of the Winking Buddha* was published soon after. Neither book sold well at the time and that was the end of the "picture novel" as far as St John Publications was concerned.[4]

The term "graphic novel" as used currently remains slippery. Most of Will Eisner's books marketed under that designation, for example, consist of collections of shorter works. Similarly, many of the graphic novels currently marketed are actually hardcover or trade paperback collections of previously published comic book stories. In many cases, an ongoing series of fifty or more issues will be collected in a run of trade editions. Vertigo, an imprint of DC Comics (itself a property of Time/Warner/AOL) is a prolific publisher of these works, both in periodical and hardcover and/or trade paperback form. A typical Vertigo series is *100 Bullets* by writer Brian Azzarello and Eduardo Risso. In this series, various individuals with reasons for seeking revenge meet a stranger, Mr Graves, who gives them a satchel containing an unregistered gun and 100 bullets that he promises can never be traced.

The drama in the early books of *100 Bullets* revolves around each protagonist's decision whether to use the gun and bullets, and also the identity of the mysterious Mr Graves and the "Minutemen," the shadowy organization he represents. As the series continues, focus shifts from the moral and ethical conundrums of the people receiving the guns and bullets to an account of a battle between the Minutemen and their former employers, the Trust, a group of 13 aristocratic European families who wield vast power behind the scenes. As is often the case with graphic novels, what appeared at first to be a crime story evolves into a huge pulp fantasy epic.

During the past ten years three graphic novels about crime have been particularly influential, serving as the basis for critically acclaimed motion pictures. Their appearances on cinema screens, broadcast and cable television stations and in DVD format have brought them to a far larger public than the people who initially read the novels on which they were based.

A History of Violence, by writer John Wagner and artist Vince Locke, was published in 1997 by Paradox Press, a predecessor of DC's Vertigo imprint.[5] The story begins when McKenna, the middle-aged owner of a small-town coffee shop in Michigan, thwarts a robbery by two gun-wielding thugs with his bare hands. His feat draws the interest of the national media, and is seen by gangsters in New York City who recognize him as one of two young neighborhood hoodlums who committed a daring robbery against them many years earlier. This puts McKenna and his family, who know nothing of his past, in danger, and he is forced to return to New York to settle old scores with skills in violence he thought he left behind when he fled the city and his old identity decades before.

True to its title, *A History of Violence* is a very violent story, even more so than David Cronenberg's 2005 film adaptation, which has a completely different and slightly softer ending. Vince Locke's black and white art ranges from pretty to uncomfortably graphic, and the reader is in the position, as is frequently the case in crime literature, of rooting for one violent man, a reformed criminal, against other men who are even more brutal. A similar situation prevails in *The Road to Perdition*, a 1998 graphic novel by writer Max Allan Collins and artist Richard Piers Rayner.

The protagonist of *The Road to Perdition* (Collins 2005) is Depression-Era hoodlum Michael O'Sullivan, a World War I hero and the enforcer for a gang of Irish-American hoodlums in the Quad Cities of Eastern Iowa and Western Illinois. O'Sullivan is a criminal with his own set of ethics: he prides himself on never attacking civilians, considering himself a soldier in the gang headed by the elderly John Looney, his father figure. When Looney's biological son murders O'Sullivan's wife and younger son, Michael, who was also nearly killed on orders of the elder Looney, must find a way to avenge their deaths while protecting his older, pre-teen son, also named Michael. Beautifully illustrated with fine period detail by the English artist Richard Piers Rayner, *The Road to Perdition* is a tough, lurid story with a sentimental undertone. Like *A History of Violence*, it is best described as the story of a bad man who redeems himself through devotion to his family. In 2002 Sam Mendes directed a film version starring Tom Hanks as O'Sullivan and Paul Newman as John Looney.[6]

Frank Miller published his first *Sin City* graphic novel, *The Hard Goodbye*, in 1991, after an unhappy experience as co-scripter of the second *RoboCop* movie. Seven subsequent *Sin City* volumes have appeared since that time. In *The Hard Goodbye* Miller established a distinctive high-contrast black-and-white graphic style that can be photographic at times, but more often is highly abstract. Some panels almost require readers to stop and puzzle out what they are seeing. Miller's techniques are among the most sophisticated ever employed in graphic storytelling.

Another of Miller's strengths is his familiarity with various forms of crime fiction outside of his background in graphic fiction. He has said that he sees it as a duty to bring to his work some of the qualities of related forms, particularly in his case the qualities of hard-boiled fiction (Miller 2003). He has read widely in the works of Chandler, Hammett, and Spillane and draws on film noir and neo-noir (see Simpson, chapter 14 in this volume), as well as on the history of the comic book medium. He had a particularly close relationship with Will Eisner, the leading theorist and teacher of graphic storytelling.

Miller's indebtedness to Eisner is evident in one of his recent forays into directing: he was instrumental in bringing to the screen a big-budget version of Eisner's *Spirit*, released in the US on Christmas Day, 2008, and starring Scarlet Johansson, Samuel L. Jackson, Eva Mendes and Gabriel Macht. Miller directed the film as well as writing the script, based on Eisner's comic book stories. His work as a director began with the film adaptation of *Sin City*. In 2005, when his graphic novel came to the screen, he shared director credits with the veteran Robert Rodriguez (Figure 26.1). A script for a second *Sin City* film has been written, and is scheduled to be filmed in 2010; a third is scheduled for 2011. Once again, Miller will co-direct with Rodriguez.

In an age of show-business synergy, Miller's transition from comic book creator to director of a major Hollywood film shows the potential influence of the graphic storytelling medium. The cinematic appeal of the comics was evident to visionaries like Will Eisner over 70 years ago, but the full potential of film adaptation has rarely been realized: with only a few exceptions, the Hollywood studios continued to regard graphic stories as nothing more than a source of exciting plotlines and colorful costumes. Miller's rise in particular suggests that may be changing, and that graphic storytelling and cinema are increasingly seen as related – and co-equal – arts.

Figure 26.1   The film adaptation of *Sin City* (2005, dir. Frank Miller and Robert Rodriguez; produced by Elizabeth Avellán) brought Frank Miller's graphic novel to the screen.

NOTES

1   These origins of the Joker and Two-Face were changed in the highly successful 2008 film, *The Dark Knight*, but they have been standard in the various Batman comic books since the early 1940s.

2   Although artist Bob Kane initially conceived the idea of Batman, and negotiated legal rights to the character with DC Comics, recent investigations have shown that his friend, writer Bill Finger, contributed so much to the origin of the Batman mythos as to be virtually a co-creator. A third cartoonist, Jerry Robinson, devised the Joker.

3   Eisner's *Spirit* stories have been reprinted several times, most recently by DC Comics as part of the DC Archives editions.

4   *It Rhymes with Lust* was reprinted in replica form by Dark Horse Books (Baker et al. 2007). It is a graphic work many years ahead of its time, and worth reading.

5   *A History of Violence* is currently in print as a Vertigo title (Wagner and Locke 2004).

6   Since the film appeared Collins has written two additional novels depicting O'Sullivan's time on the road in the Midwest with his son, robbing banks that hold mob money and plotting revenge. Richard Piers Rayner was not involved with either project.

27

Criminal Investigation on Film

Philippa Gates

Detecting the Genre

A crime film can be defined as a film that centers on committing a criminal act – whether it be a crime against the laws of nature such as murder, or against the laws of society such as embezzlement (Thompson 2007: 1–2). Although that definition may seem straightforward, the crime film as a genre includes many different types of narratives and protagonists depending on what type of crime is committed (for example, theft as opposed to murder), whether the film focuses on the execution of the crime or the aftermath (the heist film, say, versus the prison film), and what type of protagonist occupies the center of the narrative. The most significant distinction among the subgenres of the crime film is the nature of the protagonist: he – and the protagonist is most often male – is either the perpetrator of the crime (e.g., in the heist or gangster film) or the investigator (e.g., in the murder-mystery or courtroom drama), and his alignment with one side of the law over the other will affect the film's themes and conclusion. A central theme of the crime film is an exploration of the social aspects of crime, whether cause, investigation, or punishment – particularly the restrictions and/or failings of the criminal justice system (as in the courtroom or prison drama). While heist or gangster films may allow their protagonists to get away with their crimes, the detective film tends to have a conservative conclusion in which justice being served means the apprehension or elimination of the criminal. It is the detective film with which this chapter is concerned.

A genre is a body of films that share a set of conventions, including formal elements – such as themes, types of action, and character types – and visual elements – such as settings, costume, and props. While critics and scholars may not agree on what constitutes the genre of the detective film, the subgenres and specific cycles that occur within the overarching category of the detective film are readily definable. Contemporary detective films may have much in common with the cycles of the genre that have preceded them – sharing conventions, character types, and narrative structures.

Nevertheless, the themes they express, the social concerns with which they engage, and the narrative and stylistic variations they present are distinctly the product of our specific social moment. According to Nick Browne, film genre criticism has often only attempted to regulate, classify, and explain film through genre; instead, he argues that we should consider film genres as gravitating toward "specific assemblages of local coherencies – discreet, heterotopic instances of a complex cultural politics" (1998: xi). In a negotiation of social change, the varieties of the detective film have evolved and intersected with other subgenres. This is a hybridization that allows the genre to be current and innovative. Thus, although all detective films may deliberate themes of law and order, heroism and villainy, and social and political attitudes towards crime, the commitment to one side of the debate over the other changes in relation to shifting social opinion and is manifested through the popularity of a particular subgenre as a cycle of films with common characters and themes.

The Classical Sleuth

The detective genre appeared in the fiction of the mid-nineteenth century as a response to the fears arising from urbanization, industrialization, and the working class and it continues into the twenty-first century in various forms of popular culture in the same vein: our increasingly complex and alienating society makes us the potential victims of criminals – or potentially the criminals ourselves. Edgar Allan Poe created the amateur sleuth with Auguste Dupin in the short story "Murders in the Rue Morgue" (1841) and Sir Arthur Conan Doyle's Sherlock Holmes and Agatha Christie's Hercule Poirot solidified his characterization. Robert Reiner argues that in order to alleviate the concerns of the upper classes, the classical detective in fiction was put forth as a "rational and unfailingly resourceful individual symbolising a superior ideal of self-disciplined initiative, who is symbiotically related to a well-ordered social organisation" (1985: 147). Cinematic crime serials were popular in France but tended to focus on master criminals outwitting the official investigators, as in Louis Feuillade's *Fantômas* (1913 to 1914) and *Les Vampires* (1915 to 1916). In American film, silent serials were notable for offering female crime-fighters, including "The Perils of Pauline" (1914) and "The Exploits of Elaine" (1914–15) starring Pearl White. Silent crime films focused less on complicated mysteries and investigations and more on the visual pleasure of disguises and action sequences.

It was only with the coming of sound in the late 1920s that the classical detective story could flourish on screen because of the elaborate plots that defined the genre – a puzzle that must be pieced together by clues (some meaningful, others irrelevant) into a cohesive and intelligible narrative that identifies its "author" (the criminal). Because of this focus on the puzzle element, the classical detective story is also known as the murder-mystery or "whodunit." The sleuth's popularity can be attributed to the reassurance that even if the official investigators (i.e., the police) could not identify the criminal, the amateur sleuth or private detective could. The sleuths of classical detective fiction have been intermittently popular with audiences. Sherlock Holmes, the world's most famous detective, has been played by more actors than any other character in the world, but most memorably by Basil Rathbone alongside Nigel Bruce's Dr Watson in film and on the radio (1939–46) and Jeremy Brett on British television (1984–94). Agatha Christie's Miss Marple was played by Margaret Rutherford in British film (1961–4) and by Joan Hickson (1984–92) and Geraldine McEwan (2004–7) in British television series. And Hercule Poirot was played by Peter Ustinov in films and made-for-television movies (1978–88) and by David Suchet in a British television series (1989–2008).

The amateur sleuth (also known as the criminologist) was extremely popular in Hollywood film during the 1930s and 1940s, with most studios promoting at least one successful detective as the feature character of a B-series: for example, Bulldog Drummond at Paramount, The Saint at RKO, Perry Mason at Warner Bros, The Lone Wolf at Columbia, Nick Charles at MGM, and Michael Shayne at Twentieth Century-Fox. Classical Hollywood also saw the rise of the Asian sleuth, including Charlie Chan, a police detective who starred in 44 films (1931–49); Mr Moto, an international agent, in eight films (1937–9); and Mr James Lee Wong, an amateur sleuth, in six films (1938–40). Although Charles Rzepka has noted the ways in which Chan's original creator, the novelist Earl Derr Biggers, exploited the formulaic features of the detective genre to interrogate or overturn invidious racial stereotypes, the progressive impact of Hollywood's placing of racially "othered" heroes in central positions of subjectivity on screen was tempered by featuring white actors in "yellowface" – most memorably Chan by Swedish-born Warner Oland, Moto by Hungarian-born Peter Lorre, and Wong by English-born Boris Karloff. Following the Yellow Peril-inspired demonization of the Chinese as "Oriental villain" or "Dragon Lady" in American culture, Chan and Wong appeared as "model minority" figures, representing immigrants who had assimilated into mainstream society. Chan was characterized as "Chinese" through his quiet and controlled manner, his halting English, and his tendency to offer pearls of Confucian (although sometimes more like fortune cookie) wisdom during his investigations: as Chan tells his Number One Son, "Facts, like photographic film, must be exposed before developing." Kentaro Moto, the Japanese secret agent, was presented as less benign than his Chinese counterparts; beneath a veneer of politeness and small stature was a calculating, intelligent, and often menacing man. Unlike Chan and Wong, Moto fought enemies with jujitsu and coolly dispatched them with knives and guns. And, while the Chan series proved popular throughout the 1940s, the equally popular Moto series saw its demise in 1939 with anti-Japanese sentiment on the rise on the eve of World War II.

Female detectives, prolific during the Great Depression, have again become more prevalent and popular since the 1980s. The female detective of 1930s B-films and series was an independent woman who put her career ahead of the traditionally female pursuits of marriage and a family and who chased crime as actively as – and with greater success than – the men who populated the police department or the rival paper's staff. As girl reporter Florence Dempsey (Glenda Farrell) tells her friend in

The Mystery of the Wax Museum (1933), "You raise the kids, I'll raise the roof! I would rather die with an athletic heart from shaking cocktails and bankers than expire in a pan of dirty dishwater." Occasionally, the female sleuth was a private detective (e.g., Jane Wyman in *Private Detective* [1939]) or an undercover government agent (e.g., Constance Worth in *China Passage* [1937]); however, outnumbering the official investigators who were paid to solve mysteries were those who sleuthed out of curiosity. These were the amateur detectives popular enough to star in their own series: girl reporter Torchy Blane (most memorably, Glenda Farrell) in nine films (1937–9), teenager Nancy Drew (Bonita Granville) in four films (1938–9), and schoolteacher Hildegarde Withers (played most notably by Edna May Oliver) in six films (1932–7).

Hard-boiled Private Eyes

The hard-boiled detective was an adaptation of the British sleuth to the environment and anxieties of urban America but also the evolution of the frontier and dime novel hero. Rather than a cop, he was most often a private detective who relied on smarts learned from the mean streets rather than from books (like the sleuth) or the academy (like the cop). The hard-boiled detective appeared in 1930s film in a "soft-boiled" form. The Production Code – Hollywood's system of self-censorship, introduced in 1930 but not strictly enforced until 1934 – prohibited the sex, violence, and language of hard-boiled fiction and so the detectives of American authors like Dashiell Hammett and Raymond Chandler were portrayed on screen as suave sleuths like Philo Vance and Nick Charles (both played by William Powell) who operated among America's urban elite. The American detective would not appear as truly hard-boiled until *film noir* during World War II, when he was epitomized by Humphrey Bogart in films like John Huston's *The Maltese Falcon* (1941) and Howard Hawks's *The Big Sleep* (1946).

"*Noir*" is a label that cuts across generic lines, including the Gothic melodrama *Gaslight* (1944), the criminal-adventure thriller *Double Indemnity* (1944), the gangster film *White Heat* (1949), and investigative thriller *The Big Sleep* (1946) (see Simpson, chapter 14 in this volume). *Film noir* offered a critique of wartime and postwar society, especially the problems that ex-servicemen faced, from unemployment to broken homes to physical disability. Frank Krutnik links *noir's* appropriation of the hard-boiled tradition to the popularization of Freudian psychoanalysis in American culture at the time: rather than regarding crime as organized or the result of social problems, it was attributed to individuals with psychological problems (1991: xii). The changing international climate with America's entry into World War II saw a redefinition of heroism and villainy. In *The Maltese Falcon*, Cairo (Peter Lorre) and Gutman (Sydney Greenstreet) are identified as wealthy and homosexual, as in Hammett's novel, but also specifically European in order to highlight Sam Spade (Bogart) as a working-class, heterosexual, American hero.

Film noir also saw a handful of female investigators, reflective of the renegotiation of gender roles in the wake of the war, including Ella Raines in *Phantom Lady* (1944), June Vincent in *Black Angel* (1946), and Ann Sheridan in *Woman on the Run* (1950). It is surprising that the female detective appears in *film noir* since the independent woman tended to be branded as the dangerous *femme fatale*; however, the threat, it would seem, was not the woman replacing the male detective but replacing him as the breadwinner and head of the household. In marked contrast to her independent, fast-talking, and career-driven sisters of the 1930s, the 1940s female detective wants to be a dutiful wife rather than an independent career woman and her only motive to unravel the mystery is to save the man whom she loves. After 1950, the female detective leaves the big screen, except for a couple of rare outings, until the 1980s.

Disillusioned private detectives returned in 1970s retro- and neo-*noirs* in a reaction to the aftermath of a new war – Vietnam – as well as in response to such social upheavals as the Watergate scandal and the Women's and Civil Rights Movements. As Linda Dittmar and Gene Michaud note, "What is important about this particular historic moment is that it deeply divided the country's population and brought about a profound crisis in the American imagination" (1990: 6). Rather than the *chiaroscuro* contrast of shadows and night in black and white, the new *noir* films – including Roman Polanski's *Chinatown* (1974), Robert Altman's *The Long Goodbye* (1973), and Ridley Scott's *Blade Runner* (1982) – whether set in the past, present, or future, respectively – brought the anxieties of masculinity into broad daylight. These films, as well as Francis Ford Coppola's *The Conversation* (1974) and Arthur Penn's *Night Moves* (1975), both starring Gene Hackman, questioned the heroic abilities of their protagonists, who ultimately fail as detectives. For example, *Chinatown*, set in the age of classic *noir*, exposes the impotence of the hero, Jake Gittes (Jack Nicholson), in the face of political corruption – as water officials scam the city – and familial corruption – as patriarch Noah Cross (John Huston) commits incest with his daughter and the film concludes with the suggestion that he will repeat the offence with his granddaughter. While some neo-*noir* films in the 1980s and 1990s featured a private eye, such as in *Angel Heart* (1987), or a police detective, as in *Basic Instinct* (1992), the focus was less on investigating a mystery and more, as Alain Silver and Elizabeth Ward suggest, on "the need to find love and honour in a new society that tenders only to sex and money" (1988: 370).

The popularity of the female hard-boiled private eye would not come until the 1980s in the fiction of Sue Grafton and Sarah Paretsky and only one of their characters made it to the big screen: Paretsky's V. I. Warshawski in the film of the same name (1991) starring Kathleen Turner.

The Police Detective

The police procedural (see Messent, chapter 13 in this volume) appeared in the mid-1940s as a reflection of the professionalization of real-life crime detection in an attempt to combat organized crime. By the mid-twentieth century, the upper and middle classes no longer regarded the police as a necessary evil but as the embodiment of social good; in a reflection of this shift, the police detective came to be the dominant hero in the detective film. The police procedural – in a response to the disillusionment and paranoia of the Cold War period – offered a reassuring detective who was effective, if conservative and unexciting. The subgenre's distinguishing feature was the emphasis on procedure: entire scenes were devoted to surveillance and tailing, pounding the pavement for leads, fingerprints and ballistics analysis, and technologies like the Photostat. The police detective (or other law enforcement agent) of this period did not need the superior intellect of the sleuth or the street smarts of the hard-boiled private eye; instead, he relied on the teamwork and procedures of the police force in films like Henry Hathaway's *The House on 92nd Street* (1945) and Jules Dassin's *The Naked City* (1948).

The 1950s was the decade of containment in the aftermath of World War II with a precipitant rise in divorce rates, public debates regarding homosexuality, the rise of psychoanalysis, and the recognition of the physical and emotional burdens that men experienced as they attempted to fulfill their traditional male roles (Peek 1998: 74). While Jimmy Stewart had played the stable and dependable detective in the procedural *Call Northside 777* (1948), by the mid-1950s he embodied the contradictions and anxieties of postwar masculinity, playing detective-figures who were vulnerable, feminized, or disillusioned in Alfred Hitchcock's *Rear Window* (1954) and *Vertigo* (1958) and Otto Preminger's *Anatomy of a Murder* (1959) (see Haeffner, chapter 45 in this volume). The detective of the 1950s – as the product of the McCarthy era, the Cold War, and a materialistic society in which the end justifies the means – was not only vulnerable or cynical but often corrupt and violent in *noir* films like *Detective Story* (1951), *Kiss Me Deadly* (1955), and Orson Welles's *Touch of Evil* (1958). The female cop, on the other hand, although she became an increasing presence on television with series like "Decoy" (1957–9) and "Honey West" (1965–6), was absent from the big screen until the 1980s.

The Cop Action Hero

The detective film all but disappeared in the late 1950s, with criminals returning as the focus in crime films like *The Killers* (1964) and *Point Blank* (1967). The few films that did center on the efforts of the detective – such as *The Chase* (1966) with Marlon Brando, *Tony Rome* (1967) with Frank Sinatra, and *Madigan* (1968) with Richard Widmark – saw an increasing focus on pursuing criminals rather than on the mystery of "whodunit." The replacement of the Production Code with the Ratings System by 1968 meant that graphic violence and sexuality could be explored and a new era of detective films appeared. In a period when President Nixon's hard-line politics on crime and the widespread loss of confidence in law-enforcement were dominating American society, the vigilante cop film featured a lone enforcer who annihilated

Figure 27.1   Richard Roundtree's private investigator in *Shaft* (1971, dir. Gordon Parks, produced by Joel Freeman): the black detective has become increasingly popular and pervasive in the new millennium.

crime with extreme violence in films like *Bullitt* (1968) with Steve McQueen, *The French Connection* (1971) with Gene Hackman, and *Dirty Harry* (1971) with Clint Eastwood. Similar vigilante crime-fighters also appeared in B-grade "blaxploitation" films – named for the fact that they exploited black subculture and black audiences. *Cotton Comes to Harlem* (1970) and *Shaft* (1971) featured black male cops and a private investigator, respectively (Figure 27.1); *Coffy* (1973) and *Foxy Brown* (1974) featured black female vigilantes seeking justice for loved ones; *Cleopatra Jones* (1973) featured a black female secret agent; and *Sheba, Baby* (1975) a private detective. These black women, embodied by Pam Grier and Tamara Dobson, were empowered – using guns and martial arts to defeat the villains. Even if objectified (they often appeared scantily clad or topless while undercover), they are notable, particularly as white women had no such models in film until the late 1980s.

The detective of the 1980s followed in the vein of Dirty Harry as an action hero; however, his heroism was linked directly to his body, which was presented as stripped-off and on display. Susan Jeffords argues that, in the 1980s, conceptions of masculinity were in flux due to changes in the economy, gender relations, race relations, and the workforce; Hollywood's response was the hard-bodied hero (1994: 11–12). Or, as

Mark Gallagher argues, while capitalist society severely limited the middle-class male's ability to establish his identity through physical action, the action film provided him with fantasies of heroic omnipotence (1999: 199). Epitomized by Mel Gibson in *Lethal Weapon* (1987) and Bruce Willis in *Die Hard* (1988), the cop action hero represented an idealized image of Americanized heroism and masculinity and a solution to law and order made impotent by bureaucracy. In *Die Hard*, the class, race, and masculinity of John McClane (Willis) are emphasized in the light of personal crisis – the imminent loss of his wife and family – and national threats – Japanese corporations and German terrorists. In *Lethal Weapon*, Martin Riggs (Gibson) is established in opposition not only to his buddy, a middle-class, domesticated, African-American, but also to his *doppelganger*, the villainous, hyper-white (described as albino) Mr Joshua. The hard body of the white male became the site upon which masculine crisis, personal and often national, could be articulated but, more importantly, resolved through physical action.

A popular trend within the cop action film was the "buddy cop film" in which two characters of opposite backgrounds (in terms of race, class, or personality) were thrown together. Beginning with Eddie Murphy and Nick Nolte in *48 Hrs* (1982), the buddy cop film has continued to draw audiences with an increasing emphasis on comedy in films like the *Rush Hour* series (1998, 2001, and 2007) starring Jackie Chan and Chris Tucker.

The Lawyer

After the detective has identified the criminal, it is left to the district attorney's office to prosecute, and the defense lawyer to defend, the criminal in court. Nicole Rafter argues that the lawyer film or courtroom drama explores the tension between immutable "natural" law and fallible "man-made" law, and that the hero of such films is a "justice figure" who attempts to close the gap between the two – from manipulated law to the ideal (2000: 93–4). Norman Rosenberg notes that the first phase of the courtroom drama in the early 1930s was experimental and that the critical "law *noir*" questioned what was exposed as a fallible system (1994: 345). The lawyer-as-justice-figure is a repeated focus of the genre as evident in films such as *Marked Woman* (1937) starring Humphrey Bogart, *The Young Philadelphians* (1958) starring Paul Newman, and Hitchcock's *The Paradine Case* (1947) and *To Kill a Mockingbird*, both starring Gregory Peck. The 1960s and 1970s saw only occasional lawyer films rather than a steady cycle. On television, Raymond Burr starred as the world's best-known lawyer, Erle Stanley Gardner's Perry Mason (1957–66 [series] and 1985–93 [specials]).

The female lawyer appeared as a detective searching for the truth in the late 1980s and early 1990s. Played by Glenn Close in *Jagged Edge* (1985), Cher in *Suspect* (1987), and Mary Elizabeth Mastrantonio in *Class Action* (1991), the female lawyer *appeared* to be a feminist model; however, as Cynthia Lucia explains, like the *femme fatale* of the neo-*noir* erotic thriller, the female lawyer was presented as "dangerously ambitious" and "personally and professionally deficient" (1992: 33). In terms of their professional lives, these women were presented as incompetent lawyers, often proved wrong by their male colleagues, and, in terms of their personal lives, they were married to their jobs and could not attain fulfillment without love interests or children. These themes still dominated the genre in more recent television series like "Ally McBeal" (1997–2002), although with a more comedic tone.

By the mid-1990s it was the youth who played the lawyer in the courtroom in what Keith Bartlett refers to as the "Grisham cycle" (Bartlett 2003). Films based on John Grisham bestsellers like *The Firm* (1993) starring Tom Cruise, *A Time to Kill* (1996) starring Matthew McConaughey, and *The Rainmaker* (1997) starring Matt Damon, offered a young male lawyer as a detective full of ambition and a desire for the truth. The themes of the lawyer film shifted to a concern with morally bankrupt lawyers defending wealthy (often guilty) clients for money and fame, reducing the courtroom to a three-ring circus in which lawyers sold their version of the truth. The idealistic youth brought hope that natural, rather than human-made, justice would determine guilt or innocence.

The Criminalist

While the 1980s were dominated by a backlash against feminist and civil-rights gains in the cop action and neo-*noir* film, the early 1990s experienced a shift to "sensitive" and "thinking men" heroes. The crime film thus saw heroism redefined as involving brains rather than brawn: an intelligent sleuth-like hero once again attempted to assemble the puzzle-like narrative of the crime committed but this time with a focus on police procedure as the key to bringing the criminal to justice. In a relocation to the middle class, the 1990s detective was an educated and professional hero – a criminalist – trained in crime scene investigation and forensic science. And with the criminalist came an interest in specific kinds of crime. On the one hand, the cop action hero often chased criminals involved in drug deals, heists, terrorism, or political corruption; on the other hand, the criminalist always investigates homicide and often that committed by a serial killer. In the criminalist film, the spectacle of the body shifts from the *femme fatale* of *film noir* and the male hero of the cop action film, to the murder victim – the "work" of the killer put on display. The body is a text that can be "read" by the detective in order to identify its "author" – the killer. Just as in the case of the classical detective story, part of the pleasure of the criminalist film is the invitation to read the signs alongside the detective and to try to solve the mystery before the detective does. A decade after *The Silence of the Lambs* (1991) made the criminalist film popular, successors like *Murder by Numbers* (2002) and *Blood Work* (2002) saw killers, in a postmodern play, stage their "work" in order for it to be read in a specific way, with their audiences – the detectives – in mind.

The attraction of the serial killer is that he is elusive, potent, and violent. The association of homosexuality and villainy persisted in Hollywood film until recently:

for example, "Buffalo Bill" in *The Silence of the Lambs* is presented as "abnormal," as a transsexual who longs to transform his male body through a "dress" made of his female victims' skin. The serial killer of the last decade, however, is not defined by obvious external markings of "otherness" – femininity, homosexuality, or foreignness. Instead, as Philip Simpson suggests, the contemporary serial killer disguises his true nature behind a masquerade of normalcy (2000: 4). Despite Linnie Blake's assertion that "the serial killer is nothing less than the last American hero" (2002: 208), only a very few of these onscreen criminals are presented as in any way admirable – for example, John Doe in *Se7en* (1995) and Hannibal Lecter (as embodied by Anthony Hopkins) in *The Silence of the Lambs, Hannibal* (2001), and *Red Dragon* (2002). But while both are intelligent and intriguing neither is technically the "hero" of the film: the detective is and the serial killer is there to offer the hero a challenging adversary. Because Western culture mythologizes bandit figures like Robin Hood, we tend not to mind the clever thief getting away with his crime; however, we fear the serial killer, and it is thus the triumph of the detective as hero that we desire. Lecter, as the star of a series of the films, is somewhat of an exception; however, since he only kills those who cross him, we do not fear – as we do with those who kill randomly – that we could be his next innocent victim. Along with this focus on serial killers has come a dramatic increase in the depiction of horrific violence – what Jane Caputi and Diana Russell term "gorenography" (1992: 18) and I, "the spectacle of the gross" (Gates 2006: 167). The appeal of the criminalist – in an era defined by information technology – is his/her reliance on science and technology to solve crime, an appeal reflected in the proliferation of criminalists in films like *Kiss the Girls* (1997) and *Untraceable* (2008) and on television with series like "CSI: Crime Scene Investigation" (2000–) and its spin-offs. No longer is the process of detection a game of chance, brute force, or solving a puzzle; it is, we are led to believe, an exact science.

"Other" Detectives

The black detective had certainly become more popular and pervasive by the new millennium. Famous precursors include Sidney Poitier's Mr Tibbs in *In the Heat of the Night* (1967), Richard Roundtree's private investigator in *Shaft* (1971), and Eddie Murphy's comedic *Beverly Hills Cop* (1984, 1987, and 1994). More recently, Denzel Washington played a private eye in *Devil in a Blue Dress* (1995) and Morgan Freeman, the criminalist in *Se7en, Kiss the Girls,* and *Along Came a Spider* (2001).

Although the two silent Charlie Chan films starred Japanese actors, Hollywood seemed reluctant to have an Asian detective played by an Asian-American actor with the move to sound. The exceptions include Keye Luke who, made famous in the role of Chan's "Number One Son" opposite Warner Oland in the 1930s, played Mr Wong in *Phantom of Chinatown* (1940); James Shigeta who played a police detective in *Crimson Kimono* (1959); and Wood Moy and Marc Hayashi who played cabbies trying to solve a mystery in Wayne Wang's independently produced *Chan Is Missing* (1982). More recently, Jackie Chan has portrayed crime-fighting heroes in the *Rush Hour* series and the *Shanghai* films (2000, 2003). On television, black, Hispanic, and Asian-American detectives are included in some ensemble cast series, such as "CSI" and "CSI: Miami" (2002–).

While the genre has been dominated by men – as detectives and criminals – the female detective has become increasingly common, especially in television ensemble casts and with the emphasis on brains, experience, and education over physical prowess. Ever since Jodie Foster paved the way as an FBI agent-in-training in *The Silence of the Lambs*, the female detective has starred in criminalist films such as *Copycat* (1995) and *Untraceable*. On television, the female detective stars in series such as "Crossing Jordan" (2001–7), "Law and Order: Special Victims Unit" (1999–), "CSI," and "Prime Suspect" (UK 1991–2006). While the white, heterosexual female detective is more common these days, the lesbian and woman of color are rare. Television shows including "CSI: Miami" (2002–), "Diagnosis Murder" (1993–2002) "Law and Order: SVU," and "Women's Murder Club" (2007) do present black women in secondary roles – most often as a pathologist.

While fiction has seen more detectives with disabilities, film has seen only one adapted to the screen – Jeffrey Deaver's quadriplegic detective, Lincoln Rhyme, in *The Bone Collector* (1999) played by Denzel Washington. Television has seen a few, including "Ironside" (1967–75), starring Raymond Burr in a wheelchair and, more recently, "Sue Thomas: F.B. Eye" (2002–5) featuring Deanne Bray, a deaf actress, as a deaf detective. In terms of psychological impairments, Tony Shaloub's sleuth in "Monk" (2002–) is obsessive-compulsive as a result of the trauma of his wife's unsolved murder. Adrian Monk updates the comedic fussiness of the classical sleuth such as Hercule Poirot to the streets of present-day San Francisco.

The current emphasis on education and experience has all but excluded the youth from the detective film: young men have had not the time, opportunity, or inclination to gain or hone their observational and deductive skills. In the contemporary detective film, it is the wisdom of age and experience that succeeds where the folly of youth fails. The occasional appearance of young detectives in the genre is, therefore, notable – for example, the roles of Brad Pitt in *Se7en* (1995), Johnny Depp in *Sleepy Hollow* (1999) and *From Hell* (2001), and Josh Hartnett in *Hollywood Homicide* (2003). The appeal of the youth as the contemporary detective is, in many ways, that we watch him struggle and fail as a detective. The ensemble casts of the three "CSI" shows include one young male to highlight the experience, patience, and self-control needed to do the job well, since the youth tend to lack these qualities.

In contrast, since knowledge and wisdom are the weapons that the contemporary detective must possess in order to defeat the ingenious criminal, advanced age is considered an asset where in the past it was regarded as an impediment. In the same vein, the "Baby Boom" generation is providing Hollywood with a new, viable, audience demographic to cater to. On television, Angela Lansbury in "Murder, She Wrote," Andy Griffith in "Matlock" (1986–95), David Jason in "A Touch of Frost"

(UK 1992–), and Dick Van Dyke in "Diagnosis Murder" are senior citizens. Morgan Freeman was a sexagenarian when he starred as Alex Cross in *Kiss the Girls* and *Along Came a Spider* and so too was Clint Eastwood when he returned to investigative roles in films like *True Crime* (1999) and *Blood Work*.

Conclusion

The detective film appeared almost as soon as the medium of cinema was born and became popular in the early 1930s, when sound could first do justice to its complicated plots and characters and the Depression and Prohibition made its themes regarding crime and justice increasingly relevant. Each decade has seen the dominance and proliferation of different trends in the genre: the British classical sleuth and the soft-boiled versions of American hard-boiled private investigators dominated the screen in the 1930s; the 1940s saw both replaced by *film noir*'s hard-boiled private eye; he, in turn, was replaced by the police detective who shifted from conservative and stable in the late 1940s to neurotic and often corrupt during the 1950s. This figure all but disappeared from the screen in the 1960s and reappeared as a violent vigilante by the early 1970s. The hard-boiled private eye and *noir*-hero returned in the late 1970s and early 1980s, but the cop as action hero became the dominant type of detective by the mid-1980s. The 1990s and 2000s, however, saw the return of the sleuth in the educated, intelligent, middle-class criminalist. The secret to the continuous popularity of the detective genre is its malleability: it evolves and alters with shifting social attitudes and anxieties towards the law, crime, gender, and heroism.

Part III
Artists at Work

Fiction

Film

Fiction

28
William Godwin (1756–1836)

Philip Shaw

Caleb Williams, the first novel by the radical philosopher William Godwin, is a significant landmark in the history and genre of early crime fiction. Originally titled *Things as They Are; or, The Adventures of Caleb Williams*, the novel was composed in 1793, the year of Britain's entry into the war against revolutionary France, and was published the following year amid a political climate of paranoia and persecution. When Godwin began *Caleb Williams* he had recently completed an *Enquiry Concerning Political Justice and its Influence on General Virtue and Happiness*, a searching critique of the effects of political processes and institutions on human behavior and the potential for social reform. What complicates any easy alignment of the earlier treatise with the novel that followed it, however, is the latter's emphasis on action and incident. As Charles Rzepka notes, the appeal of the novel comes not from its presentation of abstract, philosophical ideas but rather from its investment in "the terror and mystery of crime; the obsessive thrills of flight, pursuit, arrest, and escape; and the daring use of incognito and disguise" (2005: 55). Yet as we shall see, while *The Adventures of Caleb Williams* owes a considerable debt to the popular vogue for true-crime tales, the novel's interest in criminal psychology, its fascination with the allure of transgression and its concern with miscarriages of justice are extraordinarily prescient. *Caleb Williams* can thus be read as a foundational text for the deductive preoccupations of the nineteenth-century "detective" novel *and* as a harbinger of the existential concerns of twentieth-century *noir* or hard-boiled fiction (see Simpson, chapter 14 and Pepper, chapter 10 in this volume).

In his 1832 preface to the "Standard Novels" edition of *Fleetwood*, a novel first published in 1805, Godwin provided an account of the literary influences that had informed the composition of his earlier book. Somewhat surprisingly, the first texts Godwin mentions are religious: *The History of Mademoiselle de St Phale* (1690) and *God's Revenge against Murder and Adultery* (1770). The first is a polemical tale of Catholic oppression peppered with lurid accounts of kidnap and torture, the second a compilation of "tragical histories" in which an omniscient and jealous God is shown "perpetually pursuing the guilty, and laying open his most hidden retreats to the light of day" (Godwin 2000: 449). Both works have an important bearing on *Caleb Williams*'s treatment of the themes of moral integrity and the hounding of the innocent, but they also provide a template for the author's proto-Freudian insights into the complex relations between love and hate.

Godwin goes on in the preface to cite two rather more predictable influences, stating that he was "extremely conversant with the 'Newgate Calendar,' and the 'Lives of the Pirates'" (2000: 449). The *Newgate Calendar* or, to give it its formal title, *The Malefactor's Register; or The Newgate and Tyburn Calendar … from the Year 1700 to Lady-Day 1779*, was a collection of criminal tales, intended for moral instruction but enjoyed by many for its sensationalism. Notwithstanding the ubiquitous use of the "Providential Plot" (Kayman 1992: 62), in which crime is always followed by punishment, it was the extravagant accounts of trickery and evasion that elicited delight in the majority of readers. The "Lives of the Pirates" was a title given to Daniel Defoe's *A General History of the Robberies and Murders of the Most Notorious Pyrates* (1724), a similarly arresting account of criminal derring-do. As will become apparent, both works contain material bearing on the more adventurous aspects of Godwin's novel.

In addition to these influences, *Caleb Williams* is often read in relation to two major cultural trends of the eighteenth century: the Gothic and sensibility. In terms of the former, *Caleb Williams*'s atmosphere of suspense and terror, often set in strange, secret chambers, dank prison cells and crumbling ruins, owes much to the popular Gothic fictions of Horace Walpole (1717–97), William Beckford (1744–99) and Ann Radcliffe (1764–1823). Like many of these writers, Godwin betrays a fascination with the more extreme aspects of Calvinist and Catholic doctrine, particularly Calvinism's stress on the paranoia-inducing notion of omniscience and omnipresence, and Catholicism's emphasis on mystery, concealment and the inscrutable power of the supernatural. From the culture of sensibility Godwin adapted the theme of class conflict, using the psychological terrain of sensibility, with its stress on emotional responsiveness and extreme states of feeling, as a medium for exploring the relations between tyrannical landowners and their powerless servants. Samuel Richardson's *Pamela* (1740–1) is a particularly important text for Godwin in this respect, but Godwin goes further than Richardson in allowing his novel to become a staging ground for the exploration of radical political ideas. In light of this, Godwin can be linked with "Jacobin" contemporaries like Robert Bage (1728–1801), Elizabeth Inchbald (1753–1821) and Thomas Holcroft (1745–1809), all of whom wrote novels, stories, and plays in support of social and political reform. While *Caleb Williams* avoids, for the most part, the overly didactic ambitions of these writers, the novel shares their concern with psychological realism by showing, rather than stating, "the effects of social circumstance upon individual thought and behaviour" (Godwin 2000: 35). For Godwin, as I will go on to explain, fiction serves as a "lower" court of appeal, granting a voice to those denied a hearing by the "higher" legal framework.

Let us consider now how the influences outlined above are manifested in the novel's plot, which centers on the intense and violent relationship between Ferdinando

Falkland, a powerful figure of authority, and Caleb Williams, his naive and culpable disciple. From the outset Falkland is portrayed as a man of exquisite sensibility. Described as "kind, attentive and humane" (Godwin 2000: 61), Falkland uses his wealth and power for the advancement of the general good. With his devotion to reason, Falkland is, in many ways, the embodiment of the socially progressivist ideals set out in Godwin's *Enquiry*. As Falkland's history is recounted, however, it soon becomes apparent that reason is not the only principle to which he adheres. A misplaced sense of honor and an excessive attachment to archaic notions of chivalry are shown to be in conflict with the Enlightenment pursuit of truth and justice. Falkland's benignity, moreover, is not consistent: "his disposition," we are told, "was extremely unequal ... sometimes he was hasty, peevish and tyrannical ... sometimes he entirely lost his self-possession, and his behaviour was changed into frenzy" (2000: 63). In his position as Falkland's secretary, Caleb Williams, a talented young man of humble origins, becomes witness to his master's strange fits of passion. Possessed by an insatiable curiosity, fueled in part by "an invincible attachment to books of narrative and romance," Caleb, in one of many references within the novel to the power of fiction, confesses that he "panted for the unravelling of an adventure" (2000: 60). When, early on in his employment, he stumbles upon his master hastily shutting the lid of a mysterious trunk, his curiosity is naturally aroused, the more so when Falkland reacts to his servant's discovery with a torrent of paranoid invective. The trunk, the contents of which are never revealed, functions in the narrative as a Hitchcockian McGuffin, an empty plot device around which the desires of the central characters circulate and towards which they are inexorably drawn.

With his taste for Gothic adventure whetted by this incident, the secretary learns more about the origins of his master's erratic behavior through listening to the account of Falkland's steward, Mr Collins. It is from Collins that Caleb discovers his employer's involvement in a lengthy and tempestuous dispute with his nearest neighbor, the boorish and brutal Barnabas Tyrrel. Tyrrel and Falkland are presented in the novel as diametrical opposites: the one physical, conservative, instinctive, and tyrannical; the other cerebral, liberal, rational, and benevolent. In many ways, Tyrrel – the name suggests "tyrant" – embodies the very forces of ignorance and prejudice that Godwin's concept of political justice was designed to dispel. Tyrrel, however, is immovable and no amount of reasoning on the part of his perceived antagonist, Falkland, can prevent him from pursuing his destructive course. It is at this point that the fiction provides a somewhat gloomy commentary on the *Enquiry's* advocacy of social progressivism. With echoes of the regressive Calvinistic doctrine of damnation, Falkland's subsequent downfall is described by Collins as being the result of "the uninterrupted persecution of a malignant destiny" (2000: 74) and, in a revealing moment, Falkland is described by Tyrrel as haunting him like a "demon" (2000: 90).

Matters come to a head between the antagonists as a result of Tyrrel's cruel treatment of his orphaned cousin, the sensitive and good-natured Emily Melville. Noticing that Emily has developed an attachment to Falkland, Tyrrel resolves to commit her to a wholly unsuitable marriage with the son of a local farmer. Repulsed by this proposal, Emily, who by this time has become a virtual prisoner in Tyrrel's home, determines to escape. Following a dramatic pursuit, she is eventually taken under the protection of Falkland, only to succumb to the effects of a grave illness brought on by the stresses of her recent trials. When Emily dies, the community turns against Tyrrel; he is publicly humiliated at a local assembly presided over by Falkland. Ashamed of his defeat, Tyrrel takes revenge on his accuser by violently and publicly assaulting him. It is this event, a social catastrophe for a man as strongly attached to notions of chivalry and honor as Falkland, that motivates him, in the end, to give vent to his repressed feelings of rage and murder Tyrrel.

What renders Falkland's act doubly ignoble is his calculated endeavor to protect himself from suspicion; the author, it should be noted, conspires at this point with the perpetrator by rendering the question of his guilt or innocence ambiguous. When rumors begin to circulate that Falkland is indeed the murderer of Tyrrel, he defends himself with sublime eloquence at a magistrate's hearing. Falkland's speech, greeted with "applause and involuntary transport" by "all ranks and degrees" (2000: 172–3), dispels these rumors, but the charge is definitively quashed following the discovery of a bloody parcel of clothes belonging to a Mr Hawkins who, like Emily, was a victim of Tyrrel's tyranny. Eventually, following the discovery of further evidence, Hawkins and his son are tried and executed. Although the reader is not told that Falkland has anything to do with this sudden turn of events, he is shown from this moment to be a significantly changed man: "[h]e now made himself a rigid recluse ... [t]here was a solemn sadness in his manner ... a stately coldness and reserve in his behaviour," interrupted, as Collins observes, by sporadic outbursts of "furious insanity. At these times his language is fearful and mysterious, and he seems to figure to himself by turns every sort of persecution and alarm which may be supposed to attend upon an accusation of murder" (2000: 175).

It is this behavior that arouses the suspicions of Caleb Williams. "Was it possible," he asks, "that Mr. Falkland should be the murderer?" (2000: 180). Having resolved to keep watch on his patron, Caleb gives in to his taste for intrigue and adventure. The delight he takes in observing Falkland is presented in a manner reminiscent of the febrile intensity of Gothic romance:

> To be a spy upon Mr. Falkland! That there was danger in the employment, served to give an alluring pungency to the choice. I remembered the stern reprimand I had received, and his terrible looks; and the recollection gave a kind of tingling sensation, not altogether unallied to enjoyment. The farther I advanced, the more the sensation was irresistible ... The more impenetrable Mr. Falkland was determined to be, the more uncontrollable was my curiosity. (2000: 180–1)

From here on Caleb taunts his master with his suspicions, conveyed indirectly through literary allusions and suggestive anecdotes. Throughout this deadly game, the two men are linked by "magnetic sympathy" (2000: 186), for behind the game there is real love. It must be emphasized at this point that Godwin's novel provides an acute insight into the relations between curiosity and desire. In a manner prefiguring the highly sexualized writings of Raymond Chandler (1888–1959) and Dashiell Hammett (1894–1961), the language in which Caleb expresses his fascination with his master's secret is distinctly erotic in tone: significantly, the "more impenetrable" the master determines to be, "the more uncontrollable" is the servant's curiosity. (For more on the writings of Chandler and Hammett, see Panek, chapter 32 and Hall, chapter 36 in this volume.)

Significantly, it is through literature, and specifically through the reading of a hidden or forbidden text, that Caleb is led, inexorably, into a confrontation with Falkland. The text in question is a letter, written by Hawkins, which casts doubt over the man's involvement in Tyrrel's murder. When Caleb presents this evidence, the master responds with a typically elevated speech, the effect of which is to prompt Caleb to declare, "Sir, I could die to serve you! I love you more than I can express. I worship you as a being of superior nature" (2000: 197). Godwin draws here on the link between sublime expression and physical or emotional "rapture," a link articulated in the first century CE by Longinus in *Peri Hupsous* or *On the Sublime*. In Longinus's account, sublime rhetoric "ravishes" or "transports" the listener; it exerts "an irresistible force and mastery, and get[s] the upper hand with every hearer" (Longinus 1965: 100). The sublimity of Falkland's speech is checked, however, by the return of Caleb's readerly curiosity. In a passage reminiscent of Edmund Burke's contemporary exposition of the sublime (Burke 1990), Caleb describes his curiosity as "a principle that carries its pleasures, as well as its pains, along with it" (Godwin 2000: 199). His painful pleasure, it should be noted, is informed by and focused on the reading of texts.

What the novel thus constructs is a conflict between two competing accounts of the sublime: a classical version focused on the persuasive powers of speech and a modern version centered on the act of reading. While the former posits a relationship between master and slave, the latter takes for granted the right of the individual to determine the truth for him or herself. For Caleb, sublime reading thus becomes a painful pleasure because it throws his mind into perpetual restlessness. No sooner has the servant experienced the regressive delight of giving way to the force of his master's speech than, as self-enfranchised reader, he turns, once again, to question the veracity of that speech:

> The fluctuating state of my mind produced a contention of opposite principles that by turns usurped dominion over my conduct. Sometimes I was influenced by the most complete veneration for my master ... at other times the confidence ... began to ebb (2000: 198).

Eventually, following another incident that forces Caleb to doubt, definitively, Falkland's protestations of innocence, he experiences for himself "a kind of rapture," a "soul-ravishing calm," a "state of mental elevation." Yet, despite having internalized the master's power, Caleb clings, incessantly, to the object of his desire: "I felt ... that it was possible to love a murderer" (2000: 207–8).

In anticipation of Thomas De Quincey's 1827 essay, "On Murder Considered as One of the Fine Arts" (De Quincey 2006), Godwin conveys here a profound insight into the psychological underpinnings of the crime genre. Caleb is motivated not out of sympathy for the murder victim but rather out of a fascination with the murderer, the sublime "artist" whose genius is manifested in the execution and concealment of transgression. What Caleb the reader desires is precisely the *je ne sais quoi* that enables the master to present himself as a self-authorizing figure, above and beyond the law. When an opportunity to discover Falkland's secret presents itself, the servant does not hesitate to seize it. The climactic moment occurs when, in the chaos and confusion of a house fire, Caleb is directed "by some mysterious fatality" (2000: 210) to return to the mysterious trunk, his discovery of which, earlier in the narrative, had aroused Falkland's wrath. Here again Caleb's endeavors to disclose the truth are frustrated by the sudden entrance of the master; with his appearance "the lid dropt down" and the trunk's contents remain forever concealed (2000: 211). In the aftermath of the incident, which Caleb calls "the crisis of my fate" (2000: 212), Falkland confesses to his crime. But his confession only serves to tip the balance of power between the two men, with the employer vowing to kill his servant in the event of any disclosure (2000: 215). Subsequently Caleb becomes a virtual prisoner in Falkland's house, his movements observed, his every word and gesture scrutinized.

Following a failed attempt to extricate himself from his master's grasp, Caleb is framed for robbery and is committed to jail. It is at this point that Godwin indulges his enthusiasm for *The Newgate Calendar*. Inspired by the *Calendar*'s account of the jail-breaker Jack Sheppard, he shows Caleb mounting a series of daring escapes from prison, eventually finding temporary refuge with a gang of outlaws. The gang is led by Captain Raymond, a character based on "the justified criminal rebel" Dick Turpin. Raymond is an articulate and rational man with a taste for radical polemic. "Our profession," he announces, "is the profession of justice ... We who are thieves without a licence ... are at open war with another set of men who are thieves according to law" (2000: 307). Although admiring the energy and enthusiasm of the outlaws, and even sharing, to some extent, their rejection of established codes of behavior, Caleb questions the identification of thievery and class war, arguing along utilitarian lines that crime is ultimately to the detriment of human society. The political debate is terminated when, following the threat of betrayal by the unscrupulous gang member Gines and a subsequent attack by the gang's presiding matriarch, Caleb is forced on the run again.

From here on, *The Adventures of Caleb Williams* justifies its title as the hero endeavors, through increasingly daring and elaborate means, to evade capture. Once again the *Newgate*'s influence is notable, as Caleb becomes an expert in disguise, passing first as an Irish beggar, then as a Jew and finally as an invalid. The identities the hero assumes are in themselves significant, as they serve to highlight the plight of the poor and dispossessed, and the victims of racial and religious prejudice, linking the novel, once again, with the revolutionary counter-currents of the 1790s. But even as the novel lays stress on the rational causes and logical consequences of social injustice, Caleb frequently casts himself as the victim of a malignant spirit. His pursuit by Gines, a former gang member now working in the service of Falkland, thus has an air of unreality to it, with the pursuer demonstrating an almost superhuman ability to track his quarry. Although clearly inspired by the *Newgate Calendar's* account of the notorious "thief-taker" Jonathan Wilde (1689–1725), a thief himself whose fortune was founded on the extortion and coercion of other thieves, Godwin imbues Gines with metaphysical significance, depicting him as the instrument of an omniscient deity whose "power reach[es] through all space" and whose "eye penetrate[s] every concealment" (2000: 335–6).

But Gines is not the only instrument of Falkland's will. The other principle shaping Caleb's destiny is literature itself. This principle is materialized in the hand-bill Gines uses to menace his prey. Giving details of Caleb Williams's "crime," the hand-bill, which has been deliberately printed and circulated, first, by Forester, Falkland's relation and magistrate, and then, in a more elaborate form by Gines himself, prompts Caleb to experience an uncanny feeling of disassociation as he becomes the subject of a narrative outside his control. Styled "as the notorious housebreaker, Kit Williams" (2000: 330), Caleb overhears a conversation in which he is described as "a devilish cunning fellow"; despite the fear of discovery, he admits to feeling "enjoyment" when a young woman confesses that she "loved him for his cleverness" (2000: 331–2). Here again curiosity is freighted with erotic overtones, further emphasizing the links between narrative, criminal, and sexual desire.

The sense in which the hero's fate is determined by the conventions of popular crime fiction is sustained when, in London, having taken on the identity of a Jew, Caleb determines to make his living through literature. In a passage reflecting Godwin's own recent history, Caleb relates how he becomes a crime writer, drawing on his enthusiasm for "the histories of celebrated robbers" (2000: 357) to peddle incident-filled tales for the readers of a popular newspaper. This proves, in the end, to be his undoing as, following a chance encounter with the publisher, Gines is able to track him down. In a further meta-fictional gesture Caleb, having escaped capture, overhears a street hawker attempting to sell "*the* MOST WONDERFUL AND SURPRISING HISTORY AND MIRACULOUS ADVENTURES OF CALEB WILLIAMS" (2000: 368). Even when Caleb gains what appears to be a permanent reprieve from his pursuer, the text returns, like the Freudian repressed, to dash the fantasy of self-determination.

It may be that Godwin's ambivalent feelings towards the genre of crime fiction are revealed in Caleb's bitter reflection that his "fame" is "miserable": "to have my story bawled forth by hawkers and ballad-mongers, to have my praises as an active and enterprising villain celebrated among footmen and chambermaids" (2000: 374). Godwin, it seems, is troubled by the low cultural status of the genre, and it may be that he too fears becoming the prisoner of his own creation: in any case, towards the end of the story Caleb confesses that "[w]riting, which was at first a pleasure, is changed into a burthen" (2000: 409). But despite this admission the hero reaffirms his faith, right up to the end, in the ability of textual evidence to convey the truth. "I will tell a tale," Caleb announces, "[t]he justice of the country shall hear me! ... [Falkland] may hunt me out of the world. – In vain! With this engine, this little pen, I defeat all his machinations; I stab him in the very point he was most solicitous to defend!" (2000: 421–2).

Godwin's original draft for the novel's "Postscript" has Caleb committed to a prison, his mental health deteriorating following a disastrous attempt to indict his master in a court of law. Dissatisfied with this pessimistic conclusion, Godwin redrafted the scene, granting Caleb a moving soliloquy, poured out with such "uncontrollable impetuosity" that "[e]very one that heard me was petrified with astonishment ... [and] melted into tears" (2000: 432). In what amounts to a repetition of the court room scene enacted earlier, the transference of sublimity from master to servant prompts Falkland to repent and to honor Caleb's claim to justice: "'Williams,' said he, 'you have conquered! I see too late the greatness and elevation of your mind'" (2000: 432). But the idea that elevated speech alone should settle a matter of guilt or innocence is highly dubious, not least when it is founded on a neo-Longinian association between noble rhetoric and noble character. Thus the novel suggests, somewhat despairingly, that only those capable of sublime powers of persuasion will be granted recognition in an aristocratic system of law. In the end it is left to Caleb to articulate this feeling, announcing to Falkland with rueful candor:

> I began these memoirs with the idea of vindicating my character. I have now no character that I wish to vindicate: but I will finish them that thy story may be fully understood; and that, if those errors of thy life be known which thou so ardently desired to conceal, the world may at least not hear and repeat a half-told and mangled tale. (2000: 434)

29

Edgar Allan Poe (1809–1849)

Maurice S. Lee

From the beginning to the end of his career in prose fiction, Edgar Allan Poe is obsessed with crime. His first story, "Metzengerstein" (1832), describes the punishment of a prince who burns down a rival's palace. His final tale, "Hop-Frog" (1849), is about a court jester who dresses a king and his ministers as apes before chaining them together and setting them on fire. In between are other lurid crimes: the potential poisoning of a wife in "Ligeia" (1838); the stabbing of a twin in "William Wilson" (1843); the disfiguring of a cat and (somehow less shocking) axing of a wife in "The Black Cat" (1843); the entombing of a drunken nemesis in "The Cask of Amontillado" (1846). Less murderously, Poe's essay "Diddling Considered as One of the Exact Sciences" (1843) catalogs various confidence scams, and "The Man of the Crowd" (1840) attempts (somewhat unsuccessfully) to portray "the type and the genius of deep crime" (Poe 1984: 396). Poe is justly famous for Gothic tales that focus on the dark side of human nature; and he certainly hopes to shock his audience at a time when literature was often expected to comfort readers with moral lessons. Yet as much as Poe's fiction revels in the grotesque details of crimes, it is more interested in the drama of such crimes coming to light. "The Tell-Tale Heart" (1843) and "The Imp of the Perverse" (1845) take the form of a murderer's confession, while "Berenice" (1835) and "'Thou Art the Man'" (1844) spectacularly expose criminal acts. Poe's most sustained narratives of crime and revelation are his detective stories, which in many respects represent his greatest literary achievement.

As much as works of detective fiction are driven by the desire to uncover a culprit, detective fiction as a genre has no single mastermind. With various roots in classical literature, Gothic novels, and popular crime narratives, detective fiction in even its earliest forms cannot be limited to one lineage or set of conventions. That said, if anyone can be taken to be the inventor of detective fiction, it is Poe, whose crime-solving protagonist, C. Auguste Dupin, appears in three short stories – "The Murders in the Rue Morgue" (1841), "The Mystery of Marie Roget" (1842–3), and

"The Purloined Letter" (1844). Written before the word "detective" was coined in 1847, what Poe called his "tales of ratiocination" established a new form of crime fiction.

The Dupin stories have been broadly influential since their first appearance in American popular magazines in the early 1840s. Charles Dickens's *Bleak House* (1853) and Fyodor Dostoevsky's *Crime and Punishment* (1866) have characters indebted to Dupin. In Britain in the later nineteenth and early twentieth centuries (as Martin Kayman 1992 has shown), Poe's tales helped shape the detective fiction of Wilkie Collins (see Mangham, chapter 30 in this volume), G. K. Chesterton, and Arthur Conan Doyle (see Hodgson, chapter 31 in this volume). Emile Gaboriau in France and Edogawa Rampo in Japan also drew from the Dupin stories when pioneering detective writing in their native tongues. And though Poe's influence may be less direct in the hard-boiled and golden age detective fiction of the early and mid-twentieth century, it resurfaces in postmodern detective works (see Merivale, chapter 24 in this volume) from such authors as Eco Umberto (Italy), Paul Auster (the United States), and especially Jorge Luis Borges (Argentina – see Borinsky, chapter 37 in this volume). Matthew Pearl's novel, *The Poe Shadow* (2006), is just one recent example of the many texts that continue to re-imagine Poe's detective fiction. Like one of Poe's corpses that will not stay dead, the presence of Dupin haunts modern culture – from the "high" realm of academic literary criticism and poststructural theory to more popular forms such as comics, film, television, and song lyrics. Poe sometimes suffered from delusions of grandeur, but even he did not anticipate a remarkable fact about his detective writing: no set of tales has had more impact on literature and culture in the English-speaking world and beyond.

One reason for such influence is that the Dupin stories introduce but do not exhaust the possibilities of detective fiction, offering later writers a generative model open to improvisation. Recognizable conventions of detective fiction appear in one or more of the Dupin tales – the genius investigator, the astonished sidekick, the doppelganger-villain, the extraordinary crime, the locked room scenario, the dramatic unwinding of clues and conclusions. Poe also pursues thematic interests that survive in modern crime fiction in general and detective writing in particular – anxieties over race and sexuality, concerns about ethics and social control, commentaries (and meta-commentaries) on the reading of signs, the status of language, and the psychology of conspiracy and fear. Yet for all the conventions that Poe helps to establish, the Dupin tales are not conventional. Poe bombards the reader with literary allusions, extraneous facts, and apparent digressions. The narratives, as compelling as they may be, are not as smoothly executed or logically precise as some later examples of detective writing. To the modern reader of the genre, the Dupin stories can seem like old family photos: Strange in their historical distance and yet powerfully, oddly familiar. To better understand Poe's achievement and difference, this chapter will take a Dupin-like approach by moving from facts toward conjectures. First, we will examine the stories themselves, paying particular attention to the trials and errors of Poe's experimentation. Then we will address a more speculative question: How is it that Poe happened to become the primary founder of detective fiction?

"The Murders in the Rue Morgue"

At the center of "The Murders in the Rue Morgue" is an improbable plot: an orangutan escapes from the sailor who owns him, climbs through a fourth story window, and kills a mother and daughter in their seemingly locked room, thus baffling the city police. Poe has certainly (to use one of Dupin's favorite words) imagined an "*outré*" situation, and yet at first glance the tale does not appear to be a work of fiction at all. Poe begins in an expository mode with a challenging (if somewhat haphazardly rendered) set of philosophical problems. The most basic of these – that the "analytic" powers themselves are "but little susceptible of analysis" – foregrounds the longstanding Cartesian paradox that the mind, which performs operations of knowing, cannot accurately know itself (Poe 1984: 397). Like much of Poe's writing, "The Murders in the Rue Morgue" explores the limits of human reason, in this instance subordinating the mechanical logic of chess to a method that Poe associates with whist (a card game similar to bridge). The method of the whist player is not fully explained: it seems like "intuition" (Poe 1984: 397), is "inaccessible to the ordinary understanding" (Poe 1984: 398), and involves "observations and inferences" (Poe 1984: 399). But if the vagueness of Poe's description supports his point that the analytic powers cannot be analyzed, Poe also makes clear that he is not seeking simply to mystify or thrill, for at the outset he envisions his story as a kind of thought experiment.

The introduction of C. Auguste Dupin shows that "The Murders in the Rue Morgue" is an experiment of much imaginative license. Living in Paris, a city Poe did not know firsthand, Dupin's character is marked by a lack of family, employment, and even sunshine. Like many protagonists of detective fiction, his status on the margins of traditional social structures is analogous to his ability to think "outside the box" and thereby outperform official investigators such as the Prefect of Police. This is to a lesser extent the case with the story's unnamed narrator, who himself lacks history, family, and employment and is in many ways a mirror image of Dupin. Indicating their shared position on the borders between isolation and community, crime and convention, the narrator says of himself and Dupin, "We existed within ourselves alone" (Poe 1984: 401).

As critics from Jacques Lacan to Jacques Derrida to John Irwin have shown, the trope of doubling that appears throughout the Dupin tales is open to much interpretation. Philosophically, Poe is interested in the problem of other minds: Can we ever really know another person, or is our perception of the outside world merely a reflection of our own point of view? Psychologically, doubling can involve projection – the displacing of socially unacceptable desires onto other people or agents. Leland Person (2001) has shown how Poe's fiction frequently exerts violent control over women; and it is not difficult to find in "The Murders in the Rue Morgue" projected misogyny and sexual aggression. Other readers, including J. A. Leo Lemay (1982), have detected a homosocial or homosexual dynamic between Dupin and the narrator, who expresses passionate attachment for his fellow bachelor and roommate as they walk arm in arm through the nights of a city associated with sexual license. It is also possible to speculate that Poe found in Dupin a more general object of wish fulfillment. Like Poe, Dupin is a well-read genius raised in wealth but fallen on hard economic times. Unlike Poe, who (justifiably) felt under-appreciated by his culture, Dupin in "The Murders in the Rue Morgue" is a conquering hero.

Other doublings in the story implicate readers themselves. Like the narrator, we witness Dupin's investigations and listen at length to his discourses. Like Dupin, we attempt to uncover hidden meanings, so much so that the role of the literary critic becomes eerily similar to that of the detective. We can even feel like the horrified sailor who cannot help but watch the murders through the window of the apartment. We may actually want to be that sailor, to know precisely what took place, even though – or rather, especially because – the knowledge is so terrible. Fiction in general and detective writing in particular invite readers to assume the place of another. But whereas identification in nineteenth-century sentimentalism is marked by benevolent sympathy, in Poe's world of guilty pleasures, it can feel more like voyeurism with all the potential for exploitation and sensationalism that the term connotes. With doubling everywhere in the tale, "The Murders in the Rue Morgue" is like a hall of mirrors in which possible reflections, projections, and identifications cannot be stabilized.

Only Dupin seems capable of navigating the labyrinth of the story. After his intro-duction, one might expect the murders to be announced, though Poe offers instead a curious section describing how Dupin reads the narrator's mind, again returning the reader's attention to Dupin's "method – if method there is" (Poe 1984: 402). Whether or not the scene is believable, it plays an important role in the tale. When Dupin claims that men wear "windows in their bosoms," he foreshadows the solution to the Rue Morgue case (Poe 1984: 401). The individual steps in the narrator's thought process are also thematically suggestive: the would-be actor Chantilly and the *Théatre des Variétés* highlight the malleability of identity, while the Latin quote about letters losing their sounds points toward the inaccuracy of words (a problem evident when witnesses mistake the orangutan's screams for various foreign languages). Additionally, Dupin's mind-reading dramatizes the psychological theory of associationism. For eighteenth- and nineteenth-century mental philosophers, thoughts follow other thoughts according to set laws. Dupin has clearly mastered this theory, though his suppositions – seemingly the result of his preternatural intuition – are in part based on and corroborated by his empirical observation of the narrator. Only after this example of Dupin's method does Poe begin the main plot of his tale, which offers Dupin a more dramatic opportunity to demonstrate his investigative genius.

The grisly facts of the Rue Morgue murders showcase Poe's crafted sensationalism. A bloody razor is disturbing, but one placed on a chair with seeming care in the midst of "wildest disorder" is chilling (Poe 1984: 405). A corpse is bad, but a "quite warm" one is worse, just as a "fearfully mutilated" head is more fearsome when it falls off its body (Poe 1984: 406). Particularly in nineteenth-century America, where domestic ideology made a kind of religion out of the sanctity of the home and the sexual purity of women, "The Murders in the Rue Morgue" is especially horrifying as a kind of home invasion. That the bloody tresses of hair are gray emphasizes that neither gender nor age spared Madame L'Espanaye. That the body of her daughter was "forced up the narrow aperture" of the chimney, hints not only at images of rape, but also suggests the violation of the hearth, a main symbol of domestic life. As Elise Lemire (2001) and others have shown, race also figures in the tale. Racist ideology of the period associated Africans with apes; African-Americans in the North and South often worked as barbers and grooms; and the fears of supposedly rapacious blacks and the impurities of race mixing formed a powerful subtext in the slavery debate, which had already reached a fevered pitch by the early 1840s. From Thomas Dixon's racist depictions of African-Americans to William Faulkner's Joe Christmas to Richard Wright's Bigger Thomas – and including real-life sensational cases such as the Scottsboro Boys and O. J. Simpson – the specter of black violence on the white female body has gripped the imagination of many Americans well beyond Poe's time.

Another unnerving aspect of "The Murders in the Rue Morgue" is that the authorities and even reason itself seem helpless. As Michel Foucault has famously argued, social control requires not only the physical containment of crime; it also needs to demonstrate – that is, perform and narrate – that containment for the general populace. In this sense, the murders in the Rue Morgue publicly demonstrate the failure of authority: the Paris newspapers call it a "spectacle" and "{t}ragedy" and complain that "[t]he police are entirely at fault" (Poe 1984: 405, 406, 411). Even worse, the harder the police work on the crime, the more it seems to be beyond human reason. Other Poe works – for instance, *The Narrative of Arthur Gordon Pym* (1838) and "The Facts in the Case of M. Valdemar" (1845) – turn to supernatural forces to explain impossible events. "The Murders in the Rue Morgue" differs in that rational solutions are possible; and Poe goes to great lengths to discuss and dramatize what the appropriate methods of detection are.

Dupin is a better investigator than the police, because he is willing to follow his intuition. The police make "a vast parade of measures" but err in examining objects "too close" (Poe 1984: 412). They are over-committed to empiricism and induction (reasoning from facts to general principles). Dupin is also a careful empiricist: he examines the crime scene with "a minuteness of attention" and "scrutinize[s] every thing" (Poe 1984: 413). But if his "inductions" follow the lead of the police (Poe 1984: 418), he also makes "deductions" that move his thinking from general principles to facts (Poe 1984: 416), even if his principles are hypotheses or, as he later says, "guesses" (Poe 1984: 425). As logicians of the eighteenth and nineteenth centuries showed, induction must be guided by some form of deduction; for without a set of governing rules or assumptions, there is no way to decide what facts to gather or how to arrange them in meaningful patterns. Dupin's trick is to combine induction and deduction, empiricism and theory, in a dialectical process that – as David Van Leer (1993) notes – can generally be identified as the scientific method. Dupin observes the apartment, hypothesizes that something is wrong with the nail, and tests his conjectures with further evidence. As a result, the orangutan is captured and placed in the *Jardin des Plantes* – a renowned museum of natural science and a symbol of enlightenment order. After all the brutal killing and chaos of the tale, reason appears to triumph.

However, as skeptical readers note, it is hard to explain a step in Dupin's method. Where do his hypotheses come from? How does he make the leaps in logic that lead to an escaped orangutan, particularly because the evidence he finds does not point solely to this conclusion? It is at this moment that Dupin's analysis cannot itself be analyzed. As he abruptly declares when reconstructing the details of the murders: "I will not pursue these guesses – for I have no right to call them more – since the shades of reflection upon which they are based are scarcely of sufficient depth to be appreciable by my own intellect" (Poe 1984: 425). Suddenly Dupin's method seems more like intuition, something beyond the realm of self-conscious reason. Just as the head of the nail is separated from its body – indeed, just as Madame L'Espanaye is practically decapitated and the Prefect of Police is "all head and no body" (Poe 1984: 431) – "The Murders in the Rue Morgue" suggests that the intellect is distinct from more intuitive ways of knowing (as when one has a "gut feeling"). We will return to the question of intuition, but for now a final point should be made: Though Dupin solves the murders in the Rue Morgue and subordinates racialized, sexualized violence to scientific reason, the origins of intuition remain murky. The enduring mystery is how exactly the mystery was solved.

"The Mystery of Marie Roget"

What little success Poe enjoyed in his life often went to his head. "The Murders in the Rue Morgue" was quite popular after appearing in *Graham's Magazine* in 1841. The story was even reprinted in French journals, helping to establish Poe's enduring reputation. But instead of writing another detective story that would allow him to solve a puzzle of his own devising, Poe took on an actual mystery – the case of Mary Rogers, whose body was found in the Hudson River in 1841. Like the tabloid and (increasingly) mainstream press of the twenty-first century, newspapers of the time reported at length on the sensational facts of the case. In "The Mystery of Marie Roget," Poe attempts to account for Rogers's death in a thinly disguised fictional form – moving the setting to Paris, changing names to French equivalents, and voicing his conjectures through Dupin. That Poe sets Dupin on a real world case suggests how seriously he believed in the methods employed in "The Murders in the

Rue Morgue"; and that Poe was willing to test his ratiocination so publicly indicates how confident and imprudent he could be.

Poe was not entirely misguided in thinking that he might help to untangle the Mary Rogers mystery. In an early essay, "Maetzel's Chess-Player" (1836), Poe correctly surmised that a touring chess automaton actually contained a hidden dwarf; and in a review from May, 1841, he predicted the murderer in Dickens's *Barnaby Rudge* (1841) before the novel was fully serialized. As Shawn Rosenheim (1997) has discussed, Poe considered himself an accomplished cryptologist, challenging readers to send him coded messages (which, according to Poe, never once stumped him). Unfortunately, "The Mystery of Marie Roget" did not work out so nicely. The story appeared in three parts between November 1842 and February 1843. But between the second and third installments, the deathbed confession of an innkeeper revealed that Rogers died from a botched abortion – a possibility that Poe had not considered, and one that showed some of his earlier conclusions to be false (most notably, that a jealous ex-lover was the culprit). As Laura Saltz (1995) has pointed out, Poe is strangely and powerfully silent on the discovery of the deadly abortion. The final installment of "The Mystery of Marie Roget" offers some vague disclaimers, and Poe added footnotes to a later edition to make his mistakes less egregious. Yet if "The Mystery of Marie Roget" remains a flawed (though for some, riveting) performance, it also sheds light on the evolution of Poe's detective fiction.

In some respects, "The Mystery of Marie Roget" follows the example of Poe's first detective story. "Roget" explicitly mentions "The Murders in the Rue Morgue" and adopts a similar narrative form. After some initial philosophical exposition and the reporting of facts through quoted newspaper articles, Dupin's analytic powers are brought to bear and explained to the appreciative narrator. Poe continues to contrast the plodding efforts of the police to Dupin's brilliant method of "inductions" and "intuition" (Poe 1984: 508). The story also discusses sensational subjects, such as how long it takes a decomposing body to float. Before Poe even learned of Rogers's abortion, he emphasized sexualized details – the "youth and beauty of the victim" (Poe 1984: 509), the "charge against her chastity" (Poe 1984: 516), the possibility of rape, the amount of hair and type of garters used to identify the corpse. As with "The Murders in the Rue Morgue" – and anticipating Poe's infamous statement that the death of a beautiful woman is the most poetic subject – "The Mystery of Marie Roget" lingers over the body of its female victim.

What most distinguishes "Roget" from "The Murders in the Rue Morgue" is the nature of the crime. As Dupin emphasizes, the death of Roget is not an *outré* event; for while a razor-wielding orangutan is more or less unexpected, women disappear with "great frequency, in large cities" (Poe 1984: 510), making the Roget case an "*ordinary*" one (Poe 1984: 519). Mark Seltzer (2004) has shown how this increases the horror of the story: how many others have suffered the same end as Roget? At the same time, the very typicality of the crime poses an analytic challenge. "The Murders in the Rue Morgue" calculates according to chance and probability, which is one reason Poe prefers whist to chess: whereas the chess-like logic of the police makes them incapable of imaginative speculation, Dupin is more open to explanations that include unlikely and even random events.

"The Mystery of Marie Roget" departs from this specific line of reasoning as Dupin practices a method more sociological than psychological and more interested in averages than anomalies. Poe continues to present Dupin as an expert in the "Calculus of Probabilities" (Poe 1984: 507). But because cases like Roget's occur often in big cities, Poe uses what statisticians and probability theorists call a "frequentist" model that bases predictions, not on intuitive leaps, but on large samples of data. When estimating how long bodies stay underwater, Dupin wishes that he could draw his conclusions from "fifty instead of five examples" (Poe 1984: 523); and he discusses Roget's "probable" routes and the "average diversity" of her walks (Poe 1984: 533). Dupin also speculates regarding odds: the chances are "ten to one" that Roget had eloped (Poe 1984: 537); general opinion is correct in "ninety-nine cases from the hundred" (Poe 1984: 539); the chances are "one thousand to one" that someone would find Roget's discarded clothes (Poe 1984: 543). At the beginning of the story, Poe (through Dupin) praises the calculus of probabilities: "[M]odern science has resolved to *calculate upon the unforeseen.* ... We subject the unlooked for and unimagined to the mathematical *formulae* of the schools" (Poe 1984: 534). Yet by the end of the story, Poe and Dupin recognize the "mistakes which arise in the path of Reason through her propensity for seeking truth *in detail*" (Poe 1984: 554). For all its careful argumentation and forensic evidence, the method of "The Mystery of Marie Roget" proves fallible in the real world. Frequentist logic may predict average outcomes in the long run, but it will not necessarily solve the individual case, which for Poe and the reader of detective fiction is the most important one.

"The Purloined Letter"

As if chastened by "The Mystery of Marie Roget," Poe's final tale of ratiocination returns to what works in "The Murders in the Rue Morgue" – a fully imagined story, a locked room in Paris, a sexually charged crime, and a challenge tailored, not for the number crunching frequentist, but for the intuitive genius. "The Purloined Letter" is in many ways a refinement of "The Murders in the Rue Morgue": the pacing is quicker; there are fewer red herrings; Poe begins immediately in a fictional mode, embedding sections of exposition within the action of the story. The economy of the tale is so efficient that it lacks the slowly realized suspense associated with detective fiction, making it difficult for readers to participate imaginatively in the solving of the crime. "The Purloined Letter" is a quick read. But as a text of surprising psychological, moral, and philosophical sophistication, it continues Poe's exploration of the possibilities of detective writing.

Dupin in this instance is up against, not an orangutan or medical accident, but rather an antagonist who has become a familiar presence in detective fiction – the villain who mirrors and thereby complicates the character of the investigator. In fact, "The Purloined Letter" is the only Dupin tale in which a definite culprit and crime exist: the Minister D— has been blackmailing the queen with a stolen letter he has hidden in his apartment. As in "The Murders in the Rue Morgue," the police are unable to solve the case because they rely too much on chess-like logic and empirical scrutiny. As the Prefect says: "We divided [the building's] entire surface into compartments, which we numbered, so that none might be missed; then we scrutinized each individual square inch throughout the premises" (Poe 1984: 685). By contrast, Dupin uses a less systematic method that "The Purloined Letter" associates with "'even and odd,'" a game similar to whist insofar as chance and intuition come into play (Poe 1984: 689). Dupin mentions a boy who has mastered the game through "an identification of the reasoner's intellect with that of his opponent," a process not entailing rational analysis so much as a kind of doubling that involves mimicking facial expressions and "wait[ing] to see what thoughts or sentiments arise in [the] mind or heart" (Poe 1984: 690). This method is remarkably modern in that Poe suggests that psychological states are driven by physiological causes and that the mind/body split of "The Murders in the Rue Morgue" is not as clean as sometimes supposed. By following his embodied intuitions achieved by mirroring his opponent, Dupin correctly concludes that the stolen letter is hidden in plain sight.

One reason Dupin's identification is so successful is that he and the Minister D— are so alike. Both are mathematicians and poets who anticipate their opponents; both are haughty geniuses with a love of the classics and an eye for telling clues. By doubling Dupin with the Minister D—, Poe not only makes a psychological point about intuitive processes, he also reveals the moral ambiguities of Dupin. More than in his previous adventures, Dupin in "The Purloined Letter" is openly hostile to authority figures. Moreover, his motives are far from pure. In "The Murders in the Rue Morgue," he is glad to exonerate an innocent man who once did him a favor. In "The Purloined Letter," he is driven by monetary gain, practically extorting fifty thousand francs from the Prefect. And – as we learn at the end the story – Dupin seeks revenge from the Minister D— who once did him an unspecified "evil turn" (Poe 1984: 698). "The Purloined Letter" smudges the line between detective and criminal, champion of truth and self-interested genius, particularly when Dupin steals back the stolen letter by committing forgery and faking the shooting of a child. In this sense, Dupin is aptly named: he shares the same initial (that is, *letter*) with his antagonist; both men attempt to *dupe* the other; and in a story of puns and hidden messages, Dupin's full initials spell "cad." Americans of the time might even have questioned whether Dupin fights on the right political side, for (as Irwin has shown) by returning the letter he helps the queen and royalists of France keep down their more democratic rivals.

Another important aspect of "The Purloined Letter" is its commentary on language, which critics in the traditions of Lacan and Derrida have explored in dense philosophical terms. As mentioned, "The Murders in the Rue Morgue" shows that words are subject to misunderstanding, for language is not directly representative of reality but instead is contingent on shifting contexts (such as the different linguistic backgrounds of the witnesses who differently interpret the orangutan's sounds). "The Purloined Letter" further exposes the gap between signs and things. The stolen letter can be taken as a written text and a symbol for all writing; and the fact that it eludes the empirical police suggests that language cannot be fully understood within the framework of scientific positivism. When Dupin makes an imperfect copy of the letter and forges its royal seal, the story further indicates that words are not entirely representative (even of words themselves) and that the authority of written language is by no means absolute. Perhaps most provocatively, Poe never reveals what the letter is actually about. It seems to have something to do with infidelity, continuing Poe's pattern of sexual subtexts, but the actual contents of the letter are never explicitly named. From Lacan's perspective, the meaning of the letter can be said to reside in its absence of meaning, for the power of blackmail requires that truths are not broadly communicated or known.

Poststructuralist readings of "The Purloined Letter" have, among other things, done much to expose the text's intricate linguistic play – the complicated deployment of classical allusions, the use of "odd" to mean both strange and uneven (Poe 1984: 680), the bilingual puns (for example, Dupin forges the seal with a piece of bread, and his own name echoes bread in French). Such readings also tend to suggest that interpretation of the story will never be complete, for – as with the stolen letter itself and all language in general – the meaning of "The Purloined Letter" will depend on whoever possesses it. Poe's last detective story can thus stand as a culmination of his tracing of the limits of reason. In "The Murders in the Rue Morgue," Dupin's methods remain beyond analysis. In "The Mystery of Marie Roget," Poe cannot solve his crime. Though Dupin in "The Purloined Letter" clearly emerges the victor, we do not know the contents of the letter, the fractious history of Dupin and the Minister D—, or (as Poe suggests in the language of gaming) whether their struggle will take yet another "turn." Poe never wrote another Dupin tale, though he lived for five years more, leaving the legacy of detective fiction to later authors and critics.

Why Poe?

The epigraph to "The Murders in the Rue Morgue" claims that even the most difficult mysteries "are not beyond *all* conjecture," a statement that can apply to the question of why Poe of all people invented detective fiction (Poe 1984: 397). Potential answers include biographical, literary, and cultural speculations, none of them mutually exclusive. Poe's fascination with crime is apparent in almost all of his fictional works; and stories like "The Imp of the Perverse" are highly attuned to the psychology of transgression, so much so that Poe can seem to anticipate uncannily Freudian thought. Poe also had a longstanding interest in puzzles, which we can see in tales like "The Gold-Bug" (1843), coded poems such as "Enigma" (1833), and essays like "A Few Words on Secret Writing" (1841). Poe even published coded messages that were not solved until the end of the twentieth century.

In addition to his insights into puzzles and crime, Poe also had an educational background that helped him think about detection from various perspectives. Poe was well schooled by his adopted family; and his exposure to classical literature and languages is evident in the Dupin tales, as is his training in mathematics (a subject in which he did well). Poe was also a follower of science – editing a book on conchology (the study of mollusk shells), writing a column on scientific advances, and publishing a cosmological work, *Eureka* (1848), near the end of his life. Poe was not only an early practitioner of what we now call science fiction, he joined in larger intellectual debates about the limits of logic and empiricism (see Dauncey, chapter 12 in this volume). These debates included philosophical thinkers; and though Poe was never a rigorous student of philosophy, his interest in transcendentalism helped him think critically about intuition and mind/body dualisms. The Dupin stories draw on Poe's reading in various disciplines, enriching his discussion of analysis, method, and detection.

Yet as much as Poe's "high" intellectual background helped him write about a fantastically knowledgeable investigator, much of the inspiration for the Dupin tales emanates from "low" sources. After dropping out of college because of gambling debts, Poe was disinherited and thrown into poverty. Meredith McGill and David Reynolds have shown how Poe's subsequent work as an editor and reviewer brought him in close contact with the Gothic mysteries and crime narratives that were everywhere in antebellum print culture – not only from luminaries like Dickens, but also from less remembered figures such as George Lippard and George Thompson. As an industry insider in financial straits, Poe drew on these popular traditions; and he specifically credited William Godwin's *Caleb Williams* (1794 – see Shaw, chapter 28 in this volume) for teaching him how to write a narrative backwards (that is, to envision the ending first and then work toward the beginning, a method Poe used in the Dupin tales). At the same time, Poe was keenly aware of the marketability of new subjects and narrative styles. Sharing the romantic urge for originality, Poe also had economic motives for his literary innovations.

Changing social conditions figure as well. In the decades before the Civil War, Poe lived in Richmond, Baltimore, Philadelphia, and New York City, witnessing firsthand the related phenomena of increasing urban density, growing city crime, and the rise of professional police forces. Obviously the "Mystery of Marie Roget" is grounded in an actual crime; and "The Murders in the Rue Morgue" mentions the real life crime-solver Eugène Vidocq, an ex-criminal who began the first private detective agency in 1833 in France. Drawing on intellectual and social discourses unavailable a generation before, Poe's Dupin tales are distinctly modern formally and thematically. So much does Poe reflect the concerns of his time one might argue that his tales of ratiocination come less from individual inspiration and more from a set of cultural forces: if Poe had never invented detective fiction, Dickens or Victor Hugo would have.

Of course, the Dupin tales remain distinctly Poe's own; for if Poe is not as singular a genius as he sometimes presents himself to be, no one in his time or since has written detective fiction in quite the same way. As an expansive thinker with interests ranging from philosophy to science to cryptology, as a student of psychology with no small streak of perversity and paranoia, as an orphan adopted by an aristocratic family who lived most of his life in urban poverty, and as a professional writer with aesthetic and economic desires for originality, Poe was the right person at the right place and time to establish a new kind of crime fiction.

30
Wilkie Collins (1824–1889)

Andrew Mangham

The Crime Sensation

Wilkie Collins's contribution to the genre of crime fiction is an important one: some would even say he practically invented the full-length British novel of detection. T. S. Eliot famously suggested as much in 1927, pointing to *The Moonstone* (1868) as the first and the greatest of English detective novels (Eliot 1960b: 413). Although this opinion remains the subject of an ongoing debate on literary criticism, most commentators tend to agree that the publication of *The Moonstone* gave a crucial turn to the shaping of crime fiction in English.

The genre to which this novel properly belongs is sensation fiction (see Pittard, chapter 7 in this volume), a style of writing that Collins spearheaded with *The Woman in White* in 1860. Throughout the 1860s Collins and his fellow Sensationists incurred a good deal of critical censure because they made crime one of their key preoccupations. Henry Mansel complained in 1863, for example, that if "a crime of extraordinary horror figures among our *causes célèbres* the sensationist is immediately at hand to weave the incident into a thrilling tale, with names and circumstances slightly disguised." There is, he continues, "something unspeakably disgusting in this ravenous appetite for carrion, this vulture-like instinct which smells out the newest mass of social corruption, and hurries to devour the loathsome dainty before the scent has evaporated" (Mansel 1863: 499, 503). "Murder, conspiracy, robbery, fraud, are the strong colours upon the national palette" (Oliphant 1863: 169), agreed Margaret Oliphant that same year, and Wilkie Collins was leading the way in exploiting this unseemly taste for blood.

Born in 1824 to an advantaged and artistic family, Collins trained as a lawyer in the 1840s before becoming an in-house writer for Dickens's *Household Words*. After closing the magazine down following a dispute with his publishers, Dickens launched the new periodical *All the Year Round*, featuring *The Woman in White* as its flagship serialization. It was after this publication that Collins's literary career truly took off.

He was always happy to admit that he drew much of his inspiration from the details connected with real crimes of the nineteenth century. He once wrote:

> I was in Paris wandering about the streets with Charles Dickens [... We were] amusing ourselves by looking into the shops. We came to an old bookstall – half shop and half store and I found some dilapidated volumes of records of French crimes, a sort of French *Newgate Calendar*. I said to Dickens "Here is a prize." So it turned out to be. In them I found some of my best plots. *The Woman in White* was one. (Baker 2002: 26)

His open appropriations of real crime stories are crucial to a full understanding of Collins's contribution to the genre of crime fiction. As we have seen, the author was criticized for a perceived morbid obsession with crime. Yet, what his critics seemed to have understood only partially is that the author took advantage of morbid sensitivities *already widespread* in the nineteenth century. When *The Woman in White* exploded onto the scene in 1860, audiences had already developed a keen taste for criminal fare. Real crimes were reported in the daily newspapers and read episodically in ways that prefigure the ways modern audiences consume soap operas. Figures such as William Palmer, Madeline Smith, and Constance Kent, all three of whom were tried for murder, became national celebrities; courtrooms were packed with spectators.

Like Dickens, Wilkie Collins worked as a journalist before becoming a novelist. As an employee of *Household Words*, he would have seen – first hand – how the public's imagination was gripped by actual criminal indictments. His legal training had given him the expertise to follow the minutiae of litigious procedure and many of his plots exploited actual loopholes in criminal and civil law. What he appeared to have noticed in these early years was that, unlike events in the "penny dreadful" literature and Newgate novels, the real cases were attracting a new, middle-class audience. By the time he was asked to contribute to *All the Year Round* in 1860, Collins had realized how ingrained crime, in particular, had become in bourgeois culture. *The Woman in White* thus combined Gothic melodrama with secret crimes within the "respectable" modern family. And so was born the formula that has dominated crime fiction ever since.

So why did the Victorians enjoy crime stories? And how did this become pivotal to their sense of their own culture? The answer is not as simple as we might expect. Crime stories, at first glance, appear to allow the reader to stake a claim to moral high ground that is palpably different to the lower footings occupied by the likes of Bill Sikes. In reading about such rogues, we may rest assured that we are simply better than they are. When it comes to the Wilkie Collins novel, however, there emerges a problem with this convenient supposition: here all of the major criminals appeared to be from the middle or upper classes. Palmer, Smith, and Kent were all middle class, while the villains of *The Woman in White*, Elizabeth Braddon's *Lady Audley's Secret* (1862), and Mrs Henry Wood's *East Lynne* (1862) were all aristocratic (or so it seems). The 1860s was a decade that shifted criminality, with the aid of Collins and his contemporaries, from the slum districts of London to the comfortable firesides of nineteenth-century suburbia. Henry James famously wrote of sensation fiction: 'Instead of the terrors of Udolpho, we [are] treated to the terrors of the cheerful country house, or the London lodgings. And there is no doubt that these [are] infinitely the more terrible' (Pykett 1994: 6). Worrying though this shift might seem, it actually formed part of a powerful machinery of surveillance. Figuring crime to be a possibility in every home was a sure-fire method of turning that environment into a place of observation, stricture, and control. Looking at instances of unmotivated domestic crime, Forbes Winslow wrote in 1860 that there exists "the supreme importance of cultivating in early life the habit of looking within, the practice of rigidly questioning ourselves as to what we are, and what we are doing" (Winslow 1868: 142). The Victorian age was the first period to open its household doors to the scrutiny of professionals like police detectives, forensic examiners, and psychologists.[1] This process formed part of the era's habit of "looking within." The family home was a precious retreat. Conceived as central to the maintenance of Britain's political power, it required protection and maintenance; reasons were needed for sending in the professionals whose job it was to guard and preserve the sanctity of British households. Cue the body in the drawing room.

Wilkie Collins was much more than a passive recorder of these cultural changes. Mansel and Oliphant were correct when they suggested that he exploited crime to create his novels but they were wrong when they implied that this is the sum of Collins's powers. The author wrote crime novels that were *about* crime; his texts offer an exploration of the way in which murder mysteries operated within the complex strands of Victorian culture. He is not content with simply retelling felony stories but also uses his radical new style of writing as the basis for an intricate commentary on his culture's obsession with murder.

The Murder of Francis Savile Kent

Murder was certainly a vivid color on the nation's palette in the years immediately preceding the publication of Collins's *The Moonstone*: the population was obsessed with the so-called Road Murder, the killing of Francis Savile Kent, in 1860. On the 3 July of that year the *Times* reported how "a shocking murder was perpetrated at Road, a village about four miles from Frome":

> About 7 o'clock, it was found that one of [Samuel Savile Kent's] sons, a fine lad of just four years of age, was missing from his cot in the nurse's room, in which he usually slept, and after an hour's search his body was found stuffed down the seat of a privy on the premises, the throat being cut so as almost to sever the head from the body, and a large stab being apparent near the heart, evidently inflicted after death, as no blood had flowed from it. The body was wrapped in a blanket belonging to its bed, and he appears to have been killed while still asleep. (Anon 1860a: 12)

Discussing the murder's possible wider significance, the newspaper's first reaction was to invoke the popular notion of the home as "sacred" and to cast the murder as a shocking encroachment on its values:

> It is certain that the value of human life, the security of families, and the sacredness of English households demand that this matter shall never be allowed to rest till the last shadow in its dark mystery shall be chased away by the light of unquestionable truth. (Anon 1860b: 5)

A. D. Hutter (1998) suggested that crime was often figured, in the mid-Victorian period, as a foreign energy – infecting the lifeblood of the family from outside its established parameters, a view that is clearly supported by the *Times*'s characterization of the Road Murder as a slur on the untainted profile of British domesticity. Yet, as Anthea Trodd and Elizabeth Rose Gruner have rightly observed, the Road controversy also generated an impression that crime was no alien introduction to the family, but a factor generated from within the home itself (Trodd 1989: 19–25). The death of Francis Kent, Gruner writes, "suggested that the Victorian family [... was] itself the source of many of its complexities and dangers" (Gruner 1998: 222). Paradoxically, this is also supported by the *Times*'s reporting of the murder: "We cannot divest ourselves of the belief," the newspaper admitted, "that the child suffered death at the hands of some one belonging to the house." It concludes: "It is evident that the guilty person must have been in the house over night, for all the fastenings were exactly as they had been left the previous night, when Mr Kent himself saw they were secure" (Anon 1860a: 12). Originally viewed as a monstrous breach of the home's traditional parameters, the newspaper was now willing to admit that the crime was generated from within the Kent home itself. Readers of crime fiction will recognize one of that genre's main characteristics here: the murder took place in a contained and isolated environment, thus implicating a limited number of people.

Following an inconclusive inquest into the Road Murder, the Home Secretary commissioned Sergeant Whicher, a Scotland Yard detective, to investigate the case. Within days of his dispatch, the *Times* announced Whicher's "apprehension of Miss Constance Kent," Francis's 16-year-old stepsister. In the preliminary Magistrates inquiry into her arrest, Whicher testified:

> I am an inspector of detectives. I have been engaged since Sunday last in investigating the circumstances connected with the murder of Francis Savile Kent. ... I have made an examination of the premises, and believe that the murder was committed by some inmate of the house. ... I sent for Constance Kent on Monday last to her bed room, having previously examined her drawers and found a list of her linen ... in which were enumerated, among other things, three night dresses as belonging to her. ... I said, "Here are three night dresses; where are they?" She said, "I have two; the other was lost at the wash the week after the murder". ... This afternoon I again proceeded to the house and sent for [Constance] into the dining-room. I said, "I am a police officer, and

I hold a warrant for your apprehension, charging you with the murder of your brother Francis Savile Kent" (Anon 1860c: 5)

This scene appears to prefigure the dénouements of later crime fictions. Like Sherlock Holmes or Hercule Poirot, Whicher assembles the family in order to announce his deductions. Based on the evidence of a missing nightgown, and that evidence alone, he confined Constance to the county jail. Magistrates agreed with an overwhelming public opinion that there was not enough evidence against her and ordered the prisoner's release. After many investigations, and investigations into those investigations, the Road Murder seemed to remain a mystery. The case never left the pages of British newspapers between 1860 and 1865 because many correspondents wrote in to voice their opinions on what might have occurred. In April 1865, however, Whicher's original conclusions appeared to find validation:

> The proverb "murder will out" has often been discredited in our time by the lasting mystery which has enveloped great crimes, but an event has now occurred which will recall it to every mind. The "Road Murder", that dark deed which filled the country with amazement and painful curiosity five years ago, and the incidents of which were studied as a dreadfully fascinating problem in every household, seems now likely to receive a full explanation. Yesterday, Miss CONSTANCE EMILY KENT, one of the unfortunate family, a young lady of only 21 years of age, surrendered at Bow-street and made a voluntary confession of the crime. (Anon 1865: 8)

Constance claimed that she used her father's razor to cut the boy's throat because she was enraged by an ongoing dispute with her stepmother. In the July of the same year, she was arraigned for murder and found guilty. Despite receiving the death sentence, she was reprieved by the Home Secretary and served 20 years of penal servitude.

The Moonstone

The Moonstone was serialized, weekly, in *All the Year Round* from January to August 1868, three years after the sentencing of Constance. Collins had corresponded with Dickens on the subject of the Road mystery, which seemed to bear an uncanny resemblance to many of the former's sensational plots. If we look upon Collins's fiction and the Road mystery – for the moment – as commercial enterprises, it appears that Collins and Constance kept each other in business. The Road Murder saga owed a great deal, in its journalistic format, to the sensational tales of popular writers like Collins. Similarly, sensation novelists were eager to spin the details of this new scandal into fictional stories that were sure to find a substantial audience.

As with the Road Murder story, which emerged through a series of fragmented and often contradictory journalistic articles, *The Moonstone* is narrated through a string of testimonies concerned with a crime committed within the confines of a bourgeois home. In both the Road Murder and *The Moonstone*, there are indications that one of the house's inmates is responsible and a Scotland Yard detective arrives on the scene to become preoccupied with discovering a stained nightdress.

Yet Collins's narrative also explores how far such events became the foundations for unhealthy, reactionary fixations on professional and unprofessional detection. Like Constance Kent's bloodstained nightdress, the Moonstone becomes the object of a frenzied investigative search, and Collins even adds a missing, paint-stained incriminating nightshirt to the intrigue for good measure. The preliminary suspicions of Sergeant Cuff, a professional detective modeled on Whicher, tend towards Rosanna Spearman, a former thief rehabilitated into a housemaid. "It was plain that Sergeant Cuff's suspicions of Rosanna had been raised" (Collins 1998b: 125), admits the head butler, Gabriel Betteredge, by the fact that she had a criminal history:

> The upshot of it was, that Rosanna Spearman had been a thief. … There was certainly no beauty about her to make the others envious; she was the plainest woman in the house, with the additional misfortune of having one shoulder bigger than the other. (Collins 1998b: 34–5)

Betteredge admits that Rosanna is considered a suspicious woman, not only because of her criminal history, but because of her physical deformities as well. Notice how the investigative, male gaze moves seamlessly in the above passage from issues of criminality to those relating to female biology. With her criminal propensities and physical deformities, Rosanna personifies the delinquent proclivities and somatic incapacities that were central to mid-Victorian definitions of womanhood, characteristics that had appeared also to be embodied in the figure of Constance Kent. What we see in *The Moonstone*, however, is no objective process of deduction, but a less impressive, but quite deliberate on Collins's part, demonstration of male prejudice.

The connections between the investigation of the theft and conservative male interpretation are most obviously negotiated in Collins's depiction of the Shivering Sands, whose uncanny behavior firmly associate them with femininity and the site of the novel's most fascinating moments of crime investigation. "Having now told the story of Rosanna," Betteredge moves on "to the story of the sands":

> The sand-hills here run down to the sea, and end in two spits of rock jutting out opposite each other, till you lose sight of them in the water. One is called the North Spit, and one the South. Between the two, shifting backwards and forwards at certain seasons of the year, lies the most horrible quicksand on the shores of Yorkshire. At the turn of the tide, something goes on in the unknown deeps below, which sets the whole face of the quicksand shivering and trembling in a manner most remarkable to see, and which has given to it, among the people in our parts, the name of The Shivering Sand. (Collins 1998b: 36)

The description seems to employ images of the female body and its psychosomatic symptoms. The sands are located between two rocks "jutting out opposite to each other," mimicking images of the female genitalia between extended legs. References to the "unknown deeps below" recall the images of the Moonstone as having "unfathomable depths" (Collins 1998b: 74) of its own, as well as British domesticity as divided between outer calmness and dangerous, unknown interiorities. The sands shiver and tremble as though manifesting corporeal reactions to a mental stimulus:

> The horrid sand began to shiver. The broad brown face of it heaved slowly, and then dimpled and quivered all over. "Do you know what it looks like to *me*?" says Rosanna, catching me by the shoulder again. "It looks as if it had hundreds of suffocating people under it – all struggling to get to the surface, and all sinking lower and lower in the dreadful deeps! Throw a stone in, Mr Betteredge! Throw a stone in, and let's see the sand suck it down!" (Collins 1998b: 38–9)

Like a vulnerable body, the sands shiver, heave, dimple, and quiver as though suffering from a loss of control. Like the Kent home, the Sands appear to have ghastly secrets and the flow and ebb of the tide echoes Victorian associations of the female body with the sea (Moscucci 1993: 33). It is hardly surprising, therefore, that Rosanna (a personification of criminality and somatic disability) feels a strong connection with the landscape: "Something draws me to it," she admits, "I try to keep away, from it, and I can't. ... I think that my grave is waiting for me here" (Collins 1998b: 38). Circumstances later compel her to commit suicide by jumping into the quicksand.

It is Rosanna's attachment to the Sands that leads the amateur detective figure Franklin Blake, not knowing himself to be the thief, to search for the Moonstone there. He understands from Rosanna's suicide note that she has hidden something beneath them and, if we bear in mind how similar the portrait of the Shivering Sands is to the image of the female body, we can see his investigation as a highly sexualized activity:

> The bared wet surface of the quicksand itself, glittering with a golden brightness, hid the horror of its false brown face under a passing smile. ... I saw the preliminary heaving of the Sand, and then the awful shiver that crept over its surface – as if some spirit of terror lived and moved and shuddered in the fathomless deeps beneath. ... The sight of it so near me, still disturbed at intervals by its hideous shivering fits, shook my nerves for the moment. A horrible fancy that the dead woman might appear on the scene of her suicide, to assist my search – an unutterable dread of seeing her rise through the heaving surface of the same, and point to the place – forced itself into my mind, and turned me cold in the warm sunlight. I own I closed my eyes at the moment when the point of the stick first entered the quicksand. (Collins 1998b: 312–13)

Again, the description of the landscape is replete with psychosomatic symptoms and the suggestion of hidden depths. The search for clues to a woman's crime, or a crime that Blake *believes* to be a woman's, becomes a sexual act of penetrating the surface to get to hidden "realities." Like the detective and journalistic searches for the missing link in the Road Murder scandal, Blake's inspection of the Sands seems to be a compulsive, figurative search of sacred spaces for secret conclusions. He avoids looking into the sand as his stick begins to penetrate it, which reads like an anticipation of Freud's identification of the "vagina dentata" phobia, in which men are terrified by the prospect of gratifying their desires. This aversion could be driven by the fact that, like the investigators of the Road Murder, Blake is searching for evidence he is half-afraid to discover – evidence that crime and violence reside within the "fathomless deeps" of nineteenth-century respectability, and the Victorian reader's own mind. Whether or not those links exist, the narrative suggests that the process of searching for them is an unhealthy business.

If additional support were needed to highlight similarities between the Road Murder and the plot of *The Moonstone*, it can be found in the fact that the search for the diamond becomes synonymous with the search for a stained nightdress. When Sergeant Cuff begins to investigate the crime scene, he notices a smear on a painted panel of the door to Rachel's room. Local policemen believe the smear to be inconsequential but Cuff maintains:

> "I made a private inquiry last week, Mr Superintendent", he said. "At one end of the inquiry there was a murder, and at the other end there was a spot of ink on a tablecloth that nobody could account for. … Before we go a step further in this business we must see the [garment] that made the smear, and we must know for certain when the paint was wet." (Collins 1998b: 109)

Cuff's suspicions are correct; Franklin, the true but unwitting thief, creates the smear, which leaves a stain on his nightgown. Catherine Peters has written that the change from blood to paint is evidence of Collins's attempt to neutralize the Road Murder of its bloody details (Peters 1992: 309). Yet I propose that, in changing the stain from blood to paint, Collins better engages with the complex issues swirling around sexuality, domesticity, crime, and detection. The stain on the nightgown in Collins's narrative is caused by the amateur detective figure himself, and so, when Franklin finally recovers the box Rosanna has hidden in the Shivering Sands, he discovers that his search has been self-referential – a search for his *own* responsibility:

> Putting the case between my knees, and exerting my utmost strength, I contrived to draw off the cover. … [Inside] it was a nightgown. … [I] instantly discovered the smear of the paint from the door of Rachel's boudoir!
>
> My eyes remained riveted on the stain, and my mind took me back at a leap from the present to the past. … I had discovered the smear on the nightgown. To whom did the nightgown belong? … The nightgown itself would reveal the truth; for, in all probability, the nightgown was marked with its owner's name.
>
> I took it up from the sand, and looked for the mark.
>
> I found the mark, and read –
>
> MY OWN NAME.
>
> There were the familiar letters which told me that the nightgown was mine. … I had penetrated the secret which the quicksand had kept from every other living creature. And, on the unanswerable evidence of the paint-stain, I had discovered Myself as the Thief. (Collins 1998b: 313–14)

If, as several critics have observed, the theft of the Moonstone from Rachel Verinder's bedroom is replete with "seduction symbolism" (Rzepka 2005: 105), Franklin's search of the Sands is similarly imbued with violent sexual connotations: he places the box between his knees and refers to himself as having "penetrated the secret" of *that night* in Rachel's boudoir. There are also indications that Franklin's search is not the work of an entirely objective mind. The soiled nightdress reveals no evidence of female culpability but links the detective *himself* directly to the crime.

In this fascinating retelling of the Road Murder mystery, the investigation has revealed, like that of Oedipus, more about the investigator than it has about his object. Observe how the fragmented, broken sentences of this passage suggest hysteria. This is a scene that exposes Franklin, not Rosanna or Rachel, as the unhealthiest character in the novel. The very object linking him to the crime, a smeared blotch of paint, is also sexually symbolic: it came from the still-wet panel of the door to Rachel's room that Franklin and Rachel, apparently destined to be engaged, had painted together just before the theft, and its appearance on Franklin's nightdress raises unsettling associations with the semen stains often cited, in the so-called "hygenic" anti-masturbatory literature of the day, with nocturnal emission. In short, the stained nightdress suggests that the male, investigative process which seeks out crime is a distorted and perverse act, like Blake's irrationally fearful poking of the Sands that hides his own guilty but unconscious complicity in the crime.

Wilkie Collins thus uses images from the Road Murder to form the basis of a complex investigation into the Victorian, masculine obsession with discovering and defining crime. Blake's blameworthiness not only suggests that the era's concept of crime was the fictive work of a conservative process, but that the act was itself beset with faults, problems, and unhealthy reasoning. Such thought-provoking recolorings are Collins's legacy to crime fiction.[2]

NOTES

1   Ronald R. Thomas has written on the links between *The Moonstone* and forensic investigation (1999, 2007). Anthea Trodd also mentions *The Moonstone* in her discussion of the encounters between the professional police and domestic order (1989: 19–25).

2   This work has been informed by my previous research, particularly *Violent Women and Sensation Fiction* (Basingstoke: Palgrave Macmillan, 2007).

31

Arthur Conan Doyle (1859–1930)

John A. Hodgson

Sherlock Holmes and the Detection of Cultural Values

"'I trust that age doth not wither nor custom stale my infinite variety,' said he, and I recognized in his voice the joy and pride which the artist takes in his own creation" ("The Empty House," Doyle 1986: 1.673). Like Cleopatra, whose praise by Enobarbus in Shakespeare's *Antony and Cleopatra* he is here happily claiming for himself, Sherlock Holmes has become a figure for the ages, a literary archetype. He is as universal a literary presence as Odysseus or Don Quixote, and as widely known as they for a series of adventures, always with a common theme, but infinitely varied.

In the late 1880s and early 1890s Arthur Conan Doyle, a young, recently married "penniless doctor" and struggling writer, made two breakthroughs that together forever changed the literary landscape. First, he created a new kind of protagonist, a detective who, going beyond the mental acuteness of Poe's Dupin and the dawning professionalism of Gaboriau's Lecoq, would "reduce this fascinating but unorganized business to something nearer to an exact science." Second, he hit upon the idea of using a recurrent protagonist in a series of independent but interrelated stories tailored to the needs of the increasingly popular monthly magazines:

[I]t had struck me that a single character running through a series, if it only engaged the attention of the reader, would bind the reader to that particular magazine. On the other hand, it had long seemed to me that the ordinary serial might be an impediment rather than a help to a magazine, since, sooner or later, one missed one number and afterwards it had lost all interest. Clearly the ideal compromise was a character which carried through, and yet instalments which were each complete in themselves, so that the purchaser was always sure that he could relish the whole contents of the magazine. (Doyle 1989: 95–6)

The first Sherlock Holmes short story, "A Scandal in Bohemia," appeared in the monthly *Strand Magazine* in July 1891. The resonances of that advent continue to be felt today.

Cleopatra's special power, Enobarbus added, was that "she makes hungry where most she satisfies." The formula is particularly apt for the hero of a series of adventures: each individual tale should satisfy the reader but also whet the appetite for more. Doyle early developed a particular skill in stimulating this hunger. After the editor of the *Strand Magazine* accepted his first two Holmes stories and asked for more, Doyle began introducing into each new story brief allusions to some of Holmes's other cases. Early in the first of this next batch of four stories ("A Case of Identity"), for example, Watson instances a randomly chosen newspaper article as predictably commonplace, only to learn that he has lit upon the highly eccentric "Dundas separation case" and that Holmes had been "engaged in clearing up some small points in connection with it." Then, as Holmes offers Watson a pinch of snuff, Watson marvels over Holmes's splendid new "snuffbox of old gold, with a great amethyst in the centre of the lid" – "a little souvenir from the King of Bohemia in return for my assistance in the case of the Irene Adler papers," Holmes notes (an allusion to "A Scandal in Bohemia"; Doyle 1986: 1.252). In the third of these stories ("The Five Orange Pips"), the device has matured into a standing promise of great riches forever in store: "When I glance over my notes and records of the Sherlock Holmes cases between the years '82 and '90," Watson begins, "I am faced by so many which present strange and interesting features that it is no easy matter to know which to choose and which to leave." For 1887 alone, he has accounts

> of the adventure of the Paradol Chamber, of the Amateur Mendicant Society ... of the facts connected with the loss of the British bark *Sophy Anderson*, of the singular adventures of the Grice Patersons in the island of Uffa, and finally of the Camberwell poisoning case. (Doyle 1986: 1.289–90)

From a very early stage, in other words, the introductory incidentals of most of Holmes's tales serve not so much to tighten up the subsequent plot (as we would expect in an independent story) as to tighten up the series and develop the Sherlock Holmes myth.

The myth, as myths do, has taken on a life of its own. Growing from a base of enthusiastic readers in England and America, and formalized especially by the efforts of Ronald Knox and Christopher Morley in the 1920s and 1930s, myriads of Holmes-centered societies – it would be accurate to call them fan clubs – have formed worldwide and continue to thrive today. The members, "Sherlockians," are particularly known for their devotion to Holmesian exegesis and speculation, proceeding from a set of critical tenets ("the Game") established by the founding fathers – that Holmes and Watson were real people, Doyle merely their literary agent, and the stories disguised accounts of actual historical events. Sherlockians seek to fill in the details of Holmes's and Watson's biographies and explain inconsistencies in the canon. As Ed

Wiltse has aptly noted, the Sherlock Holmes stories "took [the] communal experience of culture to a new level," and "Sherlockiana is itself a kind of founding text in the genre of fan community-based writing, particularly that organized around serial television" (Wiltse 1998: 108, 120 n. 8).

While Sherlock Holmes "scholarship" – really, gamesmanship – continues to pour forth at an impressive pace from the Game's participants, however, Doyle's status in the academy has for some time been curiously uncertain. As an archetypal "dead white male" author – an outspoken defender of the Empire, a role model of Victorian ethics and chivalry – Doyle naturally received relatively less critical attention as scholars turned increasingly to the stories of women, of social outsiders, of the colored and subjugated and colonized, although he is now receiving relatively more attention from a second generation of colonial studies scholars interested in analyzing how the countercurrents of colonialism, racism, and patriarchy in turn influenced and changed English society. All the while, however, Sherlock Holmes has been but a modest and minor presence on the syllabuses of college and university courses, widely known but little taught, frequently invoked but only occasionally studied.

Joseph McLaughlin has suggested that "in academic discourse, the Holmes tales have been less popular [than with general audiences], ignored because they lack the stylistic complexity, moral ambiguity, and intricate psychology that are the commonplaces of modernism" (McLaughlin 2000: 27). McLaughlin's own analysis of the works – notably sensitive as it is to their complexity, ambiguity, and psychology, and placing them firmly in the modernist tradition – privileges the four novellas, as if these qualities require the extended scope of a longer work for their effective development, thus implying that academe's relative disregard of the Holmes stories springs more from their brevity than from their innate literary qualities. Perhaps. But a more likely explanation is that too often the Holmes stories incidentally sound notes that jar contemporary sensibilities, distracting from the story and the issues at hand. The same present-day reader who can cherish (at least on the page) the Victorian atmosphere of fog and gaslight and tobacco smoke and hansom cabs might nevertheless balk at that other, equally Victorian atmosphere of class, gender, ethnic, national, and racial consciousness so casually apparent in the Holmes narratives. A client describes to Holmes his encounter with a "dark-haired, dark-eyed, black-bearded man, with a touch of the sheeny about his nose" ("The Stock-Broker's Clerk," Doyle 1986: 1.497). A suspect confronted by Holmes and invited to explain himself blurts out, "I'll chance it. ... I believe you are a man of your word, and a white man, and I'll tell you the whole story" ("The Abbey Grange," Doyle 1986: 1.898). Holmes himself observes didactically to Watson,

> One of the most dangerous classes in the world ... is the drifting and friendless woman.
> She is the most harmless and often the most useful of mortals, but she is the inevitable
> inciter of crime in others. She is helpless. ... She is a stray chicken in a world of foxes.
> When she is gobbled up she is hardly missed. ("The Disappearance of Lady Frances
> Carfax," Doyle 1986: 2.401)

Do we react with embarrassment? With irritation? With condescension? And are we reacting to a fictional character, to a particular author, or to the ethos and mores of an entire culture?

Doyle himself was both a man of his age and a critic of his age, not to be casually stereotyped or labeled. We would do well to remember that, for example, he was an outspoken defender of British actions in the Boer war but also a supporter of Irish Home Rule; or again, that he was an opponent of women's suffrage but also a supporter of divorce law reform. His Sherlock Holmes stories could be highly formulaic, but his own sensibilities were hardly so. And even what seem to be pure polemics always serve the purposes of the Holmes stories, not vice versa. Concluding the paragraph about "the drifting and friendless woman" quoted just above, for example, Holmes continues simply, "I much fear that some evil has come to the Lady Frances Carfax," and Watson responds dryly, "I was relieved at this sudden descent from the general to the particular."

All too often, critics of the Sherlock Holmes stories have not followed that descent from the general to the particular carefully enough. Some of the most influential criticism of the 1980s and 1990s emphasized Sherlock Holmes as a maintainer of imperialist, patriarchal, and orthodox values, an agent of Foucauldian disciplinarity, "a kind of *ur*-policeman who is all the more effective in his disciplinary function for being separate from the official police" (Wiltse 1998: 107). More recently, however, critics have begun recognizing him as also a questioner of values. As Leslie Haynsworth suggests, "the Holmes stories actively create the kind of narrative space that invites interrogation of, rather than complicity with, the various cultural values and beliefs that shape our ideas about normative and deviant subjectivity" (Haynsworth 2001: 463). In what follows, I shall use two stories – one that is little read and lightly regarded, one that is widely recognized as among the very best – to suggest just how Doyle's cultural self-awareness expresses itself.

Unorthodox Thinking in "Wisteria Lodge"

Critical subtlety and complexity disguised by social stereotypings everywhere inform Doyle's treatment of race in a little-noted story, "The Adventure of Wisteria Lodge." Its writing and publication in 1908 broke a long sabbatical from the Holmes stories dating back to the appearance of "The Adventure of the Second Stain" in late 1904 and the publication of *The Return of Sherlock Holmes* in 1905. The intervening period had been a stressful one for Doyle: his wife of 21 years, Louise, died of tuberculosis after a 13-year decline in 1906, he took up the cause of the unjustly accused and convicted George Edalji in 1907, and he married his long-time friend and soul-mate, Jean Leckie, in 1908. The story itself, moreover, is structurally distinctive. Alone among the Holmes stories to that point, "Wisteria Lodge," appears in two parts, in a form reminiscent of *A Study in Scarlet* and anticipatory of *The Valley of Fear*. It is also unique in presenting a second detective – Inspector Baynes, of the Surrey Constabulary – who conducts a parallel and (herein lies its uniqueness; Baynes is no Lestrade or Gregson) equally capable investigation, so that Holmes and Baynes, working separately, cooperatively assemble a complete solution of the mystery. This very cooperativeness, with its doubling of perspectives, offers a hint about how to read the story.

Doyle had increasingly been attentive to racial issues in English society and elsewhere during this time. The Edalji case, to begin with, had a strong racist tinge. George Edalji was the son of a Sikh father (the Vicar of Great Wyrley) and an English mother, and the family had been the object of sustained persecution: in Doyle's words, "The appearance of a coloured clergyman with a half-caste son in a rude, unrefined parish was bound to cause some regrettable situation" (Doyle 1989: 216). Too, the Belgian rape of the Congo was then very much in the news, and Doyle was already following with horror reports of Belgian-sponsored atrocities that he would soon (in 1909) be persuaded to publicize and decry to the world in *The Crime of the Congo*. "Wisteria Lodge" is notable as a story in which the issue of race is not only foregrounded but even obtruded.

Yet the emphasis is subtle: the case's more insistent theme is not race, but the grotesque. The story opens with Holmes's evocation of the word, taken from a prospective client's telegram:

> "I suppose, Watson, we must look upon you as a man of letters," said he. "How do you define the word 'grotesque'?"
> "Strange – remarkable," I suggested.
> He shook his head at my definition.
> "There is surely something more than that," said he; "some underlying suggestion of the tragic and the terrible. If you cast your mind back to some of those narratives with which you have afflicted a long-suffering public, you will recognize how often the grotesque has deepened into the criminal." (Doyle 1986: 2.293–4)

And it ends with Holmes's return to this theme as he concludes his explanation of the case: "It is grotesque, Watson, … but, as I have had occasion to remark, there is but one step from the grotesque to the horrible" (Doyle 1986: 2.320). The word's burden, however, has changed considerably in the interim.

This pattern occurs frequently in the Holmes stories: the tragic, the horrible, the criminal emerges from what had seemed initially only grotesque, odd, strange. The first of his own earlier cases adduced here as an example of the grotesque – "The Red-Headed League," with its fantastic advertisement to fill a vacancy in the League of the Red-Headed Men and its absurd task of copying out the Encyclopedia Britannica by hand – is no more than "strange – remarkable" at first; only later does the hint of criminality emerge. The same is true of several cases Holmes does not cite here. "The Adventure of the Six Napoleons," for example, opens with news that someone is breaking into houses and establishments to destroy plaster busts of Napoleon: the facts, Holmes notes, "are singular, not to say grotesque" (Doyle 1986: 1.808), although the crimes at first seem trivial. So it is, too, with the "absurd little figures dancing across the paper" in "The Adventure of the Dancing Men" – "so grotesque an object," but at first glance seemingly only "some childish prank" (Doyle 1986: 1.705) And the account at hand in "Wisteria Lodge," despite his client's overwrought language ("Have just had most incredible and grotesque experience," the telegram reads), seems at the outset quite mundane: Mr Scott Eccles, spending a night as the house guest of a new acquaintance, is not awakened as requested at eight the following morning, and rises late to find the house empty of both host and servants. Only someone as sheltered, stolid, and "conventional to the last degree" (Doyle 1986: 2.294) as the very dull and very respectable Mr Scott Eccles would call this experience "most incredible and grotesque."

But this mildly farcical episode proves the prelude to a case of violent murder, and soon enough instances of the grotesque lie thick on the ground. All of these, moreover, cluster around the figure of the host's remarkable and exotic cook. At the scene of Mr Eccles's stay, Inspector Baynes found "one or two *very* remarkable things" (Doyle 1986: 2.302); and a return visit there quickly produces another, in the on-site constable's panicky account of a recent intruder:

> "Lord, sir, what a face it was! I'll see it in my dreams. ... It wasn't black, sir, nor was it white, nor any colour that I know, but a kind of queer shade like clay with a splash of milk in it. Then there was the size of it – it was twice yours, sir. And the look of it – the great staring goggle eyes, and the line of white teeth like a hungry beast." (Doyle 1986: 2.306)

The constable, we later learn, has caught a glimpse of the host's foreign cook, soon described in a newspaper account as "a man of most remarkable appearance – being a huge and hideous mulatto, with yellowish features of a pronounced Negroid type" (Doyle 1986: 2.309). The very remarkable things that Inspector Baynes found in the house all wait in this exotic cook's special province, the kitchen. In the sink are the savagely torn fragments of a white cock; under the sink, a pail of blood; in the fireplace, the charred bones of a lamb or kid; and on the dresser stands "an extraordinary object," a "sinister relic":

> It was so wrinkled and shrunken and withered that it was difficult to say what it might have been. One could but say that it was black and leathery and that it bore some resemblance to a dwarfish, human figure. At first, as I examined it, I thought that it was a mummified negro baby, and then it seemed a very twisted and ancient monkey. Finally I was left in doubt as to whether it was animal or human. A double band of white shells was strung round the center of it. (Doyle 1986: 2.307)

In these hints of violent sacrifice and images of ambiguous, monstrous figures – the face at the window, "the queer thing in the kitchen" – the grotesque makes its real appearance in the story:

"The fellow is as strong as a cart-horse and as fierce as the devil. He chewed Downing's thumb nearly off before they could master him. He hardly speaks a word of English, and we can get nothing out of him but grunts" (Doyle 1986: 2.310)

The story's subsequent emphases on the animalistic savagery of this monstrous cook and on the vileness of his religion (a worship of "unclean gods," even involving "human sacrifices followed by cannibalism" [Doyle 1986: 2.320]) simply fill in a set of associations that seem a textbook instance of a colonial encoding of the Other: this animal-like, Negroid, mixed-race idolator represents all that is foreign and inferior to white, civilized, moral, rational English society and culture.

But then, in a stunning reversal, Holmes's solution of the mystery upsets this entire reading. Mr Scott Eccles, he observes, "orthodox and conventional to the last degree" (Doyle 1986: 2.294), had been caught up in this plot (as an establisher of an alibi) precisely because he so typifies proper English society: "He is the very type of conventional British respectability, and the very man as a witness to impress another Briton" (Doyle 1986: 2.303). But the exotic cook with his apparently bizarre idol and actions – "all the mystery of that weird kitchen" (Doyle 1986: 2.320) – is equally a type of orthodoxy and convention. The "relic" is his religious fetish, which, after it had been left behind, he had been driven by "his piety or his superstition" to try to recover, even at great personal risk. "The torn bird, the pail of blood, the charred bones" (Doyle 1986: 2.320) are simply the remnants of his highly conventional sacrament, as Holmes, fresh from a research trip to the British Museum, documents with a quotation from the implicitly authoritative "Eckermann's *Voodooism and the Negroid Religions*." The deeper point here, as Holmes emphasizes to Watson, is that "our savage friend was very orthodox in his ritual" (Doyle 1986: 2.320). The mulatto cook and the pompously respectable Mr Scott Eccles (whose very name evokes "church"), apparently the extreme opposites of this tale, are actually types of each other: whose religion is piety and whose is superstition, or even which is the good citizen and which the savage, is entirely a matter of perspective – although it takes an unconventional, unorthodox thinker such as Holmes to perceive this.

Rosemary Hennessy and Rajeswari Mohan have argued that Sherlock Holmes functions in his stories "to present as obvious and natural a hierarchy that protects the interests of the middle-class, western, white male" (Hennessy and Mohan 1989: 337). In "Wisteria Lodge," at least, this conclusion seems untenable: here Holmes, while he works to protect the interests of his middle-class, Western, white male client, dramatically calls both the obviousness and the naturalness of that hierarchy into question. Indeed, to take that hierarchy for granted is to think like Scott Eccles and Watson and Inspector Gregson: it is to be unable to solve the crime.

Distressingly few of Doyle's critics have been willing to credit him with this ability to see beyond the cultural values that he so prominently represented and championed. But increasingly some have at least recognized that the stories persistently hint at depths that Watson, Gregson, and Holmes's various clients cannot fathom. Catherine Belsey, for example, has noted that the Holmes stories are "elusive concerning both sexuality and politics" (Belsey 1994: 387). As "Wisteria Lodge" shows, they can be elusive concerning race and religion, too.

Confidence and Honor in "The Second Stain"

Belsey's comment on the Holmes stories' sexual and political elusiveness particularly refers to "The Adventure of the Second Stain" – as it happens, the last Holmes story to have been written and published before "Wisteria Lodge." Doyle himself regarded "The Second Stain" as "one of the neatest of the stories," and one of the best (Doyle 1989). "Neatest" might seem a curious commendation, but it is entirely apt: the story's remarkable, economical symmetry of plot at once shows Holmes to advantage and encourages a reconsideration of British mores and values.

The "second stain" of the title is a bloodstain on the floor beneath a bloodstained carpet on which a man has been stabbed to death. The two stains are found not to be aligned – a sign, of course, that the carpet has been moved since the murder occurred ("it is simple enough. The two stains did correspond, but the carpet has been turned round" [Doyle 1986: 1.916]), and thus a crucial clue that prompts the eventual solution of the mystery. But the title also hints at a fundamental doubleness that governs the entire story. For "The Second Stain," like Poe's "The Purloined Letter," tells tales both of domestic and of political intrigue, with threats of "stains" on both personal and national honor; and only by recognizing how these two tales essentially correspond before they get turned round in the telling will we become able to discover their deeper message.

The two levels of "The Second Stain" are early characterized by Lord Bellinger, the Premier who seeks Holmes's assistance, as "public duty" versus "the most intimate domestic ties" (Doyle 1986: 1.903); by Lady Hilda, later, as "a matter of politics" versus "a matter of love and trust" (Doyle 1986: 1.922). The political story is a tale of diplomacy and intrigue: a "potentate who has been ruffled by some recent Colonial developments of this country" has written a hot-headed, indiscreet letter to the British government without consulting with his Ministers, and now regrets it and (like the British government) hopes to suppress it. The letter is "couched in so unfortunate a manner" that its publication would inevitably involve both countries in a war (Doyle 1986: 1.905). But the potentate's leagued enemies would gain great advantage by securing and publishing it, "so as to make a breach between his country and ours" (Doyle 1986: 1.906) and weaken both. And now the letter has disappeared; apparently it has been stolen, although it has not yet been published.

The second story, meanwhile, gives a very similar plot in a different register (on some of the parallels, see Belsey 1994: 386–7; Metress 1994 42). A young lady, "an impulsive, loving girl" (Doyle 1986: 1.921), has written an "indiscreet," "foolish" letter (implicitly to a man). Later she loves and marries another man, and "had thought that the whole [earlier] matter was forgotten" – only to learn that her letter has been stolen or otherwise acquired by a blackmailer. Its threatened transmission to her husband would, she feels sure, involve her marriage in "certain ruin" (Doyle 1986: 1.922).

This quick synopsis only begins to sketch the parallelisms of the story's two subplots. Connected through the marriage of the Right Honourable Trelawney Hope, Secretary for European Affairs (from whose possession the potentate's letter has disappeared) and Lady Hilda Trelawney Hope (who had written that "letter of an impulsive, loving girl"), the subplots are brought to correspond by the figure of Eduardo Lucas, the secret agent who comes to possess both letters, acquiring the domestic one so that he might be able to exchange it for the political one. Ultimately, they are also brought to correspond by the figure of Holmes himself – like Lucas, a private agent who deals in secrets. By forcing us to consider what to make of this ultimate correspondence, "The Second Stain" puts some of the fundamental assumptions of British society into question.

Thematically uniting the two subplots of "The Second Stain" is the issue of confidence. Early in the story, Holmes insists, in a dramatic moment, that the Premier take Holmes into his confidence. Holmes asks exactly what the missing document is and why its disappearance is so important; the Premier, in response, begins cautiously to describe its physical appearance ("the envelope is a long, thin one of pale blue colour. There is a seal of red wax, stamped with a crouching lion"). (This is exactly the kind of entirely superficial identification, we later realize, that Lucas had provided Lady Hilda when he required her to "bring him a certain document which he described in my husband's despatch-box" [Doyle 1986: 1.922].) When Holmes persists – "My inquiries must go more to the root of things. What *was* the letter?" – the Premier puts him off: "That is a state secret of the utmost importance, and I fear that I cannot tell you, nor do I see that it is necessary" (Doyle 1986: 1.904). Whereupon Holmes declines the case, to the momentary anger of the Premier, who nevertheless soon cedes the point: "No doubt you are right, and it is unreasonable for us to expect you to act unless we give you our entire confidence" (Doyle 1986: 1.905). The importance of this scene is soon reemphasized when Lady Hilda unexpectedly visits Holmes to probe for information. As she describes her situation to him, "There is complete confidence between my husband and me on all matters save one. That one is politics. On this his lips are sealed. He tells me nothing." Now, she realizes, an important document has disappeared from their home. "But because the matter is political my husband refuses to take me into his complete confidence." Yet it is important, she insists, that she be informed. Will Holmes tell her what is going on? "Let no regard for your client's interests keep you silent, for I assure you that his interests, if he would only see it, would be best served by taking me into his complete confidence" (Doyle 1986: 1.910).

Holmes of course declines, as he must. But this scene between Holmes and Lady Hilda repeats itself near the end of the story, when we come to a better and a different understanding of her marital confidences. The foolish, girlish letter with which Lucas was blackmailing her, she says, would have destroyed her marriage had her husband seen it: "I meant no harm, and yet he would have thought it criminal. Had he read that letter his confidence would have been forever destroyed. ... What was I to do?" To which Holmes answers, "Take your husband into your confidence," and she rejoins, "I could not, Mr. Holmes, I could not! On the one side seemed certain ruin, on the other, terrible as it seemed to take my husband's paper, still in a matter of politics I could not understand the consequences, while in a matter of love and trust they were only too clear to me" (Doyle 1986: 1.921–2).

So there is not, after all, "complete confidence between my husband and me on all matters save one." Or rather, we need to reinterpret that "between." A fairer statement of Lady Hilda's claims would be that her husband confides in her in all matters save one (politics), while – a misalignment that she had left unspoken in her first interview with Holmes – she similarly confides in him in all matters save one (love). Confidence, we are reminded, is not always a reciprocal relationship. Indeed, we are always reminded of this in a Holmes story, for the detective – like the detective story author – is one in whom confidence must be placed but from whom confidences can never be expected. Even in "The Second Stain," "Inspector Lestrade had taken [Holmes] into his confidence in the case" (Doyle 1986: 1.913), although the reverse is certainly not true.

Holmes's absolute insistence, in their second interview, on Lady Hilda's confidence if he is to help her, however, also sounds a series of disturbing echoes. These are anticipated in their first interview when she states, "You are the only other person, save only these politicians, who knows the true facts" (Doyle 1986: 1.910). Not so, as she (although not yet Holmes) is well aware: Lucas also knows them. And in the second interview, the parallels between Holmes and Lucas become unmistakable. When Holmes issues his ultimatum, "If you will work with me I can arrange everything. If you work against me I must expose you" (Doyle 1986: 1.920), the phrases might easily be those Lucas had already spoken to her; when she responds, "You are trying to frighten me. It is not a very manly thing, Mr. Holmes, to come here and browbeat a woman," she is speaking from recent experience. When she begs for mercy (" 'Oh, spare me, Mr. Holmes! Spare me!' she pleaded, in a frenzy of supplication" [Doyle 1986: 1.921]), she is but reenacting her first interview with Lucas ("I implored his mercy" [Doyle 1986: 1.922]). We cannot ignore these persistent hints that Holmes and Lucas, however different their motives and their values, are in certain respects counterparts. Like Holmes, Lucas deals in confidences; like the detective, the secret agent or the blackmailer is one in whom confidence must be placed but from whom confidences can never be expected.

Eduardo Lucas, we eventually learn, was a man who shared no confidences with anyone. He was "Well known and popular" (Doyle 1986: 1.909), but "He kept his life in water-tight compartments" (Doyle 1986: 1.915) and indeed led a double life – the married M. Henri Fournaye in Paris, the unmarried Mr Eduardo Lucas in London. As this doubleness suggests, he was particularly careful to keep his personal life separate from his professional one. Without any allegiances either political or personal – "it is a question of money with these fellows," Holmes observes (Doyle 1986: 1.907–8) – his relations with countries and associates, like those with women, are "promiscuous but superficial" (Doyle 1986: 1.912). His downfall comes, as Trelawney Hope's almost does, when his private life breaks into his professional one. His insanely jealous wife, Mme Fournaye, tracks him to his residence in London, mistakes a professional visitor (Lady Hilda, bringing the letter stolen from her husband's dispatch-box) for a private mistress, and follows her into Lucas's residence to exact revenge for what she takes to be her betrayal. Lucas, for his part, when he hears the intruder's steps, anticipates a professional rather than a personal threat: his concern, accordingly, is to secrete the newly acquired document rather than to worry immediately about his safety. He is undone, as the Trelawney Hopes are almost undone, by the consequences of a breakdown of marital confidence.

Certainly we should not interpret "The Second Stain" as too broad a warning about the dangers of withholding confidence. Hope is right not to confide in his wife about matters of politics (significantly, his last words to her in this story are, "As to you, my dear, I fear that this is a matter of politics. We will join you in a few minutes in the dining-room" [Doyle 1986: 1.923]) – but right also in his impulse to share with her the implications for his own situation ("Where is my wife? I must tell her that all is well. Hilda! Hilda!" [Doyle 1986: 1.924]). The consequences of confiding too broadly can be as devastating – blackmail or war, for example – as the consequences of confiding not at all – isolation and death.

While Holmes is linked to Lucas as a receiver of confidences, however, he even more significantly resembles the Premier himself in the carefulness of his own confidings. The point is lightly driven home early in his first meeting with the Premier and Hope, in one of those subtle touches Doyle carries off so well, conveying worlds of social significance in a simple, passing gesture. Holmes has just won his point that he must have the Premier's entire confidence, and Lord Bellinger has accordingly described the nature of that missing letter from "a certain foreign potentate" and the likelihood of war should the letter be published:

> Holmes wrote a name upon a slip of paper and handed it to the Premier.
> "Exactly. It was he. And it is this letter – this letter which may well mean the expenditure of a thousand millions and the lives of a hundred thousand men – which has become lost in this unaccountable fashion." (Doyle 1986: 1.905)

Why does Holmes not simply speak the name? What is the point of this little scene? Although Watson makes no comment on it, there can be only one answer: to exclude Watson from an unnecessarily full knowledge of the situation. Similarly – and the point this time is simply to exclude Watson and Lestrade from the direction and progress of Holmes's ongoing investigation – Holmes reenacts this gesture late in the story in an incident that constitutes the very *anagnorisis*, or recognition moment, of the plot. Holmes and Watson are leaving Lucas's residence, where Inspector Lestrade has just shown Holmes the uncorresponding second stain and the constable on duty has confessed to having momentarily admitted a young lady to the crime scene:

> As we left the house Lestrade remained in the front room, while the repentant constable opened the door to let us out. Holmes turned on the step and held up something in his hand. The constable stared intently.
> "Good Lord, sir!" he cried, with amazement on his face. Holmes put his finger on his lips, replaced his hand in his breast pocket, and burst out laughing as we turned down the street. (Doyle 1986: 1.918–19)

Only later do we learn that Holmes has shown the constable a photograph of Lady Hilda, and that the constable's recognition of her as the young lady he had admitted to the crime scene has confirmed his theory about her role in purloining the letter.

Holmes's relation to Watson, his housemate and partner, reflects the full mutual confidence that was entirely lacking in Lucas's relations with his estranged wife and imperfectly honored between the Trelawney Hopes. But while Holmes relies absolutely on Watson (and vice versa), he does not confide in Watson inappropriately or prematurely. His caution in such matters is matched by that of Lord Bellinger, the consummate diplomat, who, "with twinkling eyes," waits until Hope has left the room before inquiring of Holmes, "There is more in this than meets the eye. How came the letter back in the box?" (Doyle 1986: 1.924) – his pointed "back" signaling that he, unlike Hope, is not fooled by the story Holmes has just given (that the letter had remained in the dispatch-box all along, somehow overlooked after becoming misplaced among the other papers therein), just as his twinkling eyes suggest he realizes that Holmes is gallantly protecting Hope from some unpleasant truth and, therefore, probably screening Lady Hilda. But Holmes, appropriately, as he "turned away smiling from the keen scrutiny of those wonderful eyes," turns away the question even as he acknowledges its force: "We also have our diplomatic secrets."

While Doyle in the Sherlock Holmes stories reflects the values of his culture, then, he also, repeatedly and persistently, reflects on them. And surely this is one important reason for Holmes's sustained popularity beyond Doyle's own time and into our own very different era. Holmes's investigations do not merely found themselves on cultural assumptions, they often probe and test those assumptions. The fundamental honorableness of both Holmes and Watson, for example, established and demonstrated in story after story, can be taken for granted in "The Second Stain," as it is by Lord Bellinger when he takes them into his and the nation's confidence. But honor, although a signal virtue, is also a point of weakness in the Right Honourable Trelawney Hope, for it stymies his wife's confidence: "[H]is own honour stands so high that he could not forget or pardon a lapse in another" (Doyle 1986: 1.921). In a very real sense, then, Hope's rigid and oblivious sense of honor is the indirect cause of his wife's crime; and Holmes's recognition of this cultural blindness (for his actions show that he agrees with Lady Hilda's analysis of her husband) lies at the crux of the story. Although Holmes never overtly challenges the validity of Hope's conception of honor, the entire thrust of "The Second Stain" nonetheless works powerfully to call that conception into question. The narrowness of Hope's thinking about how honor can be stained is part and parcel of his cultural unreflectiveness, the quality that also makes him, like all the other exemplars of conventional thinking in the stories, incapable of deeper analysis (and thus ineffective at detection). But Holmes, like Lord Bellinger, stands at the head of his profession, and represents an aspect of England at its quirky best, because he knows not to take even his own most deeply held cultural values for granted.

32
Raymond Chandler (1888–1959)

Leroy Lad Panek

It all began when Florence Dart Thornton left Ireland to visit her sister in Nebraska and met Maurice Benjamin Chandler, a charming but peripatetic and alcoholic railroad man. Before her new husband permanently decamped, their only son, Raymond Thornton Chandler, was born in Chicago on July 23, 1888. For seven years Raymond and his mother spent their summers near her sister and her husband, Grace and Ernest Fitt, in Plattsmouth, Nebraska, of which Chandler retained not-always-idyllic memories. In *The Little Sister*, Chandler's most famous detective, Philip Marlowe, would direct a cynical laugh at "small towns" like Plattsmouth, adding, "I grew up in one" (Chandler 1995a: 2.405). In 1895 Chandler's parents divorced and mother and son left the United States for England. There, the boy and his mother moved in with her mother and sister in an establishment supported by the boy's maternal uncle, Ernest Thornton. Uncle Ernest provided his young American nephew with a classical prep school education at Dulwich College, whence another popular British writer, P. G. Wodehouse, had recently graduated. The curriculum at Dulwich would later enrich the writing that made Chandler famous with numerous allusions to British medievalism and classical literature.

From 1907, when he became a naturalized British subject and sat for his civil service exams, until the publication of his first detective story in 1933, Chandler knocked about from one career to another. Adept at languages, ancient and modern, and chafing at the bureaucratic routine of the civil service, he soon left government work to try earning his living as a newspaperman, an art critic, a short story writer, and a poet, before returning to the US in 1912 (with a loan from Uncle Ernest), where he landed jobs as a bookkeeper and a reporter. Taking several years out to serve with the Canadian Army's Gordon Highlanders during World War I in some of the worst fighting on the Western Front, Chandler eventually secured a place with the Dabney Oil Syndicate in Los Angeles, where he rose to the position of vice president only to be fired for alcoholism, absenteeism, and skirt-chasing in 1932, three years into the Depression. Meanwhile, in 1919, he had begun an affair with the multiply divorced

Pearl Eugenie "Cissy" Hurlburt Pascal. An emphatically "liberated" woman of the age, "Cissy" was interested in music and art, and was also 18 years Chandler's senior. They married in 1924 after the death of Chandler's mother, who had opposed the marriage.

When he was fired by Dabney, Chandler quite consciously set about becoming the professional writer he had long aspired to be. He listed himself in the city directory as a writer, took a correspondence course in the subject, and devoted four hours a day, every day, to mastering the craft. Inevitably, given his personal circumstances and his background in business, Chandler paid as much attention to selling what he wrote as he did to writing itself:

> I began to read pulp magazines, because they were cheap enough to throw away and because I never had any taste for the kind of thing which is known as women's magazines. This was in the great days of the *Black Mask* (if I may call them great days) and it struck me that some of the writing was pretty forceful and honest, even though it had its crude aspect. I decided that this might be a good way to learn to write fiction and get paid a small amount of money at the same time (Chandler 1995a: 1040).

Printed on inexpensive wood "pulp" paper, magazines like *Black Mask* had, since the 1890s, developed into venues for a wide range of popular genres – including science fiction, war stories, Westerns, romances, and detective stories. By 1930, however, detective fiction had come to dominate the world of the pulps, and when Chandler turned to writing professionally there were dozens of them exclusively devoted to detective stories, magazines like *Detective, All Detective, Detective Action Stories, Detective Library, Detective Weekly*, and the following year, *Spicy Detective*. At the top of the heap were the magazines Chandler chose to zero in on: *Dime Detective*, founded in 1931, and *Black Mask*, begun as a general fiction magazine in 1920 but by 1933 exclusively devoted to detective stories.

Chandler turned first to *Black Mask*, the magazine that introduced the reading public to hard-boiled fiction (see Pepper, chapter 10 in this volume) with a double debut in 1923 of Carroll John Daly's "Three Gun Terry" in May and Dashiell Hammett's first Continental Op story, "Arson Plus," the following October. *Black Mask* editor Harry Sutton presided over the creation of this new kind of fiction with its tough loner hero, violence, and terse, slangy prose, but it was Joseph Shaw who saw it through to maturity. Shaw came to *Black Mask* in 1926 and inherited writers Daly, Hammett (see Hall, chapter 36 in this volume), and Erle Stanley Gardner. It was Shaw who first articulated the aims of what came to be called hard-boiled fiction: "We wanted simplicity for the sake of clarity, plausibility and belief," and "We wanted action, but we held that action is meaningless unless it involves recognizable human character in three dimensional form" (Shaw 1946: viii).

By the time Chandler was casting about for a place to sell his work, Shaw had made *Black Mask* into a popular and profitable enterprise, increasing the circulation of his magazine from 66,000 when he became editor to 130,000. As Chandler was preparing to move into the world of pulp fiction, Dashiell Hammett was achieving celebrity as a hard-boiled writer and moving away from his old tough-guy heroes. By 1933, when Chandler sold his first story, Hammett had long since made the transition from short stories to novels, nearly given up writing about his tough, middle-aged fat detective the Continental Op, and made his tough-guy heroes Sam Spade and Ned Beaumont more intriguing. He would write only one more novel, *The Thin Man* (1934), a book replete with jazz age repartee.

With writing for the pulps and their "forceful and honest" prose in mind, Chandler, in his characteristically meticulous way, invented exercises to teach himself how to write pulp detective stories. As he would later tell Gardner, "I simply made an extremely detailed synopsis of your story and from that rewrote it and then compared what I had written to yours, and then went back and rewrote it some more, and so on" (Chandler 1981: 8). But it was not simply the "forceful and honest" technique of the pulps that appealed to Chandler. By the time he turned to writing, detective stories in general and Hammett's in particular were beginning to become accepted as literature – at least by *avant garde* American critics like Dorothy Parker and then abroad by the likes of Andre Gide and Robert Graves. And that meant something to Chandler. He turned to the detective stories because they were on the verge of becoming legitimate literature, but he also turned to them because pulps in general and Hammett in particular had come to embody the kind of stoic romanticism that Chandler had favored in the poetry and criticism he wrote as a young man in England. On top of that, he turned to hard-boiled detective fiction because of the allure of the new kind of prose he found in Hammett's stories.

In 1944, a decade after he had begun writing detective fiction, Chandler enumerated the virtues of the kind of literature he took up in 1933 in an essay entitled "The Simple Art of Murder," published in *The Atlantic Monthly* and then rewritten and published again in 1950. For Chandler, Hammett stood at the center of his thinking about the hard-boiled detective story. First of all, he singled out Hammett for avoiding the artificiality of the British detective story: he "gave murder back to the kind of people who commit it for reasons" (Chandler 1995a: 989). And then there was Hammett's style, which was colloquial, American, strikingly original, and "at its best could say almost anything" (Chandler 1995a: 989). That was the kind of prose Chandler was to teach himself how to write.

In December 1933 *Black Mask* published Chandler's "Blackmailers Don't Shoot." It took him five months to write this long short story – and to type it with both margins justified. Captain Shaw paid him the standard rate of a penny a word. Written in the third person like *The Maltese Falcon*, the story introduces Chandler's first detective hero, an import from Chicago to California, Mallory – perhaps named for Sir Thomas Mallory, author of *Morte D'Arthur* and patron saint of modern notions of chivalry. Apropos its Southern California setting, the story bristles with nightclubs, movie stars, sleek suave gangsters, glamorous worldly women, underworld patois, and most of all, plenty of action. One of the police detectives recounts some of the mayhem to Mallory at the end of the story this way:

You looked pretty fast to him, and not knowing you was a dick he gets kinda nervous. His gun went off. You didn't shoot right away, but the poor sap lets off another round and plugs you. Then, by – you drilled him in the shoulder, as who wouldn't. ... Then the shotgun boy comes bargin' in, lets go without asking any questions, fogs Mardonne, and stops one from you (Chandler 1995b: 50–1).

It took seven months for Chandler's second detective story, "Smart Aleck Kill" to appear – once again in *Black Mask*. Although he changed the name of the hero in reprints, the *Black Mask* original featured a return of Mallory, his private eye detective hero from the first story. As in "Blackmailers," the people and the problems are connected with Hollywood, the movies, and the ambience and personalities Hollywood and the movies create.

In October 1934 a new kind of Chandler story appeared in *Black Mask*. For "Finger Man" he centered on politics rather than the cinema, abandoned the name Mallory for his hero and named him Carmady, and made his detective more proletarian. There would be five more Carmady stories: "Killer in the Rain" (January 1935, *Black Mask*), "The Man Who Liked Dogs" (March 1936, *Black Mask*), "Goldfish" (June 1936, *Black Mask*), "The Curtain" (September 1936, *Black Mask*), and "Try the Girl" (January 1937, *Black Mask*).

Up to this point, one of the elements that marked Chandler's heroes was their sophisticated appearance, especially their clothes. It is something that stands out from the first paragraph of "Blackmailers Don't Shoot":

The man in the powder-blue suit – which wasn't powder blue under the lights of the Club Bolivar – was tall, with wide-set gray eyes, a thin nose, a jaw of stone. He had a rather sensitive mouth. His hair was crisp and black, and ever so faintly touched with gray, as by an almost diffident hand. His clothes fitted him as though they had a soul of their own, not just a doubtful past. His name happened to be Mallory (Chandler 1995b: 5)

In "Finger Man," however, Chandler colors his hero much more proletarian, which helps to align him more with workers than with the leisure class. As in the later works, the detective's office helps to define him.

There was nothing there but an old red davenport, two odd chairs, a bit of carpet, and a library table with a few old magazines on it. The reception room was left open for visitors to come in and sit down and wait – if I had any visitors and they felt like waiting. (Chandler 1995b: 95)

Even more than the locale, however, it is the narrative voice that focuses Chandler's conception of his heroes and changes the reader's relationship to them from "Finger Man" onward. In "Finger Man" the third-person perspective of his earlier stories changed to the first-person narrative of the hero himself. The effect can sometimes approach that of reading a case report or a deposition:

Miss Glenn made a clean getaway and was never heard of again. I think that's about all, except that I had to turn the twenty-two grand over to the Public Administrator. (Chandler 1995b: 1.145)

At this point, Chandler's narrative structure supposes an implicit listener – whether a police official or some other neutral but interested party – and has yet to be spiced with the personal asides and striking figurative language that were to become hallmarks of the later stories.

After "Finger Man" Chandler occasionally experimented with point of view – returning to third person for "Nevada Gas" (June 1935, *Black Mask*), "Spanish Blood" (November 1935, *Black Mask*), "The Guns at Cyrano's" (January 1936, *Black Mask*), and "The Noon Street Nemesis" (May 1936, *Black Mask*). In these pieces, too, Chandler brought in heroes with different names – successively DeRuse, Delaguerra, Malvern, Anglich – who possess most of the same personal attributes as Mallory or Carmady. Late in 1937 Chandler changed publishers from *Black Mask* to *Dime Detective*, and for that pulp he wrote five stories in which the first-person detective narrator is John Dalmas: "Mandarin's Jade" (November 1937), "Red Wind" (January 1938), "Bay City Blues" (June 1938), "The Lady in the Lake" (January 1939), and "Trouble Is my Business" (August 1939).

While Chandler sometimes noted that all of his early heroes shared the same attributes and were, essentially, the same person, this is not entirely true. Certainly, from first to last, Chandler's heroes are all private eyes, and he took pains to fit them into the pattern that readers of Daly, Hammett, and others expected from their hardboiled detectives. But for Chandler the concept of being hard-boiled grew to become more complex and nuanced than it had been in the hands of his predecessors. There is, for instance, Chandler's handling of the hero as outsider. Mallory, his first hero, is literally an outsider – he comes from Chicago to Los Angeles to work. But after Mallory Chandler's heroes are all long-standing Californians. Chandler creates our sense of their isolation and alienation by giving them minimal and transient places of residence or business, or from the nature of their employment, making them strangers in the land of opulence and excess exhibited in the mansions and nightclubs where they must go to find a job or to do it. The same is true for Chandler's use of the knightly archetype. He began with Mallory, a name clearly associated with knights and chivalry, and then used a number of names with less powerful associations – Dalmas, DeRuse, Delaguerra, Malvern, Anglich, and Carmady – and finally ended by naming his detective hero after the brooding, misanthropic, mysterious Elizabethan loner who perfected dramatic blank verse, created heroes unfit for their worlds, and ended up stabbed in the eye in a tavern in Deptford. And at the same time Chandler distributed his references to knighthood among incidental details in the narrative, such as chess playing or the stained glass window at the Sternwood mansion in *The Big Sleep*.

Chandler's heroes are anything but cold-blooded and distant, however. While they come in contact with a lot of despicable men and women, from the first story onward they display a consistent sympathy with honest, honorable, and genuine people, people on both sides of the law and of both sexes. Nonetheless, they are never comfortable with authority figures. In "Blackmailers Don't Shoot" Mallory's employer is a gangster for whom he has more respect than for the police detective who does the legal wrap-up at the end of the story, "a big shabby Irishman with a sweaty face and a loose-lipped grin. His white moustache was stained in the middle by nicotine. His hands had a lot of warts on them" (Chandler 1995b: 48–9). By "Finger Man" the detective hero is an independent agent working on behalf of the district attorney, a relationship defined by exploitation and marginalization: "He allowed me two hundred fee and nine dollars and twenty cents mileage. Sometimes I wonder what he did with the rest of it" (Chandler 1995b: 145).

But for Chandler, being hard-boiled had less to do with callous relationships with people and more to do with attitude. And it was decidedly more psychological than physical. Indeed, Chandler's heroes rarely engage in violence and in fact receive a lot more than they give when it comes to physical abuse. In this respect their hardness comes from their ability to take punishment and bounce back, persist, and finish what they started. Significantly Chandler also links "hardness" to a particular kind of attention or perception:

> There was death in the big room. Dalmas went towards it slowly, walking softly, listening. There was a hard light in his gray eyes, and the bone of his jaw made a sharp line that was pale against the tan of his cheek (Chandler 1995b: 160).

While Chandler attaches the term "hardness" to the attitudes of both his heroes and his villains, he links the hardness of his heroes to expressions of satisfaction or even joy. Thus,

> He spread his hands and looked down at them. A faint, metallic smile showed at the corners of his lips. (Chandler 1995b: 168)

> [Malvern] lifted a hand and drew his fingers slowly down her cheek, down the angle of her tight jaw, his eyes held a hard brown glitter, his lips a smile. (Chandler 1995b: 265)

Finally, tough and realistic as they may be, Chandler's detectives are also sentimental.

> You think you're hard-boiled but you're just a big slob that argues himself into a jam for the first tramp he finds in trouble. (Chandler 1995b: 282)

By 1938, Chandler had fashioned the basics of his hard-boiled world: his hero was in place, his first person narration was maturing, and he had created the essentials of the prose style that would become the pattern for legions of future writers. All he had to do was turn from short stories to novels. *The Big Sleep* came first, in 1939.

Chandler was never very good at making up plots, and in order to write novels he reused plots he had invented for his early short stories – with *The Big Sleep* he turned principally to "Killer in the Rain" and "The Curtain." From "Killer in the Rain" Chandler picked out the loopy, doped out nymphet Carmen Dravec, H. H. Steiner's dirty book business, Steiner's murder, the hijacking of Steiner's stock of porn, and the search for the missing naked pictures of Carmen. From "The Curtain" Chandler appropriated the plot thread of the aged General Slade Winslow hiring the hero to find his missing son-in-law, Dud O'Mara, who "married General Slade Winslow's rickety-rackety divorcee daughter," and Carmady's discovery that the missing man had been murdered. He also used the episode of the hero seeking a gangster's missing wife and being mugged by a garage mechanic and threatened with death by a professional killer who always wears brown clothes. For *The Big Sleep* Chandler also exchanged O'Mara's creepy young stepson, the murderer in "The Curtain," for the equally emotionally unbalanced Carmen Dravec from "Killer in the Rain."

After he finished *The Big Sleep*, Chandler planned to mine, or as he termed it "cannibalize," more of his short stories and turn them into novels. In his next three books Chandler reached pretty far back for two of these mining expeditions – the first yielded *Farewell, My Lovely* (1940), and the second gave him the material for *The High Window* (1942). For the last novel of this period, *The Lady in the Lake* (1943), Chandler drew on more recent short fiction "Bay City Blues (1938)," "The Lady in The Lake" (1939), and "No Crime in the Mountains" (1941).

Few people have much good to say about the plots Chandler stitched together for these novels. At best their loose construction might be considered as a metaphor for his view of the world as a confusing, contradictory place in which loose ends are never tied up. Be that as it may, Chandler's long fiction gave him not just an opportunity to tell stories, but also a chance to flesh out his hero through his narrative voice and, perhaps more importantly, to exercise his craft as a writer.

The passages below serve as a miniscule sample of the ways in which Chandler perfected his craft in making his novels. In "The Curtain" Carmady describes General Winslow's greenhouse:

The air steamed. The walls and ceiling of the greenhouse dripped. In the half light enormous tropical plants spread their blooms and branches all over the place, and the smell of them was almost as overpowering as the smell of boiling alcohol. (Chandler 1964: 93)

In *The Big Sleep* this became:

It opened on to a sort of vestibule that was about as warm as a slow oven. He came in after me, shut the outer door, opened an inner door and we went through that. Then it was really hot. The air was thick, wet, steamy and larded with the cloying smell of tropical orchids in bloom. The glass walls and roof were heavily misted and big drops of moisture splashed down on the plants. The light had an unreal, greenish color, like light filtered through an aquarium tank. The plants filled the place, a forest of them, with nasty, meaty leaves and stalks like the newly washed fingers of dead men. They smelled as overpowering as boiling alcohol under a blanket. (Chandler 1995b: 592)

The 42 words of the short story became 122 in the novel. In *The Big Sleep* Chandler added a significant amount of sensory detail to the passage, expanding the one reference to the sense of smell in the short story to include the temperature and the humidity, the color of the light in the greenhouse, and the "cloying" smell of the orchids in particular. More importantly, when Chandler rewrote the piece about the General's greenhouse, he laced it with figurative language. And it is not just figurative language, but vivid, surprising, and even shocking figurative language.

To be sure, Chandler paid attention to making details from the stories more particular and vivid in the novels. But his principal object was to rework the prose – to perfect the rhythm of the sentences and augment or sharpen the tropes of the original short stories. In the four novels he wrote between 1938 and 1943 Chandler established what, for many, would become the essentials of hard-boiled prose style.

Before Chandler began his novels, the basic elements and the virtues of hard-boiled style had been developed and demonstrated by Hammett in his late short stories and novels. They consisted of slang and other kinds of non-standard diction, short declarative sentences relying on active verbs, first person narration with asides to the listener/reader, and occasional wisecracks. Chandler focused his efforts to refine these elements. In his notebooks he compiled lists of different kinds of slang (railroad, Hollywood, pickpocket, and San Quentin Prison Slang) to use in his dialogue. He also elevated overstatement and understatement into standard features of the new style, drawing on the working class "wise crack" popularized by writers like Damon Runyon. Indeed, in the opening paragraphs of both *The Big Sleep* and *Farewell, My Lovely* Chandler used this device to help establish the wry tone – and Marlowe's character – for the ensuing narrative. Thus, early in *The Big Sleep* Marlowe describes the entrance doors of the Sternwood mansion as being wide enough to "have let in a troop of Indian elephants," and in the first paragraph of *Farewell, My Lovely* he describes Moose Malloy as being "a big man but not more than six feet five inches tall and not wider than a beer truck."

Most importantly Chandler made the simile a standard feature of hard-boiled style. His narrators use similes both to explain events and people to their reader/listeners and to characterize the narrator by his range of reference and his original, shocking, or at least novel juxtapositions. Indeed, in rewriting his short stories into novels, Chandler paid particular attention to even the smallest details and rhythms of his similes: for example, "he looked about as unobtrusive as a tarantula on a slice of angel food" in "Try the Girl" became "he looked about as inconspicuous as a tarantula on a slice of angel food cake" in *Farewell, My Lovely*.

On one level Chandler used similes to help create the background of the marginal world in which his detectives live, similes like these from *The Big Sleep*:

as black and shallow as the enamel on a cafeteria tray
as false as an usherette's eyelashes
as empty as a headwaiter's smile

But Chandler's similes also serve to characterize his narrator/heroes and to make manifest in the prose style his prescription in "The Simple Art of Murder" that the hero "must be a complete man and a common man and yet an unusual man" (Chandler 1995a: 992). First of all, Chandler used similes to demonstrate the hero's wide range of knowledge and awareness. Thus at the same time that his private investigators can draw upon the kind of experience that would lead them to describe things as being as "tasteless as a roadhouse blonde" ("Spanish Blood"), as "tough as an ingrown toenail" ("Guns at Cyrano's"), and as "empty and deserted as a closed theater" ("The King in Yellow"), they can also casually refer to elements of high culture such as Marcel Proust (*The Big Sleep*), Isadora Duncan (*Farewell, My Lovely*), a Cremona violin (*Farewell, My Lovely*), Cardinal Richelieu (*Farewell, My Lovely*), or Chopin (*Little Sister*). In nearly every case, Chandler's similes demonstrate his hero's wit and *joie de vivre*. Sometimes they seem to serve no other purpose:

As eyebrowless as a French roll ("Try that Girl")
As hot as a bartender's bunion ("Mandarin Jade")
As crazy as a pair of waltzing mice ("Killer in the Rain")

At their best, Chandler's similes set off reverberations which amplify and deepen the reader's understanding of the narrator and his world. Thus, for example, in *Farewell, My Lovely* when Marlowe tells readers that his cigarette tasted like "a plumber's handkerchief" the comparison functions both as a witty remark and ignites an immediate recognition of what the comparison means – given knowledge both of the general functions of handkerchiefs and the materials in which plumbers immerse their hands. From the 1940s well into the next century Chandler's similes would serve as the model and inspiration for dozens upon dozens of writers.

While Chandler was working on his first group of novels in Los Angeles, in neighboring Hollywood filmmakers were using the hard-boiled story as the basis of what would come to be called *film noir* (see Simpson, chapter 14 in this volume). John Huston's 1941 Warner Brothers version of Hammett's *The Maltese Falcon* led the way. Shortly after Bogart's appearance as Sam Spade, two of Chandler's novels were used to make films: *The Falcon Takes Over* (1942) with a screenplay by Lynn Root, Frank Fenton, and Michael Arlen, was loosely based on *Farewell, My Lovely*, and *A Time to Kill* (1942) was based on *High Window*. In 1943 Paramount pictures hired Chandler as their own in-house hard-boiled writer to work with Billy Wilder on the film version of James M. Cain's novel *Double Indemnity* (see Marling, chapter 34 in this volume). Released in 1944, the film received eight Academy Award nominations including Best Picture, Best Actress, Best Director, Best Screenplay and Best Dramatic Score. Chandler would go on to collaborate on the screenplays of *And Now Tomorrow* (1944) and *The Unseen* (1945) before he served as the sole writer of the screenplay for *The Blue Dahlia* (1945), which received another nomination for an Academy Award for Best Screenplay. The next year saw the Warner Brothers film version of Chandler's *The Big Sleep*, with screenplay by Leigh Brackett, Jules Furthman, and William Faulkner. In 1950 Chandler wrote his last screenplay, *Strangers on a Train*, for Alfred Hitchcock, based on Patricia Highsmith's novel.

After World War II Chandler came to be recognized as America's leading mystery writer and spokesman for the hard-boiled school. He would write only three more novels, *The Little Sister* (1949), *The Long Goodbye* (1954), and *Playback* (1958). All are sadder and darker, and *The Long Goodbye* in particular less concerned with actual detection and more deliberately literary than Chandler's earlier work. Moving away from his pulp origins, Marlowe in these books is, as Anthony Boucher put it in *The New York Times Book Review*, "less a detective than a disturbed man of 42 on a quest for some evidence of truth and humanity" (Boucher 1949: vii.24). *The Little Sister* was also the first of his novels to provide an insider's view of the film industry, based on his experiences as a screenwriter during the preceding 6 years. In many ways it epitomizes Chandler's *oeuvre*, which in addition to its lone, self-mocking, sentimental hero with his wise-cracking colloquialisms, has come to stand for a certain fixed array of personality types, cultural attitudes, and geographical locales branded the world over as "Chandlerian."

The very title of *The Little Sister*, reminiscent of Bible-belt evangelical salutations and down-home familial sentiment, harkens back to Chandler's early childhood summers in Nebraska. Orfamay Quest, a mousy but religious young lady from Manhattan, Kansas, hires Philip Marlowe to find her missing brother, Orrin, who has come to California during the postwar aeronautics boom to find work. Chandler milks Orfamay's teetotaling and anti-tobacco prejudices for a few chuckles, using the whiskey-swigging pipe-smoker Marlowe as straight man. But it does not take long for the reader to begin to suspect Orfamay of knowing more than she is letting on about Orrin's disappearance and the shady schemes by which he got himself into trouble. Against the myth of sod-busting uprightness that Orfamay and Orrin seem to represent, Chandler sets the story of their older stepsister, Leila Quest, an up and coming Hollywood starlet going by the screen name of Mavis Weld. Reversing the expected, and sentimental, contrast of honest midwestern family values with phony Hollywood display, Chandler writes Mavis as a hard-working and deserving professional whose career is ultimately jeopardized by her atavistic desire to protect her "little sister," while ostensible hicks Orrin and Orfamay turn out to be cold-blooded blackmailers and murderers.

That is not to say that Hollywood and metropolitan Los Angeles in general get off lightly. Chandler's behind-the-scenes vignettes on studio lots and in agents' offices, among stars, starlets, directors, producers, and owners, lift the rock off a world of venality and eccentric self-indulgence bordering on the surreal. On his arrival at the studio where Mavis is shooting her next picture, Marlowe first encounters the owner of the studio, Jules Oppenheimer, in a secluded patio, all but mesmerized by his three boxer dogs' precisely choreographed peeing ritual. "Always the same," he tells Marlowe. "Even in my office."

> I figured it was just Hollywood. I lit a cigarette and sat down on the bench. "In your office," I said. "Well, every day has its new idea, hasn't it." (Chandler 1995a: 305)

The entire sequence, which goes on for some three pages, has the same sense of waking unreality, centered on a similarly elderly, narcissistic male figure, as the hothouse scene that opens *The Big Sleep*. And Hollywood also helps Chandler to some excellent one-liners. On arriving at the studio, Marlowe is curious about the bulletproof glass enclosing the guard's desk. "I never heard of anybody shooting his way into the picture business," he quips. To which "a girl in slacks with a red carnation" behind him responds, "Oh brother, if a gun was all it took" (Chandler 1995a: 304).

The Little Sister is in some ways, then, very much of a piece with Chandler's earlier work. The world through which Marlowe navigates is still full of desperate grifters and gangsters, fugitives from the law, alcoholics pushing reefers and crooked doctors pushing heroin, corrupt cops and honest if cynical cops doing their best in a corrupt world; blackmailers, hit-men, and call-girls; hypodermics, doped cigarettes, filed ice-picks, and pistols of various makes and calibers; and that staple of Chandler's gender Manicheeism, the alluring but deadly *femme fatale*. Besides Orfamay herself, B-actress Dolores Gonzales, a purported friend of Mavis's, takes the type about as far as it can go without collapsing into outright self-parody with her tight-fitting black outfits, door-blocking breasts, and come-hither hysterics. Backing away from Dolores, who is holding a gun on him, Marlowe sums her up in the penultimate chapter: "Slim, dark and lovely and smiling. Reeking with sex. Utterly beyond the moral laws of this or any world I could imagine" (Chandler 1995a: 414).

But if *The Little Sister* remains a recognizably Chandlerian novel, it also reveals a significantly more jaundiced and weary resignation to the accelerating commercial sprawl and consumerism of postwar LA, a tawdriness we can now recognize, a half-century later, as an indelible part of the American landscape we all inhabit. Leaving Mavis Weld's apartment on Sunset Strip, Marlowe embarks on an odyssey through the neon-lit fast-food freeway ganglia of the new southern California, "the department store state. The most of everything and the best of nothing" (Chandler 1995a: 268). Punctuated by the refrain, "Here we go again. You're not human tonight, Marlowe," it is the same long journey to the end of night that Marlowe has occasionally taken in previous books, like *Farewell, My Lovely*. Never before, however, has it seemed so bleak, used-up, and hopelessly out of touch with itself.

> I smelled Los Angeles before I got to it. It smelled stale and old like a living room that had been closed too long. But the colored lights fooled you. The lights were wonderful. There ought to be a monument to the man who invented neon lights. … There's a boy who really made something out of nothing. (Chandler 1995a: 269).

The sleaze and corruption lying just below the surface of Chandler's previous novels are still there, like the bloated corpse of Crystal Kingsley snagged beneath calm mountain waters in *Lady in the Lake*. But now the surface itself seems oily and iridescent, smeared with vulgarity, "a neon-lighted slum" (Chandler 1995a: 357). "I used to like this town," Marlowe tells Dolores at one point:

> A long time ago. There were trees along Wilshire Boulevard. Beverly Hills was a country town. Westwood was bare hills and lots offering at eleven hundred dollars and no takers. Hollywood was a bunch of frame houses on the interurban line. Los Angeles was just a big dry sunny place with ugly homes and no style, but goodhearted and peaceful. (Chandler 1995a: 357)

In Marlowe's wistful voice we can hear, perhaps, the intonations of a young Doughboy returning from the Western Front to a golden land fresh with promise, and a new job at Dabney Oil with lots of room for advancement and nothing to regret.

At the end of 1954, the year *The Long Goodbye* made its American debut, Cissy Chandler died and Chandler began to enter his last alcoholic, self-destructive spiral. *Playback* was published in 1958, the year before he died.

His second life as an inspiration for successive generations of hard-boiled detective writers began soon afterward. In the mid-1960s and early 1970s Ballantine reissued three collections of Chandler's short stories: *Killer in the Rain* (1964). *Trouble Is my Business* (1972) and *Pickup on Noon Street* (1972), the precursors to Frank MacShane's biography, *The Life of Raymond Chandler* (1976) and his two-volume Library of America collection *Raymond Chandler: Stories and Early Novels* and *Raymond Chandler: Later Novels and other Writings* (1995). Directly or indirectly the hard-boiled revival that began in the 1970s and extended to the end of the century was inspired by Chandler – in the development of its heroes, in its implicit and explicit romantic worldview, in its attention to place, and most of all in its style. It began with Ross Macdonald, who said that Chandler wrote like "a slumming angel" (Macdonald 1981: 27). It took off with Robert B. Parker's dissertation "The Violent Hero, Wilderness Heritage and Urban Reality: A Study of the Private Eye in the Novels of Dashiell Hammett, Raymond Chandler, and Ross Macdonald" (1970), with his Spenser novels and his rewrite of Chandler's unfinished novel *Poodle Springs*. It continues with contemporary writers like Earl Emerson and Robert Crais. Indeed, in the half-century since his death Chandler's works have become part of our nation's literary legacy to the world.

33

Agatha Christie (1890–1976)

Merja Makinen

For the greater length of her critical reception, Agatha Christie has been praised as an ingenious puzzle-plotter. "Agatha Christie had the intellect and technical skill to make of the clue-puzzle" the ideal narrative mode for her time, argues Stephen Knight. "She isolated in her technically brilliant plots, her restrained characterization and subtle thematic nuances just what a dedicated reader could hope for as a fictional defence against feared crime" (2004: 89). The golden age "whodunit" presents all the clues needed to solve the murder, alongside a plethora of "red herrings" to confuse the issue. Typically, it involves a closed community of suspects (a train, a girl's school, a village) most of whom could be the murderer, as revealed through the process of the detection. "Each character is of interest to us, for each is a genuine suspect. No-one can be fully developed, however, for the very nature of the game requires that Christie spread her attention about equally among her relatively large cast" (Merrill 1997: 89). The pleasure of such a text is in trying to solve the puzzle by analyzing all the information and arriving at the murderer before the unmasking in the denouement (see Rowland, chapter 8 in this volume).

And the narrative is inclusive with regards to the reader. In *Cards on the Table* (1936) Christie literally does lay all her cards on the table by reproducing typographically the four bridge scores of the suspects because Poirot insists that they hold the key to solving the murder. In *The Mysterious Affair at Styles* Christie first gives a diagram of the murdered woman's room (with door openings and significant furniture), has Hastings note in minute detail all the clues Poirot finds there and then has Poirot delineate five of his six important things (though not why they are significant). Here the reader is being addressed and invited to engage in the puzzle by a supremely readerly narrative. An awareness of the reader is included within the parameters of the process of narration. Pierre Bayard argues in *Who Killed Roger Ackroyd?* (2000), citing Roland Barthes's "Death of the Author," that not only does the attentive reader becomes an active participant in the narration but that Christie's strength lies in her ability to hide from his or her notice the facts in plain view on the page, a phenomenon that he allies to the Freudian concept of "psychic blindness."

This combination of pleasurable activity in the reader and ingenious plot-twists has proved phenomenally successful. Christie has sold over two billion copies world-wide, half of them in translations, her work having been translated into more than 44 languages: Sova claims that "only Shakespeare and the Bible have outsold her" (1996: xiii). However, for the majority of the twentieth century the critical con-sensus has been that her plotting was her major claim to fame, since her texts presented a cosy, conservative Englishness inhabited by stock characters in a mid-dle-class community, which is restored to order by the elimination of the murderer. "The general critical consensus regarding golden age fiction is that the plot is elevated above all other considerations (often including credibility) and that realistic character development takes a back seat to the construction of the puzzle" (Scaggs 2005: 35). While acknowledging her influence as a crime figure, such criticism tends to dismiss the texts themselves as less interesting because less literary than those of her compatriot Dorothy Sayers. This critical view has, however, been revised during the last decade of the twentieth and the first decade of the twenty-first century.

The most important element in the critical shift has been the acknowledgement of Christie's complexity. So, for example, one of Christie's narrative tropes is her manipulation of cultural stereotypes: the major uttering imperialist views, the old maid distrustful of young people, the nurturing nurse companion. The texts deploy these stereotypes against the reader and the text's investigator, invoking erroneous prejudices that "blind" them to the more complex masked depths. Hastings, Poirot's earliest sidekick, was used to this effect as the "idiot friend," but Luke Fitzwilliam plays much the same role in *Murder Is Easy* (1939), finally realizing at the close that his unthinking sexism has made him look in the wrong direction for the killer, "Not a *man* – she never mentioned a *man* – *you* assumed it was a man" (1972: 215). Rather than invoke these stock characters, Christie examines how her characters masquerade within the conventional expectations, thereby reconfiguring the instability and slip-periness of social identities. As Richard York observes,

> Christie's novels are sustained experiments in how people cannot be who they say they are. People are disguised, they are reduplicated, they adopt other selves. ... Most confus-ingly, perhaps, they pretend to be themselves. (York 2007: 35)

Or as Poirot puts it, in *Peril at End House*: "They were a shade too 'typical' ... was it not playing a part just a little too thoroughly?" (1973a: 55). York argues that while Christie's texts are not postmodern, since the novels close with the presentation of a truth, they do revel in playing with "the seductive power of the perspectives we take for granted" (2007: 22).

Christie's use of the generic format is not formulaic either, but similarly parodic and playful. Lee Horsley argues that the author is questioning and self-reflexive in relation to the genre and turns her "preoccupation with the form to more deconstructive ends" (2005: 41). Christie's novels systematically broke each of the ten rules of the "Detection Club" and Van Dine's twenty rules, most famously in *The Murder of Roger Ackroyd* (1926), the furore around which brought her to the world's attention. Although Christie flouted the "rules" of golden age fiction, she practiced a playful deconstruction rather than wholesale destruction. In the Beresford novel, *Partners in Crime* (1929a), the two partners deliberately pastiche twelve of Christie's contemporary detectives, sometimes with the star detective and at other times with the sidekick solving the crime. Christie's ability to critique self-reflexively the genre's conventions points to a complex engagement with the development of the golden age genre.

The biased nature of Raymond Chandler's analysis of the golden age as safe and cozy has become increasingly evident, with critics arguing persuasively for the disturbing consequences of setting the crimes in such known, domestic environments. Christie's murderers do not lurk "out there" in the unknown urbanized world of crime but are ensconced within the circle of friends and family. Surely this is more destabilizing to any concepts of the known and safe? Knight suggests that the "intimate danger" is exactly what is disturbing about her texts: "The cause of disorder in her novels is consistently a matter of personal betrayal ... and this sense that you cannot trust anyone at all is a threatening message coded into the whole 'golden age' form" (2004: 91). For Knight Christie's sinister aura derives precisely from this "capacity to realise, in formulaic, repeatable mode a sense of personal unease and possible danger that emerges even in – especially in – a world secluded from social and international disorder" (2004: 92). He challenges commentators who see golden age fiction as "a sunny account" of a stable, coherent society because they "overlook the repetitive traumas of betrayal that are central to the form" (2004: 92–3).

Indeed, one could argue that the unsettling frisson of anxiety surrounding Christie's crime fiction is the deadly potential embedded in even the most mundane domestic situation. Parents, children, spouses all prove to be lethal family members, while apparent bastions of society – doctors, politicians, wealthy manufacturers, through to the humble "companion" – could also be dangerous. Christie's texts assume that anyone can be a murderer, no one is exempt, no one totally to be trusted. As Linden Peach argues, the "English middle class between the wars ... was not a coherent group" and the novels' denouements cannot solve the divisions that have been elaborated between the classes, the generations, and the genders. England is not "reaffirmed at the close" but revealed as fragmented. "The detective story is something of a masquerade. Setting false trails for the reader and presenting them with what is not as it might appear, [it] has at its heart duplicity and performance" (2006: 105–6). It is a "duplicity" that Peach believes extends to the author, determined to fool the reader as an effective "whodunnit" writer.

Christie's output was phenomenal. During her 57 years of writing she produced 68 crime or mystery novels and over 100 short stories (not to mention the

6 romances, 19 plays and 3 volumes of poems). Given such an oeuvre, perhaps the one thing that can be confidently asserted is that, despite the formulaic similarities of much of her crime fiction, it is unwise to attempt to make monolithic statements about her work as whole. Certainly to compare *The Mysterious Affair at Styles* (1920) to *Endless Night* (1967) or *Hallowe'en Party* (1969) is to encompass a wide variation in types of detective novel and in worlds of detection, from the almost cheerful sifting through the different alibis at the country house by a semi-comic Poirot, where the villain does prove to be the outsider, to the much darker first person narration of a youthful, swinging-sixties psychopath or the unconventional single mother and daughter family at the center of the drowning of a child at an apple-bobbing Halloween party. These murders are less explicable, less reasonable and the denouement more fraught. Christie's last two published novels, *Curtain* (1975) and *Sleeping Murder* (1976), cannot be used for such a comparison since she had been counseled to write the "final" case for both Poirot and Miss Marple during the 1940s and file them away for later publication. Even so, as Robin Woods argues in " 'It was the mark of Cain': Agatha Christie and the murder of mystery," *Curtain*, with its motiveless murders, foreshadows the true crime genre that would come to supersede the golden age puzzle-plots. "Christie portrayed, and in a sense foresaw a new kind of crime that would lie beyond the detective's control" (Woods 1997: 103).

It would, then, be more accurate to acknowledge the ways in which Christie's novels shift and change over 50 years. By the end of World War II, many of Christie's cases are more motiveless and less comforting in their denouement, for all that the killer is apprehended or punished. Certainly the re-evaluation of her work argues for a much more complex, unsettling assessment of Christie's oeuvre and for a recognition that her characterization, her use of the generic expectations and her domestic settings are all anchored in an unfounded trust. Christie's 68 novels have a variety of detectives but she is most closely associated with three enduring serial detectives. I will first examine the novels centering on Poirot and Miss Marple, and then, in the final section, will consider the Beresford novels, which are usually categorized as thrillers rather than detective novels. Christie herself differentiated between them, seeing the former as more pleasurable and less rigorous to write, but the Beresford series and the other thrillers in fact contain some of Christie's most interesting dissections of gender, cultural change, and social instability.

Poirot

Hercule Poirot is the longest running of Christie's detectives, introduced in her first novel, *The Mysterious Affair at Styles* (1920) and making his final appearances in *Elephants Can Remember* (1972) and *Curtain* (1975). He is featured in 33 novels and 65 short stories: as Bargainnier points out, he appears in 17 novels during the 1920s and 1930s, 11 during the 1940s and 1950s and only 5 in the 1960s and 1970s, suggesting that Christie was getting progressively tired of his idiosyncrasies (1980: 44). Yet in some of his final appearances (e.g., *Third Girl* [1966], *Hallowe'en Party* [1969], and *Elephants Can Remember* [1972]), Poirot's relationship with Ariadne Oliver (whom Gill calls Christie's "story-writing alter ego" [1990: 73]) enriches his character with an affectionate and amused friendship.

Poirot's traits are well summed up by Sally Munt:

> He is a parody of the male myth; his name implies his satirical status: he is a shortened Hercules and a *poirot* – a clown. He is narcissistic, emotive, feline, apparently irrational, eccentric, quixotic, obsessed with the domestic, and socially "other" in that he is a Belgian. … He is a feminine hero. (1994: 8)

In creating the detective as foreigner in *Styles*, Christie initially developed the stereotype of "otherness," stressing his dandyism, his outrageous moustaches, and his overbearing conceit. Hastings, as the invalided war-hero sent home from the Front (where Poirot was a passive refugee), is contrasted as the man of action voicing an English distaste for Poirot's alien status. He is shocked at Poirot's slow and immaculate dressing, patronizingly amused by his emotional over-reactions and finds his complacency "absurd." In later novels he will disapprove of Poirot reading private letters as "unsporting" behavior. Poirot's effete correctness of attire is deliberately linked to an ordered thought-process that metonymically also becomes inappropriate for English heroic masculinity. Tidiness of dress and of domestic surroundings links via its foreign "otherness" to femininity in Poirot. However, the character does not long remain outlandish. He references the European modernity influencing Britain, the modern exemplar compared to whom Hastings is old-fashioned and out-of-touch.

By the 1930s, Poirot's behavior is less alien, as his tidiness is linked to the clean lines of modernist interiors and his penchant becomes both more familiar and more fashionable. Comments are still made about his being "sartorially ambitious" (*Hallowe'en Party* 1969) but this reads as familiar difference rather than alienated otherness. In Alison Light's interpretation this is a positive attempt to think through the cultural possibilities for a new masculinity after the horrors of World War I.

> In his own small way, Agatha Christie's Poirot was part of the quest for a bearable masculinity which would make what had previously seemed even effeminate preferable to the bulldog virtues of 1914. Christie, like Sayers, recognised the impossibility of creating a confident, British middle-class hero in the old mould. (Light 1991: 43)

Rowland links this less heroic masculinity to the burgeoning form of the golden age puzzle plot in both Sayers and Christie, associating the absence of an autocratic characterization with the formal aspects of a readerly text. "Fracturing the heroic mould of masculinity transforms both the detectives and the reader's relation to the novel.

No longer exhibiting a mastery of events, the loss of Holmesian confidence democratises the form" (Rowland 2001: 19).

Poirot, in the prolific interwar years, predominates as Christie's chosen detective. As Merrill suggests, "Poirot is almost always introduced early, usually with the task of solving a murder committed within the first one hundred pages" (1997: 94), although the variations within the first hundred pages differ widely from his being summoned immediately to view a body to a more developed story before the murder occurs. The detective's investigation forms the major part of the narrative, sifting through all the relevant clues with "periodical recapitulations of the more important details" (Merrill 1997: 94). His investigations rely predominately on a careful piecing together of the facts in an explicable chain, ignoring no detail, however small and domestic (*The Mysterious Affair at Styles* is partially solved by observing how spills to light a fire are stored on a mantel piece). Simultaneously the detective relies on his knowledge of psychology in relation to the type of killing involved. Some characters, he explains, could perform a timid, panicked murder, others would only perform a dashing and audacious one, while a third type would be methodical and premeditated. While he assumes everyone is capable of murder, Poirot is adamant that no one could commit a murder outside of their "character," and dismisses false confessions on this very ground. In *Cards on the Table*, he rejects Mrs Lorrimer's confession immediately: "I am willing to believe that you killed Mr Shaitana – *but you cannot have killed him in the way you say you did.* No-one can do a thing that is not *dans son charactère*" (Christie 1993: 191). His concentration on the psychological aspect necessarily focuses attention on the minutiae of the characters' behavior, though Christie's use of psychology is not developed to any great extent. (An exception is *Appointment with Death* published in 1938 during the rise of fascism and Nazism, where Poirot, aided by a famous psychologist, meditates on the propensity of people to allow themselves to be tyrannized over.)

It is true that the Poirot of the later novels evidences a less confident grasp of the British 1960s and his out-of-datedness may have influenced Christie's choice to deploy him less often. The effete dandy of *Styles* is less able to comprehend the new dandyism of the Carnaby Street generation in *Third Girl* (1966). Although he is well aware that women would find "The Peacock," as Mrs Oliver dubs one male character, "exotic and beautiful," he does not condemn him as the other elderly characters do and instead attempts to explain him via the past, by linking his appearance in silks and satins, with shoulder-length chestnut curls, to Van Dyck's paintings of cavaliers. He is less comfortable with the young "beatnik" women who reject the glamorous allure of his own prime and acknowledges that he is "too old" to help one "because he did not understand her, because it was not even possible for him to appreciate her" (2002: 301). While the ending belies this acknowledgement and seeks to assert his continuing validity, the claim is not completely effective and Poirot's sense of being outside of things carries a psychic wound, since the young people are unaware of his fame and importance.

Poirot's overweening pride in his success, his concern for his immaculate appearance, even to physical discomfort – much is made of ill-fitting patent shoes or impractical suits – are important parts of his characterization and though they are modulated through the 50 years from alien to familiar, they always remain because they are a necessity of his characterization. Rowland suggests that one "factor in the anti-heroic detective is the way personal weaknesses and vulnerabilities are not external to the success of investigations but intrinsic to them," going on to assert that while Poirot is often mocked and despised for "his attention to domestic details and gossip ... his espousal of what are characterised as 'feminine' methods of investigation ... prove crucial" (Rowland 2001:19).

These human fallibilities, seen through other's amused eyes, inject an important element of humor into the Poirot texts that is often absent from the Miss Marple novels. On the whole, and I take into account here my earlier admonition not to try to span Christie's enormous output with a monolithic statement, the Poirot novels have a lightness that stems from the detective's fallible comedic qualities. The later Poirot novels have darker overtones, whether of the gathering world war in *Appointment with Death* (1938) or the horrific drowning of a child in order to create a garden in *Hallowe'en Party* (1969). The motives are often less explicable and the surrounding milieu more fractured, because the world Christie depicted was changing and the expectations about detective fiction along with it. But the familiarity of Poirot's weaknesses reassures us that not all has changed and that the famous Belgian detective, for all the xenophobic dismissal of the unappreciative characters, will prevail both in solving the crime and in surprising the reader in the denouement.

Miss Marple

The character of Miss Jane Marple is featured in fewer books than Poirot. Introduced in a series of short stories in 1928 and appearing two years later in her first book-length adventure, *The Murder at the Vicarage* (1930), Miss Marple ended her career with *Nemesis* (1971) and the 1940s-composed *Sleeping Murder* (1976), having assumed the role of detective in 12 novels and some 20 short stories. Gill notes that 12 years separate the first two novels of the series "and another ten years separate the second from the third and fourth" (1990: 181), until Christie was closer to her creation's age.

Where Poirot is the foreign outsider, Miss Marple is the village insider, conversant with all the community. The literary antecedent to Miss Marple, the character of the nosy old spinster with nothing better to do than spy on her neighbors, is found in Anna Katherine Green's Miss Butterworth in *That Affair Next Door* (1897), her second novel after the famous *The Leavenworth Case* (1878) that Christie remembers affectionately in her *Autobiography* (1977). It is in *The Murder of Roger Ackroyd* that Christie initially creates the elderly spinster, the sister of the narrator who enjoys amateur sleuthing, subsequently recognizing the character's potential as a series detective.

Christie's Miss Marple is a bourgeois character, living frugally on an annuity, though still able to employ a maid and then, as the social mores change, a daily help and, finally, as her health deteriorates, a live-in companion. Shaw and Vanacker examine Miss Marple's clothing in the various novels and conclude that "Although they change, Miss Marple's clothes are always out of date, as one would expect of an elderly spinster lady of limited means" (1991: 46). Where Poirot uses his foreignness to his own advantage, subtly exaggerating it to misguide English characters into dismissing his acumen, Miss Marple manipulates the sexist and ageist prejudices about old ladies being worthless to society, lacking in intellectual ability and outmoded in their assumptions and expectations, adopting the persona society expects as effective camouflage.

Like Poirot, Miss Marple's character modulates over the years. She is transformed from a rather waspish introduction in *Murder at the Vicarage* (1930) to a gentler, mellower figure in *The Body in the Library* (1942) and *The Moving Finger* (1943), with pink cheeks and twinkling blue eyes, and then to a more vengeful detective in the final novels, taking pleasure in the fact that the culprit will be punished – which, of course, means being hanged since capital punishment remained in force for the majority of Christie's writing career. Poirot tends to engage in detection to show off his abilities and because he "disagrees" with murder, while Miss Marple sees a more personal affront in the killings. Shaw and Vanacker suggest that this stems from her insider status, that her integration into the community fuels the force of her retribution (1991: 2). There is less humor employed in the Miss Marple cases: her "weaknesses" are less clear since her elderly, frail, female status is not portrayed as comic and is never countenanced as anything but an overlooked strength in the texts. As such, these detective novels – despite the comic enjoyment of women traducing the masquerade – tend to have the darkest tone of Christie's detective and thriller fiction. Light, Rowland, and Peach suggest the later ones contain elements of Gothic sensibility.

Robert Merrill argues that the Marple novels are "a very different kind of game" (1997: 95), since she appears more intermittently within the text and is never the main investigator. We thus follow the male investigator for most of the narrative while appreciating that his interpretation of the facts will need to be rewritten by Miss Marple during the denouement:

> The game is therefore very un-Poirotish. The relevant clues are only sometimes before us ... and the lines of inquiry actively pursued by the police can be assumed to be inaccurate ... There are fewer suspects and clues, as indeed there must be, given our distance from the crucial evidence, but arriving at Miss Marple's solutions is still much more difficult than arriving at Poirot's. (Merrill 1997: 95–6)

Indeed, Merrill claims that it is well nigh impossible for the reader to arrive at the solution since the Marple plots stress "mystification rather than deduction" (1997: 96). This closed, less playful, invitation to engage in the narrative game perhaps helps to create the more serious tone of her series. It is noticeable that the Miss Marple stories do not offer the reader such overt clues as card scores, diagrams of a room's layout, or typographically reproduced handwritten notes.

Critical attention has focused on the way Miss Marple manipulates cultural expectations that old women in a village community will be ignorant of the seedier aspects of modern life, playing up to these expectations in a manner that lends itself to theorizing as a feminine masquerade, performing the role culturally expected without quite owning it as she shuttles between identities: "an old lady with a sweet, placid, spinsterish face, and a mind that has plumbed the depths of human iniquity and taken it all as a day's work" (*The Body in the Library* 2002a: 101). Cultural prejudices are dismantled to demonstrate how, behind the fluffy, frail exterior and the rather meandering, inconsequential talk, is an astute, shrewd, and knowledgeable woman whose expertise places her in the center of social occurrences, rather than at the excluded margins. Her characterization quietly challenges and rewrites the expectations of women of a certain age who are unmarried and live alone. "The figure of Miss Marple herself is clearly important as a trope in which conventional assumptions about gender are contested" (Peach 2006: 109). Christie also attaches an importance to the way women talk to each other, re-evaluating the dismissively termed "gossip." Gossip is shown to be a subversively pleasurable communal activity, which men fail to police in book after book, and also Miss Marple's main way of collecting the facts that will rid society of its disruptive villain. Like Poirot she also focuses on the small, domestic, feminine minutiae of life, whether nails are bitten (*The Body in the Library*), how a hat is worn (*They Do it with Mirrors*), or why someone takes an umbrella on a fine day (*Sleeping Murder*). Despite the darker tones of the Marple novels and stories, the pleasure available in the text's uncovering of the erroneous expectations of phallocentric ageism should not be overlooked.

Miss Marple's main process of detection has some similarities to Poirot's use of "psychology," although, since she classifies characters into "types," it is more rigid. Where Poirot can accommodate an infinite variety of characters, though they may not step outside of their specific nature, Marple insists there is a small, finite number of types to which all characters conform, so that a multinational banker might remind her of an odd-job man she knew personally because of similar character traits. "You'd be surprised if you knew how very few distinct types there are in all" (1982: 163), she states in *Murder at the Vicarage*. Such a thesis neatly side-steps the issue of her passive insularity, since the whole world can be reduced to the confines of the village community she knows so intimately. As Shaw and Vanacker argue, where Poirot creates a pattern from the available facts and characters, Miss Marple uses a preexisting pattern of humanity and hence holds a more "deterministic view of human nature" (1991: 74). They point to Miss Marple's rejection of psychology or environmental factors, in favor of a belief that some people are predisposed towards evil. This more fatalistic, fixed conception of the world perhaps further explains her more pitiless apprehending of the murderers and her vindication of the innocent. In *A Caribbean Mystery* (1964) and again in *Nemesis* (1971), the last written of her novels, Miss Marple is delineated as Nemesis – in classical mythology the daughter of Night and Vengeance – who measures out happiness and punishes the wicked. In the cause of "justice," Miss Marple acknowledges, she could be "ruthless," quoting the biblical passage "Let Justice roll down like waters/ And Righteousness like an everlasting stream" (Christie 1984: 189). Behind the mask of her fluffy pink shawl and pearls, Miss Marple is as vengeful as a Greek Fury.

Thrillers

Christie's thrillers, as she acknowledged, were less rigorous novels to write, although they also have similarities in their quest to unearth the villain veiled behind the array of acquaintances and suspects. Christie wrote both a series of five novels with Tommy and Tuppence Beresford, and a number of individual novels almost invariably with bright young women as the protagonists. In both, Christie's examination of the social expectations of femininity and the array of available cultural formations becomes even more overt than in the Poirot and Marple series, and closer to some of the questioning of gendered configurations found in her romance fiction published under the pseudonym of Mary Westmacott (e.g., *Unfinished Portrait*, 1934, and *Absent in the Spring*, 1944, which explore the damage to the feminine psyche of attempting to inhabit the masquerade of dutiful domesticity).

Christie often included romance plots in her detective fiction, allowing Poirot and Marple to preside over denouements that not only involve apprehending the culprit but also bring together the young lovers in a dual-facetted happy ending. In the thrillers, romance becomes more central and often proves the driving impetus for the action. Anne Benningfield, in *The Man in the Brown Suit* (1924), travels to South Africa on a whim to catch up with a man she glimpsed in England because of her sexual attraction to him. Victoria Jones meets a young man on a London park bench and resolves to follow him to Baghdad because of a similar desire in *They Came to Baghdad* (1951). Courageous, reckless, and active, these young women name their own sexual desires and search for a love relationship of equal agency. They are the true heroines of Christie's re-negotiating of what Light, discussing Poirot, terms impossible: "the confident, British middle-class hero in the old mould" (1991: 43).

Christie bridges the impossible by switching genders to create a heroic femininity, located in the "bright young things" of the 1920s Jazz Age, breaking "the old mould" and replacing it with a more modern, twentieth-century formation. In the *Seven Dials Mystery* (1929), Bundle, the madcap and intrepid young woman, is contrasted to the much slower and duller Bill who, like Hastings, undercuts the effectiveness of the masculine action figure during the 1920s. "In general, Christie looks upon her bright young women with indulgence, enjoying their chic, admiring their spunk, understanding their boredom and pique" (Gill 1990: 86). The plots of the thrillers are less distinctive, with foreign agents threatening the stability of

Britain in a variety of ways, from selling top secrets to fomenting fascist conspiracies. The real interest of these novels, often dismissed as silly by the critics of detective fiction, is in the exploratory de-stabilizing of gendered expectations in the characterization. The style is light-hearted and determinedly bright, as befits both the modern tone rejecting Edwardian solemnity and the parodic questioning of the texts.

Charles Osborne argues that Christie created a new genre of thriller in the "comedy-adventure," analogous to the best-selling "adventure-romance" of 1920, *The Prisoner of Zenda* (2002: 134). Tommy and Tuppence Beresford also conform to this redrawing of the gender map in a relationship similar to Bundle and Bill, where she is an active, quick-witted and intuitively brilliant investigator and he is a more passive and considered partner (though not in the "idiot friend" position of Hastings). The texts consistently stress the complementarities of their gendered characterizations. The two novels of the 1920s, *The Secret Adversary* (1922) and *Partners in Crime* (1929), examine their "joint venture" as "adventurers" as they try to settle to a job after the excitement of the war; Tommy returns from service abroad and Tuppence refuses to return to the family home and the role of dutiful daughter. They are insatiable for excitement. At the end of the first novel Tommy proposes marriage and the opening of the second sees them as newly-weds. *N or M?* (1941), set during World War II, has Tommy too old to fight but enlisted to uncover the fifth column of German sympathizers and agents working in Britain. Tuppence outwits the attempts of the authorities to keep her away from the action and assumes an equal role in the investigation.

The Beresfords are unusual in ageing appropriately to the chronology of publication, so that by the 1940s they are middle-aged, in *By the Pricking of my Thumbs* (1968) they are both "elderly" and going grey, while in the final novel, *The Postern of Fate* (1973), Tuppence is over seventy. This device allows Christie to redraw their relationship through the changing years and different social periods. In the last two novels they also investigate murders and hence straddle the boundary from thriller to detective fiction, the mystery exploiting the sinister liminal potential of an old people's home in both cases. The Beresford texts span Christie's oeuvre: the first was her second novel, after *Styles*, while *Postern of Fate* was the last she wrote. The couple proved enduring if not overly prolific and Gill suggests this longevity derives from the nature of their mutual relationship. "Their panache – the combination each has of being hot and cool, humorous and sexy, needful and independent – offers an unusual and vital form of male-female professional and private cooperation" (1990: 74).

As must be increasingly obvious, a major part of the revisioning of Christie's fiction has come from critics interested in gender. Exploring in detail her hundreds of characters allows a fuller awareness of the more challenging aspects of her fiction. The earlier view of Christie's characters as stock stereotypes ignores the whole range of unexpected persons, from sympathetic unmarried mothers (*After the Funeral, Cat among the Pigeons, The Hallowe'en Party*) and mistresses (*The Hollow*) to lesbian couples (*Murder Is Announced, Nemesis*), as I have expounded in *Agatha Christie: Investigating Femininity* (2006). Christie wrote over a period of 50 years and during this period her writing reflects on and explores the cultural changes occurring between the 1920s and the 1970s. Detective fiction, in its unveiling of the instabilities and fractures within society, proves an ideal process for a quiet exploration of how these changes impact on character and cultural expectation. Both Poirot and Miss Marple similarly raise questions about feminine activity and investigation through their reification of the more feminine, domestic codes of comprehension. Such critical re-examinations suggest that, while Christie's political assumptions may remain conservative, her detective novels and thrillers cannot be so simply pigeonholed.

34

James M. Cain (1892–1977)

William Marling

James M. Cain was not a detective novelist per se, but he changed forever the way American detective fiction is written. His first-person confessional narrators, his frank portrayal of lust and greed, and his deft stylistic touches raised several of his novels, and the films made from them, to the status of classics, influencing generations of writers.

Born in 1892 to an Irish family in tidewater Maryland, Cain grew up in an atmosphere that he once described as "feinschmecker Catholicism," meaning that his parents were "gourmets of religious ritual." They attended mass regularly because "the services were mounted in a manner worthy of Ziegfeld." By the age of 13, Cain did not believe a word of the "whole mumbo-jumbo, especially the confessional, where I was faking and suddenly knew that the priest knew it" (Hoopes 1982: 20). Not surprisingly, Cain's narratives are essentially "faked confessions."

As a young man, Cain tried teaching, inspecting roads, singing, and selling insurance, before getting on as a police reporter at *The Baltimore American*. In 1917 he moved to *The Baltimore Sun*, one of the best papers in the US and the catbird seat of critic H. L. Mencken. Drafted in 1918, Cain served with a headquarters' troop during World War I and edited *The Lorraine Cross* during the occupation of Europe. On his return, he married childhood sweetheart Mary Clough, whom he offended by dressing sloppily, treating Prohibition as a joke, and speaking a tough-guy lingo out of the side of his mouth. A job awaited Cain at *The Sun* and he finally met Mencken, whose icon-smashing books, brusque style, and editorship of *Smart Set* made him a powerful influence on the writers of this generation.

Cain began to specialize in his reportage, covering the West Virginia coal field battles, even becoming a member of the United Mine Workers. He placed articles on this topic in *The Atlantic* and *The Nation*. He developed his own deft handling of dialogue during a stint of teaching at St John's, and eventually he found a job through his Baltimore connections at the *New York World*, where he ended up writing "light" pieces for the editorial page of Walter Lippmann.

Cain moved to New York City alone in 1924, leaving Mary in Annapolis. These were the declining days of the *World*, a paper purchased and groomed by Joseph Pulitzer in 1883. Besides Lippmann, the editorial pages printed Maxwell Anderson, Allan Nevins, Arthur Krock, Franklin P. Adams, and Heywood Broun. Cain specialized in the offbeat editorial – praise for man-eating sharks or jazz in church, denunciation of federal regulation of baseball and of Americanized opera (Hoopes 1982: 122–3).

He lived mostly with Elina Tyszecka, a Finn whose husband, like Cain's wife, was elsewhere, but he dated five or six women. According to one reporter, Cain "was almost aggressive about wanting you to know he was living in sin." When Elina went on a long trip, he moved in with yet another woman, a reporter at his paper (Hoopes 1982: 126–7). Cain drank prodigiously with Mencken when the latter was in town, and otherwise with the *World*, *New Yorker* or Algonquin Round Table crowds. They all had a cynical view of relations between the sexes. "Love is the illusion that one woman differs from another," Mencken thundered. Cain thought himself romantic when he countered, "Love is the discovery that one woman *does* differ from another" (Hoopes 1982: 527).

In 1925 Cain wrote several debunking pieces for *American Mercury*. He attacked altruists in "The Pathology of Service" and Seventh Day Adventists in "Servants of the People." In "The Pastor" he wrote, "[T]he typical American man of God in these our days is so loathsome, such a low, greasy buffo, so utterly beneath ridicule, so fit only for contempt" (Hoopes 1982: 129). In 1926 Cain wrote a play, *Crashing the Pearly Gates*, about economic conflict and sexual temptation in the coal fields, but it closed after a week. If Cain saw sex everywhere, it was with reason. He was seeing yet another woman when Elina returned, expecting to marry him; he finally divorced Mary and married Elina, adopting her children.

The most sensational news story of 1927 and 1928 was the trial and execution of "Tyger Woman" Ruth Snyder and her lover Judd Gray for the murder of her husband Albert. Gray's situation was eerily like Cain's and it tapped strong national fears about the 1920s "flappers," and sexuality. Ruth, 31, was a striking blonde with "a gaze of Scandinavian iciness," who supposedly convinced corset-salesman Judd Gray, her lover, to bludgeon her husband with a sash weight and then to strangle him with picture wire (Anon 1927). Though a mother, Ruth dressed like a flapper, stocked her basement with Prohibition booze, and liked to gamble. She focused public fears about flappers as mothers. Gray was so short and dejected, the *New York Times* reported, that spectators thought him a dupe and compared him to Charlie Chaplin's "Little Tramp." He testified that, after sex, Ruth would claim her husband beat her: "I'd like to kill the beast," he'd respond heroically. "Do you really mean that?" she asked with interest. Beneath her cool surface, the newspapers detected a fiery "Tyger Woman." A circulation war among East Coast newspapers helped to keep the story on the front page for eight months and a sensational photo of Ruth Snyder's electrocution in the *New York Daily News* in 1928 later shocked the nation.

Gray, like Cain, had gone to World War I an innocent and returned having tasted Europe's alcohol and freer sex. Prohibition was in force when he returned, with boyish, revealingly dressed flappers everywhere. When he married the woman his parents liked, she bored him. Rather than let life pass him by, Gray cultivated a series of women, until he found Ruth. They kept a permanent suitcase at the Waldorf, where they met three times a week. The sex was apparently a revelation, and afterwards they shopped at Macy's or danced in nightclubs. It was an affair full of bad dialogue, an excuse for not missing what the "Jazz Age" had to offer (Marling 1995: 121).

Three aspects of the trial especially caught Cain's attention. Without his knowledge, Snyder took out personal injury insurance on her husband for fifty thousand dollars and double indemnity in case of death. She instructed the postman to deliver payment coupons only to her, ringing the doorbell twice as a signal. This sign and "double indemnity" became symbols of sexual duplicity for newspaper readers. The third aspect that Cain recalled later was apocryphal: that after the murder Snyder sent Gray off on the train to establish his alibi in upstate New York with a bottle of relaxing wine that was in fact laced with cyanide. But this added detail made the "double" threat of the *femme fatale* explicit.

Cain did not use this plot until he left New York in 1931 to become a Hollywood screenwriter. After the Stock Market Crash in 1929, the *World's* ad revenues dropped, and it was sold to Scripps-Howard in 1930. Cain worked next as managing editor of *The New Yorker*, but when Paramount offered him $400 a week, he, Elina, and her children packed up for Hollywood.

Despite his gift for dialogue, Cain was never a great scriptwriter, but he loved the Paramount commissary and the writers' talk there. Released after his first studio contract, Cain drove around southern California – one of the chief forms of recreation there – looking for magazine articles to write. In his early pieces Cain could not find enough praise for the friendly Californians, their excellent schools, and extensive roads (for example, see "Paradise," *American Mercury*, March 1933). One place he liked was a lion farm that supplied animals to movies (Hoopes 1982: 225; Marling, 1995: 162). He combined this admiration with tensions he attributed to a young couple running a nearby gas station: "Always this bosomy-looking thing comes out – commonplace, but sexy, the kind you have ideas about. We always talked while she filled up my tank. One day I read in the paper where a woman who runs a filling station knocks off her husband. Can it be this bosomy thing? I go by and sure enough, the place is closed. I enquire. Yes, she's the one – this appetizing but utterly commonplace woman" (Hoopes 1982: 225).

In Cain's sensational narrative "The Baby in the Icebox" (1933), the husband lets the 500-pound lion loose in the house to kill her. She puts the baby, possibly illegitimate, in an unplugged freezer for safety, and then locks her husband in the house. After he shoots her through a window, the cat turns on and kills him. The house catches on fire, but the baby survives in the freezer.

Encouraged by Knopf, Cain then began a novel he called *Bar-B-Que*. The basic plot came from the Snyder-Gray case, which he discussed with screenwriter Vincent

Lawrence. Lawrence introduced Cain to the Hollywood principle of the "love rack" – that the audience had to *care* about characters, that love stories were the best plot to make them do so, and that one of the lovers had to be a "losing lover". It took Cain six months to write the story of Frank Chambers, a drifter who finds work at the roadside gas station/sandwich joint of Greek immigrant Nick Papadakis and his steamy wife Cora – he made Judd Gray into a California hobo.

Crisp and pastel, California seemed like the perfect setting for a retelling of the Snyder-Gray murder, one in which the lovers' mutual betrayal would be a figure for the social and economic "guilt" that Cain sensed in his own and the nation's disgust with the hedonism of the 1920s. Since he was most comfortable with the first-person point of view, he would "confess" for Judd Gray. Newspapers had suggested Chaplin's persona of the Little Tramp: Gray could be a hobo, folding in social anxieties about the unemployed. The account of Frank and Cora's torrid sex, their decision to murder Nick, the initial botched effort, the success in a faked auto accident, and her confession under pressure follows the sequence of the Snyder-Gray case. Cain got his characters to the stage of arrest and confession, but once they were "racked" he stopped. Lawrence diagnosed the problem: the love element stalled with Cora in jail. "Get her out of there," he advised. "Your story doesn't move until she's free and they start up their lives again" (Hoopes 1982: 233).

Cain struggled with the second half of the novel for months before remembering either the insurance job he held briefly or the "double indemnity" details of the trial. He saw that the insurance worldview made an ironic economic contrast with the initial world of sexual temptation: a figure for the kind of economy emerging in the Depression. He invented a defense lawyer named Katz whose rivalry with the district attorney leads him to trick the prosecution into a squeeze play between three insurance companies. As plotting, this may remind us of O. Henry's devices, but ideologically it shows that justice is pure economic efficiency. Since it is cheaper for the companies, they reverse their testimony, making "justice" into an economy of scale. So Frank and Cora are thrown back together after having betrayed one another. The power that each thought to have attained over the other actually resides in the alliance of the law, insurance companies, and police. Cora and Frank become two "losing lovers", growling in one cage.

Then Cora becomes pregnant, and Frank reticently proposes marriage, but in an accidental repetition of the original crime, he kills her in an unintended auto accident. This time he is convicted and sent to death row, where he discovers God and writes the confession we have been reading.

Some readers find this ending, indeed the whole relationship after Frank and Cora's release, unsatisfactory. For them, the melodrama of lust and crime breaks; there is a narrative rift, after which the characters show a cynicism and suspicion at odds with the speed and eroticism of the novel's first part. And the late revelation of the confessional form imparts a more conventional morality to the closure than anticipated, as Joyce Carol Oates noted in comparing the novel to Dostoevsky's *Crime and Punishment* and Camus's *L'Etranger* (Oates 1977: 111–12).

But in the 1930s, this constrictive, punitive second part explained the way life was going to be in the future. The possibility of being a prodigal son or daughter and returning to the largesse of a forgiving father was past. Cain had, in fact, larded the novel with details from Luke's parable, with Mexico functioning as a "far country" and Nick Papadakis as Frank's "father" (Marling 1995: 165–8). But Cain overturned the parable's mercy. The emerging positive values cluster around Cora, who changes from an ingénue who believes that "Hollywood" will make her a star into the kind of economic realist that the Depression economy required. She tells Frank:

> They gave me a screen test. It was all right in the face. But they talk now. The pictures, I mean. And when I began to talk, they knew me for what I was, and so did I. A cheap Des Moines trollop, that had as much chance in pictures as a monkey has. (Cain 1934: 12)

For Cora, emerging forms of technology and economy are truth; the uncomprehending Frank only knows this: "Whole goddam country lives selling hotdogs to each other" (Cain 1934: 96).

It is Cora's program that triumphs, at least economically. She urges Frank to help her to "make something" of the Greek's roadside restaurant, adding refrigerated draft beer and Tivoli lights and "radio music" under the trees; and indeed, business picks up. But when Cora announces her pregnancy, Frank goes off philandering with Madge, who captures and trains big cats. On his return, he meets not Nick's gruff mercy, but Cora's icy comment, "I couldn't have this baby and then have it find out I let its father hang for murder" (Cain 1934: 122). It is of significance in the male psychodrama that the legal threat she poses to Frank is voiced at the same moment that she confronts him with his paternity. For Frank the imaginary solution to this conflict is Cora's "accidental death" in the car accident, a substitute gratification that Cain lays before male readers audaciously.

"*Postman* was probably the first of the big commercial books in American publishing," writes biographer Roy Hoopes, "the first novel to hit for what might be called the grand slam of the book trade: a hard-cover best-seller, paperback best-seller, syndication, play *and* movie. It scored more than once in most of these mediums and still sells on and on, even today." The novel set a new standard of hard-boiled-ness; it was so tough that the *New York Times*'s reviewer called it a "six-minute egg" (Hoopes 1982: 244; see also Pepper, chapter 10 in this volume).

After making only $3,000 in 1933, Cain was suddenly rich and in demand. He was able to quit a column he had been writing for the Hearst papers. Reprint and movie rights to *Postman* sold; the studios called. Cain next wrote an eight-part serial, "Double Indemnity," for *Liberty* magazine in 1936. Part reworking of *Postman*, part recollection of his youth selling insurance, *Double Indemnity* portrayed a corporate/legal control of life that amounted to "double jeopardy" and appealed to Depression readers' sense of helplessness (Hoopes 1982: 248).

This time Cain stayed even closer to the Snyder-Gray trial, making his protagonist an insurance salesman. Walter Huff meets Phyllis Nirdlinger just as Ruth Snyder met her beau, when he comes to her door selling insurance. She asks questions that make him suspicious, but her intentions complement his desire to dupe his employers, and he joins her in a plot to murder her husband. Huff explains his plan to collect on the double indemnity feature offered in case of death on a railroad journey. But after the two commit the perfect murder, a faked suicide, they are estranged, because Huff's employers – led by Keyes, the claims chief – shadow Phyllis's every move. Like Frank Chambers, who pursued Madge, Huff moves on to a new lust object – Phyllis's stepdaughter Lola. But Lola makes known Phyllis's complicity in a series of grisly murders and also reveals that she is secretly dating Lola's former boyfriend Nino Sachetti. Since Huff is the only father-figure left in the narrative, he grows appropriately paranoid: have Phyllis and Nino duped him into committing murder on their behalf? Will Nino, the new prodigal son, kill him? Has he been a sap? He plots to murder Phyllis, but she ambushes him first. Waking in a hospital with police about to blame Lola, Huff confesses. After some ends are wrapped up with Keyes in boy-to-boy fashion, he then commits suicide with Phyllis.

For *Double Indemnity* Cain scaled back his religious motifs, but the central features of confession remain. Huff begins on the word I and addresses the reader directly a dozen times in the first forty pages. His references to "this House of Death, that you've been reading about in the papers" establish a degree of anteriority, and his asides – "Getting in is the tough part of my job, and you don't tip what you came for till you get where it counts" – give his account the retrospection and moral weight of confession (Cain 1936: 29). The final pages reveal it to be just that – a notarized testament he has traded for temporary freedom.

Lust, in *Double Indemnity* as in *Postman*, is the sin by which other sins gain admission: sexual desire persuades Huff to stay and draw out Phyllis's proposition of murder. But his desires constantly change: he wants Phyllis, he wants to outwit the system, to have Lola, to save himself, and then to kill Phyllis. This continually renewed consumptive capacity seems to be what made Huff an appealing *film noir* hero: he is an existential rebel in a consumer economy. But his lust is actually less important than his desire to outwit the statistical system of the insurance industry: "I'm going to put it through, straight down the line," he says, "and there won't be any slips" (Cain 1936: 23).

> I'm a croupier in that game. I know all their tricks, I lie awake nights thinking up tricks, so I'll be ready for them when they come at me. And then one night I think up a trick, and get to thinking I could crook the wheel myself if I could only put a plant out there to put down my bet. (Cain 1936: 29)

Huff is the first high-tech, white-collar criminal in American literature. But the emerging economy needed to limit his kind of aggressive rationality rather than let it "crook the wheel." That Huff works in one of the Depression's growth industries may have offended intellectuals, for reviewers of 1936 treated him as reviewers might treat a Wall Street arbitrager of 2008. But popular audiences seem to have sympathized with him more, and a glance at the issues of *Liberty* magazine in which the novel was serialized shows how widespread was the reach of the system that Huff problematizes. Each article in *Liberty* has a suggested reading time, statistics pepper the pages, and the ads celebrate the mechanical icons of the novel – cars, trains, and ships. To be certain, Cain still used religious imagery. Huff's early confession that he stands fascinated at the edge of a precipice "looking over the edge" (1936: 18) recalls Calvinist preacher Jonathan Edwards's "Sinners in the Hands of an Angry God." And later when Huff returns home so rattled he cannot think, he recites the Lord's Prayer. On discovering his fear of Phyllis, he says, "I did something I hadn't done in years. I prayed" (1936: 79). But his prayers have a wooden quality: religion does not mean much in the life of a protagonist who chooses to commit suicide, actual, or economic.

The movie of *Double Indemnity* (1944) became one of the masterpieces of *film noir*, but Cain had little to do with it. As a conjunction of eccentric talents, however, it is probably unrivaled: James M. Cain's novel as co-scripted by Raymond Chandler (who said that Cain was "every kind of writer I detest, a *faux naif*, a Proust in greasy overalls, a dirty little boy with a piece of chalk") and Billy Wilder, who called Chandler "a virtuoso alcoholic" (McShane 1981: 23; Sikov 1999: 341). But Wilder's casting – he hounded Fred MacMurray, who had never played any but personable roles, until he consented to play Walter Huff – and his outsider's eye for the unique in California settings, combined to produce a work of genius. It is a distinctly Los Angeles movie and one that exhibits *film noir*'s central motifs.

The film's opening shot shows a car running a red light, a metaphor for all that follows, and the remainder of the night-time urban montage leaves no doubt where we are. Not until five minutes into the movie does Wilder allow the sunny Hollywood hills of Cain's first page to appear. The outside of the Nirdlinger house is as Cain described it, but inside it is cool and Gothic, rather than the tacky Tijuana decor that Cain satirized. The initial meeting between Walter and *femme fatale* Phyllis lasts much longer than in the novel, and when MacMurray leaves the second time he stops at a drive-in, where he orders a beer, and then later at a bowling alley to "roll a few lines and calm my nerves."

These scenes are not in the novel but are brilliant additions, expanding on a minor theme in Cain, the extent to which Walter is also a consumer. For Wilder (and Chandler), California was the epitome of marketing; Huff lives in a consumer setting that has anticipated even his leisure needs. For Cain, on the other hand, a good "California setting" was a nationally known oddity, such as a moonrise over the Pacific. Wilder discarded such scenes, indeed he dispensed with nature altogether. He substituted a supermarket, where Walter and Phyllis meet repeatedly to discuss their crime amid pyramids of cans and boxes of baby food. Murder, the movie suggests, is a series of marketing decisions combined with lucky breaks, such as whether your product appears at eye-level. A passing patron, in fact, grumbles to Walter about her difficulty in reaching the baby food.

Wilder also discarded Cain's ending (Walter and Phyllis commit suicide on a cruise ship) and made the technological theme overt: first he filmed Walter dying in the Folsom gas chamber, a set that cost Paramount $150,000 and took five days of shooting. Then he decided to make the same statement less emphatically: Walter completes his confessional Dictaphone roll just as his boss and pursuer, Keyes, walks in. Keyes allows Walter to flee, predicting that he "won't make it as far as the door," where indeed the salesman collapses (Sikov 1999.) Wilder, following the predictive, statistical portrait of life underlying Cain's novel, simply extends the novel's underlying theme of technological determinism. Most earlier *film noir* offered some way out of this fatalism. *Double Indemnity* does not. Instead of man creating himself from/against a landscape, technology composes or reduces character on the field of its possibilities.

With their bank account replenished, Cain and Elina moved to Belden Drive, near LA's Griffith Park, and with Henry Meyers began hosting genteel, musical Friday evenings, where everyone played or sang as well as discussed events. Cain was delighted with his "counter-attack" on Hollywood, which he felt was philistine, especially the studios. Meanwhile a theatrical version of *Postman* remained unwritten and magazine assignments piled up (Hoopes 1982). The Cains visited Mexico, where an idea seized him, a tale of sex and music that harked back to his early interests: he would write about an opera singer and his sex drive. *Serenade* (1937) is a novella about John Howard Sharp, a tenor who loses his voice and only gets it back when he beds Juana, a Mexican prostitute, in a storm-stricken chapel. The recharged Sharp then sings in Hollywood musicals, which Cain clearly detested, until the New York Metropolitan calls, setting up a showdown with his nemesis, composer-director Winston Hawes. In the melodramatic ending, Juana figures out that Hawes is homosexual (and Sharp's ex-lover) and will again cost Sharp his voice, so she kills him. Then she and Sharp flee to Mexico. The plot really is as bad as it sounds, and the novella is interrupted by long digressions on Puccini and other composers and marred by asides about "Japs" and "Spigs," as well as homophobia.

In the next few years, Cain was bothered by medical problems and his father's death. He worked in Hollywood and traveled, placing "Two Can Sing" in *American* magazine (1938). It later appeared as *Career in C Major*. He worked on a play titled *7-11*. Since the early 1930s Cain had wanted to write about "the great American institution that never gets mentioned on the Fourth of July, a grass widow with two small children to support" (Hoopes 1982: 305). But Hollywood called, and he traveled, and then he stopped to write *The Embezzler* for Knopf, which appeared in *Liberty* (1940) as "Money and the Woman." There was also an operation for gallstones before Cain could return to the "grass widow." She may be modeled on Cain's grandmother but is more likely to be a version of Kate Cunningham, whom Cain was seeing regularly (Hoopes 1982: 305). Despite Kate's help, Cain found it difficult to write in the third person, or "straight" as he termed it. He finally finished *Mildred Pierce*, his longest work, in 1941.

Not a crime novel per se, *Mildred Pierce* is the most realistic of Cain's major works, with a complex plot and flashes of brilliance. It follows the lives of Bert and Mildred Pierce through the Depression in Glendale, California, relentlessly examining their lives, their taste, their work, and their children. It does so through a lens worthy of Thorstein Veblen, but one that admires self-sacrifice and coopera-tion. The narrative opens with the leggy Mildred throwing her vain, unemployed husband, Burt, one of the builders of the subdivision she lives in, out of his own house:

> She had little to say about love, fidelity, or morals. She talked about money, and his failure to find work; and when she mentioned the lady of his choice, it was not as a siren who had stolen his love, but as the cause of the shiftlessness that had lately come over him. (Cain 1941: 7)

The emasculation felt by jobless men in the Depression is depicted elsewhere in the era's literature; what is new in this novel is the grudging admiration that Cain yields up for Mildred as she takes a series of menial jobs, from baking cakes and pies to waiting tables, to make ends meet for her daughters Ray and Veda. She embodies many qualities of Cora from *Postman*. Employing an intuitive genius about cooking and kitchens, not to mention restaurants (which Cain researched thoroughly), and leveraging a few financial breaks and favors, Mildred finally opens her own restaurant.

Just as she does so, she meets Monty Beragon, a suave Pasadena polo player whose family owns stock in a bank, citrus groves, and packing houses. They spend a weekend at Lake Arrowhead, during which Mildred's daughter Ray falls ill unbeknownst to her, and on Mildred's return dies of an elevated fever. Grief-stricken, Mildred decides to succeed for her other child, the haughty, superficial Veda, who idolizes "society."

Mildred's initial "loans" to Monty for his polo expenses soon become an entitle-ment, but her business acumen makes her restaurant and pie business successful. The more Mildred condescends to him, the more Monty comes to regard himself as a gigolo, and their lingua franca becomes "wanton ... shamefully exciting" sexual intercourse (Cain 1941: 171). With the end of Prohibition in sight, Mildred adds a bar to her operations, but the expense denies Veda her Christmas present, a new grand piano.

As Mildred spends more and more time on her business, expanding to Laguna Beach and Pasadena, 17-year-old Veda begins to stay out late, to date many men, and to become "fast" in hopes of a film role. Mildred's old friend Wally reenters the plot to fix one such incident, over the objections of Bert. Estranged from everyone, Mildred begins to drink away her days. Six months later Bert informs her that Veda will sing on a nationwide radio program. They listen. Her voice flawless, Veda is a hit as – that worst of all things for Cain – a coloratura soprano.

Mildred schemes to get back Veda through Monty, but when she returns, Mildred ignores the demands of work to attend to her. Wally Burgan, it develops, forces her into a bankruptcy from which, in a typical Cainian twist, he figures to gain. When Mildred catches Veda and Monty in bed she chokes her, apparently crushing her voice box. But Veda uses this injury to get out of one recording contract and into a better one. Mildred divorces Monty and remarries Bert. She starts making pies again, and the novel ends on a "better off without 'em" moment, as they decide to get drunk.

The much-changed film version of *Mildred Pierce* (dir. Michael Curtiz, 1945) starred Joan Crawford, who won the Oscar for Best Actress. It was nominated in five other categories. The cast included Jack Carson, Zachary Scott, Eve Arden, and Ann Blyth. Randall MacDougal, who received the nomination for Best Screenplay, modeled his script on *Double Indemnity* – the story is a retrospective confession. The film opens with Mildred visiting Monty's beach house (not in the novel) where he is killed, then moves to the police offices of Inspector Peterson, where the story is told as a murder investigation. The middle of the film does focus on the economic details of Mildred's restaurants, especially the rise of an auto-and-dining-out culture. In its use of voice-over and its combination of "classic" and noir lighting styles, the film is highly inventive. At the end, in a masterfully choreographed scene, Inspector Peterson reveals that Veda killed Monty.

Reprints, serials and movie royalties kept the Cains living well. Cain then had a long overdue operation for gallstones and an ulcer. He fielded questions from Edmund Wilson, who included him in the first major critical piece on the hard-boiled school, "The Boys in the Back Room," for the *New Republic* in 1941. "The poets of the tabloid murder," wrote Wilson, all "stemmed originally from Hemingway" (Hoopes 1982: 313). Possibly because of this essay, the press expected *Mildred Pierce* to be hard-boiled. But it wasn't and the reviews were disappointing. Cain, his stomach repaired, began to drink too much again. Although he worked for Hollywood in the late 1940s and had some of his scripts and novels filmed, he wrote no important hard-boiled fiction for the rest of the decade. He did write an introduction to a collection aimed at soldiers called *For Men Only* (1943), in which he stated: "The world's great literature is peopled by thoroughgoing heels, and in this book you will find a beautiful bevy of them, with scarcely a character among them you would let in the front door. I hope you like them. I think they are swell" (Hoopes 1982: 339).

In 1946 Cain published *Past All Dishonor*, a historic novel set in the Nevada of the 1850s with an incest plot. Historic settings and this plot were to dominate Cain's work for the next two decades, during which he published another nine books, none of which could be termed hard-boiled. Cain married twice more: to Aileen Pringle in 1944, and to Florence McBeth in 1947. He and Florence moved to Hyattsville, Maryland, and they spent the rest of their lives there. Cain died on October 27, 1977 at the age of 85 (Hoopes 1982: 498).

Cain's legacy is very different today from what it would have been fifty years ago, when Raymond Chandler disparaged him. He was a scandalous author back then.

Today he is read not so much by fans of the detective novel (or prurient readers) as by aficionados of *film noir* and the *roman noir*, and by students of creative writing. Even though he did not write the film scripts of his novels, he provided two of the most compelling motifs of *film noir*: the first-person confessional point of view and the theme of sexual desire trapped by consumerism and used against itself. He also distilled the massive change in the US economy during the Depression and its aftermath into a gripping narrative form. Stylistically, he crystallized certain economies in narrative form, begun by Modernists such as Stein, Hemingway, Joyce and Dos Passos, and brought them into popular fiction. In fact he went well beyond them in his ability to represent character through dialogue, to connote sexuality by metaphor, and to impart the impression of speed to prose.

35
Dorothy L. Sayers (1893–1957)

Esme Miskimmin

Introduction

Dorothy L. Sayers is often grouped with her "golden age" contemporaries, Agatha Christie, Margery Allingham, and Ngaio Marsh as one of the "Queens of Crime," and is best known for her detective stories featuring the aristocratic sleuth, Lord Peter Wimsey, who features in eleven of her twelve detective novels and appears in four collections of short stories (see Rowland, chapter 8 in this volume). Nonetheless, Sayers's crime writing is only a small part of her wide-ranging oeuvre, which includes poetry, letters, essays, criticism, theological scholarship, and drama, all of which are arguably underpinned or influenced by her role as a theologian, and which demonstrate her intellectual and academic abilities in addressing religious, political, social and literary issues. Most of the critical material on Sayers, however, has focused on her best-known work, her detective fiction, and until recently there has been a tendency to make a clear and mutually exclusive division between this and Sayers's other writings. By placing the crime fiction within the context of her wider writing, and considering Sayers's literary career as a whole, we can identify within it a number of themes and purposes that matured and developed as it progressed. In her later works of detective fiction, themes such as faith versus scientific empiricism, social responsibility, or female emancipation are developed to the point that they are arguably in tension with the generic requirements of the works that they appear in. These tensions, acknowledged and explored by Sayers in several metatextual episodes, take her detective fiction beyond the formulaic "puzzle" story and generate some of the most complex and interesting writing within the genre.

Education and Early Career

Dorothy L. Sayers was the only child of the Reverend Henry Sayers, headmaster of the Christchurch Choir School, Oxford, and Helen Mary Sayers (née Leigh). In 1897, the family moved to Bluntisham-cum-Earith, Huntingdonshire, where Henry Sayers had been offered the living. This was the beginning of Sayers's lifelong attachment to East Anglia, later to become the fictional home of Wimsey's family seat, Duke's Denver, and the setting for her dark and intricate detective story *The Nine Tailors* (1934). Sayers was educated at home until the age of 15, when she was sent to Godolphin School, Salisbury, to prepare for entrance to Oxford. She went up to Oxford in 1912 to study Modern Languages at Somerville and gained a first, although like other female students she was not actually awarded her BA and MA until the university conferred degrees on women in 1920. While at University, Sayers wrote and published a number of poems. She continued to write poetry throughout her life and, although they are largely overlooked and perhaps not the most successful of her literary endeavors, she had two early volumes published after coming down from Oxford: *Op 1* (1916) and *Catholic Tales and Christian Songs* (1918). These early poetic works demonstrate a lyricism that is also very evident in her later prose style and that contributed to the success of her translation of Dante's *Divine Comedy* later in her life. Her poems also establish the spiritual and theological themes that pervade all of her writing, including her detective novels, whether as abstract theological discussions or as expressions of personal faith.

After leaving university in 1915, Sayers took various jobs including teaching, a brief post at Blackwell's publishers, some time in France as an assistant to the head of a schools exchange scheme and, like many individuals in the postwar years of depression, periods of unemployment. In 1922 she moved to London, having secured a job as a copywriter at the advertising firm of Benson's, where she remained until 1931. In 1921, Sayers began writing her first detective novel, *Whose Body?*, published in 1923 by Gollancz, in which she introduced the character of Lord Peter Wimsey.

Public Success and Personal Crisis

Sayers's first few detective novels sold well, and Wimsey caught the public imagination. Despite having a secure job and the beginnings of a career as a writer of detective fiction, however, Sayers's personal life was less satisfactory. In 1922, she began a relationship with a neighbor, Bill White, which resulted in an unplanned pregnancy. White could not marry Sayers – he was already married – and did not want to acknowledge the baby. Sayers decided to conceal her pregnancy and in 1924 she gave birth to her only child, John Anthony White (later Fleming), subsequently placing him in the care of her cousin, Ivy Shrimpton. The existence of Sayers's son remained a secret from nearly all of her family and friends, and certainly her reading public, until after her death.

A further development in Sayers's personal life took place in 1925 when she met a reporter on crime and motor-racing, Oswold Arthur "Atherton" Fleming, known to everyone as "Mac." Mac was divorced, but that did not dissuade Sayers from marrying him on April 13, 1926 in a registry office – another instance of her personal experiences conflicting with her deeply felt Christian beliefs and upbringing. Mac was aware of the existence of Sayers's son and for a while she cherished hopes of the boy living with them. This never happened and as the marriage progressed it became increasingly unhappy. The situation was made worse by Mac's ill-health, a result of being gassed in the trenches of World War I, and Sayers's consequent position as the main bread-winner for them both. The physical and psychological after-effects of the war on ex-soldiers are explored in her novel *The Unpleasantness at the Bellona Club* (1977a [1928]), and several biographers have drawn parallels between Mac and the character of George Fentiman, a bitter victim of Mustard Gas who must rely on his wife's income (Brunsdale 1990: 106). With the expense of supporting a child and an increasingly invalid husband, the extra money to be earned from writing popular detective fiction became more significant. Despite her talents in this direction, her novels show evidence of the increasing tensions between Sayers's need to write for the requirements of her book-buying public and her desire to focus on more intellectual subject matter and develop her literary style.

The "Game" of Detection

Before the publication of *Whose Body?*, Sayers wrote to a friend, acknowledging that the impulse to write crime fiction was generated in part by financial need: "there is a market for detective literature if one can get in and [it] might go some way towards providing bread and cheese" (B. Reynolds 1995: 181). Sayers was right about the "market": detective fiction was a boom genre in the interwar years, and *Whose Body?* demonstrates her proficiency at the golden age formula that was so popular with its readership, meeting generic prerequisites such as the relatively "closed" environment and cast of characters, the "puzzle" mystery, and the larger-than-life aristocratic sleuth.

Sayers was fully aware of the appeal and nature of the formula. In her introduction to *Great Short Stories of Detection, Mystery and Horror*, she comments on the great popularity of "puzzle" activities in the interwar years: "The pages of every magazine and newspaper swarm with cross-words, mathematical tricks, puzzle-pictures, enigmas, acrostics, detective-stories …" (Sayers 1928: 9). Part of the appeal of the golden age stories was the potential for the reader to solve the mystery alongside the detective, having been provided with all the necessary clues by the author. Initiates to the Detection Club (of which Sayers was president from 1949–57) had to "solemnly swear never to conceal a Vital Clue from a reader," and in 1929, Ronald Knox produced his "Ten Commandments" of detective fiction, which would ensure this idea of "fair play" for the reader-detective. Commandment eight, for example, states that, "The detective is bound to declare any clues upon which he may happen to light" (Knox 1929: xi–xiv).

While Knox's "rules" are to some extent tongue-in-cheek, the decalogue demonstrates the general attitude both to and of the golden age detective novel, reinforcing the idea that it is a cerebral pastime for amusement, governed by rules in the way that any other game is, and Sayers enters into the club spirit, particularly in her short stories and earlier novels. She stresses the parallels between detective fiction and puzzle games through constant references to other activities of a similar nature: for example, in *The Unpleasantness at the Bellona Club*, Anne Dorland comments that "a detective story keeps your brain occupied. Rather like chess" (Sayers 1977a: 217). In fact, in some of Sayers's short stories, a game or puzzle is central to the plot. In "Nebuchadnezzar" (1939, Sayers 1975: 148–58), for example, the solution to a murder is revealed during the process of a game of charades, and in "The Fascinating Problem of Uncle Meleager's Will" (1928, Sayers 1979: 39–59), the whereabouts of the eponymous uncle's hidden fortune can only be discovered through the solution of a crossword by both the detective and the reader, who is provided with a blank grid for the purpose.

From the first, these self-conscious acknowledgements of the boundaries of her chosen genre, represented by the literal "boundaries" and rules of the games it is paralleled with, are contrasted with the development of her style and subject matter beyond these conventions. It is in her characterization of Lord Peter Wimsey that we can initially identify the tensions that become increasingly apparent in Sayers's detective fiction. On one hand, Wimsey is a caricature, with his "long, amiable face [which] looked as if it had generated spontaneously from his top hat" (Sayers 1977b: 9), his now-trademark monocle, and his affected speech patterns. From the beginning of his characterization in *Whose Body?*, however, Sayers has already begun to invest her detective with a deeper psychological dimension which manifests itself in two ways: Wimsey's postwar neurasthenia and, linked to this, his troubled conscience about his role as a detective. In *Whose Body?*, Wimsey's shell-shock returns once he has gained confirmation of the identity of the murderer. As he dwells on this, his mind returns to his experiences in the trenches and he imagines himself there once again, believing that he can hear the "noise of the guns," and the "Tap, tap, tap" of the German sappers (1977b: 132). Sayers places the roots of Wimsey's psychological difficulties in issues of responsibility: in the war, when he spent "four years' "giving orders ... to people to go and get blown to pieces" (Sayers 1977c: 379), and in his role as a detective, where he must accept the personal and social consequences of his investigations.

In *Whose Body?*, for example, Sir Julian Freke has no characteristics that draw Wimsey or the reader to him personally, and he has, moreover, murdered a relatively harmless man for reasons of personal pride. Nonetheless, Wimsey still suffers a crisis of conscience, as, although Freke has no personally redeeming features, he is of vital social importance as an eminent nerve specialist who does significant good in the treatment of neurasthenia sufferers, such as Wimsey himself. Wimsey goes to call on Freke at his surgery and falls into conversation with the mother of a child who is being treated there, and who describes Freke as "un saint qui opère des miracles! ...

and he does it all, cet homme illustre, for nothing at all" (1977b: 165). Despite being a murderer, Freke is something of a philanthropist, and Wimsey's bringing him to justice will mean that society loses his expertise, as another doctor comments: "heavens, Lord Peter, you don't know what a blow you have struck at the profession – the whole civilised world" (1977b: 177). Thus, in benefiting society through the reinforcement of justice and the restoration of order, Wimsey is simultaneously removing a character capable of significant social good, a problem that clearly highlights the ethical difficulties he faces as a detective.

In developing the character of her detective in this way, Sayers takes crime fiction beyond the features and functions of a puzzle and potentially encourages her vicarious reader-detective to engage with the moral complexities inherent within a genre that essentially revolves around the themes of good and evil, crime and punishment, retribution and justice. As the inquiry in *Whose Body?* progresses, Wimsey complains to Inspector Parker (the professional foil to his amateur sleuth): "It *is* a game to me, to begin with and I go on cheerfully, and then I suddenly see that someone is going to be hurt, and I want to get out of it." (1997b: 123). Parker's response to Wimsey's problem is to tell him to get "this playing-fields-of-Eton complex out of [his] system once and for all":

> "You want to hunt down a murderer for the sport of the thing and then shake hands with him and say, 'Well played – hard luck – you shall have your revenge tomorrow!' Well, you can't do it like that. Life's not a football match. You want to be a sportsman. You can't be a sportsman. You're a responsible person" (1997b: 123).

The key issue in Parker's argument is the choice (or absence of choice) that Wimsey has between personal feeling and social responsibility, a theme that is sustained throughout Sayers's detective fiction, and also in her later theological dramas. In Sayers's final detective novel, *Busman's Honeymoon* (1937), Wimsey's new wife Harriet asks him why he must investigate the murder that has occurred in their home, because "It's such a beastly little crime – sordid and horrible." Wimsey's response is that he cannot pick and choose:

> "I can't wash my hands of a thing, merely because it's inconvenient to my lordship, as Bunter says of the sweep. I hate violence! I loathe wars and slaughter, and men quarrelling and fighting like beasts! Don't say it isn't my business. It's everybody's business" (Sayers 1977c: 128).

Once again, the conclusion to the investigation brings about an attack of neurasthenia, as he waits for the execution of the man he has effectively condemned through his investigations, musing on whether "if there is a God or a judgment – what next? What have we done?" (1977c: 395). Wimsey's recurrent difficulties with detection allow Sayers to explore of the dichotomy between a genre that is essentially a "game," and the morally complex subjects that that genre deals with. The inherent tensions in the characterization of Wimsey reflect the wider tensions in Sayers's crime writing between an adherence to genre and the frustrations created by the generic restraints placed upon her literary impulses, as her stories develop into discussions of themes and ideas beyond those required for a popular detective novel.

Pushing the Boundaries of Genre

By the early 1930s, Sayers's dissatisfaction with formulaic genre-writing were becoming more evident, but the more "literary" elements that appeared in her detective fiction displeased her reading public, who felt that they compromised the detective narrative. Her seventh novel, *Five Red Herrings* (1931), is a somewhat dry, textbook exercise in the form, revolving around timetables and alibis. Her deliberate adherence to genre with this novel is important, as it was a response to criticism of the previous novel, *Strong Poison* (1930), which had deviated from the formula and moved towards a further psychological development of Wimsey in the form of a romantic interest (Plain 1996: 52). As a result, *Five Red Herrings* was written with the intention of its being, as she put it, a "pure puzzle story," where her readers could play "spot the murderer" (B. Reynolds 1995: 312).

As a writer, Sayers encountered the dichotomy later identified by Todorov in his seminal essay "The Typology of Detective Fiction" (1966) in which he discusses how, in popular fiction, there is no "dialectic contradiction between the work and its genre." He argues that "detective fiction has its norms; to 'develop' them is to disappoint them: to 'improve upon' detective fiction is to write literature, not detective fiction" (Todorov 1977: 43). Sayers is aware of this dichotomy and acknowledges that the detective story "does not, and by hypothesis never can, attain the loftiest levels of literary achievement." A detective story, she tells us:

> does not show us the inner workings of the murderer's mind – it must not; for the identity of the murderer is hidden until the end of the book. The victim is shown rather as a subject for the dissecting-table than as a husband and father. A too violent emotion flung into the glittering mechanism of the detective-story jars the movement by disturbing its delicate balance (Sayers 1928: 37–8).

Close readings of Sayers's detective fiction reveal any number of dialectic contradictions between her works and their genre and, more importantly, a self-consciousness and occasionally metatextual acknowledgement of this imbalance. This is particularly true of the novels *The Documents in the Case* (1930), a "collaborative" novel with Robert Eustace (who provided the scientific input), and *Gaudy Night* (1935).

The Documents in the Case

The Documents in the Case is certainly not the most satisfying detective novel in terms of meeting generic expectations: there is a murder, granted, and a group of suspects, and several "clues," but the detective story is often interrupted or replaced by a dialogue between scientific "reasoning" and Christian beliefs about the nature and origins of life, to the extent that this discussion arguably becomes a secondary narrative. This theme is largely explored through the character of Munting, chief narrator and somewhat reluctant amateur detective. It is interesting that, in this latter role, Munting expresses the same doubts about detection as Wimsey:

> People write books about murders, and the nice young men and women in them enjoy the job of detecting. It is a good game and I like reading the books. But the emotions of the nice young people are so well regulated. ... They don't seem to suffer from fits of retching terror for fear they should find out something definite. (Sayers and Eustace 1978: 201–2)

This self-reflexive moment has a dual function, drawing the reader's attention once more to the potentially difficult focuses of crime and detective writing, but also raising a metatextual awareness of the role of the writer, compounded by Munting's own occupation as an author.

Most of the "documents" that comprise the novel are statements and letters written by Munting, many of which are focused on his need for an explanation of the origins of life, whether this is provided by faith or by science. For example, in one letter he dwells on a visit to a scientist friend who is working on "synthetic gland-extracts":

> So far, however they don't seem to have been able to make synthetic life – the nearest they have got is stimulating frog-spawn into life with needles. But what of the years to come? *If*, as the bio-chemists say, life is only a complicated chemical process, will the difference between life and death be first expressible in a formula and then prisonable in a bottle? (Sayers and Eustace 1978: 73–4).

This theme is returned to repeatedly by Munting, and is given greater scope in the novel by the presence of Perry, a vicar, who provides a theistic perspective on Munting's arguments.

At the end of the novel, this dialogue becomes pertinent, as the criminal is caught out by a fundamental difference between the naturally occurring version of the fungal poison muscarine and the laboratory-synthesized version, but until this point, and even accepting it, it can be quite difficult to justify the devotion of so much of the text to abstract scientific/theological discussion as necessary to the progression of the detective-narrative. The denouement begins at a supper-party given by Perry, at which there is a working through of the information needed to close both the detective narrative and the questions regarding science and faith that have been the focus of the novel. The supper party consists of people who might potentially provide answers to Munting's investigations: Hoskyns, who is a physicist; Matthews or "Stingo," who is a biologist; and Waters, the chemist. In addition there is Perry, representing the Church, and Munting, representing the arts in his capacity as a writer. The function of the conversation between these characters, with regard to the detective narrative, is to reach a point where it becomes clear to Munting that there can be a difference between naturally synthesized muscarine and a version of the chemical created in a laboratory, if the synthetic muscarine is in its "racemic" form, which would mean that his friend Lathom can be proved guilty of murder.

The conversation that Sayers presents between the characters up to this point is exceptionally long, overly technical, and, as Paton Walsh observes, lacking in "fictional zap" (Miskimmin 2004: 278). Reynolds argues that, at the end of *The Documents in the Case*, "Dorothy L. Sayers rises to the height demanded by the theme. Her intellect and her imagination are fused and the writing is brilliant. But so light-weight and at times jaunty is the handling of the rest of the work that this profoundly interesting section seems almost an intrusion" (B. Reynolds 1998: 253). Arguably, it is not just this section that is intrusive (and the "jaunty', "light-weight" nature of the rest of the text is debatable): in giving her themes their full academic and artistic scope, Sayers develops the novel beyond its generic boundaries, resulting in a text that cannot succeed as a detective novel, but is equally frustrated in its literary aspirations by the necessary presence of generic convention.

To some extent, Sayers acknowledges these frustrations through the device of Munting as a writer-character, using him to develop a metatextual discussion of the processes of writing, specifically the tensions between writing for a popular readership and pursuing more "literary" aspirations. At the beginning of the novel, Munting is engaged in writing for money, "quill driving," a publication titled *Life* (1978: 21). He complains to his fiancé, also a writer, of having to write this rather than his "own stuff' (1978: 22), which is more "highbrow" poetry and novels. In addition to exploring the tensions between writing for money and writing to satisfy a literary or creative urge, Sayers acknowledges the role of the reading public in the process. In the flat below Munting and Lathom live the Harrisons, suburban middlebrows whom Munting mocks for their indiscriminate consumption of "culture." The Harrisons invite Lathom and Munting to a number of "soirees" and Munting demonstrates his intellectual snobbery as he describes their "appalling sitting room, all arty stuff from Tottenham Court Road, with blue and mauve cushions and everything ghastly about it" (1978: 20). He then goes on to detail the pseudo-intellectual conversation that takes place between himself and Margaret Harrison:

"No sooner had I got there than I was swept into a discussion about this 'wonderful man Einstein.' Extraordinarily interesting, wasn't it, and what did I make of it? Displaying all my social charm, I said I thought it was a delightful idea ..." (1978: 28)

In conversation, Margaret Harrison shows very little understanding of the subjects that she discusses with Munting, using the conversation instead to show off her "fashionable" ideas and her interest in topical issues, of which she has a limited knowledge gleaned from the Sunday papers and popular-press versions of events. Munting mocks these sources in a letter to his fiancé, when he discusses the prevalence of articles such as "What does the Unconscious mean to me?" – "Is Monogamy Doomed?" – "Can Women Tell the Truth?" – "Should Wives Produce Books or Babies?" – "What Is Wrong with the Modern Aunt?" – and "Glands or God – Which?" (1978: 71). He acknowledges, however, that this is what the general public seem to want to read and that his writing will be received and judged by the same audience: "These are the people who read the books, Bungie. And what are we to do about it, you and I, if we want to live by bread?" (1978: 35), a lament that echoes his creator's comment about writing detective fiction to provide "bread and cheese."

Sayers also explores these themes through another, more significantly developed writer-character, Harriet Vane. She appears in four novels as Wimsey's love-interest, gaining in textual presence and depth of characterization as they progress, and is considered by most biographers to be semi-autobiographical (Coombes 1992: 9, 115; Rowland 2001: 9; Reynolds 1998: 26). Vane, like Sayers, writes detective novels and Sayers arguably makes use of this detail to present some of her frustrations about achieving a balance between the detective narrative, with its necessarily formulaic approach, and the more "literary" element to her writing. This is most apparent in *Gaudy Night*, a novel in which the detective story again takes something of a "back seat" to other narratives: in 450 pages there are a handful of anonymous notes and spiteful practical jokes and a somewhat muted attempt at murder. The real investigation may be Sayers's own into the obligations of creative or intellectual minds.

Gaudy Night

Gaudy Night is another novel in which Sayers arguably creates a dialectic contradiction between the work and its genre. It is not so much, as in *The Documents in the Case*, that she allows a sociological or theological discussion to become the chief focus of the text, although she does address the contemporary issues of female emancipation and education, but perhaps that, in her own words, she allows her characters to develop "too violent emotion[s]" which then disturb the "delicate balance" or "glittering mechanism" of her detective story. In *Gaudy Night*, the relationship between Wimsey and his love interest, Harriet Vane, is finally resolved. They meet in *Strong Poison* (1930), in which Wimsey has Harriet acquitted of murdering her lover. Although this novel perhaps begins with Wimsey as a "knight errant," it becomes clear that Sayers cannot reconcile Harriet with the "damsel" in need of rescue: she is sexually experienced, financially independent and not about to make gratitude the basis for a relationship. Wimsey in his generic "role" is incompatible with the psychological development of Vane, and in the next two novels charting their relationship, *Have his Carcase* (1932) and *Gaudy Night*, the lovers "struggle … to reach equilibrium" (Rowland 2001: 7).

This is finally achieved in *Gaudy Night* when, in returning to their alma mater, Oxford, they recognize that an emotional harmony can be obtained through their intellectual equality. Sayers employs a series of symbolic episodes to make this academic parity clear, such as when Wimsey takes Harriet's gown instead of his own and she observes that it does not matter, as their gowns are identical: "And then it struck her as strange that it should be the same thing" (1970: 273), or when Wimsey completes a sonnet that Harriet has begun (the subject of which, is, appropriately, love described through the metaphor of a balanced spinning-top) (346). Finally, Wimsey "allows" Harriet to risk her life for the investigation, which, he argues, negates any obligations she may feel for his having previously saved it, allowing them to "clear all scores" and form a relationship (436). The academic and emotional are combined in Wimsey's final proposal of marriage, couched in formal Latin: *"Placetne, magistra?"* and Harriet's response: *"Placet"* ("Does it please you, mistress?" "It pleases me": the term "magistra" is the female equivalent of "master," as in the academic title, "Master of Arts").

"Equilibrium" is the key to *Gaudy Night*, both textually and metatextually. As well as bringing the love story to a conclusion where its protagonists achieve a degree of equality, Sayers uses the setting of the women's college, "Shrewsbury," to explore the changing roles of women in the interwar period as they struggle to reconcile public lives and careers with the domestic sphere, marriage, and motherhood. In addition, she addresses the imbalance between genre and literary development through Harriet Vane's increasing frustrations with her latest detective novel *"Death 'twixt Wind and Water"* – a title that perhaps reflects the many "balances" sought in this novel. Vane outlines to Wimsey her concerns that, "academically speaking," her hero, Wilfred, "is the world's worst goop." Wimsey comments that "from a purely constructional point of view [he doesn't] feel that Wilfred's behavior in the novel is sufficiently accounted for," and suggests that Harriet "make[s] Wilfred one of those morbidly conscientious people, who have been brought up to think that anything pleasant must be wrong … Give him a puritanical father and a hell-fire religion." This re-creation of "Wilfred" with a psychological dimension would obviously develop Harriet's book beyond its genre. She complains that if she rewrites her character, with "violent and life-like feelings, he'll throw the whole book out of balance," to which Wimsey replies that she would "have to abandon the jig-saw kind of story and write a book about human beings for a change" (1970: 291).

All three tensions – between the two lovers, between women's roles and expectations, and between the popular and the serious arts – are explored in an episode similar to the dinner party in *The Documents in the Case*. The main protagonists assemble in the Senior Common Room after dinner and engage in an academic discussion focused on the themes of the novel. In terms of the detective narrative, the episode serves to establish the "back story" behind the crime, an incident in the past involving an academic who stole and suppressed a valuable document which would have destroyed the premise of his doctoral argument, and finally committed suicide when he was discovered and stripped of his doctorate and his livelihood, leaving his widow to take revenge on the academic community that destroyed him. Wimsey approaches his investigations by posing the hypothetical problem of "the artist of genius who has to choose between letting his family starve and painting pot-boilers to keep them" (Sayers and Eustace 1978: 325). In this episode Sayers returns once more to the theme of responsibility, social, moral, and personal, but the main focus seems to be that of the responsibility of the artist to his or her creative potential: as the group concludes, "A bad picture by a good painter is a betrayal of truth – his own truth" (1978: 326).

While the discussion is not directly about writers and writing, the themes reflect those explored in Harriet's earlier conversation with Wimsey and, although it is dangerous to make assumptions about authorial intention, Sayers's textual preoccupations with creative responsibility seem to reflect the growing inclinations in her own writing to develop her themes, characters and style beyond the requirements of a "pure puzzle story." This is not to say that Sayers felt that in writing detective fiction she was a "good painter" making "bad pictures," but that she found that what she wanted to do with her writing was impossible within the horizons of the genre she was writing in.

Wartime and After

Sayers's collection of short stories, *In the Teeth of the Evidence* (1939), was the last of her detective writings to be published in her lifetime (*Striding Folly* was published posthumously in 1972), and by the time it was in print she had already completed several projects entirely unrelated to the detection genre, including a religious drama for the Canterbury Festival, *The Zeal of Thy House* (1937). The beginnings of a final Wimsey novel, *Thrones Dominations*, were in existence but Sayers declared her intention to write no more detective fiction, at least until the war was over, and in fact never returned to it. The novel was completed for publication by Jill Paton Walsh in 1998.

By the outbreak of World War II in 1939, Sayers and Mac had been living for nearly a decade in Witham, Essex, although Sayers was still making frequent visits to London for work. Sayers was becoming recognized as a theological writer and scholar: she had been invited to write several essays for publication, including "The Greatest Drama Ever Staged" for the *Times* Passion Sunday edition and a radio nativity play for children, *He that Should Come* (1938). During the war she wrote a range of essays, talks, and pamphlets, many of which had a Christian basis, and she served briefly on the Ministry of Information Authors' Planning Committee. She also wrote to help the war effort in a less direct and more popular format: from November 1939 to January 1940 she resurrected the characters of her detective novels for one last appearance in a series of fictional letters in the *Spectator* (now referred to collectively as "The Wimsey Papers"), in which the various members of the Wimsey family discussed the war with the aim of disseminating information and boosting public morale.

After the end of the war, and after Mac's death in 1950, Sayers continued to write within the public domain – essays, papers, letters – but her chief project was her translation of Dante's *Divine Comedy*, a culmination of all her intellectual, linguistic and poetic passions. She completed the first two volumes, *Hell* (1949) and *Purgatory* (1955) but left *Paradise* unfinished at her death from heart failure on December 17, 1957. It was completed by her friend and biographer, Barbara Reynolds.

36
Dashiell Hammett (1894–1961)

Jasmine Yong Hall

In the history of detective fiction, Dashiell Hammett is seen as the founder of the hard-boiled school; he has been widely credited with establishing a style of writing both quintessentially American, and, in sharp contrast to the English tradition, based on material from actual, lived experience (see Pepper, chapter 10 in this volume). Howard Haycraft describes him as the creator of the "lean, dynamic, unsentimental narrative" (Haycraft 1994: 161) while Julian Symons adds that he took the writing of the 1920s pulps and by adding in his own experience as a Pinkerton detective gave that style a foundation in reality (Symons 1985: 2). From the beginning, Hammett's style and his real life experience confuse his realism with his reality. This confusion is interestingly apparent in Raymond Chandler's assessment in which he contrasted Hammett with the English style of writing:

> [Hammett] wrote ... for people [who] were not afraid of the seamy side of things; they lived there. Violence did not dismay them; it was right down their street.
>
> Hammett gave murder back to the kind of people that commit it for reasons; not just to provide a corpse ... He put these people down on paper as they were, and he made them talk and think in the language they customarily used for these purposes. (Chandler 1995a: 989)

The "people" Chandler refers to first, the audience for Hammett's novels, eventually become the "people" who are put down on paper, his characters. The source of Chandler's confusion lies in the need to suggest that the American style provides a transparent medium for the real as against English fictiveness. Hammett gives murder a reason; it is not just to provide a device around which to build a story. By insisting that the detective story is meaningful rather than merely an entertaining puzzle, Chandler is also attempting to take the detective story out of the genre of pop culture as a product of mass consumption. In this way, he wants to ally his own writing with that of the modernists and their attempt to establish a separate artistic value for writing removed from the values of the market.

If we can place Chandler in the context of modernism, Hammett himself, with his frequent undercutting of the reality of the stories he tells and the ways in which he draws attention to both writing and detection as businesses rather than forms of art, denies modernism's attempt to find value through transforming the real into art. His own description of his writing emphasizes that the language of the detective story "originated in the mind of some professional worker with words" and that what seems like "common speech" is produced by "skillfully editing, distorting, simplifying, coloring the national tongue and not by reporting it verbatim" (Panek 2004: 63). This did not prevent Hammett from using his experience with Pinkerton's to establish his own bona fides as a detective story writer. Symons, for example, points to Hammett's advice to be as accurate as possible in the presentation of details: "a pistol, to be a revolver, must have something on it that revolves" (Symons 1985: 61). His professional experience helped create verisimilitude, a verisimilitude that sold more stories. He did not aspire to an artistic form of writing which would create a value that transcended his time, but rather saw writing as something shaped by the time in which it was created. In his praise of Anatole France, for example, he notes that France "condemned the semicolon, a hangover from the days of lengthy sentences, as not suited to an age of telephones and airplanes" (Panek 2004: 96).

The historical context that most influenced Hammett's own writing was early twentieth-century capitalism and the Depression. If modernists reacted to this context by attempting to construct an alternative to exchange value through art, Hammett created a world filled with meaningless objects. The most emblematic of these may be the Maltese Falcon, whose blackened exterior does not hide the countless riches which its false advertising purports, but only more blackness. In place of the alienated figure of the individual artist standing against the corruption of society, Hammett offers a much less morally defined central character. In fact his first detective undercuts the very notion of individuality (usually associated with the private in private detection, and in the hard-boiled style of first person narrative) by remaining nameless.

This character's designation, "The Continental Op" (short for operative), reduces our sense of individual agency. In contrast to the word "detective," which implies the more active role of perceiving and investigating, an operative is more a functionary of the agency he works for. He is both less private in being attached to a business, and less of a self (two related conditions): "When I say me, I mean the Continental" (Hammett 1999: 39). In this way, Hammett brings into question one of the most important ways in which the hard-boiled detective might be the site of meaning in the detective story — as the upholder of his own individual code of honor. The Op's moral agency is also called into question by the growing sense, over the course of the 28 short stories and 2 novels in which he appears, that he is very much a part of a more general social corruption, particularly in his increasing and indiscriminate use of violence. In the Op stories, investigation is a business, and as a business it differs from the more general capitalist system only in making violence more explicit.

The moral decline apparent in the Op has already come to fruition in his boss: "The Old Man's voice and smile were as pleasantly polite as if the corpse at his feet had been part of the pattern of the carpet. Fifty years of sleuthing have left him with no more emotion than a pawnbroker" (Hammett 2001: 523). Chandler faulted the English school for treating corpses merely as elements in a puzzle, but Hammett's metaphor implies that this is just how detectives react to corpses, as part of a pattern. The fact that death holds no meaning after a number of years in the business is likened to the job of being a pawnbroker – someone who receives objects and replaces them with slips of paper which represent them. In a reading of the *Maltese Falcon*, I suggested that Hammett had created an analogy between stories and money (Hall 1994). Writing in the context of the stock market crash, he saw money as unconnected to any actual value; similarly, detective stories failed either to represent the world as it really is, or to give that world a moral order or meaning. The detective as pawnbroker, a man who gives out slips of paper in place of objects, and through whom objects can be endlessly exchanged, can be read in the same terms.

Another description of the Old Man, this one from "The Big Knock Over," shows that Hammett's detectives are characterized not by an ability to read the world properly, à la Sherlock Holmes, but by a kind of skepticism that such a reading could ever take place: "he was one of those cautious babies who'll look out the window at a cloudburst and say 'It seems to be raining,' on the off chance that somebody's pouring water off the roof" (Hammett 2001: 548). Reality is always subject to con-artistry – storytelling in fact. So reading the world is not a means to knowledge; it is a means to power.

The disjunction between the world and meaning, and the relation of this disjunction to capitalism and violence, all play a central role in the first Op novel, *Red Harvest*. Hammett was drawing upon a real life experience with Pinkerton's in which he had been called in to the town of Anaconda, Montana as a union-buster. In the novel, the struggle between the union and management, Elihu Willsson, is already over. Willsson had hired thugs to shore up his power base. Having invited them in, though, he cannot get rid of them, and the town has devolved into open warfare between the criminals and the corrupt police department, with Willsson connected to both sides. Willsson's son Donald hires the Op at the beginning of the novel but is killed before he can explain what the job is. A short time later, Elihu pays the Op to clean up the town, though it is clear that this is not his real motive; when the Op reveals to Elihu the name of his son's killer, Robert Albury, Elihu tries to remove him from the case. The Op then uses the fact that he has received a $10,000 retainer as a means to do "a complete job or nothing": "The check has been certified, so you can't stop payment. The letter of authority may not be as good as a contract, but you'll have to go into court to prove that it isn't" (Hammett 1999: 57).

This is the principle that initially motivates the Op, loyalty not to client, but to "the job." This principle gives the Op a veneer of neutrality in a violently divided town. Unlike a code of honor, though, the code of business is founded on a certified check. The emptiness of this foundation is revealed by what the Op says immediately after the quotation cited above:

> Your fat chief of police tried to assassinate me last night. I don't like that. I'm just mean enough to want to ruin him for it. Now I'm going to have my fun. I've got ten thousand dollars of your money to play with. I'm going to use it opening Poisonville up from Adam's apple to ankles. (Hammett 1999: 57)

The Op's initial neutrality gives no connection to others and no meaning to the world. Lacking any anchor, objectivity quickly evolves into violence. What defines the self becomes physical attack – a relation to others through vengeance.

Hammett's critique of capitalism, which led to his imprisonment during the Red Scare of the 1950s, does not appear directly in his novels. John G. Calweti's analysis of *Red Harvest* states there is no optimistic vision of change through a proletarian hero, but rather "the discovery that the comforting pieties of the past – belief in a benevolent universe, in progress, in romantic love – are illusions and that man is alone in a meaningless universe" (Cawelti 1994: 11). But I think this reading implicitly registers Hammett's critique of capitalism, which produces a world of objects without meaning. The connection between objective style, realism, and violence is also implicit in the way that Symons's description of the Op's development makes violence and realism interchangeable: "The Op's behavior becomes steadily more vicious, callous, or realistic. (The terms are optional)" (Symons 1985: 37).

In this world, people become bodies and one relates to them as a consumer either with violence or with sexuality. In *Red Harvest*, the Op's female counterpart, Dinah Brand, is an object of sexual fascination while her own fascination is with money: "She's so thoroughly mercenary, so frankly greedy, that there's nothing disagreeable about it" (Hammett 1999: 26). Like the Op's job ethic, Dinah's explicit interest in money gives her a neutrality which makes her universally desirable. Gender difference in the novel is registered in the fact that while the Op is the alienated worker in the capitalist system, Dinah is its product. Interestingly Dinah's sexuality is conveyed by the way in which her physicality escapes the limits of her clothing: " 'Your legs are too big,' I told her. 'They put too much strain on the material' " (Hammett 1999: 74). The incipient rips and tears in Dinah's clothing are signs of violence, opening seams in the material world in order to suggest something beyond it. But like violence, these signs pointing to a value lying beyond the objective surfaces of life undermine the sense of value precisely to the extent that they are pursued. Robert Albury, one of Dinah's lovers, notes how desire loses its value in the face of death: "When I was in danger, facing the gallows, she didn't – didn't seem so important to me." To which the Op replies "I couldn't find anything to say except something meaningless ..." (Hammett 1999: 55).

In the end what gives the Op a bargaining chip against the one last powerful man in town left alive, Elihu, is the fact that the detective possesses love letters Elihu had written to Dinah. He cannot use them, though, either to implicate Elihu in Dinah's death, or to bring any real change to the town. As David Bazelon notes, for the Op to truly combat evil "he would have to fight his client directly ... The question of doing or not doing a job competently seems to replace the whole larger question of good and evil" (Bazelon 1994: 170–1). In bringing closure to the novel through the love letters, which the Op describes as ranging from "silly" to "goofier" (Hammett 1999: 160), we are brought back again to meaningless slips of paper.

It is an ending in which Hammett implicates his own writing. Again Bazelon points to the connection: "the Op has the same relation to the experience of his job, its violence and excitement ... as has the ordinary consumer of mass culture to the detective stories and movies he bolts down with such regularity and in such abundance" (Bazelon 1994: 171). The next Op novel, *The Dain Curse*, places an even stronger emphasis on this parallel as the novel focuses not so much on the Op's relation to his job, but on various fictions and the process of constructing them. As Sinda Gregory points out, the book can be described as a stringing together of three types of traditional detective story plots: a country-house mystery, a gothic novel, and a "small-town potboiler" (Gregory 1994: 61). Add to this the fact that the Op is given a side-kick in the character of Owen Fitzstephan, a friend and writer with whom he discusses the case in terms that continually compare it to writing detective stories, and the self-reflexive nature of the novel becomes apparent.

Each of these genre-inflected sections of *The Dain Curse* ends with the Op identifying the killer(s) and reconstructing what actually happened, although the first two "solutions" are shown to be false. Hammett's most parodic effect arises from the first false closure as the Op rounds up the usual suspects and reveals the killer's identity in melodramatic fashion. The Op's solutions are contrasted with Fitzstephan's in that Fitzstephan attempts to interpret events through the structure of a well-crafted story while the Op realizes that reality does not function this way. But the artifice of Fitzstephan's narrative is most brought into play by the fact that he is not just the detective's sidekick, but also the murderer. Thus, the writer's attempts to turn reality into a story are finally revealed as an act of deliberately misleading the detective.

This would seem to point to the Op as the contrasting heroic figure who challenges the fabrications of the writer with the truth. However, the very style of the novel – its parodies of various detective genres, the ambiguous identity of the criminal, and the excesses apparent in its elements of spiritualism and drug addiction – all make the reader aware that the Op himself and the truth he discovers are fictions too. The denouement of the story also casts doubt on the Op's ability to know the truth. An important fact that has eluded him all along is that the killer is himself a member of the Dain family. Fitzstephan uses this fact along with the excessive number and manner of the killings to argue that he is not guilty by reason of insanity. While

Fitzstephan sees the insanity plea as yet another bit of con-artistry, the Op actually believes in it:

> as a sane man who by pretending to be a lunatic, had done as he pleased and escaped punishment, he had a joke – if you wanted to call it that – on the world. But if he was a lunatic, who ignorant of his craziness, thought he was pretending to be a lunatic, then the joke – if you wanted to call it that – was on him. (Hammett 1999: 379)

What is most important here is not truth, but power: who controls the irony and who is the butt of the joke. As Bruce Gatenby concludes, quoting the Op, "he made a long and laughable story of it. Maybe some of it was the truth" (quoted in Gatenby 1994: 64).

Stories and storytellers are the central theme in Hammett's most famous novel, *The Maltese Falcon*. The conflict between the detective, Sam Spade, and his two main opponents, Brigid O'Shaugnessy and Caspar Gutman, revolves not so much around the question of good and evil, or truth and falsehood, but around who tells the best stories. Much of this verbal dexterity, which was carried across to the 1941 film version in Humphrey Bogart's fast paced delivery, is apparent in the novel in the sparring dialogues between Spade and Brigid and Spade and Gutman.

The power of storytelling is especially clear in a chapter entitled "Horse Feathers" in which the police intrude upon a chaotic scene between Spade, Brigid, and Joel Cairo that has erupted into physical violence between Brigid and Cairo. In order to rid themselves of the police, each of the three then tells a version of what happened, with Cairo telling a version closest to the truth and Spade the most outlandish. (The chapter's title is the description given by Lieutenant Dundy to Spade's story.) What Spade tells the police is that everything they have just witnessed is a prank the three are playing on the dunder-headed cops (note Hammett's play on the Lieutenant's name). So Spade's story is both a lie, and a lie which says that what has taken place is also a lie. In using this story, Spade gains control of both criminals and police. Dundy, unable to cope with his frustration in sensing that Spade is putting one over on him, lashes out physically. And it is this violence which in facts marks his defeat – a defeat which allows Spade to escape police questioning.

The novel's literariness is marked not only by verbal power plays but by close associations with classical literature, in particular stories of the Grail quest. That quest is alluded to in tales of the Falcon's origins in the crusades and also directly invoked by the similarity of Hammett's plot to traditional quest romance. As I have pointed out elsewhere, unlike the original Grail story, no transcendent system of belief gives Hammett's story meaning (Hall 1994). Instead the only foundational value is money: "We didn't exactly believe your story ... We believed your two hundred dollars" (Hammett 199: 416). Without a transcendent value, stories become meaningless pieces of paper endlessly exchanged. And if the exchange comes to a stop it is not in truth, but in a world which resists interpretation – an ending not in an afterlife, but in the material reality of death.

What makes traditional detective stories powerful is that they take the inhuman, objective world and turn it into "clues." The story of the investigation is a necessary delay between the moment when death has robbed the body of meaning, and the moment when the detective returns it to meaning by making it a signifier of someone's guilt. But in *The Maltese Falcon* Hammett makes the delay itself arbitrary. Spade knows from the moment that he sees Archer's corpse that Brigid is the killer. The purpose of the delay is never clear.

There is an analogy to what Spade is doing in the Flitcraft story that Hammett has Spade recite to Brigid (with no apparent connection to the plot). Flitcraft, a man Spade was hired to find, had run away from his life when a beam falling from a building almost killed him, taking a bit of flesh off his cheek when a chip of flying concrete strikes him. After a brief period in which he drifted from place to place, he settled down again, recreating exactly the life he had left behind. The falling beam reveals the randomness of the world, that people die for no reason. Flitcraft reacts to this reality by giving up on trying to make his life fit a particular narrative – the narrative of the respectable married man with a job downtown and a wife and kids in the suburbs. But then after a time he returns to a very similar version of the same story. Likewise, the entire middle of the novel involving the pursuit of the Falcon becomes just an arbitrary pause in Spade's narrative as detective.

The purpose of stories is not truth but distraction, a distraction from the fact of death that, as Charles Rzepka has observed, only leads those who come under its spell closer to the death they cannot bear to think about (Rzepka 2005: 192–5). It is this fact that seems to be uncovered when the black patina of the Falcon is chipped away to reveal not the fascinating treasure that Gutman's distracting stories represent, but lead, an element Hammett must have chosen to make the connection to violent death, either by the metal's association with lead bullets, or lead coffins. The way in which the Falcon serves as a diversion is encapsulated in the scene in which it is delivered to Spade's office by the dying Captain Jacoby. Spade and Effie's reaction to the Falcon is described between the moment that Jacoby dies, and the moment that both of them remember that his corpse is lying on the floor of the office. Effie at first is in shock, but as Spade unwraps the Falcon "excitement began to supplant nausea in her face." That same excitement expresses itself in Spade as a kind of sexual possessiveness: "Spade laughed. He put a hand down on the bird. His wide-spread fingers had ownership in their curving. He put his other arm around Effie Perine and crushed her body against his. 'We've got the damned thing, angel,' he said" (Hammett 1999: 530).

As the novel draws to a close there seems to be a need to have story and world come together, for the Falcon to be what it promises to be. That desire to translate the symbolic into the real, though, comes through in this scene not as a way of giving the object human meaning, but taking what is human and objectifying it, so that Spade's fondling of the Falcon is equivalent to his man-handling of Effie Perrine (the girl and the bird linked by the similarity of her last name to the word "peregrine").

This point is further emphasized as Spade backs up to admire the bird and we are reminded that Jacoby's dead body is beneath him: "Effie Perine made a horrified face and screamed, pointing to his feet. He looked down at his feet. His last backward step had brought his left heel into contact with the dead man's hand, pinching a quarter-inch of flesh at a side of the palm between heel and floor" (Hammett 1999: 530). Not only does Gutman's beguiling story of the Falcon's fabulous provenance thus lead Spade to step straight into the hand of death, but the pinched bit of flesh, like the scar on Flitcraft's face, like the chip taken off the Falcon, is also a reminder of the gap between world and meaning. That gap is never closed, and so the bird and its promised value remain divided, as does Brigid and any possible role for her in a romance narrative (she never reassumes the "Miss Wonderly" character she played at the novel's opening). And when one realizes that Spade's story itself is not justified by the need to uncover Archer's murderer, then the novel is revealed to be like its namesake, an entertaining diversion hiding nothing beyond its patina of black ink except meaninglessness.

In *The Glass Key*, detective story and romance narrative elements are even more obviously artificial, and the motives of the main character, Ned Beaumont, more mysterious. Beaumont is the right-hand man of political boss, Paul Madvig, his closest friend. Madvig is engaged to marry Janet Henry, the daughter of a senator who is a more socially acceptable politician than Madvig, but equally corrupt. Beaumont despises the hypocrisy of the upper-class Henry family and warns Madvig of the consequences of accepting the Senator's "pound of flesh" (Hammett 1999: 596) in return for political support. After the Senator's son is killed, suspicion falls on Madvig, and Beaumont is deputized to assist in clearing him.

As Madvig loses control of the city, a struggle for power emerges – much like the conflict in *Red Harvest*. In that struggle, Madvig's political rival, Shad O'Rory, tries to obtain damaging information on him, first by attempting to bribe Beaumont, and then, in an excruciatingly brutal scene, by having him beaten over and over again. The extreme level of violence is contrasted with the lack of any depiction from Beaumont's point of view of the emotional effect of what he is suffering. The full realization of how unrelenting the beatings have been comes in a description in which Beaumont crawls into the bathroom of the apartment where he is being held and spots a razor behind the washstand pedestal:

> Getting it out from behind the pedestal was a task that took him all of ten minutes and his nerveless fingers failed a dozen times before they succeeded in picking it up from the tile floor. He tried to cut his throat with it, but it fell out of his hand after he had no more than scratched his chin in three places. He lay down on the bathroom-floor and sobbed himself to sleep. (Hammett 1999: 669)

Not having access to the character's thoughts here, we could at first think he is after the razor as a means of defending himself. The fact that he is trying to kill himself and lacks the ability to do even that conveys an almost unimaginable degree of existential despair, but wholly from the outside, from our attention being focused on the effects of violence on the body.

In fact, through most of the novel, Hammett represents Beaumont's use of his own body as the material he employs to create a story that is not really about him:

> "Ned Beaumont made his eyes blank." (Hammett 1999: 593)
> "He put thoughtfulness on his face." (Hammett 1999: 595)
> "Ned Beaumont grinned crookedly at the blond man and made his voice drawl." (Hammett 1999: 598)

As with Spade, Beaumont's character is most clearly defined by control. In Spade, that control is primarily shown through verbal manipulation. When Spade gives Brigid to the police because he won't "play the sap" for her, we also see a self-control which places a higher value on not becoming a mark than on the satisfaction of any desire. In Beaumont that kind of self-control seems to be Hammett's main focus. Beaumont uses his own body as if it is a puppet that he "makes" perform certain actions. Who the performer is behind the mask remains largely a mystery.

Beaumont's most important self-description may be the one he offers Paul Madvig at the beginning of the novel, that he "can stand anything [he's] got to stand" (Hammett 1999: 593). As a kind of play on the Cartesian definition of self, Beaumont's is an "I" whose proof of being rests not on thinking but on the passive ability to withstand abuse. The self is that which remains aloof from the vulnerability of the body. Only when physical violation becomes so extreme that death is preferable does the body display a real emotion – real, but still disconnected in that it is shown through physical action rather than through a description of an inner psychological state.

If *The Glass Key* is a psychological novel, it is one in the same way that *The Maltese Falcon* is a detective story. In fact it draws attention to the gap between object and meaning in a much more stark way since the body most resistant to meaning is not a reified object like the Falcon, or a corpse, but the living body of the main character. That resistance is shown by the way in which the novel's closure seems completely inexplicable in terms of Beaumont's character. If he has the kind of loyalty which leads him to put his life at risk for Madvig, why is he unable to accept Madvig's apology at the end and remain in his service? What is it that they have fought about? He and Janet leave town together – are they in love? She "impulsively" asks to go with him when she hears that he is leaving, to which he responds that he will "take you if you want to go" (Hammett 1999: 774). Again there is a kind of passivity here which refuses to give anything away about the character's inner life.

Like his previous re-workings of genre literature, Hammett's take on the psychological novel is a somewhat parodic one, as his choice of title makes clear. The glass key has no part in the story's plot but features in a dream Janet Henry relates to

Beaumont. In the dream, she and Ned, both hungry, discover a locked room containing a table of food they can see through a window. They find the key to the room, but when they unlock it, snakes emerge and attack them. Janet at first says that they were able to relock the door, climb onto the roof, unlock it from above to release the snakes, and then satisfy their hunger. However, this version, Janet later reveals, is false. The key, being made of glass, shattered, the snakes were uncontained, and Janet woke screaming.

At one level, Hammett uses the "key" to imply that if it seems to reveal what is hidden through its transparency, it is nevertheless too fragile to release anything of value. If it "unlocks" meaning, it is only such an exaggeratedly Freudian one that its artifice draws attention to itself. The case for Hammett's satirical use of Freudian imagery is strengthened by an account of the title's origin. Will Murray relates the story as told by one of Hammett's contemporaries. F. Orlin Tremaine, the editor of *The Black Mask*, would ask writers for the titles of works in advance of their being written. "Thinking of a tricky title, [Hammett] said 'The Glass Key' and then, when he had to write the thing, he couldn't figure out how to get the glass key in the title into the story. And he had his character have a dream. And of course when the key went into a lock, it shattered" (Murray 1994: 116). The title, then, comes not out of any need to explain something about Janet's character, about her relationship to Ned, or anything else integral to the novel. Its origin lies in the need for a writer to satisfy his employer so that the book can be publicized and sold.

This kind of mockery of Hammett's own "art," which dates back at least to *The Dain Curse*, reaches its culmination in *The Thin Man*. Here, too, it is useful to begin with the title. *The Thin Man* refers to Clyde Wynant, who, up until the very end of the novel, is assumed to be the murderer. However, it turns out that Wynant is actually the first victim. The real murderer, Herbert MacCauley, dismembers Wynant's body and dissolves the flesh by burying it in lime in order to disfigure its identity – so *The Thin Man* is thin indeed.

This eating away of the flesh is part of an ongoing theme of cannibalism in the book. There is both metaphoric cannibalism in the portrayal of the physical/sexual abuse in the Wynant family, and actual cannibalism in the story of Alfred G. Packer which the detective, Nick Charles, gives Gilbert Wynant to read. (This is an actual case from the *Celebrated Criminal Cases of America* which is reprinted in the novel for the reader to follow along with Gilbert.)

Opposing this picture of humanity eating its own is both the generally light-hearted tone of the novel, and also the intimate and playful relationship between Nick and Nora Charles (which became the basis for the series of *Thin Man* movies). There is playfulness in the verbal dueling between Spade and Brigid in *The Maltese Falcon* and in Ned Beaumont's self-deprecating humor, but in *The Thin Man* that playfulness is more prominent, and, more importantly, does not disappear at the end with some attempt to make language attach itself to the world in a meaningful way. Thus, the "thin man" could be the murderer, turns out to be the victim, but has also been taken to be the writer or the detective. The lack of a body, thin to the point of not being there, is not important. Truth is not the main value, but preserving relationships with others through language and through social codes is. As Nick explains to Nora after lying to a crook he had once put in jail (and who has become a friend who runs a speakeasy): "To a mugg like him, once a sleuth, always a sleuth, and I'd rather lie to him than have him think I'm lying" (Hammett 1989: 81).

This attitude toward truth extends to the solution of the novel. When Nick finishes explaining it to Nora, she is dissatisfied with the lack of certainty: "'But this is just a theory, isn't it?' 'Call it any name you like. It's good enough for me.'" (Hammett 1989: 195). This cheerful disregard for the truth has been taken as a failing by several of the novel's critics. Bazelon compares the main character unfavorably to Ned Beaumont whose "weakness was at least to some degree a product of moral consciousness"; in Nick Charles this becomes "the weakness of deliberate unconsciousness" (Bazelon 1994: 173). George Thompson is similarly critical: "Charles's hardboiled exterior covers only emptiness" (Thompson 1994: 143). But I think these critics miss the point by looking for moral certainty in the connection between the interior and the exterior, between meaning and the objective world. Instead, this novel finds morality lodged firmly in human exchange – through language, stories, and polite fictions.

At the heart of the novel is the relation between Nick and Nora. One way to conceptualize what has happened to the lone protagonist of Hammett's earlier fiction (or of the hard-boiled detective generally) is that the sarcastic monologue has become a dialogue, and by becoming a dialogue has sacrificed some of sarcasm's isolating effect to playful romantic exchange. Many of the jokes shared by the married couple have to do with each spouse's attraction to others:

> Nora said: "She's pretty."
>   "If you like them like that."
>   She grinned at me. "You got types?"
>   "Only you, darling – lanky brunettes with wicked jaws."
>   "And how about the red-head you wandered off with at the Quinns' last night?"
>   "That's silly," I said. "She just wanted to show me some French etchings." (Hammett 1999: 782)

These exchanges come across as romantic because they evince a confidence that is born of separating the body from the affections. The witty repartee of romance can thus play with the idea that the body might wander because the wandering body has, for those who engage in this banter, no meaning.

What Hammett achieved in his last novel was in direct opposition to the model of good writing that Chandler saw him representing. It is also an interesting inversion of *Red Harvest* in which objectivity leads to violence. In all of his novels, Hammett suggests – in opposition to Chandler's ideal – that the objective world represented by the murdered body resists any attempt to reconnect it to humanity by giving it meaning. Instead, the murdered body is primarily a device to sell stories – stories that enter a marketplace of exchange that never eventuates in contact with reality. In his final novel, Hammett seems to embrace this view more fully than ever. And by subordinating the meaningful body to the shifting meanings of the story he also embraces the idea that it is in stories that human relationships and morality lie:

> "Listen: remember those stories you told me? Were they true?"
> "Probably not." (Hammett 1999: 781)

37

Jorge Luis Borges (1899–1986)

Alicia Borinsky

Friendship

In 2006, Adolfo Bioy Casares, a long-time friend and collaborator of Jorge Luis Borges, published *Borges*, a chronicle of his conversations with the renowned Argentine writer dating from 1947 to Borges's death in 1986. The two had first met in 1931. Bioy's entries record Borges's assiduous dinner visits to the residence of Bioy Casares and his wife, Silvina Ocampo, and provide a unique opportunity to glance at the making of a sensibility based on today's unfashionable category of taste. Gossip, language play, recitations of poems known by heart, condemnations of both friends and foes, chit-chat about literary competitions, dismissal of academics, parodies and the rare burst of admiration reveal the depth of an association that produced a great deal of writing out of the sheer delight of decades of partaking in literature, art, and philosophy. These elements of Borges and Bioy's shared lives also recall the figure of the nineteenth-century dandy or *flaneur* that provides the template both for our earliest examples of the detective as impassioned amateur, such as Poe's Auguste Dupin, and for the original creators and critics of the new genre in which he debuted: not just Poe himself, but also the English essayist that Poe and Borges both admired, Thomas De Quincey. Bioy authored a detective novel, *Los que aman odian* (1946, *Those who Love, Hate*), with his wife, Ocampo, and wrote fiction that Borges held in great admiration, saying of Bioy's *La invención de Morel* (1940, *Morel's Invention*) that it had a perfect *trama*, a word that conveys both plot and design.

Bioy and Borges were part of a cenacle considered somewhat aloof and detached by outsiders. Like Dupin, and like Poe, they offered the world an aristocratic shrug of the shoulders that defied the popular trends and received wisdom of the day – especially, for the two Argentines, the experimental enthusiasms of the Avant-Garde – in favor of the classicist's search for transparency and brevity. Among those humbled by their *Je ne sais quoi* attitude, Julio Cortázar refers in *Diario para un cuento* to his own incapacity to tell a story with the kind of distance that he admires in Bioy's prose and, in *La vuelta al día en ochenta mundos* (1967) wonders how he should address Borges in a letter, since doing it as a peer would ignore the considerable difference in the quality of their work: for him, Borges was unmatchable. Another member of this group, Victoria Ocampo, Silvina's older sister, founded a journal she named *Sur*, which published James Joyce, Rabindranath Tagore, and Virginia Woolf among others, together with Spanish-speaking writers such as Borges. She was romantically involved with a few of the writers she invited to collaborate in *Sur* and whom she hosted in Argentina, acquiring a reputation for her independence in both love and letters. Victoria's house in San Isidro was allegedly the site for Borges's "The Garden of Forking Paths" (*El jardín de los senderos que se bifurcan*, Borges 1962).[1]

This is the world in which Borges lived and worked. He had come from the middle class and, although he had distinguished ancestry, his financial situation was not prosperous – in this respect, again, he resembled Poe's Dupin. Bioy's household and Victoria's friendship brought Borges into a literary society oblivious of financial concerns where intellect and style prevailed over all other considerations.

It was Bioy who convinced his friend to devote himself exclusively to literature. Over the years, before he attained the readership that would make his financial existence easier, Borges earned a living as a teacher, translator, editor, and as Director of the National Library of Argentina, all positions consistent with his writing that appear, as well, as occupations of some of the characters in his work. Other jobs, however, he considered distinctly humiliating. Among the resentments that Borges nursed against the Argentine dictator Juan Perón was the fact that he had appointed him Poultry Inspector of the Market of Buenos Aires. It was, of course, an insult, but Borges's enduring shock shows the extent to which he considered literature something of a sacred calling.

As is evident from their conversations, Borges and Bioy did not equate vulgarity with lack of money or social standing. Quite the opposite. As happens frequently in Borges's writing, high profile academics, as well as politically engaged artists, tend to be the target of ridicule along with various characters said to be members of the international upper crust, in particular women like the Countess of Bagnoregio in *Pierre Menard, Author of Don Quixote* (*Pierre Menard, autor del Quijote*, Borges 1962) and Teodolina Villar in *The Zahir*. In real life, though, Borges appears to have been cowed by the authority exuded by Victoria Ocampo and the persistent influence of his mother, whose power over him is well documented in Estela Canto's *Borges a contraluz*.

The irreverence that permeates the conversations recorded by Bioy and the earliest parodic detective stories that Bioy and Borges published under the pseudonym "H. Bustos Domecq" (*Seis problemas para don Isidro Parodi* [1942, translated 1981 as *Six Problems for Don Isidro Parodi*] and *Dos fantasías memorables*, 1946 [*Two noteworthy fantasies*]) were a form of rigorous engagement with art and literature because the two of them, following the example of Borges's master, the absurdist Macedonio Fernández, understood the deadening power of solemnity. One of Bioy's entries (Saturday, August 26, 1960) tells of a conversation in Bioy's apartment as the two were reading works submitted to a short story contest for which they were part of the jury. Borges says, "People don't laugh anymore at any artwork. They know how badly those who mocked the Impressionists ended up and they are afraid of being judged poorly by posterity. Why that fear of posterity? As Wilde said, so far posterity has done nothing for us." Then he comments, reading a title, "*University culture*, oxymoron" (Bioy Casares 2006: 678–70, my translation).

Neither posterity nor academia. Nor for that matter, politics: while the members of *Sur* were anti-Nazi and anti-Fascist during World War II, which made them anti-Peronist by default, their anti-Peronism was rooted in a total dismissal of nationalism and populism that is evident in the shaping of characters in Borges as well as in the works he authored with Bioy. The position appears to echo that of Dada and Surrealism. But it would be a mistake to confuse the early Borges with the numerous avant-garde practitioners of art and literature with whom he associated earlier in his career. Although the collaboration with Bioy bespeaks a will to tinker with established genres through multi-tonal and eccentric literary constructions, his dismissal of the earnestness of the avant-garde is clear in his essays and poetry. The detective fiction he wrote with Bioy is, in many ways, an implicit inscription of the avant-garde problematic in a parodical vein. While Avante-Gardists like the Ultraistas, Creacionistas and some of the original members of the Generación Martín Fierro advocated invention, Borges was more attracted by sheer intelligence. His conservative skepticism about finding new forms of writing was a constant during his life and is, to a great extent, a paradox given the impact that he has had as an innovator.

As young men Borges and Bioy worked on a task involving two other famous collaborators, Frederic Dannay and Manfred B. Lee, who together wrote under the "Ellery Queen" pseudonym. Borges and Bioy founded the Colección del Séptimo Círculo where they published Ellery Queen and authors featured in the Ellery Queen magazine. They also published an anthology of detective fiction where, in addition to Queen, they featured authors such as Hawthorne, Simenon, Peyrou, Conan Doyle, Stevenson, and Chesterton (Borges and Bioy Casares 1981). Thus, together with Poe, Ellery Queen is a vital reference for the understanding of their detective fiction.

As his admiration for Queen suggests, a see-sawing between popular and high culture is omnipresent in Borges, and it is nowhere more evident than in his collaborations with Bioy under the pen name H. Bustos Domecq. From their point of view, literature emerges from leisure. This perspective is paramount to an understanding of the special tone that they strike both in their literary collaboration and conversations, and gives a clue to the kind of detective they preferred: an idle character stemming from the Dupin tradition. Free time and seemingly boundless attention to details are part of the capacities for observation of such detectives and lend them the aura of a particular kind of intelligence. L. B. Jeffries, the disabled photographer in Hitchock's *Rear Window* (1954) who, sitting in his wheelchair, can see the crime neatly framed by his window, is among the classical examples of the type.

Cosmetic Intelligence and the Idle Detective

Borges's and Bioy's first collaboration as "H. Bustos Domecq," *Six Problems for don Isidro Parodi*, features six connected stories written between 1941 and 1942 framed as cases to be solved by an unfairly jailed detective, Isidro Parodi. Each of the cases is called a *problem*, and the six that compose the volume have a similar structure: a different character visits Parodi, the jailed detective, proposing to him an unsolved crime in which the visitor somehow is implicated. Parodi considers the "problem" and offers a resolution using the few available details. Clearly, Borges and Bioy have ironically recreated, through Parodi's forced incarceration, the milieu of the "armchair detective" who solves cases entirely in his head without having to visit the scene. Parodi's classical predecessors include Jacques Futrelle's S. F. X. van Dusen, the Baroness Emma Orzcy's "Old Man in the Corner," Sherlock Holmes's older brother, Mycroft, and, in *The Mystery of Marie Roget*, Dupin himself.

Six Problems is framed by a preface by another character, Gervasio Montenegro, and a biography of the fictional author, H. Bustos Domecq, attributed to a schoolteacher, Miss Adelma Badoglio. This complex labyrinth of authorship and transmission is essential to the sly humor of Bioy's and Borges's detective parody.

Gervasio Montenegro, who appears again in *Chronicles of H. Bustos Domecq*, represents one target of this parody. "From the fresco of what I do not hesitate to call 'contemporary Argentina' is missing the silhouette of the gaucho on horseback," he writes, "and in his place stands – and I expose the phenomenon in all its repulsive crudeness – the – the Jew, the Israelite" (Bustos Domecq 1980: 11). Montenegro's prejudices are representative of an anti-Semitic portion of Argentine society despised by Borges and Bioy, and particularly relevant to the war period during which the book was written and published. Asked about his political involvement at the time by Edgardo Cozarinsky for his documentary film *Boulevards du Crépuscule* (*Sunset Boulevards*) in 1992, Bioy implies that he did not think of it as particularly political since, in his words, there were only the good and the bad, and it was easy to tell one from the other.

Borges kept working on characters like Montenegro as a problematic cultural and philosophical issue raised by World War II. Unlike Bioy, however, he was interested in a territory in which differences become blurred, not more distinct. Later texts such as "The Secret Miracle" (Borges 1943), "Deutsches Requiem" (1949), "Three Versions of Judas," and "The Mirror of the Enigmas" (1952) give us a sense of the philosophical possibilities of changing positions within the original labyrinthine narrative structure of *Six Problems for don Isidro Parodi*.

One of the sins of Gervasio Montenegro appears in his signature: he belongs to the Argentine Academy of Letters, a sure proof of pompousness and ignorance for Borges and Bioy. Nevertheless, the preface is peppered with references alluding to a body of literature that Borges and Bioy took seriously. The inclusion of these works in the statement of the much-parodied Montenegro suggests a second level of representation in which the invented author, H. Bustos Domecq, seems a parodic composite of Borges and Bioy themselves. This implicit self-mockery, a recurrent device in Borges, saves the two authors from appearing arrogant in their relentless and punishing humor.

Montenegro mentions the forerunners of the genre, among them Poe's Dupin, who, he notes, captured the ape responsible for the troubles in the Rue Morgue. This reference to Poe, much admired by Borges is, like Montenegro's characterization of Domecq, double edged. Montenegro privileges the one story about which he and his creators might have reservations because of its resolution, as we read in Bioy's inventory of everything that he and Borges considered impermissible in literature. While "The Purloined Letter" is about intelligence, logic, and patterns, the ape in the Rue Morgue cuts short the inquiry with a surprising and whimsical solution.

"Such sedentary sleuths, such strange *voyageurs autour de la chambre*[2] are, if only in part, forerunners of our Parodi," writes Montenegro. "Perhaps an inevitable character in the development of detective fiction":

> Parodi's appearance, his *trouvaille*, is an Argentine achievement, produced – it should be noted – during the presidency of Dr. Castillo. Parodi's lack of mobility is the symbol and epitome of intellectuality, and it stands as a challenge to the pointless, frenetic action of American detective stories, which an overcritical yet quite accurate mind might compare with the celebrated squirrel of legend. (Bustos Domecq 1980: 12)

Montenegro's French affectation and political opportunism (he attempts to credit the presidency of Castillo for the book) is matched by his fervent xenophobia. Nevertheless, the implication here is that he is part of a group that shares some of Bioy's and Borges's tastes.

In addition to making a self-deprecatory joke, the biographical note about H. Bustos Domecq places the isolation of the jailed detective in the context of an interpretive community. The schoolteacher to whom the biographical note is attributed reveals a high degree of social affectation from the outset by referring to the book's fictitious author as *Dr* H. Bustos Domecq. The title of "Dr" is a common derogatory device for Borges, pointing to its owner's distance from literature, as was the case of the derided poet Arturo Capdevila whom Borges and Bioy called *Dr* Arturo Capdevila in the journal *Revista Martín Fierro*. The fact that the author of the note in *Six Problems* is identified as a female teacher further denies her credibility since neither women nor schoolteachers hold any literary prestige for Borges.

If this were all that is at play here, the book could be regarded as a minor exercise, a sophisticated pastime. However, its wealth of allusions gives us a means by which to unfold what is only implied in Borges's often cryptic writing.

"The Twelve Figures of the World," the first of the six problems, serves also as our introduction to Parodi, and is representative of the Domecq tales as a group. The story features him as having already spent 14 years in jail accused of a crime that was in fact committed by a member of a gang with the kind of influence that came from producing votes in political elections, the accuser being a police officer who owed Parodi money. Parodi is jailed in the now demolished Las Heras prison, which at the time sat atop a small elevation in the area called Palermo–Recoleta, a part of the city frequently mentioned in Borges's work. In the poem "The Mythical Foundation of Buenos Aires," Borges even suggests, against historical evidence, that it was in that neighborhood that the city was first erected. The Las Heras jail was a huge structure with a multilayered population that mirrored the functioning of Argentine society as a whole. It is portrayed as just such a microcosm in the novel.

Parodi is bald and fat, and he drinks the native *mate* – a brew made by steeping the dried leaves of the *yerba mate* plant – thereby striking a very Argentine pose. When we first encounter him, he is ranting against foreigners who, he tells Molinari, his first visitor, have now almost overtaken the prison. These people of dubious pedigree and uncertain origins, says Parodi, parrot the opinions of those who think of themselves as "true Argentines," a subject on which Borges consistently expressed skepticism. In his 1931 essay "Our Inabilities" (Borges 1999: 56–8) he deplores the Argentine's self-importance, his lack of imagination that mistakes irregularity for monstrosity and disdains anything non-Argentine and, above all, his pride in his cleverness. All these characteristics Borges sees as prevalent in the city of Buenos Aires, which was at that time even more of an immigration site than today. Resentment and false confidence in one's capacities for unveiling the truth behind apparent realities are proof of the self-deluding shrewdness he derides, and they offer him broad targets. Molinari visits Parodi because he believes that he has killed a man. In the end, the detective's investigation reveals that he is not only mistaken, but was the unwitting victim of a hoax that preyed on his ultra-nationalism.

Molinari finds no difficulty in augmenting Parodi's putdowns of non-Argentine newcomers:

> Molinari, who was prone to nationalistic sentiments, joined battle to say that he was fed up with Italians and Druses, not to mention English capitalists, who had filled Argentina with railways and meat-packing plants. Only yesterday he'd walked into the All-Star Pizza Parlor, and the first thing that he set eyes on was an Italian. (Borges 1999: 19)

In 1931, under Uriburu's presidency, two men of Italian origin, Severino di Giovanni and Paulino Scarfo, were accused of anarchism and executed at Las Heras. By posturing as anti-foreign, Parodi, whose name suggests Italian origins as well as an inclination to mockery, subtly ridicules Molinari's nationalistic prejudices. The game he plays is a variation on Borges's "El indigno," in which a Jew betrays the confidence of an Argentine gang member out of a sense of duty. He is put in his place, however, when the very policeman who should have been pleased by his turning informant asks if the Jew is going straight only to be accepted as a real Argentine. Clearly, the bond between the gang member and the policeman is stronger than that between the policeman and the Jew, because it is based on a common birthplace. But while the Jew in "El indigno" is only suspected of play-acting, Parodi is deliberately assuming a role. Molinari wants to get Parodi on his side, but Parodi puts him off with seemingly irrelevant questions: "'Tell me,' said don Isidro, 'this Italian that's on your mind – is it a man or a woman?' 'Neither,' replied Molinari, getting to the point, 'Don Isidro, I have killed a man'" (Borges 1999: 19). Parodi dismisses the seriousness of the accusation by facetiously citing himself as an example of wronged innocence, a more than dubious proof, since he is in jail. However, Parodi gives signs of being fully aware of the nature of Molinari's problem when the Druses, an ancient and secret sect and an offshoot of Islam, appear to lie at the heart of the case.

The Druses are a community whose members, it is supposed, hide their beliefs when necessary and often appear secular with the option to be religious. Considered Muslim by some and an independent monotheistic faith by others, they are close to Jews; some are even Israeli citizens. Borges and Bioy portray the Druses as both part of mainstream Argentine society and members of a secret, and impenetrable, organization. Their jobs as drivers of frozen meat trucks show them to be part of everyday Argentine reality while their practices bespeak the secrecy of a brotherhood with strict rules. The truck carrying frozen meat to be delivered to butchers is a common sight in Buenos Aires and pertains to Argentine folklore, closely associated as it is in the popular imagination with *gauchos* (cowboys): to have a man behind the wheel who is not a full-blooded Argentine is thus tantamount to a usurpation.

Molinari's tale of his initially casual association with the Druses translates their exoticism into quotidian Argentine realities. He is interested in their rituals in the same disconnected way as he is curious as to the cost of the bull's statue he sees in one of their homes. Price, not purpose, establishes the value of the sect's relics for the community of non-believers. Similarly, the exoticism of Druse names is combined with daily details that flatten everything into the banal mentality of Buenos Aires. The story emphasizes this cultural divide and stresses that Molinari's curiosity builds a distance because it defines him as an outsider. As Molinari gets entangled in a mystery that involves a tea diet for three days and the learning of some words as signs, he is made to believe that he has killed the treasurer of the group, its bookkeeper. When he visits Parodi, he wants to confess, but Parodi's resolution of the case exonerates him of the crime he believed he had committed.

Parodi begins his explanation by asking Molinari to pick certain cards from a marked deck and earns Molinari's admiration when he guesses which one he will choose at each successive turn. The same predetermined result, says Parodi, occurred with the Druses, who played an elaborate "numbers game" by sending the gullible Molinari on a wild goose chase for members of the sect that were ordered systematically, like marked cards. Parodi's conclusion, although seemingly deductive, is not a product of sheer analytical intelligence, however; it is a hunch based on national prejudices because his main conclusion is that most of the Druses were "satisfied to make fun of a native Argentine" (1999: 35). As it turns out, Molinari was taken in by the exotic nature of Druses, believed he was an inductee, and thought that the "books" on which one of them was working were part of the cult when, in fact, they were merely account books. The death of the treasurer, for which Molinari blamed himself, was caused by somebody else from the group in an effort to cover up a crime of embezzlement through arson.

Parodi's solution appears to depend upon a knowledge of patterns or recursive algorithms to explain the mechanisms causing Molinari's false perception of his own guilt. But while Molinari may not have been to blame for murder, he is, nevertheless, guilty of something else. He was the victim of a practical joke because he was not aware of the role he played in the Druse community. Attracted by what he perceived to be their differences from Argentines, he sought to know them and got caught in a plot having little to do with religion, but everything to do with being Argentine. A timeless national penchant for corruption and cover-ups displaces the neatness of the numerical patterns adduced by Parodi, and posturing, xenophobia, snobbishness, and opportunism insure Molinari's blindness to his own condition. In trying to know the Druses he misses himself. Instead of penetrating an alien culture, he has sunk deeper into his own limitations, the least knowledgeable agent in the plot.

The number game unveiled by Parodi is a cosmetic version of intelligence because although the card pattern shows Molinari's lack of involvement in the crime, it tells, as well, how far he was from understanding his own role in the plot. Being part of a game, a rivalry, a war in which unknowing opponents become interchangeable or expendable is one of the recurrent themes in Borges's work. *Six Problems for Don Isidro Parodi*, at the start of his narrative career, posits that a practical joke based on a misunderstanding of the role played by nationalities may demand the subtleties of intuition as opposed to the logical certainties of intelligence. Through parody, Parodi re-enacts one of the dichotomies not only enunciated by Poe in his distinction between numerical "acumen" and intuitive "analysis" in "The Murders in the Rue Morgue," but also observed frequently, in religious terms, by Chesterton's Father Brown, an atypical sleuth much admired by Borges. In this case, however, the choice of intuition over intelligence, played out in Chesterton as the triumph of faith over logic, is made evident to readers as a humorous wink, an invitation to laugh at nationalism and xenophobia.

Universal Patterns and Local Readings

Concerned about the trivializing effects of local color, Borges expressed mixed feelings about some of his writings, particularly *El hombre de la esquina rosada* (*The Man from the Pink Corner*) in which he uses local dialogue and stereotyped Argentine characters. Preoccupation with the relationship between the local and the universal traverses his work, which tries to be hospitable to Argentina without becoming picturesque. Time and again he reclaims a universal cultural tradition in a multilingual context.

Six Problems for don Isidro Parodi is an extreme representation of a certain kind of hyper-Argentine error seemingly doomed by nationalistic posturing. "Death and the Compass," published in 1944 as part of *Artificios*, was considered by Borges to be his most Argentine story, its very lack of specific local references helping readers to sense the unreality of Buenos Aires much more accurately than they could in any other of his texts. The representation of Lönnrot, whose intellect is taxed to solve a series of bloody murders, does not involve characterization by voice in the form of direct speech quotations, or any prior mention of his background. We are led, instead, in a seamless manner to the villa of Triste-le-Roy, impregnated with a fragrance of eucalypti, recalling, for some Borges commentators, Villa Ocampo, Victoria's home in San Isidro.

Lönnrot, unlike Parodi, is not inclined to claim cultural insertion as a clue to the resolution of a mystery. He thinks of himself, instead, as "a pure reasoner, an Auguste Dupin" (Borges 1943: 76). The reference to Poe is not mere homage but an intervention by which Lönnrot is included in the history of detection as a Dupin *with a difference*. He has a story that makes him unpredictable and an object of curiosity himself since he is described as having "something of the adventurer in him, and even a little of the gambler" (1943: 76). The intertextual relationship with Poe implies a dialogue in which Borges rewrites Dupin as a point of interest, thereby creating another source of uncertainty for the reader in the figure of the elusive detective. Instead of being the neutral point in the pursuit and investigation, Lönnrot is part of the mystery.

For Borges, Buenos Aires was a universal site for secrets embedded in the conflicting cultural codes of immigrants and their languages. The Druses confused Molinari by letting him believe that the accounting books were sacred. Jewish but not quite, Argentine but not quite, Italian but not quite, the many characters in the world of *Six Problems for don Isidro Parodi* turn dogmatically affirmed nationalities into a practical joke when made an object for detection. In much the same manner, *Death and the Compass* provides us with a broad register of Jewish sources, both high and low, only to deflate their significance in the end: the *Ydische Zeitung*, the *Tetragrammaton*, a *History of the Hasidic Sect* and the word *goyim*, Yiddish for naturalized non-Jews. As often happens in Borges, he proposes with one stroke what he undoes with another.

The serious use of numerical and geometrical solutions alluding to sacred sources is in counterpoint with that in *Six Problems for don Isidro Parodi*. Philo-Semitism appears in "Death and the Compass" with its numerical hypotheses without a hint of parody and the mind that posits them has a non-trivial intelligence. The Jewish textual tradition attracted Borges for its capacity to include interpretation at the core of reading. Detection and reading more generally are identified in *Death and the Compass* as almost identical exercises. If in *Six Problems* the hypothesis of the jailed detective suggests incarceration as a source for his shrewdness and relative objectivity in analyzing situations, here the image of detective as scholar intensifies the implied positive value given to detachment from hands-on experience.

Lönnrot is described as initiating his search as though he had suddenly become a bibliophile or Hebraist. He does not pay attention to the police investigation about the murder plot he tries to elucidate. Instead, he plunges into studying the Baal Shem Tov, the *Tetragrammaton* (the unutterable name of God), and other obscure Jewish and Persian sources. In doing so, he acts as a Jewish man dedicated to serious and committed study, a rabbi eschewing the need to obtain immediate results characteristic of a police action. A journalist from the *Ydische Zeitung*, a daily newspaper more inclined to secular and straightforward concerns, provides the reader with a necessary but false summary, claiming that Lönnrot had dedicated himself to the study of the texts in an effort to discover the name of the murderer. But if this summary is indeed false, we are forced to ask ourselves why the search for the name of the culprit would be wrong.

The purpose of the story is to displace the idea behind a detective's investigation from the need to punish a crime by finding its perpetrator, to recognizing the repetition of patterns. In this respect Borges repeats, but with a difference, the shift of focus in his earlier *Six Problems* from Molinari's supposition of his own guilt to the recursive algorithm that has brought him to that mistaken conclusion: there the confessing criminal turned out to be the dupe of his own prejudices. In "Death and the Compass," too, detection becomes a way of understanding the transcendental logic of a history of repetitions through the recognition of patterns, in this case, patterns arising from an examination of books rather than from a series of isolated experiences. Here, however, the patterns uncovered by the investigation make the smug investigator, not the confessing criminal, their victim. In this story, the patterns are metaphysical as well as numerical. They take us back to the Hebrews and the Greeks as they move from concrete events to mathematical relations, philological allusions, and notions of the divine. The *Ydische Zeitung* offers a less abstract solution – an anti-Semitic plot (sadly a common event in Argentina) – and Inspector Treviranus a less elegant one – a jewel heist gone wrong – than the answer that Lönnrot discovers encoded in the mystery of the Tetragrammaton. It leads him to the mastermind behind the killings, but also to his own death.

Just before Red Scharlach fires the shot that ends the story, he promises Lönnrot, for the "next time," a labyrinth consisting of a single invisible and unceasing line. Scharlach's linear labyrinth is susceptible of many possible interpretations, including the narrative of the story itself, or of the history in which we live. How successive events may retain their particularity and yet create a labyrinth in which readers, and readers of detective fiction in particular, can get lost remained a question for Borges himself, who often wondered about the interplay between the local and the universal, the rigidity of the text and the suppleness of the reader's imagination, the isolated detail and the larger pattern to which it contributed.

Throughout his career, Borges strove to include reading as the great adventure, the unveiling of a mystery regarding sources and the fight among interpreters to lay a claim to truth.

History, Culture, and Crimes

While Borges is probably best known to fans of the postmodern detective genre for his three Poe tribute stories – "Death and the Compass," "The Garden of Forking Paths," and "Ibn Hakkan al-Bokhari, Dead in his Labyrinth" – he has also contributed significantly to the wider category of crime literature, particularly in his close studies of the psychology of evil (see Merivale, chapter 24 in this volume, on Borges and postmodern detective fiction). Two stories especially, *The Secret Miracle* and *Deutsches Requiem*, provide an occasion for gauging Borges's sense of an individual's capacity for acting and stating the unpleasant truths about our conventional bifurcated moralism in a limiting historical situation.

Deutsches Requiem relates in the voice of a character named Otto Dietrich zur Linde the beliefs of a devoted Nazi on the eve of his execution. He asks for no forgiveness because he feels devoid of guilt. His tastes are given in a dispassionate tone: Brahms, Schopenhauer, Shakespeare. About these he notes that he wants all of those who admire them to know that he shares in the wonder at their work. This moment implicates Borges directly in the mind of the character he has created, since these are crucial names in his own genealogy as a writer. In *Sobre los clásicos* (*On Classics*) Borges says that a classic is a text that keeps recurring in the hopes and discussions of a community (Borges 1952), and he adds that he can imagine drawing the same implications and associations from works in languages he does not know, thereby stating that the foreignness of experience is not a stumbling block for the recognition of the power of a text to serve as a prism reflective of the human condition.

In *Deutsches Requiem* he suggests that the re-interpretation of the shared classics, the canon, involves us inextricably and intimately with the enemy in our midst. Like Borges himself, his protagonist is interested in Nietzsche and Spengler. His adherence to the Nazi Party stems from true conviction, not passionate comradeship:

> I will say little of my years of apprenticeship. They were more difficult for me than for others, since, although I do not lack courage, I am repelled by violence. I understood, however, that we were on the verge of a new era, and that this era, comparable to the initial epochs of Islam and Christianity, demanded a new kind of man. Individually my comrades were disgusting to me; in vain did I try to reason that we had to suppress our individuality for the lofty purpose that brought us together. (Borges 1964: 142–3)

Otto zur Linde stands before death not as a murderer who has found an ideological justification for his violent instincts and social resentments but as an individual who has acquiesced to violence and to participation with the Nazi party out of a deep historical conviction. When he lays out the basis of his convictions he does so by mentioning the same sources of thought by which Borges chooses to define himself. We are told that zur Linde diligently performed his tasks as sub-director of the concentration camp at Tarnowitz and, among references to Whitman and Shakespeare, he tells how he drove to suicide a Sephardic Jew named David Jerusalem because that seemed the best way to destroy the compassion that he felt for him. A convinced Nietzschean, he expects the advent of the new man and refuses to see his crimes as self-indulgence. They are, rather, a form of abnegation, of self immolation: "Many things will have to be destroyed in order to construct the New Order; now we know that Germany also was one of those things. We have given more than our lives, we have sacrificed the destiny of our beloved Fatherland. Let others curse and weep; I rejoice in the fact that our destiny completes its circle and is perfect" (Borges 1964: 146–7). He feels that the Nazis have won because those striking them, the winners, have, in fact, adopted the Nazis' own methods of violence and, in so doing, are preparing the advent of the New Man. Germany has, in fact, won through its defeat but the victors do not know it.

Otto zur Linde is honest; he is presenting a deeply held opinion. No lying here. But in his authenticity he may be mistaken about Shakespeare, Schopenhauer, and Nietzsche – the very names with which he has built his identity. Even if he were right about them, his sense of who they were and what they wrote has directed him towards a path questioned by others with the same personal investment. The truth that Otto zur Linde is able to tell about himself does not illuminate anything but his own circumstances, although it is strong enough to justify his destiny and, in his view, give a full account of the course of history.

An additional story again brings in the question of history and an intimate understanding of one's fate during the same period. A character named Hladik in "The Secret Miracle" (Borges 1964: 90–1) awaits execution under charges of Philo-Semitism. A middle-aged writer and scholar, Hladik was working on a play, *The Enemies*, which he had been unable to finish. Awed by the possibility of dying without having achieved its completion he says to God: "If in some fashion I exist, I am not one of Your repetitions and mistakes, I exist as the author of *The Enemies*. To finish this drama, which can justify me and justify You, I need another year. Grant me these days. You to whom the centuries and time belong" (Borges 1964: 92). The execution, scheduled for nine o'clock, takes place on schedule but, nevertheless, Hladik is able to finish his play as he experiences a moment of plenitude and density of reference new to him. The story concludes by telling us that before dropping dead Hladik found the one phrase he had been missing.

The completion of Hladik's play *The Enemies* had been rendered possible by his executioners, his enemies. Like Otto zur Linde he died having been able to turn his demise into a triumph. For his executioners he was a victim; for himself he had realized what he had always wanted, even to the point of having been inscribed in his own play. Each man had a direct, unmediated relationship to his goals. One cannot but think that they were truthful. And yet, being truthful, being anchored by a stable identity, is not enough.

The German who believes he has won the war and the Philo-Semite who triumphs as he is murdered bear their destinies as a secret. To all eyes, these men have been defeated. These stories tell us that we do not know how history is lived and interpreted by those who make it, any more than the characters in "Death and the Compass" can understand or interpret the narrative that animates them in a reader's imagination. The opposing groups die and triumph blind to the nature of their conflict and no amount of individual devotion and authenticity can make up for that radical ignorance of what is at stake.

Who is to resolve these issues? Who will give shape to stories that demand that victims be recognized as such and those responsible be punished? The sorter of details, the builder of taxonomies and hierarchies is the reader who, engaged in detection here as in every specimen of the detective genre *per se*, has to give meaning to stories of the past. Throughout World War II, and beyond, Borges posed his most intense questions about the meaning of historical events and the impact of culture on our understanding of them. The world is his crime scene, whose interpreter and frustrated detective is none other than the reader.

Notes

1   The text is dedicated to Victoria Ocampo.

2   An allusion to the meditation *Voyage autour de ma chambre* by Joseph de Maistre (1753–1821).

38
Chester Himes (1909–1984)

Stephen Soitos

Introduction

Chester Himes was one of the most prolific, problematic and neglected African-American writers of the twentieth century. He wrote 17 novels, dozens of collected and uncollected stories and essays, and a significant two-volume autobiography over a long and difficult life split between his native United States and self-exile in Europe. While receiving recognition and awards for his writing in France, Himes was largely unknown to American readers during most of his lifetime.

Part of this neglect can be attributed to the discriminatory attitude of American publishers and mainstream readers towards black writers during Himes's lifetime. But Himes was also an author of irascible honesty and deep complexity. His unflinching view of racism and its physical and psychological toll on both blacks and whites alienated many who were unwilling to face the frightening aspects of violence and hatred that infused all of his work.

Himes was one of a very few crime and mystery story authors who actually committed crimes, having been an inmate at the Ohio State Penitentiary from 1929 to 1936. His harsh prison internment and its psychological effects, expressed so brutally in his prison stories and novel, might be considered a foreshadowing of the monumental institutionalized racism that has been inflicted on black males to this day. Himes was 19 when he went to prison for armed robbery and 26 when he was released. His outlaw persona, conforming to the "Badman" of black vernacular culture, was a proud stance and an instrumental tool in his survival both in prison and in the outside world. He later claimed that he learned to write in prison partly as a defensive ploy and a way to give voice to the invisible members of society.

After prison Himes continued to be thwarted in his goals by the destructive forces of racism, poverty, and unemployment, as well as artistic neglect. He moved with his wife, Jean Johnson, to California and wrote two books about his experiences working in the LA wartime industry of shipbuilding.

If He Hollers Let Him Go (1945) and *Lonely Crusade* (1947) were both poorly received and widely misunderstood by critics and readers. The negative reaction to these brutally honest novels brought retribution from his publishers, who arbitrarily cancelled publicity and support after publication of *Lonely Crusade*. Himes wrote his prison novel *Cast the First Stone* (1952) from a white male viewpoint to facilitate publication. Many passages were deleted and the result was an unfocused book that only regained its vitality when a reissued version entitled *Yesterday Will Make You Cry* (1998) restored its original black protagonist and deleted passages.

Chester Himes's early work depicted one of the most unforgiving and disturbing visions of the African-American male experience in contemporary literature (see Bailey, chapter 21 in this volume). His first five novels are often grouped together unfairly under the rubric of protest novels. *If He Hollers Let Him Go*, *Lonely Crusade*, *Cast the First Stone*, *The Third Generation* (1954), and *The Primitive* (1955) provide a shocking social history of race relations in the United States from World War I through the Depression and World War II to the days of the black urban rebellion of the 1960s.

At age 44, after writing five novels, Himes found himself working as a busboy in a New York cafeteria. His long marriage with Jean Johnson was over and he had been falsely accused of reckless driving in an accident with a white woman, which led to more jail time. His life in the United States having come to an end, he left for Europe in 1953 with the encouragement of the African-American author Richard Wright, who was then living in Paris. Himes was also attracted by French critical acclaim for his writings. In 1952 reviewers selected Himes's *Lonely Crusade* as one of the five best books by an American author published that decade in France.

In 1956 Himes was offered a contract to write a mystery novel by the French publishers Gallimard for their Serie Noire imprint, which published hard-boiled American writers such as Dashiell Hammett and Raymond Chandler. Himes published his first mystery novel, *For Love of Imabelle*, in 1957, and the following year the French translation won the prestigious *Grand prix de la littérature policière* award for best mystery of 1958.

Between 1957 and 1969, Himes wrote his Harlem cycle of nine crime novels: *For Love of Imabelle* (1957); *The Real Cool Killers* (1959); *The Crazy Kill* (1959); *The Big Gold Dream* (1960); *All Shot Up* (1960); *Cotton Comes to Harlem* (1965); *The Heat's On* (1966); and *Blind Man with a Pistol* (1969). These books, set in Harlem, featured two black New York City police detectives, Coffin Ed Johnson and Gravedigger Jones. With a cast of all black characters they revolutionized African-American detective fiction, a tradition that stretched back to Pauline Hopkins's *Hagar's Daughter* (1901–2) and John E. Bruce's *The Black Sleuth* (1907–9). (See Bailey, chapter 21 in this volume.)

The mystery novels proved to be a perfect vehicle for Himes's sardonic and absurdist vision of American culture. They also "signified" (to use the black vernacular for "parodied") and expanded on the hard-boiled tradition of the lone private eye. Himes was able to work important "Blues Detective" tropes (Soitos 1996: 27–51) into his socially aware and highly critical texts, including black detective personas working as teams rather than as individuals, "Double Conscious Detection" that used "blackness" as a disguise or mask in the detective process, and the use of black vernaculars (musical as well as linguistic) and "hoodoo" practices and beliefs drawn from black spiritual and religious traditions.

Besides the mystery novels featuring Gravedigger and Coffin Ed, Himes also wrote the superb suspense novel *Run, Man, Run* (1969), which also takes place in Harlem, and two satiric novels dealing with white and black sexual relations, *Pinktoes* (1961) and *Case of Rape* (1963). A film version of *Cotton Comes to Harlem* in 1970 further increased Himes's standing internationally. In 1972 he published the first volume of his autobiography *The Quality of Hurt* and in 1976 the second volume, *My Life of Absurdity*. In 1993, his unfinished apocalyptic novel of violent black revolution, *Plan B*, appeared posthumously. Chester Himes died on November 12, 1984 in Spain.

The Man

Himes's reputation as a mystery and crime writer is often attributed to the substantial achievement of his Harlem series of crime novels. It is not generally realized how integral to his work are the notion of crime and the exclusion of the criminal from society. Himes's fascination with crime writing has its roots in his early reading of mystery and crime stories, but the genre was also a perfect means for expressing Himes's worldview, particularly his assessment of the African-American male's condition in a racist society. In Himes's fiction an individual's outrage at blatant prejudice and subtler violations of his personal integrity often lead to violence and social rebellion against dominant white authority figures and racist power structures.

Crime fiction was not just a literary puzzle or game to Himes. For him, crime gave voice to the voiceless as well as providing them with a means of revenge. Given the crucial similarities between his own life and those of his fictionalized selves, both the earlier novels he wrote in the United States and much of his later fiction appear to be highly autobiographical.

One might say that the writer in Chester Himes was conceived in fire and born in prison. On Easter Monday, April 21, 1930 a prison wing at Ohio Penitentiary caught on fire. The blaze was quick and merciless, racing up five tiers of the huge cellblock in punishing waves of heat and smoke. Prison guards caught unawares were unable to enter the blazing inferno to unlock the cells. Prisoners in the other wings of the huge building watched helplessly as the fire grew. In desperation they broke from their surrounding cellblocks and attempted to free the trapped men beating on the bars of their cells. Himes, prisoner and would-be writer, was among this milling crowd of helpless would-be rescuers tormented by the screams of the dying men. Only a few badly burned prisoners were removed before the cellblock was consumed and 317 prisoners lost their lives dying like animals in locked cages.

This event forced Himes to confront the horror of prison life and became the basis of one of his earliest short stories, "To What Red Hell" (1934). The story was a graphic and harrowing indictment of the consequences of centralized institutional power and provides a frightening description of prisoners abandoned and helpless. The story was instrumental for Himes in defining and giving expression to his rage over what it meant to be a black male in America. In writing it he became conscious of his inferior status – "'furious boiling with all that hot rebellion I'd been feeling of late against the least thing that appeared to jeopardize my rights" (Himes 1973: 177). Himes emerged from the infernal world of the prison fire with a new authorial voice. Possessed with a growing political consciousness, he sought an evolving and coherent definition of himself as a free person. He would dedicate his life to depicting this dilemma in incendiary prose that shocked his readership.

Another crucial story from this period featured a black protagonist. "The Night's for Crying" (1937), Himes's story of a black man on death row, emphasizes the man's intense isolation and his unquenched resistance against discriminatory society to the end. This later version of "Blackie" is an alienated man nursing his hatred of white authority, but he also represents the innumerable suffering black men excluded and discriminated against in all aspects of American life. He is the very essence of a black man trapped in the core of his country who insists on dying the way he lived: in utter and total defiance of a prejudiced society and judicial system.

Cast the First Stone (1952), Himes's third novel after *If He Hollers Let Him Go* and *Lonely Crusade*, deals with prison life and the behavior patterns necessary for survival in prison. Featuring white characters, it was rewritten to artistic death from an original manuscript Himes's had started in prison. Jim Monroe, a white inmate serving 20–25 years for armed robbery, is involved in a prison riot, a fire, gambling, numerous intrigues, and a significant love affair with another prisoner, Dido. But this prison memoir, inhibited by its white point of view, is dry and ineffectual. The nexus of confinement is ambiguous and the reader is more tantalized by what was left out than by what was included.

This novel was later reissued with the black viewpoint restored and revelatory passages concerning white and black relations, including male love, deeply analyzed. *Yesterday Will Make You Cry*, Himes's original manuscript version of his prison years, is an overwhelmingly revealing indictment of institutionalized racism and the growing state-sponsored prejudice that would later erupt in the 1950s and 60s into a civil war over civil rights in the inner cities of the United States.

Himes's writing was influenced not only by his experiences in prison, but also by his knowledge of and fondness for pulp crime fiction published in such early detective magazines as *Black Mask*. He directed the conventions of the hard-boiled genre to his own ends, reworking the tough, detached, cynical viewpoint of the hard-boiled crime narrative into a commentary on the oppressed black male in white America. Crime and violence, motivated by generic temptations in their original pulp contexts, became connected in Himes's imagination with revolt, defiance, and the validation of blackness.

Besides the use of pulp fiction motifs in his writing, Himes also utilized a primarily black vernacular cultural form. This was the idea of the bad black, the "Badman," an incorrigible rebel of folklore who generated numerous folk ballads and songs in the black oral tradition. Himes was familiar with this vernacular role, which was often performed in prison environments by black inmates.

This Badman heroic tradition emphasized the inherent powers of the black hero triumphant over white oppression. This was a stance similar to the Trickster tradition in which the intellectual and conjuring skills of the black outwitted the Man. One such Badman figure was Bras Coupe, who lived in Louisiana in the 1830s. Coupe was a native African sold as a slave who escaped to the Louisiana swamps, where he formed a Marron (from the French, "marronage," for "fugitive") colony. He raided plantations, murdered whites and defied capture with the use of hoodoo or conjuration. Another legendary Badman was Morris Slater, commonly known as Railroad Bill, who appeared in 1893. He robbed trains and supplied poor blacks along the tracks with the goods he appropriated. His ability to elude capture created the myth that he was a powerful shape-shifter who could change his form at will.

These folk legends were captured in the vibrant and energizing song heritage of the African-American folk tradition. Songs about such real-life Badmen have parallels in the toasts or *signifying* ("cutting") contests attributed to Stagolee, a mythical figure, who like earlier heroic ballad figures was a fast-talking, action-oriented, and violent defender of his natural rights. These heroic Badman forms have also had a strong impact on the Blues, that other bastion of black secular expression, and more recently on Rap music, where modern avengers brag and list poetically their powers and accomplishments.

Early Life

Himes's writing was crucially shaped by a disturbing family dynamic, which had a profound psychological effect as well. He was born on July 20 in Jefferson City, Missouri. His father Joseph Sandy Himes headed the mechanical arts department at a local black college. Chester was the youngest in his family with two older brothers, Joseph and Edward. His mother, Estelle Bomar, was light-skinned and claimed that her family was descended from English nobility through the paternity of her family's southern plantation owner.

Estelle's social-register fantasy and aristocratic attitudes betrayed a very serious and debilitating form of color prejudice within the black community that was to affect Chester Himes's image of himself throughout his troubled life. Her attitudes were a source of conflict between her husband and her three sons. Perhaps of all of them, Chester was affected the most, torn between his mother's assimilation creed and his natural need to rebel and determine his own identity as a black man in racist America.

His fourth novel, *The Third Generation* (1954), deals specifically with this dilemma and others associated with a black family growing to maturity in the segregated South at the beginning of the twentieth century. Himes maintained that he was the product of two opposing traditions, the body-servant tradition, represented by his light-skinned mother, and the field-hand tradition represented by his father, a very dark man whose ancestors worked in the fields. Himes respected his father, but he maintained that Joseph Sandy Himes "was born and raised in the tradition of the southern Uncle Tom … [an] inherited slave mentality, which accepts the premise that white people know best" (Himes 1970b: 26) The attitudinal conflict embodied by his parents seems to be reflected in the constant friction between a white female (or near-white female) and a black male that appears in four of Himes's first five novels. Himes later recalled how deeply hurt his mother was by knowing he could not have straight hair. As a young man he remembered "the tenderness of doing her nails, the soft delight of her hair, the passion of her whippings" (Himes 1954: 235).

This schism over racial identity in Himes's family had parallel repercussions in the environment of his youth. Early racial incidents contributed to his sense of guilt and unworthiness, sometimes compounded with personal or family tragedies. On one early occasion, Chester and his older brother Joseph planned to demonstrate the use of explosives to an assembly at their father's college, but Chester's mother forbade him to participate. Performing the experiment alone, Joseph made a mistake and was blinded. Unable to be admitted to a white hospital, he never received the medical care required to save his sight. Chester, suffering from survivor's guilt, blamed himself for his older brother's blindness.

Another incident occurred in early 1926 when Chester was working as a busboy at the Wade Park hotel in Cleveland. He fell down an open elevator shaft and suffered a back injury that plagued him for the rest of his life. White doctors would not care for him and the hotel discriminated against him by firing him and refusing to pay compensation.

In September 1926 Himes enrolled in Ohio State University, where he did poorly in part because of the racist environment. "I was tired of [the university's] policy of discrimination and segregation, fed up with the condescension, which I could never bear. … [I]t was much later in life that I came to understand I simply hadn't accepted my status as a 'nigger'" (Himes 1972: 28). What Himes would not accept was being relegated to the status of a lower-class citizen because of color. In reaction, he created a new persona that was the reverse of the role being imposed on him. He now acted out the part of the Badman and he did it with a flair and vengeance that surprised even him.

After dropping out of school Himes returned to Cleveland and took up the street life. He associated with members of the black underworld, where he gambled and pimped and learned something of the hustling world. "Little Katzi," as Himes was affectionately called by his friends, was arrested for burglary and forgery; he took drugs and became notorious for his violence. "I discovered that I had become very violent," he later wrote. "I saw a glimmer of fear and caution in the eyes of most people I encountered. Squares, hustlers, gamblers, pimps, even whores. I had heard that people were saying 'Little Katzi will kill you.' I can't say what I might have done" (Himes 1972: 47).

Himes met Jean Johnson, his future wife, during this period, but although she provided some stability to his life, Himes was launched on a trajectory of self-destruction and could not be stopped. In November 1928 he broke into the home of a rich, white Cleveland couple and robbed them at gunpoint of $20,000 in cash and $28,000 in jewelry. He fled to Chicago, where he was arrested.

At the detective bureau his feet were bound, his wrists handcuffed behind his back, and he was hung upside down on an open door and pistol-whipped on the face and testicles until he confessed. In December 1928 he was tried, found guilty, and sentenced to serve 20–25 years at hard labor. The sentence was severe, even for the times, but an earlier, even more serious crime Himes had committed might have influenced his sentence. A few months before his arrest, he and an accomplice had broken into a State Armory and stolen cases of guns that Himes had sold to Cleveland mill workers and criminals in his neighborhood.

Himes later claimed that he grew to manhood in the Penitentiary, where he learned how to survive for 8 years in a very dangerous environment. "On occasion, it must have seemed to others that I was bent on self-destruction," he wrote (Himes 1972: 61). Himes was also intent on developing a writing career, which created an aura of power around him in the eyes of the other inmates and even the guards. They learned to treat him with cautious respect for his writing skills, a source of mysterious allure in a prison population where inmates fought to the death with knives over whether France was in Paris or Paris in France.

In May 1936 Chester Himes was paroled, and he and Jean Johnson married the next year. Although he thought of himself as a writer, he could not make a living with his pen. Instead, he supported himself and his wife by working as a part-time waiter and contributing to an Ohio writer's project for the WPA program.

In 1941 Chester and Jean moved to California. He worked at 23 jobs in the next 4 years in the shipyards of Los Angeles and he wrote his first two novels at the same time. Himes was later to say that "Los Angeles hurt me racially as much as any city I have ever known – much more than any city from the South" (Himes 1972: 73). The anger, frustration and sense of rejection Himes experienced in Los Angeles were readily transferred to *If He Hollers Let Him Go* (1945) and *Lonely Crusade* (1947). Both books are told from the viewpoint of a black male who is involved with the shipyards as a welder in the first book and as union organizer for a black union in the second.

In the first book Bob Jones comes to California from Cleveland to work because at home he was being refused work while white men were being hired ahead of him. In California, however, he finds a more insidious species of discrimination that gives him repetitive nightmares in which he is falsely accused of crimes and hunted down by angry mobs of white people. Bob Jones finds himself in a racial trap. He is hounded by his white superiors in the shipyard and forced to work like a machine in the worst conditions. His interior sense of persecution assumes an outward form when a white southern woman on his worksite accuses of him rape. In the end Jones is run off his job by white workers and forced to join the US army.

In *Lonely Crusade* Lee Gordon is involved in a complicated political game between Communists, black workers and the owner of the Shipyards. The black union is being sold out and Lee Gordon is presented with the moral dilemma of standing up for what he knows is right or accepting a permanent management position. In the middle of this conundrum Gordon strives to keep his manhood intact. Class warfare and economic subjugation of black workers are constant themes here: Gordon must reject the Communist party line and confront the manipulative capitalist manager. In the end, Lee Gordon heroically leads the union parade straight into a police cordon that has orders to shoot him on sight.

In these early novels the protagonists are always planning retaliatory violence against whites who have insulted and humiliated them, but they rarely put these plans into action. Instead, ferocities of hate multiply and disdain for the hypocritical American system drives Himes's protagonists into a terrible personal anguish that destroys their lives and the lives of those around them.

Himes's publisher Knopf had lined up radio appearances and book signings at the book department at Macy's and Bloomingdales in New York City on the day *Lonely Crusade* was published. Getting cold feet at the last minute, Knopf canceled the signings and Himes was also dropped from an interview planned for a CBS network show. Himes believed he was being punished for his unsympathetic portrayal of Communists in the black community and in the labor movement, as well as for his discomfiting critique of racism at all levels of society. After these publishing failures and lack of public response to his novels, Himes was discouraged enough to stop writing for a few years. He wondered whether literature could meaningfully articulate the difficult truths of a black male's absurd existence in the American system.

He and Jean settled on the East Coast where Himes worked in a series of menial jobs in and around New York City – caretaker, porter, janitor, dishwasher, bellhop. In 1948 he delivered a speech at the University of Chicago entitled "The Dilemma of the Negro Novelist."

His brutally honest assessment of the situation for black writers in the United States was not well received. White Americans, he maintained, only wanted to be entertained by the black experience. Mainstream America did not take black literary artists seriously. It was no wonder, therefore, that black people should feel angry. "To hate white people," he said, "is one of the first emotions an American Negro experiences. ... He must of necessity hate white people. He would not be, and it would not be human if he did not, develop a hatred for his oppressors" (Himes 1966b: 56). Furthermore, the black writer had to deal with the reaction of the black middle class, a mixture of caution laced with antagonism. Himes portrayed African-Americans as soul-sick after centuries of oppression: writing as he did was "opening old wounds ... an agony ... to be reviled by ... negroes and whites alike" (Himes 1966b: 53).

Himes essential message was that a black writer cannot free himself of race consciousness because he cannot free himself from race. This constant pull and tug on the black consciousness, what W. E. B. Du Bois characterized as the Double Consciousness dilemma, drove Himes into serious depression and alcoholism. His life was a series of mishaps, broken relationships and no-end jobs. Himes had come to the conclusion that to be an observant recorder of the racial atmosphere in mid-century America could only lead to anti-social behavior and eventual self-destruction. His assessment was startling. "If this plumbing for the truth reveals within the negro personality homicidal mania, lust for white women, a pathetic sense of inferiority, paradoxical anti-Semitism, arrogance, Uncle Tomism, hate and fear and self-hate," he said, "this then is the effect of oppression on the human personality" (Himes 1966b: 57).

In 1951 Chester and Jean separated, and towards the end of his New York period he was involved in an affair with a white woman that became the principal inspiration for the novel *The Primitive*. The novel covers a period of seven days in which Jesse Robinson, an unsuccessful black writer, becomes the lover of the unstable Kris Cummings. Jesse and Kris are symbols of the destructive force of prejudice and racism. Kris sees in Jesse an exotic savage who is always capable of satisfying her physical appetites, while Jesse sees in Kris the ideal of feminine beauty and will sell his soul to make love to her. Both are caught and deluded by the stereotypical myths of black men and white women. Eventually, Jesse kills Kris in a drunken rage on a Sunday night, but he does not realize she is dead until Monday, when he is caught and arrested. Both lovers, it seems, are destroyed by racism. Himes has stated in relation to the novel: "the final answer of any black to a white woman with whom he lives in a white society is violence" (Himes 1972: 137).

One element of the book is common to almost all of Himes's work: his use of autobiographical incident as a means of exploring and relieving his personal anguish. Himes later said that everything in the book was true except that he did not kill the white woman. Writing this inter-racial love story acted as a catharsis for him and allowed him to continue his writing.

Himes was convinced that the African-American was a new species of human being because of the hybrid quality of his identity. The "negro problem" as he saw it was a manifestation of cultural and racial prejudices and misconceptions so complicated that it was inexplicable and always resulted in farcical tragedy – a tragedy shared by millions. In his writing he struggled with how difficult it was to earn respect in the United States as a free-born African American.

Himes returned to the theme of sexual power and control in inter-racial relationships in two other novels, *Pinktoes* (1961) and *A Case of Rape* (1963). In these novels social taboos prevent any positive relationship from developing. Both of these books attacked racial stereotyping and lambasted black generational infighting and color discrimination within the race.

Pinktoes parodies race relations with vicious glee. Mamie Mason is a Chicago black political activist and socialite determined to resolve the race issue single-handedly. As an egotistical social meddler she engineers elaborate mixed-race get-togethers, but the guests come not to solve the race problem but to enjoy inter-racial sex. This respectable group of people have deluded themselves into believing that they are improving black-white relationships when, in reality, all they are doing is playing out sexual stereotypes.

Himes declared that *A Case of Rape* was written in order to reveal the preconceptions and humiliations to which black Americans were subjected in Paris during the Algerian war. The main characters are exiles mordantly self-conscious about race and sex. The book serves as an expose of the judicial and social prejudices of a French society deeply split by its own buried and often denied racism.

Europe

Himes was an expatriate African-American in the last half of his life. He went to Paris at the same time as Richard Wright and James Baldwin, where he joined a long list of African-American writers and musicians seeking redemption, if not sanity, by living in Europe. However, he never became a member of any expatriate community, moving over the years from France to Sweden to Spain and traveling throughout much of Western Europe. Himes's major achievement in the second half of his life spent in Europe was the series of detective novels he wrote during his last two decades.

Detective fiction has proven to be a dynamic literary device for the implementation and testing of cultural worldviews. Its continuous popularity supports this contention, as does the frequency of experimentation with the form. The conventions of the genre were effectively challenged by African-American authors who transformed them for their own use, infusing the text with black tropes that led to the creation of an African-American detective tradition. Rather than focusing simply on the crime and capture of the suspect, "blues detectives," as I choose to call them, are interested in the social and political atmosphere, often to the exclusion of detection. This social and political atmosphere is suffused by racial prejudice. Recognizing his or her own blackness, as well as what blackness means to the characters in the text, the Blues Detective is a new creation in the detective literary landscape, representing a complex amalgam of African American cultural signs.

In 1956 Himes met Marcel Duhamel, the editor of *La Serie Noire*, a mystery/crime imprint published by Gallimard. The French publisher suggested Himes write a detective novel and Himes agreed to write one because he was broke. In the early 1930s Himes had published his crimes stories in *Esquire* and *Abbot's Monthly*, and he had subscribed to *Black Mask*, the foremost detective pulp of the era. Thus, when Duhamel suggested to Himes that he read Dashiell Hammett and Raymond Chandler, two classic American hard-boiled writers, Himes was already ahead of him.

In the nine novels of the Harlem series, Himes staked out radical territory in the annals of American crime fiction and became an important contributor to the African-American Blues Detective tradition. The novels form a bridge from Rudolph Fischer's *The Conjure Man Dies* (1932), once considered the first African-American authored black mystery novel, to the unbridled success of black crime writing, both male and female, that erupted in the late twentieth century with such names as Walter Mosley (see Gruesser, chapter 44 in this volume) and Barbara Neely. In detective fiction Himes found a vehicle that helped him elucidate the peculiar conditions of racism in America. His economic and political critique of American society is honed to a razor's edge in the novels he wrote featuring his two black detective characters, Coffin Ed and Gravedigger, double-conscious detectives who must use trickery and violence to survive. Drawing on the folk tradition of the black Badman, they use their guns on white and black citizens alike and their blackness to get into places that white officers fear to approach, like the inner sanctum of Sister Heavenly's dope den in *The Heat's On* (1966).

Himes's descriptions of Harlem, a city within a city, are laced with indictments of the white power structure. Desperation in Harlem is the engine of numerous scams and rip-offs, part of the paradox that is Harlem and that contributes to the complex behavior of its inhabitants. The catalog of religious charlatans and swindlers is long, including Sweet Prophet Brown in *The Big Gold Dream* (1960), who works his flock for money, to the Reverend Sam in *Blind Man with a Pistol*, who uses a harem of black nuns for material gain and sexual release, to Tomsson Black, who creates chaos on a grand scale in *Plan B*. Inherently critical of white power structures, Himes indicates that racism and one of its offspring, poverty, are directly responsible for the craziness of his Harlem world. His worldview suggests that there is little hope for improvement.

It is important, however, that we do not associate critique with negativity. Himes was proud of black people and black culture and proved himself a pioneering detective writer through his use of black detective tropes as well as his willingness to satirize black behavior. The important point is that Himes was aware of the shared values that help define African-American culture that he hoped, through satire, to promote and strengthen.

Interestingly, Himes's satiric vision came to rest on a rather drastic solution to America's racism. His new solution evolved out of his fascination with a characteristic of detective novels in general – their use of violence. Speaking about the detective form, Himes says, "It's just plain and simple violence in narrative form" (Williams 1973: 314). Himes's use of violence in the novels evolves from comic vision to serious confrontation. Often the two are mixed in a way that makes them hard to distinguish. In *Real Cool Killers*, a man whose arm is cut off with an axe yells at his assailant, "Wait a minute, you big mother raper, till Ah finds my arm! … It got my knife in his hand" (Himes 1966a: 8). Early in the detective series Coffin Ed and Grave Digger function as ordering devices in the novels, but as the series progresses, attitudes change. The detectives lose control and other forces outside and inside Harlem take over. Ultimately, Grave Digger and Coffin Ed are unable to solve crimes in a world spinning out of control. At the end of *Blind Man with a Pistol*, Himes's last complete novel, the two detectives take potshots at rats fleeing a burning tenement while a race riot engulfs the Harlem community.

Many incidents in the novels suggest that the violence in Himes's work moves from a random pattern of absurdist incidents towards a more pointed political message. In *Cotton Comes to Harlem*, a black attendant to the Reverend Deke O'Malley is gunned down by a white gang wearing black masks, and "human brains flew through the air like macabre birds" (Himes 1970a: 11). Himes's theory of detective narration based on violence also becomes more sophisticated in the later works. In the last novels and in *Plan B*, Himes's ultimate statement on racial conditions in America, the violence reaches new heights.

Interestingly, however, the violence in these stories differs from that of his earlier work in that it now reflects a coherent viewpoint. Forced into extremes of behavior by racist practices, American blacks now answer back in bursts of violent activity. In *Plan B* this culminates in armed black revolution.

In 1972 Himes said, "It is an absolute fact that if the blacks in America were to mount a revolution in force with organized violence to the saturation point, that the entire black problem would be solved" (Fuller 1972: 18). *Plan B* describes this black revolution in graphic detail. Many whites are killed and the result is repression on a grand scale by the American authorities, including the internment of black Americans in concentration camps, an outcome considered quite real at the time among many members of the black community. Himes's latent anger expressed itself in ever more vivid forms over the course of his career, from echoes of slave revolts through the Badman mystique to organized violent revolution.

In his final years, after the completion of his two-volume autobiography, Himes's energies were reduced by illness. Retiring to his house in southern Spain he lived out his last days in relative comfort with his second wife, Lesley Packard. He died and was buried in Spain in 1984.

39
David Goodis (1917–1967)

David Schmid

Despite a 30-year career, during which he published 18 novels, many of them classics of *noir* crime fiction (see Simpson, chapter 14 in this volume), the magnitude of David Goodis's achievement and the distinctiveness of his contribution to the genre have not been adequately appreciated. In contrast with Hammett's Sam Spade or Chandler's Philip Marlowe, who move purposefully in a corrupt world, the archetypal Goodis hero is more acted upon than active, a man trapped by both a haunted past and a sordid present. No other writer in the genre matches Goodis's empathetic obsession with the lives of losers, victims, drop-outs, and has-beens. Although the archetypal Goodis hero tries to cheat his fate, his attempt to live a decent life is doomed to failure, and Goodis lovingly examines the destruction of hopes and dreams that defines his hard-boiled universe.

Goodis's originality is not exclusively a product of his difference from the other major *noir* writers; indeed, he has much in common with Dashiell Hammett, Raymond Chandler, James M. Cain, and Cornell Woolrich. Like them, Goodis makes extensive use of urban settings; includes frequent descriptions of graphic violence; focuses on people entangled in crime and murder through bad luck, accident, or mistaken identity; and thematizes urban angst, alienation, and paranoia. Rather than exploring new ground, Goodis instead puts his narratives under pressure by exaggerating characteristic *noir* features. His urban settings are grim and squalid almost to the point of absurdity and episodes of violence are so frequent and graphic that they approach the parodic. His protagonists are so hounded and attacked by fate, so wounded by both physical and existential violence, that they almost cease to exist. Goodis walks a fine line between intensifying the recurrent obsessions of *noir* and deconstructing the genre altogether.

What enables Goodis to pull off this balancing act is the most distinctive feature of his work, namely the consistent yet evolving understanding of masculinity that runs throughout his fiction. Goodis's obsession with testing the limits and redefining the characteristics of masculinity both gives coherence to his work and comprises his most original contribution to the *noir* genre. Rather than using two-dimensional tough guys, Goodis rewrites *noir* conventions by peopling his novels with wounded and vulnerable male protagonists.

Many *noir* writers share Goodis's interest in masculinity, and a number of critics have discussed the relationship between *noir* narratives and masculinity. In particular, Frank Krutnik in his 1991 book, *In a Lonely Street: Film Noir, Genre, Masculinity*, uses Freud's account of how the Oedipus complex produces male subjects to argue for the instability of male authority. Krutnik emphasizes that "the phallic regime of masculine identity is by no means a secure option that can be taken for granted once it is set in place." Given its vulnerable status, Krutnik argues, masculinity "has to be consolidated and perpetually protected against various forms of deviance and disruption" (Krutnik 1991: 85).

Krutnik's work sheds much light on the challenges faced by Goodis's protagonists, and the ability of his novels to generate suspense. Contrary to Krutnik, however, I want to emphasize how unusual Goodis's examination of vulnerable masculinity is in the *noir* genre. Krutnik acknowledges that many *noir* narratives, especially the private-eye-dominated narratives of Hammett and Chandler, assert and consolidate masculine law in a relatively unproblematic manner by having the detective hero affirmed as "potent, invulnerable, undivided, and also uncontaminated by both the machinating *femme fatale* and the corrupted male figures" (Krutnik 1991: 125). At the same time, however, Krutnik argues that *noir* narratives *in general* articulate anxiety about the instability of masculine subject formation. I believe that what Krutnik describes as the "conventional affirmation of heroic masculinity" (1991: 88) is far more widespread in *noir* narratives than he acknowledges. *Noir* writers other than Hammett and Chandler – including Chester Himes, James M. Cain, William McGivern, and Gil Brewer – subscribe to the same view of a masculinity under siege from deviant others and in need of both protection and assertion. In this respect, David Goodis is especially significant because he is the exception that proves the rule about the depiction of *noir* masculinity.

In Goodis's work, the constitution and maintenance of dominant understandings of masculinity are deeply problematic. Whereas protagonists such as Sam Spade and Philip Marlowe are able to maintain the appearance of masculine competence and toughness (albeit at the cost of denying emotional connections with others), Goodis's protagonists spectacularly fail to maintain a tough masculine facade because they are open, vulnerable, and desperate to break out of their isolation and establish a physical and/or emotional connection with another person.

This emphasis on vulnerability rather than toughness, on openness rather than isolation, is enough in itself to demonstrate how Goodis intensifies anxieties about masculinity. But Goodis's originality extends further than this. According to conventional patriarchal standards, Goodis's protagonists are "failed" men, unable to defend themselves from physical or emotional pain; but Goodis never criticizes them. Although his heroes are frequently punished for attempting to connect with others, the reader is meant to admire them for the attempt, not condemn them for their lack of success. Rather than taking refuge behind an emotionally isolated facade of tough-guy masculinity, Goodis's heroes revise the *noir* genre by personifying a different understanding of masculinity: wounded but open, vulnerable but connected.

The potentially risky desire for connection is an important theme in Goodis's work from the beginning of his career as a *noir* writer. His first two *noir* novels, *Dark Passage* (1946) and *Nightfall* (1947), both feature protagonists whose desire to connect with others is dangerous, possibly even fatal. The hero of *Dark Passage*, Vincent Parry, begins the novel in prison, having been wrongly convicted of the murder of his wife. After he escapes from prison, the rest of the novel is divided between his efforts to find a safe place to stay and his attempts to discover his wife's real murderer and thus clear his name. The most immediately noticeable characteristic of the novel is its paranoia. Given Parry's situation, such paranoia is understandable, but Goodis sees paranoia as a more generally appropriate reaction to an unstable and dangerous world. Goodis believes Parry's fear of constant betrayal to be a sensible attitude, but this view is complicated by the fact that Parry also desperately wants and needs to trust and love someone. *Dark Passage* thus presents an archetypal Goodis hero who is torn between the desire for self-preservation and the desire for human contact. As is typical in his work, by the conclusion of the novel neither of these desires is unambiguously fulfilled – the open-ended conclusion being another Goodis trademark. Goodis is less interested in the eventual fate of his characters than he is in analyzing their emotional isolation and their efforts to overcome that isolation.

Like Parry, Donald Vanning begins *Nightfall* in a state of enforced isolation. The book opens with Vanning hiding in New York City and living under an assumed identity. While on his way to a new job in Chicago, he has the bad luck of running into a gang of bank robbers who force Vanning to help them. After he escapes with the gang's money, killing a member of the gang in self-defense in the process, he is hunted by both the police and the gang, necessitating anonymity and subterfuge.

Vanning is an even more representative Goodis protagonist than Parry, because his decision to break out of his isolation is a product of choice rather than necessity. Although, like Parry, Vanning lives in fear that he will be recognized and that his true identity will be revealed, Goodis makes it clear that he has hidden himself successfully; if he had been willing to remain isolated, there is every reason to believe that he would have remained undiscovered. But isolation is precisely what Vanning cannot endure. Vanning gives in to his need for human contact when he strikes up a conversation in a bar with a woman named Martha, even though he knows it is a foolish thing to do. Indeed, Vanning's decision turns out to be incredibly unfortunate, because Martha is connected with the gang, and through his association with her, Vanning falls into their hands.

At first glance, it seems that both Vincent Parry and Donald Vanning are punished for transgressing the bounds of normative masculinity by admitting to vulnerability and the need to connect with another person. Ultimately, however, both *Dark Passage* and *Nightfall* end on an upbeat note that validates their protagonists' decisions to reach out to others. While these happy (or, at least, not unambiguously sad) endings may seem to contradict what I have said about the ("unmasculine") desire for contact always leading to punishment, two points need to be made about the conclusions to *Dark Passage* and *Nightfall*. First, these upbeat conclusions, when viewed in the context of Goodis's entire *oeuvre*, are highly unusual. Second, these endings illustrate the importance of highlighting the differences among three distinct stages of Goodis's literary career.

Goodis started his career like so many other *noir* writers, with an apprenticeship in pulp magazines, followed by a stint in Hollywood as a screenwriter. After experiencing initial success, however, Goodis's association with the film industry came to a rather abrupt end and in 1950 he returned to his hometown of Philadelphia, where he moved back in with his parents. The return to Philadelphia marked the beginning of the third and final part of Goodis's career. Between 1950 and his death in 1967 at the age of 49, Goodis published 13 paperback original novels, most of them written for an advance of about $1,500. Not only do these "Philadelphia novels" make up the bulk of Goodis's fiction, they also represent his most distinctive contribution to the genre. If the work Goodis produced during his time in Hollywood, when he enjoyed success and prestige, was characterized by upbeat endings, everything changed in the Philadelphia novels. Lee Server has argued that some writers saw paperback originals as a dependable living or as a stepping stone to bigger and better things, whereas for others, paperbacks were "the last or near-last stop on a downward spiral from previous literary successes or ambitions" (1994: 35). One could not find a more succinct description of the final stage of Goodis's career, and the intricacies of Goodis's downward spiral find eloquent expression in the male protagonists of his paperback novels. Goodis's dramas of beset-manhood take on a new intensity to match the destruction of his own hopes and dreams, leading to an exploration of wounded masculinity unparalleled in popular literature.

The Philadelphia stage of Goodis's career got off to a spectacular start with the publication of *Cassidy's Girl* (1951), easily the most commercially successful of Goodis's novels, reportedly selling over one million copies, and another good example of the role played by the tension between isolation and contact in his understanding of masculinity. Like so many of Goodis's heroes, Cassidy is on the run from his past. He is a former airline pilot whose life fell apart when the plane he was piloting crashed through no fault of his own, killing most of the passengers. Driving a bus for a living gives him some feeling of control in his life, but his security is thoroughly undermined by his sadistic and seductive wife Mildred, who is a fantasy figure for Cassidy. Mildred knows that Cassidy is obsessed with her voluptuous body, and she uses her physical charms to keep reasserting her control over him. In trying to break away, Cassidy chooses someone who is the complete opposite of Mildred. Where Mildred is dominating, the young alcoholic Doris is passive; and where Mildred is almost impossibly voluptuous, Doris is skinny and anemic. The opposition between the sexually aggressive woman and the shrinking waif appears again and again in Goodis's fiction. Although the hero is attracted to the waif, he normally ends up with the sexual aggressor, and indeed, Cassidy eventually returns to Mildred.

There is more at stake here, however, than Cassidy's choice of a particular type of woman. Goodis uses his character to dramatize one of his most fundamental beliefs, namely, that people who want more out of life and who believe that they can assert some control over the direction of it are usually doomed to fail. For Goodis, true "happiness" lies in accepting the hand that fate has dealt. Although Cassidy believes that he and Doris can build a new life together, when Cassidy's bus crashes, again through no fault of his own, he realizes that Doris needs whiskey more than she needs him. Cassidy then decides to follow his friend Shealy's advice to "Just slide down and enjoy the trip" (1967: 102). Yet, no matter how sensible the advice to surrender to fate appears, Goodis's heroes rarely follow it willingly. They instead put themselves through mental and physical torture in order to exorcise the past rather than simply acquiesce. In this sense, Goodis's protagonists are idealists who are faced with a choice between involvement and noninvolvement. Even though it is easier and safer to stay uninvolved, they consistently choose to do the right thing, to get involved, in spite of the costs to themselves.

Two novels where Goodis presents the tension between involvement and withdrawal in its clearest and most sustained form are *Street of No Return* (1954) and *Down There* (1956). Whitey, the protagonist of *Street of No Return*, begins the novel in a state of fatalistic disengagement from life, as the opening words of the novel indicate:

> There were three of them sitting on the pavement with their backs against the wall of the flophouse. It was a biting cold night in November and they sat there close together trying to get warm. The wet wind from the river came knifing through the street to cut their faces and get inside their bones, but they didn't seem to mind. They were discussing a problem that had nothing to do with the weather. In their minds it was a serious problem, and as they talked their eyes were solemn and tactical. They were trying to find a method of obtaining some alcohol. (Goodis 1991: 3)

Before taking refuge in the bottle, Whitey was a successful singer by the name of Eugene Lindell, but then he became involved with a girl named Celia, who was dating the leader of a criminal gang, Sharkey. When Whitey refused to stop seeing Celia, Sharkey had him beaten nearly to death by fellow gang members Chop and Bertha, thus ruining his singing career and precipitating his decline into alcoholism.

Like Cassidy, Whitey has learned to enjoy his decline, but this all changes one night when he sees Chop walking down the other side of the street. Whitey is now faced with a choice: should he stay where he is, rendered invisible by the bottle, and safe in the security of his fellow lushes, or should he follow Chop on the offchance that he will see Celia again and thus risk both further beatings and reopening the psychic wounds of the past? As wrenching as this revisiting of the past will inevitably be, Whitey cannot resist its pull. By the end of the novel, the bruised and battered Whitey has seen Celia again but that is all; he does not even get to speak with her. As if to emphasize the fruitlessness of his attempt to re-engage himself with life, at the end of the novel Whitey is in the same place he began, sitting in a doorway with his friends, drinking:

> The three of them walked across the street. They sat down on the pavement with their back against the wall of the flophouse. The pavement was terribly cold and the wet wind from the river came blasting into their faces. But it didn't bother them. They sat passing the bottle around, and there was nothing that could bother them, nothing at all (Goodis 1991: 168).

By the standards of conventional *noir* narratives, Whitey is a conspicuously "failed" man. Not only did he fail to speak to Celia, he was regularly beaten for his troubles, failing even to defend himself properly. Characteristically, though, Goodis does not see Whitey as a failure. Although he feels that Whitey is none the wiser for his decision to follow Chop, Goodis wants his reader to admire Whitey's indomitability, no matter how foolish it seems.

In his last major novel, *Down There*, filmed in 1962 by François Truffaut as *Shoot the Piano Player*, Goodis elaborates the connection between masculinity and emotional connection in even greater detail. In this novel, however, Goodis adds an explicit consideration of the role of violence in defining masculinity. Consistent with his emphasis on vulnerability as a defining element of masculinity (almost to the point of masochism), *Down There* contains a moving disavowal of the link between masculinity and violence and of the use of violence as a form of conflict resolution.

There are many similarities between *Street of No Return* and *Down There*. Like Whitey, Eddie, the piano-playing protagonist of *Down There*, begins the novel defeated and cut off from life. Eddie, whose real name is Edward Webster Lynn, is a former concert pianist who walked away from his career after his wife committed suicide. Racked with guilt over his wife's death and scared by the anger he feels for his manager, the man he holds responsible for her death, Eddie has tried to escape from his past and take refuge in an anonymous present. However, just as Whitey was confronted with a figure from his past, Eddie is confronted by his brother Turley, who is in trouble and needs Eddie's help.

Despite his premonition about the consequences of helping Turley, Eddie does of course become involved, and his decision to break out of his emotional isolation unleashes a tragic chain of circumstances, including a painful revisiting of his past, the death of a woman he was beginning to love and his murder of another man in self-defense. Eddie's complicated status as the agent rather than the victim of violence indicates that his situation is both more dangerous and more complicated than Whitey's. *Down There* places great stress on the connection between vulnerability and masculinity, between the willingness to be hurt and what it means to be a man, through presenting and critiquing another model of masculinity. After his wife's death, Eddie goes into a rapid downward spiral, which culminates one night when three men attack him. At this moment, a "wild man" erupts in Eddie and he beats his three attackers nearly to death:

> Then something happened. They weren't sure what it was, but it seemed like propeller blades churning the air and coming at them. The one with the lead pipe had made a rapid departure, and they wondered why he wasn't there to help them. They really needed help. One of them went down with four teeth flying out of his mouth. The other was sobbing, "gimme a break, aw, please – gimme a break," and the wild man grinned and whispered, "Fight back – fight back – don't spoil the fun." (1990: 82)

If Goodis adopted the traditional definition of "tough" *noir* masculinity, Eddie would embrace his capacity for violence, and indulge it by killing his manager, the man he blames for his wife's death. Instead, Eddie is deeply disturbed by his violent outbursts. Eddie's ambivalence about his capacity for violence means that he does everything possible to avoid a confrontation with Plyne, the bouncer at the bar where Eddie plays the piano, and Eddie is horrified when he kills him. Eddie's immediate reaction to Plyne's death is to distance himself from it: "Eddie sat there in the snow and looked at the dead man. He said to himself, Who did that?" (1990: 113). Eddie's distancing is dictated not only by his desire to avoid guilt or punishment, but also by his need to disavow his capacity for violence. Such a disavowal speaks volumes about the distance between Goodis's fiction and conventional representations of masculinity in *noir* fiction.

By this point in his career, Goodis had published 15 novels, 10 of them in the 6 years he had been living in Philadelphia. After 1956, the frenetic pace of Goodis's literary production slowed dramatically: he published just two more books, *Fire in the Flesh* (1957) and *Night Squad* (1961) before his death in 1967. A single posthumous novel, *Somebody's Done For* (1967), followed, but it does nothing to change the impression that Goodis's talents were at a low ebb in his final years, with banal gunfights and unambiguously positive endings tending to replace the psychological analysis and open-ended conclusions that characterize his best novels. But the other distinguishing feature of Goodis's most accomplished work, as I have argued in this chapter, is his treatment of masculinity (see also Pepper, chapter 10 and Gavin, chapter 20 in this volume). Although much *noir* crime fiction written after World War II expresses postwar anxieties about both male and female gender roles, the genre is usually not fatally destabilized by such anxieties because, at the center of these narratives, is a stabilizing force, a vision of masculinity encapsulated in Chandler's famous words from "The Simple Art of Murder":

> But down these mean streets a man must go who is not himself mean, who is neither tarnished nor afraid. The detective in this kind of story must be such a man. He is the hero; he is everything. He must be a complete man and a common man and yet an unusual man. He must be, to use a rather weathered phrase, a man of honor, by instinct,

by inevitability, without thought of it, and certainly without saying it. He must be the best man in his world and a good enough man for any world (Chandler 1995a: 991–2).

The conventional *noir* man, no matter how beset by anxieties about his identity, is still able to persuade himself that he is a hero. He is competent, strong, willing (perhaps even happy) to use violence and, above all, he retains a certain distance from the environment he inhabits that guarantees his inviolability.

David Goodis's most important contribution to the *noir* genre consists in his very different understanding of *noir* masculinity, but despite these differences, Goodis's work has one striking similarity to the dominant definition of what it means to be a man: just as Chandler *et al.* see their protagonists as heroes, so Goodis heroizes his wounded, vulnerable protagonists. Rather than dismissing them as "unmanly" failures, Goodis celebrates their indomitability, their willingness to prioritize vulnerability over toughness, openness over isolation. In doing so, Goodis definitively rewrites the *noir* tradition of masculinity and makes a decisive and lasting contribution to the genre.

In spite of its undoubted importance Goodis always had a low opinion of his own work. In a 1966 letter to William Sherman, Goodis said of his first novel, "It was nothing, and the same applies to most of the sixteen others since then" (Sherman 1968/9: 41). The underwhelming response to Goodis's death seemed to confirm the accuracy of Goodis's words. After his death, Goodis and his books fell into obscurity for 20 years, with none of his novels being reprinted until Black Lizard republished novels such as *Black Friday* and *Nightfall*, starting in 1987. Since then, a new generation of readers actively interested in resurrecting the pulp fiction of the 1940s and 1950s has become familiar with Goodis's work. As a result, his reputation has steadily improved, and he is currently regarded as among the most important and inventive American hard-boiled crime fiction writers.

40

P. D. James (1920–)

Louise Harrington

Phyllis Dorothy James is one of Britain's most successful and highly regarded novelists, yet oddly there is not a great deal of critical material on her work available. Despite the fact that almost all her novels are concerned with the detection of a crime, she has, in many ways, transcended the crime fiction genre. Born in Oxford in 1920, James did not publish her first novel, *Cover her Face*, until 1962, and her early writing career was combined with a successful career in the Civil Service, initially as an administrator in the National Health Service until 1968 and then in the Home Office where she worked for both the Police Department and the Criminal Policy Department. This administrative experience has provided a background for many of her novels. A full-time novelist since retiring from the Civil Service in 1979, she has, as of 2008, published 16 crime novels: *Cover her Face*, *A Mind to Murder* (1963), *Unnatural Causes* (1967), *Shroud for a Nightingale* (1971), *An Unsuitable Job for a Woman* (1972), *The Black Tower* (1975), *Death of an Expert Witness* (1977), *Innocent Blood* (1980). *The Skull beneath the Skin* (1982), *A Taste for Death* (1986), *Devices and Desires* (1989), *Original Sin* (1994), *A Certain Justice* (1997), *Death in Holy Orders* (2001), *The Murder Room* (2003), *The Lighthouse* (2005) and *The Private Patient* (2008). She has also written the dystopian novel *The Children of Men* (1992), and an autobiography, in diary form, entitled *Time to Be in Earnest* (1999).

As a writer, James is particularly influenced by Jane Austen, Dorothy L. Sayers (see Miskimmin, chapter 35 in this volume), Graham Greene and Evelyn Waugh; she has often been called the natural successor to Sayers. James remembers that when she decided to try writing professionally, "[i]t didn't occur to me either to begin with anything other than a detective story. They had formed my own recreational reading in adolescence and I was influenced in particular by the women writers: Dorothy L. Sayers, Margery Allingham, Ngaio Marsh and Josephine Tey" (James 1999: 12). She also believes that while the "construction of a detective story may be formulaic; the writing need not be" (James 1999: 12). James's detective fiction (or "crime novels," the term she prefers) famously combines traditional golden age characteristics (see Rowland, chapter 8 in this volume), such as the enclosed community with a limited number of suspects, with the psychological and social realism associated with mainstream fiction. Her debut novel, *Cover her Face*, which introduced James's poet-policeman Adam Dalgliesh, is very much in the tradition of British detective fiction, and can be viewed as a deliberate attempt to engage with the "country house" conventions of golden age writers like Christie (see Makinen, chapter 33 in this volume) or Allingham (Rowland 2001: 5). Like them, James makes use of these crime conventions with the majority of her plots taking place within isolated and often claustrophobic communities: a country house in *Cover her Face*, a nursing school in *Shroud for a Nightingale*, a forensic laboratory in *Death of an Expert Witness*, a psychiatric clinic in *A Mind to Murder*, an isolated religious community in *Death in Holy Orders* and a quasi-monastic one in *The Black Tower*. Although a number of James's later novels, such as *Innocent Blood*, *A Taste for Death* and *Devices and Desires* move away from the closed circle trope into the terrain of the realist novel, taking place in a wider social, moral and geographical universe, in her more recent novels James appears increasingly to have returned to golden age conventions: the murders take place in a small, private museum in *The Murder Room* and on a privately owned island in *The Lighthouse*.

But James's work fundamentally differs from golden age crime fiction like Agatha Christie's in one salient respect. In Christie's world, the detective restores the troubled traditional middle-class order to its previous serenity/complacency: it establishes that the disruption is not, superficially at least, in the social order itself, but in the individualized motives of certain characters. This is most heavily emphasized in Christie's Miss Marple series, where the eponymous heroine repeatedly solves crimes by comparing characters to people, mostly untrustworthy, she has known in the past; the murderers are "types," almost inevitably born bad, a fact that exonerates society from any blame or responsibility. In James's world, the murder contaminates and permanently alters all aspects of the community. While echoing the style and conventions of classic British detective fiction, these closed, often suffocating, communities also serve to highlight the social and existential isolation of many of James's characters, most notably Dalgliesh himself. In *A Taste for Death*, Dalgliesh recognizes that he has "a splinter of ice in the heart" (James 1986: 260), a line that originated with Graham Greene, a writer James admires and resembles. James herself notes that even as a child, a part of her would observe both pain and happiness "with a disinterested ironic eye" (James 1999: 67).

A conservative Anglican, James's work conveys a great sense of tragedy and this parallels one of her major themes: the moral emptiness of modern secular life. This awareness of the cultural absence of God informs all James's work, and is underlined by the echoes of the Holocaust central to both *Shroud for a Nightingale* and *Original Sin*. *Shroud for a Nightingale*, while superficially maintaining the golden age conventions with its emphasis on place and enclosed communities, unveils the terrible motive for the murders to be an attempt to conceal Matron Taylor's former identity as a young German nurse, Irmgard Grobel, who inadvertently assisted in the killing of mentally ill patients under the Nazi regime. This revelation, as well as providing the motive, is also the culmination of one of James's central questions in this novel: what makes a good nurse? Is it merely obedience to higher authority (which is the defense that exonerates Taylor/Grobel) or is it imagination and a sense of responsibility? The characters of the various nursing students are examined by James and Dalgliesh, not just as likely murderers but also as good nurses: while Sister Brumfett insists that if you teach the students obedience and loyalty, "you've got a good nurse," Sister Gearing observes that, rightly in her eyes, "these kids ask whether the orders are reasonable before they start obeying" (James 1971: 149). James uses these golden age conventions to examine both professional and social ethics and cultural stereotypes, such as the naturalness of feminine nurture. The killer is after all a nurse, dedicated to her profession and her patients, and contemporary witnesses testify to Grobel's kindness, gentleness, and skill as a nurse. The author concludes, however, that obedience to the rules is not enough: it cannot replace moral integrity and ethical awareness.

James can be viewed as a condition of England author, a successor not only to Christie and Sayers, but also to Gaskell and Dickens: all of her work is concerned with the state of modern Britain, the decline of traditional Englishness, and an elegiac recognition of the willful absence of faith. In her autobiography, she mourns the decline and fragmentation of the Church of England, which she sees as

> the visible symbol of the country's moral and religious aspirations, a country which, despite great differences of class, wealth and privilege, was unified by generally accepted values and by a common tradition, history and culture (James 1999: 88).

James is an avid supporter of the Book of Common Prayer and the Anglican liturgy. Religion and the absence of faith in modern Britain play a central role in her work. Dalgliesh is the son of a Church of England minister, but believes only in the absence of God. Unable to have faith in a higher power, Dalgliesh seeks comfort in the rigid strictures and formal rules both of the criminal justice system and of his poetry, only for them to fail him at various stages. In *A Certain Justice*, he is unable to apprehend the killer of Venetia Aldridge, not through lack of knowledge but through lack of evidence, while in *A Taste for Death* there are repeated references to his lack of poetic output.

The church and its rituals make many appearances in James's novels: *Death in Holy Orders* takes place in an Anglican seminary threatened with closure, the religious conversion of murder victim Sir Paul Berowne is central to *A Taste for Death*. In the latter, although the main storyline concerns the hunt for the murderer of Berowne and Harry Mack, an ultimately unfinished subplot revolves around Berowne's sudden "experience of God," and the presence of stigmata on Berowne's wrists. These signs, which confuse and even repel Dalgliesh, are ultimately never explained, as neither Dalgliesh, nor perhaps the realist fiction form, can deal with something that is so opposed to what is "documented, demonstratable, real" (James 1986: 55). All of her books reveal James's fascination with the structured rituals of work (the law, medicine, the police force) that supposedly are contemporary substitutes for God, but which ultimately fail. In *The Black Tower*, the community that Dalgliesh investigates is quasi-religious, a home for disabled men and women run in monastic style by the spiritual and charismatic Wilfred Anstey. But not only is the Grange revealed to be the convenient cover for a drug-smuggling operation, Anstey's miraculous recovery from a degenerative disease is due to a medical misdiagnosis. Not only is there no God, but medicine has proved to be fallible as well.

Feminism is also a conflicted subject in James's work. This is apparent in the portrayal of her two most important female characters, Cordelia Gray and Kate Miskin. Cordelia Gray is the protagonist in two of James's non-Dalgliesh novels, *An Unsuitable Job for a Woman* and *The Skull beneath the Skin*. The former makes an early contribution to a modern subgenre of crime fiction, the feminist detective novel, and can be seen as part of the tradition that includes professional female investigators such as Sue Grafton's Kinsey Millhone and Sara Paretsky's V. I. Warshawski. In the first Gray novel, Cordelia, left to run the Pryde detective agency after the suicide of her employer and mentor, is both independent and self-reliant. But *The Skull beneath the Skin* fails to advance the narrative of the ambitious and empowered female detective; instead, James presents a Cordelia who makes silly mistakes, fails to solve the central mystery, and has to be rescued from almost certain death by a passing sailor. Depicted as a much weaker feminist protagonist in this text than in its predecessor, Cordelia is ultimately presented as better, and more importantly, happier, at finding lost cats than solving murders. Furthermore, even in the earlier text, as Sally Munt observes, Cordelia's story is framed by the appearance of Dalgliesh, which serves as a validation of the judicial and patriarchal establishment (1994: 53). Since *A Taste for Death*, it appears that James is more comfortable with a female professional who works within the strictures of the police service and under the direct jurisdiction of Dalgliesh: Detective Inspector Kate Miskin, despite her intelligence, independence, and ability, looks to Dalgliesh as her masculine authority/father figure, and in both *The Lighthouse* and *The Private Patient*, James implies that Miskin nurses an unrequited love for Dalgliesh.

It is not the case that James is simply anti-feminist or anti-working women. Many of her Dalgliesh books contain successful and sympathetic professional women such as Mary Taylor, Kate Miskin (who appears in all the Dalgliesh novels from *A Taste of Death* onwards), and Dr Emma Lavenham, a lecturer in English literature at Cambridge and, as of *The Private Patient*, Dalgliesh's second wife. But the latter two are defined mostly in terms of their relationship to Dalgliesh. In *Death in Holy Orders*, Emma is a major character; she discovers one of the bodies, and much attention is given to portraying her background, her intellectual ability and her beauty, the latter being "a puzzle, sometimes almost a torment" (James 2001: 92). In the last three books, she is depicted solely as Dalgliesh's love interest, albeit a sympathetic and well-drawn one. In these latter narratives, she is associated with the feminine and the irrational: in *The Private Patient* for example, she drives through the night to visit

Dalgliesh who is in the middle of a murder case in order to plead with him to assist in apprehending the attacker of one of her friends. Often, for James, professional women are portrayed as romantically unfulfilled, unsympathetic or downright villainous: in *A Certain Justice*, defense barrister Venetia Aldridge, in spite of her intellectual brilliance and oratorical skill, is ultimately condemned as all three, while Clarissa Lisle in *The Skull beneath the Skin* is unfeeling and manipulative, qualities that lead to her murder.

Emma, meanwhile, is undoubtedly clever and gifted, but it is worth noticing how much James focuses, in *Death in Holy Orders*, on her physical beauty. Beauty, especially in the female, is of great importance to James. In *Unnatural Causes*, Dalgliesh admits how much he values beauty in women in his reaction to crippled Sylvia Kedge: "He had discovered that he did not like her, and was the more ashamed of the emotion because he knew that its roots were unreasonable and ignoble. He found her physically repellent" (James 1967: 9–10). At first this fixation can appear superficial and slightly irritating in its apparent insistence on equating a woman's worth with physical attractiveness. But it is more that female beauty, for James, along with physical attractiveness in men, restores some kind of sensual pleasure in the modern, godless world. She also, cleverly, recognizes how physical attractiveness has replaced the worship of God. While the beauty of women like Emma, *Cover her Face*'s Deborah Maxie, Mary Taylor or elegant, murdered Jo Fallon brings pleasure to Dalgliesh, a man who values the finest quality, whether it be in wine, interior decoration or women, it rarely offers the women any comfort.

Women's relationship to motherhood is also a major concern in James's writing. James's belief is that easier divorce inflicts suffering upon children (Rowland 2001: 197), and throughout her career as a novelist she paints vivid portrayals of lonely and inadequately mothered children, most notably Octavia in *A Certain Justice* and Philippa Palfrey in *Innocent Blood*. In her autobiography, James writes of her disapproval of easy divorce, of her feeling that the lack of a father is largely responsible for the breakdown of the family in modern British society. Strangely the traditional nuclear family, as well as single motherhood, is often, in James's texts, shown to be lacking. In *The Murder Room*, Tally Clutton is aware that when visiting her married daughter, she was "received with a scrupulous politeness and a strict adherence to accepted social norms which didn't hide the absence of real warmth or genuine affection" (James 2003: 48). Similarly, Emma is painfully aware of her elderly academic father's overwhelming love for her dead mother and sister, a love that leaves little space for his living child. Kate Miskin, meanwhile, is an illegitimate orphan, grudgingly raised by her maternal grandmother in miserable social surroundings. Incestuous and near-incestuous families are another key trope in James's work: Domenica and Howarth in *Expert*, Alex and Alice Marr in *Devices and Desires*, Dominic Swain and Barbara in *Taste* are all disconcertingly close, while Eric and Karen Surtees in *Holy Orders* are openly in an incestuous relationship, and Philippa Palfrey admits to losing her virginity to her adoptive father in *Innocent Blood*. This preoccupation of James's, while seemingly melodramatic and distasteful on initial reading, is in actuality shorthand for what

James perceives as the fragility of the family in modern, secular Britain. The dissolution of sexual boundaries mirrors the erosion of social class boundaries and social perceptions of right and wrong.

Pregnancy and motherhood are similarly almost always fraught in James's fiction, with female characters regularly giving birth outside matrimony or coping with the effects of illegitimate birth: Kate, Sally Jupp in *Cover her Face*, Raphael and Clara Arbuthnot in *Death in Holy Orders*. James has been criticized for her conservative rendering of modern maternity: Susan Rowland points out that "[t]he impression gained by a first reading of *A Certain Justice* is that James's tragic sense of the professions failing to assuage the social fragmentation of secular modernity is finely honed here to criticise working mothers" (Rowland 2001: 176). *Innocent Blood* is perhaps one of James's most interesting explorations of motherhood. The central character, Philippa, was adopted as a young child, and the text starts with her decision to trace her biological parents, only to discover that she is Rose Ducton, whose natural mother is in prison for the murder of the child that her husband had raped. The novel deals with Philippa's simultaneous horror at her mother's crime and her atavistic need for her birth mother, who is portrayed clearly but sympathetically by James. Mary Ducton has committed a terrible crime and been party to what is in Western society's eyes an even more monstrous one, but she is neither vilified nor victimized. Bravely, in a society that refused to countenance Myra Hindley, a notorious sexual abuser and serial killer of children in the early 1960s, as anything other than a monster, James portrays Mary not as evil, but as a woman unable to cope with children. Philippa/Rose slowly comes to realize that she was placed for adoption *prior* to the murder, not as a result of it, and not because of fears of what her father's pedophiliac desires would mean for a female child, but because of her mother's physical abuse.

Indeed, James's work is overtly pessimistic about all human relationships, not just those between parent and child. Dalgliesh is a widower; his wife and son died in childbirth, and we never learn their names. Until *Death in Holy Orders*, which introduces his second wife Emma, he is resolutely unattached and solitary. James regularly places unmarried or widowed women at the center of her novels, women such as Tally Clutton, Miss Blackett in *Original Sin* and Emily Wharton in *A Taste for Death* who are snubbed, patronized and often bullied. There is no room for the gentle spinsters of the golden age in James's glittering and heartless, godless modern world.

Throughout James's novels, place and setting are vitally important, creating atmosphere, providing clues and illustrating character. James herself notes that "for me, setting, character, narrative are always interdependent" (James 1999: 4). *The Black Tower*, for example, began with the author's visit to the Dorset coast, and a visit to an Oxford church inspired *A Taste for Death*, while a brief glimpse of Sizewell nuclear power station dominating the Suffolk coastline inspired *Devices and Desires*. Gothic settings are a particular favorite of James, from the Victorian mansion in *Shroud for a Nightingale* and the island castle in *The Skull beneath the Skin*, to the London house of the Berownes in *A Taste for Death* and Innocent House in *Original Sin*. Here, the familiar and the ordinary are made strange and terrible, emphasizing the dislocation of modern life:

> On the second floor rose three very high, curved windows ... between the windows, mounted on incongruous corbels which looked more Gothic than neo-classical, were stone caryatids, whose flowing lines, reinforced by the typically Soanian pilasters at the corners of the house, drew the eye upwards ... There was a moment of extraordinary silence in which even the muted roar of the traffic in the avenue was stilled and in which it seemed to him that two images, the shining façade of the house and that dusty blood-boltered room in Paddington, were held – suspended out of time, then fused so that the stones were blood spattered, the caryatids dripped red. (James 1986: 102–3)

The town house of the Berowne family is obviously a relic from a vanished world, a world of aristocracy, hierarchy and established religious faith. The splendid house is now a museum piece: Dalgliesh muses on the "melancholy unbreathed atmosphere of a seldom-visited country house drawing-room" and expects to see "a white looped cord marking off the area where tourists' feet were forbidden to tread" (James 1986: 116).

James's strong sense of place, and her juxtaposition of the mundane with the horror and alienation of murder is one of her greatest strengths as a writer and is demonstrated in the opening sentences of *Shroud for a Nightingale*: "On the morning of the first murder Miss Muriel Beale, Inspector of Nurse Training Schools to the General Nursing Council, stirred into wakefulness soon after six o'clock and into a sluggish early morning awareness that it was Monday, 12th January, and the day of the John Carpendar Hospital inspection" (James 1971: 1). That first murder, which the reader knows with increasing trepidation will come, but not how and to whom (the victim is, counter-intuitively, herself a nurse), is thus described:

> [T]here was something pathetic and disturbing about that rigid white-faced figure on the bed, eyes tight closed, bibbed like a baby, the thin tube dragging, and wriggling like a worm from the corner of her mouth ... There was a squeal, high-pitched, horribly inhuman, and Nurse Pearce precipitated herself from the bed as if propelled by an irresistible force. One second she was lying, immobile, propped against her mound of pillows, the next she was out of bed, teetering forward on arched feet in a parody of a ballet dancer, and clutching ineffectually at the air as if in frantic search of the tubing. And all the time she screamed, perpetually screamed, like a stuck whistle. (James 1971: 17, 19)

James's precise, clear and almost pitiless description, ornamented with incongruous artistic and mechanical tropes, gives the reader an uncomfortable sense of both immediacy and estrangement. Nurse Pearce, the first murder victim, is transmogrified from a nervous, flesh and blood girl, into an inhuman, parodic figure. This extract demonstrates one of the central theses of James's fiction: how quickly humanity is stripped away from us. Civilization is only ever a thin veneer.

As a writer, James scrupulously abides by the distinct rules of the detective fiction genre. The plot frequently unfolds among a limited number of possible suspects. Like Christie, she provides readers with the clues they need to deduce the killer – Dalgliesh and his team never know more than the readers, and often less. And, like her golden age predecessors, James is most comfortable in middle-class surroundings, with middle-class characters and preoccupations. She finds the detective fiction form comforting because of its strictness: "[t]he catharsis of carefully controlled terror, the bringing of order out of disorder, the reassurance that we live in a comprehensive and moral universe, and that, although we may not achieve justice, we can at least achieve an explanation and a solution" (James 1999: 13). But it is that final inability to administer full moral and social justice that sticks in the craw: while we, and she, can take comfort in knowing the finite rules of detective fiction, fundamentally in her novels, the dead can never find justice nor the living experience catharsis in a world where God is absent. Human justice as administered by the place and the law can never make true reparation. James's bleak vision of our modern world can best be summarized in Matron Taylor's words in *Shroud for a Nightingale*: "we are all alone, all of us from the moment of birth until we die. Our past is our present and our future" (James 1971: 81).

41
Patricia Highsmith (1921–1995)

Bran Nicol

Patricia Highsmith was an American writer, born in 1921 in Fort Worth, Texas. In 1963 she left the United States for Europe and never returned, living in France, Italy, and Switzerland, where she died, in Locarno, in 1995. Highsmith was the author of 22 novels and numerous short stories, and her books were commercially successful throughout her life. Only recently, however, has her work begun to garner critical acclaim, with some regarding her as belonging to a macabre tradition in American writing stretching back to Poe, and others as the literary equivalent of film directors like Alfred Hitchcock (see Haeffner, chapter 45 in this volume) or even David Lynch.

Highsmith is considered one of the finest exponents of suspense writing and plotting, an activity central to the various modes of crime fiction, and she is especially adept at portraying the disturbing criminal impulses which can erupt in ordinary life – or perhaps even provide its foundation. The novelist Graham Greene, a great admirer of Highsmith, singled out her ability to defamiliarize the everyday, explaining that her world "is not the world as we once believed we knew it, but it is frighteningly more real to us than the house next door" (Greene 2000: ix). More precisely, Highsmith's importance in crime fiction comes from the part she played in the postwar development of what is known as "the *noir* thriller" (Priestman 1998; Horsley 2001), a relative of the hard-boiled crime genre (see Pepper, chapter 10 and Simpson, chapter 14 in this volume), but one that pushes the figure of the private eye and his investigation into the background or leaves it out completely, and focuses instead on anti-heroes who deliberately and consciously choose to exceed the law.

In her preoccupation with showing how crime can emerge out of the most mundane situations, Highsmith's fiction has been considered an example of what the philosopher Hannah Arendt (referring to Nazi war criminals) termed the "banality of evil" (Knight 2004: 148). Rather than professional criminals, her novels tend to focus on ordinary people who choose crime as a way of resolving a situation in which they find themselves, or simply as the most effective means of getting what they want, or commit crime by accident and then find they have to continue doing so to avoid discovery. At the heart of her plots, then, is an emphasis on the destructive power of individual desire (though the exact motivations behind this often remain mysterious), and an exposure of how fragile and inconsequential are the moral codes that structure liberal-democratic society.

This is clear from her first novel, *Strangers on a Train* (1950), which focuses on Guy Haines, an ordinary, decent young man who has embarked on a respectable but difficult career as an architect, yet is stuck in an unhappy marriage. On a train journey, he encounters a disaffected young man named Charles Bruno, who proposes to him a Faustian pact: he will kill Guy's wife, if Guy will kill Charles's despised father. Because the police will be unable to establish a connection between the two apart from a single meeting it will be "the perfect crime." Guy never quite agrees to the plan, but is appalled when he hears that his wife has been killed, a crime apparently obligating him to fulfill his side of the bargain. Bruno continues to intervene more and more uncomfortably and aggressively in Guy's life, eventually drowning himself while drunk on a boating party, leaving Guy with no real option but to turn himself in.

The success of this novel and its author's career was assured once *Strangers on a Train* was made into a film by Alfred Hitchcock in 1951, with a screenplay by Raymond Chandler. (Hitchcock tricked Highsmith into accepting a paltry sum of $7,500 for the rights by negotiating with her anonymously through an intermediary.) Highsmith's next novel, however, *The Price of Salt* (1952), departed from the crime genre, marshaling her talent for creating suspense and portraying anxiety to represent an illicit lesbian love affair between a shopgirl and a married customer. The novel has been described as anticipating Nabokov's controversial *Lolita* (Castle 2003). It originally appeared under the nom de plume Claire Morgan but was reissued in 1984 under Highsmith's own name and with the title *Carol*. Following Andrew Wilson's 2003 biography, which made publicly available for the first time material from Highsmith's personal notebooks, the authorial motivation behind the novel became clear.

Wilson uncovers a central episode that sheds light on more than just Highsmith's character and sexuality and illuminates the impulses that drive all of her fiction. In December 1948, when Highsmith was working temporarily in the toy department of Bloomingdale's store, she encountered Kathleen Senn, a customer in a mink coat who bought a doll for one of her daughters and gave Highsmith her name and address and delivery details. So sick with desire did Highsmith feel that on two occasions (in June 1950 and January 1951) she traveled by train to the woman's house in New Jersey to spy on her. Highsmith noted at the time how close her desire felt to murder:

> Murder is a kind of making love, a kind of possessing. (Is it not, too, a way of gaining complete and passionate attention, for a moment, from the object of one's attentions?) To arrest her suddenly, my hands upon her throat (which I should really like to kiss) as if I took a photograph, to make her in an instant cool and rigid as a statue (A. Wilson 2003: 2).

The peculiar combination of sexual desire and aggression contained in this statement is common in her fiction, which is dominated by the motif of people who want to become or to destroy someone else.

Carol is a direct playing-out of Highsmith's fantasy that she and Senn had become lovers. However, the ambivalent desire which motivated Highsmith's stalking of Senn, and also the kind of following and spying she put into practice in this biographical episode, features in many typical examples of Highsmith's fiction. *Strangers on a Train* contains a scene where Bruno stalks Guy's wife Miriam before killing her, while Highsmith describes Bruno's thoughts: "If he could just get her alone and clap his hand over her mouth – or would she be able to bite? He squirmed with disgust at the thought of her wet mouth on his hand" (Highsmith 1998: 72). One of her finest novels, *Those Who Walk Away* (1967), tells how Ed Coleman, convinced his son-in-law Ray Garrett is to blame for the suicide of his daughter Peggy, tries to kill Ray in Rome. He fails and instead follows him to Venice where Ray is staying with his girlfriend Ines. There, in a dreamlike replaying of the main crisis-point of Highsmith's most famous novel, *The Talented Mr Ripley*, both men end up on a motor-boat in the lagoon. Ray pushes Ed overboard, Ed pretends he has died, and for the rest of the novel lives an alternative life under an assumed name.

In an essay on Highsmith, the journalist Susannah Clapp labeled the author "a balladeer of stalking," because her fiction tends to revolve around "[t]he fixation of one person on another – oscillating between attraction and antagonism" (Clapp 1999: 96). She quotes the playwright David Hare's admission that what he loves about Highsmith's work is the fact that "behind it lies the claim that, once you set your mind to it, any one human being can destroy any other" (Clapp 1999: 95). This is the kind of logic that informs the suspense and appeal of Highsmith's novels, the fact that one individual can easily terrorize or destroy another, once he or she chooses.

The logic is demonstrated chillingly in one of Highsmith's most representative, strangely personal and yet underrated novels, *This Sweet Sickness* (1960). She described the original "germ" of the novel as a variation on the idea of cashing in on "the old insurance game": a man wants to insure himself, then "die" or disappear in order to collect the money. She originally conceived of her hero setting himself up "in a different house with a different name, a house into which he could move permanently when his real self was presumably dead and gone." However, it was only when she thought of a "better motive" for the scam than insurance money that the idea really came to life. What if "[t]he man was creating his second house for the girl he loved but never won"? What if he was interested in neither insurance nor money but was instead "obsessed with emotion" (Highsmith 1983: 5)?

David Kelsey is such a man, so deeply in the grip of an erotomanic delusion that he is convinced the woman he is in love with, Annabelle Delaney, loves him in return – even though she is married and clearly though politely rejects his advances. This is what he calls "The Situation," which weighs on him "like a rock, say a five-pound rock, that he carried around in his chest day and night" (Highsmith 2002: 11). He spends his days living modestly in a guesthouse and working in a scientific lab. On weekends, however, under the pretence of visiting his sick mother in a nursing home, he lives in a house that he has bought in another town, and pretends Annabelle is there with him. To facilitate the self-deception he has bought the house under another name, "William Neumeister," and, when in the house, fantasizes that he really is this person – essentially a more successful, wealthier, more powerful version of himself.

We can recognize some distinctive Highsmith motifs in this outline: in particular the fascination with characters who live double lives and who become obsessed with another person. From the opening the reader knows that nothing good can come of this, and Highsmith gradually, patiently, and in detail describes how things get worse, keeping the suspense building. This is why Greene described her as "the poet of apprehension rather than fear. Fear after a time ... as we all learned in the Blitz, is narcotic, it can lull one by fatigue into sleep, but apprehension nags at the nerves gently and inescapably" (Greene 2000: x). David's acting-out of his fantasy becomes more and more overt and his behavior towards Annabelle more intrusive. His letters become more frequent and insistent, and he starts to telephone and then visit her, much to her chagrin and the annoyance of her husband. Eventually when the husband, Gerard, comes to David's secret home to warn him off, a fight breaks out and David accidentally kills him. It is at this point that the advantage of having another identity, hitherto latent in David's mind, becomes clear to him. He lays tracks to ensure that "Neumeister" appears the major suspect, but of course the police find this alter-ego to be untraceable. However, like Guy Haines, David is increasingly driven into madness by his predicament. Eventually he is responsible for another death and at the end of the novel his life is over. He fully assumes the identity of Neumeister and while on the run in New York lapses into psychosis, hallucinating that Annabelle is accompanying him around New York, sharing meals with him at restaurants and visiting his friends.

The implication is that the delusion, his "sweet sickness," is unshakeable; it can only intensify and increase. This psychotic element partly accounts for the novel's disturbing effect because it is as if David is incapable of resisting his breakdown – even when another girl's love for him (Effie Brennan's) offers an escape from his delusion staring him in the face. Typically for Highsmith, the novel's disturbing effect is enhanced because David is *not* suffering from a more clearly debilitating form of psychosis, but, up to a point, remains aware of the effects of his behavior. Indeed this is why he is able to continue the deceit about his double life, because he is so sensitive to how other people might see him. This is a typical Highsmith motif: David's "human" side is what enables his "subhuman" side to operate, by providing a cover. To label the murderous Highsmith hero simply "evil," monstrous, or "a psycho" would be to ignore the most disturbing implications of her fiction.

This is true of her best-known character, Tom Ripley, who murders so often and coldly over the course of several novels as to become a serial killer – though to persist with that label would diminish the complexity and appeal of his character. He first appears in *The Talented Mr Ripley* (1955), Highsmith's most famous, as well as critically analyzed and filmed, novel. The story tells how the eponymous protagonist is asked by rich magnate Herbert Greenleaf, who mistakenly believes Tom was at Princeton with his son Dickie, to go and "rescue" Dickie from his decadent, slothful sojourn in Italy so that he can assume his rightful position in the family business. In Europe, however, Tom becomes fascinated by Dickie's easy-going lifestyle in the upper-class expatriate community and carefully ingratiates himself into this society. Realizing that the fickle Dickie, while at first delighted with his new friend, will quickly grow weary of him, Tom kills Dickie on a boat trip, assumes his identity and uses his ability to forge signatures to ensure that he continues to receive Dickie's stipend. Once this plan has started to bear fruit Tom makes the "new" Dickie disappear, leaving behind a suicide note that praises Tom Ripley. He then reappears as Tom and manages to prevent the police and Dickie's suspicious family from finding out the truth. By the end of the novel, when he leaves Italy for Greece, Tom has gotten away with two murders, having killed Dickie's suspicious friend Freddie as well.

Although, of the four film versions of the Ripley novels, Anthony Minghella's 1997 *The Talented Mr Ripley* is perhaps the closest to the original in spirit, Minghella decided to make Ripley's apparent latent homosexuality explicit, giving the killings a sexual motivation. In the novel, however, Tom's homosexuality is presented simply as the most efficient method Tom can employ to win over Dickie. He murders Dickie not because he realizes Dickie will never love him, as the film implies, but because it is the most effective way of continuing the lifestyle he wants. As Slavoj Žižek has put it, "the repeated sidelong glances he casts at Dickie betray not a desire to have him, but to be like him" (Žižek 2003: 14).

The fact is that Ripley is incapable of love – incapable, in fact, of any moral discrimination whatsoever. He kills to get what he wants. His appeal is undoubtedly based on his epitomizing the moral relativism of the acquisitive, aspirational, late twentieth century. John Scaggs suggests that Ripley lives out the "flip-side of the American Dream by displaying ambition, selfish ruthlessness, and a lack of moral baggage in order to become rich and successful" (Scaggs 2005: 116). Žižek thinks he embodies the cloudy moral universe of postmodern culture, "today's rewriting of the Ten Commandments as recommendations which we don't need to follow too blindly. Ripley stands for the final step in this process: thou shalt not kill, except when there is really no other way to pursue your happiness" (Žižek 2003: 14).

Highsmith followed *The Talented Mr Ripley* with four further novels, *Ripley under Ground* (1970), *Ripley's Game* (1974), *The Boy who Followed Ripley* (1980) and *Ripley under Water* (1991). In these we see Ripley getting married to a rich Frenchwoman and running an art-forgery business while continuing with deceptions, evasions, and murder in order to preserve his successful and respectable status. That the series was not all produced in a burst of activity, in successive years, but with gaps of several years between each installment (during which Highsmith wrote many other novels), suggests that the appeal of the Ripley novels for Highsmith was not the opportunity to capitalize commercially on a successful formula. Rather Ripley was a character who kept returning to Highsmith, like an enduring obsession, not least because of his personal associations. Like her, a woman who specialized in the masculine genre of the crime thriller, he was an outsider figure. He also shared with his creator a complex, partially hidden sexuality, the desire to "hide" in Europe, and a deep scorn for bourgeois pretentions. As much as he can be seen as a dark "everyman" for the late twentieth century, Ripley is also someone who rebels against the very ordinariness and philistinism of late twentieth-century culture. As Lee Horsley has argued, very often Ripley's attitudes to those he kills or contemplates killing are motivated by contempt for their lack of imagination or artistic taste. In this sense, he amounts to a variation on a tradition as old as crime fiction itself, which sees murder, to quote Thomas De Quincey, "as One of the Fine Arts" (Horsley 2005: 136–8).

Highsmith's fiction is clearly rooted in its author's personal experience and psychology. Yet its preoccupations and style can also be read as an implicit critique of crime fiction. Crime fiction has always been dedicated, in different ways, to producing a kind of realism. Yet Highsmith's ability to place criminality at the very heart of everyday life eclipses even the realism of Chandler's "mean streets," exposing – as Greene noted – the inherent romanticism of the hard-boiled tradition (Greene 2000: ix). Highsmith's crime fiction is never romantic.

Her ability to inject a new kind of realism into her fiction results from more than just her characters and plotting: it also comes from the quality of the writing itself. Although she once confessed that "style does not interest me in the least" (cited in Dupont 1988), what sets Highsmith apart from other crime writers is her distinctive, measured, emotionless style, which maintains the same pace and detached perspective no matter what she is describing. Susannah Clapp has noted that "her narratives suggest a seamlessness between bumbling normality and horrific acts" without the reader being able to "hear the gears shift when the terrible moment arrives" (Clapp 1999: 96–7). An example is the chilling moment in *The Talented Mr Ripley* when Tom murders Dickie, just as the victim is getting ready to jump off their rowing-boat for a swim:

> … "I'll go in if you will!" Tom shouted. "Will you?" He wanted Dickie to slow down.
>
> "Will I? Sure!" Dickie slowed the motor abruptly. He released the tiller and took off his jacket. The boat bobbed, losing its momentum. "Come on," Dickie said, nodding at Tom's trousers that were still on.
>
> Tom glanced at the land. San Remo was a blur of chalky white and pink. He picked up the oar, as casually as if he were playing with it between his knees, and when Dickie was shoving his trousers down, Tom lifted the oar and came down with it on the top of Dickie's head. (Highsmith 1999: 91–2).

In a complementary argument, Žižek suggests that the key to Highsmith's achievement is the fact that she "takes the most narrative genre of all, crime fiction, and imbues it with the inertia of the real, the lack of resolution, the dragging-on of 'empty time' characteristic of life itself" (Žižek 2003: 13). More than just the unfolding of a narrative, Highsmith's fiction dwells on the moments when "nothing happens," when there is no "narrative" at all, or when narrative goes wrong. This is true of the murder scene in *The Talented Mr Ripley*. Tom has to hit Dickie, clumsily and savagely, eight more times with the oar before the victim loses consciousness. During the attack Tom is frightened by the sheer noise and strength of Dickie's groans. The scene thus gives the reader an appalling sense of how messy and complicated real murder must be.

Highsmith regarded the fascination with justice in conventional detective and crime fiction as boring, and was quite uninterested in making her anti-heroes pay. As Tony Hilfer puts it, one of the distinguishing features of Highsmith's plotting is the way she "deliberately and shamelessly evades the conventional morality of crime and punishment" (Hilfer 1990: 136). Her characters either escape police investigation, like Ripley, or turn themselves in, like Guy Haines in *Strangers on a Train*. Often the absence of justice provides the novels with an extra sense of despair, as at the end of *This Sweet Sickness*, where the reader feels that David Kelsey's capture by police would be a relief.

At one level, Highsmith's distinctive "flat" style effectively squeezes the suspense out of her narratives by avoiding the typical pattern in crime fiction where a dramatic event is carefully built up to and then followed by a period of calm. Instead the atmosphere of apprehension, as Greene called it, is constant. At another level, Highsmith's writing preserves the suspense of crime narrative, but routes it through a different circuit to that of the "logic-and-deduction" novel. Instead of anxiously wondering whether the detective can figure it out in time to prevent further murders, Highsmith's readers find themselves guiltily hoping that her heroes can continue to get away with it. Even though Ripley continues to remain at large, he is never free of the fear that he might be apprehended soon – and this means the suspense continues to the very end of the novel.

The logic of identification is central to Highsmith's achievement – not just in the way that her anti-heroes perversely or maliciously identify with other people, but because Highsmith so clearly identifies with her characters that she ensures her readers do too. She once wrote of Charles Bruno in her diary, "*I love him!*," and at times signed her name as "Pat H., alias Ripley" (A. Wilson 2003: 194). While she acknowledged them as "psychopathic or neurotic," she also claimed that her antiheroes are all "fairly likeable, or at least not repugnant" (Highsmith 1983: 46). In concentrating our attention on the minds of the protagonists, narrating their thought processes and reasoning so we experience their dilemmas, desires, and amorality from the inside, she makes us complicit in their crimes, and aware of how close we are to the amorality of the late twentieth century embraced by its supercilious Tom Ripleys.

42

Elmore Leonard (1925–)

Charles J. Rzepka

Critics and biographers who, like undertakers, prefer subjects that do not move around much once they are put in a box, must find Elmore "Dutch" Leonard a frustrating challenge to their powers of summation. As this book goes to press, Leonard has interrupted the writing of his forty-third book – featuring a documentary filmmaker and a group of Somali pirates – to plug his latest, *Road Dogs*, during a promotional tour to six states. He is halfway into his eighty-fourth year and is not about to take a nap in anybody's box.

At first glance, Leonard seems easy to summarize: he is, at this moment, the best-known writer of crime fiction in America – perhaps the world. His books and stories are populated with a well-trained ensemble of gangbangers and dope-dealers and shysters and an intriguing assortment of psychopaths, female professionals from hookers to airline attendants all looking to move up, honest cops hampered by legal niceties and crooked cops on the take, Hollywood phonies and Delta mobsters, hanging judges and hit-men, and dozens of eccentric blue-collar, beer-drinking extras. In Leonard's world, stupidity is a crime when pride persuades the stupid they are smart. Not surprisingly, his most compelling hero-protagonists are intelligent (but never intellectual), modest, and conscientious if not necessarily law-abiding: while looking to make the big score or get revenge or just survive, they nevertheless try to hold onto their souls. "You haven't made up your mind yet, have you?" Robert Taylor asks Dennis Lenahan, the high diver he is trying to enlist as a money-launderer in *Tishomingo Blues*. "To sell my soul? No, I haven't," replies Dennis (Leonard 2002: 197).

A liberal Catholic and a recovering alcoholic since the late 1970s, Leonard believes in free will and the power to change one's life (Devlin 1999: 104, 106; Grella 1998: 36). Accordingly, and as incongruous as it may seem in light of his obvious debts to *noir* (Horsley 2001: 206–7; see also Simpson, chapter 14 in this volume), his view of the world is a comedic rather than tragic one. If, as Charles McGrath believes, "the Hollywood types" burn with a "zeal for Leonard's novels … in inverse proportion to their ability to make anything but turkeys out of them" (McGrath 2005: 1), the fault may lie here. "My books haven't been easy to shoot," says Leonard, because "they've been taken too seriously" (Grobel 2001: 270). He tries to make even his scariest characters "a little funny" (Skinner 1987: 42). Above all he believes in authenticity, if not authority, whether legal or ecclesiastical, and there is more than a peck of satiric humor in Leonard's fiction at the expense of his inauthentic losers for every bushel of *noir* violence they dish out.

Stylistically, as well, Leonard should be easy to put in a box. He is famous for his "cinematic" prose, his attention to the *mise en scène* and the telling visual detail, as well as his unerring ear for the "voices" of his characters, a stream of discourse into which his own narrative murmur typically disappears. This is a skill he worked hard to develop, helped along by the examples of Ernest Hemingway's *For Whom the Bell Tolls* during an early phase of writing Westerns – "his dialogue went straight down the page," says Leonard (Grobel 2001: 255–6) – and, in turning to crime fiction in the early 1970s, George V. Higgins's *The Friends of Eddie Coyle* – "the best crime book there is" (Grobel 2001: 284). "For the most part I'm copying a sound of speech," says Leonard, "so that my 'sound' or style or attitude is the sound of the characters. You never hear *me*. You're never aware of words used by an author because I never use a word that my characters wouldn't or couldn't" (Skinner 1987: 41). By now, Leonard's handling of the pace and arc of dialogue and the curtain-dropping one-liner seems instinctual. It is thus no surprise that, despite their unimpressive track record in the cinema, dozens of his books have been optioned by Hollywood and more than twenty, as of this writing, have made it to movie or TV screens.

Like Leonard's filmic feel, his geeky obsession with the minutiae of gizmos, trades, and professions has become legendary: not just law-enforcement protocols and gun-specs, but ironworking (*Killshot*), the music industry (*Be Cool*), movie making (*La Brava, Get Shorty*), and casino gambling (*Glitz*), to name just a few. He has a special affinity for the data of place and time: not just Civil War battles, for instance, but present-day Civil War re-enactments (*Toshomingo Blues*). His voracity for facts is matched by the assiduous efforts of his principal researcher of the last three decades, Gregg Sutter, who sees it as intimately connected to the driving force behind his boss's seemingly haphazard but organically emergent plots: "What Dutch is looking for in research is a series of 'triggers' that inspire scenes or characters ... a single fact, a gesture, or a backdrop; once he had it he'd be off and running again" (Sutter 1986: 10). As Leonard has repeatedly insisted, "plot doesn't interest me that much" (Grobel 2001: 269). The choices his characters make, how well they "audition" and "play their role" (Skinner 1987: 42), shape the books they are in: free will, not predestination, runs the Elmorean universe.

A summary like this, however, reflects only the bright, expansive surface glare of Leonard's best-known work. In addition to crime novels and screenplays unfolding in Detroit, Miami, and Hollywood, his top three locales, he has set tales in present-day Italy and turn-of-the-century Cuba, and many Westerns, early in his career, in the Arizona Territory. One book, *Touch* (1987), examines the place of miracles in the modern world. He has written essays (including "Ten Rules of Writing"), short stories (his most recent collection, *When the Women Come Out to Dance*, appeared in 2002), and a children's book, *A Coyote's in the House* (2004), dedicated to his grandchildren. As one biographer, James E. Devlin, suggests, any classificatory scheme for so prolific and diverse a writer must, finally, be an arbitrary choice (Devlin 1999: 50). It might be wise, therefore, to simply begin at the beginning.

Learning to Write

Leonard wrote Westerns for many years before first trying his hand at crime fiction in *The Big Bounce* (1969). His first tale, "Trail of the Apache," appeared in 1951 in *Argosy*. Leonard, a Navy veteran, was working for an ad agency in Detroit that handled the Chevrolet account. Born in New Orleans in 1925 to a peripatetic family (his father traveled the country scouting GM dealerships), he had been raised for part of his early childhood in Oklahoma, to which he returned imaginatively in his Depression era gangster tale, *The Hot Kid* (2005). In 1934, his family settled down in Detroit. There, Elmore attended Blessed Sacrament Academy, a Catholic elementary school, and the Jesuit run University of Detroit High School, where he played on the varsity baseball team and received the nickname "Dutch," after the Washington Senators' pitcher, Dutch Leonard. It was at the University of Detroit that he later earned his bachelor's degree in English and Philosophy.

Leonard was never a fan of sagebrush sagas. "When I think of the nineteenth century, it has no appeal to me," he says. "I hadn't even read many westerns. When I picked up Zane Grey I couldn't believe it was so bad" (Grobel 2001: 255). Nor did he particularly like guns, except as a plot device. To this day, despite his encyclopedic knowledge of firearms, he does not own one. Rather, the Western seemed to him an uncomplicated genre for someone just getting the hang of writing. As biographer David Geherin puts it, "It seemed a good place to learn" (Geherin 1989: 4). Leonard's approach to writing, in short, was strictly professional, and remains so: methodical, disciplined, thorough, and highly skilled through the habituation of painstakingly acquired techniques. Despite his distaste for Zane Gray, he admires James Fenimore Cooper's frontier tales – at least in screen versions like *Last of the Mohicans* starring Daniel Day Lewis (Grobel 2001: 288) – and fell in love with movie Westerns as a boy. References and allusions to classic "oaters" like *Stagecoach*, *The Plainsman*, and *The Gunfighter* pepper the pages not only of his Western fiction, but also many of his works in the crime genre, especially "eastern-westerns" (Grobel 2001: 275) like *City Primeval: High Noon in Detroit* (1980) and *Killshot* (1989).

From the very beginning Leonard was drawn, not to the traditional Old West cowpokes and gunslingers, but to the Apaches resisting settlement or confinement to reservations, and to those outrunners of the white man's civilization – especially cavalry scouts – who, like Cooper's Natty Bumppo, shared something of the Native American's disgust with modernity, respect for cultural tradition (however appalling to white sensibilities), and intuitive connection to the natural world. Few of Leonard's Apaches are "noble" in the Rousseauean sense, however: in fact, most are conniving, treacherous, gullible, superstitious, and violent, especially when they have drunk too much "tizwin" (corn beer). But nearly all of them are nothing but themselves, and that seems to earn them Leonard's respect throughout his Western period. Like the white heroes he holds up for our admiration, beginning with Indian agent Eric Travisin of "Trail of the Apaches," who is "one-quarter Apache" after all (Leonard 2004: 2), Leonard's "savages" nearly all know what they are supposed to do in any given situation – whether tracking buffalo or roasting a kidnapped settler alive over an open fire – and they commit themselves single-mindedly to doing it, and doing it right.

Leonard's style has evolved radically since his earliest Old West stories, from a primary reliance on descriptive prose and a vaguely defined narrative persona to a greater use of unadorned dialogue, narrative transparency, and, most intriguingly, free indirect discourse and interior monologue as expository devices. Although the latter have attracted critical notice (see, e.g., Rhodes 2008: 145), they are rarely considered significant in their own right, and tend to get swallowed up in commentary on Leonard's way with point of view or stunning manipulation of "voice" in general. One can find robust examples of free indirect discourse, however, just two years after "Trail of the Apache," in Leonard's increasing reliance on verbs of sensation and then thought or belief to introduce passages of mental discourse. In "Blood Money" (1953), bank robbers Rich Miller, "the boy," and Eugene Harlan, an ex-con, have been cornered by a posse:

> Rich Miller watched Eugene move back to the table along the rear wall and pick up the whiskey bottle that was there. The boy passed his tongue over dry lips, watching Eugene drink. It would be good to have a drink, he thought. No, it wouldn't. It would be bad. You drank too much and that's why you're here. That's why you're going to get shot or hung. (Leonard 2004: 269)

By 1989, Leonard could dispense with such markers of interiority, plunging us from the first line of *Killshot* directly into the self-deluding rationalizations of Armand "Blackbird" Degas, a half-Ojibway, alcoholic hit-man from Toronto, and one of Leonard's most compelling, and oddly moving, portraits of homicidal psychopathy:

> The Blackbird told himself he was drinking too much because he lived in this hotel and the Silver Dollar was close by, right downstairs. Try to walk out the door past it. Try to come along Spadina Avenue, see that goddamn Silver Dollar sign, hundreds of light bulbs in your face, and not be drawn in there. Have a few drinks before coming up to this room with a ceiling that looked like a road map, all the cracks in it. (Leonard 1989: 7)

It is not just Leonard's subsequent experiences as an alcoholic, or his discovery of Higgins's way with "voices," that accounts for the differences here. The voice in

Armand's head belongs to him in a way that Rich Miller's cannot, intimately connected in its rhythms and diction and defensive imperatives with the mental demons that, since his parentless boyhood on the Walpole Island reservation, have cut him off from any possibility of identifying with another person and, thereby, beginning to transform his monologic rants into dialogic understanding – and ultimately, self-understanding.

This aspect of Leonard's achievement, his manipulation of free indirect discourse so as to convey not just a kaleidescopic shift in points of view, but also a polyphonic series of distinct, interiorized voices, obviously cannot translate well to the screen. Its resistance to cinematic treatment suggests another reason why so many of Leonard's otherwise promising "products" result in indifferent or even disappointing films. To judge from recent reviews of the movie version of *Killshot* (2009), just released to DVD after a vexed sojourn tracing the labyrinths of Hollywood "options," this history has just repeated itself. The comments of blogger "station909 from Israel" are typical: "I asked myself if the plot wasn't about the action but about [Armand Degas] (played by Mickey Rourke)," writes "station909," "but I found that the character was inconsistent – either he is a professional killer or some guilt haunted brother. But both don't go together" (station909 2009). Armand's interior monologues go a long way toward reconciling the two.

Growing Up

There is, finally, something childlike about Armand, just as there is about his garrulous sidekick, Richie Nix, whose maternal girlfriend, Donna Mulry, a retired prison cafeteria worker and Elvis worshipper, buys his clothes and cooks his meals as though he were her little boy. "I picture most of my characters as children," says Leonard. "I see them as they were at a certain age. ... And as they grow up, they're still children" (Grobel 2001: 282). This is a sentiment often expressed in Leonard's books: Mrs Pierce in *Gunsights* thinks of her lover, Bren Early, as "a little boy" (Leonard 1998: 406); Carolyn Wilder thinks the same about both Clement Mansell, the "Oklahoma Wildman," and his antagonist, Lieutenant Raymond Cruz, in *City Primeval* (Leonard 1980: 164, 202). The honor game into which these men have been drawn closely resembles the code of the schoolyard, where young males must either bully or be bullied.

If we take seriously what Leonard is saying about his childlike characters, we begin to see that for him "growing up" is not a matter of accumulating years, but of successfully negotiating the passage through what Lacanian psychoanalysts would call "the mirror stage," that point in an infant's development or an adolescent's life (the latter a more advanced recapitulation of the former) when he or she first "assumes an image," becoming preoccupied by the self as an object in the gaze of others who inhabit and understand a world with which the child is initially unfamiliar (Lacan 1977: 2). For the infant this world is bounded by the family, and authoritative confirmation of the self comes to be lodged in the parents; for the adolescent, this world lies in the wider society of strangers outside the family, where it is often difficult to locate the site of authoritative self-confirmation in any single individual. In both cases, successful self-integration or "deflection of the specular I into the social I" (Lacan 1977: 5) – which is to say, "growing up" – depends upon the interiorization of the authoritative gaze, and a consequent ability to dispense with overt, external mediations of self-awareness. The primary emotions governing those who fail the task of interiorization are shame and rage, the quintessential affects of projected self-doubt and externalized self-construction.

Leonard draws upon a wide range of devices, including mirroring surfaces, to register a character's arrest at this stage, which is marked by an inability to mediate self-awareness except through an externalized image of the self. Teddy Magyk in *Glitz*, the momma's boy whose obsession with getting back at detective Vincent Mora for sending him to jail dominates nearly every waking moment of his life, is a case in point. Going to the bathroom in the middle of the night after stalking Vincent for days, Teddy stops before the mirror and grins, "turning his head to look at the grin from different angles":

> "Hi"
> "Hi, yourself."
> "Haven't I seen you someplace before?"
> "Now you do, now you don't."
> "Wait."
> He stared at himself in silence, not grinning now.
> "When you gonna do it?"
> "What?"
> "You know what."
> He stared at himself in silence.
> "Tomorrow. Didn't I tell you?" (Leonard 1985: 241)

Teddy's degree of dissociation is extreme, but not unusual in Leonard's universe, and every such case of dissociation, whether mild or severe, reveals a commensurate degree of inauthenticity, a preoccupation with "playing the game" or acting the role to which one feels inescapably assigned, often expressed in cinematic terms. Wayne Colson, the ironworker in *Killshot* whose life, along with that of his wife, Carmen, is under threat from Degas and Nix, can do little more than reprise classic movie scripts of catching the bad guys by surprise when they decide to invade his house. High among the I-beams of a construction project, Wayne (named by his parents after John Wayne) sits down to run and re-run ambush scenarios from old movies through his head, oblivious to the world, and his fellow workers' safety, until the walking boss and the raising-gang foreman, alarmed by his "frozen" posture, climb up to awaken him out of his trance (Leonard 1989: 132–5).

Wayne's next move speaks directly to Leonard's ideal of authenticity:

> From where he was now he could take ladders down to each floored level. Maybe he was going to and changed his mind, favoring the express route. They watched him slide down the column where the guys were standing around watching, and head for the steel-company trailer. (Leonard 1989: 136)

Wayne is most himself when he is not looking at himself playing a role scripted by someone else – in this case, the *mano a mano* face-off featured in traditional Westerns – but rather doing a task he is trained as an ironworker to do, here, sliding down I-beams rather than taking the stairs like a neophyte or, in the jargon of the trade, "a punk." He knows he is being watched, perhaps even showing off, but does not watch his audience watching him. Instead, he lets his professional training take over his behavior: he becomes what he is doing.

Authenticity for Leonard is nearly always a function of getting absorbed in performing a task that one is used to or getting the hang of, not becoming preoccupied with how well one is performing it or how others are evaluating it, let alone with playing a pre-scripted role. This is very much in synchrony with Leonard's disciplined absorption in the craft of writing: "I'm a serious writer," he says, "but I don't *take* it seriously, if that makes any sense. I don't stew over it, I try and relax and swing with it" (Grobel 2001: 281). Like a good jazz musician, a true professional has to master his trade "in the shed," then put what he has learned out of his mind when he wants to "swing with it."

Rules, Roles, Reflections

Paying too much attention to "the rules" or "the role" indicates a fall into self-conscious disintegration, a Lacanian *Spaltung* or splitting of the self that is the hallmark of Leonardian inauthenticity. In Leonard's novels, movies and television exacerbate this process and figure it thematically.

Leonard's pop cultural and mass media references are so ubiquitous as to draw the focused attention of postmodernist critics and social scientists. In each instance, according to Chip Rhodes, readers learn that "identity is always already a simulation, a performance, a fiction – with no mooring in bodies, histories, ontologies" (Rhodes 2008: 152). Leonard introduced this idea as early as his first crime novel, *The Big Bounce*, which opens with several police officers watching a brutal beating that just happened to be captured on film by a documentary filmmaker interested in the plight of migrant workers. It is particularly evident, however, in those books that thematize the self-alienating effects of mass mediation and replication, such as *Split Images*, *La Brava*, and *Get Shorty*. In the first two books particularly, writes Glenn Most, "reality is imitating art and we can no longer confidently draw the line between what is fiction and what is truth." So involuted is the process that the lives led by Leonard's characters come to look like "the lives we are led, by television and the other mass media, to believe we actually lead" (Most 1988: 109).

For Leonard, however, this dynamic is nothing new. His last Western novel, *Gunsights* (1979), set in 1893, ends with a traditional stand-off between good guys and bad guys that peters out when a flock of newspaper reporters arrives, complete with tripod cameras, to record the event for "history" – and for their eager metropolitan readers, who have been riveted for weeks by the reporters' Wild West hype. The reporters are accompanied by Captain Billy Washington, a celebrity cowboy, who has come to ask Leonard's two protagonists to join his Wild West show. In Leonard's view, our place in history is always a mediated one, in every place and time, whether by movies and television, by newspapers and daguerrotypes, or by legend and myth. The trick is not to get taken in by the hype and estranged from who you really are by pretending to be a hero who never was. The younger protagonists of his Western fiction, like Lieutenant Duane Bowers in *The Bounty Hunters* or Bran Early in *Gunsights*, must often be taught the difference between the Civil War stories they heard at West Point and the dirty, tedious, and often inglorious realities of real combat on the frontier. Their dark avatar a century later, Richie Nix, does not just want to rob banks like his hero, Billy the Kid, but surpass him by robbing a bank "in every state of the union – or maybe just forty-nine, fuck Alaska" (Leonard 1989: 22). In "Cavalry Boots," (1952), Leonard's first-person narrator (a rarity), sets out to tell the embarrassing truth behind the story of Bud Nagle, a malingering greenhorn volunteer whose cowardice and incompetence resulted, through a series of improbable accidents entirely beyond his control, in the Third US Dragoons' surprise defeat of Cochise and his band of renegade Apaches at Dos Cabezas. Nagle had become a hero only because the Third's "regimental pride" (Leonard 2004: 147) could not admit any other interpretation of events.

Punks and Pros, Performers and Professionals

In general, Leonard does not care much about ordinary morality, let alone legality. Victimless crimes do not interest him, and his dominant ethic is the golden rule – "Do unto others" – often interpreted in retributive as well as altruistic terms. What seems most often a matter of concern to him is not whether a protagonist is good or bad, but whether he can answer the challenges to authenticity or resist the temptations to inauthenticity that life inevitably brings. And, as I have suggested, Leonard's understanding of the authentic is essentially a performative one.

I say "he" when referring to Leonard's protagonists because they are preponderantly male. While his female characters have come a long way from their first appearances in his early Westerns, few can be considered as dominating the action. At the same time, it would be too harsh to say that he portrays even his frontier women "almost always as victims" (Most 1988: 104). Indeed, ever since the transformation of complacent housewife Mickey Dawson into the "new Mickey" in *The Switch*

(Leonard 1978: 244), Leonard has been drawn to female characters like Jackie Burke in *Rum Punch* (1992) ("Jackie Brown" in Quentin Tarantino's eponymous movie version of 1997) who, like his favorite males, demonstrate agency and ambition. Many of his heroines, like US Marshall Karen Sisco in *Out of Sight* (1996) and singer Linda Moon in *Glitz* and, later, *Be Cool*, are also dedicated professionals. By the time we get to *Up in Honey's Room* (2007), set in World War II Detroit, Louly Webster (a reputed former gangster's moll) is showing Marine recruits "how to fire a Browning machine gun from the backseat of a Dauntless dive-bomber without shooting off the tail" (Leonard 2007: 46). But make no mistake: it is not Louly's violence that Leonard admires, but her sheer prowess and technical savvy. "Louly's having all the fun," says her husband Carl, who's been honorably discharged after being wounded in the Pacific Theater. Mrs Webster gets to "swing with it." She is a proud professional.

It will be interesting to see how the female protagonist of Leonard's next book, who is filming Somali pirates in action, will fare. In any case, Leonard's male characters are easier to type than his females, perhaps because their numbers help recurrent personalities emerge more clearly. There are the young hot shots and the seasoned vets, the maniacs and the cool customers, the talkers and the silent types, and (always) the stupid and the less-stupid. But it might be more useful to organize them according to a few recurrent patterns of relationship that seem to shape his male protagonists' struggles for authenticity. In his "eastern westerns" particularly, we can discern two recurrent axes defining characters positionally, whether we think of them as bad guys or good.

The first axis runs between the apprentices or "punks" and the "old pros." The apprentices are unseasoned and inexperienced to one degree or another, but eager, often rash and spontaneous, with something to prove. They may be violent or working hard to contain their violent tendencies, or they may be obsessed, like the West Pointers in Leonard's Westerns, with doing things strictly by the book, but in nearly all cases they are faced with the task of learning how to be themselves rather than someone from a novel or a movie or a training manual. "You can keep up the spit and polish if you want," Eric Travisin tells young Lieutenant De Both in "Trail," "but I'd advise you to relax and play the game without keeping the rule book open all the time" (Leonard 2004: 7). Sometimes apprentices are "naturals" at what they do, like police lieutenant Raymond Cruz in *City Primeval*, who is gifted with what amounts to second-sight in his intuitive reading of clues, or US Marshall Carl Webster as he first appears in *The Hot Kid*, where his quick draw earns him feature status in *True Detective* magazine. Webster is in fact so gifted that he can teach the old pros a thing or two, and by the time he reappears in *Up in Honey's Room* he has become a legendary "old pro" himself, "with a gaunt face who wasn't even forty" (Leonard 2007: 69). Even with their gifts, however, Leonard's apprentices have yet to lose their self-awareness in performing the professional tasks that face them. Cruz, who at 36 has not yet "established his image" (Leonard 1980: 36), pictures himself as Gregory Peck in *The Gunfighter*. Carl Webster, when starting out in *The Hot Kid*, keeps a running count of his kills just like Richie Nix in *Killshot*. Richie plays apprentice to old pro Armand Degas, whose rules of the trade – "One shot, one kill," "never talk to them before," "don't think about it," and never leave witnesses (Leonard 1989: 86, 88, 105, 382) – seem to have been lifted from a mob training manual.

Armand, however, like every other old pro, knows the rules in his bones. It is only in the face of Richie's infuriating arrogance and recklessness that he is obliged to spell them out. He is not self-conscious when doing his job, but only when he isn't. That is when the bottle beckons and he gets crazy ideas like starting over again and becoming a new person in partnership with Richie, who has begun addressing "The Blackbird" as "Bird": "The Bird. New name for the beginning of a new time in his life. ... He liked the way Richie Nix said it, the guy sounding proud to know him, wanting to show him off" (Leonard 1989: 59).

Armand, beginning to triangulate his sense of identity through the fun-house mirror of Richie Nix's admiration, exemplifies the challenges and difficulties besetting nearly all of Leonard's seasoned professionals: you get old, you get bored, you get set in your ways or you lose a step, and before you know it, you are second-guessing or irrelevant or out on your ass or, like Armand, you are dead. Perhaps, like Vincent Moro in *Glitz*, you take a long detour from your regular job in Miami when you find yourself feeling bad about killing a mugger who severely wounded you, and you get lucky, ending up in Atlantic City where you solve three murders, kill the sociopathic murderer (who is out to get you, too), and fall in love with a rock singer – and wonder if you will ever go back to your old job. For a brutal ex-cop like Walter Kouza in *Split Images* (1981), the detour is even longer: he ends up as henchman for a sociopathic millionaire who likes to videotape himself killing people.

In *City Primeval*, this axis of relationship running between apprentices and masters, "punks" and "old pros," is lightly but distinctly etched. Early in the book, Raymond Cruz tells an obnoxious young female reporter for *The Detroit News* that what influenced him most, coming onto the force, was "the old pros" (Leonard 1980: 25), and it is not long before we find him sizing them up as ego-ideals: "He *was* a police officer. But what kind?"

> He could be dry-serious like Norbert Bryl, he could be dry-cool like Wendell Robinson, he could be crude and a little crazy like Jerry Hunter ... or he could appear quietly unaffected, stand with hands in the pockets of his dark suit, expression solemn beneath the gunfighter mustache ... and the girl from the *News* would see it as his Dodge City pose: the daguerrotype peace officer. (Leonard 1980: 35)

But the newspaper reporter has it right. Cruz thinks he is individuating himself – "quietly unaffected ... with hands in the pockets of his dark suit, expression solemn" – among the "old pros" who have already "established [their] image[s]" and thereby staked out the available territory of "police officer" identities. But in fact he is only falling unwittingly into mythic typicality: his "gunfighter moustache" betrays the

Gregory Peck role Cruz denies playing. "Why would she tell him he was posing? Playing a role, she said. You had to know you were doing it before you could be accused of posing" (Leonard 1980: 35). But "knowing you are doing it" is the mark of maturity, Leonard's ironic sign of self-integration, because it involves some degree of self-knowledge: deliberation, free choice, play. It is not the same as watching yourself doing it. You know who you are when you *choose* to be somebody, not when the mirror of celebrity or myth *tells* you who you are.

Mirrors, Mirages

It is Cruz's appropriation by, rather than of, Peck's *Gunfighter* archetype that makes him vulnerable along the horizontal axis often transecting the vertical relationship between punks and pros in Leonard's fiction: the axis of mirroring antagonists. In *City Primeval* Cruz's nemesis, Clement Mansell, exploits the lieutenant's weakness for sagebrush heroics by repeatedly inviting him into the personal honor "game" that distinguishes the traditional genre of the Old West. In fact, Cruz feels "a strange rapport" (Leonard 1980: 77) with Clement, who not only gets his own mirror scene, like Teddy Magyk (Leonard 1980: 168), but also manages to inveigle Cruz into mirroring him by the end of his initial interrogation: "Me and you," he tells Cruz, "we're sitting here looking at each other, sizing each other up, aren't we?" (Leonard 1980: 91). Alluding to Cruz's failure to put him away three years previously due to a legal technicality, the Oklahoma Wildman says, "See, now it *does* get personal. Right?"

> "Well, I have to admit there's some truth to what you say."
> "I knew it," Clement said. "You've got no higher motive 'n I do. ... You don't set out to uphold the law any more'n I set out to break it. What happens, we get in a situation like this and then me and you start playing a game." (Leonard 1980: 88)

Cruz's reply gives nothing away: "Some other time – I mean a long time ago – we might have settled this between us. I mean if we each took the situation personally." He could be rejecting Clement's understanding of their relationship because it is anachronistic, but he could also be admitting its legitimacy by citing restraints that, upon reflection, seem arbitrary rather than axiomatic. Significantly, it is not the laws that Cruz is sworn to uphold that prevent the two of them from playing Mansell's "game," but their being born in the wrong place and time, as well as (Cruz implies) any lack of personal motivation, at least on his part. But when your self-understanding has been mediated by Hollywood Westerns, historical constraints soon weaken, and making others "take it personally" is something that Leonard's bad boys are supremely good at.

As the novel unfolds and Clement, protected by legal technicalities, gets away with ever more outrageous behavior, including armed robbery and a vicious beating of his own defense attorney, who has become Cruz's new girlfriend, the police finally decide they have no choice but to make the "Oklahoma Wildman" disappear by sealing him up alive in a hidden vault beneath the apartment of Skendar Lulgjaraj, his last victim. "It's done, Raymond thought. Walk away" (Leonard 1980: 210). But Cruz knows that this solution is neither legal nor, more importantly, honorable. Later that night he returns to the vault alone, opens the door, walks out before Clement sees him, and waits in the outlaw's apartment, where he has arranged to settle things face to face by placing two guns within arm's reach on the dining room table. But Clement, suspicious now, refuses to go for his gun, checkmating Cruz in his attempt to kill Clement outside the law, but with honor, like a Hollywood gunfighter. Instead, Clement goes into the kitchen for some drinks and returns with a bottle of beer for Cruz. When he reaches into his pants to get an opener, the detective shoots him three times, thinking he is going for a hidden gun.

> Clement said, "I don't believe it ... what did you kill me for?"
> Raymond didn't answer. Maybe tomorrow he'd think of something he might have said. After a little while Raymond picked up the opener from the desk and began paring the nail of his right index finger with the sharply pointed hooked edge. (Leonard 1980: 222)

That final gesture is pure Leonard, for it exactly replicates the scene from *The Gunfighter* that most impressed Cruz (and apparently Leonard himself) as a boy: when the outlaw catches Gregory Peck sitting in a barber's chair without his gun, Peck bluffs him into backing down by suggesting there might be a gun under his neck cloth pointed directly at the man's chest. In fact, Peck turns out to be paring his nails.

As often happens with Leonard's pop cultural allusions, however, the meaning of this scene has been turned upside down and inside out. In *The Gunfighter* the good guy bluffed the bad guy into backing down, and two lives were saved. In *City Primeval* the good guy is drastically mistaken in his reading of the bad guy's intentions and ends up killing an unarmed man under an illusion fostered by his obsession with Hollywood stereotypes. In fact, the good guy ends up playing the trigger-happy bad guy, and the bad guy the unarmed good guy, with fatal results. When Cruz pares his nails after killing Clement in cold blood, his imitative behavior seems as much a suppression of personal awareness and responsibility as a sign of cool bravado, an aping of cinema self-possession belied by his inability to come up with an answer to Clement's question. Maybe tomorrow *will* bring the answer, but probably not, because Hollywood has no answers to provide. While we come away from the end of *City Primeval* relieved that Clement is dead, we are also left wondering about the state of Raymond Cruz's soul, a site now haunted by a "Gregory Peck" who never existed, except as an image on the silver screen.

Did Cruz have any other choice? None that was not dishonorable or unprofessional, except to keep working at it until he got it right, which was simply not feasible. In the end, neither Cruz's gifts nor his training are enough to rid the world of Clement Mansell, which makes his killing of Clement outside the law a practical necessity, but also a professional failure. In Leonard's world we are all free, but some of us have fewer choices that will let us keep our souls. Cruz is not as lucky as Dennis Lenahan, for instance, at the end of *Tishomingo Blues,* when dope-dealer Robert Taylor, impressed by Lenahan's cool, quiet self-possession on the diving platform, admits that selling one's soul for big bucks is not, after all, the path to success. Take the great blues guitarist, Robert Johnson, says Taylor: he played so well everyone thought he had sold his soul to the devil. They were wrong. "What he did," says Taylor, "was leave the Delta ... and went to the woodshed":

> "You know what's meant by woodsheddin'? It's getting off by yourself and finding your sound, your chops, what makes you special. ... You understand what I'm saying?"
> "You want something," Dennis said, "work for it. If I want to run a diving show, get off my ass and make it happen." (Leonard 2002: 302)

Then just swing with it.

43

Sara Paretsky (1947–)

Malcah Effron

Sara Paretsky is the author of the V. I. Warshawski detective stories and two stand-alone novels, *Ghost Country* (1998) and *Bleeding Kansas* (2008). While the Warshawski series and *Ghost Country* deal with Paretsky's adopted hometown of Chicago, *Bleeding Kansas* returns to her childhood home near Lawrence, Kansas. Paretsky grew up as one of five children and the only daughter of a University of Kansas professor of bacteriology (Paretsky 2007: xiv). In *Writing in the Age of Silence*, a collection of autobiographical essays, she describes her parents as civil activists outside the home but participants in a strict patriarchal structure that suppressed and subsumed the only daughter inside the home (2007: 7,11). In response to this unhappy life at home in Kansas and motivated by positive summer work experiences on Chicago's South Side, Paretsky adopted Chicago as her new home and uses the South Side as the childhood home of her detective. Paretsky's adult life is largely based in Chicago where she worked her way up in the insurance business, earned a doctorate in history from the University of Chicago, and now lives with her husband (2007: 11, 36). She cites the feminist movement of the 1960s and 70s as important in freeing her from familial expectations and allowing her to leave the domestic realm to create the independent character that is the feminist private investigator V. I. Warshawski (2007: 57–62). Paretsky is particularly influential on women's writing in crime fiction not only as a writer but also as an activist, one of the founding members (some would say the founding mother) of the organization Sisters in Crime (2007: 69), which seeks to reveal and to redress gender inequalities in the crime fiction marketplace.

Paretsky's hard-boiled series chronicles Chicago private investigator V. I. Warshawski. Warshawski's biography parallels that which has come to typify fictional female private investigators. At the start of the series in *Indemnity Only* (1982), Warshawski is in her early thirties, has lost her parents, and has lost her desire to participate in the patriarchal structures of the American workplace in the 1970s and 80s. Born to a working-class family on Chicago's South Side, Warshawski escapes her background through a basketball scholarship to the University of Chicago and then University of Chicago Law School. Her mother, an Italian refugee whose singing career was cut short by the Nazis, died of uterine cancer when Warshawski was in high school, but not before instilling in her daughter an intense sense of pride, a strong work ethic, and a love of opera. Her father, a Polish-American police-man who died a few years later, imparted a sense of honesty and justice. With this background, Warshawski found the patriarchal systems of the American legal system and marriage intolerable, so she has left her position at the public defender's office and has divorced her husband by the start of the first novel, when she has already established herself as a private investigator. These background details inflect all the novels in the series, explaining Warshawski's increased access to the police through her father's former colleagues, particularly his best friend Bobby Mallory, her cli-entele of family and friends, and her abiding values. She also establishes her own network of friends, including various female associates and male lovers, but espe-cially her friend Dr Lotty Herschel, who helps her find herself as a feminist in the 1970s and who supports her both physically and emotionally through the traumas of her investigations.

With this back-story and cast of characters, Paretsky's Warshawski series has received critical attention as a feminist intervention in the hard-boiled genre, particu-larly in association with its class overtones. However, Paretsky's interventions are not only consciously feminist rewritings of the genre but also conscious generic writing. Paretsky admits to her feminist interpolation of the hard-boiled form, noting that "[w]hen I started writing, it was in conscious emulation of the private eye myth" (2007: 103). In her "conscious emulation," Paretsky not only follows the basic formula of Raymond Chandler's Philip Marlowe (2007: 103), but also acknowledges generic precursors through allusions to specific generic tropes and to other fictional detectives, even those outside the specific hard-boiled subgenre in which her series participates. Thus, Paretsky's important social commentaries can be understood both as a revision of the genre and through its revisions of the genre.

Paretsky and Gender (Performance)

The detective genre as a whole, and particularly the hard-boiled subgenre, has tradi-tionally been understood as a masculine genre, as highlighted in Raymond Chandler's definition of the hard-boiled detective in "The Simple Art of Murder" (1944):

> [D]own these streets a *man* must go who is not *himself* mean, who is neither tarnished nor afraid. The detective in this kind of story must be such a *man* ... The story is this *man*'s adventure in search of hidden truth, and it would be no adventure if it did not happen to a *man* fit for adventure. (Chandler 1995a: 991–2)

With this underlying formula, critics have debated women's ability to function as convincing hard-boiled detectives. Kathleen Gregory Klein suggests that:

When transferred straight from the male private eye to the female, the role fits poorly [and] establishes the conditions of her failure as either an investigator or a woman – or both. (1988: 162)

However, Klein regards Paretsky's V. I. Warshawski as one of the hard-boiled female detectives who excels at revealing the complications of translating gendered positions, showing that "[t]he tensions between the demands of the detective novel and the feminist ideology require a careful balancing act" (1988: 216).

Maureen Reddy agrees with Klein's argument, reading Warshawski as a key contributor to the feminist counter-tradition of the hard-boiled genre (1988: 2). In particular, Reddy notes that women tend to define themselves in term of relationships, "valuing affiliations with others over autonomy and perceiving relationships in terms of balancing needs and negotiating responsibilities in order to maintain the relationship" (1988: 10), as Warshawski does with what Reddy calls her "chosen family" (1988: 109). Warshawski's chosen family includes Dr Lottie Herschel, reporter Murray Ryerson, bartender Sal Barthol, neighbor Salvatore Contreras, and the other recurring characters who help her both physically and emotionally with her investigations. Though her "chosen family" dominates her social circle, Warshawski frequently solves cases for family members and Paretsky retains Warshawki's mother in the cohort through frequent dream interludes. In one dream, for instance, that Warshawski says often occurs in times of stress,

I'm trying to reach my mother behind the maze of equipment in which her final illness wrapped her, but the tubes keep sprouting and spreading like plant roots, knitting a plastic thicket that keeps me from her. (1994: 276)

Not only do such dreams allow Gabriella, Warshawski's mother, to remain a supportive force in her life, but they also show insight into the detective's emotional state, providing her with an interiority not common in the male versions of the hard-boiled genre.

Paretsky also uses these issues of family, as Reddy argues, to bring "feminist concerns from the edges of the texts to its center," (Reddy 1988: 12). For instance, when confronted with her alcoholic cousin Elena in *Burn Marks*, Warshawski states that "I did not have to be a Victorian angel and go sit with her. I didn't, I didn't, I didn't" (1990: 237) and in *Blacklist* (2003), she refuses to wait inactively like Homer's Penelope for her lover Morrell to return from Afghanistan. She also comments on the "he-men [who are] disgusted by talk of real women's real bodies" (2003: 204). These moments invoke and complicate traditional images of womanhood that, despite the women's movements in the 1960s and 70s, still seem to have mythic resonance in contemporary culture. While these moments clearly evoke Paretsky's feminist commentary in the series, ultimately, as Kenneth Paradis suggests, Warshawski's position as a woman enables her to behave as the hard-boiled detective and still engage with the balancing act that Klein and Reddy outline:

[w]hile Marlowe has to be an *extraordinary* individual to perceive the diffuse, endemic corruption ... one only has to be a *normal woman* to have an experience of corruption and injustice. (Paradis 2001: 91, emphasis in original).

In this respect, Warshawski's active participation in the hard-boiled genre preconditions her gendered social commentary, but Paretsky ensures active – rather than traditionally female passive – engagement.

However, Warshawski must also balance the roles of the classic (i.e. masculine) hard-boiled hero and the feminine roles that temper this performance. While Paula E. Johnson acknowledges the overt feminist rhetoric in the Warshawski series and critical acceptance of it, she also sees the detective as "imitat[ing] a male model almost to a tee" (1994: 97), even down to its deliberately performative features: "V. I. *enacts* the traditional hard-boiled detective's response" (1994: 104). Sally Munt revisits the notion of performativity in relation to femininity rather than masculinity. Noting "Warshawski's constant changes of dress" and preference for outfits that "are often silk and almost always are expensive", she suggests that "[t]he fetishization of clothes in Paretsky's work implies the 'draggish' imperative of femininity, signalling its artifice" (1994: 47). Paretsky is clearly aware of the performative nature of gender roles underscored in Johnson's and Munt's arguments. For instance, Warshawski says in *Bitter Medicine* that her responses come "with Sam Spade toughness" (1987: 90), associating toughness here with masculinity, as when she similarly claims that "[b]ecause I'm a woman in a man's business people think I'm tough" (1987: 56). As the adjectival form of "Sam Spade" and the verb "think" reveal, for Warshawski the masculine trait of "toughness" is a performance rather than an inherent characteristic. However, her portrayal of classic femininity is equally performative, as when she describes giving "my most ingratiating smile – Lauren Bacall trying to get Sam Spade to do her dirty work for her" (1993: 419). Warshawski's gendered behavior comes from appropriating various roles rather than exhibiting her own preferences. Despite her gender performances, Warshawski summarizes her view of her role in society with reference to social position, not gender: she is "just the garbage collector, cleaning up little trash piles here and there" (1987: 293).

Paretsky and Class

While stereotypical notions of class tend to imagine greater criminal activity in poorer, urban areas, the central locus of crime in the Warshawski series is in the upper classes, particularly in big business and Chicagoland suburbia. While the series does not deny the dangers of certain urban environments, the crimes that come from within these impoverished communities tend to be petty crimes, such as public intoxication and minor harassment. Conversely, in the 12 Warshawski novels published to date, the wealthy have always turned out to be the villains, using and disposing of the lower classes to aid their criminal enterprises. In this, Warshawski's version of the hard-boiled narrative does not differ significantly from those written by her main generic role model, Raymond Chandler, whose Philip Marlowe often uncovers how the rich exploit economic and political systems. However, while Chandler seems to employ the rich as villains to deplore the decay of patriarchal power structures, Paretsky uses this decadence to indicate the problems inherent in these structures (Walton and Jones 1999: 210). By tying critiques of patriarchal structures to wealthy corporate executives and politicians, Paretsky outlines power displacement not only between genders but also between classes.

Warshawski expresses the essence of Paretsky's social commentary when she responds in *Blacklist* (2003) to a rich client complaining that bad things often happen to good people:

> No one ever writes about all the good things that happen to bad people, like how the rich and powerful walk away from the messes they make, and people like me, like my neighbor, like my parents, pay for the clean up. (2003: 414)

Here Warshawski equates "bad people" with "rich and powerful," showing that, in Paretsky's books, rather than using the poor as a scapegoat for their problems, the rich become the goat sacrificed to restore the ideology of American egalitarianism. This ideology and ideal of egalitarianism allows Warshawski to combat the power of class differences. She asserts the democratic rights of all American citizens to equal recognition under the law. In *Tunnel Vision* she challenges a senator's assumption of authority over her when she says, "Hey, I'm a voter and a taxpayer. If he can say the same, we're equals" (1994: 422). Here, Warshawski not only asserts her equal status with the senator under American law, but also implies that his position is in fact inferior if he does not adhere to the laws of the country, by not paying his taxes, for instance. While these relationships are shaped by notions of class, class in the Warshawski series also appears as a further symptom of patriarchy. Thus, the corporate heads of the corrupt enterprises behind the criminal networks are not only rich members of the upper classes, but also predominantly men. Where women are the criminal masterminds, as in *Blacklist*, they instigate the crimes to protect men from the law.

Paretsky's social commentary appears not only in the plot structure, but also in Warshawski's first-person narrative style. In particular, her use of the traditional form of the hard-boiled "wise crack" identifies the inherent power inequality between the villains and the victims. Scott Christianson (1995) and others have carefully examined how feminist hard-boiled fiction seeks to appropriate the "wise crack" to allow women to talk back to the system, but in Paretsky's novels, these comments are not gender restrictive and often serve to undermine class differences created by power inequalities. For instance, when recovering from a concussion, Warshawski responds to a nurse's standard questions:

I told her [my name] and the date, and who the president was. If he got hit on the head they'd have to keep him for observation because he wouldn't know who I was. (1994: 263)

Warshawski's witty retort epitomizes the hard-boiled wisecrack, and in cracking wise she brings herself and the leader of the United States to the same level. Through Warshawski's witty language here, Paretsky underscores her commentary about class power disparity by recalling the supposed equality of all citizens according to American ideology.

Ultimately, criminality in relation to class in Paretsky's detective novels is summarized in Linda Wells's characterization of Warshawski as "willing to confront … ruthless power brokers" (1989: 53). As the term "power broker" suggests, the Warshawski series combats those who treat power as a commodity to be bought and sold rather than as something earned. Because the criminals treat power as something to be purchased, initially the power divides along American class lines – those defined by wealth. By inverting the standard middle-class fears of the lower classes, the Warshawski series redefines the problems that lead to criminality in terms of relations to power and to what enables empowerment.

Paretsky and Genre (Performance)

While presenting what Reddy calls the feminist counter-tradition in her hard-boiled narratives (1988: 2), Paretsky carefully responds to and embeds herself in the detective fiction tradition. She acknowledges that her first plot closely parallels that of Raymond first Philip Marlowe novel, *The Big Sleep* (1939), but she also explicitly signals how she responds to the genre in her frequent allusions to generic tropes and other generic icons from the hard-boiled and other schools. These allusions tend to take one of two forms: either comparing or contrasting Warshawski's behavior with that of her fictional counterparts. Because these allusions are not restricted to the hard-boiled tradition, Paretsky's novels can be understood to read and interpret the wider range of the Anglo-American detective tradition in general and Warshawski's place in it.

Warshawski as narrator establishes parallels through deliberate comparison and iconic allusions. For instance, in *Deadlock*, her detective methods force her down "on hands and knees, just like Sherlock Holmes" (1993: 485). Such descriptions as this invoke classic figures of detective fiction and classic detective fiction methods. By referring to these characters, Paretsky indicates her familiarity with generic expectations and situates herself within them. Though these moments articulate Paretsky's adherence to certain generic conventions, the self-conscious, ironic tone with which she makes these comparisons indicates the intentionality behind them and moderates Paretsky's social and generic critique. Paretsky further indicates her entrenchment in the detective genre at the end of *Tunnel Vision*, when she signals the novel as potentially the final one in the series – or at least a breaking point – by alluding to Arthur

Conan Doyle's (intended) method to dispose of Sherlock Holmes, of whom he had become weary: "lately I'd been studying travel brochures for Reichenbach Falls" (1994: 461). In Warshawski's considering a vacation in the location Doyle intended for Holmes's final resting spot, Paretsky aligns her predicament with Doyle's, an alignment reinforced by the fact that no Warshawski novels were published for five years after *Tunnel Vision*. Such allusions show that Paretsky not only uses generic markers to begin her series, but also uses generic precedent to contemplate its end.

While the comparisons between Warshawski and other detectives begin to indicate how Paretsky situates herself in relation to the larger tradition of fictional detective narrative, the contrasts better show her interventions into the genre. The effect is generally to humanize the genre by undermining the superhuman qualities of her fictional colleagues. With regard to the whodunit genre, Paretsky generally works to diminish the idea of the detective as a supremely intelligent being. She establishes her detective as intelligent, giving her two degrees from the highly ranked University of Chicago, but through her contrasts with the classic whodunit detectives, she under-cuts the fantastic superiority associated with the position of the detective protagonist. For instance, in *Bitter Medicine*, Murray Ryerson, a journalist who helps Warshawski with her investigations, says that "[i]f you're looking for Sherlock Holmes or Nero Wolfe doing some fancy intellectual footwork, forget it" (1987: 286). In this, Ryerson highlights the difference between Warshawski and the classic whodunit investigative methods, suggesting that Paretsky's detective does not base her investigations simply on the ratiocination that dominates the strand of detective fiction that stems from Edgar Allan Poe's Dupin stories. In some cases, Warshawski disparages herself in comparison with the whodunit detectives, as when she suggests that "[n]o doubt Gervase Fen or Peter Wimsey would immediately have grasped the vital clue reveal-ing the identity of the murderer" (1987: 47). While these moments present Warshawski as less phenomenally intelligent than her counterparts, they also make her appear more aware of her own limitations. Furthermore, such awareness and such limitations suggest that her intelligence is closer to that of her reader, who might also miss the importance of minutiae as clues at first reading. In this way, Paretsky creates a greater sympathetic understanding between her protagonist and her audience.

With regard to the hard-boiled genre, Paretsky tackles the toughness embedded in the form and undercuts it in the contrasts with Warshawski. For instance, when offered drinks, Warshawski frequently refuses, but her refusals always relate to the generic image of the hard-boiled detective as a drunkard:

> I opted for sherry – Mike Hammer is the only detective I know who can think and move while drinking whisky. Or at least move. Maybe Mike's secret is he doesn't try to think. (1993: 354).

In this moment, Warshawski not only indicates that she does not have an extraordi-nary alcohol tolerance, but also criticizes misogynistic forms of the hard-boiled text, as represented by Mickey Spillane's Mike Hammer, whose intellectual capabilities she clearly disparages. Warshawski also notes the contrasts between her behavior and hard-boiled conventions when she ironically observes that "[o]f course, a hard-boiled detective is never scared. So what I was feeling couldn't be fear" (1993: 703). In Reddy's feminist reading, "the detective mocks both herself and the hard-boiled tradition" (1988: 96), so her wider range of emotions than her 1930s counterparts challenges the conventional limitations of the genre. In such direct contrasts, Paretsky indicates that she directly intervenes in the hard-boiled conventions so that they are no longer necessarily dictated by the detective's bravado, again undermining the machismo that typically identifies the hard-boiled trope as indicative of a masculine genre.

With these overt indications of her responses to detective fiction's generic tropes, Paretsky signals that she deliberately manipulates the detective fiction genre to serve her social agenda. She counters the fantastic qualities of the form to highlight social problems related to inequalities in both gender and class. By showing the generic tropes to be incredible genre conventions, she implies that investigative methods restricted to the independent upper echelons of the wealthy classes or to the potent working-class male may conform to generic – and social – expectations, but they are not, for that reason, the only plausible version of the detective formula. In the feminist revisions that deliberately overturn class stereotypes, Paretsky intervenes in the classic forms of the detective genre to call attention to social inequalities through both the cases and the charisma of her hard-boiled detective, V. I. Warshawski.

44
Walter Mosley (1952–)

John Gruesser

For the black writer of any era, crime fiction presents at least two challenges. As a popular form with clearly recognizable conventions, detective and mystery writing would seem a restrictive vehicle for an African American author aspiring to do more than simply entertain readers by satisfying their expectations. Moreover, because the genre requires the detective to solve the crime or crimes and thereby restore the established order, the mystery is notoriously conservative. As a result, the question for black crime writers becomes how to preserve the integrity of their detectives. No matter how brilliant or brave they are, black sleuths in the pay of white clients or the white power structure risk coming off as lackeys. In short, African-American mystery writers must strike a difficult balance between genre conformity and genre subversion. Like other black authors dating back to the early 1900s, Walter Mosley (who initially failed to find a publisher for his non-mystery stories about heroic yet flawed African-American males) has turned to detective fiction as the means to make social, political, and moral statements that might not otherwise have found an audience (see Bailey, chapter 21 in this volume).

The Easy Rawlins Series

By setting his Easy Rawlins mystery series in the corrupt, violent, and ethnically diverse milieu of postwar Los Angeles, Mosley, who was born in that city in 1952 to a black World War II veteran father and a white Jewish mother, places his protagonist on the familiar turf of the hard-boiled detective. Like his white counterparts created by writers such as Raymond Chandler, Easy, short for Ezekiel, is tough, street smart, fiercely independent but vulnerable to the attractions and deceptions of women. Yet, like Rudolph Fisher's Perry Dart and John Archer and Chester Himes's Coffin Ed Johnson and Grave Digger Jones, Mosley's signifying detective, Easy Rawlins, operates in a distinctly black environment, having access to nightspots and organizations the police and white operatives cannot infiltrate. In the eleven Easy books that have been published to date – *Devil in a Blue Dress* (1990), *A Red Death* (1991), *White Butterfly* (1992), *Black Betty* (1994), *A Little Yellow Dog* (1996), *Gone Fishin'* (1997), *Bad Boy Brawly Brown* (2002), *Six Easy Pieces* (2003), *Little Scarlet* (2004), *Cinnamon Kiss* (2005), and *Blonde Faith* (2007) – which span the years 1939 through 1967, Mosley draws on African American folk culture and innovatively uses the mystery genre to illustrate the conflict between personal and racial freedom.

Although *Devil in a Blue Dress* adheres quite closely to the hard-boiled formula, it casts Easy as a black detective, adept at juggling linguistic and social codes to deceive and outwit both white and black characters. Easy lives, at least initially, in Watts, belonging to an extensive network of black Houstonians transplanted in Los Angeles and coming to regard his role as a sleuth as a matter of doing "[p]rivate investigations" for "[p]eople I know and people they know" (2002: 262) rather than a strict fee-for-services-rendered form of employment. In each installment of the series, Easy tells his own story in his idiosyncratic voice from a vantage point at a considerable temporal distance – internal evidence suggests the 1980s – from the events he describes. This enables Easy to reflect on how things (and he himself) have changed in the intervening years and thereby either overtly or subtly comment on the progress or lack thereof made by African-Americans in the last 40 years. Apart from his use of an African-American detective who operates in a black environment, Mosley remains remarkably faithful to hard-boiled crime writing. However, he uses the detective genre to depict how Easy's decision to become a private investigator complicates his relationship with his friends and the black community generally.

Comparing Easy to a prime example of the hard-boiled detective, such as Chandler's Philip Marlowe, reveals how closely Mosley adheres to the conventions of the tradition while infusing the white American detective story with distinctly black themes. Although tough-guy private eyes frequently disguise their actual intentions to achieve their goals, Easy deceives people and wears masks to an even greater extent than Marlowe and his cohorts. Because the hard-boiled hero operates in a world where appearance and reality seldom mesh, the detective, by definition a seeker of truth, is himself not always truthful in achieving this end. A hard-boiled sleuth such as Marlowe will normally identify himself and his profession; however, the seediness of his office and his lower middle-class standard of living can cause people to underestimate him, and he occasionally finds it expedient and prudent to disguise his true intentions when gathering information or pursuing a criminal. Nevertheless, the hard-boiled lifestyle and moral code perfectly suit a man like Marlowe. Easy, in contrast, adopts the role of a detective as more of a consciously chosen pose than an expression of his true nature. Not only in relation to whites but especially in his dealings with blacks, Easy acts in ways that link him to the trickster figures common in African American folk tradition.

In Mosley's 1948 Los Angeles, a black man does not acquire a detective's license and hang a shingle advertising his services as a private investigator. With no models on which to pattern himself, Easy must invent a detective persona that will work in his milieu. When DeWitt Albright, a veritable Moby Dick of murderous whiteness, surfaces in Joppy's bar asking Easy to do some investigative work for him, Easy knows he has sailed into deep, uncharted waters; nevertheless, the one hundred dollars Albright offers is too tempting for the recently unemployed Easy to refuse. Unlike Marlowe, to survive and succeed Easy must invent the means for dealing with not only Albright, and the corrupt, white power brokers who employ killers like him, but also the violent, oppressed black community in which he lives. The method Easy chooses is based on the well-established African-American strategy of signifying.

As Easy explains at the end of the second chapter of *Devil*, he can speak in two languages: "I always tried to speak proper English in my life, the kind of English they taught in school, but I found over the years that I could only truly express myself in the natural, 'uneducated' dialect of my upbringing" (2002: 54). This ability links him to the great trickster, the Signifying Monkey, a figure that, as Henry Louis Gates (1998) observes, dwells between the European-American and the African-American linguistic domains. In the many versions of the story of the Signifying Monkey, the mischievous Monkey persuades his friend the Lion that their friend the Elephant has insulted him. When the Lion seeks satisfaction from the innocent Elephant, he is soundly thrashed. The Lion returns to punish the Monkey but cannot reach him in the trees. Thus, through words alone the Monkey succeeds in diminishing the status of the King of Beasts.

Mosley may in fact be slyly alluding to the Signifying Monkey tales in the remarkable seventeenth chapter of *Devil* when Easy, in desperate straits, penetrates the facade of white power and respectability in search of answers and a means of changing the rules of a game that is rigged against him. Convinced that once Albright has what he wants he will kill him, Easy violates both the social and linguistic codes that segregate whites and blacks when he goes to a company significantly named Lion Investments in search of Maxim Baxter, whose card Albright has given him. Things come into clearer focus for Easy when a bronze plaque informs him that Todd Carter, Daphne Monet's former boyfriend and the person who has hired Albright to search for her, is the president of the firm. The rules of propriety dictate that a poor black man like Easy has no business entering the offices of Lion, much less demanding to speak to its senior officers. These rules also dictate that menials should never discuss the personal lives of the kingpins. Easy, however, has no intention of observing propriety. By exposing the hypocrisy of such niceties when people have been killed and more lives are on the line and by deftly switching from standard English to slang to black vernacular, he cuts through the layers of subordinates insulating the president and gains direct access to Carter, which proves crucial to his success and survival.

However, Easy's signifying does not occur exclusively or even primarily in his dealings with white people. What makes him a successful detective in Watts is his ability to exploit his southern roots and manners to gain information from people, often without their realizing his true objective. In an extended passage in Chapter 18 of *Devil*, Easy explicitly acknowledges his role playing in a description of his unsuccessful search through the shadiest places in Watts for the man he assumes is Daphne's current lover:

During the next day I went to the bars that Frank Green sold hijack to and to the alley crap games that he frequented. I never brought up Frank's name though. Frank was skitterish, like all gangsters, and if he felt that people were talking about him he got nervous; if Frank was nervous he might have killed me before I had time to make my pitch.

It was those two days more than any other time that made me a detective.

I felt a secret glee when I went into a bar and ordered a beer with money someone else had paid me. I'd ask the bartender his name and talk about anything, but, really, behind my friendly talk, I was working to find something. Nobody knew what I was up to and that made me sort of invisible; people thought they saw me but what they really saw was an illusion of me, something that wasn't real. (2002: 175)

Easy's ability to signify is his greatest asset as a detective. In a world where appearance rarely reflects reality, Easy creates masks for himself more consistently and consciously than his hard-boiled predecessors like Marlowe in order to deceive others and find the truth. Unlike Sadipe Okukenu, the protagonist of John Edward Bruce's *The Black Sleuth*, whose invisibility, which foreshadows that of the protagonist of Ralph Ellison's *Invisible Man*, is imposed by and limited to the white world in which he operates, Easy deliberately makes himself invisible in the black world as well as the white. In Pauline Hopkins's *Hagar's Daughter*, Venus Johnson dresses as a boy to uncover the place where her father, one of the villains, is hiding her kidnapped grandmother; Easy likewise disguises himself to fool people. However, where Venus's disguise is physical, Easy's is linguistic and rhetorical.

Although the active, autonomous life of a signifying private investigator provides Easy with a degree of freedom he has never experienced before, the role playing that it entails complicates his relationship with his friends and other members of the black community. The question for Easy comes to be whether he must live disengaged from his fellow blacks in segregated, postwar America in order to be a detective. Although *Devil* does not definitively provide an answer, it presents Easy with two major foils that help to clarify his position – one who for many years seems like he will never change and one whose compulsion to deceive others ensnares her. Easy's ambivalent relationship with his deadly old friend Raymond Alexander (aka Mouse) and his encounters with the *femme fatale* Daphne Monet underscore the tensions caused and the dangers posed by his new profession. In contrast to the static Mouse, who represents the past from which Easy tries to but can never quite escape, Easy has gone through many changes, having served in World War II, moved to Los Angeles, worked as a machinist, bought a house, and become a detective. Daphne, like Easy, disguises herself, but her role as a seductive white woman for white and black men imprisons rather than liberates her. Although he survives and even prospers at the end of *Devil*, subsequent novels will return to the question of whether Easy Rawlins the detective can maintain his friendships and remain engaged with the black community.

In *Devil's* final chapter, Easy remains troubled about the imperfect justice that has been meted out and the role he has played in effecting it. Sitting with his longtime friend Odell, Easy expresses his concern that because of him one killer, his old friend Mouse, will once again escape retribution while another will be punished:

"Odell?"

"Yeah, Easy."

"If you know a man is wrong. I mean, if you know he did somethin' bad but you don't turn him in to the law because he's your friend, do you think that's right?"

"All you got is your friends, Easy."

"But what if you know somebody else who did something wrong but not so bad as the first man, but you turn this other guy in."

"I guess you figure that other guy got ahold of some bad luck." (2002: 263)

Although the sustained laughter of the two men that follows suggests that Odell has mollified Easy's troubled conscience, Mosley will make sure that such moral dilemmas continue to confront Easy. Having lost Joppy and Dupree in solving the mystery in *Devil*, in the next novel, *A Red Death*, Easy will see his friendship with Odell evaporate because of his detective work. This leaves him with the one friend he feels the most ambivalent about, Mouse, a living reminder of Easy's past, a man whose words and actions in *Devil* deny the validity of Easy's efforts to better himself and lead the independent life of a signifying detective.

The Fearless Jones Series

Beginning with the short story "Fearless" (1995) and continuing through the novels *Fearless Jones* (2001), *Fear Itself* (2003), and *Fear of the Dark* (2006), Mosley has created a second set of detective stories that is both highly entertaining and socially and politically significant. On the surface, the Easy Rawlins and Fearless Jones series appear quite similar. Each takes place in postwar Los Angeles, each stresses white racism and police brutality, and each features a pair of starkly contrasting black male friends and transplanted Southerners who work together to solve mysteries and mete out their own brand of justice. Yet whereas the Rawlins series trades in moral ambiguity epitomized by the recurrent clash between personal and racial freedom, the Jones series frequently evokes classical myth to explore the permutations of black male friendship and heroism.

A committed bibliophile and an admitted coward, Paris Minton serves as the narrator of the Fearless Jones series, and thus his thoughts, actions, and particularly his fears dominate the stories. A man of great strength, boundless self-confidence, uncanny personal magnetism, and an unerring sense of right and wrong, Fearless Jones contrasts with but also complements the bookworm and puzzle-solver Minton. Their relationship begins in San Francisco when Paris buys the recently returned war hero Fearless a drink, mainly to get close to the women surrounding the bigger, more popular man. As recounted in "Fearless", when Paris is later harassed by two racist policemen and Fearless intervenes, the ensuing fight leaves the two white cops dead and Fearless badly injured. In 1949, three years after Paris nurses Fearless back to health and the latter relocates to Los Angeles, Fearless asks Paris to come down to his new town to help him out with a problem involving his girlfriend Deletha. After murder, mayhem, considerable anguish for Paris, and the duo's acquisition of a tidy sum of money – elements present in each installment in the series – Paris decides to stay in Los Angeles. By the time *Fearless Jones* opens in 1954, Paris, who vividly recalls being denied access to the local library as a child in Louisiana and explains that he came to California because the libraries there were open to everyone, has realized his dream of owning a bookstore.

A key difference between the Rawlins and Jones series is that whereas Easy chooses to be a detective because of the personal, and at times financial, freedom it affords him, Paris and Fearless are accidental or, as Mosley has described them "amateur sleuths," solving mysteries to save themselves or because of a sense of duty they feel to others. It is significant that Paris, unlike Easy, never refers to himself as a detective, and when Whisper Natly, Watts's only bona fide black private eye, suggests a partnership between himself and Paris in *Fear of the Dark*, set in 1956, Paris refuses the offer. Moreover, unlike the amoral and anachronistic Mouse who causes moral dilemmas for Easy, Fearless, with his "smart heart," counterbalances Paris and his "smart head." After what happened in Pariah, Texas in 1939 (as described in *Gone Fishin'*), Easy has profound reservations about Mouse, fleeing from him, first to the war and then to Los Angeles. Yet when he embarks on his career as a detective, Easy needs Mouse at times for his firepower and deadly reputation, although he insists on calling the shots himself. Paris, however, has no qualms about Fearless, even though the latter is often in a jam and Paris worries about the consequences of the promises that his friend makes. Significantly, *Fearless Jones*, like *Devil in a Blue Dress*, ends with a reference to friendship. However, whereas the tension between Easy's newfound profession and his relationships with his fellow African-Americans troubles him at the end of *Devil* (and will continue to do so), Paris has absolutely no misgivings about Fearless, as seen in the final paragraph: "He hasn't gotten in any trouble, and I'm hoping that he doesn't. But I know that if he does, I'll have to help him, because Fearless is my friend" (2002: 312).

Paris and Fearless enjoy a more equal partnership than Easy and Mouse do. Although Mosley never uses the term, Mouse has been described as Easy's "sidekick." Fearless, however, cannot be seen this way, and, despite the fact that Paris's voice and actions dominate the series, Paris sees himself as playing the secondary role. Certainly Fearless's self-assurance links him to Mouse; moreover, like Mouse, who lacks the morals with which Easy wrestles, Fearless experiences none of the trepidation that Paris so palpably feels, readily acknowledges, and vividly describes. However, there is much more to Fearless than this, as Paris repeatedly points out and Mosley underscores by connecting the titles of the stories to him rather than Paris. In each of the novels, once Paris has finally figured out the mystery, Fearless, with his unerring moral compass, makes the right choices and saves Paris from his baser instincts. In *Fear Itself*, set in 1955, Paris discovers a priceless diary that has been written by members of and passed down within an African-American family since the beginning of the eighteenth century. Initially he wants it only for his own intellectual gratification; however, once he learns that it may be worth $100,000, he itches to sell it. Fearless brilliantly finesses the situation by borrowing photographic equipment from Jackson Blue (one of a handful of characters who are mentioned in both the Rawlins and Jones series) to photograph the book before he returns this remarkable treasure to the family that produced and rightfully owns it so that Paris will have access to its contents.

Allusions to myth pervade Mosley's second detective series. Not only does Fearless's nickname function as a Homeric epithet but his real first name, Tristan, links him to medieval romance and the Knights of the Round Table, a connection underscored by Paris's reference to his friend as "the Lancelot of South L.A." Meanwhile, like his namesake who abducted Helen of Argos, Paris, without thinking of the consequences, frequently succumbs to the attractions of women who are involved with other men. *Fear of the Dark*, in particular, teems with references to myth and literature. The plot turns on Paris and Fearless's search for the former's cousin, Ulysses S. Grant IV (otherwise known as Useless), one of whose fellow extortionists is named Hector. Moreover, early in the book Paris reads James Joyce's *Ulysses* and later recites from memory the first book of *The Odyssey*.

Mosley himself has aptly stated, "Fearless is one of those old kind of heroes like Achilles, and Paris is more like Ulysses" (Mudge 2001). A war hero, Fearless is all about honor, like Achilles, but he comes off as much more likeable than the *Iliad's* protagonist. Although Paris lacks Odysseus's swagger, he has his cunning, ability to lie, and instinct for self-preservation. Moreover, Paris is often in trouble (which is one of the ways that Odysseus's name has been translated), remarking in "Fearless", "I remember thinking that I owed Fearless something – and that trouble was my only currency" (1995: 150). In addition, despite acknowledging how afraid he is all the time and criticizing himself for cowardice, Paris acts courageously on many occasions, physically confronting stronger men and bluffing his way through encounters with powerful people by means of assumed identities and prepared or spur-of-the moment lies. Fearless, in fact, regards Paris as the braver man because he takes great personal risks despite his fears while Fearless, as his name suggests, never feels threatened by anything.

Mosley does not see myth merely as something African-Americans can read about and make reference to but rather as something they can create and embody. Paris says of Fearless in *Fear Itself*, "He was like some mythical deity that had come down to earth to learn about mortals. Maybe that's why I stayed friends with him even though he was always in trouble. Because being friends with him was like having one of God's second cousins as a pal" (2003: 102). In connection with a confrontation with Bubba Lateman, a huge man who owns a parking lot guarded by vicious dogs, Paris remarks in *Fear of the Dark*,

"*Bulfinch's Mythology* came to me then. It seemed to me that this tableau belonged in those pages. Fearless was the hero, I was the hero's companion, Useless was the mischievous trickster, and Bubba was the ogre or giant. We were playing out roles in a history that went back before anyone could remember. The river Styx might have lain to our left, and this was just a step in our journey" (2006: 283).

Through such memorable descriptions, Mosley, a black Jewish writer well versed in the Western literary tradition, depicts his 1950s African-American characters as legendary figures.

Had Walter Mosley only written the Easy Rawlins series, with its signifying protagonist and emphasis on the tensions between personal and racial freedom, he would have indelibly left his mark on crime fiction. With the creation of the Fearless Jones series, which highlights black male friendship and connects his characters to classical myth, Mosley has added to his stature as one of the most significant late twentieth- and early twenty-first-century authors of detective and mystery writing.

Film

45

Alfred Hitchcock (1899–1980)

Nick Haeffner

While Alfred Hitchcock's films have featured many forms of crime including robbery, smuggling, kidnapping, espionage, and fraud, their recurrent crime motif is undoubtedly murder. Indeed, it did not take long for Hitchcock to become so identified with murder that he famously said, "if I was making Cinderella, everyone would look for the corpse" (Gottlieb 1995: 145). In a letter to François Truffaut, Hitchcock complained of the way in which audiences had imprisoned him in the crime genre and expressed envy at the Frenchman's relative freedom in this regard: "How lucky you are not to be categorized and stamped as I am, for this is the root of my difficulties in acquiring a good subject, especially in respect to acceptance by audiences" (in Truffaut 1986: 513).

A distinctive blend of humor, romance, suspense, and aestheticism defines the singularity of Hitchcock's approach to crime, with humor often strongly associated with his treatment of murder. Of his most famous film, Hitchcock himself said: "[T]o me, *Psycho* was a big comedy. Had to be" (Gottlieb 2003: 107).

Hitchcock's approach to crime fiction, including his celebrated sense of humor, originated in England. On several occasions he expressed his view that the link between crime and art, or at least aesthetics, was deeply rooted in English culture:

> Crime is much more literate in England than in America. In England, unlike America, crime novels are first rate literature. Not only are the English more attracted by crime, but the crimes themselves are more bizarre. (Gottlieb 2003: 138)

When the interviewer Charles Samuels asked Hitchcock, "What do you think differentiates the British interest in crime from the American?" Hitchcock replied: "The British interest is aesthetic" (ibid.).

Similarly, Hitchcock tells Arthur Knight:

> Go back as far as you like, right up to the present day, crime has always interested the English litterateurs. They write books on the most recent *cause célèbre* and it's always taken seriously. ... I follow in that tradition." (Gottlieb 2003: 167)

Hitchcock was, however, not only interested in crime fiction as literature. He was also keenly aware of the circumstances surrounding real life crime and criminals of his own day. For example, he was intrigued by the Crippen case, a notorious instance of serial killing, and his interest in it was characteristically filtered through the culture industry, mediated by Ernest Raymond's novelization of the event, *We the Accused*. The Crippen case is mentioned in *The 39 Steps* (1935) when a member of a music hall audience asks Mr Memory "when was Crippen hanged?"

In his youth, Hitchcock had been a regular visitor to the Old Bailey in London where he was an avid spectator at murder trials. In a courtroom, justice frequently depends on small details, considered by others to be trifling. The jury, however, is easily swayed by compelling stories, told by barristers or witnesses, which may not be true, but which have considerable power to manipulate the public. Neither lesson was lost on Hitchcock's filmmaking, with its obsessive eye for detail and ability to take in the audience with a well-crafted tale. His experience of formal justice in action also helped to persuade the director that the law was by no means coterminous with the good (one of many points of convergence with the worldview of Dickens to be found in Hitchcock's work). Hitchcock soaked up many highly detailed accounts of murder cases, which he drew on throughout his career. When interviewed in later life by Huw Weldon he was asked: "Is it true you are yourself a great expert on crime?" Hitchcock replied:

> I suppose one has at one's fingertips all the details of the famous cases of the past. For example, in the film *Rear Window* there are two passages in it which come from famous English crimes. The Crippen case – I used a bit of that; and the Patrick Mahon case – a man who killed a girl and then cut her up into pieces and threw the flesh out of the window of a train. But his great problem was what to do with the head, and that's what I put in, in *Rear Window*, with the dog sniffing the flowerbed. (Gottlieb 2003: 71)

When asked about his film *Frenzy* (1972), which marked a return to the London street markets of his youth, Hitchcock drew on his memories of Crippen once again: "A man who is impotent and only gets satisfaction out of killing. You have the prime example of the Crippen case – he killed eight women and buried them all over the house" (in Gottlieb 2003: 108).

Another real life influence on *Frenzy* was the serial killer Reginald Christie who was executed in 1953 after having been found guilty of murdering his wife, his mistress, a neighbor and her baby and prostitutes. Several of the bodies were found buried in the garden and cellar of Christie's house. What particularly fascinated Hitchcock was the sexual aspect of the killings (Hitchcock believed, evidently correctly, that audiences would share his interest in sexual perversions of all kinds): "The amazing thing about the case is that Christie was a necrophile. In other words, he killed women to get sexual satisfaction. I remember reading the transcript of the trial" (Gottlieb 2003: 108). The case crops up in the film as two well-dressed gentlemen, discussing the work of a rapist and serial killer, note that England has not had a juicy sex murderer since Christie, adding with heavy irony that "tourists expect the streets to be wreathed with fog and littered with ripped whores."

Hitchcock had a less well-known preoccupation with Adelaide Bartlett, who was accused of the murder of her husband by chloroform poisoning in 1886. Bartlett had struck up an unconventional relationship with a clergyman named George Dyson. Adelaide's husband Thomas appears to have known that the relationship was more than platonic but, at the same time, encouraged it. Hitchcock's plans to film the story were never realized but elements of it found their way into *I Confess* (1953). Hitchcock's detailed account of Thomas Bartlett's slow demise also echoes the long, lingering poisoning of Alicia Huberman in *Notorious* (1946), with its domestic setting and perverse, triangular relationship based on a loveless marriage (Hitchcock 1953).

Hitchcock's English Films

What Hitchcock seems to have learned from the case of Jack the Ripper may provide the most important clues to the development of his later preoccupations. Hitchcock's first serial killer story based on the Ripper, *The Lodger* (1926), drew on the successful West End play of the same name by Marie Belloc-Lowndes. As she explains,

> The story of *The Lodger* was written by me as a short story after I heard a man telling a woman at a dinner party that his mother had a butler and a cook who married and kept lodgers. They were convinced that Jack the Ripper had spent a night under their roof. (Belloc-Lowndes 1971: 97)

The sense of a story being relayed through a series of Chinese whispers (Belloc-Lowndes overhearing a man tell a woman about something his servants had told him about), is carried over into the film, where it is *talk about* the killings, relayed from one person to another (with the help of modern mass communications) which causes the fear, rather than the mere fact of the killings themselves. As Allen (2002) notes, the representation of the murders in the popular press at the time was particularly important. Indeed, Hitchcock himself devotes an extended sequence near the start of *The Lodger* to the process by which the press and radio report one of the killings in the story.

As Rothman observes,

> In one of the most remarkable sequences of the film, Hitchcock dissolves from a radio announcer reading the story of the murder to one solitary listener after another: a man who rolls his eyes, an angry woman who yowls like a cat, a man who listens taut with excitement, a woman so aroused that she runs her tongue sensually over her lips. (Rothman 1982: 10)

The fecundity of the Ripper case as a basis for compelling storytelling has prompted at least one scholar to see it as a kind of cultural engine, producing endless narratives: "we can see Jack the Ripper not just as a killing machine but as a narrative machine that can only produce more versions, more stories" (Warwick 2007: 85). In Hitchcock's case, the persona adopted by the Ripper himself in his letters to the police seems to have a peculiar congruence with the elements of the Hitchcockian thriller since, as Bloom notes,

> The ripper letters are a form of true life confession heightened to the level of a fiction which embraces a cockney persona, a sense of black humour, a melodramatic villain and a ghoul and mixes it with a sense of the dramatic and a feeling for a rhetorical climax. (2007: 95)

The Lodger is also one of many of Hitchcock's English films notable for the homely settings of their murders. Among the most well-known examples is *Blackmail* (1929), where a young woman, Alice White (Anny Ondra), is lured to the flat of an artist who then attempts to rape her. Alice kills the man with a bread knife in self-defense and wanders the streets of London in a guilt-ridden daze, seeing images all around her that remind her of the stabbing. The film is notable for its use of subjective vision and hearing, taking us into the mind of a woman who has killed and revealing a perception of reality heightened and distorted by the emotional experiences that she undergoes.

Murder! (1930) also contains images of a woman in trance, this time accused of a murder she did not commit. The murderer is finally revealed as a "half-caste," an ambiguous term which appears to be a euphemism in the film for homosexual. Handel Fane (Esme Percy) is one of a number of killers coded as gay in Hitchcock's work. Much critical discussion has been generated by Hitchcock's preoccupation with apparently homosexual murderers, among the most important contributions being Robin Wood's (1992) essay on the topic. *Murder!* also contains a formally experimental trial sequence which highlights Hitchcock's skeptical view of the law and the criminal justice system.

Sabotage (1936), based on Joseph Conrad's *The Secret Agent,* contains an instance of a woman who murders at home using a kitchen knife. In this case, it is Winnie Verloc (Sylvia Sidney) who can no longer contain her rage and anguish at the discovery that her husband (Oscar Homolka) is working for terrorists and has been responsible for the accidental death of her brother Stevie (Desmond Tester). As with *Psycho* (1960) some years later, Hitchcock filmed the murder sequence as a montage of very short close-ups and edited them together to achieve an effect of rare intimacy and intensity.

Sabotage is one of several of Hitchcock's English films that bear comparison with the work of Fritz Lang (Sylvia Sidney had also worked on the latter's *Fury* [1936]). However, while Hitchcock was undoubtedly influenced by Lang's fusion of crime and the everyday as exemplified in films such as *M* (1931), he does not share the latter's interest in organized crime or crime as a social system, interests most apparent in Lang's *Dr Mabuse* films. In addition, by the time he got to America, Hitchcock had become the model for Lang to imitate (see Gunning 2000).

Hitchcock's American films deal much more consistently with crime, especially murder, than does his British output. It's easy to lose sight of the fact that it took many years before Hitchcock became "Hitchcock" and that before emigrating to the US he had directed 24 feature films which included a melodrama (*The Manxman*, 1929), a musical biopic of Johann Strauss (*Waltzes from Vienna*, 1933), a gentle romance (*The Farmer's Wife*, 1928) and a boxing film (*The Ring*, 1927).

The critic Charles Barr (1999) has described the six British films beginning with *The Man Who Knew too Much* (1934) and concluding with *The Lady Vanishes* (1938) as Hitchcock's "thriller sextet," arguing that it is with this cycle of films that the director finally realizes his true vocation as a crime thriller director after a long period of experimenting with different genres.

Hitchcock in Hollywood

Donald Spoto, in his 1988 biography *Alfred Hitchcock: The Dark Side of Genius*, goes farther than this, arguing that Hitchcock grew ever bolder in his project to realize his personal murderous feelings towards women on celluloid, culminating in the brutal rape and murder of Brenda Blaney in *Frenzy*. In this teleological view, Hitchcock gradually moved towards the realization of an inner essence and the indulgence of a personal obsession with murder throughout the American films, with one, perhaps minor exception, the romantic comedy *Mr and Mrs Smith* (1941).

However, Hitchcock's association with the crime thriller may have been as much a millstone around the neck of a much more versatile and complex director as an expression of his personal preferences. Certainly, the Hollywood film industry regarded Hitchcock first and foremost as a highly accomplished and professional director for hire. After all, if history had turned out a little differently, Hitchcock's American debut under producer David O. Selznick would have been *Titanic*, not *Rebecca* (1940). Among the other films he might have made are such incongruous projects as *Hamlet* (starring Cary Grant), *Intermezzo, Mein Kampf, Letter from an Unknown Woman, How Green Was my Valley, The Lost Weekend, Les Miserables* and *Treasure Island*. Hitchcock was reportedly also approached to finish directing *Cleopatra* (Gottlieb 2004: 89).

It is also easy to overlook the fact that Hitchcock proved himself a very accomplished director of romantic comedy. Lesley Brill (1988) has argued that Hitchcock's films are primarily concerned not with murder but with romance: "the great majority of Hitchcock's films have elements of both romance and irony, with outcomes that usually favour romance" (1988: 200). Richard Allen (2008) links the films to the German idealist tradition of Romantic irony. The films frequently deal with love and romance in all its forms, both "normal" and "pathological," although, like Freud, Hitchcock seems not to have observed a clear-cut distinction between the two.

Certainly, there is an unstable movement between romantic love (supposedly "normal") and murder (pathological) in much of Hitchcock's work. In this context it is worth recalling Truffaut's celebrated observation that in Hitchcock's films "the love scenes were filmed like murder scenes, and the murder scenes like love scenes" (1969: 533). This observation is perhaps most memorably illustrated in *Strangers on a Train* (1950), where the killer stalks his prey through the tenebrous Tunnel of Love and strangles her on Love Island, filmed in the reflection of her fallen, cracked glasses, one of the director's most disturbingly beautiful cinematic moments.

The lengths to which Hitchcock went to in order to achieve these lovingly created murders have been well documented in interviews with the director. For *Strangers on a Train*, Hitchcock explains,

> We took a large concave mirror and photographed the murder scene in it. Next, we photographed the glasses as they lay on the grass. Then the image filmed in the concave mirror was diminished and printed into the frames of the glasses. (In Gottlieb 2003: 36)

The idea that murder naturally lends itself to theatrical (sometimes operatic and spectacular) treatment was not invented by Hitchcock, of course. It goes back at least as far as Aristotle's *Poetics*, and received its modern and perhaps most eloquent justification in Thomas De Quincey's *On Murder Considered as One of the Fine Arts* (1827), where the author praises the aestheticization of killing as an art readily appreciated by the public:

> People begin to see that something more goes toward the composition of a fine murder than two blockheads to kill and be killed, a knife, purse and a dark lane. Design, gentlemen: grouping, light and shade, poetry, sentiment, are now deemed indispensable attempts of this nature. (2006: 10)

The murder of Juanita de Cordoba (Karin Dor) in *Topaz* (1969) was another occasion for Hitchcock to demonstrate how much he had learned from De Quincey's precepts. In the film, Juanita de Cordoba is a Cuban resistance fighter whose treachery is exposed by a Cuban official, Rico Parra (John Vernon). As Hitchcock explains, the operatic staging of her death was both elaborate and highly aestheticized:

> I had attached to Karen Dor's dress five cotton threads that were controlled by five men placed out of the camera range. At the moment when she collapsed, the men drew the strings and the dress spread like a flower that was opening. It was a counterpoint. Even though it depicted a death, I wanted it very beautiful. (In Gottlieb 2003: 125)

But the most De Quincean film in Hitchcock's oeuvre is surely *Rope* (1948), in which two college students strangle a fellow student, David Kentley (Dick Hogan), for kicks and conceal his body in a trunk that then forms the centerpiece of a theatrically staged dinner party to which David's parents are invited.

Rope is one of a number of Hitchcock's films from the 1940s which, rather than simply condemning fascism, also explore its allure. Perhaps the most extreme example of this tendency in Hitchcock's work would be the position pieces put in the mouth of Uncle Charlie (Joseph Cotton) in *Shadow of a Doubt* (1943), whose dinner table conversation includes the following speech:

> The cities are full of women, middle-aged widows, husbands dead, husbands who've spent their lives making fortunes, working and working. And then they die and leave their money to their wives, their silly wives. And what do the wives do, these useless women? You see them in the hotels, the best hotels, every day by the thousands, drinking the money, eating the money, losing the money at bridge, playing all day and all night, smelling of money, proud of their jewelry but of nothing else, horrible, faded, fat, greedy women. ... Are they human or are they fat, wheezing animals, hmm? And what happens to animals when they get too fat and too old?

When his niece protests to her uncle that elderly widows who live complacent lives on their husband's money "are alive, they're still human beings," he turns full face, in big close up, to the camera and asks, "are they?" This chilling question, addressed effectively to the audience, is simply left hanging.

Such subversive amorality is a defining feature of a style of filmmaking with which Hitchcock has often been linked: film noir (see Silver and Ursini, chapter 4 in this volume). Clearly, many of Hitchcock's films (most obviously, perhaps, *Strangers on a Train* [1951]) share features in common with film noir, such as the use of shadows, graphic composition within the film frame, subjective shots and characters who exhibit perverse sexuality (Figure 45.1). In their classic *Film Noir: An Encyclopaedic Reference to the American Style* (1996), Silver and Ward list only *Notorious, Shadow of a Doubt, Strangers on a Train* and *The Wrong Man* (1957) as Hitchcockian examples. However, other Hitchcock films that have been cited as noir include *Rebecca* (1940), *Suspicion* (1941), *Rope* (1948) and *Vertigo* (1958) and *North by Northwest* (1959) (Brion 1992; Borde and Chaumeton 1955). There are direct links between some Hitchcock films and the literary tradition of hard-boiled crime fiction upon which film noir was based. For example, Hitchcock offered the job of directing *Strangers on a Train* first to Dashiell Hammett and then to Raymond Chandler. *Rear Window* (1954) and the television film *Three O'Clock* (1951) are both based on short stories by Cornell Woolrich.

However, as Naremore argues, there are at least four elements which distinguish Hitchcock's American films from the mainstream of film noir. The first is Britishness: "most of his films took place in a prosperous, virtually all-white milieu that was characterized, at least outwardly, by a feeling of whimsy, sophistication and good manners – in other words, by qualities that the typical American associated with upper-class Britishness" (Naremore 1999: 267). Unlike a number of noir classics set in a seedy underworld, "his American work seldom bears the marks of poverty" (Naremore 1999: 270). Secondly, Naremore points out that Hitchcock's work, unlike classic noir, prefers clarity to disorientation. "Hitchcock's images are composed with the directness and simplicity of a storyboard or cartoon, and their sequential organisation is intended to lead the audience step by step through the action." Thirdly,

Figure 45.1   Strangers on a Train (1951, directed and produced by Alfred Hitchcock) shared
such features with film noir as the use of shadows, graphic composition within the film frame
and subjective shots and characters who exhibit perverse sexuality.

Hitchcock's films deal with material considered "feminine": "he was a practitioner of
the female Gothic – a director who, in collaboration with Selznick, specialised in
glossy, romantic, 'women's pictures'" (1999: 271–2).

Finally, Hitchcock's films return again and again to nostalgia for a lost nineteenth-
century world, often through villains such as Uncle Charlie in *Shadow of a Doubt* and
Gavin Elster in *Vertigo*. The seductive but dangerous charms of the old world are
contrasted with the brash modernity of American life, as in *Psycho*, where the sleek
modern design of the Bates motel is set against the towering gingerbread Gothic of
the Bates mansion, home of Hitchcock's most terrifying murderer, "Mrs Bates." The
scene in the film where Lila Crane (Vera Miles) searches the bedroom of Mrs Bates
and encounters a perfectly preserved world of Victoriana is among the most creepy in
the film. Among other examples not mentioned by Naremore we could also include
Rope's Brandon, Phillip and Rupert with their fascination for Nietzsche's nineteenth-
century aristocratic philosophy of the *Übermensch* as an antidote to the democratic,
leveling tendencies of modernity, and the Nazis in *Notorious*, still living out a fantasy
of old world gracious living while hiding out in 1940s Rio.

However, the new world fares little better in Hitchcock's pessimistic outlook. Modern American living comes under the director's critical gaze in *Shadow of a Doubt*, *Strangers on a Train*, *Rear Window*, *North by Northwest* and *The Birds* (1963), but perhaps even more so in Hitchcock's work for television, where the crime story meets Hitchcock's sense of humor at its most biting. Hitchcock frequently complained that his American films had not given him the opportunity to exercise his sense of humor sufficiently. The constraints placed on him in this regard have been well documented in his comments about working on *Rebecca* (1940) with producer David O. Selznick. Hitchcock cited *Shadow of a Doubt* as one of the few American films to capture the particular blend of humor and suspense that he required. *The Trouble with Harry* (1955), a black comedy concerning a corpse which is repeatedly disinterred, was conceived, in part, as a vehicle for Hitchcock's darkly comic sensibility and to prove that American audiences could respond to his particularly English preoccupation with irony.

Hitchcock on Television

The experiment helped to pave the way for *Alfred Hitchcock Presents*, a half-hour television series which was first broadcast on CBS (1955–60), then NBC (1960–2) after which the episodes were increased in length and the show ran as *The Alfred Hitchcock Hour* (1962–5). Hitchcock himself directed only 17 of the 268 episodes of *Alfred Hitchcock Presents* and only one episode ("I Saw the Whole Thing" [1962]) out of 93 from *The Alfred Hitchcock Hour*. The show was effectively a business venture for Hitchcock who franchised out the directing to a number of different individuals. The selection of the stories, even those directed by Hitchcock himself, was the job of Joan Harrison, with the director merely approving or rejecting synopses prepared for him. It has been suggested by Leitch that "a disinterested observer would be hard pressed to find any sign of any Hitchcock touch either thematic or technical, that distinguished the seventeen episodes of *Alfred Hitchcock Presents* directed by the master of suspense from the 251 that were not" (1999: 60).

However, close examination of the Hitchcock-directed episodes reveals some evidence of thematic continuity with the feature films and there are occasional stylistic flourishes which hint at the director's presence. For instance, in "Banquo's Chair" (1959) there is an extreme close-up of a character's face turning from profile to full face, a "bird's eye view" of a dinner table shot from the ceiling and a long shot of a character walking into close-up (much as Madam Sebastian does to make her entrance in *Notorious*). In these ways, Hitchcock could be said to have left his cinematic signature. Although ostensibly dedicated to crime stories, the series contains a number of episodes in which no crime is actually committed, e.g. "Poison" (1958), "Breakdown" (1955), "Mr Blanchard's Secret" (1956), "The Crystal Trench" (1959), "Dip in the Pool" (1958), "Bang! You're Dead" (1961), "The Case of Mr Pelham" (1955), and "The Horseplayer" (1961). Nevertheless, episodes such as "Revenge" (1955), "Arthur",

"Wet Saturday" (1956), "Banquo's Chair" (1959), "Lamb to the Slaughter" (1958) and "Back for Christmas" (1956) are excellent examples of Hitchcock's famous comment that "television has brought murder back into the home – where it belongs" (Gottlieb 1995: 58).

"Wet Saturday" provides a good example of a homely domestic setting for a murder story. Millicent (Tita Purdom), the splendidly dotty daughter in an eccentric English family, dispatches a teacher on whom she had a crush. Her father (Sir Cedric Hardwicke) then sets about heartlessly incriminating a friend of the family by planting his fingerprints on the murder weapon and samples of his hair at the scene of the crime. The father threatens to shoot the family friend if he fails to co-operate with their scheme, while the doltish son takes great delight in roughing up the fall guy to make it appear that he has been in a fight with the murder victim.

Hitchcock seems to take considerable pleasure in revealing the ruthless and brutal nastiness of this apparently respectable upper middle-class English family. Even the kindly mother seems to take in her stride the whole plan to frame the family friend for murder. But Hitchcock is only playing true to form in his treatment of so-called civilized bourgeois families. In *The 39 Steps*, for instance, Richard Hannay believes himself delivered from his pursuers at the well-to-do home of a prominent justice of the peace. The judge's wife walks into the drawing room just as his host reveals that he is a foreign spy and pulls a gun on Hannay. Seeing the gun, the wife asks politely whether Mr Hannay will be staying for dinner. "I don't think so," replies the husband, at which the wife retires graciously, leaving her husband to shoot the hapless Hannay.

The theme of eating and murder developed in feature films such as *Rope* and *Frenzy* is carried over into the Hitchcock-directed TV specials. In the aforementioned "Wet Saturday," Millicent alternately sobs because she has murdered someone and eats sandwiches compulsively, leading her father to admonish, "I will not compete for your attention with a sandwich." In "Arthur," the urbane protagonist (Laurence Harvey) confesses that he is a murderer as he takes a lovingly prepared roast chicken out of the oven. It transpires that he has turned his fiancée into chicken feed in order to dispose of her strangled corpse. "Banquo's Chair" takes its inspiration from the "play within a play" in *Hamlet* as a murderer is led to confess his guilt during a staged performance which takes place over a pheasant supper.

But no consideration of the commingling of murder and eating in Hitchcock would be complete without mention of "Lamb to the Slaughter." Based on a story written by Roald Dahl (who also contributed the stories for "Dip in the Pool", "Poison", "Mrs Bixby and the Colonel's Coat" [1960] "Man from the South" [1960] and "The Landlady" [1961]), "Lamb to the Slaughter" tells of a man who returns home from work to deliver the crushing news to his pregnant wife that he is leaving her for another woman. His wife Mary (Barbara Bel Geddes), clubs him to death in a semi-trance with a large frozen leg of lamb. She then fakes a crime scene and calls the police to report a murder. On arrival, the police are mystified at their inability to find a murder weapon. Mary serves up the cooked leg of lamb to the police and, in another room laughs to herself as one of the officers suggests that the murder weapon must be "under our very noses." What makes the drama affecting and slightly disturbing is Bel Geddes's performance, which manages to suggest that Mary's actions are motivated by trauma and a kind of surrealist *amour fou* as well as revenge.

"Lamb to the Slaughter" exemplifies De Quincey's approach to crime, which prized erudition, outrage, irony, and extremity, combining urbanity and elitism with what he described as "a spirit of jovial and headlong gaiety" (2006: xiii). Charles Dickens, in a passage from *Great Expectations*, shows how influential De Quincey's style had become and at the same time demonstrates the phenomenon, frequently exploited by Hitchcock, whereby the audience might be led to identify with both victim and perpetrator. Dickens writes:

> A highly popular murder had been committed and Mr Wopsle was imbrued in blood to the eyebrows. He gloated over every abhorrent adjective in the description, and identified with every witness at the inquest. He faintly moaned "I am done for", as the victim, and he barbarously bellowed, "I'll serve you out", as the murderer. ... He enjoyed himself thoroughly, and we all enjoyed ourselves and were delightfully comfortable. (Quoted in De Quincey 2006: xxvi)

The tone of irony in this style of writing finds its fullest expression in the memorable introductions and epilogues provided for *Alfred Hitchcock Presents* and *The Alfred Hitchcock Hour*, scripted by James Allardice. As Olsson notes:

> The encounter between Allardice's tongue-in-cheek scripts and Hitchcock's peerless delivery proved to be a perfect fit. Even outside the shows, Allardice contributed to many of Hitchcock's public performances and scripted trailers featuring Hitchcock, including those for *North by Northwest*, *Psycho* and *The Birds*, up until the writer's death shortly after the end of the television run. (Olsson 2007: 66)

As the show's stories often ended with virtue unrewarded and villains left unpunished, leaving the network's censors appalled, the epilogues provided by Hitchcock were used to supply perfunctory and sometimes completely implausible resolutions wherein the perpetrators of crime received their just deserts. Such adjuncts were transparently only there to appease the censor, their ridiculousness only serving to make more of a mockery of the rules.

The studied amorality of Hitchcock's persona in the introductions and epilogues led to an even greater emphasis on the macabre, the jokey and the perverse than was outwardly evident in the feature films. Instead, the television output is perhaps best approached as a further example of Hitchcock the pragmatist at work, exploiting different, and not necessarily consistent, aspects of himself to further his career. In the mind of the public, however, the many Hitchcocks that co-existed inside that ample frame are associated with a single concept: murder. While Hitchcock's films have featured many forms of crime, including robbery, smuggling, kidnapping, espionage and fraud, he appears strikingly uninterested in such transgressions. Recently,

Hitchcock Blonde, a successful theatre production about a lost Hitchcock film from the 1920s, which turns out to be a home movie of the director strangling one of his leading ladies, once again reinforced the perception that Hitchcock had a monomaniacal obsession with murder. *Hitchcock Blonde* could be viewed as part of an ongoing attempt to pathologize Hitchcock himself by suggesting that his interest in murder was abnormal and that his films were realizations of violent revenge fantasies against women.

However, the personal psychology of this extremely complex and paradoxical character remains a matter of (not always helpful) speculation. Hitchcock was only able to make the films he did because audiences wanted to see them. *Psycho* broke box office records mainly because audiences (both male and female) were fascinated by the dark subject matter. Hitchcock's own preferences were always heavily influenced by his understanding of what, in his estimation, audiences would pay to see. "I know very well," Hitchcock explained, "that when the public goes to see a Hitchcock film, they will be very disappointed if they don't find one or more crimes in it" (Gottlieb 1995: 119).

46
Martin Scorsese (1942–)

Mark Desmond Nicholls

Martin Scorsese and the Hollywood Gangster Melodrama

Howard Hawks's 1932 film *Scarface* and Francis Ford Coppola's *The Godfather*, released forty years later, stand out as beacons of the Hollywood gangster picture, but no individual director has a more substantial association with the genre than Martin Scorsese. From his early New York University short, *It's Not Just You, Murray!* (1964), through *Mean Streets* (1973), *Raging Bull* (1980), *GoodFellas* (1990), *Casino* (1995), *The Gangs of New York* (2002) and *The Departed* (2006), Scorsese has defined both the scope and the essence of the gangster film with a focus on the genre unequalled in cinema history. Ranging from petty thief to police chief, Scorsese has applied an anthropologist's discipline to his representation of the full range of customs and manners of those who engage in the business of crime and punishment. Suggesting the work of the psychologist, Scorsese's films provide a detailed account of the popular and deep-seated attraction towards the sense of criminality that we all possess and seek out through various forms of popular culture. Grounded in the traditions of the cinematic past, the greatest contribution of these films to crime fiction in the cinema is the unavoidable conclusion that very few gangster films (or television programs) made since the late 1970s can be said to have escaped Scorsese's influence.

The Anthropology of the Mob

As a filmmaker, Martin Scorsese employs melodrama as a method of formal cinematic expression. That is to say, he manipulates the elements of cinematography, editing, sound, and *mise en scène* to conjure an emotional response in the spectator to his themes of male desire. It is as a result of the essentially melodramatic nature of these films that a substantial part of Scorsese's anthropological analysis of Italian-American mob-based organized crime points to the domestic and the everyday. These are not films about women; in no way can they be read in terms of the domestic entanglements of matrimony and motherhood common to the women's melodrama as we might experience it in films such as *Steel Magnolias* (Herbert Ross, 1989). Nevertheless, ideas of the domestic sphere, home and family play a signature role in Scorsese's gangster films. In *Mean Streets,* Charlie's (Harvey Keitel) mother is absent from the film but a freshly pressed and laundered shirt lying on his bed waiting for him with a note is enough to signal the perhaps uncomfortable, but certainly indispensable role of the mother and the domestic sphere for the Scorsese "wise guy." Nothing marks the heights of the Scorsesean domestic absurd like the midnight supper scene in *GoodFellas*. In this scene Scorsese's own mother, Catherine, plays mother to Tommy (Joe Pesci), Jimmy (Robert De Niro) and Henry Hill (Ray Liotta), pushing plates of food on the trio while one of their bleeding victims lies half dead and struggling in the boot of the car outside. However much women in these films are relegated to the role of mother or whore, however much the domestic sphere is embarrassingly tolerated as a necessary complement to the life of an Italian American gangster, such scenes leave a lasting impression on the spectator and help to establish the entire gamut of mundane things of gangster life with which Scorsese's films are concerned.

Scorsese's version of the gangster film can be read as melodrama because it inclines towards the mundane, what Robert Heilmann sees as the genre's distinguishing conflict between "men and things" (Heilmann 1968: 79). In Scorsese's pursuit of this vision, he achieves almost anthropological detail in his depictions of everyday life among certain parts of New York's Italian American community (Mortimer 1994; Friedman 1997: 23). In his review of *GoodFellas* Maurizio Viano even goes so far as to indicate Scorsese's ability to represent "the truth of ethnic situations and concerns" (Viano 1991). Scorsese himself has spoken of the importance he places on the representation of "seemingly unimportant details" (Keyser 1992: 200–1), "how people live, what they ate, how they dressed" and the way that such representations produce the all-important impression of the "real" in his gangster pictures (Smith 1990: 28). It is this mundane vision that gives substance to the representation of the lives of the street level criminals that are so central to his work. While Frances Ford Coppola's *Godfather* films chart the activities of Cosa Nostra royalty all the way to the Kefauver Committee hearings of the US Congress, and indeed to the Papal Curia itself, Scorsese's gangsters have their feet more firmly planted on the Little Italy sidewalk. These wise guys will quite simply do anything for a buck. Charlie and Michael (Richard Romanus) in *Mean Streets* are not so self-important or high-minded that they cannot take time out to swindle a couple of green college kids out of five dollars. Even Sam "Ace" Rothstein in *Casino* can easily go back to the relatively low dollar-value realm of sports handicapping, once the keys to the Tangiers Casino and, indeed, Las Vegas itself are taken from him.

What Scorsese shows us to be important about these largely unremarkable street criminals is that they represent a vital part in the organization of the mob. An understanding of their lives and the frequently banal nature of their work is central to a key aspect of Scorsese's anthropological approach: his painstaking elaboration of almost every single detail of the business of crime. This is no better expressed than in the elaborate montage sequences of *GoodFellas*, *Casino* and *The Gangs of New York* where we see every facet of each particular criminal organization, its activities and interrelationships, from the smallest criminal transaction to the management of sophisticated and highly lucrative crimes. The elaborate 33 minute sequence at the beginning of *Casino* best illustrates the range of activities, and their varying importance, that are subject to Scorsese's scrutiny. From Sam's own punctiliousness over the placement of chips at the casino tables, to the relentless methods used to keep millionaires playing and to keep casino cheats at bay, all the casino operations are portrayed. In addition, details of entities seemingly extraneous to the casino business, such as the eating habits of Kansas City mob bosses and the kickbacks that Las Vegas hookers must give in order to operate, reveal such entities to be intimately related to the operation under consideration. The fast-flowing river of coins on a conveyer belt and the brick-sized stacks of dollar bills seen in the Tangiers Casino count-room point to the basic motivation behind all the detail in all of Scorsese's crime films: money. Robert De Niro's voice-over in the film reminds us that the whole point not only of the Tangiers, but also of Las Vegas itself, is to "get your money". As represented by *Casino*, in Scorsese's gangster pictures money is the reason for everything. The assassination of Tommy in *GoodFellas* may look like some grand retribution for his taboo murder of a "made man," but as Ray Liotta's voice-over makes clear, it was also for "a lotta other things." As Scorsese points out, "a gangster's job is to make money. ... Someone gets out of line, and it ruins the money making for everybody. So he has got to go" (Keyser 1992: 200). From this perspective Tommy is "whacked" because he is no longer "a good earner." His excesses of behavior are not forbidden in themselves, but in so far as they threaten the smooth flow of cash, they are viewed in mob circles as unpardonable offenses. Similarly Joe Pesci's character in *Casino*, Nicky Santoro, is finally deemed expendable because his excessive lifestyle stops the flow of money to the bosses "back home." As an ace handicapper who can still "make book" Sam Rothstein remains useful, but only as long as he can bring in a dollar.

Raging Bull, perhaps Scorsese's most critically respected film, places its focus on its central protagonist, Jake La Motta (Robert De Niro) and is generally less interested in the detail of mob organization than are Scorsese's subsequent films. The role of the mob in Jake's story, however, and the largely subjective way in which Scorsese tells it, allows him to concentrate on the one aspect of mob business involved in the sport – fight fixing. Popularized in Hollywood cinema by Elia Kazan's *On the Waterfront* (1954), the story of the hapless Neanderthal ordered by the mob "to take a dive for the short-end money" was a well-known consequence of mob interference by the time Scorsese released his film in 1980. The practice of a boxer throwing a fight is not particularly sophisticated and hardly needed to be exposed by Scorsese's forensic lens. Indeed, what the film tells us about this practice is that it is a small detail of mob life. Although the prospect of having to perform such a task takes on an existential significance for Jake, its wider significance to the organization is almost miniscule. In fact, given the obviousness of Jake's eventual compliance in carrying out the order, we learn later that the fight purse was actually withheld pending investigation by the district attorney. Accordingly, the return to the bosses from Jake's "dive" must have been minimal and yet, having made the gesture, Jake is granted his wish and a shot at a title fight. Not only is "a dollar a dollar" in this context, but the incident tells us a great deal about authority in Scorsese's mob. In one sense, it shows us that the mob is concerned about authority, that the dollar value of any activity, while highly important, is not the final consideration. In another sense we can see that the situation shows the mob to be desperate to acquire earners as well as cash. Forever struggling with the sense of its own decline, Scorsese's mob in *Raging Bull* demonstrates the way in which an almost token gesture of allegiance is enough to satisfy its rules concerning membership. However much Sicilian origins, notions of authority and the myth of omertà (manly obligation) are asserted as important in this connection (Keyser 1992: 207), ultimately it is money and the details of how it comes in that count. If Scorsese's melodrama conforms to Heilmann's formula for the genre, it is as a struggle between men and money. All the banal details of mob life that we see in Scorsese's films, from pick-pocketing techniques in the Five Points, to Paulie's (Paul Sorvino) expert system for slicing garlic, ultimately point to that very basic struggle.

New York Histories

Ever since the sober title cards introducing the original 1932 *Scarface* called on the government and the people to act, and the confrontation between the film's protagonist and his mother and sister became Oedipal, the relationship between the gangster melodrama and the social message picture has been a viable cinematic notion. For all the local and domestic emphasis in Scorsese's gangster films, the director's interest in the broader narratives of history, and the history of New York City in particular, is obvious. In his reverie of the "glorious time" of his youth, Henry Hill in *GoodFellas* firmly places his introduction to mob life in 1955 as part of the relative freedom that existed before the New York gang wars and the famous Cosa Nostra convention and subsequent FBI raid at Apalachin in 1957. Henry's involvement in the Air France robbery of 1967 may be represented in *GoodFellas* in a purely local context, but along with the film's portrayal of the record-breaking Lufthansa Heist of 1978, it operates to place the narrative of the film within the context of events of national significance. The use of documentary footage of building implosions in *Casino* has a similar effect, as does Scorsese's portrayal of Tammany Hall politics and the New York draft riots of the early 1860s in *The Gangs of New York*.

Such a backdrop approach, where historical and political events are interpreted by, and invoked as context to, interpersonal struggles, is a standard technique of the melodrama. It is often a technique that is subject to criticism on the grounds of trivializing significant historical issues and events (Sobchack 1995). Taking this critical point further, I would argue that in Scorsese's films such historical and political contexts are even taken for granted. However vague and imprecisely drawn such historical meta-narratives may be in these films, I suggest that the very presence of these public events lends their private struggles the status of social history. In this way, playing behind Scorsese's finely drawn but somewhat parochial worlds, we find some of the major events of nineteenth- and twentieth-century New York and United States history.

The gangster movie, taking a cue from the Western itself, has always marked the closing off of the west, demonstrating the city of modernity as the essential site for the resolution of dramas of power and male anxiety (Schatz 1981: 45–110). The claustrophobia of Scorsese's *mise en scène* – think of the predominance of the narrow corridor shots in *Taxi Driver* – shows just how far these films are from Monument Valley. Charlie in *Mean Streets* cannot even feel comfortable at the beach. The pimp, Sport (Harvey Keitel), in *Taxi Driver* once had a horse, but it was run over by a car at Coney Island. These incidents suggest that Scorsese's landscape provides none of the room that was available to John Ford and John Wayne in which to bring resolution to traditional problems of order and authority. Given the history of the gangster film, there is, however, nothing outstanding about Scorsese's predominantly urban settings for his gangster films. The only exception to this lies in the way in which films such as *Who's that Knocking at my* Door (1968), *Taxi Driver,* and *Casino* refer to the John Ford Western in order to emphasize the point.

The way that Scorsese places his gangsters in such specific and local contexts, without totally divorcing them from the broader context of society, demonstrates the social history idea that these stories are simply a few among many. The same effect is achieved by the way Scorsese so frequently portrays his gangsters as crowded in. With its huddled, polyglot masses and "top of the heap" reputation for being at the heart of national and international affairs, this is also a particularly New York idea. It is an old cliché of the movies that in New York "there are a million stories out there" but Scorsese's films demonstrate that there is a particularly New York fashion to telling them. What Scorsese's "New York historical gangster melodrama" does is to demonstrate that the world of the gangster is one of a pattern of many such little New York histories. Not only does Scorsese's approach to crime fiction tell us about the history of the Italian American mob, but it tells us the history of New York and both stories are told in a particularly New York way. The anthropology of the mob achieved in Scorsese's gangster films may be fascinating, but each of these films seems to suggest so many other stories. This is particularly the case in *The Gangs of New York*, which brings together the worlds of upper and lower Manhattan. Assuming that half the number of these associated tales bears any relationship to Scorsese's stories, New York itself is revealed through Scorsese's work as a place of great complexity and infinite possibility. Scorsese's gangster films thus play a role in the historiography of New York, but these films also line up beside *Who's that Knocking at my* Door (1968), *Taxi Driver* (1976), *New York, New York* (1977), *After Hours* (1985), *Life Lessons* (1990), *The Age of Innocence* (1993) and *Bringing Out the Dead* (1999), not to mention films by directors such as Woody Allen and Spike Lee, as part of a wide-ranging, post World War II, New York City filmic subgenre. Woody Allen's *Manhattan* (1979) may stand out as the quintessential New York movie in this category, but such a category or subgenre would hardly exist without the definition given to it by Scorsese's gangster pictures.

The Same Hypocrisy

When in *Casino* Nicky Santoro threatens to "bust open" a banker's head it provides a rare moment in Scorsese's films before *The Gangs of New York* in which organized crime and the legitimate world intermingle. Francis Ford Coppola summoned the chutzpah to have Michael Corleone assassinate a police captain in *The Godfather* and the connection between the two worlds in Coppola's gangster films is eloquently represented, once again by Michael, when he tells a corrupt senator in *The Godfather Part Two* that they are "both part of the same hypocrisy." Until the new millennium, however, Scorsese has largely kept these two worlds apart. In *GoodFellas* we see mobsters paying off cops, but this is simply a case of low level insurance paid to officers on the beat to avoid minor but annoying complications to the smooth flow of underworld business. As Henry Hill says in his voice-over narration, the mob was really just a police force for those who could not go to the cops. Scorsese's films up until the release of *The Gangs of New York* emphasize this point by placing almost all aspects of the legitimate world, and what Henry calls "good government bullshit," at a distance.

The separation of powers in Scorsese's films before *The Gangs of New York* is not, however, suggestive of some inviolable barrier between organized crime and the legitimate world. In many ways, although apparently distanced from the apex of power in society, Scorsese's twentieth-century films are highly suggestive of the ultimate and absolute corruption of power that may exist at any level of society. It is the mundane and the domestic nature of Scorsese's subject matter that makes it so easy to infer the basic vices of greed and corruption that occur in any individual, in any class or social context. The sense of nostalgia for the fat times expressed by characters like Henry Hill and Sam Rothstein, as well as the rise, decline and fall narrative of these films, further indicate that power and greed in Scorsese's films are highly relative concepts.

One element that further serves as evidence of the thinness of the line between power and its pale shadow in Scorsese is the notion of organized crime. There is very little of the "organized" about Scorsese's picture of crime in Mobsville, USA. *Mean Streets, Raging Bull, GoodFellas,* and *Casino* are all about the decline of the organization as a result of the actions of highly disruptive and self-indulgent individuals. The anarchic Johnny Boy (Robert De Niro) in *Mean Streets*, Jake La Motta, Tommy, Henry Hill, and Nicky Santoro all have such disrespect for authority and the expected way of doing things that their stories are very much about the point when organization breaks down. In *The Gangs of New York*, where the connections with the legitimate world are much more directly drawn, it is at the point when Bill Cutting's (Daniel Day-Lewis) excesses of violence and parochialism get out of hand that his connections

Figure 46.1   Boss Tweed (Jim Broadbent) maintaining the appearance of the law, especially when it is being broken, in *Gangs of New York* (2002, dir. Martin Scorsese, produced by Alberto Grimaldi and Harvey Weinstein).

to Tammany and the agencies of authority in the larger world are severed. Nevertheless, despite the comedy of disorganization in Scorsese's cinematic world, particularly in *GoodFellas* (I. Christie 2003), the evidence of enduring success and of the establishment of firm connections with legitimacy abounds in these films. While Scorsese concentrates on the story of how such success is squandered, these films clearly indicate that success and legitimacy are only as far off as the achievement of a moderate degree of organization. The more localized the picture of greed and power gets in these films, the more broadly an audience can apply its message.

Boss William Tweed's (Jim Broadbent) trailer-ready line, "the appearance of the law must be maintained, especially when it is being broken," perfectly demonstrates the way that *The Gangs of New York* more literally extends Scorsese's vision of the scope and reach of organized crime into the legitimate world in his films released after 2002 (Figure 46.1). Nothing in American folklore brings these two worlds together like Tammany Hall. In the picture of fire-fighting corruption, "early and often" voting, the bribing of elected officials and the employment of a Five Points gang's "muscle" to match the Tammany family "spirit," we seem to be watching a kind of official super-text accounting for an implied narrative of official and legitimate corruption in Scorsese's mob films reaching back to 1968. Relocating the traditional focus of this story from New York to Boston, *The Departed* further demonstrates the essential interdependence between the worlds of crime and law enforcement. As the head of the local dominant crime syndicate, Frank Costello (Jack Nicholson), places his creature, Colin Sullivan (Matt Damon), at the top of the police force investigating his actions, so too does the force place Billy Costigan (Leonardo DiCaprio) in Nicholson's crew. These worlds, and the federal superstructures that hover above them, are thus shown to be so interwoven that no one, cop or hood, remaining inside either organization manages to come out alive. Only Dignam (Mark Wahlberg), who withdraws from the police force in the confusion of values, is left alive – isolated and unauthorized, but with the moral license to dispense justice.

The mutual dependence of blue and white collar crime may well have been inferred in earlier Scorsese films, as I have indicated, but the activities to confirm the association were happening somewhere else, further up the food chain and therefore of no immediate interest or use to Scorsese's gangster. Nevertheless, in these more recent films much of that ground is explored. Starting from the point of low level, street hood, nickel-and-dime crime in *Mean Streets*, Scorsese has widened his picture of organized crime to take in the activities of bosses well beyond the neighborhood reach of Paulie in *GoodFellas* and Bill Cutting in *The Gangs of New York*, to elected officials, police officers and, as is implied in *The Departed*, the FBI. In expanding his picture of crime in recent films, Scorsese has heightened our consciousness, not so much about the origins of crime, but about our understanding of its ultimate beneficiaries. If the US Federal Government through the FBI, or the Democratic Party through Tammany Hall, are shown to be the ultimate winners in these films, Scorsese nevertheless paints their fortunes as equally vulnerable to the mundane vicissitudes of human error, despite their exalted status.

The Law in Crisis

The inevitability of this connection between Scorsese's mundane world and the world of Olympian deities is best indicated in those films that nod to the lone vigilantism of Dignam in *The Departed*. Dignam's personally motivated assassination of Colin Sullivan suggests that the interpenetration of these two worlds is so great that the only hope for justice lies in the lone and arbitrary actions of the individual. This is the solution of the classical Western and it is essentially the key dilemma of Scorsese's most famous and controversial film, *Taxi Driver*. Travis (Robert De Niro), the loner of the film, can find no solution to his personal existential dilemmas in the spectacle of the city or the unreflective urban crowd that inhabits it. Nor are the social evils he perceives from his paranoid perspective solved by the vacuous platitudes of presidential candidate Charles Palantine (Leonard Harris). In the absence of a viable moral or ethical authority, the only solution for Travis lies in unilateral violence and the bloody rescue of a teenage prostitute, Iris (Jodie Foster), from her questionable servitude at the hands of her pimp and various underworld characters.

The national celebrity gained by Travis in *Taxi Driver* demonstrates the extent to which Scorsese's films, more broadly, are about a crisis of the law. This is also evident in the casual corruption of lawyers and the confusing impartiality of the law in *Cape Fear*, as well as in the portrait of the conflict between custom and law in *The Age of Innocence*. Inevitably, as in the case of Dignam and the police department in *The Departed*, Scorsese's films clearly indicate the idea that the legitimate world must come to terms with the criminal, or extra-legal, world if it is to maintain its hegemony. In *Cape Fear* middle-class lawyer and family man, Sam Bowden (Nick Nolte), needs to go beyond the law in order to escape pursuit by Max Cady (Robert De Niro), a ghost from his dubiously ethical past. As a lawyer himself, in *The Age of Innocence* Newland Archer (Daniel Day-Lewis) must advise Ellen Olenska (Michelle Pfeiffer) against relying on the law of divorce in favor of acceding to the unwritten rules of nineteenth-century New York society. In so doing, and shunning divorce as a means to their Romantic fulfillment, Newland and Ellen highlight the moral claims of another, higher law of "love over everything" that is perhaps even more threatening to notions of law as a sign of civic order and stability.

Thus it is in Scorsese's non-gangster films, where notions of that law and its fragility seem more prescient, that we can find the most revealing commentary on Scorsese's crime fictions. At the apex of power in New York/American society, the law seems so fickle that it is only in the street crime of *Mean Streets* and *GoodFellas* that we can see a viable outcome. Scorsese's characters may come to an unhappy, or excessively mundane end, but in the legal, moral and ethical world in crisis portrayed by these films, we see that, nevertheless, something must pay; that is to say, something must pay off. Scorsese's characters, and his audiences, are hungry for the satisfaction of their desires. What all his films show us, whether they are melodramas or gangster melodramas, is that if one is to have any hope of the satisfaction of desire, crime (expressed in one form or another) is the only way.

47
John Woo (1946–)

Karen Fang

Many Western admirers of the celebrated Hong Kong film director John Woo were first exposed to his distinct brand of high octane crime dramas as fans of action cinema, a generic category popularized during the 1980s and early 1990s by video rental.[1] The reasons for this common association are the fast-paced, highly choreographed, and high caliber action favored by film audiences during this period, and at which Woo is an undoubted genius. But this label obscures the actual classification in which his films were originally marketed. Films in this category, known in Hong Kong as *ying xiong pian*, or "hero movies," differ from Hollywood action films in that they are interested less in action sequences than in the character attributes that motivate them, and in fusing a contemporary interest in gunplay and pyrotechnics with a narrative focus upon traditional and even anachronistic values. Woo's films develop this contrast between traditional and modern sensibilities to a degree that distinguishes him even among other Hong Kong directors working within the same tradition, and it is this thematic and stylistic concern, largely overlooked in the early Western reception of Woo's films, that should take priority in any assessment of the trio of crime films upon which his reputation is based.

Ying Hung Boon Sik (1986), or as it is known by its English title, *A Better Tomorrow*, provides an exemplary introduction to Woo's aesthetics and concerns. A breakthrough film for both the director and the star, Chow Yun-fat, who would go on to headline Woo's other prominent Hong Kong crime dramas, *A Better Tomorrow* portrays two counterfeiters who are betrayed by a colleague, and follows their story first as one of them, Mark (Chow), is injured in a revenge attack, and later as the other, Mark's partner and friend, Ho (Ti Lung), comes to Mark's support upon Ho's release from prison. With such a plot of honor and treachery, *A Better Tomorrow* puts the moral concerns typical of the *ying xiong pian* at the center of the film, a point that is further illuminated by the film's original Chinese title. "Ying Hung Boon Sik" translates as "true colors" or "essence of hero," a phrase which clearly articulates its continuity with the "hero" tradition of the *ying xiong pian*.[2]

A Better Tomorrow further emphasizes the precariousness of honor and respect in modern society through a generational plot. Shing (Waise Lee), an associate who betrays Mark and Ho, is a young and ambitious upstart with no respect for tradition, while Mark, who appears to be between Shing and Ho in age, remains a fierce and loyal agent of traditional values, who repeatedly comes to injury – and ultimately dies – because of his loyalty to Ho. The film's dialogue only reinforces this theme. Ho's father admonishes Ho and his younger son that their fraternal bonds should override the professional conflict embodied in the fact that Ho is a criminal while his younger brother Kit (Leslie Cheung) is a cop; in an early scene in a bar and in the film's climactic action sequence, Mark delivers memorable speeches on loyalty; and at one point the uncle of the man who betrayed Ho and Mark apologizes to Mark on behalf of his wayward nephew, remarking that "brotherhood and ethics do not seem to exist in our world anymore."

This lament for past values makes *A Better Tomorrow* a particularly overt instance of the *ying xiong pian*, and is also evident in the film's relationship to martial arts and especially swordsman films, that distinctly Asian genre depicting feudal or chivalric tradition in pre-modern China or Japan. Traditional martial arts films often follow a novice who gradually apprehends the teachings of his master; similarly, in Woo's films, the many speeches about honor and respect might be considered part of this convention, merely updated with modern weaponry. And in an even more conspicuous display of his debts to these antecedent genres, Woo, who apprenticed with the legendary swordsman director Chang Cheh, casts Ti Lung, a former swordsman star, as one of the film's leads.

Yet at the same time that Lung's presence in the film imbues the story of resilience and survival with a uniquely intertextual poignancy, the film also asserts its stark differences from these earlier genres. *A Better Tomorrow*, of course, is not set in medieval China but in the modern urban metropolis of Hong Kong, and the film calls attention to this topicality through a variety of visual and artistic devices. The interior and exterior locations of buildings feature the glossy surfaces often associated with contemporary architecture, and it is fitting that Ho and Mark counterfeit American dollars, reflecting Hong Kong's status as a global financial capital. Where swordsman films often used the long sleeves of medieval robes to accent swordplay, *A Better Tomorrow* dresses its actors head-to-toe in Armani, using the sleek, closely tailored business attire to signify the cosmopolitan success of the protagonists. (At the time of the film this use of Armani was particularly resonant, given the recent prominence of the Italian luxury label in the 1980 Hollywood hit, *American Gigolo.*) All these details revise the swordsman film by presenting an intriguing new kind of hero. If Ho, as played by Ti Lung, embodied the film's chivalric origins within the outmoded swordsman genre, it was Mark, in the six-foot-tall, Armani-clad body of Chow Yun-fat, whose glamorously modern sensuality updated what remained an essentially traditional notion of romantic heroism, and who personified Woo's distinct cinematic sensibility.

Woo's style, as can be seen in *A Better Tomorrow*, is thus a hybrid, which merges traditional values and elements of a fundamentally Eastern genre with a modern and often distinctly Western aesthetic. For its audience this mix proved a winning formula: the film dominated the local box office for three months, and became the territory's highest-grossing film of the decade. But if the extraordinary commercial success of this apparent action film might suggest its parallels with trends in contemporary Western markets, where star-driven action spectacles increasingly were dominating production and consumption, Woo's movie also remains notably different from the Hollywood action films to which it is often compared. As Yvonne Tasker (1993) points out, Hollywood actioners often are vehicles for individual stars, and cast the actor as the rugged loner prized by American individualism. By contrast, *A Better Tomorrow* has an ensemble cast, composed of three different actors who shared equal billing. Such an emphasis upon collective talent rather than a singular star within *A Better Tomorrow* has notable affinities with the film's plot, as it reinforces the emphasis upon fraternity and cooperation that the film's story espouses, and is again typical of the traditional values within the *ying xiong pian*. Indeed, if Tasker sees American action movies of the 1980s espousing a neoconservative Reaganite ideology of charismatic authority, Woo's films seem to offer a truly different perspective. Instead of a topical, highly politicized ideology, movies like *A Better Tomorrow* uphold a timeless, particularly cultural worldview, and instead of responding to that perception with a reactionary vigilantism, they imagine the consequences of their imminent demise.

It would be easy to say of *A Better Tomorrow* that its emphasis on the collective rather than the individual is typical of Asian culture. Such a comment, of course, voices a particularly suspect kind of orientalism, and probably assumes that the film's differences from American action movies are those typical of Hong Kong films in general. But just as the *ying xiong pian* differ from Hollywood action movies, Woo's films also deviate from their local contemporaries, as is particularly visible in the director's unique visual style. Hong Kong films are widely noted for their frenetic pacing, which moves relentlessly from one scenario to another, and rarely exceed nine reels (a half-hour shorter than conventional Hollywood pictures). As David Bordwell (2000) and Stephen Teo (1997) point out, this compressed and highly accelerated pace to Hong Kong cinema distinguishes it from classical Hollywood, and remains one of its defining attributes. This temporal acceleration in Hong Kong movies, moreover, is particularly obvious in action and crime films, where the grammar of the action sequences distills the difference between these two traditions. Aside from the obvious differences between martial arts and gunplay genres, Hong Kong films often use real-time medium shots, to better portray the kinetic accomplishments of their martial arts-inspired forms of action. Yet Woo's films, by contrast, are full of slow-motion close-ups, which fix on Chow's face or the faces of the other characters, both when they are sighting a target and when they are concerned for each other's welfare. Such scenes arrest the velocity usually associated with Hong Kong film and, in the latter case, reinforce the traditional values typical of the *ying xiong pian* through their privileging of emotion over action.

The Killer (*Dip huet seung hung*, 1989) provides an interesting version of Woo's penchant for close-ups. In the film, Chow plays a hired assassin, and in elaboration of the romantically chivalric character that the actor brought to the film with his fame from *A Better Tomorrow*, the plot follows his character as he undertakes jobs to fund a surgery that will repair the eyesight of a lounge singer he inadvertently injured during a gunfight. As in *A Better Tomorrow*, *The Killer* blends its traditional values with a distinctly modern and even moodily noirish ambiance. Chow remains in Armani, and in this film is shown living in an austerely elegant apartment; the film even puts chivalric conventions literally into modern dress, as the silk hand-kerchief traditionally handed from a lady to her knight is ingeniously reinvented in *The Killer* as the silk scarf that the assassin ties around the singer when she is blinded in the gunfight, and which the killer later caresses in her apartment. Most importantly, *The Killer* expands upon the identification of cop and criminal that was a crucial element of *A Better Tomorrow*, and which would become a central theme of Woo's trilogy of crime films with Chow. Just like the climax of *A Better Tomorrow*, in which Ho's estranged brother, the cop, must cooperate with his criminal brother, *The Killer* includes a detective who becomes increasingly fasci-nated with the assassin that he is tracking. These characters collaborate in the film's final sequence, and Woo depicts their bond through a series of lingering glances, whose florid emotionality is further underscored by the musical motif accompanying the scene.

Such male-to-male gazes, common in Woo's films, can be discomfiting for Western viewers unaccustomed to the *ying xiong pian*, and indeed, some Western scholars, like Jillian Sandell (1996) and Julian Stringer (1997), have interpreted the scenes for their homoerotic appeal. Such readings are supported by the marginal and passive roles accorded women in Woo's films, and indeed may resemble the homoerotic gaze that Tasker and others have noted in Hollywood action films, but the difference between Woo's scenes and comparable moments in Western film also highlights their role in bolstering the narrative emphasis upon loyalty and honor. Where Hollywood actioners place their solitary protagonist at the center of a frame, Woo's films favor two-shots, in which the inclusion of two characters within a shared space emphasizes cooperation and mutual commitment. Indeed, in contrast to the rather static slow-motion shots of action stars in Hollywood movies, Woo's slow-mo sequences often are combined with the shot-reverse-shot structure traditionally used for dialogue, and thereby dynamically portray the bonds between characters. A formal precedent for this pecu-liar film grammar of Woo's may again originate with swordsman films, which often cut in to characters' faces during battle sequences, but Woo's films still distinguish themselves in the duration for which he is willing to linger on the sequence. As the film cuts back and forth between the faces of Chow and the cop who once was his pursuer but now is his accomplice, *The Killer* illustrates the cooperative union between the two characters that the film portrays. As the literal translation of the film's Chinese

Figure 47.1   The Killer [*Dip huet seung hung*] (1989, dir. John Woo; produced by Hark Tsui [as Tsui Hark]): Woo's film is about the "Bloodshed of Two Heroes."

title more accurately proclaims by emphasizing the plurality of protagonists within the film, *The Killer* is about the "Bloodshed of Two Heroes" (Figure 47.1).

The peculiar blend of old-fashioned values and contemporary stylistic techniques that Woo introduced to Hong Kong crime cinema therefore occurs on a variety of levels, and extends from the merely narrative interest in honor in the modern world to include the very aesthetic means by which it considers those issues. Woo's films often distill a story into a series of paired opposites. In addition to the general mix of old and new typical of Woo's films, for example, *The Killer* also explores the paradoxical affinities between crime and policing, examines the coexistence of innocence and experience in the debased modern world (where experienced figures, such as the assassin and detective, must cooperate to protect the innocent, such as the singer), and portrays these issues through a unifying motif of vision versus blindness. The latter theme, in particular, is an organizing trope of the film. After her injury the singer's blindness emblematizes her innocence, and the killer and the detective both exploit that attribute by not disclosing to her that her benefactor is also the assassin who injured her. By contrast, the killer and detective are both identified with acute vision, an attribute of their worldly experience that is portrayed both literally (such

as when the killer spies a distant glint that warns him of an ambush), and metaphorically (as the detective is the sole figure at the bureau who really understands the killer's
moral psyche). These themes come to dramatic climax in the film's tragic conclusion,
when the killer is blinded and fatally injured, and collapses before he is able to reunite
with the singer. As the film allows viewers to see what neither the singer nor the
killer can see, Woo's film foregrounds cinema as a modern technology invaluable for
its ability to depict traditional and fundamentally old-fashioned concerns. By the end
of *The Killer*, it is the audience who is put in the position of experience, and as we
watch this last knight expire, film's modern technology reminds viewers of the traditional values that are increasingly at peril in our world.

This is not the first reflexive allusion to the cinematic arts that Woo has incorporated into his films. As a teenager Woo had been an extra in local film shoots, and as
a young director Woo occasionally stood in for actors in his own films (see his 1975
swordsman flick, *Hand of Death*). In *A Better Tomorrow*, the director plays a detective
investigating the criminal syndicate in which the characters are involved; in his introductory scene in the film, the director appears in a close-up tracking shot that has
him tracing the path that Mark had walked during a gunfight, and thereby uses the
cop-criminal comparison so common in Woo's films to add a third category that allies
those characters with cinematic talent. As in *The Killer*, this scene in *A Better Tomorrow*
identifies cinema as a modern technology of vision, and uses the body of Woo to
portray an ability to see what others in this increasingly blinded modern world cannot.
By casting himself as a cop in *A Better Tomorrow*, or by placing the audience in a
privileged position at the end of *The Killer*, Woo foregrounds film as a resource capable
of preserving a morality increasingly at peril in modern society. Indeed, *A Better
Tomorrow* revives the novice-*sifu* plots of the martial arts films from which the *ying
xiong pian* originated, and presents Woo as the gifted artist-teacher from whose vision
the audience can learn.

Although *Hard Boiled* (*Laat sau san taam*, 1992) is not as critically celebrated as
the two other films in the trilogy, this later crime drama presents an intriguing and
even overblown version of the themes and characteristics that define Woo's unique
vision. The two-hour movie, Woo's last film to be shot in Hong Kong, features several
long and expensive set-pieces, such as the 30-minute shootout at a hospital with which
the film concludes, and was widely thought to be Woo's calling card for Hollywood.
It certainly demonstrates what the director could achieve when given free rein. The
first part of the film resembles *The Killer* and *A Better Tomorrow* in its situational
concern with traditional values of loyalty and honor. The plot, which centers on the
cautious alliance between a plainclothes and undercover cop, who at first are unaware
of each other but eventually cooperate in an effort to stop a vicious and violent young
arms dealer, includes an important early scene when the undercover cop (Tony Leung)
must assassinate the courtly older arms dealer for whom he works while undercover
and whom, despite his criminal affiliation, the cop has come to see as a benevolent
paternal figure. The scene is presented as a moment of agonizing moral confusion for
the undercover cop, whose estrangement has caused him to cherish the arms dealer's

more kindly attributes. (After the arms dealer releases the cop to kill him – and even urges him to, noting with an old-world grace that he "can see that here is where I check out" – the cop goes berserk and mows down the young assistants that the arms dealer had hoped to save with his own death.) This early scene thus sets the tone for the subsequent plot, which follows the growing cooperation between the undercover cop and the hard-boiled detective played by Chow, who both see themselves as last resorts against an increasingly immoral and unscrupulous society.

Like *The Killer* and *A Better Tomorrow*, then, *Hard Boiled* uses its modern setting and plot of contemporary arms dealing only as a guise for a traditional and even anachronistic concern with old world values. Indeed, anachronism is a notable motif within the film. The film's opening credits take place over a montage of newspaper headlines mourning a police force outgunned by increasingly violent gangs, and the first sequence in the film features a shoot-out at Hong Kong's famed Wyndham Teahouse, which was slated for demolition at the time of the film's production. As in the two earlier films, Chow embodies the mélange of urban sophistication with tra-ditional values typical of Woo's interests, but *Hard Boiled* also builds upon the other films, and particularly the director's appearance in *A Better Tomorrow*, by including Woo as a retired cop and current proprietor of the jazz bar where Chow's character occasionally performs, and a mentor with whom Chow's character consults. In Western films jazz often symbolizes a sophistication and estrangement associated with cutting-edge modernism, but in this Hong Kong film the jazz elements have a notably nos-talgic feel, literally suggesting the different rhythm to which these characters are attuned. In this film, Woo's appearance as a retired cop puts him in the same civilian dress as Chow's plainclothes detective and the undercover cop (here the bearer of Armani), and underscores his shared sense of the erosion of police power upon which the film dwells. But because Woo is also, of course, the film's director, this diegetic commentary works, as in *A Better Tomorrow*, to conflate cinema with the social func-tion of the police, and therefore presents film as the source of cultural wisdom and tradition once enforced by that institution, but now only resident in these retired, unofficial forms. "What a shame, what a pity," says Woo in his opening lines in the film. Although his ostensible reference is to the violence at the teahouse shootout, the dialogue also summarizes the moral sensibilities that distinguish Woo's unique brand of Hong Kong crime film. Lamenting the developments of contemporary culture, Woo both voices – and visually portrays – a fading code of justice and honor that is increasingly marginalized in contemporary society.

As an overblown but highly accessible version of John Woo's most characteristic artistic concerns, *Hard Boiled* therefore provides an important corrective to widespread Western notions of his films. For many Western converts to Woo's brand of crime cinema, the quintessential John Woo scene is a moment of action or physical tension, such as when a character explodes forward with guns pumping in both hands; when two or three characters are caught in a stand-off with guns pointed at each other; or when two gunfighters, once at odds, combine forces and advance abreast while shoot-ing side by side, as occurs at the climax of each of these three films. But while images like these undoubtedly account for his films' prominence among Western categories of action cinema, they are secondary to the emotional drama that is the core of the *ying xiong pian*, the genre in which those films were conceived. The real image that must be recognized as the "typical John Woo scene" thus occurs in the moment before that iconic action, a moment that brings former antagonists to fragile cooperation, or when a character who has temporarily lost his ethical bearings is restored to his code and summons his energy in a heroic, often fatal assault. Unlike Woo's action scenes, these moments depend more upon dialogue than physical action, and often unfold in slow motion, introducing into the otherwise hyperkinetic pace of Hong Kong cinema an unusual instant of stillness or visual arrest. Indeed, such scenes – like the slow-motion reaction shot of Chow Yun-fat's head recoiling from the fatal bullet wound that interrupts his harangue of the young cop in *A Better Tomorrow* and jolts the survivor into action – have a notably different effect from the moments of slow-mo during Hollywood action sequences. In their temporal expansion of the emotional content of Woo's films, such scenes reiterate his films' formal and narrative emphasis on the fate of traditional values within a violent and increasingly valueless society. As Woo himself has described it, his movies "created a new kind of style in action, production design and cinematography," but only to bring out the "old-fashioned, the true value of … morality" (Elder 2005: 50).

NOTES

1 For the role of video in the Western discovery of Hong Kong cinema, see Desser (2005).

2 In fact, Woo's film was inspired by a 1960 film of the same name. Note how the chivalric reso-nances of the Chinese title compare with Hollywood action movies like *Lethal Weapon* or *Die Hard*, whose ballistic titles emphasize mayhem and violence.

Conclusion

Charles J. Rzepka and Lee Horsley

"I've read that people never have figured out Hamlet, *so it isn't likely Shakespeare would have made* Macbeth *as simple as it seems."*
I thought this over while I filled my pipe. "Who do you suspect?" I asked, suddenly.
"Macduff," she said, promptly.
"Good God!" I whispered, softly. (Thurber 1965: 33)

The narrator of James Thurber's parody, "The Macbeth Murder Mystery," while staying at an English country hotel, meets a lady "murder specialist" who has made the "stupid mistake" of reading *Macbeth* under the misapprehension that it is a detective story. "The person you suspect of the first murder should always be the second victim," she tells him. Bringing to bear the scholarly apparatus of a devoted student of Shakespeare ("the Third Murderer has puzzled 'Macbeth' scholars for three hundred years"), he questions her closely about the quite different set of critical assumptions that she deploys in her own reading of *Macbeth*: "'Is that so?' I murmured. 'Oh, yes,' said my informant. 'They have to keep surprising you.'" Thurber's parody raises in its brief compass several of the questions addressed in this collection of essays on the history and the nature of crime fiction: What divides "serious literature" from genre fiction? How close is the relationship between the two? What are the conventions that define the various subgenres of crime fiction? What expectations do we bring to our reading of popular fiction and what demands does it make on our critical faculties?

In his Introduction to this *Blackwell Companion*, Charles Rzepka notes that we have not had space to give close attention to the various forms of comedy and parody to which the genres of crime and detection have given rise, and both editors find, at the end of the day, that we particularly regret this omission. Parody, as Dwight Macdonald suggests, is to be enjoyed as "an intuitive kind of literary criticism, shorthand for what 'serious' critics must write out at length" (Macdonald

1960: xiii), and crime fiction has been a rich source of comic and parodic reworkings which have functioned both to assist in the process of generic transformation and to crystallize the conventions of its main subgenres. In novels that work to modify the paradigms, the impulse to parody has often been quietly in play in the details that have shifted our understanding of one well-established narrative form or another – Christie's *The Murder of Roger Ackroyd*, Hammett's *The Tenth Clew* and Hjortsberg's *Falling Angel* can all, for example, be seen as transformative texts that deliberately exaggerate an aspect of the established form in order to challenge our habits of reading and change our generic expectations. Alison Light observes that the whodunit has, from the outset, been "a self-conscious form given to self-parody" – so much so that by the end of a decade Ronald Knox "was able to draw up a list of its mock rules" (Light 1991: 74). Patricia Merivale, in her contribution to this *Companion*, notes that parody and its near-relation pastiche have been important ingredients as well in more "serious" postmodern adaptations of crime fiction.

Working with bolder strokes on a broader canvas, contemporary cinema has fixed in the minds of popular audiences the key elements in a range of subgeneric variants. Classic detection is parodied, for example, in *The Adventures of Sherlock Holmes' Smarter Brother* (Gene Wilder, 1978); *Zero Effect* (Jake Kasdan, 1997), with Daryl Zero as the Holmes figure whose work "relies fundamentally on two basic principles: objectivity and observation, or 'the two obs'"; *Clue* (Jonathan Lynn, 1985), with its accumulating bodies and three different endings; and the long-running series of Clouseau films, from the early Peter Sellers *Pink Panther* (Blake Edwards, 1963) to the recent (2006 and 2009) Steve Martin remakes. The gangsters of the great sagas are reduced to children in Theodore Huff's short film *Little Geezer* (1932) and, more famously, in Alan Parker's *Bugsy Malone* (1976), which opens with "Someone once said if it was raining brains, Roxy Robinson wouldn't even get wet." Hard-boiled private eye films are sent up in *Dead Men Don't Wear Plaid* (Carl Reiner, 1982) and *Who Framed Roger Rabbit* (Robert Zemeckis, 1988); police procedurals in the "Naked Gun" series; Hitchcock films in Mel Brooks's *High Anxiety* (1977) and Danny DeVito's *Throw Mama from the Train* (1987).

Parody and pastiche of crime film conventions have become increasingly pervasive during the last two decades. Generic knowingness and liberal borrowing (ranging from "homage" to parody) have characterized the work of many of the best contemporary filmmakers, and dozens of films have played with established character types, plots and images. Among the period's distinctive reworkings of the formulas and materials of earlier crime narratives we find, for example, the Coen brothers' *The Big Lebowski* (1998) and *The Man Who Wasn't There* (2001); *Serial Mom* (John Waters, 1994); *Get Shorty* (Barry Sonnenfeld, 1995); *One Night at McCool's* (Harald Zwart, 2001); *Kiss Kiss Bang Bang* (Shane Black, 2005); and David O. Russell's *I Heart Huckabees* (2004), in which existential detectives keep everyday life under surveillance and a *femme fatale* played by Isabelle Huppert tells the protagonist, "It is a losing game mankind has played for more than a century. Sadness is what you are, do not deny it. The universe is a lonely place, a painful place. This is what we can share between us, period."

As Hupert's eloquent existential gloom suggests, to parody a form isn't just to make its formal qualities highly visible; it is, generally speaking, to juxtapose conventional elements of style, structure and characterization with the way in which the text creates meaning. Part of the effect often resides in the implication that there is a gap between serious intent and generic fixity – and this is, of course, a difficulty with which writers of genre fiction frequently contend. In reading the explorations of crime fiction published in this volume one is struck by how often it is an acute awareness of this possible disjunction that has led writers to modify the form. Important turning points examined by our contributors repeatedly adjust the genre in response to the anxieties of any given time. This may include, of course, modifications that mask a society's deepest anxieties, as when golden age fiction turns away from a traumatized landscape and rejects the heroic wartime model of male behavior (see Rowland, chapter 8 in this volume). But it more often entails generic transformations conceived as ways of rewriting conventions to make them more responsive to contemporary socio-political preoccupations: Chandler's often-quoted defense of the hard-boiled ethos, implying – somewhat problematically, as Andrew Pepper argues – the creation of a form "more realistic and more politically radical than other forms of crime writing" (chapter 10 in this volume); Chester Himes's introduction of larger-than-life black detectives, Coffin Ed and Grave Digger, who "understood the links between white oppression and crime and violence in the black ghetto" (Bailey, chapter 21 in this volume); female crime writers like Muller, Paretsky, and Grafton, who created a counter-tradition in first-person narratives that "reveal women's experiences in the face of patriarchal systems of both crime and justice" (Gavin, chapter 20 in this volume)

These particular innovations by Chandler, Himes, and female hard-boiled writers are not meant to draw a laugh, of course, because they are focused on legitimating and empowering, rather than undermining through ridicule, a new kind of protagonist that will challenge the dominant cultural presuppositions of the genre they inherited. But laughter, even self-directed laughter, is often not far away. Chandler's Philip Marlowe expresses surprise at managing to light a match on his thumbnail, just like a real tough-guy – "for once it lit" (Chandler 1995b: 601); in Himes's *Real Cool Killers*, as Stephen Soitos notes, a one-armed man tells his assailant to "wait a minute … till Ah finds my arm! … It got my knife in his hand"; in Sue Grafton's *"F" is for Fugitive* PI Kinsey Millhone – crack shot, cynical liar, and tough as nails – confesses that hypodermic needles make her queasy. In scenes like these, we can recognize the wide range of purposes – from self-deprecation to surreal slapstick – that humor answers in a formulaic genre, even when the point is not to make us laugh at the limitations of the genre itself.

The essential elements of humor, writes psychologist Ron A. Martin, are "incongruity, unexpectedness, and playfulness" (Martin 2006: 6). Of these three, critics of crime fiction and detection tend to concentrate on the first two, perhaps because the incongruous and the unexpected offer so much more scope than the ludic for reflection on the ideological contradictions and psychological evasions inevitably engaged by the emergence, integration, and eventual ubiquity of an extremely popular genre. Playfulness is typically overlooked: "play" is for children and is never innocent, at least in the eyes of adult critics. But it might be salutary, intellectually, to consider our very ancient instinct for play – our attraction to role-playing and "dressing up," our speculative trying out of ideas, our love of verbal wit and situational ironies, our disentangling of narrative alternatives – less as a means of evading our cultural or tribal anxieties than as an ever-open doorway into their deepest shadows. We love to laugh, which makes the unbearable bearable, yes, but also, like the mirroring shield of Perseus, lets us look upon the face of Medusa without turning to stone.

If crime and detective fiction have perpetuated a wide range of class, gender, and racial prejudices over the centuries, legitimizing imperialism, capitalist exploitation, and discrimination against women and minorities through some very creative forms of ideological mystification, then the genre's inherent tendencies toward self-parody, reflexive humor, and limit-case comedy, allied with its Protean malleability in the hands of parodists working in other genres, "high" as well as "low," have contributed to its redemption. Its appropriation by the dominant culture of its time and place was a foregone conclusion, but what other popular genre – the Western? science fiction? the romance novel? the adventure tale? – has evinced, from so early on, as sharp and unerring an instinct for play at its own expense, and ideologically critical play at that? When the unjustly accused fugitive Caleb Williams, aka "Kit Williams" of broadsheet notoriety, ends up in London writing "histories of celebrated robbers" because there is no money in poetry, Godwin means for us to smile even as we deplore the "Things as They Are" that put Caleb in this ironic situation.

Perhaps no better epilogue to our *Companion* could be found than the following lines, from one of Godwin's most famous admirers, on the incongruous – the "simple" and the "odd" – and laughter: even better for our purposes, dying of laughter. The next (and the last) voice you hear will be that of Prefect G –, from Edgar Allan Poe's "The Purloined Letter":

> "The fact is, the business is very simple indeed, and I make no doubt that we can manage it sufficiently well ourselves; but then I thought Dupin would like to hear the details of it, because it is so excessively odd."
>
> "Simple and odd," said Dupin.
>
> "Why, yes; and not exactly that, either. The fact is, we have all been a good deal puzzled because the affair is so simple, and yet baffles us altogether."
>
> "Perhaps it is the very simplicity of the thing which puts you at fault," said my friend.
>
> "What nonsense you do talk!" replied the Prefect, laughing heartily.
>
> "Perhaps the mystery is a little too plain," said Dupin.
>
> "Oh, good heavens! who ever heard of such an idea?"
>
> "A little too self-evident."
>
> "Ha! ha! ha! – ha! ha! ha! – ho! ho! ho!" – roared our visitor, profoundly amused, "oh, Dupin, you will be the death of me yet!" (Poe 1984: 681)

References

Abbott, Megan (2002). *The Street Was Mine: White Masculinity in Hardboiled Fiction and Film Noir*. New York: Palgrave Macmillan.

Abbott, Megan (2005). *Die a Little*. New York: Simon and Schuster.

Abbott, Megan (2007). *Queenpin*. New York: Simon and Schuster.

Abe, Kobo (1977). *Secret Rendezvous*. Trans. Juliet Carpenter. New York: Knopf.

Ackroyd, Peter. *Hawksmoor*. (1985). London: Abacus.

Ainsworth, William Harrison (2007). *Jack Sheppard* [1839]. Peterborough: Broadview Press.

Allen, Grant (1898) *Miss Cayley's Adventures*: "The Adventure of the Cross-Eyed Q.C.," *The Strand Magazine* 16: 688–98.

Allen, Grant (1980). *An African Millionaire* [1897]. New York: Dover.

Allen, R. (2002). "The Lodger and the Origins of Hitchcock's Aesthetic," in *Hitchcock Annual*, 2001–2 (10): 38–78.

Allen, R. (2008). *Hitchcock's Romantic Irony*. New York: Columbia University Press.

Allison, Hughes (1948). Corollary. *Ellery Queen Mystery Magazine*, July.

Allsop, Kenneth (1968). *The Bootleggers: The Story of Chicago's Prohibition Era*. London: Hutchinson.

Altick, Richard D. (1970). *Victorian Studies in Scarlet*. New York: Norton.

Ambler, Eric (1999). *The Mask of Dimitrios*. London: Pan Books.

Amis, Kingsley (1965). *The James Bond Dossier*. London: Jonathan Cape.

Andelman, Bob (2005). *Will Eisner: A Spirited Life*. Milwaukie, OR: M Press.

Anon. (1828). *The Florida Pirate, or, An Account of a Cruise in the Schooner Esparanza; With a Sketch of the Life of Her Commander*. New York: S. King.

Anon. (1837). *Confessions, Trials, and Biographical Sketches of the most Cold Blooded Murderers, who have been Executed in this Country from its First Settlement down to the Present Time*. Boston: George N. Thomson.

Anon. (1840). "William Ainsworth and Jack Sheppard." *Fraser's Magazine for Town and Country*, February 21: 227–45.

Anon. (1846). *The Lives of the Felons, or American Criminal Calendar, Compiled in Part from the New-York "National Police Gazette," and Corrected, Enlarged and Revised on Careful Comparison with the Criminal Records of the Various States*. New York: George F. Nesbitt.

Anon. (1860a). "Barbarous Murder," *Times*, July 3: 12.

Anon. (1860b). "The Recent Murder at Road," *Times*, July 11: 5.

Anon. (1860c). "Apprehension of Miss Constance Kent," *Times*, July 21: 5.

Anon. (1865). Untitled Report, *Times*, April 20: 8.

Anon. (1887). "Strange Adventures of Ascena Lukinglasse," *Punch*, September 10: 109.

Anon. (1888). "The Author of Madame Midas," *Illustrated London News*, October 6: 410.

Anon. (1890). "Crime in Fiction," *Blackwood's Magazine* 148: 127–89.

Anon. (1895). "Martin Hewitt, Investigator." Review, *Bookman* 7: 156.

Anon. (1927). Various articles on Snyder case. *New York Times*, May 22–24 and April 26–28.

Anon. (1976). *Richmond: Scenes in the Life of a Bow Street Runner* [1827]. New York: Dover.

Arrington, A. W. (1849). *Illustrated Lives and Adventures of the Desperadoes of the New World Containing an Account of the Different Modes of Lynching, the Cane Hill Murders, the Victims, the Execution, the Justification, Etc., Etc.* Philadelphia: Peterson.

Asbury, Herbert (2002). *The Gangs of New York* [1927]. London: Arrow Books.

Ascari, Maurizio (2007). *A Counter-History of Crime Fiction: Supernatural, Gothic, Sensational.* Basingstoke: Palgrave Macmillan.

Atwood, Margaret (1996). *Alias Grace.* New York: Doubleday.

Auden, W. H. (1988). "The Guilty Vicarage," in R. W. Winks (ed.), *Detective Fiction: A Collection of Critical Essays* (rev. edn, pp. 15–24). Woodstock: Foul Play Press.

Auster, Paul (1990). *The New York Trilogy* (*City of Glass* [1985]; *Ghosts* [1986]; *The Locked Room* [1986]). New York: Penguin.

Baden-Powell, Robert Stephenson Smyth (2004). *Scouting for Boys* [1908]. Oxford: Oxford University Press.

Bailey, Frankie Y. (1991) *Out of the Woodpile: Black Characters in Crime and Detective Fiction.* Westport, CT: Greenwood.

Bailey, Frankie Y. (2008). *African American Mystery Writers: A Historical and Thematic Study.* Jefferson, NC and London: McFarland.

Bailey, Frankie Y. and Green, Alice P. (1999). *"Law Never Here": A Social History of African American Responses to Issues of Crime and Justice.* Westport, CT: Greenwood.

Baker, Brian (2007). "Gothic Masculinities," in Catherine Spooner and Emma McEvoy (eds.), *The Routledge Companion to Gothic* (pp. 164–73). London: Routledge.

Baker, Matt, Arnold Drake, and Leslie Waller (2007). *It Rhymes with Lust.* Milwaukie, OR: Dark Horse Books.

Baker, William (2002). *Wilkie Collins's Library: A Reconstruction.* London and New York: Greenwood Press.

Bakhtin (1984). *Rabelais and his World.* Trans. Hélène Iswolsky. Bloomington and Indianapolis: Indiana University Press.

Baldick, Chris (ed.) (1992). *The Oxford Book of Gothic Tales.* Oxford: Oxford University Press.

Baldick, Chris, and Robert Mighall (2000). "Gothic Criticism," in David Punter (ed.), *A Companion to the Gothic* (pp. 209–28). Oxford: Blackwell.

Bannorris, A. (1847). *The Female Land Pirate: Or Awful, Mysterious, and Horrible Disclosures of, Amanda Bannorris, Wife and Accomplice of Richard Bannorris, a Leader in That Terrible Band of Robbers and Murderers, Known Far and Wide As the Murrell Men.* Cincinnati: E.E. Barclay.

Bargainnier, Earl F. (1980). *The Gentle Art of Murder: The Detective Fiction of Agatha Christie.* Ohio: Bowling Green Press.

Barr, C. (1999). *English Hitchcock.* Dumfriesshire: Cameron and Hollis.

Bartlett, K. (2003). "Grisham Adaptations and the Legal Thriller," in S. Neale (ed.), *Genre and Contemporary Hollywood* (pp. 269–80). London: BFI Publishing.

Barzun, Jacques (1965). "Meditations on the Literature of Spying," *American Scholar* 34 (2) Spring: 167–78.

Bayard, Pierre (2000). *Who Killed Roger Ackroyd? The Murderer Who Eluded Hercule Poirot and Deceived Agatha Christie.* London: Fourth Estate.

Bazelon, David (1994). "Dashiell Hammett's Private Eye: No Loyalty beyond the Job," in Metress (ed.), *The Critical Response to Dashiell Hammett* (pp. 167–73).

Beare, Margaret E. and Naylor, R.T. (1999). "Major Issues Relating to Organized Crime: Within the Context of Economic Relationships," Nathanson Centre for the Study of Organized Crime and Corruption. Available at: http://epe.lac-bac.gc.ca/100/200/301/lcc-cdc/major_issues_org_crimes-e/nathan.html

Bell, Florence Eveleen Eleanore (1969). *At the Works: A Study of a Manufacturing Town* [1907]. New York: Augustus M. Kelley.

Belloc-Lowndes, M. (1971). *Diaries and Letters of Marie Belloc Lowndes* [1911–47]. London: Chatto and Windus.

Belsey, Catherine (1994). "Deconstructing the Text: Sherlock Holmes," in John Hodgson (ed.), *Sherlock Holmes: The Major Stories with Contemporary Critical Essays* (pp. 381–88). Boston and New York: Bedford St. Martin's.

Bender, John (1987). *Imagining the Penitentiary: Fiction and the Architecture of Mind in Eighteenth-Century England.* Chicago: University of Chicago Press.

Bennett, D. (1979). "The Detective Story: Towards a Definition of Genre," *PTL: A Journal for Descriptive Poetics and the Theory of Literature* 4: 233–66.

Bernstein, Stephen (1999). " 'The Question Is the Story Itself': Postmodernism and Intertextuality in Auster's *New York Trilogy*," in Merivale and Sweeney (eds.), *Detecting Texts* (pp. 134–53).

Bhabha, Homi K. (1994). *The Location of Culture.* London: Routledge.

Billman, Carol (1986). *The Secret of the Stratemeyer Syndicate: Nancy Drew, the Hardy Boys, and the Million Dollar Fiction Factory.* New York: Ungar.

Bioy Casares, Adolfo (1940). *La invención de Morel.* Buenos Aires: Emecé.

Bioy Casares, Adolfo (2006). *Borges.* Barcelona: Editorial Destino.

Black, Joel (1991). *The Aesthetics of Murder: A Study in Romantic Literature and Contemporary Culture.* Baltimore: The Johns Hopkins University Press.

Black, Joel (1999). "(De)feats of Detection: The Spurious Key Text from Poe to Eco," in Merivale and Sweeney (eds.), *Detecting Texts* (pp. 75–98).

Blackbeard, Bill, Dale Crain, and James Vance (eds.) (2004). *100 Years of Comic Strips.* New York: Barnes and Noble.

Blake, L. (2002). "Whoever Fights Monsters: Serial Killers, the FBI and America's Last Frontier," in S. Gillis and P. Gates (eds.), *The Devil Himself: Villainy in Detective Fiction and Film* (pp. 197–210). Westport, CT: Greenwood Press.

Bleiler, E. F. (1976). "Introduction," *Richmond: Scenes in the Life of a Bow Street Runner.* New York: Dover.

Bleiler, E. F. (1978). "Introduction," in E. F. Bleiler (ed.), *Three Victorian Detective Novels* (pp. vii–xvi). New York: Dover.

Bloom, Clive (2007). "The Ripper Writing," in A. Warwick, and M. Willis (eds.), *Jack the Ripper: Media, Culture, History.* Manchester: Manchester University Press.

Boone, Troy (2001). "The Juvenile Detective and Social Class," in Adrienne E. Gavin and Christopher Routledge, *Mystery in Children's Literature: From the Rational to the Supernatural* (pp. 46–63). New York: Palgrave.

Borde, R. and Chaumeton, E. (1955). *Panorama du Film Noir Americaine 1941–1953.* Paris: Editions du Minuit.

Bordwell, David (2000). *Planet Hong Kong: Popular Cinema and the Art of Entertainment.* Cambridge, MA: Harvard University Press.

Borges, Jorge Luis (1943). *Artifices*. Buenos Aires: Emecé.

Borges, Jorge Luis (1952). *Other Inquisitions* [*Other Inquisitions.*] Buenos Aires: Sur.

Borges, Jorge Luis (1962). *Ficciones*. New York: Grove Press.

Borges, Jorge Luis (1964). *Labyrinths*. New York: New Directions.

Borges, Jorge Luis (1999). *Selected Non-Fictions*. Trans. Eliot Wienberg. New York: Viking.

Borges, Jorge Luis, and Adolfo Bioy Casares (1981). *Los mejores cuentos policiales*. Buenos Aires: Emecé.

Botting, Fred (1996). *Gothic*. London: Routledge.

Boucher, Anthony (1949). "Chandler Re-Valued," *New York Times Book Review*, September 25: vii.24.

Boucher, Anthony (1958). "Introduction," in Edgar Lustgarten, *The Murder and the Trial* (pp. ix–xi). New York: Charles Scribner's Sons.

Boucher, Anthony (1962). "Afterword," in A. Boucher (ed.), *The Quality of Murder: Three Hundred Years of True Crime Compiled by Members of the Mystery Writers of America* (pp. 253–4). New York: Dutton.

Bourdieu, Pierre (1989). *Distinction: A Social Critique of the Judgement of Taste*. Trans. Richard Nice. London: Routledge.

Bradford, W. (1856). *History of Plymouth Plantation*. Boston: Little, Brown & Co.

Brantlinger, Patrick (1982). "What Is 'Sensational' about the 'Sensation Novel'?" *Nineteenth-Century Literature* 37: 1–28.

Brauer, Stephen (2003). "Jay Gatsby and the Prohibition Gangster as Businessman," *The F. Scott Fitzgerald Review*, 2 (1), (January): 51–71.

Breu, Christopher (2005). *Hard-Boiled Masculinities*. Minneapolis: University of Minnesota Press.

Brill, L. (1988). *The Hitchcock Romance: Love and Irony in Hitchcock's Films*. Princeton: Princeton University Press.

Brion, P. (1992). *Le Film Noir*. Paris: Editions de la Martiniere.

Brite, Poppy Z. (1996). "The Poetry of Violence," in Karl French (ed.), *Screen Violence*. London: Bloomsbury.

Brite, Poppy Z. (1997). *Exquisite Corpse*. London: Phoenix.

Bronski, Michael (2005). "The Return of the Repressed: Leo Frank through the Eyes of Oscar Micheaux," *Shofar: An Interdisciplinary Journal of Jewish Studies* 23 (4): 26–49.

Browne, N. (1998). "Preface," in N. Browne (ed.), *Refiguring American Film Genres: History and Theory* (pp. xi–xiv). Berkeley: University of California Press.

Browne, Ray B., and Lawrence A. Kreiser, Jr (2000). *The Detective as Historian: History and Art in Historical Crime Fiction*. Vol. I. Bowling Green: Popular Press.

Browne, Ray B., and Lawrence A. Kreiser, Jr (2007). *The Detective as Historian: History and Art in Historical Crime Fiction*. Vol. II. Newcastle-upon-Tyne: Cambridge Scholars Press.

Bruccoli, Matthew J. and Judith S. Baughman (eds.) (2004). *Conversations with John Le Carre*. Jackson: University Press of Mississippi.

Bruce, John E. (2002). *The Black Sleuth* [1907–9]. Ed. John Cullen Gruesser. Boston: Northeastern University Press.

Brunsdale, Mitzi (1990). *Dorothy L. Sayers: Solving the Mystery of Wickedness*. Oxford: Berg.

Buchanan, H. G. (1848). *Asmodeus: or Legends of New York*. New York: Munson & Co.

Buckley, Matthew (2002). "Sensations of Celebrity: *Jack Sheppard* and the Mass Audience." *Victorian Studies* 44: 423–63.

Buckley, William F. Jr (1994). *The Blackford Oakes Reader*. New York: William Morrow.

Bulwer-Lytton, Edward (1833). *Eugene Aram: A Tale* [1832]. London: Richard Bentley.

Bulwer-Lytton, Edward (1835). *Paul Clifford* [1830]. London: Richard Bentley.

Bulwer-Lytton, Edward (1846). *Lucretia; or, The Children of Night*. London: Saunders and Otley.

Bulwer-Lytton, Edward (1896). "Preface to the Edition of 1840," *Eugene Aram: A Tale*. In *The Novels of Lord Lytton* (Vol. 7). New York: Athenaeum Society.

Buntline, N. (1848). *Mysteries and Miseries of New York*. New York: Berford.

Burke, E. (1990). *A Philosophical Enquiry into the Origin of our Ideas of the Sublime and Beautiful*. Ed. A. Phillips. Oxford and New York: Oxford University Press.

Burnett, W. R. (1968). *High Sierra* [1940]. London: Flamingo.

Burnett, W. R. (1984). *Little Caesar* [1929]. London: Zomba Books.

Bustos Domecq, H. (1980). *Six Problems for Don Isidro Parodi* [1942]. Trans. Norman Thomas di Giovanni. New York: Dutton.

Butts, Dennis (1997). "How Children's Literature Changed: What Happened in the 1840s?" *The Lion and the Unicorn* 21 (2), April: 153–62.

Caillois, R. (1984). *The Mystery Novel*. Trans. R. Yahni and A.W. Sadler. Bronxville, NY: Laughing Buddha.

Cain, James M. (1934). *The Postman Always Rings Twice*. New York: Knopf.

Cain, James M. (1936). *Double Indemnity*. New York: Knopf.

Cain, James M. (1937). *Serenade*. New York: Knopf.

Cain, James M. (1940). *The Embezzler*. New York: Liberty magazine.

Cain, James M. (1941). *Mildred Pierce*. New York: Knopf.

Cain, James M. (1985). *The Five Great Novels of James M. Cain*. London: Picador.

Calinescu. M. (1993). *Rereading*. New Haven: Yale University Press.

Canto, Estela (1989). *Borges a contraluz*. Madrid: Espasa Calpe.

Caputi, J. and D. E. H. Russell (1992). "Femicide: Sexist Terrorism against Women," in J. Radford and D. E. H. Russell (eds.), *Femicide: The Politics of Killing Women* (pp. 13–24). New York: Twayne.

Carcaterra, Lorenzo (2001). *Gangster*. New York: Ballantine Books.

Carlson, Marvin (1993). *Deathtraps: The Postmodernist Comedy Thriller*. Bloomington: Indiana University Press.

Carr, John Dickson (1935). *The Three Coffins*. London: Hamish Hamilton.

Carr, John Dickson (2002). *The Hollow Man* [original publication *The Three Coffins*, 1935]. London: Orion.

Castle, Terry (2003). "The Ick Factor," *The New Republic*, November 10.

Cawelti, J. G. (1976). *Adventure, Mystery, and Romance: Formula Stories as Art and Popular Culture*. Chicago: University of Chicago Press.

Cawelti, John (1994). "From *Adventure, Mystery, and Romance*," in Metress (ed.), *The Critical Response to Dashiell Hammett* (pp. 6–11).

Cawelti, John G. and Bruce A. Rosenberg (1987). *The Spy Story*. Chicago: University of Chicago Press.

Chamoiseau, Patrick (1999). *Solibo Magnificent*. Trans. Rose-Myriam Réjouis. New York: Vintage.

Chandler, James (1998). *England in 1819: The Politics of Literary Culture and the Case of Romantic Historicism*. Chicago: University of Chicago Press.

Chandler, P. W. (1841). *American Criminal Trials*. Boston: Little and Brown.

Chandler, Raymond (1964). *Killer in the Rain*. New York: Ballantine.

Chandler, Raymond (1981). *Selected Letters of Raymond Chandler*. New York: Columbia University Press.

Chandler, Raymond (1995a). *Later Novels and Other Writings*. Ed. Frank MacShane. New York: Library of America.

Chandler, Raymond (1995b). *Stories and Early Novels*. Ed. Frank MacShane. New York: Library of America.

Chesterton, G. K. (1911). *The Innocence of Father Brown*. London: Cassell & Co.

Chesterton, G. K. (1936). *Illustrated London News*, June 13.

Chesterton, G. K. (2003a). "The Head of Caesar" [1913] in *The Wisdom of Father Brown* [1914]. *Complete Annotated Father Brown*, I (pp. 227–34). Ed. John Peterson. Shelburne ON: Battered Silicon Dispatch Case.

Chesterton, G. K. (2003b). "The Invisible Man" in *The Innocence of Father Brown* [1911]. *Complete Annotated Father Brown*, I (pp. 185–95). Ed. John Peterson. Shelburne ON: Battered Silicon Dispatch Case.

Chesterton, G. K. (2003c). "The Sign of the Broken Sword" in *The Innocence of Father Brown* [1911]. *Complete Annotated Father Brown*, I (pp. 303–14). Ed. John Peterson. Shelburne ON: Battered Silicon Dispatch Case.

Christianson, S. (1995). "Talkin' Trash and Kickin' Butt: Sue Grafton's Hard-boiled Feminism," in Irons (ed.), *Feminism in Women's Detective Fiction* (pp. 127–47).

Christie, Agatha (1926). *The Murder of Roger Ackroyd*. London: Collins.

Christie, Agatha (1929). *Partners in Crime*. London: Collins.

Christie, Agatha (1967). *Endless Night*. London: Collins.

Christie, Agatha (1973a). *Peril at End House* [1932]. London: Fontana.

Christie, Agatha (1982). *The Murder at the Vicarage* [1930]. London: Fontana.

Christie, Agatha (1984). *Nemesis* [1971]. London: Fontana.

Christie, Agatha (1987). *The Mysterious Affair at Styles* [1920]. New York: Bantam.

Christie, Agatha (1991). *The ABC Murders* [1936]. New York: Berkley.

Christie, Agatha (1993). *Cards on the Table* [1936]. London: HarperCollins.

Christie, Agatha (2002a). *The Body in the Library* [1942]. London: HarperCollins.

Christie, I. (2003). "Manhattan Asylum", *Sight and Sound*: 20–3.

Clapp, Susannah (1999). "The Simple Art of Murder," *The New Yorker*, December 10: 94–7.

Clarke, Donald Henderson (1929). *In the Reign of Rothstein*. New York: Vanguard Press.

Clarke, Donald Henderson (1949). *Louis Beretti* [1929]. New York and Chicago: Diversey Publishing.

Clarke, Donald Henderson (1950). *Man of the World: Recollections of an Irreverent Reporter*. New York: Vanguard Press.

Cobley, Paul (2000). *The American Thriller: Generic Innovation and Social Change in the 1970s*. Basingstoke: Palgrave Macmillan.

Cohen, D. A. (1988). *Pillars of Salt, Monuments of Grace: New England Crime Literature and the Origins of American Popular Culture, 1674–1860*. New York: Oxford University Press.

Cohen, Patricia C. (1998). *The Murder of Helen Jewett: The Life and Death of a Prostitute in Nineteenth-Century New York*. New York: Alfred A. Knopf.

Collins, J. (1989). *Uncommon Cultures: Popular Culture and Post-Modernism*. New York: Routledge.

Collins, Max Allan (2005). *Road to Perdition*. New York: DC Comics.

Collins, Philip (1992). *Dickens and Crime*. London: Macmillan.

Collins, Wilkie (1996). *The Woman in White* [1859–60]. Ed. J. Sutherland. Oxford: Oxford University Press.

Collins, Wilkie (1998a). *The Law and the Lady* [1875]. Harmondsworth: Penguin.

Collins, Wilkie (1998b). *The Moonstone* [1868]. Ed. Sandra Kemp. London: Penguin Books.

Conquergood, L. D. (2002). "Lethal Theatre: Performance, Punishment, and the Death Penalty," *Theatre Journal*, 54 (3): 339–67.

Conrad, Joseph (1983). *Under Western Eyes.* Oxford: Oxford University Press.

Coombes, David (1992). *Dorothy L. Sayers: A Careless Rage for Life.* Oxford: Lion.

Corber, Robert J. (1997). *Homosexuality in Cold War America: Resistance and the Crisis of Masculinity.* Durham, NC: Duke University Press.

Cornwell, Patricia. (1995). *The Body Farm.* London: Time Warner.

Cornwell, Patricia (1996). *From Potter's Field.* London: Time Warner.

Cornwell, Patricia (1997). *Unnatural Exposure.* Great Britain: Little, Brown.

Cornwell, Patricia (2001). *The Last Precinct* [2000]. London: Warner Books.

Coveney, Peter (1957). *Poor Monkey: The Child in Literature.* London: Rockliff.

Craig, P. and M. Cadogan (1981). *The Lady Investigates: Women Detectives and Spies in Fiction.* London: Victor Gollancz.

Crispin, Edmund (1944). *The Case of the Gilded Fly.* London: Victor Gollancz.

Crofts, Freeman Wills (1925). *Inspector French's Greatest Case.* London: William Collins.

Dacre, Charlotte (1997). *Zofloya, or the Moor* [1806]. Ed. Kim Ian Michasiw. Oxford: Oxford University Press.

Dahmer, Lionel (1994). *A Father's Story.* New York: Morrow.

Danforth, S. (1674). *The Cry of Sodom Enquired Into; Upon Occasion of the Arraignment and Condemnation of Benjamin Goad, for His Prodigious Villany.* Cambridge: Marmaduke Johnson.

Davis, Mike (1990). *City of Quartz: Excavating the Future in Los Angeles.* London: Vintage.

De Quincey, Thomas (2006). *On Murder Considered as One of the Fine Arts.* Ed. Robert Morrison. Oxford: Oxford University Press.

Décuré, N. (1999). "In Search of Our Sisters' Mean Streets: The Politics of Sex, Race, and Class in Black Women's Crime Fiction," in Klein (ed.), *Diversity and Detective Fiction* (pp. 158–85).

Defoe, Daniel (1725). *The True and Genuine Account of the Life and Actions of the Late Jonathan Wild.* In Fielding, *Jonathan Wild* (pp. 221–57).

Della Cava, F. A. and M. H. Engel (1999). "Racism, Sexism, and Antisemitism in Mysteries Featuring Women Sleuths," in Klein (ed.), *Diversity and Detective Fiction* (pp. 38–59).

Della Cava, F. A. and M. H. Engel (2002). *Sleuths in Skirts: Analysis and Bibliography of Serialized Female Sleuths.* London: Routledge.

Denning, Michael (1997). *The Cultural Front: Laboring of American Culture in the Twentieth Century.* London and New York: Verso.

Derrida, Jacques (2000a). "'A Self-Unsealing Poetic Text': Poetics and Politics of Witnessing." Trans. Rachel Bowlby. In Michael P. Clark (ed.), *Revenge of the Aesthetic: The Place of Literature in Theory Today* (pp. 180–207). Berkeley: University of California Press.

Derrida, Jacques (2000b). *Demeure: Fiction and Testimony.* Trans. Elizabeth Rottenberg. Stanford, CA: Stanford University Press.

Desser, David. (2005). "Hong Kong Film and the New Cinephilia," in Meaghan Morris, Siu Leung Li and Stephen Ching-kiu Chan (eds.), *Hong Kong Connections: Transnational Imagination in Action Cinema* (pp. 205–21). Durham: Duke University Press.

Devlin, James E. (1999). *Elmore Leonard.* New York: Twayne.

Dexter, Colin (2007). *The Jewel that Was Ours* [1991]. Basingstoke and Oxford: Pan Books.

Dickens, Charles (1998). *Oliver Twist* [1838]. Oxford: Oxford University Press.

Didion, Joan (1968). *Slouching towards Bethlehem.* New York: Farrar, Straus & Giroux.

Dittmar, L. and G. Michaud (1990). "Introduction," in L. Dittmar and G. Michaud (eds.), *From Hanoi to Hollywood: The Vietnam War in American Film* (pp. 1–15). New Brunswick, NJ: Rutgers University Press.

Donovan, Dick (1892). *A Romance from a Detective's Case Book.* "The Jewelled Skull." *Strand Magazine* 4: 70–82.

Dorfman, Ariel (1990). *Hard Rain [Moros en la costa* 1973]. Trans. George Shivers. London and Columbia LA: Readers International.

Douglas, John, and Mark Olshaker (1998). *Obsession: The FBI's Legendary Profiler Probes the Psyches of Killers, Rapists, and Stalkers and their Victims and Tells How to Fight Back.* New York: Scribner.

Dove, George N. (1982). *The Police Procedural.* Bowling Green, OH: Bowling Green University Popular Press.

Doyle, Arthur Conan (1986). *Sherlock Holmes: The Complete Novels and Stories.* Ed. Loren D. Estleman. 2 vols. New York: Bantam Books.

Doyle, Arthur Conan (1989). *Memories and Adventures* [1924]. Oxford: Oxford University Press.

Drew, Bernard A. (1986). *Hard-Boiled Dames: Stories Featuring Women Detectives, Reporters, Adventurers, and Criminals from the Pulp Fiction Magazines of the 1930s.* New York: St Martin's Press.

Dulles, Allen (ed.) (1968). *Great Spy Stories from Fiction.* New York: Harper Collins.

Dupont, Joan (1988). "Criminal Pursuits," *New York Times Magazine,* October 12.

Eco, Umberto (1979). *The Role of the Reader: Explorations in the Semiotics of Texts.* Bloomington: Indiana University Press.

Eco, Umberto (1984). *The Name of the Rose* [1980]. Trans. William Weaver. New York: Harcourt, Brace, Jovanovich.

Eco, Umberto (1987). "Narrative Structures in Fleming," in *The Role of the Reader: Explorations in the Semiotics of Texts.* London: Hutchinson.

Eisner, Will (2001). *The Spirit Archives,* Vol. 4. New York: DC Comics.

Elder, Robert K. (2005). "John Woo: Movie by Movie, 1968 to 1990," in Robert K. Elder (ed.), *John Woo: Interviews* (pp. 16–58). Jackson: University Press of Mississippi.

Eliot, T. S. (1951). "Wilkie Collins and Dickens" [1934], in T. S. Eliot, *Selected Essays, 1917–32* (pp. 460–70). London: Faber.

Eliot, T. S. (1960a). "The Wasteland" [1921], in *The Collected Poems of T.S. Eliot.* London: Faber & Faber.

Eliot, T. S. (1960b). "Wilkie Collins and Dickens", in *Selected Essays of T. S. Eliot.* New York: Harcourt, Brace and World.

Ellis, Bret Easton (1991). *American Psycho.* London: Picador.

Ellison, Harlan (1980). "Shatterday," in *Shatterday* (pp. 319–32). Boston: Houghton Mifflin.

Ellroy, James (1992). *White Jazz.* London: Arrow.

Ellroy, James (1994). *"The American Cop,"* British Channel 4 Television Programme.

Ewert, Jeanne C. (1999). "'A Thousand other Mysteries': Metaphysical Detection, Ontological Quests," in Merivale and Sweeney (eds.), *Detecting Texts* (pp. 179–98).

Fabre, Michel and Robert E. Skinner (eds.) (1995). *Conversations with Chester Himes.* Jackson: University Press of Mississippi.

Fiedler, Leslie A. (1970). "Introduction," in George Lippard, *The Monks of Monk Hall.* New York: Odyssey Press.

Fielding, Henry (1986). *Jonathan Wild.* Ed. David Nokes. London: Penguin.

Filreis, Alan (1997). "Introduction," in Ira Wolfert, *Tucker's People* (pp. vi–xliv). Urbana and Chicago: University of Illinois Press.

Forter, Greg (2000). *Murdering Masculinities: Fantasies of Gender and Violence in the American Crime Novel.* New York: New York University Press.

Foucault, Michel (1975). *I, Pierre RiviPre, Having Slaughtered My Mother, My Sister, and My Brother …: A Case of Parricide in the Nineteenth Century* [1973]. Trans. Frank Jellinek. New York: Pantheon.

Foucault, Michel (1977). *Discipline and Punish: The Birth of the Prison* [1975]. Trans. Alan Sheridan. New York: Pantheon.

Frank, Lawrence (2003). *Victorian Detective Fiction and the Nature of Evidence: The Scientific Investigations of Poe, Dickens, and Doyle*. Basingstoke: Palgrave Macmillan.

Freedman, Carl and Kendrick, Christopher (1991). "Forms of Labor in Dashiell Hammett's *Red Harvest*," *PMLA*, 106: 2.

Freeman, R. Austin (1923). "The Echo of a Mutiny," in *The Adventures of Dr Thorndyke* (pp. 92–125). New York: Dodd, Mead & Co.

Freeman, R. Austin (2001). *The Red Thumb Mark*. Thirsk: House of Stratus.

Friedman, L. (1997). *The Cinema of Martin Scorsese*. New York: Continuum.

Fuchs, Daniel (2006). *The Brooklyn Novels: Summer in Williamsburg, Homage to Blenholt, Low Company*. Boston: Black Sparrow Press.

Fuller, Hoyt W. (1972). "Traveller on the Long, Rough, Lonely Old Road: An Interview with Chester Himes," *Black World* 21 (March): 4–22, 87–98.

Furst, Alan (ed.) (2004). *The Book of Spies: An Anthology of Literary Espionage*. New York: Modern Library.

Gaines, Luan (2005). "Curled Up with a Good Book: An Interview with Don Winslow". Available at: http://www.curledup.com/intdwins.htm.

Galewitz, Herb (ed.), (1990). *The Celebrated Cases of Dick Tracy, 1931–1951* by Chester Gould. Secaucus, NJ: Wellfleet Press.

Gallagher, M. (1999). "I Married Rambo: Spectacle and Melodrama in the Hollywood Action Film," in C. Sharrett (ed.), *Mythologies of Violence in Postmodern Media* (pp. 199–225). Detroit: Wayne State University Press.

Gatenby, Bruce (1994). "'A Long and Laughable Story': Hammett's *The Dain Curse* and the Postmodern Condition," in Metress

(ed.), *The Critical Response to Dashiell Hammett* (pp. 56–68).

Gates, Henry Louis, Jr (1998). *The Signifying Monkey: A Theory of Afro-American Literary Criticism*. New York: Oxford University Press.

Gates, P. (2006). *Detecting Men: Masculinity and the Hollywood Detective Film*. New York: State University of New York Press.

Geherin, David (1989). *Elmore Leonard*. New York: Continuum.

Gill, Gillian (1990). *Agatha Christie: The Woman and her Mysteries*. London: Robson.

Glover, David (2003). "The Thriller," in Priestman (ed.), *The Cambridge Companion to Crime Fiction* (pp. 135–53).

Godwin, William (1998). *Caleb Williams; or, Things as They Are* [1794]. Oxford: Oxford University Press.

Godwin, William (2000). *Caleb Williams* [1794]. Peterborough: Broadview Press.

Gomel, Elana (1995). "Mystery, Qpocalypse and Utopia: The Case of the Ontological Detective Story," *Science Fiction Studies*, 22 (3): 343–56.

Goodis, David (1967). *Cassidy's Girl* [1951]. New York: Dell.

Goodis, David (1983). *The Moon in the Gutter* [1953], in *Black Box Thrillers: Four Novels*. London: Zomba Books.

Goodis, David (1990). *Down There* [1956]. New York: Vintage.

Goodis, David (1991). *Street of No Return* [1954]. New York: Vintage.

Gorrara, Claire (2003). *The Roman Noir in Post-War French Culture*. Oxford: Oxford University Press.

Gosselin, Adrienne J. (1998). "The World Would Do Better to Ask Why Is Frimbo Sherlock Holmes? Investigating Liminality in Rudolph Fisher's *The Conjure-Man Dies*," *African American Review*, 32 (4): 604–19.

Gottlieb, S. (2003). *Alfred Hitchcock Interviews*. Mississippi: University of Mississippi Press.

Gottlieb, S. (2004). "Unknown Hitchcock: The Unrealised Projects," in R. Allen and S. Ishii-Gonzales (eds.), *Hitchcock: Past and Present*. London: Routledge.

Gottlieb, S. (ed.) (1995). *Hitchcock on Hitchcock: Selected Writings and Interviews*. California: University of California Press.

Goulart, Ron (2004). *Comic Book Encyclopedia: The Ultimate Guide to Characters, Graphic Novels, Writers, and Artists in the Comic Book Universe*. New York: Harper Entertainment.

Grafton, Sue (1982). *"A" Is for Alibi*. New York: Holt, Rinehart and Winston.

Gramsci, Antonio (1971). *Selections from the Prison Notebooks of Antonio Gramsci*. Ed. Quentin Hoare and Geoffrey Nowell-Smith. London: Lawrence & Wishart.

Green, Anna Katherine (1878). *The Leavenworth Case*. New York: G. P. Putnam's Sons.

Greene, Graham (2000). "Foreword," in Patricia Highsmith, *Eleven* (pp. ix–xi). New York: Atlantic Monthly Press.

Greenfield, John (2002). "Arthur Morrison's Sherlock Clone: Martin Hewitt, Victorian Values, and London Magazine Culture, 1894–1903," *Victorian Periodicals Review* 35: 18–37.

Greenwald, Marilyn S. (2004). *Secret of the Hardy Boys: Leslie McFarlane and the Stratemeyer Syndicate*. Athens, OH: Ohio University Press.

Greenwood, James (1874). "Penny Packets of Poison," in Peter Haining (ed.), *The Penny Dreadful* (pp. 357–71). London: Victor Gollancz.

Gregory, Sinda (1994). "*The Dain Curse*: The Epistemology of the Detective Story," in Metress (ed.), *The Critical Response to Dashiell Hammett* (pp. 34–55).

Grella, George (1980). "The Hard-boiled Detective Novel," in Robin W. Winks (ed.), *Detective Fiction: A Collection of Critical Essays* (pp. 103–20). Englewood Cliffs, NJ: Prentice-Hall.

Grella, George (1998). "Film in Fiction: The Real and the Reel in Elmore Leonard," in Jerome H. Delamater and Ruth Prigozy (eds.), *The Detective in American Fiction, Film, and Television*. Westport, CT: Greenwood Press.

Gresham, William Lindsay (1946). *Nightmare Alley*. New York: Signet.

Grobel, Lawrence (2001). *Endangered Species: Writers Talk about their Craft, their Visions, their Lives*. Cambridge, MA: Da Capo Press.

Gruner, Elizabeth Rose (1998). "Family Secrets and the Mysteries of *The Moonstone*," in Pykett (ed.), *Wilkie Collins* (pp. 221–43).

Gunning, T. (2000). *Fritz Lang: Allegories of Vision and Modernity*. London: BFI.

Halberstam, Judith (1995). *Skin Shows: Gothic Horror and the Technology of Monsters*. Durham, NC and London: Duke University Press.

Hall, Jasmine Yong (1990). "Jameson, Genre, and Gumshoes: The Maltese Falcon as Inverted Romance," in Ronald G. Walker and June M. Frazer (eds.), *The Cunning Craft: Original Essays on Detective Fiction and Contemporary Literary Theory* (pp. 109–19). Macomb: Western Illinois University Press.

Hall, Jasmine (1994). "Jameson, Genre, and Gumshoes: *The Maltese Falcon* as Inverted Romance," in Metress (ed.), *The Critical Response to Dashiell Hammett* (pp. 78–88).

Halttunen, Karen (1998). *Murder Most Foul: The Killer and the American Gothic Imagination*. Cambridge, MA: Harvard University Press.

Hamilton, Lyn (1999). *The Moche Warrior: An Archeological Mystery*. New York: Berkeley Prime Fiction.

Hammett, Dashiell (1989). *The Thin Man*. New York: Vintage.

Hammett, Dashiell (1992). *The Continental Op*. Ed. Steven Marcus. New York: Vintage.

Hammett, Dashiell (1999). *Complete Novels*. New York: Library of America.

Hammett, Dashiell (2001). *Crime Stories and Other Writings*. New York: Penguin Putnam.

Hammett, Dashiell, and Alex Raymond (1983). *Secret Agent X*. New York: International Polygonics.

Harris, Thomas (1983). *Red Dragon* [1981]. London: Arrow.

Harris, Thomas (2004). *Red Dragon* [1981] *and The Silence of the Lambs* [1989]. London: Arrow.

Harrison, Kathryn (2008). "Killer Children," *The New York Times Book Review*, July 20: 1, 10.

Hart, Gail K. (2005). *Friedrich Schiller: Crime, Aesthetics, and the Poetics of Punishment*. Newark: University of Delaware Press.

Haut, Woody (1999). *Neon Noir: Contemporary American Crime Fiction*. London: Serpent's Tail.

Haycraft, Howard (1941). *Murder for Pleasure: The Life and Times of the Detective Story*. New York: Appleton-Century.

Haycraft, Howard (ed.) (1946). *The Art of the Mystery Story: A Collection of Critical Essays*. New York: Simon & Schuster.

Haycraft, Howard (1994). "From *Murder for Pleasure: The Life and Times of the Detective Story*," in Metress (ed.), *The Critical Response to Dashiell Hammett* (pp. 161–3).

Haynsworth, Leslie (2001). "Sensational Adventures: Sherlock Holmes and his Generic Past," *English Literature in Transition (1880–1920)*, 44: 459–85.

Headley, Victor (1993). *Yardie* [1992]. London: Pan.

Hegel, G. W. F. (1991). *Elements of the Philosophy of Right*. Ed. Allen Wood. Cambridge: Cambridge University Press.

Heilmann, R. (1968). *Tragedy and Melodrama*. Seattle: University of Washington Press.

Heise, Thomas (2005). "'Going Blood-Simple like the Natives': Contagious Urban Spaces and Modern Power in Dashiell Hammett's *Red Harvest*," *Modern Fiction Studies*, 51: 3.

Hendricks, Vicki (1999). *Iguana Love*. London: Serpent's Tail.

Hennessy, Rosemary, and Rajeswari Mohan (1989). *Textual Practice*, 3: 323–59.

Heyer, Georgette (1933a). *The Unfinished Clue*. London: Longmans, Green & Co.

Heyer, Georgette (1933b). *Why Shoot a Butler?* London: Longmans, Green & Co.

Heyer, Georgette (1941). *Envious Casca*. London: Hodder & Stoughton.

Higgins, George V. (1972). *The Friends of Eddie Coyle*. London: Secker and Warburg.

Highsmith, Patricia (1974). *Deep Water* [1957]. Harmondsworth: Penguin.

Highsmith, Patricia (1975). *The Talented Mr Ripley* [1956]. Harmondsworth: Penguin.

Highsmith, Patricia (1983). *Plotting and Writing Suspense Fiction*. London: Poplar Press.

Highsmith, Patricia (1998). *Strangers on a Train*. London: Vintage.

Highsmith, Patricia (1999). *The Talented Mr Ripley*. London: Vintage.

Highsmith, Patricia (2002). *This Sweet Sickness*. New York: Norton.

Hilfer, Tony (1990). *The Crime Novel: A Deviant Genre*. Austin: University of Texas Press.

Hillyard, Paddy and Janie Percy-Smith (1988). *The Coercive State*. London: Fontana.

Himes, Chester (1954). *The Third Generation*. Chatham, NJ: Chatham Books.

Himes, Chester (1966a). *Real Cool Killers* [1959]. New York: Berkley Publishing.

Himes, Chester (1966b). "Dilemma of the Negro Novelist in the United States," in John A Williams (ed.), *Beyond the Angry Black* (pp. 51–8). New York: Cooper Square.

Himes, Chester (1970a). *Cotton Comes to Harlem* [1965]. New York: Dell.

Himes, Chester (1970b). "My Man Himes: An Interview with Chester Himes," in John A. Williams and Charles F. Harris (eds.), *Armistad 1* (pp. 25–94). New York: Random House.

Himes, Chester (1972). *The Quality of Hurt*. Garden City, NY: Doubleday and Co.

Himes, Chester. (1973). *Cast the First Stone*. Chatham, NJ: Chatham Books.

Himes, Chester (1986). *If He Hollers Let Him Go*. London: Pluto Press.

Himes, Chester (1996). *Blind Man with a Pistol* [1969], in The Harlem Cycle, Vol. 3. Edinburgh: Payback Press.

Hindley, Charles (1969). *Curiosities of Street Literature* [1871]. London: Seven Dials Press.

Hitchcock, Alfred (1953). "The Chloroform Clue: My Favourite True Myster," *The American Weekly*, March 22: 10–20.

Hjortsberg, William (1987). *Falling Angel* [1978]. London: Mysterious Press.

Hoberek, Andrew (2005). *The Twilight of the Middle Class: Post World War II American Fiction and White Collar Work*. Princeton, NJ: Princeton University Press.

Hollingsworth, Keith (1963). *The Newgate Novel 1830–47: Bulwer, Ainsworth, Dickens and Thackeray*. Detroit: Wayne State University Press.

Holquist, Michael (1971). "Whodunnit and Other Questions: Metaphysical Detective Stories in Post-War Fiction," *New Literary History*, 3 (1): 135–56.

Hoopes, Roy (1982). *Cain: The Biography of James M. Cain*. New York: Holt.

Hopkins, Pauline (1901–2). *Hagar's Daughter: A Story of Southern Caste Prejudice*. In Hazel V. Carby (ed.), *The Magazine Novels of Pauline Hopkins* (pp. 1–284). New York: Oxford University Press.

Hoppenstand, Gary (1984). "Murder and Other Hazardous Occupations: Taboo and Detective Fiction," in Ray Browne (ed.), *Forbidden Fruits: Taboos and Tabooism in Culture* (pp. 83–96). Bowling Green, OH: Bowling Green University Popular Press.

Horsley, Lee (2001). *The Noir Thriller*. London: Palgrave.

Horsley, Lee (2005). *Twentieth-Century Crime Fiction*. Oxford: Oxford University Press.

Howson, Gerald (1985). *Thief-Taker General: Jonathan Wild and the Emergence of Crime and Corruption as a Way of Life in Eighteenth-century England* [1970]. New Brunswick: Transaction Books.

Hughes, Dorothy B. (1984). *Ride the Pink Horse* [1946]. New York: Golden Apple.

Huh, Jinny (2003). "Whispers of Norbury: Sir Arthur Conan Doyle and the Modernist Crisis of Racial (Un)Detection," *Modern Fiction Studies*, 49 (3): 550–90.

Hühn, P. (1987). "The Detective as Reader: Narrativity and Reading Concepts in Detective Fiction," *Modern Fiction Studies* 33 (3): 451–66.

Hume, Fergus (1898). *The Mystery of a Hansom Cab* (rev. edn). London: Jarrold.

Hume, Fergus (1985). *The Mystery of a Hansom Cab* [1886]. London: Hogarth Press.

Hunt, Peter (1994). *An Introduction to Children's Literature*. Oxford: Oxford University Press.

Hutter, A. D. (1998). "Dreams, Transformations and Literature: The Implications of Detective Fiction," in Pykett (ed.), *Wilkie Collins* (pp. 175–96).

Ingraham, J. H. (1844). *The Miseries of New York: or the Burglar and Counselor*. Boston: "Yankee" Office.

Irons, G. (1995). "Introduction," in Irons (ed.), *Feminism in Women's Detective Fiction*. (pp. ix–xxiv).

Irons, G. (ed.) (1995). *Feminism in Women's Detective Fiction*. Toronto: University of Toronto Press.

Irons, G. and J. W. Roberts (1995). "From Spinster to Hipster: The 'Suitability' of Miss Marple and Anna Lee," in Irons (ed.), *Feminism in Women's Detective Fiction* (pp. 64–73).

Irwin, John T. (1994). *The Mystery to a Solution: Poe, Borges, and the Analytic Detective*

Story. Baltimore: The Johns Hopkins University Press.

Irwin, J. T. (2006). *Unless the Threat of Death Is Behind Them: Hard-Boiled Fiction and Film Noir*. Baltimore: The Johns Hopkins University Press.

Jackson, Kate (2001). *George Newnes and the New Journalism in Britain 1880–1910: Culture and Profit*. Aldershot: Ashgate.

Jahshan, Paul (2008). "From Man of the Crowd to Cybernaut: Edgar Allan Poe's Transatlantic Journey – and Back." *European Journal of American Studies*, 2. Available online at: http://ejas.revues.org/document2293.html).

James, Clive (2007). "Blood on the Borders," *The New Yorker*, April 9: 91–6.

James, P. D. (1967). *Unnatural Causes*. London. Faber and Faber.

James, P. D. (1971). *Shroud for a Nightingale*. London: Faber and Faber.

James, P. D. (1986). *A Taste for Death*. London: Faber and Faber.

James, P. D. (1999). *Time to Be in Earnest*. London: Faber and Faber.

James, P. D. (2001). *Death in Holy Orders*. London: Faber and Faber.

James, P. D. (2003). *The Murder Room*. London: Faber and Faber.

Jameson, F. (1983). "On Raymond Chandler," in G. W. Most and W. W. Stowe (eds.), *The Poetics of Murder: Detective Fiction and Literary Theory* (pp. 122–48). New York: Harcourt Brace Jovanovich.

Jeffords, S. (1994). *Hard Bodies: Hollywood Masculinity in the Reagan Era*. New Brunswick, NJ: Rutgers University Press.

Johnson, P. (1994). "Sex and Betrayal in the Detective Fiction of Sue Grafton and Sara Paretsky," *Journal of Popular Culture*, 27 (4): 97–106.

Jones, Tobias (2006). "The Yellow and the Black," in Michael Reynolds (ed.), *Black and Blue: An Introduction to Mediterranean Noir* (pp. 25–31). New York: Europa Editions.

Joyce, Christopher and Eric Stover (1991). *Witnesses from the Grave: The Stories Bones Tell*. London: Bloomsbury.

Kayman, Martin A. (1992). *From Bow Street to Baker Street: Mystery, Detection and Narrative*. Basingstoke: Macmillan.

Kerr, Philip (1992). *A Philosophical Investigation*. New York: Plume.

Kerr, Philip (1995). *The Grid*. Toronto: Seal Books.

Keyser, L. (1992). *Martin Scorsese*. New York: Twayne.

King, Noel (2006a). "A Bridge between all these Literatures We Love: An Interview with François von Hurter of Bitter Lemon Press," *Critical Quarterly*, 49 (2): 62–80.

King, Noel (2006b). "The Main Thing We Book Publishers Have Going for Us is the Books Themselves: An Interview with Pete Ayrton of Serpent'sTail," *Critical Quarterly*, 49 (3): 104–19.

King, Stephen (1993). "Umney's Last Case," in *Nightmares and Dreamscapes* (pp. 582–626). New York: Signet.

Kinkley, Jeffrey C. (2001). "The Post-Colonial Detective in People's China," in Ed Christian (ed.), *The Post-Colonial Detective* (pp. 112–39). Houndmills: Palgrave.

Kirino, Natsuo (2008). *Real World* [2006]. Trans. Philip Gabriel. New York: Knopf.

Klaver, Elizabeth (2005). *Sites of Autopsy in Contemporary Culture*. Albany: State University of New York Press.

Klein, K. G. (1988). *The Woman Detective: Gender and Genre*. Urbana, IL: University of Illinois Press.

Klein, K. G. (1995). *The Woman Detective: Gender and Genre*. 2nd edn. Urbana, IL: University of Illinois Press.

Klein, K. G. (ed.) (1999). *Diversity and Detective Fiction*. Bowling Green, OH: Bowling Green State University Popular Press.

Knight, Stephen (1980). *Form and Ideology in Crime Fiction*. London: Macmillan.

Knight, Stephen (1988). "'A Cheerful Hardiness': An Introduction to Raymond Chandler," in Brian Docherty (ed.), *American Crime Fiction*. Basingstoke: Macmillan.

Knight, Stephen (2004). *Crime Fiction 1800–2000: Detection, Death, Diversity*. Basingstoke and New York: Palgrave.

Knox, Ronald (1929). "Introduction," in Ronald Knox and H. Harrington (eds.), *The Best Detective Stories of the Year, 1928* (pp. xi–xiv). London: Faber and Gwyer.

Koff, Clea (2004). *The Bone Woman: Among the Dead in Rwanda, Bosnia, Croatia, and Kosovo*. London: Atlantic Books.

Kreiser, Lawrence A. Jr (1999). "James Brewer: Sleuths and Carpetbaggers along the Mississippi River," *The Chicago Magazine*, February: 7.

Krutnik, Frank (1991). *In a Lonely Street: Film Noir, Genre, Masculinity*. London: Routledge.

Kungl, C. T. (2006). *Creating the Fictional Female Detective: The Sleuth Heroines of British Women Writers, 1890–1940*. Jefferson, NC: McFarland & Co.

Lacan, Jacques (1977). *Ecrits: A Selection*. Trans. Alan Sheridan. New York: Norton.

Landrum, Larry, Jr (1999). *American Mystery and Detective Novels: A Reference Guide*. Westport: Greenwood.

Lane, Roger (1999). "Introduction," in Edmund Pearson, *Studies in Murder* (pp. ix–xvi). Columbus, OH: Ohio State University Press.

Lehman, David (1989). *The Perfect Murder: A Study in Detection*. New York: The Free Press.

Leitch, T. (1999). "The Outer Circle: Hitchcock on Television," in *Alfred Hitchcock: Centenary Essays*. London: BFI.

Lem, Stanislaw (1974). *The Investigation* [1959]. Trans. Adele Milch. New York: Seabury Press.

Lemay, J.A. Leo (1982). "The Psychology of 'The Murders in the Rue Morgue'," *American Literature*, 54 (2): 165–88.

Lemire, Elise (2001). "'The Murders in the Rue Morgue': Amalgamation Discourses and the Race Riots of 1838 in Poe's Philadelphia," in J. Gerald Kennedy and Liliane Weissberg (eds.), *Romancing the Shadow: Poe and Race* (pp. 177–204). Oxford: Oxford University Press.

Leonard, Elmore (1978). *The Switch*. New York: HarperCollins.

Leonard, Elmore (1980). *City Primeval: High Noon in Detroit*. New York: Avon.

Leonard, Elmore (1985). *Glitz*. New York: Arbor House.

Leonard, Elmore (1989). *Killshot*. New York: William Morrow.

Leonard, Elmore (1998). *Elmore Leonard's Western Roundup #1*. New York: Random House.

Leonard, Elmore (2002). *Tishomingo Blues*. New York: HarperCollins.

Leonard, Elmore (2004). *The Complete Western Stories of Elmore Leonard*. New York: HarperCollins.

Leonard, Elmore (2007). *Up in Honey's Room*. New York: HarperCollins.

Light, Alison (1991). *Forever England: Femininity, Literature and Conservatism Between the Wars*. London: Routledge.

Lippard, George (1995). *The Quaker City* [1844]. Ed. David S. Reynolds. Amherst: University of Massachusetts Press.

Lloyd, David and Paul Thomas (1998). *Culture and the State*. London: Routledge.

Longinus (1965). *On the Sublime. Aristotle, Horace, Longinus: Classical Literary Criticism*. Trans. T. S. Dorsch. London: Penguin.

Lovesey, Peter (1971). *The Detective Wore Silk Drawers*. New York: Dodd Mead.

Lovesey, Peter (1976). *Swing, Swing Together*. London: Macmillan.

Lucas, Rose (2004). "Anxiety and its Antidotes: Patricia Cornwell and the Forensic Body," *Literature Interpretation Theory* 15: 207–22.

Lucia, C. (1992). "Women on Trial: The Female Lawyer in the Hollywood Courtroom," *Cineaste*, 19 (2–3): 32–7.

Lycett, Andrew (1995). *Ian Fleming: The Man behind James Bond*. Atlanta: Turner Publishing.

MacDonald, Dwight (ed.) (1960). *Parodies: An Anthology from Chaucer to Beerbohm – and After*. New York: Random House.

Macdonald, Ross [Kenneth Millar]. (1981). "Kenneth Millar/Ross Macdonald: A Checklist," in *Self-Portrait: Ceaselessly into the Past* (pp. 23–8). Santa Barbara, CA: Capra Press.

Machen, Arthur (2005). "The Great God Pan [1894]," in Roger Luckhurst (ed.), *Late Victorian Gothic Tales* (pp. 183–233). Oxford: Oxford University Press.

MacLehose, Christopher (2006). "Other Worlds," *Literature Matters*, British Council e-zine, Spring 2006: The Crime Issue. http://www.britishcouncil.org/arts-literature-literature-matters.htm

Madden, David (ed.) (1968). *Tough Guy Writers of the Thirties*. Carbondale, IL: Southern Illinois University Press.

Mailer, Norman (2003). *The Spooky Art: Some Thoughts on Writing*. London: Little Brown.

Majzels, Robert (2004). *Apikoros Sleuth*. Toronto, ON: Mercury Press.

Makinen, Merja (2006). *Agatha Christie: Investigating Femininity*. London: Palgrave.

Malmgren, Carl D. (2001). *Anatomy of Murder: Mystery, Detective and Crime Fiction*. Bowling Green, OH: Bowling Green State University Popular Press.

Mankell, Henning (2003). *The Fifth Woman*. London: Harvill [London: Vintage, 2004].

Mankell, Henning (2006). "Introduction," in Maj Sjöwall and Per Wahlöö, *Roseanna* (pp. v–ix). London: Harper Perennial.

Mansel, Henry L. (1863). "Sensation Novels," *Quarterly Review* 133: 481–514.

Marling, William (1995). *The American Roman Noir*. Athens, GA: University of Georgia Press.

Marschall, Richard (1997). *America's Great Comic-Strip Artists: From the Yellow Kid to Peanuts*. New York: Stewart, Tabori & Chang.

Martin, Ron A. (2006). *The Psychology of Humor: An Integrative Approach*. Burlington, MA: Academic Press.

Marx, Karl (2002). *Communist Manifesto*. London: Penguin.

Mason, A.E.W. (1924). *The House of the Arrow*. London: Hodder & Stoughton.

Mason, Bobbie Ann (1975). *The Girl Sleuth: A Feminist Guide*. Old Westbury, NY: The Feminist Press.

Masters, Anthony (1987). *Literary Agents: The Novelist as Spy*. Oxford: Basil Blackwell.

Mather, C. (1702). *Magnalia Christi Americana: Or, the Ecclesiastical History of New-England*. London: Thomas Parkhurst.

Maugham, W. Somerset (1948). *Ashenden or, The British Agent*. London: William Heinemann.

Mayhew, Henry (1967). *London Labour and the London Poor*, Vol. I: *The London Street Folk* [1851]. London: Frank Cass.

McBain, Ed (1999). *Cop Hater* [1956]. New York: Mass Market Paperback.

McCann, Sean (2000). *Gumshoe America: Hard-Boiled Crime Fiction and the Rise and Fall of New Deal Liberalism*. Durham, NC: Duke University Press.

McGill, Meredith L. (2002). *American Literature and the Culture of Reprinting, 1834–1853*. Philadelphia: University of Pennsylvania Press.

McGilligan, Pat (1986). *Backstory: Interviews with Screenwriters of Hollywood's Golden Age*. Berkeley and Los Angeles: University of California Press.

McGrath, Charles (2005). "The Old Master," *The New York Times Book Review*, May 8: 1, 10.

McLaughlin, Joseph (2000). *Writing the Urban Jungle: Reading the Empire in London from Doyle to Eliot*. Charlottesville and London: Fontana.

McShane, Frank (ed.) (1981). *Selected Letters of Raymond Chandler*. New York: Columbia University Press.

Meade, L. T. and Clifford Halifax (1895). "Stories from the Diary of a Doctor: 'Creating a Mind'," *Strand Magazine* 9: 33–46.

Merivale, Patricia (1967). "The Flaunting of Artifice in Vladimir Nabokov and Jorge Luis Borges," in L. S. Dembo (ed.), *Nabokov: The Man and his Work* (pp. 209–24). Madison: University of Wisconsin Press.

Merivale, Patricia (1999). "Gumshoe Gothics: Poe's 'The Man of the Crowd' and his Followers," in Merivale and Sweeney (eds.), *Detecting Texts* (pp. 101–16).

Merivale, Patricia and Susan Elizabeth Sweeney (1999). "The Game's Afoot! On the Trail of the Metaphysical Detective Story," in Merivale and Sweeney (eds.), *Detecting Texts* (pp. 1–24).

Merivale, Patricia and Susan Elizabeth Sweeney (eds.) (1999). *Detecting Texts: The Metaphysical Detective Story from Poe to Postmodernism*. Philadelphia: University of Pennsylvania Press.

Merrill, Robert (1997). "Christie's Narrative Games," in Jerome Delamere and Ruth Prigozy (eds.), *Theory and Practice of Classic Detective Fiction* (pp. 87–102). Westport, CT: Greenwood Press.

Messac, Régis (1929). *Le 'Detective Novel' et l'Influence de la Pensée Scientifique*. Paris: Champion.

Messent, Peter (1997). "Introduction: From Private Eye to Police Procedural – The Logic of Contemporary Crime Fiction," in Messent (ed.), *Criminal Proceedings*.

Messent, Peter (2000). "American Gothic: Liminality in Thomas Harris's Hannibal Lecter Novels," *Journal of American and Comparative Cultures*, 23 (4): 23–35.

Messent, Peter (ed.) (1997). *Criminal Proceedings: The Contemporary American Crime Novel*. London: Pluto Press.

Metress, Christopher (1994). "Diplomacy and Detection in Conan Doyle's 'The Second Stain'," *English Literature in Transition (1880–1920)*, 37, 39–51.

Metress, Christopher ((ed.) (1994). *The Critical Response to Dashiell Hammett*. Westport, CT: Greenwood Press.

Mighall, Robert (1999). *A Geography of Victorian Gothic Fiction: Mapping History's Nightmares*. Oxford: Oxford University Press.

Miles, Robert (2002). "The 1790s: The Effulgence of Gothic," in Jerrold E. Hogle (ed.), *The Cambridge Companion to Gothic Fiction* (pp. 41–62). Cambridge: Cambridge University Press.

Miller, D. A. (1988). *The Novel and the Police*. Berkeley: University of California Press.

Miller, Frank (2003). *The Interviews 1981–2003*. Seattle, WA: Fantagraphics.

Miller, Frank (2005). *Sin City, Vol. 1: The Hard Goodbye* [1991]. Milwaukie, OR: Dark Horse Books.

Millet, Kitty (2007). "Halakhah and the Jewish Detective's Obligations," in Linda Martz and Anita Higgie (eds.), *Questions of Identity in Detective Fiction* (pp. 59–76). Newcastle: Cambridge Scholars Press.

Miskimmin, Esme (2004). "Appendix 2: Interview with Jill Paton Walsh," in *Detective Fiction, Religion, and Dorothy L. Sayers* (pp. 263–80). PhD dissertation, University of Liverpool.

Mitchell, Gladys (1942). *Laurels Are Poison*. London: Michael Joseph.

Mitchell, Gladys (1943). *Sunset over Soho*. London: Michael Joseph.

Moore, Charles (2007). "A Tribute to the Most Famous Belgian," *Daily Telegraph*, May 26. Available online at: http://www.telegraph.co.uk/comment/3640141/A-tribute-to-the-most-famous-Belgian.html (last accessed January 28, 2009).

Moretti, Franco (1983). *Signs Taken for Wonders: On the Sociology of Literary Forms*. London: Verso.

Morrison, Arthur (1894). "The Loss of Sammy Crockett," *Martin Hewitt, Investigator. Strand Magazine* 7: 361–73.

Morrison, Arthur (1896). "The Ward Lane Tabernacle," *Adventures of Martin Hewitt. Windsor Magazine* 3: 652–64.

Mortimer, L. (1994). "*The Age of Innocence*: A Bloodless Feast", *Metro*, 97: 3–9.

Moscucci, Ornella (1993). *The Science of Woman: Gynaecology and Gender in England 1800–1929*. Cambridge: Cambridge University Press.

Mosley, Walter (1993). *A Red Death* [1991]. London: Pan.

Mosley, Walter (1995) "Fearless," in Paula L. Woods (ed.), *Spooks, Spies, and Private Eyes: Black Mystery, Crime, and Suspense Fiction* (pp. 135–57). New York: Doubleday.

Mosley, Walter (2001). *Fearless Jones*. New York: Little.

Mosley, Walter (2002). *Devil in a Blue Dress* [1990]. New York: Pocket.

Mosley, Walter (2003). *Fear Itself*. New York: Little.

Mosley, Walter (2006). *Fear of the Dark*. New York: Little.

Most, Glenn W. (1988). "Elmore Leonard: Splitting Images," in Barbara A. Rader and Howard G. Zettler (eds.), *The Sleuth and the Scholarz: Origins, Evolution, and Current Trends in Detective Fiction* (pp. 101–10). New York: Greenwood Press.

Mudge, Alden (2001). "New Crime Fiction with a Twist from Noir Master Walter Mosley: Interview by Alden Mudge." *BookPage Online*, June. www.bookpage.com/0106bp/walter_mosley.html (last accessed 10 August, 2008).

Muller, M. (1998). "What Sharon McCone Learned from Judy Bolton," in J. Grape, D. James, and E. Nehr (eds.), *Deadly Women: The Mystery Reader's Indispensable Companion* (pp. 67–9). New York: Carroll & Graf.

Munby, Jonathan (1999). *Public Enemies, Public Heroes: Screening the Gangster from Little Caesar to Touch of Evil*. Chicago: University of Chicago Press.

Munt, Sally (1994). *Murder by the Book? Feminism and the Crime Novel*. London: Routledge.

Murray, Will (1994). "The Riddle of the Key," in Metress (ed.), *The Critical Response to Dashiell Hammett* (pp. 115–17).

Nabokov, Vladimir (1996). *The Real Life of Sebastian Knight* [1941] in *Novels and Memoirs 1941–1951* (pp. 3–160). New York: Library of America.

Naremore, J. (1999). "Hitchcock at the Margins of Noir," in R. Allen, and S. Ishii-Gonzales (eds.), *Alfred Hitchcock: Centenary Essays*. London: BFI.

Nash, Ilana (2001). "Nancy Drew," in Sara Pendergast and Tom Pendergast (eds.), *St James Encyclopedia of Popular Culture*. Detroit: St James Press.

Nyman, Jopi (1997). *Men Alone: Masculinity, Individualism and Hard-Boiled Fiction*. Amsterdam: Rodopi.

Oates, Joyce Carol (1977). "Man under Sentence of Death," in David Madden (ed.), *Tough Guy Writers of the Thirties*. Carbondale: Southern Illinois University Press.

Oates, Joyce Carol (1995). "The Simple Art of Murder," *The New York Review*, December 21.

Ogdon, Bethany (1992). "Hard-boiled Ideology," *Critical Quarterly*, 34: 1.

Oliphant, Margaret (1863). "Novels," *Blackwood's Edinburgh Magazine*, 94: 168–83.

Olsson, J. (2007). "Hitchcock à la Carte: Menus, Marketing and the Macabre," in W. Schmenner and C. Granof (eds.), *Casting a Shadow: Creating the Alfred Hitchcock Film*. Evanston, IL: Northwestern University Press.

Osborne, Charles. (2002). "Appearances and Disappearances," in Harold Bloom (ed.), *Agatha Christie: Modern Criticial Views* (pp. 101–46). Philadelphia: Chelsea House.

Panek, Leroy L. (2003a). *The Police Novel: A History*. Jefferson, NC: McFarland & Co.

Panek, Leroy L. (2003b). "Post-war American Police Fiction," in Priestman (ed.), *The*

Cambridge Companion to Crime Fiction (pp. 155–72).

Panek, Leroy L. (2004). *Reading Early Hammett: A Critical Study of the Fiction prior to The Maltese Falcon*. Jefferson, NC: McFarland & Co.

Paradis, K. (2001). "Warshawski's Situation: Beauvoirian Feminism and the hard-boiled Detective," *South Central Review*, 18 (3/4): 86–101.

Paretsky, Sara (1987). *Bitter Medicine*. New York: Dell Publishing.

Paretsky, Sara (1990). *Burn Marks*. New York: Dell Publishing.

Paretsky, Sara (1991). *Indemnity Only* [1982]. New York: Dell.

Paretsky, Sara (1993). *V. I. Warshawski*. London: Penguin Books.

Paretsky, Sara (1994). *Tunnel Vision*. New York: Dell Publishing.

Paretsky, Sara (2003). *Blacklist*. London: Hamish Hamilton.

Paretsky, Sara (2007). *Writing in an Age of Silence*. New York: Verso.

Parker, Robert B. (1970). "The Violent Hero, Wilderness Heritage and Urban Reality: A Study of the Private Eye Novels of Dashiell Hammett, Raymond Chandler, and Ross Macdonald," PhD thesis, Boston University.

Peace, David (2000). *Nineteen Seventy Seven*. London: Serpent's Tail.

Peach, Linden (2006). *Masquerade, Crime and Fiction: Criminal Deceptions*. London: Palgrave.

Peachment, Chris (1994). "A Tough Old Cookie," *The Independent*, August 16. Available online at: http://www.independent.co.uk/arts-entertainment/a-tough-old-cookie-robin-cook-shook-the-crust-off-his-uppers-and-opted-for-the-underside-he-depicts-in-his-south-london-thrillers-now-hes-told-the-real-story-1540616.html

Pearson, Edmund (1930). *Instigation of the Devil*. New York: Charles Scribner's Sons.

Pearson, Edmund (1999). *Studies in Murder* [1924]. Introd. Roger Lane. Columbus, OH: Ohio State University Press.

Peek, W. C. (1998). "Cherchez la Femme: *The Searchers*, *Vertigo*, and Masculinity in Post-Kinsey America," *Journal of American Culture*, 21 (2): 73–87.

Pepper, Andrew (2000). *The Contemporary American Crime Novel: Race, Ethnicity, Gender, Class*. Edinburgh: Edinburgh University Press.

Pepper, Andrew (2009). "'Hegemony Protected by the Armour of Coercion': Dashiell Hammett's *Red Harvest* and the State," *Journal of American Studies*, forthcoming.

Perec, Georges (1969). *La Disparition*. Paris: Denoël.

Perec, Georges (1994). *A Void*. Trans. Gilbert Adair. Hammersmith: Harvill.

Person, Leland S. (2001). "Poe and Nineteenth-century Gender Constructions," in J. Gerald Kennedy (ed.), *A Historical Guide to Edgar Allan Poe* (pp. 129–66). Oxford: Oxford University Press.

Pestana, Artur (2006). *Jaime Bunda, Secret Agent: Story of Various Mysteries*. Trans. Richard Bartlett. Laverstock, UK: Aflame Books.

Peters, Catherine (1992). *The King of Inventors: A Life of Wilkie Collins*. Reading: Minerva Press.

Pfeil, Fred (1995). *White Guys: Studies in Postmodern Domination and Difference*. London: Verso.

Pileggi, Nicholas (1985). *Wiseguy: Life in a Mafia Family*. New York: Simon and Schuster.

Pirkis, C. L. (1986). *The Experiences of Loveday Brooke, Lady Detective* [1894]. Ed. M. Slung. New York: Dover.

Pizarnik, Alejandra (1992). "The Bloody Countess," [1968] in Chris Baldick (ed.), *The Oxford Book of Gothic Tales* (pp. 466–77). Oxford: Oxford University Press.

Plain, Gill (1996). *Women's Fiction of the Second World War: Gender, Power and*

Resistance. Edinburgh: Edinburgh University Press.

Plain, Gill (2001). *Twentieth-Century Crime Fiction: Gender, Sexuality and the Body*. Edinburgh: Edinburgh University Press.

Poe, Edgar Allan (1984). *Poetry and Tales*. New York: Library of America.

Porter Dennis (1981). *The Pursuit of Crime: Art and Ideology in Detective Fiction*. New Haven: Yale University Press.

Praz, Mario (1954). *The Romantic Agony* [1930]. Trans. Angus Davidson. London: Oxford University Press.

Priestman, Martin (1990). *Detective Fiction and Literature: The Figure on the Carpet*. London: Macmillan.

Priestman, Martin (1998). *Crime Fiction from Poe to the Present*. Plymouth: Northcote House.

Priestman, Martin (2003). "Post-war British Crime Fiction," in Priestman (ed.), *The Cambridge Companion to Crime Fiction* (pp. 173–92).

Priestman, M. (ed.) (2003). *The Cambridge Companion to Crime Fiction*. Cambridge: Cambridge University Press.

Pronzini, Bill and Jack Adrian (eds.) (1995). *Hard-Boiled: An Anthology of American Crime Stories*. Oxford: Oxford University Press.

Pullman, Philip (ed.) (1998). *Detective Stories*. London: Kingfisher.

Punter, David (1996). *The Literature of Terror. Vol. 2: The Modern Gothic* (rev. 2nd edn). London: Longman.

Puzo, Mario (1969, 1991). *The Godfather*. London: Arrow Books.

Pykett, Lyn (1994). *The Sensation Novel: From The Woman in White to The Moonstone*. Plymouth: Northcote House.

Pykett, Lyn (2003). "The Newgate Novel and Sensation Fiction, 1830–1868," in Priestman (ed.), *The Cambridge Companion to Crime Fiction* (pp. 19–40).

Pykett, Lyn (ed.) (1998). *Wilkie Collins*. London: Macmillan.

Pyrhönen, H. (1994). *Murder from an Academic Angle: An Introduction to the Study of the Detective Narrative*. Columbia, SC: Camden House.

Pyrhönen, H. (1999). *Mayhem and Murder: Narrative and Moral Problems in the Detective Story*. Toronto: Toronto University Press.

Queen, Ellery (1931). *The Dutch Shoe Mystery*. London: Hamlyn.

Quinn, Mary Lou and Eugene P. A. Schleh (1991). "Popular Crime in Africa: The Macmillan Education Program," in Eugene Schleh (ed.), *Mysteries of Africa* (pp. 39–49). Bowling Green: Bowling Green University Popular Press.

Radcliffe, Ann (1980). *The Mysteries of Udolpho* [1794]. Ed. Bonamy Dobree. Oxford: Oxford University Press.

Rae, W. F. (1863). "Sensation Novelists: Miss Braddon," *North British Review* 43: 180–204.

Rafter, N. (2000). *Shots in the Mirror: Crime Films and Society*. New York: Oxford University Press.

Rankin, Ian (2006). *The Naming of the Dead*. London: Orion.

Rawlings, Philip (1992). *Drunks, Whores and Idle Apprentices: Criminal Biographies of the Eighteenth Century*. London: Routledge.

Ray, Gordon N. (ed.) (1980). *The Letters and Private Papers of William Makepeace Thackeray, Vol. 1: 1817–1840*. New York: Octagon Books.

Raymond, Derek (2006). *He Died with His Eyes Open*. London: Serpent's Tail.

Raymond, Derek (2008). *I Was Dora Suarez*. London: Serpent's Tail.

Reddy, M. T. (1988). *Sisters in Crime: Feminism and the Crime Novel*. New York: Continuum.

Reddy, M. T. (1990). "The Feminist Counter-Tradition in Crime: Cross, Grafton, Paretsky, and Wilson," in R. G. Walker and J. M. Frazer (eds.), *The Cunning Craft: Original Essays on Detective Fiction and Contemporary Literary Theory* (pp. 174–

87). Macomb, IL: Western Illinois University.

Reiner, R. (1985). *The Politics of the Police.* Brighton, UK: Wheatsheaf Books.

Reynolds, Barbara (1998). *Dorothy L. Sayers: Her Life and Soul.* London: Hodder and Stoughton.

Reynolds, Barbara (ed.) (1995). *The Letters of Dorothy L. Sayers, Vol. 1: 1899–1936: The Making of a Detective Novelist.* London: Hodder and Stoughton.

Reynolds, David S. (1988). *Beneath the American Renaissance: The Subversive Imagination in the Age of Emerson and Melville.* New York: Knopf.

Reynolds, David S. (1995). "Introduction," in George Lippard, *The Quaker City; Or The Monks of Monk Hall* (pp. vii–xliv). Amherst: University of Massachusetts Press.

Reynolds, Michael (ed.) (2006). *Black and Blue: An Introduction to Mediterranean Noir* (pp. 7–12). New York: Europa Editions.

Rhodes, Chip (2008). *Politics, Desire, and the Hollywood Novel.* Iowa City: University of Iowa Press.

Riis, Jacob (1971). *How the Other Half Lives.* New York: Dover Publications.

Rippetoe, Rita (2000). "Lynda S. Robinson and Lauren Haney: Detection in the Land of Mysteries," in Browne and Kreiser (eds.), *The Detective as Historian* (pp. 11–21).

Robson, Eddie (2005). *Film Noir.* London: Virgin.

Rosenberg, N. (1994). "Hollywood on Trials: Courts and Films, 1930–1960." *Law and History Review,* 12 (2): 341–67.

Rosenheim, Shawn J. (1997). *The Cryptographic Imagination: Secret Writing from Edgar Poe to the Internet.* Baltimore: The Johns Hopkins University Press.

Ross, Alex (1996). "The Shock of the True," *The New Yorker,* August 19: 70–7.

Rothman, W. (1982). *Hitchcock: the Murderous Gaze.* Cambridge, MA: Harvard University Press.

Rowland, Susan (2001). *From Agatha Christie to Ruth Rendell: British Women Writers in Detective and Crime fiction.* Basingstoke and New York: Palgrave.

Rubin, Martin (1999). *Thrillers.* Cambridge: Cambridge University Press.

Rubin, Rachel (2000). *Jewish Gangsters of Modern Literature.* Urbana and Chicago: University of Illinois Press.

Rudd, David (1995). "Five Have a Gender-ful Time: Blyton, Sexism, and the Infamous Five," *Children's Literature in Education,* 26 (3): 185–96.

Rudd, David (2001). "Digging up the Family Plot: Secrets, Mystery, and the Blytonesque," in Adrienne E. Gavin and Christopher Routledge, *Mystery in Children's Literature: From the Rational to the Supernatural* (pp. 82–99). New York: Palgrave.

Rule, Ann (1993). *A Rose for her Grave.* New York: Pocket Books.

Rule, Ann, writing as Andy Stack (1983). *Lust Killer.* New York: Signet.

Rushing, R. A. (2007). *Resisting Arrest: Detective Fiction and Popular Culture.* New York: Other Press.

Ruth, David E. (1996). *Inventing the Public Enemy: The Gangster in American Culture, 1918–1934.* Chicago: University of Chicago Press.

Rzepka, Charles (2000). "'I'm in the Business Too': Gothic Chivalry, Private Eyes, and Proxy Sex and Violence in Chandler's *The Big Sleep,*" *Modern Fiction Studies* 46 (3): 695–724.

Rzepka, Charles (2005). *Detective Fiction.* Cambridge: Polity Press.

Rzepka, Charles (2007). "Race, Religion, Rule: Genre and the Case of Charlie Chan," *PMLA,* 122 (5): 1463–81.

Sallis, James (1993). *Difficult Lives: Jim Thompson, David Goodis, Chester Himes.* New York: Gryphon Books.

Saltz, Laura (1995). "'Horrible to Relate!' Recovering the Body of Marie Roget," in Shawn Rosenheim and Stephen Rachman (eds.), *The American Face of Edgar Allan Poe* (pp. 237–70). Baltimore: The Johns Hopkins University Press.

Saltzman, Arthur M. (1990). *Designs of Darkness in Contemporary American Fiction*. Philadelphia: Pennsylvania University Press.

Sandell, Jillian (1996). "Reinventing Masculinity: The Spectacle of Male Intimacy in the Films of John Woo," *Film Quarterly* 49 (4): 23.

Saramago, José (2004). *The Double* [2002]. Trans. Margaret Jull Costa. Orlando, FL: Harcourt.

Sawday, Jonathan (1995). *The Body Emblazoned: Dissection and the Human Body in Renaissance Culture*. London: Routledge.

Sayers, Dorothy L. (1926). *Clouds of Witness*. London: Unwin.

Sayers, Dorothy L. (1928). "Introduction," in Dorothy L. Sayers (ed.), *Great Short Stories of Detection, Mystery and Horror* (pp. 9–47). London: Gollancz.

Sayers, Dorothy L. (1930). *Strong Poison*. London: Gollancz.

Sayers, Dorothy L. (1963). *Whose Body?* [1923] London: New English Library.

Sayers, Dorothy L. (1970). *Gaudy Night*. London: Hodder and Stoughton.

Sayers, Dorothy L. (1975). *In the Teeth of the Evidence*. London: Hodder and Stoughton.

Sayers, Dorothy L. (1977a). *The Unpleasantness at the Bellona Club* [1928]. London: Hodder and Stoughton.

Sayers, Dorothy L. (1977b). *Whose Body?* London: Hodder and Stoughton.

Sayers, Dorothy L. (1977c). *Busman's Honeymoon*. London: Hodder and Stoughton.

Sayers, Dorothy L. (1979). *Lord Peter Views the Body*. London: Hodder and Stoughton.

Sayers, Dorothy L., and Robert Eustace (1978). *The Documents in the Case*. London: Hodder and Stoughton.

Scaggs, John (2005). *Crime Fiction*. London: Routledge.

Schatz, T. (1981). *Hollywood Genres*. New York: Random House.

Schechter, Harold (ed.) (2008). *True Crime: An American Anthology*. New York: The Library of America.

Schickel, Richard (1992). *Double Indemnity*. London: British Film Institute

Sears, Donald J. (1991). *To Kill Again: The Motivation and Development of Serial Murder*. Wilmington, Delaware: Scholarly Resources.

Sedgwick, Eve (1986). *The Coherence of Gothic Conventions*. Rev. edn. London: Methuen.

Seltzer, Mark (2004). "The Crime System," *Critical Inquiry*, 30: 557–83.

Server, Lee (1994). *Over my Dead Body: The Sensational Age of the American Paperback: 1945–1955*. San Francisco: Chronicle Books.

Shaw, Joseph T. (ed.) (1946). *The Hard-boiled Omnibus*. New York: Simon and Schuster.

Shaw, Marion and Sabine Vanacker (1991). *Reflecting on Miss Marple*. London and New York: Routledge.

Shephard, Richard (2006). "The Legacy of Sjöwall and Wahlöö," endnotes to Maj Sjöwall and Per Wahlöö, *Roseanna* (pp. 2–6). London: Harper Perennial.

Sherman, William David (1968/9). "David Goodis/Dark Passage," *Sight & Sound*, 38: 41.

Sikov, Ed (1999). *On Sunset Boulevard: The Life and Times of Billy Wilder*. London: Hyperion.

Silet, Charles L. P. (1994). "The 87th Precinct and Beyond: Interview with Ed McBain," *Armchair Detective: A Quarterly Journal*, 27 (4): 382–99.

Silver, A. and E. Ward (1988). *Film Noir: An Encyclopedic Reference Guide*. London: Bloomsbury.

Simpson, Philip L. (2000). *Psycho Paths: Tracking the Serial Killer through Contemporary American Film and Fiction*. Carbondale, IL: Southern Illinois University Press.

Sims, George R. (1984). *How the Poor Live, and Horrible London* [1889]. New York: Garland.

Sirvent, Michel (1999). "Reader-investigators in the Post-*nouveau roman*: Lahougue, Peeters, and Perec," in Merivale and Sweeney (eds.), *Detecting Texts* (pp. 157–78).

Skaperdas, Stergios (2001). "The Political Economy of Organised Crime: Providing Protection When the State Does Not," *Economic Governance* 2: 173–202.

Skenazy, Paul (1995). "Behind the Territory Ahead," in David Fine (ed.), *Los Angeles in Fiction* (pp. 103–25). Albuquerque, NM: University of New Mexico Press.

Skinner, Robert E. (1987). "To Write Realistically: An Interview with Elmore Leonard," *Xavier Review* 7 (2): 37–46.

Slotkin, Richard (2000). *Regeneration through Violence: The Mythology of the American Frontier, 1600–1860*. Norman: University of Oklahoma Press.

Smith, G. (1990). "Martin Scorsese Interviewed by Gavin Smith," *Film Comment*, September/October: 27–30, 69.

Sobchack, V. (1995). "'Surge and Splendor': A Phenomenology of the Hollywood Historical Epic," in B. K. Grant (ed.), *Film Genre Reader II*. Austin: University of Texas Press.

Soitos, Stephen F. (1996). *The Blues Detective: A Study of African American Detective Fiction*. Amherst: University of Massachusetts Press.

Sova, Dawn B. (1996). *Agatha Christie A to Z*. New York: Checkmark.

Spillane, Mickey (2001a). *The Mike Hammer Collection, Vol. 1: I, The Jury, My Gun Is Quick, Vengeance Is Mine!* New York: New American Library.

Spillane, Mickey (2001b). *The Mike Hammer Collection, Vol. 2: One Lonely Night, The Big Kill, Kiss Me Deadly*. New York: New American Library.

Spooner, Catherine (2006). *Contemporary Gothic*. London: Reaktion.

Springhall, John (1994). "'Pernicious Reading'? 'The Penny Dreadful' as Scapegoat for Late-Victorian Juvenile Crime," *Victorian Periodicals Review* 27: 326–49.

Srebnick, Amy Gilman (1995). *The Mysterious Death of Mary Rogers: Sex and Culture in Nineteenth-Century New York*. New York: Oxford University Press.

Stafford, David (1991). *The Silent Game: The Real World of Imaginary Spies*. Athens GA: University of Georgia Press.

station909 from Israel (2009). Available online at http://www.imdb.com/title/tt0443559/

Stevenson, Robert Louis (1992). *The Strange Case of Dr Jekyll and Mr Hyde and Other Stories*. Ed. Claire Harman. London: Everyman.

Stewart, R. F. (1980). *... And Always a Detective: Chapters on the History of Detective Fiction*. Newton Abbot: David and Charles.

Stoker, Bram (2008). "Author's Preface," in Leslie Klinger (ed.), *The New Annotated Dracula* [1901] (pp. 5–8). New York: W. W. Norton.

Stringer, Julian (1997). "'Your Tender Smiles Give Me Strength': Paradigms of Masculinity in John Woo's *A Better Tomorrow* and *The Killer*," *Screen* 38 (1): 40.

Summerscale, Kate (2008). *The Suspicions of Mr Whicher or the Murder at Road Hill House*. London: Bloomsbury.

Sussex, Lucy (1989). *The Fortunes of Mrs Fortune*. Melbourne: Penguin.

Sutter, Gregg (1986). "Getting it Right: Researching Elmore Leonard's Novels," *The Armchair Detective*, 19 (1): 4–19.

Sweeney, S. E. (1990). "Locked Rooms: Detective Fiction, Narrative Theory, and Self-Reflexivity," in R. G. Walker and J. M. Frazer (eds.), *The Cunning Craft: Original Essays on Detective Fiction and Literary Theory* (pp. 1–14). Macomb: Western Illinois University Press.

Swope, Richard (1998). "Approaching the Threshold(s) in Postmodern Detective Fiction: Hawthorne's 'Wakefield' and other Missing Persons," *Critique* 39 (Paul Auster issue): 207–27.

Symons, Julian (1985). *Dashiell Hammett*. New York: Harcourt, Brace, Jovanovich.

Symons, Julian (1992). *Bloody Murder: From the Detective Story to the Crime Novel: A History* [1972]. London: Pan.

Tani, Stefano (1984). *The Doomed Detective: The Contribution of the Detective Novel to Postmodern American and Italian Fiction*. Edwardsville and Carbondale: Southern Illinois University Press.

Tasker, Yvonne (1993). *Spectacular Bodies: Gender, Genre, and the Action Cinema*. London: Routledge.

Teo, Stephen (1997). *Hong Kong Cinema: The Extra Dimensions*. London: British Film Institute.

Tey, Josephine (1946). *Miss Pym Disposes*. London: William Heinemann.

Tey, Josephine (1953). *A Shilling for Candles*. London: William Heinemann.

Thackeray, William Makepeace (1999). *Catherine: A Story* [1839–40]. Ann Arbor: University of Michigan Press.

Thomas, Ronald R. (1994). "The Fingerprint of the Foreigner: Colonizing the Criminal Body in 1890s Detective Fiction and Criminal Anthropology," *ELH* 61 (3): 655–863.

Thomas, Ronald R. (1999). *Detective Fiction and the Rise of Forensic Science*. Cambridge: Cambridge University Press.

Thomas, Ronald R. (2007). "The *Moonstone*, Detective Fiction and Forensic Science," in Jenny Bourne Taylor (ed.), *The Cambridge Companion to Wilkie Collins* (pp. 65–78). Cambridge: Cambridge University Press.

Thompson, G. (2002). *Venus in Boston and Other Tales of Nineteenth-Century City Life* [1849]. Ed. David S. Reynolds and Kimberly R. Gladman. Amherst: University of Massachusetts Press.

Thompson, G. (n.d.). *The Outlaw; Or, The Felon's Fortunes*. New York: F.A. Brady.

Thompson, George (1994). "*The Thin Man*: The end game," in Metress (ed.), *The Critical Response to Dashiell Hammett* (pp. 137–53).

Thompson, Jim (1991). *The Killer Inside Me* [1952]. New York: Vintage Crime.

Thompson, K. M. (2007). *Crime Films: Investigating the Scene*. London: Wallflower Press.

Thurber, James (1965). "The Macbeth Murder Mystery," in *My World and Welcome to It* [1942]. New York: Harcourt Brace.

Todorov, Tsvetan (1977). "The Typology of Detective Fiction," in R. Howard (trans.), *The Poetics of Prose* (pp. 42–52). Oxford: Basil Blackwell.

Trelease, Gita Panjabi (2004). "Time's Hand: Fingerprints, Empire, and Victorian Narratives of Crime," in Andrew Maunder and Grace Moore (eds.), *Victorian Crime, Madness and Sensation* (pp. 195–206). Aldershot: Ashgate.

Trodd, Anthea (1989). *Domestic Crime in the Victorian Novel*. London: Macmillan.

Truffaut, F. (1986). *Hitchcock by Truffaut*, revised edition. London: Paladin.

Tucher, Andie (1994). *Froth & Scum: Truth, Beauty, Goodness, and the Ax Murder in America's First Mass Medium*. Chapel Hill: University of North Carolina Press.

Twain, Mark (2001). *Tom Sawyer, Detective* [1896], in *Tom Sawyer Abroad, Tom Sawyer Detective and Other Stories*. Scituate, MA: Digital Scanning.

Unsworth, Cathi (1995). "Crime and Punishment," *Melody Maker*, February 25.

Van Dine, S. S. (1926). *The Benson Murder Case*. Great Britain: Ernest Benn.

Van Leer, David (1993). "Detecting Truth: The World of the Dupin Tales," in Kenneth Silverman (ed.), *New Essays on Poe's Major Tales* (pp. 65–88). New York: Cambridge University Press.

Verissimo, Luis Fernando (2004). *Borges and the Eternal Orang-utans* [2000]. Trans. Margaret Jull Costa. London: Harvill Press.

Viano, M. (1991). "Reviews – *GoodFellas*," *Film Quarterly*, 44 (3), Spring: 43–50.

Vidocq, Eugène François (2003). *Mémoirs of Vidocq: Master of Crime* [1828]. Trans. Edwin Gile Rich. Edinburgh: A. K. Press.

von Mücke, Dorothea (1996). "'To Love a Murderer' – Fantasy, Sexuality, and the Political Novel: The Case of *Caleb Williams*," in Deidre Lynch and William B. Warner (eds.), *Cultural Institutions of the Novel* (pp. 306–34). Durham: Duke University Press.

Wagner, John and Vince Locke (2004). *A History of Violence*. New York: Vertigo.

Walpole, Horace (1968). *The Castle of Otranto* [1764]. In Mario Praz (ed.), *Three Gothic Novels*. Harmondsworth: Penguin.

Walton, P. L. and M. Jones (1999). *Detective Agency: Women Rewriting the Hard-Boiled Tradition*. Berkeley: University of California Press.

Walz, Robin (2003). "Vidocq, Rogue Cop," in Eugène-François Vidocq, *Memoirs of Vidocq*. Oakland: AK Press.

Wambaugh, Joseph (2006). *Hollywood Station*. New York: Little, Brown & Co.

Warshow, Robert (1970). *The Immediate Experience*. New York: Atheneum.

Warwick, A. (2007). "Blood and Ink," in A. Warwick and M. Willis (eds.), *Jack the Ripper: Media, Culture, History*. Manchester: Manchester University Press.

Watt, Ian (1957). *The Rise of the Novel: Studies in Defoe, Richardson and Fielding*. London: Chatto and Windus.

Weber, Max (1978). *Economy and Society* I, Ed. Guenther Roth and Claus Wittich. Berkeley: University of California Press.

Wells, L. S. (1989). "Popular Literature and Postmodernism: Sara Paretsky's Hard-boiled Feminist," *Proteus: A Journal of Ideas*, 6: 51–6.

Weyr, Tom (1993). "Marketing America's Psychos," *Publishers Weekly*, April 12: 38–41.

Williams, John (1994). "Obituary: Robin Cook," *The Independent*, August 2. Available online at: http://www.independent.co.uk/news/people/obituary-robin-cook-1380884.html.

Williams, John A. (1973). "Chester Himes – My Man Himes," in *Flashbacks: Twenty-Year Diary of Article Writing*. Garden City, NY: Anchor Press.

Wilson, Andrew (2003). *Beautiful Shadow: A Life of Patricia Highsmith*. London: Bloomsbury.

Wilson, Edmund (1988). "Who Cares Who Killed Roger Ackroyd?" in Robin W. Winks (ed.), *Detective Fiction: A Collection of Critical Essays* (rev. edn, pp. 35–40). Woodstock: Foul Play Press.

Wiltse, Ed (1998). "'So Constant an Expectation': Sherlock Holmes and Seriality," *Narrative*, 6: 105–22.

Winks, Robin W. (ed.) (1980). *Detective Fiction: A Collection of Critical Essays*. Englewood Cliffs, NJ: Prentice-Hall.

Winslow, Don (2005). *The Power of the Dog*. London: Arrow Books.

Winslow, Forbes (1868). *On the Obscure Diseases of the Brain and Disorders of the Mind* [1860]. London: John Churchill and Sons.

Winston, Robert P., and Nancy C. Mellerski (1992). *The Public Eye: Ideology and the Police Procedural*. Basingstoke: Macmillan.

Wolfert, Ira (1997) *Tucker's People* [1943]. Urbana and Chicago: University of Illinois Press.

Womack, Jack (1995). *Random Acts of Senseless Violence* [1993]. New York: Grove Press.

Wood, R. (1992). *Hitchcock's Films Revisited*. London: Faber.

Woods, Paula L. (ed.) (1995). *Spooks, Spies, and Private Eyes: Black Mystery, Crime, and Suspense Fiction of the 20th Century*. New York: Doubleday.

Woods, Robin (1997). "'It Was the Mark of Cain': Agatha Christie and the Murder of Mystery," in Jerome Delamere and Ruth Prigozy (eds.), *Theory and Practice of Classic*

Detective Fiction (pp. 103–10). Westport, CT: Greenwood Press.

Worpole, Ken (1983). *Dockers and Detectives*. London: Verso.

Worthington, Heather (2005). *The Rise of the Detective in Early Nineteenth-Century Popular Fiction*. London: Palgrave Macmillan.

Wroe, Nicholas. (2008). *"Grave Concerns,"* Guardian, February 16.

York, R. A. (2007). *Agatha Christie: Power and Illusion*. London: Palgrave.

Young, Earnie (2004). "Writing While White," *Black Issues Book Review*, July/ August, 26–8.

Zboray, R. J. and M. S. Zboray (2000). "The Mysteries of New England: Eugene Sue's 'Imitators,' 1844," *Nineteenth-Century Contexts*, 22: 3.

Ziff, Larzer (1982). *Literary Democracy: The Declaration of Cultural Independence in America*. Harmondsworth: Penguin.

Žižek, S. (1991). *Looking Awry: An Introduction to Jacques Lacan through Popular Culture*. Cambridge, MA: MIT.

Žižek, S. (2003). "Not a Desire to Have Him, But to be Like Him" [review of Andrew Wilson's *Beautiful Shadow*]. *London Review of Books*. August 21: 13–14.

Index

Note: page numbers in *italic* refer to illustrations.

Printed and bound by CPI Group (UK) Ltd, Croydon, CR0 4YY

18/12/2022

03173915-0002